CAPTAIN JOHN'S
Fishing Tackle
PRICE GUIDE

John A. Kolbeck
(aka capt.john)

Russell E. Lewis
(aka findingo)

COLLECTOR BOOKS
A Division of Schroeder Publishing Co., Inc.

On the front cover:
Clockwise from rods at top right: Very collectible early Shakespeare
Wonderods; Spinning and Baby plastic CCBC Pikies; Baby plastic
CCBC Plunker; One-of-a-kind Frank Borman (astronaut) presentation
reel, Model 408 Ultra Light by Mitchell; Early Ropher two-piece card-
board box for Fin-Dingo lures; collection of Fin-Dingo lures.

On the back cover:
Clockwise from top right: Paw Paw Plunker in early 1950s "Fire Lacquer" color; early 1950s Keel-Fish from Pacific Northwest; 1960s Heddon Sonic Kit, four lures new in kit; a perfect Randall (fish) decoy
two-piece cardboard box; a nice Bug-n-Bass by Buckeye Baits, Kansas,
in Rainbow Trout; early South Bend Vacuum Bait in cup hardware;
Lur-All Beetle Bug, papers, and two-piece box (this box became the
early Millsite box as well); a nice wooden Bear Creek, Kaleva, Michigan, ice fishing decoy; a very early (1908 – 1911) Heddon prototype
"Moonlight" type wobbler in wood with cup hardware; an early frog
spot Pflueger Neverfail five-hook.

Photos courtesy Russell E. Lewis unless otherwise noted.

Cover design by Beth Summers
Book design by Karen Smith

COLLECTOR BOOKS
P.O. Box 3009
Paducah, Kentucky 42002-3009

www.collectorbooks.com

Copyright © 2003 John A. Kolbeck & Russell E. Lewis

The current values in this book should be used only as a guide. They are not
intended to set prices, which vary from one section of the country to another. Auction prices as well as dealer prices vary greatly and are affected by condition as well
as demand. Neither the authors nor the publisher assumes responsibility for any
losses that might be incurred as a result of consulting this guide.

Searching For A Publisher?

We are always looking for people knowledgeable within their fields. If you feel
that there is a real need for a book on your collectible subject and have a large
comprehensive collection, contact Collector Books.

CONTENTS

INTRODUCTION

BY RUSSELL E. LEWIS

The most difficult question ever asked a collector is: What is it worth? I cannot talk with people about fishing lures for more than a minute before they ask that question. There is a plethora of lure identification and value guides on the market, including two which I have authored: *Modern Fishing Lure Collectibles, Volumes 1 and 2*, published by Collector Books. The strength of an identification book is that it assists one in identifying, describing and putting one's finds into historical reference. However, most of the guide books have prices that are either too high, too low, or simply inaccurate as to color or model numbers of items. My own books reflect the actual prices for which items sold or were purchased, but they only represent a limited number of lures, rods, reels, etc.

What we need in the hobby is a guide to actual sales that the collector with some experience can use either on its own or in conjunction with other references that are on the market. This is such a book! Capt. John has put together a compilation of about 10,000 prices realized in actual sales in on-line auctions, lists put out by collectors, actual auctions, antique markets, and in any other place collectible fishing tackle is sold. The prices given are not just guesses, not approximations, not maybes, but actual to the penny results for the items listed in this book. Thus, with this new guide, one can find out exactly what the same color, same model lure (or rod, or reel, or miscellaneous item) sold for in the recent past. One can also note the condition of the item and any unusual aspects of the item or the sale. Of course, this is something many of us have done on our own to a small extent. What collector does not already know that a black/white CCBC Pikie is worth far more than most other pikie colors? But, what about other nuances and color variations? My co-author and I have sold thousands of baits, rods, reels, and miscellaneous items. What we share here with the collecting public are nearly eight years of recent history selling and buying collectible fishing tackle on a fairly grand scale. Prior to my own on-line selling, I supplied hundreds of items per year to Capt. John for his own on-line business sales from my various large scale acquisitions. In turn, he kept track of most of the sales in the form of the spreadsheet used in this book. I have also kept track of each of my sales, recording them for posterity. It is through this painstaking research that we have been able to create a price guide that is exacting, correct, and up-to-date at the day of publication.

We cannot guarantee any future prices! As I write this paragraph (mid-October, 2002), the stock market has finished "up" for the first time in about fifteen weeks. The market has been close to an all time low for the past five years. There are many unsettling events that do not allow us to predict the future with precision.

However, as a social scientist and lawyer, I appreciate the lessons learned in history. This is our own personal history of lure, rod, and reel purchases and sales, and it should help define some boundaries for the buyer/seller of similar items. Our experts tell us that consumer confidence is high and spending seems to be keeping pace due to the low interest rates we are experiencing at this time. Hopefully, our prices for antique and collectible tackle will continue to enjoy the growth in pricing that we have seen in the past few years as interest in the hobby continues to grow and as items become even harder to find.

Speaking of finding items, how hard is it? Well, I recently received an e-mail from a fellow who had received his uncle's tackle box. He sent along .jpg photos of the contents and it looked like a veritable "What's What" from my Volume 2 book on fishing collectibles: nice Heddons, a Spot Tail Wood, Arbogast baits, Weber and Glen Evans flyrod baits, Al Foss metal baits, Marathon poppers, CCBC baits, Paw Paw baits, and lots more. All of the tackle was from 1950 to 1970 and in nearly mint condition throughout. The gentleman had just begun collecting and this was an early acquisition. Earlier this year I received a call to look at some tackle a gentleman was going to put in his garage sale. That grouping included dozens of early Devons and a Goodwin Granger two-tip bamboo flyrod, among other items of interest. Another recent find included the remaining lures in the original boxes (and even the original shipping cartons) from a company that closed in 1973, an unusual item called the Multi-Lure that looks a lot like an Arbogast Jitterbug, but with interchangeable lips. This find included a few gross of the original lures, mint on the cards, new in the boxes, and new in the shipping boxes. The lures are already nearly thirty years old and not very common in collector circles. I found these lures with a lead from an e-mail and I followed up with a few more e-mails until the purchase was made.

Yes, tackle is still to be found. It is hiding in garages, basements, barns, attics, rafters, storage sheds, old boats, old boat houses, marinas, antique shops, auction sales and on-line. Some of my best purchases have been made on-line. I am especially proud of a tackle box and contents that I bought a couple of years back with a number of common 1950s lures and a few reels. The box was listed by a party who really did not know much about lures. He had only taken one photo of the box and contents for his listing. Well, a close look revealed what I knew to be a Garcia reel in its leather pouch, so I bid and won the auction. When it arrived, I was tickled to find a nice Hi-Speed model that netted me $498.00 from a Japanese buyer within days of receiving the items in the mail. The box was also full of fairly decent lures, two Pflueger Supremes, and a Shakespeare fly reel. Not bad for a $160.00 purchase on-line!

Another on-line auction netted me two very rare Vom Hofe reels. It was obviously a very old tackle box, maybe a Vom Hofe itself, with a clear late nineteenth century or early twentyieth century design. The box included numerous early metal baits and a couple of early wooden lures. Again, the listing seller only placed one photo in the on-line auction site, and it was of the whole box and its contents. However, her listing indicated that one of the reels was "hard, rubber-like material." Without further ado, I figured the two reels for Vom Hofes due to the early items in the box. Sure enough, $150.00+/- and I was the owner of two Vom Hofe reels, one a very early hard rubber fly reel, the other a nice Julius Vom Hofe baitcasting reel. I also acquired a great early tackle box, some nice early metal baits, and a couple of other lures that would pay for the purchase. The box included early Devons, bobbers, floats, and other related fishing items.

My favorite find was from an antique mall. It is a favorite of mine for a number of reasons, one of them being that so many others must have missed it! In a large converted grain elevator in northwest Michigan is a huge antique mall with the typical individual sales booths. While looking for fishing items in one of the booths, I noticed a minnow bucket. It was mixed in with a bunch of household and kitchen antiques. So, I walked over to the booth (that I otherwise would have ignored) to examine the minnow bucket, which I decided to buy. I also noticed in one of the glass cases a lure with a little paper dot stuck to it that said, "Old Rubber Fish, $85.00." Well, I literally could not believe what I saw: a very rare 1890s Pflueger Muskellunge Minnow, valued at that time between $1,500.00 and $2,000.00 (shown in the Photo Gallery). Needless to say, I decided to fork out the dough for that particular Old Rubber Fish. The funny thing is that the guy with the booth next door, with only fishing items, never even looked at it, for all I know! I also bought a mint Bob-Bet worm container at the same booth. She had three fishing items, one of them the rarest find I have ever made in an antique mall, or anywhere else for that matter.

This reminds me of another bargain I found years ago. I was in an antique barn in Vermont, going over some neat old coats for sale. I picked one up, tried it on and said to the owner, "How much?"

He said, "All of the raccoon coats are $100.00."

I then said, "This is not raccoon, it is buffalo with a lamb's wool collar and beaver cuffs."

He said, "I don't care, it is $100.00."

I then said that as an archaeologist, I could assure him it was worth far more, and he said that it was still $100.00. So I bought it, and it is easily worth about $1,000.00.

The point is that if an item has a price on it, that is what it costs. If an item is not priced, be fair in evaluating it and pay the negotiated price. It is far better to be honest with people than to take advantage of them. Honest dealers will get you lots of future leads and tackle.

This does lead to an area of difficulty for most of us. How does one buy tackle from an individual who does not know the real value of his/her items? I believe that one must inform them of the actual value to the best of one's ability, and then pay a fair price. Of course, if a seller already has a price in mind, then it is ethical to pay that price (e.g., for a garage sale item or items). However, in a face to face negotiation, one should be forthcoming as to the actual value of the tackle and pay fairly for it. This will only result in more tackle coming out of the garages and attics of the seller's friends. I have always paid more for tackle than others and informed all sellers of what they had for sale. This has only resulted in my access to tackle that was denied to others.

There are many views on how to find tackle. Most of us already know that with the increasing interest in collecting, many of the traditional ways to find old items (e.g., garage sales, estate sales, farm auctions), are rapidly drying up or becoming too competitive to be fun. However, by sharing your interest with everyone you know, placing advertising in local papers, asking people if they know of any old tackle, getting your interests out to other collectors, following up possible leads in communities where defunct tackle companies once were, finding old tackle manufacturing representatives, etc., tackle will appear. After some initial correspondence with my co-author indicating that I would like him to find all of the Weber items possible for me, he was able to locate all of the original Weber archival materials, much of which I later purchased from him. I also purchased nearly fifty years of collecting and accumulating from Bud Hartman, a fishing tackle manufacturer's representative from the early '50s until the early '90s. Needless to say, this collection of six hundred plus lures had many great finds from the modern era. It is also important to note the all-important role of the "picker" in locating items for you, if you choose not to spend all of your own time on this. Actually, many of my best finds have come to me via the hard work of a good picker, out looking for items to buy to resell to me. Again, we all make a little money and the needed items end up in our possession. The Bud Hartman collection was a result of just such a find through a great picker/friend.

The key to finding tackle is simple: one needs to work hard at it and keep vigilant at all times. It is impossible to know where that rare find may pop up. I have a student who knows that I like old tackle, and she brought in her little collection to show me. There was a very rare #311 CCBC black/white Crawdad in mint condition in her display case. However, the lure was not for sale and I did not push the issue. I simply told her I would give her a few hundred dollars for it if she ever wanted to part with it. Maybe someday she will call me back. Capt. John and I find tackle all of the time; sometimes it even finds us. But, I do not know anyone who works as hard at it as Capt. John. I also spend a fair amount of time looking, and I am always willing to spend money on a good catch.

So, the two ingredients that it takes to find tackle are to work hard at it and to be fair with the pricing once it is found. On this issue, I must share one more note. At a show in Ann Arbor a few years ago, an older gentleman came in with a wooden tackle box full of really good lures. He went from table to table until he got to me, and it was my turn to pick out items to buy. Most of the others had "beat him up" on prices and were all looking to "steal" his good stuff for next to nothing. He got to me, and I simply asked what he wanted for "such and such," and he gave me a price. I then pulled out the cash and gave it to him. He left happy and I had some decent items to sell at the show. Well, the next day he walked into the show with two, not one but two, very old wooden tackle boxes just full of nice items: a Moonlight lure new in the box; Wilderdilgs new in boxes still on their cards; very rare Heddons; etc. I was located in the first corner, about ten or twelve tables into the show. He simply walked by all of the other tables and refused to stop at them when asked. He came to my tables and asked if I was interested in more lures, and I said, "Sure." We then started dealing and I spent a few thousand dollars, then and there. He sold me every good item he had with him, and I paid him the prices he asked. I then sold some of the items for a fair profit to those same individuals who had not wanted to part with their money the day before. I made money, the older gentleman made money, and some folks got some very rare lures and/or boxes that they were happy to buy at my prices. Of course, I also recorded all of my purchases and sales for tax records, as antique tackle is a business for me also.

Well, for those of you who read my other two books, you know I could go on with stories forever. However, the purpose of this book is to give you some valid pricing, so on to it. The book is organized in alphabetical fashion and should be very easy for one to use. If you have a Crazy Crawler you are wondering about, just go to the listings until you find the appropriate model and color and check it out. The same is true for a Mitchell 300, a Pikie, or anything else one can ever imagine.

Capt. John has been careful to accurately describe the condition, and this is one thing that cannot be emphasized enough in antiques and collecting: condition, condition, condition! Pricing is actually a combination of three things: condition, rarity, and the amount of desire of the purchaser. Some items indeed sell for too much because a collector just has to have it. On the other hand, some items sell for too little, because the right collector was not exposed to the item for sale. But, over all, most of the items in the book will represent the sale price realized as a result of that particular item being offered in the condition represented to a wide audience of buyers. However, from your perspective, make sure to pay special attention to the condition and the time of the sale. As timing is also important to values, items today are generally bringing in more if they are good items

with some rarity. Common items actually brought a little less in 2002 than they did in 2000, due to other economic factors. However, rare items are still tending to increase in value, so pay attention to the time of sale. I should add that author Kolbeck has indicated that recent sales of even the rarest items are not bringing prices of 2000, even though they remain fairly strong.

We have included a section of color photos showing a variety of lures and other items found within the price guide. These are only meant to be examples of some of the many types of items to be found in the price guide, and were not selected due to rarity, condition, or any other value factor. With around 10,000 entries of sales, we surely could not show them all. Hopefully the 242 photos shown will give one an example of what this price guide is all about. For more detailed photos, the reader is referred to my two volumes on lures mentioned earlier. As we have both said, this book is not intended for the raw beginning collector, but for one with some prior knowledge. It will likely be necessary for less knowledgeable collectors to use a reference book of photos in conjunction with this book. However, one thing we are certain of is that the prices shown in the following pages are the real deal!

I am always willing to appraise collections of fishing items, buy collections large or small, and sell collections for others. I also have a variety of modern fishing lure collectibles by direct sale and on eBay. I may be reached in any of the following ways and will respond to all legitimate inquiries.

Mail:
Dr. Russell E. Lewis
Bishop Hall 515
1349 Cramer Circle
Big Rapids, MI 49307

E-mail:
findingo@netonecom.net or
lewisr@ferris.edu

Website:
www.wwbait.net

Phone:
(231) 591-3581

The link found on the eBay website may be used to e-mail me via my eBay user id: findingo.

Wausau, Wisconsin, is a great place to grow up if you love fishing. I was born there in 1946, but moved to Milwaukee with my parents when I started school. Fishing left something to be desired in Milwaukee. Fortunately I had understanding grandparents, aunts, and uncles, who let me spend my summers with them in Wausau. They would often take me "up north" on weekends to fish. On days when I couldn't bum a ride, I could walk down to the Wisconsin River where my cousin and I kept an old wood rowboat tied up. I have always loved to fish but didn't start lure collecting until 1995.

After retiring from the Air Force in 1987, I took up guiding for a living. My family and I moved back to Wisconsin in 1988. Stevens Point is located in the center of the state and right on the banks of the Wisconsin River. Fishing there is some of the best in the state, so it was only natural to do something I liked and make a few doubloons while I was at it. I guided full time for ten years. Most of my clients were just regular fishermen, but I did

help with the filming of about a dozen television shows. I wrote many articles about fishing over the years.

One of my clients was an avid lure collector. He checked out some of the tackle I had been accumulating over the last fifty years. It turned out that I did have a few valuable items, but most was just old stuff not worth much. He dragged me to an antique tackle show in Neenah, Wisconsin, and I was soon hooked on collecting.

Capt. John came into being a few years later. I was really getting into the Internet chat boards that specialized in old tackle. Once in a while, I would talk in an accent. I might be Col. Kolbeck, lure Gestapo: "You vill buy dis Schmidt reel und you vill enjoy." But the one who got out of hand was Capt. John. As soon as I started talking like a pirate, it seemed like everybody joined in. It has become so bad that folks who don't know me wonder where my hook and peg leg are when we first meet!

So if'n it be true prices yer seekin, best be plunkin' down a few doubloons fer this here book.

If you are trying to identify some old tackle, this book may be a good starting place. But if you know what you have and want to find out its value, you have hit the jackpot! There are many excellent books that will help you identify old tackle. They are loaded with pictures and valuable information about the companies that produced the items so eagerly sought by tackle collectors. Pricing is another matter.

I tried to use standard reference works to buy lures at shows and on the Internet. Often this didn't work, as the prices listed were very different than those being asked. This book was originally designed for my private use. For several years, I kept records of sales and auctions that were of interest to me. A few years ago, I consolidated everything and had it bound. This was the infamous "Capt. John's Big Black Book." I put a sticker on it with the warning, "Touch and ye dies." This, of course, got attention at shows when spotted by fellow collectors. Several of them got a peek at the contents and wanted to know where I had obtained such a book and how much it cost. I didn't really want to share the information, so I would just tell them it was one-of-a-kind and not for sale. Finally, I got tired of answering all the questions. I decided I would just quote a ridiculous price and the word would soon get around. When I told the first guy $100, I was amazed that he ordered a copy! By the end of the show, I had a dozen orders.

With the help of Russ Lewis, this greatly expanded version of my price guide is now available to all at a more reasonable cost. The prices contained in this guide are real prices. They come from auctions (both live and electronic) as well as private deals. They are not wishful thinking on my part because I want to sell you my lures (too high) or because I want to buy your lures for my collection (too low).

A key ingredient for these prices is the date of the transaction. This is missing from nearly all other guides. Since prices do change, a price without a date is not of much use. The dates are listed by month and year. So 09-2002 is September, 2002.

Many times auctions end with a reserve not met (arrrgh!). As much as I hate reserve auctions, they still are valuable sources of information. They let you know how much someone was willing to pay for an item, even though the seller wasn't willing to accept it. Such auctions are noted with "NOT MET" in the description area.

I have tried to sort things into a logical order. There are many entries for more popular items. This is something missing from most other guides. Now you can actually look up what a Heddon Punkinseed sold for in any of several colors. I have tried to squeeze as much information as possible into the description area. I have used standard abbreviations plus a few of my own. Hopefully you will be able to figure out my shorthand.

If you have old tackle to sell or trade contact

Captain John
1610 Michigan Avenue
Stevens Point, WI 54481

(715) 341-5687
E-mail: jkolbeck@g2a.net

KEY TO AUTHOR ABBREVIATIONS

Abbrev.	Definition	Abbrev.	Definition
1PCCB	one-piece cardboard box	IC	in case
2PCCB	two-piece cardboard box	NIP	new in pouch
AVG or avg	average	NIT	new in tube
Banner	Heddon Banner box	NOC	new on card
Blush	chin or eye blush	NOT MET	reserve price not met in auction
BW	belly weight	NIB	new in box
COBW	chip off belly weight	NIE	new in envelope
DLT	double line tie	POBW	paint off belly weight
Down Bass box	Heddon Leaping Down Bass box	PTCB	plastic top cardboard box
EX or ex	excellent	SD	star drag
FS	free spool	toilet	Heddon toilet seat hardware
G or g	good	Up Bass box	Heddon Leaping Up Bass box
goodies	extra stuff with a reel	VG or vg	very good
HMLT	hand made line tie	x2, x3, x4, etc.	quantity of item
HPGM	hand painted gill marks		

Manufacturers' codes are used extensively when known. These are too numerous to explain in this key.

BRAND	MODEL	SERIES / MFG. CODE / DESCRIPTION	GRADE	PRICE	DATE
Abbey & Imbrie	Go-Getter	colorful 2PCCB	EX-	$32.75	11-1999
Abbey & Imbrie	Go-Getter	window style 1PCCB	EX-	$16.00	8-2002
Abbey & Imbrie	Minnow, Weedless Surface	yellow dolphin label over South Bend box, NOT MET	EX-	$294.99	7-1999
Abu		5000 Deluxe, wood, with goodies	Mint	$152.50	1-1999
Abu	Ambassadeur	black imitation leather for C reels	EX	$25.16	6-1999
AL&W		red beaver logo, bass with fly, Up Bass box	VG	$250.00	3-1999
Bass-a-Lure	BO 2 Special	bottom missing	VG	$34.85	8-1999
Bauman	Minnow, Cage Bait	all corners split	VG	$1,280.00	10-2000
Biff	Godevil & Whoopee	2 very nice early picture boxes	EX	$130.00	5-2001
Bomber	Various	3 different, 2PCCBs	VG	$10.00	1-1999
Bomber	Various	7 different, 4-2PCCBs, 3-PTCBs	EX	$23.00	1-1999
Bomber Mfg. Co.		no number	AVG	$56.00	9-2000
Buel	Minnow Gang	plain looking	EX-	$585.00	1-2001
Carter's	Bestever	picture box	VG+	$61.00	12-1999
CCBC		Deluxe Six Assortment, beater box with lures	VG+/IB	$710.00	8-2000
CCBC		large, unmarked	EX-	$40.00	10-1999
CCBC	Pikie Minnow	732 stencil	EX-	$37.00	10-2001
CCBC	Pikie Minnow, Jointed Husky	3000	EX-	$28.00	10-1999
CCBC	Pikie Minnow, Midget	2201	VG	$26.00	8-1999
CCBC	Wiggler or Crawdad	337, AL&W box with 337 stencil	EX	$28.01	11-1999
CCBC	Beetle	brown	VG	$75.00	3-1999
CCBC	Beetle	3853, 2 Down Bass boxes, H & more	Poor to VG	$118.37	2-1999
CCBC	Crawdad	intro, lure & papers, vg- box	VG-	$421.00	7-2002
CCBC	Crawdad, Baby	4000, 12-pack, empty	EX-	$300.00	11-1999
CCBC	Darter	2000, Darter insert	EX	$7.00	2-2001
CCBC	Ding Bat	5113, black Ding Bat label	EX	$76.00	3-2002
CCBC	Ding Bat	5119, Frog Ding Bat label	EX	$75.00	3-2002
CCBC	Ding Bat, Baby	V344, Baby Ding Bat in pearl chub	VG	$107.00	10-2000
CCBC	Ding Bat, Surface	5404, Golden Shiner Surface Ding Bat	VG	$37.00	12-1998
CCBC	Ding Bat, Surface	5419, Surface Ding Bat label, papers	EX	$53.00	8-2000
CCBC	Froggie	flyrod picture box	EX	$3,217.00	2-2001
CCBC	Hum-Bird	F300, flyrod picture box	EX	$3,251.00	2-2001
CCBC	Injured Minnow, Husky	3500 label	EX-	$67.00	11-1999
CCBC	Musky, Big Bomber	6701, Big Bomber Musky lure box	EX	$49.99	12-1999
CCBC	Pikie Minnow	12-pack, graphic, NOT MET	VG-	$153.51	5-1999
CCBC	Pikie Minnow	700, yellow, picture box, vg+ lure, ex- pocket catalog	EX-	$2,500.00	12-2001
CCBC	Pikie Minnow, Jointed	2631, Rainbow Fire Jointed Pikie stamp	EX	$42.00	5-1999
CCBC	Pikie Minnow, Jointed	2632, Fireplug Jointed Pikie stamp	EX	$42.31	5-1999
CCBC	Sarasota	3308	EX	$153.50	4-2000
CCBC	Wiggler	intro picture box with papers	VG	$635.00	1-1999
CCBC	Wiggler	yellow intro picture box	VG	$325.00	1-1999
CCBC	Wiggler	intro, early version?, not in Smith's book	VG-	$409.00	2-2002
CCBC	Wiggler, Creek Crab	white intro box with lure, NO BIDS	AVG	$2,250.00	10-1999
CCBC	Pocket Rocket or "Seven Thousand"	7000, 12-pack, fish pictures, grease pencil	EX	$255.00	4-2000
CCBC	Pikie, Striper or Pikie, Jointed Striper	6913, corners split	AVG	$20.00	2-2001

BRAND	MODEL	SERIES / MFG. CODE / DESCRIPTION	GRADE	PRICE	DATE
Eger	Various	5 different, blue & white, fish logo	VG	$84.00	8-1999
Etchen	Helga-Devil	nice cartoon box	EX	$16.00	8-2001
Foss	Pork Rind Flyrod	tin	VG-	$32.51	1-1999
Four Brothers	Neverfail	3167, 3⅝", minnow	VG	$546.00	7-1999
Four Brothers	Minnow, Underwater	white label, NOT MET	Ugly	$143.00	8-2000
Frost, H.J.	Otter	2WT, maroon picture box Pflueger?	EX-	$426.00	12-1999
Frost, H.J.	Senate	wood, ratty paper label, New York lure	VG	$484.00	8-2000
Garland	Cork-Head	A4, red box, text only, Florida lure	EX	$355.00	2-2001
Gateway		CR24, green	VG+	$76.00	1-2001
Guardian Brand	Shur-Strike	blue, shield, neat	VG	$31.00	8-1999
	Shur-Strike	pikie type, yellow & red, nice box, poor lure, NRA	EX	$155.50	4-1999
Heddon		Down Bass box, white border	Poor	$55.00	4-2000
Heddon		Heddon/Daisy, wood	EX	$85.00	2-1999
Heddon		no code, Up Bass box, punch through top, okay	VG-	$57.50	1-2000
Heddon		Up Bass box	EX-	$75.00	2-2001
Heddon	Bass Bug	#52, red box with white lettering	EX	$227.51	8-1999
Heddon	Bass Bug	#53, Bass Bug, Down Bass box	EX	$173.00	10-2001
Heddon	Bass Bug	#61, red box with white lettering	EX	$260.01	8-1999
Heddon	Basser	8502, Brush box	EX+	$64.55	9-1999
Heddon	Basser	8509M, Down Bass box	G	$36.00	1-1999
Heddon	Basser	8509PRH, Up Bass box	EX	$47.00	2-2000
Heddon	Basser Spook	C9859P, NOT MET	EX	$70.00	3-2001
Heddon	Chugger	9542, Brush box, catalog	EX	$29.00	4-1999
Heddon	Crab	9909NC, Brush box	VG	$16.55	3-1999
Heddon	Crab, Baby	1909L, Down Bass box	EX	$92.00	5-2001
Heddon	Crazy Crawler	2100XBW, WBH, ex lure, S-rig	EX	$101.51	6-1999
Heddon	Crazy Crawler	2100XRS, Banner box	VG	$11.50	2-1999
Heddon	Crazy Crawler	2100XRS, Banner box, catalog	EX-	$46.00	7-1999
Heddon	Crazy Crawler	2120BWH, Banner box	Mint	$41.00	3-1999
Heddon	Crazy Crawler	2120XRW, Brush box	VG	$15.50	8-1999
Heddon	Crazy Crawler	2150YRH, Banner box	EX	$97.00	4-2001
Heddon	Deep-O-Diver	white box	Fair	$280.00	4-1999
Heddon	Deep-O-Diver	white intro box, lightly soiled	EX	$503.00	3-2002
Heddon	Deep-O-Diver	white pasteboard	EX-	$450.00	12-1999
Heddon	Dowagiac	#2, wood, hung	EX	$1,712.00	1-2000
Heddon	Dowagiac Minnow	0, white pasteboard	AVG	$887.50	11-1999
Heddon	Dowagiac Minnow	00, Down Bass box, number barely visible	AVG	$281.00	4-2000
Heddon	Dowagiac Minnow	11, white intro box, casting minnow lure	VG-	$1,500.00	10-1999
Heddon	Dowagiac Minnow	100, Down Bass box	EX-	$352.00	8-2000
Heddon	Dowagiac Minnow	100, fancy back, wood, 2-way slide	EX	$1,080.00	9-1999
Heddon	Dowagiac Minnow	100, Up Bass box	EX-	$96.01	6-1999
Heddon	Dowagiac Minnow	100, wood, NOT MET	EX-	$650.00	10-2000
Heddon	Dowagiac Minnow	101, Down Bass box, later	EX	$230.00	2-2001
Heddon	Dowagiac Minnow	101, white pasteboard with vg+ lure	VG	$1,785.00	6-2000
Heddon	Dowagiac Minnow	101, white with newer vg+ lure, NOT MET	VG-	$761.00	10-2001
Heddon	Dowagiac Minnow	102, Brush box	EX-	$75.00	2-2001
Heddon	Dowagiac Minnow	102, Down Bass box, tall box, red border	VG+	$204.00	5-2000
Heddon	Dowagiac Minnow	102, wood, very nice	VG+	$688.88	1-1999

BRAND	MODEL	SERIES / MFG. CODE / DESCRIPTION	GRADE	PRICE	DATE
Heddon	Dowagiac Minnow	103 aluminum, wood	EX-	$1,675.00	9-2000
Heddon	Dowagiac Minnow	103, red 100 cup, vg+, papers, hung	Mint	$1,540.00	2-2000
Heddon	Dowagiac Minnow	103 wood, aluminum, papers	EX-	$850.90	1-2000
Heddon	Dowagiac Minnow	104, "On the metal," Down Bass box	EX-	$185.00	2-2001
Heddon	Dowagiac Minnow	105, wood, top badly faded, 4 side bold	VG	$861.00	11-2000
Heddon	Dowagiac Minnow	109A, white Down Bass box with vg- lure	VG-	$1,000.00	10-1999
Heddon	Dowagiac Minnow	109D, Down Bass box, crisp, avg lure	AVG/IB	$471.99	2-2000
Heddon	Dowagiac Minnow	109D, Up Bass box	EX	$180.00	10-2000
Heddon	Dowagiac Minnow	109L, Down Bass box, red border, tall box	EX-	$330.00	5-2000
Heddon	Dowagiac Minnow	109L, Up Bass box	EX	$128.00	5-2001
Heddon	Dowagiac Minnow	149P, Up Bass box, flipper, very faint	VG+	$170.00	12-2000
Heddon	Dowagiac Minnow	150, white, early, awful	Poor	$238.37	3-2000
Heddon	Dowagiac Minnow	150, wood, rough papers	VG	$712.00	3-2000
Heddon	Dowagiac Minnow	150, wood, very faded	AVG	$227.00	12-2000
Heddon	Dowagiac Minnow	150FG, wood, NOT MET	VG	$531.00	6-1999
Heddon	Dowagiac Minnow	151, wood, newest, super clean	EX+	$780.00	10-2000
Heddon	Dowagiac Minnow	152, white, wood, small corner chip	VG+	$711.51	6-1999
Heddon	Dowagiac Minnow	154, wood	VG+	$800.00	1-2000
Heddon	Dowagiac Minnow	154, wood	VG-	$535.00	5-1999
Heddon	Dowagiac Minnow	154, wood faded some but nice	VG+	$885.52	2-2000
Heddon	Dowagiac Minnow	154, wood, c.1905, hung	EX-	$1,576.51	7-1999
Heddon	Dowagiac Minnow	158, Down Bass box, one end flap missing	EX-	$26.00	4-1999
Heddon	Dowagiac Minnow	159BP, Up Bass box	VG-	$100.00	8-2000
Heddon	Dowagiac Minnow	159H, red scale, top only, tall box	VG+	$200.00	1-2001
Heddon	Dowagiac Minnow	159L, Up Bass box	AVG	$36.00	1-2002
Heddon	Dowagiac Muskellunge Minnow	700, large Down Bass box	EX	$375.00	2-2000
Heddon	Dowagiac Muskellunge Minnow	709R, Down Bass box, oversized		$250.00	2-2001
Heddon	Dowagiac Surface	200, Down Bass box, blue border	VG+	$1,257.00	2-2002
Heddon	Dowagiac Surface Minnow	210BM, Brush box	EX	$75.00	8-1999
Heddon	Fish Flesh	large size	VG+	$55.00	11-1999
Heddon	Fish Flesh Spook, River Runt	9109P	EX-	$27.50	4-2000
Heddon	Flaptail	7050RH, Brush box, large	VG+	$26.00	11-2000
Heddon	Game Fisher	5509D	VG+	$127.00	3-2001
Heddon	Game Fisher	5509D, Down Bass box	EX	$123.51	12-1999
Heddon	Game Fisher	5509M, Up Bass box	VG	$139.50	2-1999
Heddon	Game Fisher	Down Bass box, tall box	VG	$105.00	2-2001
Heddon	Killer	450, white, small notches, black & white picture, NOT MET	VG	$2,282.00	6-2001
Heddon	Killer	silver box, white & blue label, Patent 1902	VG	$4,050.00	9-2001
Heddon	Little Luny Frog	3409BB, Up Bass box	VG-	$57.00	8-2001
Heddon	Lucky 13	2502, Up Bass box	VG-	$32.51	4-1999
Heddon	Lucky 13	2509M, Down Bass box	EX	$70.00	5-2001
Heddon	Midget Digit	B110P, Brush box	EX-	$20.00	11-2000
Heddon	Midget Digit	B112, Brush box	VG-	$36.57	9-1999
Heddon	Minnow, S.O.S. Wounded	162, Up Bass box	EX+	$70.00	1-1999
Heddon	Minnow, S.O.S. Wounded	179M, Up Bass box, ex- dace, L-rig lure	AVG/IB	$93.00	2-2001
Heddon	Pork Rind	190NP, Banner box	EX	$22.00	2-2001
Heddon	Punkinseed	730BGL, Brush box	VG	$76.00	2-1999

BRAND	MODEL	SERIES / MFG. CODE / DESCRIPTION	GRADE	PRICE	DATE
Heddon	Punkinseed	730BGL, Brush box, "Improved" Punkinseed paper	EX-	$104.00	3-2002
Heddon	Punkinseed	740BGL, Brush box	AVG	$31.00	3-1999
Heddon	Punkinseed	740ROB	Mint	$162.50	1-1999
Heddon	Punkinseed	740ROB, Brush box	EX+	$281.00	12-2001
Heddon	Punkinseed	740SUN	VG	$36.00	1-1999
Heddon	Punkinseed	740SUN, Brush box	VG+	$67.00	4-2000
Heddon	Punkinseed	740XRY	VG	$59.00	1-1999
Heddon	Punkinseed	9630BGL, Banner box, 3 Runt boxes	EX to Fair	$51.00	5-1999
Heddon	Punkinseed, Tiny	stand up card for 6 Tinys, 3 included	NOC	$550.00	8-2000
Heddon	River Runt	9110RH, mint Runt box & pocket catalog	EX+	$22.49	4-1999
Heddon	River Runt	9119GW, Brush box	EX-	$63.00	3-2002
Heddon	River Runt	9409GW, Brush box	EX	$32.31	4-1999
Heddon	River Runt Spook	9119XRY, wall eye	EX-	$8.00	1-1999
Heddon	River Runt Spook	9330S	EX	$29.00	3-2000
Heddon	River Runt Spook	9402LUM, wall eye	VG+	$76.00	8-2001
Heddon	River Runt Spook	N9112, N9119M, No-Snag	EX-	$71.00	7-2002
Heddon	River Runt Spook	N9119L, with pocket catalog & intro paper	VG+	$46.00	4-1999
Heddon	River Runt Spook	W9119P, No-Snag, Brush box, GW	VG	$79.00	1-1999
Heddon	River Runt Spook	9439P, Brush box	EX	$42.00	4-1999
Heddon	Spoony Frog	large display box, NOT MET	EX	$2,025.00	3-1999
Heddon	Tadpolly	5009, intro box	VG-	$200.00	8-1999
Heddon	Tadpolly	5009L, Down Bass box, 1902 patent	VG	$113.50	8-1999
Heddon	Vamp	7500S, Down Bass box	EX	$126.55	11-1999
Heddon	Vamp	7509D, Down Bass box, nice	EX-	$178.51	5-1999
Heddon	Vamp	7509D, Down Bass box, ugly, big tear on top	AVG	$46.00	5-2001
Heddon	Vamp	7509L, Down Bass box	EX-	$128.49	7-1999
Heddon	Vamp	7509M, Up Bass box	EX-	$66.55	12-1999
Heddon	Vamp	Down Bass box, not numbered	EX-	$69.00	5-2001
Heddon	Vamp, Giant Jointed	7359L	EX-	$91.00	3-2001
Heddon	Vamp, Jointed	7300S, Banner box	EX	$21.00	1-1999
Heddon	Vamp, Jointed	7309M, Down Bass box	EX	$135.75	4-1999
Heddon	Vamp, Jointed	7309N, Brush box	VG	$78.00	1-1999
Heddon	Vamp, Musky	Down Bass box, no stamp, 8¾"x3" & 1¾"	EX-	$2,183.00	6-2002
Heddon	Various	1 Vamp, 7502LUMR; 1 Super Dowagiac, 9109P; 1 Dowagiac Spook, 9332XS; 2 Up Bass boxes, 1 Brush box	AVG	$56.01	8-1999
Heddon	Walton Feather Tail	#42, Down Bass box	EX	$86.00	8-1999
Heddon	Wee Willy	589XPLB, Brush box, small BX-6 Wee Willy	EX	$200.00	9-2001
Heddon	Wiggle King	intro	VG	$455.00	7-2000
Heddon	Wiggle King	intro box	EX	$621.00	3-2002
Heddon	Wiggler, Baby Crab	1902, Down Bass box	VG	$151.99	8-1999
Heddon	Wiggler, Baby Crab	1902, Down Bass box	VG-	$51.00	5-2000
Heddon	Wiggler, Baby Crab	1951, rainbow	EX	$100.99	4-1999
Heddon	Wiggler, Crab	1809B, Down Bass box, nice	EX	$340.00	7-2000
Heddon	Wiggler, Crab	1809C, Down Bass box, papers	VG+	$86.00	8-2000
Heddon	Wiggler, Crab	1902	VG	$90.00	5-2000

BRAND	MODEL	SERIES / MFG. CODE / DESCRIPTION	GRADE	PRICE	DATE
Heddon	Wiggler, Crab	Down Bass box, unmarked	VG+	$78.00	2-2001
Heddon	Wiggler, Near Surface	1705, Down Bass box, papers	VG	$152.50	7-1999
Heddon	Wiggler, Surface	1602, tall Down Bass box	VG	$167.50	3-1999
Heddon	Wilder-Dilg	#33, red letters on white box, trout size	EX	$102.51	8-1999
Heddon	Wilder-Dilg	Irvin Cobb picture box	EX-	$432.00	8-2002
Heddon	Wounded Spook	9140XRYF, 2PCCB	G	$9.99	12-1998
Holzwarth	Expert	wood, long paper label	EX-	$2,550.00	10-2000
Hurd	Supercaster	leather case	VG	$78.77	4-1999
Hurd	Supercaster reel	tube-shaped	EX	$100.00	4-1999
Immell	Chippewa	P-66, fancy, green back, NOT MET	EX	$1,402.00	9-2002
Jamison	Wiggler, Fly Rod	3"x1", one end torn	VG	$157.00	3-2001
Johnson	Automatic Striker	rough edges, picture okay	VG-	$261.00	1-2001
Kalamazoo	Bal Cli	20, reel	EX	$12.00	4-1999
Keeling		unmarked, common style	VG	$77.00	2-2000
Keeling	Tom Thumb	red on white	EX-	$178.50	8-1999
L&S	Bassmaster	12-pack, 2PCCB, gold & black	EX-	$46.00	5-2001
Meek		wood box, $1800.00 NOT MET	VG+	$1,252.97	5-1999
Millsite	Sinker	214, rainbow, 2PCCB	VG	$9.95	3-1999
Mixed	Various	9 different, nice, picture boxes	EX	$104.00	12-1998
Moonlight	Unmarked	2905	EX	$308.00	11-2000
Nieboer Flies		2"x2" picture box	VG-	$108.50	10-1999
North Channel		3-hook, wrong lure, Shakespeare?, box okay	AVG	$602.00	7-2000
Paw Paw		4W, orange & white	VG	$49.00	3-2001
Pflueger	Canoe	blue border, no code numbers	EX-	$32.00	2-2002
Pflueger	Four Brothers Neverfail	3-hook, maroon, size 3"	AVG	$106.50	1-2000
Pflueger	Four Brothers Neverfail	5-hook, maroon, size 3⅝"	EX-	$350.00	1-2000
Pflueger	Four Brothers Neverfail	3105, natural frog scale, 5-hook, 3⅝", with paper	VG+	$152.50	11-1999
Pflueger	Four Brothers Neverfail	3169, large lettering, rare	VG	$350.00	10-1999
Pflueger	Four Brothers Neverfail	3181	EX	$700.00	10-1999
Pflueger	Four Brothers Neverfail	3184, maroon target box	EX-	$820.00	10-1999
Pflueger	Four Brothers Neverfail	maroon, for 5-hook, unmarked	VG	$500.00	10-1999
Pflueger	Four Brothers Neverfail	maroon, unmarked, large lettering, rare	EX-	$600.00	10-1999
Pflueger	Four Brothers Neverfail	maroon, unmarked, "target"	EX-	$775.00	10-1999
Pflueger	Four Brothers Neverfail	maroon	EX-	$350.00	1-2000
Pflueger	Globe	maroon target logo	EX	$725.00	8-2001
Pflueger	Live Wire	7606, natural perch, 3-hook	EX-	$56.00	1-2000
Pflueger	Minnow, Neverfail Wood	wood box for 3-hook, paper label, unmarked	VG+	$920.00	10-1999
Pflueger	Minnow, Sterling Wood	wood box, partial label	Rough	$200.00	10-1999
Pflueger	Minnow, Surprise	3901, golden shiner, canoe	VG	$67.00	8-1999
Pflueger	Monarch	3181, wood box for 3-hook	EX-	$1,200.00	10-1999
Pflueger	Monarch	wood, rail damage, NOT MET	VG+	$670.00	1-2000
Pflueger	Monarch, Underwater	2171, wood box for 5-hook	EX	$1,800.00	10-1999
Pflueger	Musky Tandem Spin	maroon box, lure & card	EX-	$78.00	6-1999
Pflueger	Neverfail	3196, blue border, canoe	EX-	$100.95	5-1999
Pflueger	Neverfail	maroon target, unmarked, NOT MET	VG+	$350.00	1-2000
Pflueger	Pal-O-Mine	5004, canoe, nice paper	EX	$23.00	3-2002
Pflueger	Surprise	3970LUM, luminous, blue canoe, Surprise paper	VG+	$391.00	8-2000

BRAND	MODEL	SERIES / MFG. CODE / DESCRIPTION	GRADE	PRICE	DATE
Rhodes	Frog	wood faded, repaired	AVG	$850.00	5-2000
Rush, J.K.	Rush Tango	$50.00 prize, nice box & lure	G/IB	$75.00	3-2001
Shakespeare		54FBJ, grey box, poor label, NOT MET	VG	$120.00	1-2000
Shakespeare		#1 type, wood	EX	$650.00	10-1999
Shakespeare		#2 type, wood, faded, cleaned	VG	$350.00	10-1999
Shakespeare		#3 type, wood	EX-	$500.00	10-1999
Shakespeare		1632, 5-hook, picture, c.1905	VG	$3,400.00	10-1999
Shakespeare	Dalton Special	546, checkerboard	EX-	$10.00	2-2001
Shakespeare	Floater	172, brown & white, 2-hook, white intro picture box	EX	$3,000.00	6-2001
Shakespeare	Frog, Rhodes	wood, top faded	VG	$1,426.00	3-2002
Shakespeare	Hydroplane	709GW label	EX-	$220.00	10-1999
Shakespeare	Kazoo	590FG, fancy, green scale	VG+	$38.00	4-2000
Shakespeare	Minnow, Kazoo Wooden	avg lure	EX-	$2,500.00	10-1999
Shakespeare	Minnow, Wooden Sinker	03FG, grey	VG+	$227.50	1-2000
Shakespeare	Minnow, Wooden Sinker	03YP, grey with oval in yellow w fish	EX	$273.00	5-2001
Shakespeare	Minnow, Wooden Sinker	44, wood, end label, stamped top, c.1910	EX-	$1,000.00	6-2001
Shakespeare	Musky, Revolution	black, picture box, 6½", top only	VG-	$1,900.00	10-1999
Shakespeare	Spinner	yellow spinner, wood	VG	$300.00	2-2001
Shakespeare	Sure Lure	silver & black, intro picture box	VG	$3,500.00	8-2001
Shakespeare	Whirlwind	intro box, ex- lure	VG	$2,500.00	10-1999
Shur-Strike	Shur-Strike	0-5, yellow & red, nice	EX	$57.00	8-2001
Shur-Strike	Shur-Strike	3563G1, green & white	EX	$21.00	6-2000
Shur-Strike	Shur-Strike	3563X2, red & blue, nice	EX-	$26.25	3-1999
Shur-Strike	Shur-Strike	B2, red fish, yellow & green	EX	$52.00	5-2001
Shur-Strike	Shur-Strike	BBO-6, green & white	EX	$27.00	2-2000
Shur-Strike	Shur-Strike	BO-0, green	EX-	$23.00	4-2001
Shur-Strike	Shur-Strike	FHR-5, blue & orange	EX	$35.00	1-2001
Shur-Strike	Shur-Strike	HRT-O, blue & red	VG-	$12.30	10-1999
Shur-Strike	Shur-Strike	P6, red & yellow box & red head lure, NRA	EX	$100.18	12-1999
Shur-Strike	Shur-Strike	RR14, yellow & red, stamp, NRA	AVG	$68.89	1-2000
South Bend	Babe-Oreno	972, 12-pack, 2PCCB x12 in large 2PCCB, no lures	EX	$380.00	10-1999
South Bend	Bass-Oreno	2090R, distributed by Shakespeare	EX	$331.00	4-2000
South Bend	Callmac Bass Bug	#7 Chadwick's	AVG	$91.00	11-2000
South Bend	Callmac Bug	unusual box with flyfish papers	EX	$304.75	4-1999
South Bend	Fish-Oreno	guarantee with paper	EX	$71.00	11-2000
South Bend	Gulf-Oreno	982RHS, old style, 2PCCB	EX	$382.77	9-1999
South Bend	Minnow Surface	920RH, intro box	EX-	$265.00	1-1999
South Bend	Mouse-Oreno	949GM	EX	$51.00	3-2002
South Bend	Plunk-Oreno	929RH, script	EX-	$25.00	4-2002
South Bend	South Bend Minnow	903RSF, 3-hook	EX-	$79.00	3-2000
South Bend	Truck-Oreno	936, very faint, plain yellow box	VG-	$153.50	8-1999
Supplee-Biddle Congress		crackleback lure by Pflueger, 5-hook, vg box	EX/IB	$1,407.00	12-1999
Weber	Spiderweb	2 windows, trout, nice	EX	$26.00	5-2001
Winchester	Minnow	with papers, little rough	G	$437.00	1-1999
Woods	Deep-R-Doodle	803	EX	$5.50	1-1999
Wright & McGill	Crab, Flapper	#10, NOT MET	VG	$51.00	8-1999
Wright & McGill	Minnow, Wiggling	blue box R.M. No.3, white paper	EX-	$150.00	7-2000

BRAND	PUBLICATION YEAR	DESCRIPTION	GRADE	PRICE	DATE
Abbey & Imbrie	1897	100+ pages	VG-	$330.00	3-1999
Abbey & Imbrie	1908	supplement to 1907	VG+	$152.00	5-2001
Abbey & Imbrie	1910	super fisherman cover	EX-	$157.00	5-2001
Abbey & Imbrie	1914	cover rough	VG	$127.00	5-2001
Abbey & Imbrie	1920	160 pages, 6"x9"	EX-	$120.50	10-1999
Abbey & Imbrie	1929	binding torn	G	$75.00	10-1999
Abbey & Imbrie	1929	red cover	EX-	$77.00	5-2001
Abbott, W.W.	1884	Philadelphia, 40 pages	EX	$271.52	8-1999
Abercrombie & Fitch	1910	456 pages	G	$235.00	10-1999
Abercrombie & Fitch	1910	456 pages	VG+	$125.00	3-2001
Abercrombie & Fitch	1934	64 pages	VG	$60.07	1-1999
Abu		656754666869, last 4 in Swedish	EX	$178.50	6-1999
Action Rod	1962	13 pages	EX	$16.00	7-2000
Airex	1940s?	in envelope	NIE	$78.00	5-1999
AL&W	1920s	63 pages	VG-	$214.73	9-1999
AL&W	1933	115 pages, spring	EX-	$93.00	3-2001
Allcock	1921	165 pages, hardbound	EX	$305.00	9-2001
Bristol	1934	32 pages	Mint	$45.51	12-1999
Camp outfits & fishing tackle	1916	196 pages, color, Heddon, NOT MET	EX	$128.00	9-2000
CCBC	1919		EX	$750.00	12-2001
CCBC	1931	48 pages, NOT MET	Mint	$316.00	5-2001
CCBC	1931	mailer & order form	EXIE	$622.00	10-2000
CCBC	1936	31 pages	EX	$306.99	7-1999
CCBC	1936	31 pages	EX-	$460.71	6-1999
CCBC	1936	31 pages	VG	$204.00	12-2001
CCBC	1936	nice	EX	$280.00	11-1999
CCBC	1938	35 pages	Mint	$370.00	5-2001
CCBC	1938		EX	$280.88	12-1999
CCBC	1938	envelope, order form, return envelope	NIE	$338.00	1-2002
CCBC	1939	35 pages	EX-	$350.00	4-2001
CCBC	1940	picture, letter envelope only	EX	$71.00	6-1999
CCBC	1940	with mailing envelope	Mint	$310.00	1-2000
CCBC	1942	35 pages	EX	$227.00	5-2001
CCBC	1942	35 pages, NOT MET	EX	$198.00	4-2000
CCBC	1942		Rough	$31.00	5-2000
CCBC	1945	NOT MET	EX	$300.00	8-1999
CCBC	1949	1949 sticker over 1948	EX	$152.00	10-2000
CCBC	1950	24 pages	EX	$202.50	11-1999
CCBC	1950		VG	$350.00	5-1999
CCBC	1950	some water on pages	VG	$140.36	5-1999
CCBC	1951	24 pages	Mint	$338.00	3-2002
CCBC	1951	NOT MET	EX+	$200.00	9-1999
CCBC	1951	with price sheet	EX+	$300.00	3-1999

BRAND	MODEL	DESCRIPTION	GRADE	PRICE	DATE
CCBC	1952 – 1953	31 pages	EX	$297.50	4-1999
Chubb	1909	122 pages	Mint	$361.00	11-2000
Cummings	1937	32 pages	EX	$106.00	5-2001
Eppinger	1934	beautiful flyer	EX+	$92.00	1-2000
Fin Nor	1950s	8 pages	EX	$51.63	3-1999
Frost, H.J.	1910	14 pages	Mint	$41.00	4-1999
Garcia	1959		VG	$18.75	6-1999
Garcia	1963	annual	EX	$11.55	2-1999
Garcia	1964	annual	EX	$57.06	2-1999
Garcia	1972	annual	EX	$28.00	11-2000
Garcia	c.1965	not the annual	VG-	$31.00	5-1999
Hardy	1934	445 pages	EX	$66.00	3-2001
Heddon	1916	#14, spine shot, cover creased, ugly	AVG	$1075.00	2-2002
Heddon	1920 – 1921	#19, poor cover	EX-	$535.00	7-2002
Heddon	1922	NOT MET	VG	$162.50	1-2000
Heddon	1924		EX-	$650.00	11-2000
Heddon	1924	original mailer	NIE	$650.00	2-2001
Heddon	1924	with mailer	EX	$950.00	10-1999
Heddon	1926	23 pages, "trade" catalog	EX	$873.00	12-2000
Heddon	1926	24 bids, NOT MET	EX-	$454.12	3-1999
Heddon	1926		EX	$850.00	10-1999
Heddon	1926	color plates, 5 inserts, super	EX-	$461.00	3-2001
Heddon	1926	poster catalog, corner missing	VG	$267.00	6-1999
Heddon	1928		EX	$339.00	10-2001
Heddon	1928	all inserts	Mint	$350.00	2-2001
Heddon	1930		EX	$400.00	10-1999
Heddon	1931	36 pages	EX	$372.01	4-1999
Heddon	1931		EX	$357.00	5-2001
Heddon	1932	31 pages	EX	$500.00	12-2000
Heddon	1932	rough cover, EX inside	VG	$275.00	10-1999
Heddon	1933		EX+	$237.00	9-2001
Heddon	1934	31 pages	EX	$230.00	3-2002
Heddon	1934	31 pages	VG	$276.89	4-1999
Heddon	1934	31 pages, dealer catalog	EX	$202.00	10-2001
Heddon	1934	31 pages, NOT MET	VG+	$250.01	5-1999
Heddon	1935		VG+	$255.50	1-2000
Heddon	1936	37 pages	EX	$270.00	7-1999
Heddon	1936		EX	$340.00	10-1999
Heddon	1936	mailer, extra mail-ins	NIE	$356.00	5-2001
Heddon	1937	40 pages, large size	EX	$203.50	4-1999
Heddon	1937		EX	$250.00	2-2001
Heddon	1937		EX	$300.00	10-1999
Heddon	1938	40 pages	EX	$216.00	5-2000
Heddon	1938	42 pages	EX	$202.00	3-2001
Heddon	1939		Mint	$331.35	11-1999
Heddon	1939		VG+	$300.00	3-1999
Heddon	1941		Mint	$204.00	1-2001

BRAND	MODEL	DESCRIPTION	GRADE	PRICE	DATE
Heddon	1941		EX-	$275.00	3-1999
Heddon	1941		Mint	$610.00	3-2001
Heddon	1942 – 1943	dealers edition	EX-	$333.78	1-1999
Heddon	1948	vest pocket	EX	$41.00	2-1999
Heddon	1949	80 pages	Mint	$153.00	5-2001
Heddon	1951	30 pages	EX	$131.38	3-2000
Heddon	1951	79 pages	EX	$70.99	6-1999
Heddon	1952	31 pages, large	VG	$50.66	4-1999
Heddon	1952		VG	$25.00	10-1999
Heddon	1952	small size	EX-	$56.00	4-1999
Heddon	1952	deluxe, trout picture, envelope	NIE	$152.00	5-1999
Heddon	1953	small size	EX	$36.00	5-1999
Heddon	1953	deluxe, 76 pages	EX	$43.95	3-1999
Heddon	1954	deluxe	EX	$102.51	2-1999
Heddon	1958	deluxe, NOT MET	Mint	$87.00	5-2001
Heddon	1959	31 pages	EX-	$42.19	5-1999
Heddon	1960		EX	$39.25	2-1999
Heddon	1960	nice	EX	$51.00	12-1998
Heddon	1962	31 pages	EX	$32.01	7-1999
Heddon	1963	55 pages	EX	$45.00	4-1999
Heddon	1964	63 pages	Mint	$57.60	11-1999
Heddon	1964	63 pages, dealer trade copy	EX	$73.00	1-1999
Heddon	1964		VG+	$43.00	4-1999
Heddon	1965	63 pages	VG	$91.00	6-1999
Heddon	1965, 1970	2 different	VG	$35.75	4-1999
Heddon	1966	63 pages	EX	$36.00	7-1999
Heddon	1966		EX	$37.00	9-2002
Heddon	1968	68 pages	EX-	$40.00	2-2000
Heddon	1968		EX	$37.00	9-2002
Heddon	1969		EX	$38.00	7-2000
Heddon	1970	63 pages	VG	$41.00	6-1999
Heddon	1985		EX	$15.50	4-1999
Helin	1945		EX	$32.00	5-2001
Helin	1952	48 pages	EX	$17.00	12-1998
Helin	1962		EX	$26.00	1-1999
Horton	c.1919	Bristol rods & Meek reels, great cover	EX-	$255.00	8-1999
Jamison	c.1923	27 pages	EX	$190.00	10-1999
Johnson	1885	16 pages, Flying Helgramite ad	VG+	$787.75	4-1999
Kiffe	1925	72 pages	EX	$62.00	5-2001
Kiffe, H.H.	1895	167 pages	EX	$177.50	3-1999
Lazy Ike	1970s	color charts, Sail Shark & more	Mint	$12.00	8-2001
Marshall Field & Company	1917	144 pages	EX	$145.00	10-1999
Mills	1909	pamphlet, advice & rods only	EX-	$75.00	3-1999
Mills & Sons	1925	80 pages	EX-	$77.00	6-1999
Mills & Sons	1928	160+ pages	EX-	$87.00	3-1999
Mills & Sons	1929	154 pages	EX	$156.00	1-1999

BRAND	MODEL	DESCRIPTION	GRADE	PRICE	DATE
Mills & Sons	1929	156 pages	EX	$70.00	10-1999
Mills & Sons	1931	#131	EX	$48.25	1-2000
Mills & Sons	1933	144 pages	VG	$65.00	4-1999
Mills & Sons	1934	144 pages	EX-	$75.00	10-1999
Mills & Sons	1934		EX	$57.00	9-1999
Mills & Sons	1940	NOT MET	EX	$41.25	6-1999
Moonlight	1923	#11, 16 pages, NOT MET	EX-	$328.00	11-1999
Ocean City	1941	#41A	EX-	$26.00	5-1999
Oliver's	1989	32690	EX	$38.89	3-1999
Orvis	1957	64 pages	EX	$33.00	1-1999
Orvis	1960		EX	$47.00	2-1999
P&K	1946	32 pages	EX	$33.00	7-2000
Payne	1940s	mint with envelope	Mint	$170.00	3-1999
Peck		#46, nice	EX	$102.00	12-1998
Pflueger	1916	394 pages	VG	$660.00	8-2000
Pflueger	1919	112 pages, "Tips on Tackle"	EX	$261.00	8-2000
Pflueger	1926	133 pages	VG-	$102.50	4-1999
Pflueger	1926	#146	EX	$148.00	11-2000
Pflueger	1927	#247	EX	$46.99	7-1999
Pflueger	1928	128 pages	EX-	$113.00	9-2000
Pflueger	1928	128 pages	EX-	$134.00	5-2000
Pflueger	1928	128 pages, color	Mint	$202.50	4-1999
Pflueger	1928	#148, 125 pages	EX	$85.00	8-2002
Pflueger	1928	#148, 130 pages, NOT MET	EX-	$78.00	1-2000
Pflueger	1928	#148, NOT MET	EX-	$102.50	8-1999
Pflueger	1929	152 pages, NOT MET	VG	$55.25	5-1999
Pflueger	1929	280 pages, distributors catalog, nice	EX	$280.00	3-2000
Pflueger	1929	#149, 152 pages	EX	$225.00	10-1999
Pflueger	1931		EX	$105.00	5-2001
Pflueger	1931		EX-	$128.50	3-1999
Pflueger	1931	#151	EX	$125.00	1-1999
Pflueger	1931	#151	EX	$224.00	1-1999
Pflueger	1934	128 pages	EX	$127.00	7-2000
Pflueger	1934	154 pages	EX	$90.50	12-1999
Pflueger	1934		EX	$132.00	5-2001
Pflueger	1934	dealer, extra price lists, letter, nice	EX+	$128.50	3-1999
Pflueger	1935	128 pages	EX	$67.00	12-1999
Pflueger	1935	No. (1) 55, cover & binding torn	G	$40.00	10-1999
Pflueger	1936	130 pages, 5"x8"	EX	$132.50	3-1999
Pflueger	1936		EX	$162.00	1-1999
Pflueger	1937	#157, 128 pages	EX	$100.00	10-1999
Pflueger	1938	125 pages	EX	$76.00	4-1999
Pflueger	1938	128 pages	EX	$83.33	4-1999
Pflueger	1938	130 pages	EX	$201.00	1-2000
Pflueger	1938			$75.00	3-1999
Pflueger	1938		EX	$125.00	3-1999
Pflueger	1938	#158	EX	$65.00	12-1999

BRAND	MODEL	DESCRIPTION	GRADE	PRICE	DATE
Pflueger	1940	128 pages	EX	$167.50	4-1999
Pflueger	1940	#160	VG+	$56.00	5-1999
Pflueger	1940	nice	NM	$107.50	3-1999
Pflueger	1943	#161	EX-	$80.00	10-1999
Pflueger	1952	#88 trade, NOT MET	EX-	$44.75	6-1999
Pflueger	1959	#196, 49 pages	EX	$48.00	4-1999
Philipson Rod	1960s	12 pages	Mint	$75.00	3-2000
Richardson	1936	16 page foldout, color	EX	$12.00	3-1999
Schoverling	1911	144 pages	EX	$99.99	9-1999
Schoverling, Daly	1925	161 pages, great pictures	EX	$291.00	4-2000
Schoverling, Daly, Gales	c.1900	158 pages, lures, reels	EX-	$262.00	2-1999
Shakespeare	1912	"Art of Baitcasting"	VG	$104.56	2-1999
Shakespeare	1916	#20, 288 pages, contains Heddon & others	EX	$750.00	12-2001
Shakespeare	1919	112 pages, NOT MET	EX-	$305.00	11-1999
Shakespeare	1924	30 pages	EX	$290.00	10-1999
Shakespeare	1925	39 pages, 8 color	EX-	$355.00	2-2000
Shakespeare	1925		EX+	$264.89	12-1999
Shakespeare	1926	88 pages	EX	$430.51	1-2000
Shakespeare	1926	88 pages, NOT MET	VG+	$103.50	8-1999
Shakespeare	1926	88 pages, rough spine	VG	$157.00	4-2000
Shakespeare	1937	100 pages	EX	$105.00	7-2000
Shakespeare	1940	92 pages	EX	$44.09	4-1999
Shakespeare	1941		Mint	$87.50	3-1999
Shakespeare	1949	36 pages	EX	$43.00	4-2001
Shakespeare	1949		EX-	$18.00	11-1999
Shakespeare	1950		EX	$41.50	2-1999
Shakespeare	1951	44 pages	EX	$36.58	5-1999
Shakespeare	1951		EX-	$16.00	11-1999
Shakespeare	1952		EX	$24.76	4-1999
Shakespeare	1952		EX	$29.00	1-2000
Shakespeare	1970	with mail envelope	EX	$22.00	4-1999
Silaflex	1956	16 pages	EX	$21.50	11-1999
Skinner	c.1890s	24 pages	EX-	$158.00	1-1999
Skinner	c.1920s	nice, with illustrations	VG	$66.00	5-1999
South Bend	193?	136 pages	EX	$70.00	10-1999
South Bend	1848	52 pages	EX	$36.00	1-1999
South Bend	1920	NOT MET	EX	$493.00	9-2000
South Bend	1922	40 pages, NOT MET	EX	$144.52	11-1999
South Bend	1922	40 pages, NOT MET	EX	$272.00	10-2002
South Bend	1922	flyrod lures	EX	$354.00	6-1999
South Bend	1922	NOT MET	EX+	$227.50	6-1999
South Bend	1922 – 1923	73 pages, trade catalog, cover torn	EX-	$425.00	10-1999
South Bend	1924	nice envelope	NIE	$415.00	10-2000
South Bend	1925		EX	$173.49	5-1999
South Bend	1926	116 pages, NOT MET	VG+	$102.50	1-2000
South Bend	1926		VG+	$59.99	12-1999

BRAND	MODEL	DESCRIPTION	GRADE	PRICE	DATE
South Bend	1930	96 pages	EX	$191.94	11-1999
South Bend	1931	79 pages	EX-	$100.00	10-1999
South Bend	1931	79 pages, "What & When"	NIE	$180.27	3-1999
South Bend	1932	81 pages, boy & pole	VG	$122.50	5-1999
South Bend	1932	83 pages	VG	$52.00	1-2000
South Bend	1932	#83, 88 pages, boy & muskies	EX	$204.50	1-2000
South Bend	1932	few mouse chews	VG	$32.50	9-1999
South Bend	1932	full line	EX-	$63.00	5-2000
South Bend	1932	small	EX	$95.00	3-1999
South Bend	1933		EX-	$129.25	1-2000
South Bend	1934	92 pages	EX	$49.99	10-1999
South Bend	1934	92 pages	VG+	$43.00	8-2001
South Bend	1934		EX	$60.00	3-1999
South Bend	1934		EX-	$56.00	5-1999
South Bend	1935	full line	EX	$51.00	5-2000
South Bend	1936	112 pages, "Fish & Feel Fit"	VG	$36.32	7-1999
South Bend	1936	114 pages, "Fish & Feel Fit"	EX	$65.00	6-1999
South Bend	1937	112 pages	EX	$95.00	10-1999
South Bend	1937	full line	EX	$52.00	5-2000
South Bend	1937 – 1941	poor covers	G	$32.00	2-1999
South Bend	1939	128 pages	EX	$46.00	12-1998
South Bend	1939	128 pages	VG	$51.00	4-1999
South Bend	1939	128 pages, "Fish & Feel Fit"	EX	$41.99	7-1999
South Bend	1939		EX	$60.00	3-1999
South Bend	1939	full line	EX-	$31.00	5-2000
South Bend	1940s	48 pages	EX-	$35.00	10-1999
South Bend	1941	136 pages	EX	$56.00	5-1999
South Bend	1941	full line	EX	$47.00	5-2000
South Bend	1941	super graphics, envelope	NIE	$72.00	5-2001
South Bend	1942		EX	$55.00	1-1999
South Bend	1942	poor cover, rest ex		$37.50	2-1999
South Bend	1945	46 pages	EX	$66.00	1-1999
South Bend	1947	44 pages	EX+	$51.00	5-1999
South Bend	1947		EX-	$39.00	4-1999
South Bend	1948	48 pages, boys & bluegills	EX-	$51.00	5-1999
South Bend	1949	72 pages	EX	$45.00	10-1999
South Bend	1949		EX	$59.00	1-1999
South Bend	1949		EX	$78.00	2-1999
South Bend	1950	89 pages, trout	EX	$50.00	6-1999
South Bend	1951	104 pages	EX	$28.00	4-1999
South Bend	1952	112 pages	EX	$51.51	5-1999
South Bend	1953	full line	EX	$36.00	5-2000
South Bend	1959		EX-	$42.51	6-1999
South Bend	1970	72 pages	EX	$42.50	1-1999
V&A	1925	154 pages	EX	$100.00	3-1999
VL&A	1927		EX	$61.00	2-2000
VL&A	1932		EX	$100.00	3-1999

BRAND	MODEL	DESCRIPTION	GRADE	PRICE	DATE
Vom Hofe, Ed	1931	mailing envelope	Mint	$300.00	11-1999
Vom Hofe, Ed	1936	173 pages		$175.00	3-1999
Vom Hofe, Ed	1941		EX+	$160.00	10-1999
Weber	1935	80 pages	G	$36.00	1-1999
Weber	1938	96 pages	VG	$46.00	11-1999
Weber	1939		EX	$58.00	5-2001
Winchester	1924		VG	$152.50	8-1999
Winchester	1924	nice cover, NOT MET	VG+	$153.50	2-1999
Winchester	c.1920s	31 pages, pocket size	EX-	$77.99	4-1999
Wright & McGill	1938	74 pages	EX-	$200.00	3-1999

LICENSES

BRAND	MODEL	DESCRIPTION	GRADE	PRICE	DATE
AR	1938	papers	VG	$52.83	6-1999
AR	1938 non-resident	pin back with papers	EX-	$165.05	5-1999
AR	1939 non-resident	badge	VG	$215.00	2-1999
CA	1934	pin back, NOT MET	EX	$66.00	5-1999
CA	1934		EX	$77.00	11-2000
CA	1934		EX	$78.51	1-2000
CA	1934		EX	$86.15	9-1999
CA	1934		EX	$87.00	7-2000
CA	1941	pin	EX	$8.50	5-1999
CT	1926		EX	$132.00	4-2000
CT	1933	pin back	EX	$63.26	6-1999
CT	1943	button	EX	$61.43	4-1999
DE	1932 non-resident	pin	VG	$212.50	4-1999
DE	1932 non-resident		EX-	$504.00	7-2000
DE	1934 non-resident		EX	$392.91	8-1999
DE	1940	2½"	EX	$128.50	2-1999
FL	1927 – 1928	button, light corrosion on back, some stains	VG+	$735.00	2-2002
HI	1948 – 1949	Oahu County, 250 pin back	EX	$481.00	6-2002
ID	1909	paper	VG	$62.00	4-1999
MA	1932	pin back, problems	AVG	$47.99	4-1999
MI	1920 non-resident	paper only, ragged, no pin	AVG	$76.00	4-1999
MI	1929	trout, ugly	VG-	$100.99	9-1999
MI	1930 non-resident	White & Hoag Co., with papers	EX	$261.00	7-2000
MI	1931 non-resident	crackling under	VG	$202.49	9-1999
MI	1931 non-resident	non-resident badge	EX	$203.50	2-1999
MI	1931 non-resident	NOT MET	EX	$189.38	5-1999
MI	1931 non-resident	with paper	Mint	$300.00	5-1999
MI	1931 non-resident		EX	$214.50	9-1999
MI	1932 non-resident	pin back	EX	$257.75	6-1999
MI	1932 non-resident	with paper	EX	$227.00	5-2000
MI	1932 non-resident	with paper	Mint	$300.00	5-1999

BRAND	MODEL	DESCRIPTION	GRADE	PRICE	DATE
MI	1932 non-resident		EX	$227.50	7-1999
MI	1932	trout, with papers	EX	$164.01	9-1999
MI	1932	NOT MET	EX	$137.75	6-1999
MI	1930 – 1932 non-resident	all 3 buttons, with papers	EX+	$695.00	3-2000
MN	1927 non-resident	badge	EX	$148.50	2-1999
MN	1927 non-resident	NOT MET	EX	$100.77	3-1999
MN	1927 non-resident	NOT MET	EX-	$100.00	6-1999
MS	1937	hunting, Hinds County, NOT MET	Mint	$345.00	7-1999
MS	1938	hunting badge	EX-	$257.55	5-1999
MS	1942	family	EX	$455.00	6-1999
NC	1935 – 1936		EX-	$256.00	3-1999
NC	1937 resident	fish-shaped pin	EX	$431.00	1-1999
NC	1937 – 1938	hunting & fishing, brass badge, nice	EX	$300.00	7-1999
NC	1939	metal, curved pin	EX-	$126.00	7-1999
NC	1939	scratch on badge	VG	$163.50	3-1999
NH	1958 non-resident	rectangular metal case	EX	$31.00	4-1999
NY	1912	minnow net, aluminum	EX	$73.35	1-2000
NY	1930	hunting, fishing, trapping	EX	$18.50	8-1999
NY	1930 non-resident	pin back	EX	$229.49	6-1999
NY	1931 non-resident	pin back	EX-	$75.00	6-1999
NY	1932	fishing, hunting, trapping, button	EX	$20.50	4-1999
NY	1932	fishing, hunting	EX	$23.49	2-2000
NY	1932 non-resident		EX	$92.99	2-2000
NY	1933	fishing, hunting, trapping, pin	EX	$28.00	5-1999
NY	1935	family fishing, hunting, trapping, correct spelling	EX	$208.07	6-1999
NY	1938	fishing, hunting, trapping, button	EX	$16.05	4-1999
NY	1939 non-resident	pin	EX	$182.49	5-1999
NY	1940 non-resident	button	EX	$127.50	3-2000
OH	1940	copper pin back	EX	$11.05	5-1999
OH	1943	copper		$10.50	5-1999
Ontario	1915	canvas	VG-	$36.50	5-1999
PA	1922	sheet of paper	EX-	$610.00	8-2002
PA	1923	button, NOT MET	EX-	$280.00	4-1999
PA	1923	pin	EX	$152.66	5-1999
PA	1923 – 1959	40 different, 1 warden badge, few modern	VG- to EX	$2300.00	9-1999
PA	1924	pin badge	EX-	$177.50	5-1999
PA	1925		Mint	$255.00	3-2001
PA	1925		EX	$178.50	3-1999
PA	1925		VG	$71.00	7-1999
PA	1926	pin back	EX	$305.00	5-1999
PA	1926	pin back	VG	$76.00	6-1999
PA	1927		VG+	$28.77	11-1999
PA	1927 non-resident		EX	$350.00	7-1999
PA	1928		VG+	$41.13	7-1999
PA	1929	button	EX	$104.50	4-1999
PA	1929	button with paper	EX	$125.25	8-1999
PA	1929 non-resident	NOT MET	EX	$61.00	7-1999

BRAND	MODEL	DESCRIPTION	GRADE	PRICE	DATE
PA	1930	button	EX-	$19.50	5-1999
PA	1931 non-resident	papers	EX	$307.00	8-2000
PA	1934		EX	$64.07	2-2000
PA	1935	pin back	VG+	$26.00	6-1999
PA	1937 non-resident	with papers	EX	$283.75	6-1999
PA	1937		Mint	$61.00	3-2000
PA	1938 non-resident	3 day, NOT MET	EX	$310.00	7-2000
PA	1939 non-resident	3 day	EX	$200.00	7-2000
PA	1939	pin	EX	$20.00	4-1999
PA	1939 – 1947	9 different	EX-	$151.01	2-1999
PA	1940	resident	EX	$43.50	2-1999
PA	1940	unissued	EX	$30.00	7-1999
PA	1941 non-resident	3 day	EX	$142.00	7-2000
PA	1945 non-resident		EX	$52.00	8-2000
PA	1946 non-resident	pin	EX	$90.00	5-1999
PA	1948 non-resident	non-resident	EX	$48.00	3-1999
PA	1950	button	Mint	$29.16	5-1999
PA	1950		EX	$12.00	3-1999
TN	1934 – 1935	hunting & fishing, NOT MET	Mint	$138.50	6-1999
TN	1938 – 1939	paper license in back	EX	$164.00	4-2000
TN	1941	hunting & fishing, papers inside	EX	$142.50	5-1999
VA	1930 – 1931	hunting, fishing, trapping	AVG	$50.00	6-1999
WA	1920 non-resident	paper rectangle	EX	$38.00	2-2000
WI	1930 non-resident	NOT MET	Fair	$16.50	7-1999
WI	1930 non-resident	pin back	EX	$155.00	4-1999
WI	1930 non-resident		EX	$128.49	1-2000
WI	1930 non-resident		EX+	$145.00	7-1999
WI	1932 non-resident	pin back	EX	$88.00	6-1999
WI	1932 non-resident	pin back, NOT MET	EX	$121.50	4-1999
WV	1921	cloth	Poor	$31.00	5-1999
WV	1934	pin back, no paper	EX	$75.00	5-1999
WV	1937	NOT MET		$27.00	6-1999
WV	1938	NOT MET		$28.00	6-1999
WV	1939 non-resident	with papers	EX	$306.00	9-1999
WV	1940	hunting & fishing, papers	EX	$350.00	8-2000

LURES

BRAND	MODEL	DESCRIPTION	GRADE	PRICE	DATE
	Springhook	4", hollow metal minnow	EX	$550.00	3-2000
Abbey & Imbrie		100, Heddon crackleback, 3-hook	VG+/IB	$400.00	11-2000
Abbey & Imbrie	Bass Seeker	red head, solid, no pictures, nice box	NIB	$42.00	11-2001

BRAND	MODEL	SERIES / MFG. CODE / DESCRIPTION	GRADE	PRICE	DATE
Abbey & Imbrie	Basser	green perch scale, NO BIDS	EX	$10.00	11-2001
Abbey & Imbrie	Big Boy	green stripe	EX	$49.00	8-2001
Abbey & Imbrie	Big Boy	red, white, jointed	EX	$18.00	6-2001
Abbey & Imbrie	Flipper	Heddon, perch scale, L-rig, glass eyes, A&I props	VG+	$250.00	12-2001
Abbey & Imbrie	Frog	8, flyrod, rubber, on card	NOC	$52.00	1-2000
Abbey & Imbrie	Ghost	weird metal spinner, marked	EX	$300.00	10-2000
Abbey & Imbrie	Glowbody Minnow		EX	$70.00	4-2000
Abbey & Imbrie	Glowbody Minnow	glass body	EX	$170.00	4-2000
Abbey & Imbrie	Go Getter	red head, tack eyes, 1PCCB, great graphics	EX/IB	$50.50	12-1999
Abbey & Imbrie	Go-Getter	great window box	EX/IB	$63.31	2-2000
Abbey & Imbrie	Go-Getter	Runt type, red head, fat head, tack eyes	EX	$15.00	5-2001
Abbey & Imbrie	Go-Getter	Rush Tango type, frog, nice box	NIB	$57.00	3-2001
Abbey & Imbrie	Go-Getter	yellow flash, painted eyes, vg- box but decent	EX/IB	$88.50	9-1999
Abbey & Imbrie	Go-Getter	no code, red, white, tack eyes, window style 1PCCB	NIB	$73.00	8-2002
Abbey & Imbrie	Go-Getter	Jointed Runt type, perch scale, window box	VG/IB	$22.00	5-2001
Abbey & Imbrie	Lawrence Gang Hook	nice box with picture card inside, c.1890s	NIB	$311.00	11-2001
Abbey & Imbrie	Minnow, Underwater	green perch scale, 3-hook	EX	$66.00	11-2001
Abbey & Imbrie	Mouse, Diving	red head, painted eyes, wood checked, nice box	VG+/IB	$32.00	2-2000
Abbey & Imbrie	Octopus	rainbow, 3-hook	VG+	$780.00	10-1999
Abbey & Imbrie	Pikie	4¾", pike scale?, brown, yellow, tack eyes	Mint	$31.51	4-2000
Abbey & Imbrie	Pikie	63, red head, jointed, tack eyes, great window box	NIB	$58.00	9-2000
Abbey & Imbrie	Runt, Floating	red head, yellow, NO BIDS	EX-	$25.00	4-2001
Abbey & Imbrie	Runt, Jointed	63, red-winged blackbird, tack eyes, window box	NIB	$71.00	10-2001
Abbey & Imbrie	Slant Nose	Shur Strike, yellow, black head, glass eyes	NIB	$337.00	10-2002
Abbey & Imbrie	Spinner	on great bass & trout card	EXNOC	$19.00	4-2001
Abbey & Imbrie	Spoon Fish	Heddon metal lure	EX	$99.00	9-2001
Abbey & Imbrie	Stanley King	red, white, nice 2PCCB	EX/IB	$38.25	4-2001
Abbey & Imbrie	Torpedo	Heddon red head, glass eyes, A&I props	VG	$81.00	5-2001
Abbey & Imbrie	Torpedo, Jennings		EX	$382.00	3-2000
Abbey & Imbrie	Torpedo, Jennings	metal lures, cleaned	EX	$300.00	10-1999
Abbey & Imbrie	Vamp	frog spot, tack eyes	EX	$20.00	7-2002
Abbey & Imbrie	Vamp	green perch scale	EX	$12.50	11-2001
Abbey & Imbrie	Vamp	yellow perch scale	EX	$16.00	11-2001
Abbey & Imbrie	Vamp, Jointed	Heddon, red eyes & tail, glass eyes, L-rig	EX	$88.00	9-2001
Abbey & Imbrie	Vamp, Jointed	yellow perch scale	EX	$20.00	11-2001
Abbey & Imbrie	Vamp, Jointed	blue perch, rough belly, tack eyes, window box, nice	VG+/IB	$27.00	4-2001
Abu	Vamp, Hi-Lo	D	EX+	$81.00	3-2000
Abu	Vamp, Hi-Lo	L	EX+	$81.00	3-2000
Abu	Vamp, Hi-Lo	M	VG	$81.00	3-2000
Abu	Vamp, Hi-Lo	XBG	EX+	$92.00	3-2000
Abu	Vamp, Hi-Lo	XBW	EX	$81.00	3-2000
Abu	Vamp, Hi-Lo	XRS	EX-	$81.00	3-2000
Abu	Vamp, Hi-Lo	BGL	EX	$81.00	3-2000
Abu	Vamp, Hi-Lo	BO, brown trout	VG+	$81.00	3-2000

BRAND	MODEL	SERIES / MFG. CODE / DESCRIPTION	GRADE	PRICE	DATE
Abu	Vamp, Hi-Lo	LYS, luminous	EX	$81.00	3-2000
Acme	Minnow, Weedless	3-hook, spoon, spring, worm burn	AVG/IB	$39.00	4-2000
Action Frog	Live Action Frog		NIB	$300.00	8-2000
AL&W	Ding Bat	319, pike, ½black, rest pikie, glass eyes	NIB	$133.00	5-2000
AL&W	Pikie	pikie, 3-joint, glass eyes	EX	$90.00	10-1999
AL&W	Wiggle Fish, Baby	pikie, nice	EX+	$313.88	12-1998
Algers	Getsum	NOT MET	VG	$100.00	7-2000
Allcock	Aquatic Spider	large size on card in great tin box	NIB	$562.00	6-2001
Allcock	Aquatic Spider	on card in nice tin, rubs	NIB	$250.00	7-2001
Allcock	Kastlite	x2, one prototype & one regular, NOT MET	VG+	$240.00	8-2002
Allcock	Marvel	3" flyrod	EX	$197.00	8-2002
Allcock	Minnow, Paragon	brass, glass eyes	EX	$405.00	2-2002
Allen, Forest	Ubangi	black, white ribs	EX	$23.57	6-1999
Anderson	Minnow	perch, plastic, spring hook lure, nice box & papers	NIB	$171.00	4-2002
Arbogast	Jitterbug	½ oz., green, black spots, smooth eye	EX	$69.00	8-2000
Arbogast	Jitterbug	3 different, gold glitter	NIB	$26.00	1-1999
Arbogast	Jitterbug	⅜ oz., black, white	EX-	$71.95	3-1999
Arbogast	Jitterbug	⅜ oz., sparrow	NIB	$67.00	2-1999
Arbogast	Jitterbug	4 different, WWII	EX	$89.00	3-1999
Arbogast	Jitterbug	⅝ oz., aluminum, bubble pack	NOC	$26.00	1-1999
Arbogast	Jitterbug	⅝oz., flocked mouse, weedless trebles	NIB	$270.00	9-2000
Arbogast	Jitterbug	⅝ oz., frog, clear belly, WWII lip melted	EX-	$125.00	7-2002
Arbogast	Jitterbug	6-pack, 4 lures, great graphics, 1970s?	NIB	$212.50	4-1999
Arbogast	Jitterbug	2¾", black shore, extra heavy rig, wood	EX-	$665.00	11-2000
Arbogast	Jitterbug	white shore?	VG	$28.81	2-1999
Arbogast	Jitterbug	black, black WWII lip	NIB	$76.00	8-2001
Arbogast	Jitterbug	blue scale	NIB	$180.00	3-1999
Arbogast	Jitterbug	clear lip	NIB	$32.00	2-1999
Arbogast	Jitterbug	fluorescent yellow	EX	$13.37	1-1999
Arbogast	Jitterbug	flyrod, black, plastic lip	NOC	$32.00	10-2000
Arbogast	Jitterbug	flyrod, silver scale, plastic lip	NOC	$78.00	10-2000
Arbogast	Jitterbug	frog, age lines on belly, old wood, ugly	EX-	$39.00	8-2001
Arbogast	Jitterbug	frog, black WWII lip	VG	$39.75	1-1999
Arbogast	Jitterbug	frog, clear lip	EX	$17.00	2-1999
Arbogast	Jitterbug	frog, wood, intro box with age lines, nice	NIB	$155.00	3-2002
Arbogast	Jitterbug	frog, yellow lip	Mint	$31.00	5-2000
Arbogast	Jitterbug	frog, yellow lip	NIB	$36.00	6-1999
Arbogast	Jitterbug	frog, yellow plastic lip, wood, nice box	NIB	$152.50	4-1999
Arbogast	Jitterbug	Limited Edition, plain cedar	NIB	$105.38	8-1999
Arbogast	Jitterbug	luminous, worm burn		$28.00	12-1998
Arbogast	Jitterbug	metallic blue	EX+	$55.00	1-1999
Arbogast	Jitterbug	musky, red & white plastic	NIB	$28.50	3-1999
Arbogast	Jitterbug	orange, black spots, modern	EX	$177.50	6-1999
Arbogast	Jitterbug	perch, red WWII lip	EX	$18.58	2-2000
Arbogast	Jitterbug	perch, red WWII lip	VG	$29.00	2-1999
Arbogast	Jitterbug	perch, WWII lip	NIB	$158.01	3-2000

BRAND	MODEL	SERIES / MFG. CODE / DESCRIPTION	GRADE	PRICE	DATE
Arbogast	Jitterbug	purple CD, purple plastic lip, not WWII	NIB	$455.00	4-2000
Arbogast	Jitterbug	red head, 2PCCB, decent	EX/IB	$27.00	3-2001
Arbogast	Jitterbug	red head, plastic lip, nice box	NIB	$76.00	10-2000
Arbogast	Jitterbug	red head, red lip	Mint	$31.00	5-2000
Arbogast	Jitterbug	red head, red lip	Mint	$46.00	5-2000
Arbogast	Jitterbug	red head, white lip, no name	EX	$31.00	5-2000
Arbogast	Jitterbug	red, white, plastic lip, picture box	Poor	$17.50	2-1999
Arbogast	Jitterbug	red, white, PTCB, picture on bottom	EX/IB	$21.50	2-1999
Arbogast	Jitterbug	red, white, red lip, 2PCCB, papers	EX/IB	$41.00	3-1999
Arbogast	Jitterbug	red, white, red WWII lip	EX	$39.00	3-1999
Arbogast	Jitterbug	red, white, white WWII lip	VG-	$25.00	1-1999
Arbogast	Jitterbug	shiner scale, red lip	Mint	$42.00	5-2000
Arbogast	Jitterbug	silver scale, red lip, chips	AVG	$33.00	8-2000
Arbogast	Jitterbug	silver, red herringbone, plastic lip	EX	$963.00	9-2001
Arbogast	Jitterbug	sparrow	NIB	$67.00	2-1999
Arbogast	Jitterbug	Special Issue, bare wood	NIB	$46.00	4-2000
Arbogast	Jitterbug	WWII lip	NIB	$51.00	8-2001
Arbogast	Jitterbug	WWII shiner, red, heavy rig	EX	$32.00	2-1999
Arbogast	Jitterbug	WWII, nice box & papers	EX/IB	$41.00	3-1999
Arbogast	Jitterbug	67, clear, gold glitter	NIB	$31.51	1-1999
Arbogast	Jitterbug	x2, 4 different, clear lip	NIB	$78.50	9-1999
Arbogast	Jitterbug	x2, frog, flyrod, red head, plastic lips	NOC	$72.00	10-2000
Arbogast	Jitterbug	x2, frog, red, white, WWII	AVG- to VG	$31.56	1-1999
Arbogast	Jitterbug	x4, flyrod, 4 different colors, plastic lips	AVG	$44.00	8-2001
Arbogast	Jitterbug	XRY, red lip	EX	$29.76	2-1999
Arbogast	Jitterbug, Musky	2-hook, black scale, heavy teardrop, back stencil	VG+	$157.00	4-2000
Arbogast	Jitterbug, Musky	3-hook, plain varnish, no paint, PTCB	NIB	$79.00	8-2001
Arbogast	Jitterbug, Musky	3-pack, frog, plastic	NIB	$60.00	2-1999
Arbogast	Jitterbug, Musky	3-pack, glitter, plastic, nice	NIB	$51.00	2-1999
Arbogast	Jitterbug, Musky	black back & ribs, spots	NIB	$45.00	2-1999
Arbogast	Jitterbug, Musky	perch, PTCB	NIB	$44.05	4-1999
Arbogast	Jitterbug, Musky	plain cedar	NIB	$96.00	2-2000
Arbogast	Jitterbug, Musky	rainbow trout, side hooks, PTCB	NIB	$71.00	6-1999
Arbogast	Jitterbug, Weedless	Stanley	EX	$15.50	4-2000
Arbogast	Kicker, Weedless	frog	EX	$124.07	9-1999
Arbogast	Mopar	$100,000 contest 4-pack lures	EX	$101.00	3-1999
Arbogast	Mudbug	24, ¾ oz., 8 bids	NIB	$10.50	9-1999
Arbogast	Popper, Hula	spinning chipmunk	NIB	$34.00	9-2002
Arbogast	Scudder	big wooden lure	NIB	$39.00	8-2001
Arbogast	Skinny Minny	red head, white, yellow back, plastic	NIB	$11.00	8-2001
Arbogast	Skinny Minny	red, white	EX	$16.50	6-1999
Arbogast	Tin Liz	2½", red head, gold, glass eyes	EX	$100.00	7-1999
Arbogast	Tin Liz	2¾", glass eyes	EX	$228.00	10-2000
Arbogast	Tin Liz	3½", gold, glass eyes, nice box	NIB	$212.50	3-1999
Arbogast	Tin Liz	flyrod, painted eyes, display card with 6 mint	NOC	$120.00	1-1999
Arbogast	Tin Liz	glass eyes	Mint	$43.00	1-2000
Arbogast	Tin Liz	glass eyes, avg picture box	EX/IB	$66.00	10-2000

BRAND	MODEL	SERIES / MFG. CODE / DESCRIPTION	GRADE	PRICE	DATE
Arbogast	Tin Liz	pike	EX-	$291.00	3-1999
Arbogast	Tin Liz	silver, green, glass eyes, large	EX	$57.50	1-1999
Arbogast	Tin Liz	sunfish	EX	$351.00	7-2000
Arbogast	Tin Liz	sunfish, NOT MET	EX-	$212.50	3-1999
Arbogast	Tin Liz	walleye, huge rub on one side		$498.00	10-2000
Arbogast	Tin Liz	walleye, one side all rubbed, NOT MET	AVG	$498.00	10-2000
Arbogast	Tin Liz	crappie, 4-fin, NOT MET	EX-	$152.50	6-1999
Arbogast	Tin Liz	pike	VG+	$382.75	3-2000
Arbogast	Tin Liz	pike, crisp unmarked box & papers	NIB	$915.00	3-2001
Arbogast	Tin Liz	pike, pointers one side, NOT MET	VG-	$177.00	4-2000
Arbogast	Tin Liz	sunfish	EX	$222.50	12-1998
Arbogast	Tin Liz	sunfish, crisp unmarked box & papers	NIB	$415.00	3-2001
Arbogast	Tin Liz	sunfish, glass eyes	EX+	$456.00	1-2000
Arbogast	Tin Liz	sunfish, glass eyes, beautiful window box, NOT MET	NIB	$150.00	1-2001
Arbogast	Tin Liz	sunfish, rough unmarked box, NOT MET	NIB	$301.00	11-2001
Arbogast	Tin Liz	walleye, crisp unmarked box & papers	NIB	$1,913.00	3-2001
Arbogast	Tin Liz	walleye, NOT MET	VG	$506.00	6-1999
Arbogast	Wiggler, Hawaiian	scale, older picture PTCB, catalog	NIB	$20.50	2-1999
Arjon	Spincast	600, goodies, $200.00 NOT MET	NIB	$76.00	4-2001
Armax	Winchester	3-hook, heavy age lines	NIB	$557.50	12-1998
Arnold	Hop Along	fireplug, tack eyes	EX	$86.00	7-2000
Arntz, A.	Michigan Lifelike	chips, vg box, ex paper	GIB	$3,635.00	6-1999
Babbitt	Weedless		EX-	$375.00	10-1999
Bagley	Balsa B	B1, coach dog	EX-	$32.00	11-2000
Bagley	Balsa B	B1, yellow, green back scale, square lip	EX-	$37.00	11-2000
Bagley	Balsa B	BB2, chartreuse, black back scale, sq. lip, plastic box	NIB	$66.00	3-2001
Bagley	Balsa B	BB3 YP, yellow perch	NOC	$51.00	8-2001
Bagley	Balsa B	BB4, green scale, square lip, plastic box	NIB	$37.00	3-2001
Bagley	Balsa B	BDB1, chartreuse, black back scale, square lip	EX	$70.00	11-2000
Bagley	Balsa B	BDB1, coach dog, dent on top, square lip	VG	$15.00	11-2000
Bagley	Balsa B	BDB1, conetail, chartreuse, black back scale, square lip, small dent	VG+	$47.00	11-2000
Bagley	Balsa B	BDB1, white shad, square lip	EX	$53.00	11-2000
Bagley	Balsa B	BDB1, white shad, square lip	EX	$63.00	11-2000
Bagley	Balsa B	BDB2, chartreuse, black back scale, square lip	Mint	$89.00	11-2000
Bagley	Balsa B	BDB2, orange, black back scale, square lip	VG+	$36.00	11-2000
Bagley	Balsa B	BDB2, white shad, square lip	EX-	$42.00	11-2000
Bagley	Balsa B	DB3, 3", pearl, orange belly	EX	$68.00	11-2000
Bagley	Balsa B	common color, square lip, 15 bids	EX	$28.00	10-2000
Bagley	Balsa B	white, square lip, brass line tie	EX	$35.00	8-2000
Bagley	Kill	294, rainbow, yellow back, silver stripe over white, square lip	EX	$61.00	5-2000
Bagley	Small Fry Bass	1DSF2-LB4, bass on white	Mint	$31.00	5-2000
Bagley	Walkin Torpedo	rapala tail prop, ES (eel skin)	NIB	$60.00	5-2000
Bagley	Walkin Torpedo	rapala tail prop, GG (green on gold foil)	NIB	$50.00	5-2000
Bagley	Walkin Torpedo	rapala tail prop, RS (red on silver foil)	NIB	$51.00	5-2000

BRAND	MODEL	SERIES / MFG. CODE / DESCRIPTION	GRADE	PRICE	DATE
Bailey & Elliott	Manitou Minnow	green, papers	NIB	$2,000.00	10-2002
Bailey & Elliott	Manitou Minnow	green, white, wrench & papers	NIB	$1,725.00	4-2002
Bailey & Elliott	Manitou Minnow	green, white belly, wrench, paper	NIB	$2,500.00	8-1999
Bailey & Elliott	Manitou Minnow	green, wrench, papers	NIB	$2,812.00	1-2000
Ball, Horace	Wiggler, Floating	white, red chin, hook drags, NOT MET		$191.00	8-2001
Barracuda	Darter	frog, glass eyes, age lines	EX-	$500.00	4-2000
Barracuda	Darter	glass eyes	EX	$452.00	1-2001
Barracuda	Torpacuda	frog scale, little rusty	EX-	$75.00	8-1999
Berberisch		large, red, white, glass eyes, tail hook, no metal tail	EX	$356.00	12-2001
Biff	Go Devil	no paint left, metal, nice		$67.55	1-2000
Biff	Master	red head, decent box	EX-/IB	$156.00	10-2000
Biff	Master Plug	black, nice 2PCCB, sticky	NIB	$167.50	12-1998
Biff	Master Plug	yellow, black spots, papers	NIB	$164.50	1-1999
Biff	Master Whoopee	black, crisp papers & box	NIB	$179.00	8-2002
Biff	Musky, Spiral		EX	$76.57	8-1999
Biff	Musky, Spiral	NOT MET	EX	$38.00	4-2000
Biff	Musky, Spiral Spinner	nice crisp box, crisp papers	NIB	$375.00	4-2000
Biff	Spinner, Spiral		NIB	$175.00	10-1999
Biff	Spinner, Spiral	regular size	EX-	$64.00	7-2002
Biff	Spinner, Spiral	small size, vg box	EX/IB	$200.00	12-1999
Biff	Spiral	pike size, NOT MET	EX	$41.09	2-2000
Biff	Spiral Bait			$85.00	4-2001
Biff	Whoopee	2⅛", red, white, ugly	VG-/IB	$77.00	8-1999
Bings	Nemahbin Minnow	awful	Poor	$96.00	4-1999
Bishop	Beetle	14", CCBC replica	Mint	$264.00	1-1999
Bite-Em-Bate	Bite-Em-Bate	gold	Mint	$300.00	3-1999
Bite-Em-Bate	Bite-Em-Bate	211, red body, white head, picture box	EX-/IB	$470.00	2-2000
Bite-Em-Bate	Bite-Em-Bate	red, white, crisp box & papers	NIB	$738.00	8-2002
Bite-Em-Bate	Bite-Em-Bate	red, white, superb picture box & picture paper (7 colors listed)	NIB	$820.00	9-2001
Bite-Em-Bate	Bite-Em-Bate	red, white, great picture box	NIB	$426.00	1-1999
Bite-Em-Bate	Revolving	red & white barber pole	EX	$138.00	8-1999
Bite-Em-Bate	Revolving	red, white	EX	$142.00	5-2001
Bite-Em-Bate	Wiggler	RG, no eyes	EX-	$76.00	1-2000
Bite-Em-Bate	Wiggler, Lipped	good Diamond box (rare)	EX/IB	$600.00	10-1999
Bleeder		perch scale, NOT MET	EX/IB	$177.50	2-1999
Bleeder	Fish King	6", red head	EX	$375.00	3-1999
Bleeder	Fish King	6", red head, sparkles, papers	NIB	$1,000.00	11-2000
Bleeder	Survivor	white, green back, glass eyes, nice	EX	$101.00	8-2001
Bleeding Bait	Bleeder	2½", silver scale, white, papers	NIB	$177.00	4-2000
Bleeding Bait	Bleeder	silver scale	NIB	$255.00	11-1999
Blue Streak Tackle	Popper	301, blue	NIB	$132.00	4-2000
Blue Streak Tackle	Popper	302, red	NIB	$92.00	4-2000
Blue Streak Tackle	Popper	303, white	NIB	$138.00	4-2000
Blue Streak Tackle	Swimmer	Pikie type, blended bar perch	EX+	$46.00	4-2000
Bobel	Minnow	great box, NOT MET	NIB	$820.00	5-2001
Bolton, George	A-B-C Minnow	red, white	EX	$455.00	3-2001

BRAND	MODEL	SERIES / MFG. CODE / DESCRIPTION	GRADE	PRICE	DATE
Bomber	Bomber	6FY, wood	NIB	$57.00	1-2002
Bomber	Bomber	7 different, wood, used but some decent	AVG	$17.00	11-2001
Bomber	Bomber	100 assorted, 30 colors, plastic	NIB	$310.00	12-1998
Bomber	Bomber	313, fat forehead, #3 box	NIB	$34.00	10-2001
Bomber	Bomber	400, x2, black chrome, green chrome, wood	EX	$79.00	5-2001
Bomber	Bomber	403, earliest handmade, nose chip, otherwise nice	VG+	$106.00	10-2001
Bomber	Bomber	502, no eyes, crisp box & paper	NIB	$61.00	1-2002
Bomber	Bomber	508, PTCB	NIB	$18.50	3-2002
Bomber	Bomber	604HD, heavy duty, red head, smaller line tie	NIB	$23.00	11-2001
Bomber	Bomber	605HD, heavy duty, green perch, smaller line tie	NIB	$35.00	11-2001
Bomber	Bomber	613HD, heavy duty, green shad, smaller line tie	NIB	$42.00	11-2001
Bomber	Bomber	618HD, heavy duty, red side scale, smaller line tie	NIB	$26.00	11-2001
Bomber	Bomber	639HD, heavy duty, yellow, black spots, smaller line tie	NIB	$23.00	11-2001
Bomber	Bomber	671HD, heavy duty, purple back, glitter, smaller line tie	NIB	$26.00	11-2001
Bomber	Bomber	nude beach scene card, NOT MET	NOC	$26.55	6-1999
Bomber	Bomber	8 different, all nice, no eyes, $88.00 – $122.00 each	NIB	$122.00	11-1999
Bomber	Bomber	1st type, black, ugly	G	$85.00	10-1999
Bomber	Bomber	2 different	VG	$9.50	1-1999
Bomber	Bomber	5 common colors	EX	$45.50	2-1999
Bomber	Bomber	6 different, 1 Spinstick, PTCB	NIB	$96.05	1-1999
Bomber	Bomber	7 different, wood, 1 fluorescent yellow	EX	$57.00	4-1999
Bomber	Bomber	7 used Bombers	VG	$52.00	2-1999
Bomber	Bomber	7 used Bombers, 1-49er?	VG	$11.50	2-1999
Bomber	Bomber	8 different #5 boxes, M284 & commons	NIB	$171.50	2-2000
Bomber	Bomber	8 different, 2 sticks, 5 rip shad, 1 popper	NIB	$66.00	8-1999
Bomber	Bomber	8 different, wood, PTCB	NIB	$89.00	4-2001
Bomber	Bomber	10 different #5 boxes	NIB	$81.00	3-1999
Bomber	Bomber	10 different, wood, PTCB	NIB	$92.00	4-2001
Bomber	Bomber	12 different, some plastic, used	Poor- to EX	$15.50	4-1999
Bomber	Bomber	12 different, wood	NIB	$160.00	4-2001
Bomber	Bomber	12 different, wood, decent shape	VG+ to EX	$76.50	4-2000
Bomber	Bomber	15 different, common, 13 #3 & #4 boxes, nice	EX/IB	$204.00	12-1999
Bomber	Bomber	40 assorted, plastic	NIB	$187.50	1-1999
Bomber	Bomber	508, #5 box	NIB	$15.50	4-1999
Bomber	Bomber	514, 1949 plastic	EX	$39.00	9-1999
Bomber	Bomber	600HD, heavy duty, fluorescent red, black spots	VG	$36.88	10-1999
Bomber	Bomber	611HD, heavy duty, decent	VG+	$34.01	5-1999
Bomber	Bomber	613HD, heavy duty	EX/IB	$86.00	8-1999
Bomber	Bomber	613HD, heavy duty	NIB	$86.00	8-1999
Bomber	Bomber	617HD, heavy duty	EX-/IB	$26.00	4-2000
Bomber	Bomber	617HD, heavy duty, chips	VG-	$20.50	6-1999
Bomber	Bomber	617HD, heavy duty, rough lip, NOT MET	VG	$5.00	3-2000
Bomber	Bomber	619HD, heavy duty	EX	$39.00	6-2000
Bomber	Bomber	639HD, heavy duty	G	$20.50	4-1999

BRAND	MODEL	SERIES / MFG. CODE / DESCRIPTION	GRADE	PRICE	DATE
Bomber	Bomber	659HD, heavy duty	NIB	$70.75	2-1999
Bomber	Bomber	blue mullet, "Special" 300 box	VG/IB	$29.00	12-1999
Bomber	Bomber	clear & red bead plastic	NIB	$17.50	2-1999
Bomber	Bomber	x2; one 608HD, one 1720HD; heavy duty	NIB	$18.00	9-2000
Bomber	Bomber	3YSC	NIB	$26.50	7-1999
Bomber	Bomber	4 different, common colors, 1949 plastic, NOT MET	NIB	$22.98	6-1999
Bomber	Bomber	4 different, common colors, PTCB	NIB	$47.00	5-2000
Bomber	Bomber	4 different, modern plastic	NIB	$18.55	6-1999
Bomber	Bomber	4 different, wood, PTCB	NIB	$56.00	10-2001
Bomber	Bomber	4MO, wood	NIB	$31.00	5-2001
Bomber	Bomber	5 different, wood	VG+ to EX	$55.55	2-2000
Bomber	Bomber	6FYRB, heavy duty	NIB	$91.00	5-2000
Bomber	Bomber	6ME	NIB	$47.00	9-2000
Bomber	Bomber	6ML, awful age lines	EX+	$37.00	4-2000
Bomber	Bomber	6SC, heavy duty	VG/IB	$67.00	9-1999
Bomber	Bomber	6YSC, heavy duty	VG	$26.00	4-1999
Bomber	Bomber	10 different, plastic	NIB	$66.00	12-1999
Bomber	Bomber	207, #4 box	NIB	$47.55	3-1999
Bomber	Bomber	207, #5 box	NIB	$13.50	5-2000
Bomber	Bomber	216, #4 box, NOT MET	NIB	$31.20	2-2000
Bomber	Bomber	218	NIB	$20.00	6-2000
Bomber	Bomber	236, #5 box	NIB	$36.00	7-2000
Bomber	Bomber	237	VG+	$38.99	2-2000
Bomber	Bomber	256	NIB	$17.50	1-1999
Bomber	Bomber	259	NIB	$20.22	2-1999
Bomber	Bomber	283	NIB	$18.50	1-1999
Bomber	Bomber	283	NIB	$23.50	8-2000
Bomber	Bomber	305 F, #3 box	NIB	$30.00	11-1999
Bomber	Bomber	307, #5 box	NIB	$13.00	5-2000
Bomber	Bomber	310, #4 box	NIB	$22.01	1-1999
Bomber	Bomber	310, #5 box	NIB	$22.00	2-1999
Bomber	Bomber	312, 311 2PCCB	NIB	$30.50	1-1999
Bomber	Bomber	312, #5 box	NIB	$17.30	2-1999
Bomber	Bomber	317, #4 box, 2PCCB	NIB	$36.00	1-1999
Bomber	Bomber	320, #5 box	NIB	$13.00	5-2000
Bomber	Bomber	320, #5 box	NIB	$21.25	3-1999
Bomber	Bomber	336, #5 box	NIB	$16.00	4-1999
Bomber	Bomber	338, #5 box	NIB	$44.99	3-1999
Bomber	Bomber	340, PTCB	NIB	$15.00	11-2000
Bomber	Bomber	355, #4 box	NIB	$32.31	2-2000
Bomber	Bomber	358, #5 box	NIB	$14.49	2-1999
Bomber	Bomber	370, #5 box	NIB	$15.50	2-1999
Bomber	Bomber	373, #5 box	NIB	$13.22	2-1999
Bomber	Bomber	383, #5 box	NIB	$16.50	2-1999
Bomber	Bomber	387, #5 box	NIB	$10.00	2-1999
Bomber	Bomber	389	NIB	$19.00	3-2000

BRAND	MODEL	SERIES / MFG. CODE / DESCRIPTION	GRADE	PRICE	DATE
Bomber	Bomber	404, #3 box	NIB	$50.99	4-1999
Bomber	Bomber	406, #3 box	NIB	$31.00	1-2001
Bomber	Bomber	407	NIB	$13.00	6-2000
Bomber	Bomber	407, #3 box	NIB	$20.00	5-2000
Bomber	Bomber	414, #5 box	NIB	$13.00	5-2000
Bomber	Bomber	415, #5 box	NIB	$13.99	2-1999
Bomber	Bomber	416, #5 box	NIB	$12.49	2-1999
Bomber	Bomber	416, no eyes	EX-	$26.00	4-2000
Bomber	Bomber	417	NIB	$37.00	6-2000
Bomber	Bomber	417, no eyes	VG+	$30.00	8-2001
Bomber	Bomber	418	NIB	$21.00	4-2001
Bomber	Bomber	419HD, heavy duty	EX	$39.00	6-2000
Bomber	Bomber	420, #3 box	NIB	$12.50	6-1999
Bomber	Bomber	421	NIB	$10.51	1-1999
Bomber	Bomber	455	NIB	$10.51	1-1999
Bomber	Bomber	458	NIB	$32.05	1-1999
Bomber	Bomber	472, #5 box	NIB	$14.25	2-1999
Bomber	Bomber	484	Mint	$20.06	10-1999
Bomber	Bomber	484, huge age lines	VG	$39.00	2-2000
Bomber	Bomber	489	EX	$9.99	7-1999
Bomber	Bomber	489, #5 box	NIB	$21.00	4-1999
Bomber	Bomber	489, #5 box	NIB	$31.00	3-1999
Bomber	Bomber	504, #4 box	NIB	$23.50	3-1999
Bomber	Bomber	504, mint picture box	NIB	$22.50	1-1999
Bomber	Bomber	504, yellow eye, HMLT	AVG	$53.00	1-2000
Bomber	Bomber	505, #5 box	NIB	$10.00	3-1999
Bomber	Bomber	506	NIB	$10.00	1-1999
Bomber	Bomber	506, 2PCCB, #3 box	NIB	$33.05	2-1999
Bomber	Bomber	506, #3 box	NIB	$15.50	10-1999
Bomber	Bomber	506, #3 box, wide gap	NIB	$26.75	4-2000
Bomber	Bomber	506, #4 box	NIB	$19.50	11-1999
Bomber	Bomber	507, #5 box	NIB	$16.00	3-1999
Bomber	Bomber	509, #3 box	NIB	$27.00	2-2000
Bomber	Bomber	511	NIB	$6.00	1-1999
Bomber	Bomber	511, #3 box	NIB	$25.00	1-2000
Bomber	Bomber	515	NIB	$10.50	
Bomber	Bomber	515, no eyes	VG-	$20.01	1-2000
Bomber	Bomber	516, no eyes	EX	$56.00	11-1999
Bomber	Bomber	516, no eyes	EX+	$79.00	11-1999
Bomber	Bomber	517, lip wear, #3 box	EX/IB	$34.57	11-1999
Bomber	Bomber	517, no eyes, #2 box	EX/IB	$58.77	11-1999
Bomber	Bomber	519	NIB	$11.00	1-1999
Bomber	Bomber	520, #5 box	NIB	$12.55	3-1999
Bomber	Bomber	543	NIB	$9.99	1-1999
Bomber	Bomber	543, #5 box	NIB	$15.50	2-1999
Bomber	Bomber	555	NIB	$11.00	1-1999
Bomber	Bomber	583	NIB	$26.00	5-2000

BRAND	MODEL	SERIES / MFG. CODE / DESCRIPTION	GRADE	PRICE	DATE
Bomber	Bomber	585	EX	$19.00	5-1999
Bomber	Bomber	585	NIB	$32.260	3-1999
Bomber	Bomber	587	NIB	$26.00	5-2000
Bomber	Bomber	587	NIB	$31.00	5-2000
Bomber	Bomber	588	NIB	$20.00	5-2000
Bomber	Bomber	600HD, heavy duty, FYRB	NIB	$52.00	6-2000
Bomber	Bomber	600HD, heavy duty, x12, fluorescent, wood, early	NIB	$219.00	7-2000
Bomber	Bomber	601, no eyes	EX	$173.76	11-1999
Bomber	Bomber	603	NIB	$27.59	3-2000
Bomber	Bomber	603WG, old grey scale	EX	$11.02	11-1999
Bomber	Bomber	603WG, old grey scale	EX	$11.95	11-1999
Bomber	Bomber	606	NIB	$9.99	1-1999
Bomber	Bomber	608, no eyes	VG	$10.50	4-1999
Bomber	Bomber	608, no eyes, #2 box	NIB	$72.79	11-1999
Bomber	Bomber	609, no eyes	EX	$100.10	11-1999
Bomber	Bomber	611, #5 box	NIB	$15.00	6-1999
Bomber	Bomber	611, no eyes	EX	$150.00	11-1999
Bomber	Bomber	612, 607 #3 box	EX/IB	$20.50	1-1999
Bomber	Bomber	617, no eyes	VG+	$61.00	11-1999
Bomber	Bomber	618WG	EX+	$26.00	11-1999
Bomber	Bomber	618WG	EX-	$10.50	11-1999
Bomber	Bomber	619, #4 box, NOT MET	NIB	$18.51	2-1999
Bomber	Bomber	619, #4 box, NOT MET	NIB	$25.49	3-2000
Bomber	Bomber	619, no eyes	EX-	$30.00	2-2000
Bomber	Bomber	619, no eyes	Mint	$77.00	11-1999
Bomber	Bomber	619, no eyes, flakes on lip, otherwise nice	EX-	$10.50	11-1999
Bomber	Bomber	638	NIB	$42.50	8-1999
Bomber	Bomber	687	Mint	$20.00	6-1999
Bomber	Bomber	one 511 in #3 box, one 1781 in #5 box	NIB	$27.10	2-2000
Bomber	Bomber	one each: 300FY like 357; 606HD, heavy duty; 682HD, heavy duty	NIB	$322.00	4-2000
Bomber	Bomber	x2, no eyes, 2A boxes	VG/IB	$111.50	3-2000
Bomber	Bomber	x2; one 511, one 408; #5 box	NIB	$27.00	4-1999
Bomber	Bomber	x2; one 553HD, one 606HD; heavy duty	VG	$41.00	4-2000
Bomber	Bomber	201, #4 box	NIB	$17.08	2-1999
Bomber	Bomber	201, #5 box	NIB	$15.50	2-1999
Bomber	Bomber	204, #4 box	NIB	$17.00	3-2001
Bomber	Bomber	209, #5 box	NIB	$15.50	2-1999
Bomber	Bomber	218, #5 box	NIB	$21.00	6-2000
Bomber	Bomber	219, #4 box	NIB	$16.00	1-1999
Bomber	Bomber	220, #4 box	NIB	$19.00	10-1999
Bomber	Bomber	221, #5 box	NIB	$27.00	3-1999
Bomber	Bomber	242, #4 box	NIB	$146.00	1-2000
Bomber	Bomber	245, multi-flakes, big deal	EX	$42.00	10-1999
Bomber	Bomber	302, #5 box	NIB	$13.00	2-1999
Bomber	Bomber	304, #5 box	NIB	$30.00	4-1999
Bomber	Bomber	305, #5 box	NIB	$19.50	10-1999

BRAND	MODEL	SERIES / MFG. CODE / DESCRIPTION	GRADE	PRICE	DATE
Bomber	Bomber	311, #5 box	NIB	$12.35	5-2000
Bomber	Bomber	312, #5 box	NIB	$10.50	4-1999
Bomber	Bomber	338, PTCB, "33?"	NIB	$133.00	1-2001
Bomber	Bomber	355, #5 box	NIB	$17.50	2-1999
Bomber	Bomber	356, #5 box	NIB	$16.50	3-1999
Bomber	Bomber	382, #5 box	NIB	$25.49	3-1999
Bomber	Bomber	402, #5 box	NIB	$11.50	5-2000
Bomber	Bomber	403, wide gap	EX-	$24.99	3-2000
Bomber	Bomber	411, no eyes, 411 #2 box, patent pending	AVG/IB	$22.25	12-1999
Bomber	Bomber	412, #4 box	NIB	$41.51	2-1999
Bomber	Bomber	418, #3 box, crisp	NIB	$41.00	5-2000
Bomber	Bomber	418, wide gap, chip	VG	$31.00	2-2000
Bomber	Bomber	419, #5 box	NIB	$13.25	5-2000
Bomber	Bomber	420, #5 box	NIB	$15.00	2-1999
Bomber	Bomber	443, #5 box	NIB	$19.51	3-1999
Bomber	Bomber	457, #5 box	NIB	$12.25	5-2000
Bomber	Bomber	458, #5 box	NIB	$21.00	7-2000
Bomber	Bomber	459, #5 box	NIB	$13.01	5-2000
Bomber	Bomber	471, #5 box	NIB	$15.49	2-1999
Bomber	Bomber	489, #5 box	NIB	$15.50	2-1999
Bomber	Bomber	500ROK, fluorescent yellow, black ribs	NIB	$160.00	6-2000
Bomber	Bomber	500SB, clear plastic, colored beads	NIB	$8.00	7-2000
Bomber	Bomber	501, #3 box	NIB	$19.49	1-2000
Bomber	Bomber	502, 2PCCB, #4 box	NIB	$14.25	2-1999
Bomber	Bomber	502, no eyes, NOT MET	NIB	$75.00	9-2000
Bomber	Bomber	504, PTCB, NO BID	NIB	$15.00	11-2000
Bomber	Bomber	504, wide gap, #2c, NO BID	VG/IB	$20.00	5-2000
Bomber	Bomber	505, 2PCCB, #3 box	NIB	$18.00	2-1999
Bomber	Bomber	509, #4 box	NIB	$18.01	3-1999
Bomber	Bomber	510, 507 #3 box	NIB	$11.50	1-1999
Bomber	Bomber	511, #3 box	NIB	$31.51	4-1999
Bomber	Bomber	511, no eyes, yellow box	VG/IB	$32.99	10-1999
Bomber	Bomber	512, #5 box	NIB	$23.57	3-1999
Bomber	Bomber	516, #5 box	NIB	$14.01	2-1999
Bomber	Bomber	516, #5 box	NIB	$29.50	4-1999
Bomber	Bomber	518, #5 box	NIB	$15.49	5-2000
Bomber	Bomber	519, #5 box	NIB	$30.00	4-1999
Bomber	Bomber	520, #5 box	NIB	$12.25	5-2000
Bomber	Bomber	536, #3 box	NIB	$29.50	7-1999
Bomber	Bomber	538, #5 box	NIB	$38.00	6-2000
Bomber	Bomber	555, #4 box	NIB	$31.57	4-1999
Bomber	Bomber	585, #5 box	NIB	$36.00	6-2000
Bomber	Bomber	601, #3 box	NIB	$31.990	4-1999
Bomber	Bomber	603, 2PCCB	NIB	$17.00	1-1999
Bomber	Bomber	605, 2B box	EX/IB	$38.00	4-1999
Bomber	Bomber	605, #4 box	NIB	$23.00	3-2000
Bomber	Bomber	605, #5 box	NIB	$17.00	2-1999

BRAND	MODEL NAME	SERIES / MFG. CODE / DESCRIPTION	GRADE	PRICE	DATE
Bomber	Bomber	605, wide gap, #2C	NIB	$65.00	5-2000
Bomber	Bomber	606, #5 box	NIB	$17.79	4-1999
Bomber	Bomber	608, #3 box	NIB	$18.06	4-1999
Bomber	Bomber	608, no eyes, #2 box	EX/IB	$93.00	11-1999
Bomber	Bomber	611, 2PCCB	NIB	$31.05	1-1999
Bomber	Bomber	611, #3 box	NIB	$26.56	12-1999
Bomber	Bomber	611, no eyes	NIB	$141.00	7-2000
Bomber	Bomber	611, no eyes, box 2A	NIB	$118.50	4-1999
Bomber	Bomber	613, x12, #5 box, cellophane top	NIB	$305.00	6-2000
Bomber	Bomber	618, #5 box	NIB	$39.00	4-1999
Bomber	Bomber	640, #5 box	NIB	$12.50	3-1999
Bomber	Bomber	643, #5 box	NIB	$38.07	4-1999
Bomber	Bomber	655, #5 box	NIB	$20.57	3-1999
Bomber	Bomber	659, 12-pack, #5 boxes	NIB	$122.55	2-2000
Bomber	Bomber	671, #5 box	NIB	$14.50	6-1999
Bomber	Bomber	671, #5 box	NIB	$19.00	3-1999
Bomber	Bomber	682, #5 box	NIB	$35.87	4-1999
Bomber	Bomber	688, #5 box	NIB	$32.88	10-1999
Bomber	Bomber	689, #5 box	NIB	$31.00	3-1999
Bomber	Bomber	x2; one 511, one 515; no eyes	VG	$20.00	7-2000
Bomber	Bomber, 49er	2 different	EX	$60.99	4-1999
Bomber	Bomber, 49er	413	EX	$33.00	12-1999
Bomber	Bomber, 49er	418, 616 #2 box, nice	EX-/IB	$46.00	12-1999
Bomber	Bomber, 49er	503, NOT MET	VG-	$9.50	12-1999
Bomber	Bomber, 49er	505, 1949 plastic, wrong 2PCCB	EX	$24.07	1-1999
Bomber	Bomber, 49er	506	EX-	$36.99	1-2000
Bomber	Bomber, 49er	512	EX	$27.00	6-2000
Bomber	Bomber, 49er	512, plastic	VG-	$19.99	4-1999
Bomber	Bomber, 49er	517, 1949 plastic, papers	NIB	$164.00	8-1999
Bomber	Bomber, 49er	605, 1949, plastic	EX	$18.00	11-1999
Bomber	Bomber, 49er	605, scrapes	VG-	$20.50	6-1999
Bomber	Bomber, 49er	607, 518 #2 box	EX/IB	$56.00	12-1999
Bomber	Bomber, 49er	612	EX	$28.00	10-1999
Bomber	Bomber, 49er	612	EX	$29.00	12-1999
Bomber	Bomber, 49er	613	NIB	$40.00	1-2002
Bomber	Bomber, 49er	615	NIB	$81.00	6-2000
Bomber	Bomber, 49er	617	EX-	$46.00	1-2002
Bomber	Bomber, 49er	618, 606 #2 box	VG+/IB	$41.00	12-1999
Bomber	Bomber, 49er	620	EX	$431.75	5-1999
Bomber	Bomber, 49er	red, white, NOT MET	EX	$25.01	4-1999
Bomber	Bomberette	714	NIB	$44.00	10-2001
Bomber	Bomberette	720	EX-	$42.50	1-2000
Bomber	Bomberette	x2; one 2737, one 2747	NIB	$168.00	9-2000
Bomber	Bomberette, Midget	2739, some paint off lip	EX	$49.00	8-1999
Bomber	Bomberette, Midget	x2, 2745 box	NIB	$65.00	3-2000
Bomber	Bomberette, Midget	2733	NIB	$34.00	10-2001
Bomber	Coca-Cola	boat scene, fake, NOT MET	NOC	$41.00	6-1999

BRAND	MODEL	SERIES / MFG. CODE / DESCRIPTION	GRADE	PRICE	DATE
Bomber	Darter	candy, small size	EX	$350.00	6-2001
Bomber	Gumpy Jig	x12, display card	EX-	$10.00	7-1999
Bomber	Jerk	2 different	Mint	$62.00	3-1999
Bomber	Jerk	4 different, vg+ to ex	EX	$72.27	3-1999
Bomber	Jerk	black bee	EX	$51.75	7-1999
Bomber	Jerk	rainbow	VG	$21.76	1-1999
Bomber	Jerk	yellow dog	EX	$52.00	5-2000
Bomber	Jerk	4300 Houston	VG+	$45.00	2-1999
Bomber	Jerk	4300 Houston Special	EX	$57.00	5-2000
Bomber	Jerk	4304	EX	$21.51	6-1999
Bomber	Jerk	4304	EX	$37.00	5-2000
Bomber	Jerk	4322	EX	$27.50	2-1999
Bomber	Jerk	4351, NOT MET	NIB	$71.00	7-2000
Bomber	Jerk	4352, yellow, red stripe, glitter, #3 box	NIB	$27.26	7-1999
Bomber	Jerk	4400BJ	NIB	$120.25	4-1999
Bomber	Jerk	4400PS	NIB	$59.00	4-1999
Bomber	Jerk	4400, silver scale	EX	$9.99	8-1999
Bomber	Jerk	4400SS	NIB	$33.09	4-1999
Bomber	Jerk	4401, pearl	NIB	$62.00	7-1999
Bomber	Jerk	4404	NIB	$31.23	4-1999
Bomber	Jerk	4404, #3, red head, white, silver scales	NIB	$153.00	6-2000
Bomber	Jerk	4422	NIB	$71.00	7-1999
Bomber	Jerk	4430, NOT MET	NIB	$31.00	8-2000
Bomber	Jerk	4453	EX	$24.99	4-1999
Bomber	Jerk	4472	NIB	$42.00	10-2001
Bomber	Jerk	4500, green, white, flitter, NOT MET	EX	$37.00	12-1999
Bomber	Jerk	4504	EX/IB	$21.00	7-2000
Bomber	Jerk	4511	NIB	$54.00	10-2001
Bomber	Jerk	4515, NOT MET	EX	$20.51	6-1999
Bomber	Jerk	4519	EX	$20.00	1-1999
Bomber	Jerk	4553	EX-	$21.76	5-1999
Bomber	Jerk	4553, NOT MET	EX	$21.00	6-1999
Bomber	Jerk	4553, yellow coach dog	EX-	$41.00	2-1999
Bomber	Jerk	4584	VG+	$97.00	3-2001
Bomber	Jerk	7239, NOT MET	EX-	$15.51	12-1998
Bomber	Knothead	1204, wrong box, NOT MET	EX	$230.00	8-1999
Bomber	Knothead	1205	EX-	$143.50	1-2000
Bomber	Knothead	1205, green perch, small	VG+	$140.00	11-2001
Bomber	Knothead	1216, NOT MET	NIB	$154.00	6-2000
Bomber	Knothead	1218, ugly age lines, POBW	G	$83.00	8-1999
Bomber	Knothead	1307	EX	$178.00	5-2000
Bomber	Knothead	1307, NOT MET	NIB	$242.50	12-1999
Bomber	Knothead	1311, frog	AVG	$37.80	8-1999
Bomber	Knothead	1311, frog, large	VG-	$26.00	11-2001
Bomber	Knothead	1314, awful		$21.00	5-2000
Bomber	Knothead	1315	Mint	$250.00	9-2000
Bomber	Knothead	1316, NOT MET	NIB	$134.00	6-2000

BRAND	MODEL NAME	SERIES / MFG. CODE / DESCRIPTION	GRADE	PRICE	DATE
Bomber	Looboyle Special	perch, NOT MET	G	$71.00	6-1999
Bomber	Looboyle Special	white pearl	VG+	$515.00	4-2001
Bomber	Pinfish	2PSC	NIB	$12.00	8-2002
Bomber	Pinfish	P00-FT, fire tiger	NIB	$12.00	7-2000
Bomber	Popper	3x01, pearl	NIB	$7.00	7-1999
Bomber	Popper	FT2T	NIB	$7.55	6-2000
Bomber	Popper	x2, one large, one small	NIB	$23.00	7-1999
Bomber	Popper	x4, different colors, $15.00 – $16.00 each	NIB	$62.00	5-2000
Bomber	Slab Spoon	red, white, PTCB, papers	NIB	$26.00	3-1999
Bomber	Speed Shad	frog	NIB	$15.00	2-2001
Bomber	Speed Shad	perch?	NIB	$7.80	4-1999
Bomber	Speed Shad	x3, different colors, all metal scales	NIB	$9.00	11-2001
Bomber	Spin Stick	73RS	NIB	$12.30	1-1999
Bomber	Spin Stick	73RS	NIB	$16.50	3-1999
Bomber	Spin Stick	73RT	NIB	$67.00	8-1999
Bomber	Spin Stick	7320	NIB	$6.00	9-1999
Bomber	Spin Stick	7356	NIB	$15.50	4-1999
Bomber	Spin Stick	7356, black mullet, PTCB	NIB	$37.00	10-2000
Bomber	Spin Stick	7371	NIB	$26.00	4-1999
Bomber	Spin Stick	7386	EX/IB	$16.00	7-1999
Bomber	Spin Stick	B.A.S.S. 30 Years Commemorative	NIB	$10.51	3-1999
Bomber	Spin Stick	M7380	NIB	$43.00	8-2000
Bomber	Spin Stick, Baby	7200, 6 different	EX	$148.76	1-2000
Bomber	Spin Stick, Baby	7200, small, #4 box	EX-/IB	$37.36	11-1999
Bomber	Spin Stick, Baby	7207, 7240 #4 box	NIB	$95.00	6-2000
Bomber	Spin Stick, Baby	7239	NIB	$42.00	6-2000
Bomber	Spin Stick, Baby	7243, small #4 box	EX/IB	$46.75	6-1999
Bomber	Spin Stick, Baby	7244	EX	$31.00	2-2000
Bomber	Spin Stick, Baby	black mullet, NOT MET	EX	$18.00	1-2001
Bomber	Stick	7400, chrome coach dog, heavy age lines	EX-	$50.00	6-2000
Bomber	Stick	7406	NIB	$32.00	6-2000
Bomber	Stick	7414	NIB	$9.75	1-1999
Bomber	Stick	x2, one 7381, one 7382	NIB	$31.00	8-2000
Bomber	Top Bomber	3 different, rough	AVG	$35.00	3-1999
Bomber	Top Bomber	4004?, big black eye shadow, odd color	EX	$70.00	1-2002
Bomber	Top Bomber	4018, ugly	AVG	$35.00	12-1999
Bomber	Top Bomber	4020	EX-	$63.00	6-2002
Bomber	Top Bomber	4020	VG-	$26.00	7-2000
Bomber	Top Bomber	4040	NIB	$77.00	6-2000
Bomber	Top Bomber	6003	VG	$51.00	8-1999
Bomber	Top Bomber	6005	EX	$139.00	10-2000
Bomber	Top Bomber	6014	VG	$19.99	6-1999
Bomber	Top Bomber	6015, torn box	NIB	$100.00	1-1999
Bomber	Various	x2, one Jerk, one Spin Stick	VG	$20.50	1-1999
Bomber	Water Dog	2 plastic	NIB	$13.00	2-1999
Bomber	Water Dog	5 mixed, 3 in 2PCCB	EX/IB	$81.00	3-1999
Bomber	Water Dog	17YSC	NIB	$103.76	8-1999

BRAND	MODEL	SERIES / MFG. CODE / DESCRIPTION	GRADE	PRICE	DATE
Bomber	Water Dog	15FY, 12-pack, plastic	NIB	$25.00	3-1999
Bomber	Water Dog	15FY, 12-pack, plastic	NIB	$82.55	2-2000
Bomber	Water Dog	1573, blue mullet, 1500SB box	EX-/IB	$63.33	3-1999
Bomber	Water Dog	16SC, wood	NIB	$98.99	8-1999
Bomber	Water Dog	17MB, age lines	NIB	$27.00	6-2000
Bomber	Water Dog	17MC, heavy age lines	EX	$59.00	4-2000
Bomber	Water Dog	17MO, wood	NIB	$13.00	5-2001
Bomber	Water Dog	1501, #5 box	NIB	$16.00	2-1999
Bomber	Water Dog	1511, 2PCCB, nice	NIB	$26.00	1-1999
Bomber	Water Dog	1557, #5 box	NIB	$15.50	3-1999
Bomber	Water Dog	1606, 2PCCB	NIB	$33.00	11-2000
Bomber	Water Dog	1611, NO BIDS	NIB	$15.00	5-2000
Bomber	Water Dog	1620, 12-pack, #5 boxes	NIB	$180.00	6-2000
Bomber	Water Dog	1655	NIB	$16.50	1-1999
Bomber	Water Dog	1659, #5 box	NIB	$9.00	2-1999
Bomber	Water Dog	1671, 1 bid	NIB	$15.00	5-2000
Bomber	Water Dog	1711, #4 box	NIB	$15.00	1-2000
Bomber	Water Dog	1719, one common	NIB	$83.00	8-2000
Bomber	Water Dog	1720	NIB	$10.50	1-1999
Bomber	Water Dog	1740	NIB	$16.23	1-1999
Bomber	Water Dog	1743	NIB	$11.19	1-1999
Bomber	Water Dog	1743, #5 box	NIB	$12.50	2-1999
Bomber	Water Dog	1755, #4 box	NIB	$15.53	12-1999
Bomber	Water Dog	1771, #5 box	NIB	$10.50	2-1999
Bomber	Water Dog	1772	Mint	$7.50	3-2002
Bomber	Water Dog	1778	EX	$29.07	3-1999
Bomber	Water Dog	1780, worm burn		$2.00	2-1999
Bomber	Water Dog	1783	NIB	$32.99	1-1999
Bomber	Water Dog	1784	VG	$20.00	6-2000
Bomber	Water Dog	x2; one 1508, one 1602	NIB	$20.50	1-1999
Bomber	Water Dog	x3; one 1508, one 1511, one 1615	Mint	$25.00	1-1999
Bon-Net	Bon-Net	frog	VG+/IB	$118.00	8-2000
Bon-Net	Bon-Net	frog, 6-hook, glass eyes, NOT MET	NIB	$164.50	1-1999
Bon-Net	Bon-Net	frog, glass eyes	VG+	$108.00	11-2001
Bon-Net	Bon-Net	frog, great Hobb's box	NIB	$310.01	9-1999
Bon-Net	Bon-Net	rainbow, 6-hook, many small pointers	GIB	$242.50	2-2000
Bon-Net	Bon-Net	red, white, hardware store box	NIB	$202.50	8-1999
Brady	Fish Dinner Flyrod	frog, Eau Claire, Wisconsin	NIB	$510.00	11-1999
Breveté	Passé Partout	spring loaded, France, c.1932, NOT MET	NIB	$405.00	12-2000
Brite-Eye		medium	EX	$50.00	11-2000
British Phantom	Phantom Minnow		EX/OC	$75.00	4-2001
Brooks	Plunker, Jointed	#5, yellow, silver spots, red mouth	NIB	$36.00	3-2002
Brooks	Plunker	JSP57	NIB	$18.00	8-2001
Brown Brothers	Fisheretto	frog, painted eyes	Mint	$50.50	4-1999
Brown Brothers	Fisheretto	frog, painted eyes	Mint	$50.50	5-1999
Brown Brothers	Fisheretto	red, white, washer eyes	G	$47.87	1-1999

BRAND	MODEL NAME	SERIES / MFG. CODE / DESCRIPTION	GRADE	PRICE	DATE
Brunswick	Doll Top Secret		NIB	$22.00	10-1999
Buckeye	Bug-N-Bass		EX-	$31.00	2-1999
Buckeye	Bug-N-Bass	#1 bass, red head, sand, clear body	NIB	$90.00	3-1999
Buckeye	Bug-N-Bass	#11 crappie	NIB	$61.270	2-1999
Buckeye	Bug-N-Bass	2½", black scale	EX	$133.21	6-1999
Buckeye	Bug-N-Bass	12-pack, red head, clear	NIB	$530.55	3-2000
Buckeye	Bug-N-Bass	baby bass, large	NIB	$31.00	2-1999
Buckeye	Bug-N-Bass	bass finish		$33.00	1-1999
Buckeye	Bug-N-Bass	black, green circles	EX+	$230.50	12-1998
Buckeye	Bug-N-Bass	black, silver markings	EX	$21.75	3-1999
Buckeye	Bug-N-Bass	black, silver ribs, small	EX	$35.00	3-1999
Buckeye	Bug-N-Bass	black, silver spots, small	EX	$20.00	12-1998
Buckeye	Bug-N-Bass	rainbow trout, large	EX	$103.48	2-2000
Buckeye	Bug-N-Bass	red head, clear	NIB	$81.01	2-1999
Buckeye	Bug-N-Bass	red head, clear, black markings, no cellophane	NIB	$97.00	3-2002
Buckeye	Bug-N-Bass	silver, small	EX	$67.00	8-1999
Buckeye	Bug-N-Bass	solid black	NIB	$129.49	3-2000
Buckeye	Bug-N-Bass	white coach dog, large	EX	$33.52	3-1999
Buckeye	Bug-N-Bass	yellow & black coach dog	EX	$27.77	5-1999
Buckeye	Bug-N-Bass	yellow coach dog	NIB	$25.95	3-1999
Buckeye	Bug-N-Bass	yellow coach dog, large	EX	$36.53	3-1999
Buel, J.T.	Arrowhead	#4, 2½", "Whitehall"	EX	$150.00	3-2001
Buel, J.T.	Arrowhead Spinner	3 oz., big	VG-	$57.70	6-1999
Buel, J.T.	Arrowhead Spinner	name only, no city	EX-	$50.00	5-1999
Bumble	Bug	red, white	EX	$34.00	5-2001
Bunyan, Paul	Teardrop Spoon	red box, great	NIB	$59.00	5-2000
Bunyan, Paul	Twirl Bug Wiggler	red, white, nice 2PCCB	NIB	$100.00	7-1999
Bunyan, Paul	Weaver	1900C, NOT MET	NIB	$32.99	5-1999
Bunyan, Paul	Weaver	1900C, red head, picture box	NIB	$45.00	5-2000
Bunyan, Paul	Weaver	chrome	EX-	$47.00	9-2000
Calumet Tackle	Spiral Lure		NIB	$255.00	10-1999
Canadian Baits	Display	pretty round display with lures	EX	$86.00	1-1999
Carter's	Bestever	black, great picture box	NIB	$126.00	9-2000
Carter's	Bestever	black, nice box & catalog	NIB	$87.00	5-2000
Carter's	Bestever Flyrod	red, white, small worm burn	VG	$32.00	6-2001
Case	Rotary Marvel		EX	$493.00	2-2000
Case	Rotary Marvel		EX	$950.00	4-2001
Case	Rotary Marvel	yellow, gold spots, NOT MET	EX	$380.00	5-1999
Cats Paw	Weedless Casting	plain, crisp box	NIB	$165.00	4-2001
CCBC		flyrod, $850.00 NOT MET	EX-	$331.00	2-2002
CCBC		rainbow, silver back, 5-hook, NOT MET	EX-	$1,525.00	11-2000
CCBC	Assortment	assorted 12-pack, mixed plastics	NIB	$228.51	3-1999
CCBC	Injured Minnow	1505, red side, label, catalog	G	$49.00	5-1999
CCBC	AL&W	red, white, weedless spring hook	VG-	$650.00	8-1999
CCBC	Beetle	2½", gold, yellow, nice	EX-	$175.39	2-2000
CCBC	Beetle	3800, greenish gold, yellow wings	EX-	$102.00	5-2000
CCBC	Beetle	3800, yellow, green	NIB	$401.51	5-1999

BRAND	MODEL	SERIES / MFG. CODE / DESCRIPTION	GRADE	PRICE	DATE
CCBC	Beetle	3818, silver belly, otherwise nice	VG	$400.00	1-2000
CCBC	Beetle	3851, green, yellow	NIB	$212.50	8-1999
CCBC	Beetle	3851, yellow & green label, missing 1 spinner	EX/IB	$179.16	1-2000
CCBC	Beetle	3852	EX-/IB	$325.00	3-1999
CCBC	Beetle	3853, orange	NIB	$440.00	8-2000
CCBC	Beetle	3853, orange, label	NIB	$663.00	10-2000
CCBC	Beetle	3853, stencil	NIB	$530.00	1-2002
CCBC	Beetle	back stencil, 3851 label	NIB	$426.00	1-2002
CCBC	Beetle	black, gold	EX	$250.00	10-1999
CCBC	Beetle	black, gold	EX+	$400.00	12-1999
CCBC	Beetle	black, green spots	EX	$242.50	2-1999
CCBC	Beetle	black, label	EX-/IB	$238.00	11-2000
CCBC	Beetle	black, red wings	EX-	$228.07	3-2000
CCBC	Beetle	blue head, red, varnish flaking	VG	$179.50	6-1999
CCBC	Beetle	chain spinners, 3851 stencil	VG+/IB	$202.50	1-2000
CCBC	Beetle	crawdad finish	EX-	$415.00	1-2002
CCBC	Beetle	gold, black	VG+	$234.11	5-1999
CCBC	Beetle	gold, black wings, hook drag	EX-	$404.98	6-1999
CCBC	Beetle	gold, orange, belly stencil, NOT MET	EX	$244.00	3-2001
CCBC	Beetle	gold, yellow wings	EX+	$417.50	6-1999
CCBC	Beetle	gold, yellow wings, 1 metal spinner	VG-	$331.00	6-1999
CCBC	Beetle	green, yellow	EX	$154.00	2-2002
CCBC	Beetle	green, yellow, removable hook, no stencil	EX	$206.00	8-2001
CCBC	Beetle	metallic green, yellow wings	EX-	$177.50	2-2000
CCBC	Beetle	metallic green, yellow wings, gold stencil	EX-	$102.00	5-2000
CCBC	Beetle	metallic green, yellow, label	NIB	$515.00	9-2000
CCBC	Beetle	orange, red wings	EX-	$282.68	3-2000
CCBC	Beetle	red, white	VG-	$67.50	11-1999
CCBC	Beetle	red, white	VG-	$118.93	4-1999
CCBC	Beetle	red, white, dents	VG-	$112.51	1-1999
CCBC	Beetle	silver flash	EX	$338.99	10-1999
CCBC	Beetle	silver flash	EX	$661.00	11-2000
CCBC	Beetle	silver flash	EX-	$462.00	3-2000
CCBC	Beetle	silver flash	VG	$171.00	9-2002
CCBC	Beetle	silver flash	VG+	$455.00	1-2000
CCBC	Beetle	white, red wings	EX-	$201.50	3-2000
CCBC	Beetle	white, red wings, 3852 stencil	VG+/IB	$153.00	4-2000
CCBC	Beetle	white, red wings, might clean up	G	$67.00	3-2000
CCBC	Beetle	white, red wings, NOT MET	VG-	$69.33	6-1999
CCBC	Beetle	x2, one missing pearl, spinners	EX-	$170.00	7-2000
CCBC	Beetle	yellow	NIB	$1,313.00	6-2001
CCBC	Beetle	yellow, 3850 label	EX/IB	$438.00	1-2000
CCBC	Beetle	yellow, gold, NOT MET	Awful	$48.00	8-2000
CCBC	Beetle	yellow, green	EX	$168.00	10-2000
CCBC	Beetle	yellow, green	EX	$202.51	1-2000
CCBC	Beetle	yellow, green	EX	$230.00	10-1999
CCBC	Beetle	yellow, green	G	$100.00	3-1999

BRAND	MODEL NAME	SERIES / MFG. CODE / DESCRIPTION	GRADE	PRICE	DATE
CCBC	Beetle	yellow, green wings, rough #38 box	EX/IB	$204.00	4-2000
CCBC	Beetle, Baby	black, maroon, red eye	EX-	$370.00	12-1999
CCBC	Beetle, Baby	black, red wings, 6055 box	EX/IB	$331.00	1-1999
CCBC	Beetle, Baby	gold, black, chip on wing, shiny	VG	$130.27	2-1999
CCBC	Beetle, Baby	metallic green, green wings	EX	$200.00	4-2000
CCBC	Beetle, Baby	yellow, green, crisp label box	NIB	$354.87	2-2000
CCBC	Beetle, Baby	yellow, green wings	EX-	$187.50	3-2000
CCBC	Beetle, Baby	6000, goldfish scale, tack eyes	EX	$175.00	4-1999
CCBC	Beetle, Baby	6008 Special, rainbow, tack eyes	NIB	$230.50	11-1999
CCBC	Beetle, Baby	6025, black scale, PTCB	NIB	$120.02	10-1999
CCBC	Beetle, Baby	6034, silver flash, tack eyes, wood, PTCB	NIB	$99.00	9-2001
CCBC	Beetle, Baby	gold, yellow wings	EX	$247.00	3-2000
CCBC	Beetle, Baby	metallic, greenish wings	EX-	$187.00	3-2000
CCBC	Bomber	frog	Mint	$305.00	3-1999
CCBC	Bomber, Big	6718 label	NIB	$412.61	6-1999
CCBC	Bomber, Big	perch	Mint	$435.00	6-1999
CCBC	Bomber, Dive	6604, painted eyes, nice label box	NIB	$198.00	8-1999
CCBC	Castrola		EX-/IB	$152.50	5-1999
CCBC	Castrola	green perch	EX-	$177.00	5-2000
CCBC	Castrola	perch, glass eyes	VG	$61.00	2-2000
CCBC	Castrola	pikie, glass eyes	EX	$177.50	7-1999
CCBC	Castrola	red, white, glass eyes	NIB	$189.50	12-1999
CCBC	Castrola	silver flash, glass eyes	Mint	$283.00	3-2000
CCBC	Castrola	3118, minnow	EX+	$188.50	10-1999
CCBC	Castrola	3118, silver flash, glass eyes	NIB	$511.00	2-2002
CCBC	Champ	S30N	NIB	$95.00	2-1999
CCBC	Chautauqua Special	chub, many pointers & drags	AVG	$860.00	7-2000
CCBC	Chautauqua Special	NO BIDS	G	$1,200.00	10-1999
CCBC	Chugger	white scale, cracked eye, NOT MET	VG-	$46.00	10-1999
CCBC	Close-Pin	ugly at lead, rest nice, NOT MET		$385.00	6-1999
CCBC	Close-Pin	5000 stencil	NIB	$827.00	10-1999
CCBC	Close-Pin, Musky	5000 Special, red, white	NIB	$349.00	12-1999
CCBC	Cohokie	1000G	NIB	$26.00	6-1999
CCBC	Crab, Creek	rough intro box	EX/IB	$260.00	3-2001
CCBC	Crawdad	black, white	EX	$588.89	3-1999
CCBC	Crawdad	fair intro box, NOT MET	EX/IB	$401.50	1-1999
CCBC	Crawdad	natural crawdad, NOT MET	Mint	$50.00	4-2000
CCBC	Crawdad	silver flash	EX	$93.00	12-2001
CCBC	Crawdad	silver flash, bead eyes, NOT MET	NIB	$113.00	1-2001
CCBC	Crawdad	white, purple, NOT MET	Mint	$522.00	5-1999
CCBC	Crawdad	300 label, crisp	NIB	$102.00	10-2000
CCBC	Crawdad	300, peeler, blue tail	EX-	$97.00	3-1999
CCBC	Crawdad	315, tan, green legs	NIB	$93.50	9-1999
CCBC	Crawdad, Flyrod	red, black center, NOT MET	EX/IB	$91.00	4-2000
CCBC	Cray-Z-Fish	4 different colors	NIB	$81.00	2-1999
CCBC	Cray-Z-Fish	crab, hard plastic	EX	$17.50	2-1999
CCBC	Darter	2000 Special, BWS, painted eyes, wood, PTCB	NIB	$217.50	3-2000

BRAND	MODEL	SERIES / MFG. CODE / DESCRIPTION	GRADE	PRICE	DATE
CCBC	Darter	2005, 12-pack box, NOT MET	NIB	$685.03	12-1999
CCBC	Darter	2008W, rainbow, PTCB	NIB	$124.00	1-1999
CCBC	Darter	2009W, tack eyes, (IA?), PTCB, NOT MET	NIB	$93.00	12-2001
CCBC	Darter	2014, yellow spots, painted eyes, papers	NIB	$67.80	2-2000
CCBC	Darter	2018W, PTCB, painted eyes, rough	NIB	$17.00	11-2000
CCBC	Darter	2023W, chartreuse, black, white eye, PTCB	NIB	$101.00	3-2002
CCBC	Darter	dace, painted eyes	EX	$68.00	8-2000
CCBC	Darter	frog, painted eyes, label	NIB	$53.00	11-1999
CCBC	Darter	frog, PTCB	EX-	$15.00	1-1999
CCBC	Darter	silver flash, plastic	NIB	$18.00	5-2000
CCBC	Darter	yellow spots	EX+/IB	$30.00	10-2000
CCBC	Darter	yellow spots, painted eyes	NIB	$31.00	2-1999
CCBC	Darter, Jointed	4900M, mackerel, painted eyes, PTCB	NIB	$415.00	11-2000
CCBC	Darter, Jointed	4911W, painted eyes, PTCB, NOT MET	NIB	$157.00	5-2000
CCBC	Darter, Jointed	4938, pearl, PTCB	NIB	$97.00	6-1999
CCBC	Darter, Midget	8002W, red, white, PTCB	NIB	$26.50	1-1999
CCBC	Darter, Midget	8005, red side, painted eyes, PTCB	NIB	$204.50	10-1999
CCBC	Darter, Midget	frog, painted eyes, 8019 stencil	NIB	$51.00	6-1999
CCBC	Darter, Salt Spin	5¾", blue flash, painted eyes, stencil on back	EX	$229.00	10-2001
CCBC	Darter, Salt Spin	7702, red, white, painted eyes, stencil box, name on back	EX-/IB	$238.51	6-1999
CCBC	Darter, Spinning	9000P, frog	NIB	$14.00	5-2000
CCBC	Darter, Spinning	9000UL, ultra light	NIB	$56.00	5-2001
CCBC	Darter, Spinning	9002, PCCB	NIB	$33.88	1-1999
CCBC	Darter, Spinning	9018UL, ultra light, plastic	EX	$26.00	2-2000
CCBC	Darter, Spinning	Centennial, pike scale	NIB	$27.00	1-1999
CCBC	Darter, Spinning	dace, 12-pack box, 1 lure with box	NIB	$900.00	10-1999
CCBC	Deepster, Spinning	9633, black scale, painted eyes	NIB	$455.00	4-1999
CCBC	Ding Bat	5100	EX/IB	$86.00	2-1999
CCBC	Ding Bat	5100, glass eyes, PTCB	NIB	$47.80	4-2000
CCBC	Ding Bat	5102, 5102 label	NIB	$112.17	10-1999
CCBC	Ding Bat	5118 label	NIB	$152.50	1-2000
CCBC	Ding Bat	5118 stencil	EX-/IB	$102.00	4-2001
CCBC	Ding Bat	AL&W 3190 pikie, glass eyes	NIB	$180.00	10-2000
CCBC	Ding Bat	black	EX-	$50.00	2-1999
CCBC	Ding Bat	black	VG+	$38.88	4-1999
CCBC	Ding Bat	black, 5113 end label	EX/IB	$103.51	8-1999
CCBC	Ding Bat	frog	EX-	$49.00	6-2001
CCBC	Ding Bat	frog	VG	$32.50	1-1999
CCBC	Ding Bat	frog	VG-	$37.00	1-1999
CCBC	Ding Bat	frog, one eye	VG	$33.00	1-1999
CCBC	Ding Bat	golden shiner	EX	$75.00	8-1999
CCBC	Ding Bat	golden shiner	EX-	$58.01	5-1999
CCBC	Ding Bat	golden shiner, catalog, tag	NIB	$138.49	12-1999
CCBC	Ding Bat	golden shiner, catalog, tag, nice	NIB	$98.00	2-1999
CCBC	Ding Bat	green back	NIB	$2,025.00	7-2000

BRAND	MODEL NAME	SERIES / MFG. CODE / DESCRIPTION	GRADE	PRICE	DATE
CCBC	Ding Bat	green scale	EX	$376.00	2-1999
CCBC	Ding Bat	pearl, bad varnish	VG-	$104.00	10-2000
CCBC	Ding Bat	perch	EX	$69.00	1-1999
CCBC	Ding Bat	perch	VG	$38.00	1-1999
CCBC	Ding Bat	perch, label	EX/IB	$77.00	10-2000
CCBC	Ding Bat	pikie	EX+/IB	$56.00	2-1999
CCBC	Ding Bat	pikie	EX-	$33.52	5-1999
CCBC	Ding Bat	pikie	VG	$26.00	1-1999
CCBC	Ding Bat	pikie, worm burn, hair loss	EX	$46.00	6-1999
CCBC	Ding Bat	rainbow fire	EX-	$1,200.00	7-2000
CCBC	Ding Bat	red head	VG-	$33.00	8-2001
CCBC	Ding Bat	red, white	EX	$71.00	1-1999
CCBC	Ding Bat	red, white	NIB	$125.00	6-1999
CCBC	Ding Bat	red, white, marked	VG	$48.00	2-1999
CCBC	Ding Bat	silver flash	VG+	$41.00	1-1999
CCBC	Ding Bat	small back chip, 5101 stencil box	EX-/IB	$86.00	5-2000
CCBC	Ding Bat	small worm burn, 5102 label	EX/IB	$125.00	6-1999
CCBC	Ding Bat	white, black	EX-	$356.57	12-1999
CCBC	Ding Bat	white scale	EX	$655.01	12-1998
CCBC	Ding Bat	x2, black, frog Baby	EX	$94.00	10-1999
CCBC	Ding Bat, Baby	5218, NOT MET	EX/IB	$83.00	1-1999
CCBC	Ding Bat, Baby	back stencil, BW, NOT MET	EX	$566.00	10-2000
CCBC	Ding Bat, Baby	black, white, glass eyes	VG	$526.01	12-1999
CCBC	Ding Bat, Baby	golden shiner	EX-	$53.00	10-2000
CCBC	Ding Bat, Baby	golden shiner	Mint	$168.50	1-2000
CCBC	Ding Bat, Baby	golden shiner	VG-	$25.00	1-1999
CCBC	Ding Bat, Baby	pearl	EX-	$306.33	4-1999
CCBC	Ding Bat, Baby	perch, catalog & 2 papers, stencil box	NIB	$101.00	9-2001
CCBC	Ding Bat, Baby	pikie	EX/IB	$83.00	10-2000
CCBC	Ding Bat, Baby	silver flash	EX-	$61.00	1-1999
CCBC	Ding Bat, Flyrod	frog, (Shur-Strike?)	EX	$79.00	8-2000
CCBC	Ding Bat, Flyrod	frog, painted eyes, huge belly sliver, top nice	VG	$76.00	10-2000
CCBC	Ding Bat, Flyrod	golden shiner?	EX	$200.50	7-1999
CCBC	Ding Bat, Flyrod	pikie	NOC	$168.05	10-1999
CCBC	Ding Bat, Flyrod	pikie, on card in box, tail flaw, NOT MET	NIB	$142.51	4-1999
CCBC	Ding Bat, Flyrod	pikie, painted eyes	EX	$127.00	2-2001
CCBC	Ding Bat, Flyrod	pikie, problems		$154.52	3-1999
CCBC	Ding Bat, Flyrod	red, white, on card in box	NIB	$409.00	4-1999
CCBC	Ding Bat, Husky	frog, glass eyes	EX-	$381.00	7-2000
CCBC	Ding Bat, Husky	pikie, NOT MET	EX-	$106.49	2-1999
CCBC	Ding Bat, Husky	pikie, nothing special	VG+	$330.00	5-1999
CCBC	Ding Bat, Midget	pikie, 5200 label	NIB	$92.00	10-1999
CCBC	Ding Bat, Midget	pikie, papers	NIB	$112.55	11-1999
CCBC	Ding Bat, Surface	2 different, yellow skunk, golden shiner	VG to EX	$460.00	4-1999
CCBC	Ding Bat, Surface	5404 end label	NIB	$197.50	8-1999
CCBC	Ding Bat, Surface	5418 label	NIB	$202.50	9-1999
CCBC	Ding Bat, Surface	black, NOT MET	EX-	$75.00	5-1999

BRAND	MODEL	SERIES / MFG. CODE / DESCRIPTION	GRADE	PRICE	DATE
CCBC	Ding Bat, Surface	fireplug, huge worm burn	Poor	$103.49	12-1999
CCBC	Ding Bat, Surface	frog	EX	$61.02	3-1999
CCBC	Ding Bat, Surface	frog	EX+	$158.39	5-1999
CCBC	Ding Bat, Surface	frog	EX-	$178.49	7-1999
CCBC	Ding Bat, Surface	frog, catalog, 5419 stencil, crisp box	NIB	$205.00	11-2000
CCBC	Ding Bat, Surface	perch	EX-	$90.90	12-1998
CCBC	Ding Bat, Surface	perch, label	NIB	$225.00	8-1999
CCBC	Ding Bat, Surface	red, white, box	NIB	$122.50	3-1999
CCBC	Ding Bat, Surface	red-winged blackbird, fake stamp box	EX/IB	$634.09	12-1999
CCBC	Ding Bat, Surface	sable	EX	$526.00	12-2001
CCBC	Ding Bat, Surface	sable	EX+	$610.00	4-1999
CCBC	Ding Bat, Surface	sable, NOT MET	EX+	$406.00	1-2002
CCBC	Ding Bat, Surface	sable, NOT MET	VG	$183.52	3-1999
CCBC	Ding Bat, Surface	sable, Western Auto	VG-	$91.00	4-1999
CCBC	Ding Bat, Surface	silver flash	EX	$103.50	2-2000
CCBC	Ding Bat, Surface	silver flash	EX+	$199.99	5-1999
CCBC	Dinger	5600 label, ended 15:34 Saturday	NIB	$114.00	9-2000
CCBC	Dinger	5602, red, white, label	NIB	$167.50	9-1999
CCBC	Dinger	black	EX	$235.00	7-1999
CCBC	Dinger	chub?	VG-	$58.00	7-1999
CCBC	Dinger	dace	EX	$150.00	2-1999
CCBC	Dinger	dace	EX-	$235.39	1-1999
CCBC	Dinger	dace, hook drags but nice	VG	$145.00	9-2000
CCBC	Dinger	frog	AVG	$33.00	9-2000
CCBC	Dinger	frog, AL&W 330 #18 box	EX/IB	$192.49	4-1999
CCBC	Dinger	frog, glass eyes	G	$50.00	6-1999
CCBC	Dinger	frog, unmarked box	NIB	$197.50	4-1999
CCBC	Dinger	pikie	VG+/IB	$125.00	5-2000
CCBC	Dinger	pikie, silver plate, (unmarked?) box	NIB	$143.00	2-2000
CCBC	Dinger	red head, silver flash	EX	$500.00	7-2000
CCBC	Dinger	red head, silver flash	EX-	$280.00	10-2000
CCBC	Dinger	silver flash	EX	$128.00	1-1999
CCBC	Dinger	silver flash, label box	NIB	$250.00	7-1999
CCBC	Dinger	silver plate, 5600 label	NIB	$150.00	4-2001
CCBC	Dinger, Baby	frog	NIB	$150.00	10-2000
CCBC	Dinger, Baby	red head, glass eyes	VG	$58.00	6-2002
CCBC	Dinger, Husky	pikie	EX	$204.06	4-1999
CCBC	Dinger, Husky	pikie	VG	$203.38	9-1999
CCBC	Dinger, Husky	red head, small marked box	EX-/IB	$200.00	10-2000
CCBC	Dinger, Husky	red, white, glass eyes, thin hair	EX	$84.00	1-1999
CCBC	Dinger, Husky	silver flash	VG+	$190.37	10-1999
CCBC	Dinger, Midget	6101, nose chip	NIB	$213.00	8-2000
CCBC	Dinger, Midget	6102W, very modern, PTCB	NIB	$108.00	4-2000
CCBC	Dinger, Midget	V355 stamp, Western Auto Skunk, NOT MET	NIB	$560.00	2-2000
CCBC	Dinger, Plunking	6200 label	NIB	$159.00	1-2000
CCBC	Dinger, Plunking	black, NOT MET	EX	$82.87	5-1999
CCBC	Dinger, Plunking	golden shiner, nice	EX	$153.00	8-2000

BRAND	MODEL NAME	SERIES / MFG. CODE / DESCRIPTION	GRADE	PRICE	DATE
CCBC	Dinger, Plunking	golden shiner, NOT MET	EX	$117.50	5-1999
CCBC	Fintail Shiner	chub?, red side, all fiber fins intact, nice	EX	$1,251.00	3-2002
CCBC	Fintail Shiner	perch, metal tail	Mint	$563.32	1-1999
CCBC	Fintail Shiner	shiner scale, metal dorsal fins, POBW	EX-	$300.00	8-2002
CCBC	Fintail Shiner	white, metal tail	EX-	$617.00	3-1999
CCBC	Flip-Flap	frog, glass eyes	EX	$250.00	1-2000
CCBC	Flip-Flap	frog, gleamer, glass eyes	EX	$193.00	5-2000
CCBC	Flip-Flap	red, white, glass eyes	EX-	$127.50	6-1999
CCBC	Flip-Flap	silver flash, glass eyes	EX-	$66.00	11-2000
CCBC	Flip-Flap	silver flash, glass eyes	VG	$52.00	1-1999
CCBC	Flip-Flap	silver flash, NOT MET	EX	$132.00	11-2000
CCBC	Gar	2600GAR	NIB	$1,396.00	4-2000
CCBC	Gar	2920 stamped box, NOT MET	NIB	$1,025.00	5-2001
CCBC	Gar	a little mousy, 2900 label	NIB	$1,601.71	10-1999
CCBC	Gar	green, 2BW, some POBW, NOT MET	EX	$321.00	11-2000
CCBC	Gar	green?, paint off belly 1"		$185.00	12-1998
CCBC	Gar	green, nose chip, screw, shiny, POBW	EX-	$350.00	2-2000
CCBC	Gar	green, not awful	AVG	$120.00	3-1999
CCBC	Gar	grubby but might clean up	VG-	$210.00	7-2000
CCBC	Gar	heavy age lines, small chip, POBW, NOT MET	EX-	$511.00	5-2000
CCBC	Gar	huge belly chips, top okay	Poor	$104.00	7-2000
CCBC	Gar	natural	EX	$896.00	4-2000
CCBC	Gar	natural	VG-	$248.00	3-2001
CCBC	Gar	one eye cracked, 2900 label box	NIB	$900.00	10-1999
CCBC	Gar	pikie, many pointers around tail, NOT MET	VG-	$197.00	4-2000
CCBC	Gar	pikie, mine, end label	NIB	$1,650.00	2-2000
CCBC	Gar	rings, shin chip, top okay, BW, NOT MET	VG-	$306.00	11-1999
CCBC	Gar	stencil back, 2900 label box	EX+/IB	$1,255.00	4-1999
CCBC	Gar	stencil box	NIB	$1,224.88	9-1999
CCBC	Husky Musky	600, mullet, eye replaced	VG-	$104.00	3-1999
CCBC	Husky Musky	601 stencil	VG+/IB	$78.00	8-2000
CCBC	Husky Musky	601 stencil, NOT MET	NIB	$192.00	9-2000
CCBC	Husky Musky	603, good box	VG+/IB	$1,525.00	8-1999
CCBC	Husky Musky	607, blue, natural mullet	EX	$700.00	10-1999
CCBC	Husky Musky	607, mullet, 1 eye missing	EX/IB	$147.61	11-1999
CCBC	Husky Musky	612, white	NIB	$655.00	10-2000
CCBC	Husky Musky	5902, wrong white box, glass eyes	NIB	$242.00	11-2000
CCBC	Husky Musky	blue mullet, one side faded, glass eyes, like chub?	EX-	$280.00	10-2001
CCBC	Husky Musky	chub	VG	$136.89	4-1999
CCBC	Husky Musky	chub?	VG	$86.50	3-1999
CCBC	Husky Musky	chub, label	EX-/IB	$285.00	11-1999
CCBC	Husky Musky	flat red head, no eyes	VG/IB	$66.00	4-2000
CCBC	Husky Musky	intro picture box	EX/IB	$650.00	10-2000
CCBC	Husky Musky	mullet?	VG-	$80.00	3-1999
CCBC	Husky Musky	old lip, 600 stencil chub	VG+/IB	$151.00	10-2000
CCBC	Husky Musky	perch, box	VG	$82.75	11-1999

BRAND	MODEL	SERIES / MFG. CODE / DESCRIPTION	GRADE	PRICE	DATE
CCBC	Husky Musky	pikie, jointed, poor box	NIB	$2,025.00	6-1999
CCBC	Husky Musky	red head, no eyes, DLT	EX-	$255.00	5-2000
CCBC	Husky Musky	silver flash, glass eyes, improved	VG+	$118.00	8-2001
CCBC	Husky Musky	silver shiner, jointed, rear wire clipped off	VG+	$154.00	5-2000
CCBC	Injured Minnow		VG-/IB	$41.00	7-1999
CCBC	Injured Minnow	7 different, glass eyes	VG- to EX+	$205.00	5-2000
CCBC	Injured Minnow	1501, glass eyes	EX/IB	$51.00	6-2000
CCBC	Injured Minnow	1501, glass eyes	NIB	$104.50	4-1999
CCBC	Injured Minnow	1501, perch, glass eyes, catalog	NIB	$76.01	5-1999
CCBC	Injured Minnow	1505, blue back, glass eyes, label	NIB	$153.49	9-1999
CCBC	Injured Minnow	1505, glass eyes, label	EX/IB	$129.50	9-1999
CCBC	Injured Minnow	1505, glass eyes, PTCB	NIB	$76.00	9-1999
CCBC	Injured Minnow	1505, hang tag, papers, catalog	NIB	$672.00	2-2000
CCBC	Injured Minnow	1505 label	NIB	$124.00	4-2000
CCBC	Injured Minnow	1508, NOT MET	EX/IB	$51.50	3-2000
CCBC	Injured Minnow	1511W, puro, blue head, tack eyes, Sioux City	NIB	$306.00	5-1999
CCBC	Injured Minnow	1514, yellow spots, red ribs, glass eyes, special stencil, ex box	NIB	$474.00	8-2002
CCBC	Injured Minnow	1518 box, unmarked?	NIB	$87.00	10-2000
CCBC	Injured Minnow	1519, frog, glass eyes	EX/IB	$54.00	6-2000
CCBC	Injured Minnow	1531, glass eyes	EX/IB	$301.51	7-1999
CCBC	Injured Minnow	black, white, ultra light plastic	NIB	$29.50	5-1999
CCBC	Injured Minnow	blended red head & tail, glass eyes	G	$105.54	5-1999
CCBC	Injured Minnow	chub, glass eyes	EX-	$51.00	5-1999
CCBC	Injured Minnow	chub, red side	NIB	$74.77	6-1999
CCBC	Injured Minnow	chub, wrong box	EX/IB	$51.50	1-1999
CCBC	Injured Minnow	dace, glass eyes	EX-	$30.00	8-2002
CCBC	Injured Minnow	dace, red side scale	EX	$61.55	3-2000
CCBC	Injured Minnow	fireplug	EX-	$73.00	8-2000
CCBC	Injured Minnow	fireplug, 1531 stencil	NIB	$305.00	7-2000
CCBC	Injured Minnow	fireplug, glass eyes, decent	VG+	$88.00	10-2001
CCBC	Injured Minnow	frog, 1519 stencil	NIB	$92.00	7-2000
CCBC	Injured Minnow	frog, glass eyes	EX-/IB	$113.50	3-2000
CCBC	Injured Minnow	frog, glass eyes, PTCB	NIB	$117.00	10-2001
CCBC	Injured Minnow	glass eyes, red side label	NIB	$127.50	1-2000
CCBC	Injured Minnow	glass eyes, silver shiner label, catalog & paper	NIB	$127.50	1-2000
CCBC	Injured Minnow	golden shiner, glass eyes, 1504 label	NIB	$98.00	1-2000
CCBC	Injured Minnow	golden shiner, rubbed	VG	$29.50	1-1999
CCBC	Injured Minnow	papers, 1504 stencil	EX/IB	$166.50	8-1999
CCBC	Injured Minnow	pearl, tack eyes	NIB	$215.16	7-1999
CCBC	Injured Minnow	perch, glass eyes	EX+	$60.00	1-1999
CCBC	Injured Minnow	perch, glass eyes	EX-	$22.00	8-2002
CCBC	Injured Minnow	perch, glass eyes	Mint	$41.00	4-1999
CCBC	Injured Minnow	pikie color, glass eyes, small paint flaw	EX	$23.00	8-2002
CCBC	Injured Minnow	pikie color, plastic	NIB	$38.00	5-2000
CCBC	Injured Minnow	pikie, oil soaked box & catalog, NOT MET	EX/IB	$76.00	6-1999
CCBC	Injured Minnow	plastic, clear, purple back	EX	$364.50	3-2000

BRAND	MODEL NAME	SERIES / MFG. CODE / DESCRIPTION	GRADE	PRICE	DATE
CCBC	Injured Minnow	purple scale, white eye, plastic	EX	$88.00	12-2000
CCBC	Injured Minnow	rainbow fire, 1531 stencil	NIB	$214.00	11-2000
CCBC	Injured Minnow	rainbow fire, NOT MET	VG+	$80.00	6-2001
CCBC	Injured Minnow	rainbow fire, stencil	NIB	$395.00	3-2000
CCBC	Injured Minnow	red head, glass eyes	EX	$35.89	1-2000
CCBC	Injured Minnow	red head, glass eyes, (unmarked?) box	EX/IB	$36.00	2-2001
CCBC	Injured Minnow	red scale, broad, early type	VG	$56.00	1-2000
CCBC	Injured Minnow	red side, glass eyes	EX	$160.00	1-1999
CCBC	Injured Minnow	red side, glass eyes, hang tag, NOT MET	EX	$76.59	4-2000
CCBC	Injured Minnow	red, white, glass eyes	VG	$32.10	1-1999
CCBC	Injured Minnow	red-winged blackbird	Mint	$360.00	12-1998
CCBC	Injured Minnow	red-winged blackbird, glass eyes	AVG to Poor	$54.00	6-1999
CCBC	Injured Minnow	red-winged blackbird, glass eyes	VG	$182.00	6-1999
CCBC	Injured Minnow	red-winged blackbird, small worm burns		$65.00	1-1999
CCBC	Injured Minnow	shiner scale, black back, plastic	EX	$66.00	3-2001
CCBC	Injured Minnow	silver flash, black back, glass eyes, NOT MET	Mint	$361.00	11-2000
CCBC	Injured Minnow	silver flash, glass eyes	EX	$44.61	5-1999
CCBC	Injured Minnow	silver flash, glass eyes, rough unmarked box	EX/IB	$56.55	2-2000
CCBC	Injured Minnow	silver, flat side, glass eyes, stencil	EX	$360.00	7-2000
CCBC	Injured Minnow	strawberry, tack eyes	Mint	$910.00	4-2000
CCBC	Injured Minnow	white scale, glass eyes	EX	$357.00	5-2001
CCBC	Injured Minnow	white, black spots	EX	$2,603.00	6-2001
CCBC	Injured Minnow	white, glass eyes, stenciled name	EX-	$470.00	1-2002
CCBC	Injured Minnow	yellow spots, glass eyes	EX	$343.00	2-2001
CCBC	Injured Minnow	yellow spots, glass eyes, PTCB	NIB	$200.01	4-1999
CCBC	Injured Minnow	yellow spots, red ribs, glass eyes	Mint	$380.00	9-2002
CCBC	Injured Minnow	yellow, spots, red bloodline, glass eyes	EX	$456.51	6-1999
CCBC	Injured Minnow, Musky	3403 Special	EX-/IB	$480.00	3-1999
CCBC	Injured Minnow, Baby	1618, glass eyes	NIB	$97.00	4-2000
CCBC	Injured Minnow, Baby	1624, worm burn	VG/IB	$182.50	5-1999
CCBC	Injured Minnow, Baby	dace, glass eyes, NOT MET	EX	$58.00	9-2000
CCBC	Injured Minnow, Baby	fire lacquer rainbow fire?, glass eyes	EX-	$50.00	11-1999
CCBC	Injured Minnow, Baby	rainbow fire, glass eyes	EX	$92.00	10-2000
CCBC	Injured Minnow, Baby	red side, glass eyes	EX-	$49.15	11-1999
CCBC	Injured Minnow, Baby	red, white, glass eyes	EX/IB	$82.00	6-1999
CCBC	Injured Minnow, Baby	red-winged blackbird, glass eyes	EX	$168.00	11-2000
CCBC	Injured Minnow, Baby	white scales, glass eyes	EX-	$230.00	5-2000
CCBC	Injured Minnow, Baby	yellow spots, glass eyes	VG	$73.00	1-1999
CCBC	Injured Minnow, Baby	yellow spots, red stripe & ribs, glass eyes	VG+	$204.01	9-1999
CCBC	Injured Minnow, Husky	3501	EX-/IB	$315.00	10-2000
CCBC	Injured Minnow, Husky	3518, glass eyes, catalog	NIB	$535.99	5-1999
CCBC	Injured Minnow, Husky	blue flash, glass eyes	Mint	$1,227.00	2-2002
CCBC	Injured Minnow, Husky	golden shiner	VG+	$250.00	2-2002
CCBC	Injured Minnow, Husky	golden shiner	VG	$93.00	11-1999
CCBC	Injured Minnow, Husky	golden shiner, glass eyes	VG	$93.00	11-1999
CCBC	Injured Minnow, Husky	golden shiner, glass eyes, decent	AVG	$62.00	6-1999
CCBC	Injured Minnow, Husky	pikie, chip, heavy age lines, NOT MET	VG+	$120.00	5-2001

BRAND	MODEL	SERIES / MFG. CODE / DESCRIPTION	GRADE	PRICE	DATE
CCBC	Injured Minnow, Husky	silver flash, glass eyes	EX-	$355.00	2-1999
CCBC	Injured Minnow, Spinning	9518UL, ultra light	NIB	$66.00	7-1999
CCBC	Injured Minnow, Spinning	9518UL, ultra light, plastic bowtie props	NIB	$57.00	5-2001
CCBC	Injured Minnow, Plunker	black, black	EX-	$416.52	11-1999
CCBC	Jig-L-Worm	red, white, blue, affidavit from CCBC	EX	$424.00	3-2002
CCBC	Jigger	black, luminous head, NOT MET	EX	$415.00	3-2000
CCBC	Jigger	dace	AVG	$76.00	10-2001
CCBC	Jigger	frog, NOT MET	G	$64.00	10-2000
CCBC	Jigger	frog, ugly	VG-	$113.00	1-2001
CCBC	Jigger	red head	AVG	$77.00	7-2000
CCBC	Jigger	red head, NOT MET	VG	$130.00	4-2001
CCBC	Jigger	red, white	VG	$137.50	5-1999
CCBC	Jigger	red, white, NOT MET	VG-	$87.87	6-1999
CCBC	Jigger	silver flash, ugly	G	$88.00	2-2002
CCBC	Jigger, Baby	frog	EX	$332.00	10-2000
CCBC	Jigger, Baby	frog	EX-	$223.00	3-2000
CCBC	Jigger, Baby	frog, NOT MET	VG	$92.00	1-2002
CCBC	Jigger, Baby	frog, NOT MET	VG+	$123.00	10-2001
CCBC	Jigger, Baby	frog, numerous digs	G	$130.00	4-1999
CCBC	Jigger, Baby	luminous head, black	EX	$403.88	9-1999
CCBC	Jigger, Baby	night glow, black, white head, glass eyes	EX	$267.00	10-2002
CCBC	Lucky Mouse	3602	EX-	$362.99	10-1999
CCBC	Lucky Mouse	grey	EX-	$175.00	1-1999
CCBC	Lucky Mouse	grey, metal ears	EX	$129.00	8-2000
CCBC	Lucky Mouse	white	EX-	$180.00	11-1999
CCBC	Lucky Mouse	white, 3602 label	VG/IB	$225.40	2-2000
CCBC	Morgan Special	perch, chugger, painted eyes, long top lip	EX-	$80.00	11-1999
CCBC	Mouse	2¾", pearl, PTCB	NIB	$80.00	4-2001
CCBC	Nikie	2 perch, silver flash	Mint	$26.00	2-1999
CCBC	Nikie	9713UL, ultra light, black & white bars, plastic box	NIB	$31.01	9-1999
CCBC	Nikie	9738P, pearl	EX	$18.00	5-2000
CCBC	Nikie	red, white	NIB	$20.00	1-1999
CCBC	Open Mouth Weedless	lavender intro box, tear on top	EX/IB	$495.00	5-2001
CCBC	Open Mouth Shiner	500, vg- purple intro box	EX+/IB	$2,350.00	1-2000
CCBC	Open Mouth Shiner	red head, no eyes, worm burn, rest okay		$49.00	1-2001
CCBC	Pikie	5", red head, orange spots, glass eyes, ragged box	EX-	$456.00	4-1999
CCBC	Pikie	6", frog, tack eyes	EX	$39.99	2-1999
CCBC	Pikie	7", red head, glass eyes, papers	NIB	$45.00	1-2000
CCBC	Pikie	4½", red, white, glass eyes	EX	$33.00	2-1999
CCBC	Pikie	19", ad lure, "AL&W" on lip	EX	$1050.00	4-2000
CCBC	Pikie	700, DLT, label	NIB	$72.88	1-2000
CCBC	Pikie	700, fireplug, glass eyes	Mint	$48.00	1-1999
CCBC	Pikie	700, glass eyes, dirt common	VG+	$10.00	3-2000
CCBC	Pikie	700, golden shiner, glass eyes	EX	$35.00	1-1999
CCBC	Pikie	700, rainbow, glass eyes, one cracked	Mint	$119.00	1-1999
CCBC	Pikie	700, rainbow trout, plastic	NIB	$129.00	1-2001

BRAND	MODEL NAME	SERIES / MFG. CODE / DESCRIPTION	GRADE	PRICE	DATE
CCBC	Pikie	700, white, black, glass eyes	EX-	$129.00	4-2000
CCBC	Pikie	700, white, black, glass eyes, DLT	VG	$96.00	1-1999
CCBC	Pikie	700, white, black, no eyes, DLT	VG+	$76.00	5-2000
CCBC	Pikie	701, box	VG/IB	$20.00	1-1999
CCBC	Pikie	703, glass eyes, light mold on box	NIB	$88.51	6-1999
CCBC	Pikie	703 Special, glass eyes, PTCB?	NIB	$81.02	6-1999
CCBC	Pikie	703 Special, silver chin?, glass eyes?, PTCB	NIB	$103.50	4-2000
CCBC	Pikie	707 stencil	EX/IB	$255.00	10-1999
CCBC	Pikie	710BH, glass eyes, stencil	NIB	$460.65	10-1999
CCBC	Pikie	711, glass eyes, catalog, stencil	NIB	$237.00	2-2001
CCBC	Pikie	711 Special, black, white, glass eyes, stencil	NIB	$290.11	3-1999
CCBC	Pikie	718, glass eyes	NIB	$51.00	3-1999
CCBC	Pikie	718, glass eyes	NIB	$56.00	4-1999
CCBC	Pikie	720?, silver scale, white, purple gills, stencil box	NIB	$1424.00	9-2001
CCBC	Pikie	721, "Day & Night," glass eyes	EX-	$42.00	6-2001
CCBC	Pikie	732, rainbow fire, stencil box	NIB	$200.00	1-2002
CCBC	Pikie	733, black scale, glass eyes, PTCB	NIB	$200.00	1-2002
CCBC	Pikie	703, glass eyes	NIB	$32.00	11-2000
CCBC	Pikie	711, black, white, glass eyes	NIB	$204.00	5-2000
CCBC	Pikie	711, black, white, glass eyes, stencil box	EX/IB	$185.00	6-1999
CCBC	Pikie	711, glass eyes	EX-/IB	$203.00	4-2000
CCBC	Pikie	711, white, black, glass eyes, hang tag, catalog	NIB	$360.00	2-2000
CCBC	Pikie	721, "Day & Night"	NIB	$191.38	2-1999
CCBC	Pikie	721, night glow label	NIB	$108.15	2-2000
CCBC	Pikie	722, glass eyes	EX/IB	$107.50	2-2000
CCBC	Pikie	725, white scale, glass eyes, NOT MET	VG	$209.50	5-1999
CCBC	Pikie	731, fireplug, rainbow	NIB	$143.51	4-1999
CCBC	Pikie	731, stencil, NOT MET	EX-/IB	$100.00	1-2002
CCBC	Pikie	732, glass eyes, stencil box	NIB	$226.05	8-1999
CCBC	Pikie	733, black scale, glass eyes	EX-	$169.50	6-1999
CCBC	Pikie	2830P, 3-jointed, plastic	NIB	$90.01	9-1999
CCBC	Pikie	2434L, tack eyes, 2-hook, PTCB	NIB	$150.00	9-1999
CCBC	Pikie	6001, Sioux City	NIB	$36.00	4-1999
CCBC	Pikie	black scale, glass eyes, newer	Mint	$102.51	4-1999
CCBC	Pikie	black, glass eyes, back stencil	EX	$320.50	10-1999
CCBC	Pikie	black, white head, glass eyes, gold lettering	EX	$192.00	11-2001
CCBC	Pikie	black, white, glass eyes, DLT	VG	$125.00	7-1999
CCBC	Pikie	black, white, small touch up, pointers	VG-	$82.01	9-1999
CCBC	Pikie	blue flash, glass eyes	EX+	$103.00	4-2001
CCBC	Pikie	blue flash, glass eyes	EX-	$190.00	10-1999
CCBC	Pikie	blue head, faded	G	$81.00	6-1999
CCBC	Pikie	blue head, no eyes, DLT	VG+	$147.50	3-2000
CCBC	Pikie	blue, white, glass eyes, 710 stencil, $375.00 NOT MET	NIB	$218.00	8-2001
CCBC	Pikie	Commemorative, dace, plastic, 2PCCB	NIB	$21.50	2-2000
CCBC	Pikie	"Day-N-Night" glass eyes	Mint	$191.72	6-1999
CCBC	Pikie	"Day-N-Night" glow, glass eyes	EX	$204.52	10-1999

BRAND	MODEL	SERIES / MFG. CODE / DESCRIPTION	GRADE	PRICE	DATE
CCBC	Pikie	frog, plastic, tiny, ultra light	NOC	$46.00	1-2000
CCBC	Pikie	display, perch scale, no extra holes, NOT MET	EX	$457.00	4-2002
CCBC	Pikie	golden mullet?, glass eyes	EX-	$255.00	11-1999
CCBC	Pikie	golden shiner	EX-	$35.00	10-1999
CCBC	Pikie	goldfish, plastic	NIB	$56.00	7-2000
CCBC	Pikie	mullet, glass eyes	EX	$111.00	10-2000
CCBC	Pikie	mullet, glass eyes	EX	$175.00	7-1999
CCBC	Pikie	pickerel, gold head, flitter, red, glass eyes	EX-	$146.00	11-2000
CCBC	Pikie	pearl, tack eyes	NIB	$293.00	7-2000
CCBC	Pikie	pickerel, silver, red tail, glass eyes	G	$32.80	3-2000
CCBC	Pikie	pikie, glass eyes	EX-	$14.00	5-1999
CCBC	Pikie	pink pearl, tack eyes	Mint	$292.00	2-2000
CCBC	Pikie	rainbow fire	EX	$65.00	4-1999
CCBC	Pikie	rainbow fire, $150.00 NOT MET	EX+	$46.00	4-2001
CCBC	Pikie	rainbow, glass eyes, 708 label	NIB	$175.00	1-2000
CCBC	Pikie	rainbow, glass eyes, unmarked box	NIB	$173.00	8-2001
CCBC	Pikie	rainbow, silver back, early	Mint	$264.00	5-2000
CCBC	Pikie	rare color, silver, red, white	VG	$127.00	12-1998
CCBC	Pikie	red head, sparkles, unmarked? box	EX/IB	$167.00	8-2000
CCBC	Pikie	red head, white, CA special side screws	EX-	$69.51	4-1999
CCBC	Pikie	red horse, glass eyes, 4 red fins, DLT, nice	EX-	$2483.00	9-2002
CCBC	Pikie	silver shiner, glass eyes	NIB	$52.00	8-2002
CCBC	Pikie	tiger stripe, glass eyes	EX-	$100.00	11-1999
CCBC	Pikie	West Coast, 702 Special, 2-hook, side screw, NRA	NIB	$302.50	1-2000
CCBC	Pikie	white scale, glass eyes	VG+	$162.00	5-2001
CCBC	Pikie	white, black, no eyes	EX-	$100.00	5-2000
CCBC	Pikie	white, black, no eyes	EX-	$229.49	4-1999
CCBC	Pikie	white, black, no eyes, DLT	VG	$56.00	1-2000
CCBC	Pikie	white, blended red nose & chin, glass eyes	EX-	$249.00	2-2000
CCBC	Pikie	white, red spots , green back stripe, glass eyes	EX	$899.00	5-2001
CCBC	Pikie	x2; one 900, one 2618	NIB	$150.01	10-1999
CCBC	Pikie	x2; one 5532, one 2603; glass eyes	NIB	$212.50	8-1999
CCBC	Pikie	x2; one red & white, one black & white; no eyes	VG+	$251.76	11-1999
CCBC	Pikie	x6, all glass eyes, decent shape	AVG- to VG	$31.00	10-1999
CCBC	Pikie	x6, bought by Newbie	AVG	$91.00	7-2000
CCBC	Pikie	yellow flash, glass eyes	EX	$282.00	8-2000
CCBC	Pikie	yellow spots, glass eyes, DLT	VG-	$204.01	11-1999
CCBC	Pikie, Baby	900, 3-hook, small chips	VG-	$162.00	6-2001
CCBC	Pikie, Baby	900, white scale, glass eyes, back stencil	EX	$1,313.00	4-2002
CCBC	Pikie, Baby	908, rainbow, glass eyes	NIB	$117.00	4-2000
CCBC	Pikie, Baby	933, glass eyes, PTCB	NIB	$214.00	10-2000
CCBC	Pikie, Baby	brilliant green scale, glass eyes, DLT	VG+	$393.88	1-2000
CCBC	Pikie, Baby	fireplug, glass eyes	EX	$75.00	5-1999
CCBC	Pikie, Baby	fireplug, glass eyes, wrong 900 box	EX	$164.50	7-1999
CCBC	Pikie, Baby	fireplug, tack eyes	EX	$76.00	10-2000
CCBC	Pikie, Baby	glass eyes	Mint	$23.00	8-2000
CCBC	Pikie, Baby	glass eyes, 903 label	NIB	$83.00	4-2001

BRAND	MODEL	SERIES / MFG. CODE / DESCRIPTION	GRADE	PRICE	DATE
CCBC	Pikie, Baby	glass eyes, 9903 stencil	NIB	$76.01	10-1999
CCBC	Pikie, Baby	glass eyes, 9908 label	NIB	$156.36	3-1999
CCBC	Pikie, Baby	glass eyes, 9918 label	NIB	$49.89	11-1999
CCBC	Pikie, Baby	silver flash, glass eyes	NIB	$51.00	2-1999
CCBC	Pikie, Baby	white scale, glass eyes	VG+	$366.88	6-1999
CCBC	Pikie, Baby	yellow, red, black spots	EX-	$154.72	10-1999
CCBC	Pikie, Baby Jointed	31, rainbow fire, glass eyes	EX-	$61.26	9-1999
CCBC	Pikie, Baby Jointed	2702, label	EX-/IB	$43.05	5-1999
CCBC	Pikie, Baby Jointed	2703, glass eyes, PTCB	NIB	$153.00	8-2000
CCBC	Pikie, Baby Jointed	2704 label box	EX/IB	$60.99	5-1999
CCBC	Pikie, Baby Jointed	2708 label box	NIB	$198.00	4-1999
CCBC	Pikie, Baby Jointed	2708, rainbow, glass eyes, jointed, stencil box	NIB	$175.00	6-1999
CCBC	Pikie, Baby Jointed	2718, glass eyes, PTCB	NIB	$22.00	3-2001
CCBC	Pikie, Baby Jointed	2730, red head, orange spots, glass eyes	EX	$323.00	1-2002
CCBC	Pikie, Baby Jointed	fireplug, red, glass eyes, odd label box	NIB	$490.00	9-2001
CCBC	Pikie, Baby Jointed	rainbow fire	EX-	$90.00	10-1999
CCBC	Pikie, Baby Jointed	rainbow fire, 4232 stamped box	NIB	$127.52	5-1999
CCBC	Pikie, Baby Jointed	rainbow, glass eyes	Mint	$96.00	11-1999
CCBC	Pikie, Baby Jointed	silver flash, NRA, box	NIB	$162.50	12-1999
CCBC	Pikie, Baby Jointed	baby pickerel, 1 eye cracked, NOT MET	EX-	$78.50	4-1999
CCBC	Pikie, Baby Jointed	rainbow fire, 2731 label, mint box	NIB	$228.00	7-2000
CCBC	Pikie, Baby Jointed Deep Diver	2713DD Special, tack eyes	NIB	$108.00	4-2000
CCBC	Pikie, Baby Saltwater	938SW, 2-hook, tack eyes, PTCB	NIB	$295.00	9-2002
CCBC	Pikie, Deep Diver	703DD, catalog	NIB	$152.50	8-1999
CCBC	Pikie, Deep Diver	734DD, blue flash, tack eyes, PTCB	EX/IB	$48.50	1-1999
CCBC	Pikie, Deep Diver	737DD, tack eyes, PTCB	NIB	$270.00	10-2000
CCBC	Pikie, Deep Diver	702DD, 12-pack, wood, PTCB	NIB	$305.00	8-1999
CCBC	Pikie, Deep Diver	red head, glass eyes, crisp box	NIB	$65.00	9-1999
CCBC	Pikie, Deep Diver Baby	DD, rainbow, glass eyes, wrong box	NIB	$189.00	3-2001
CCBC	Pikie, Deep Diver Baby	DD, red head, orange, black spots, glass eyes, NOT MET	EX-	$188.00	4-2001
CCBC	Pikie, Deep Diver Jointed	700DD, glass eyes, mint box	NIB	$103.19	6-1999
CCBC	Pikie, Deep Diver Jointed	2600DD, strawberry, spots, tack eyes	EX-	$113.00	1-1999
CCBC	Pikie, Deep Diver Jointed	2603DD, tack eyes	NIB	$21.50	1-2000
CCBC	Pikie, Deep Diver Jointed	2606DD, gold scale, tack eyes, PTCB, NOT MET	NIB	$96.00	8-1999
CCBC	Pikie, Deep Diver Jointed	2607DD, glass eyes, nice	EX/IB	$100.00	8-2002
CCBC	Pikie, Deep Diver Jointed	2608DD, rainbow	EX/IB	$250.00	10-1999
CCBC	Pikie, Deep Diver Jointed	2618DD	NIB	$110.00	10-1999
CCBC	Pikie, Deep Diver Jointed	2618DD, glass eyes, crisp box	NIB	$187.00	9-2000
CCBC	Pikie, Deep Diver Jointed	2618DD, glass eyes, nice stencil box	NIB	$78.00	7-2000
CCBC	Pikie, Deep Diver Jointed	2635DD, box	EX-/IB	$40.00	2-1999
CCBC	Pikie, Deep Diver Jointed	DD, frog, tack eyes	EX	$76.00	7-2000
CCBC	Pikie, Deep Diver Jointed	DD, golden shiner, glass eyes	EX-	$22.55	1-1999
CCBC	Pikie, Deep Diver Jointed	DD, pearl, glass eyes	EX	$355.00	5-1999
CCBC	Pikie, Deep Diver Jointed	DD, silver flash, tack eyes, PTCB	NIB	$18.00	3-2001
CCBC	Pikie, Deep Diver Jointed	DD, yellow spots, tack eyes	EX	$39.25	2-1999

BRAND	MODEL	SERIES / MFG. CODE / DESCRIPTION	GRADE	PRICE	DATE
CCBC	Pikie, Deep Diver Jointed	Peters Special, 2603DD, black dot, glass eyes, metal tail, stencil box	NIB	$777.00	1-2002
CCBC	Pikie, Deep Diver Jointed	Peters Special, DD, black scale, glass eyes	EX	$122.00	8-2000
CCBC	Pikie, Flyrod	pikie, color plastic	NIB	$18.05	2-1999
CCBC	Pikie, Flyrod	red, white, plastic	NIB	$15.80	2-1999
CCBC	Pikie, Flyrod	x2, pink, orange, long lip, plastic	EX	$330.25	3-2000
CCBC	Pikie, Giant	gold scale, tack eyes, unmarked 2PCCB	EX/IB	$102.00	9-2000
CCBC	Pikie, Giant	12"	NIB	$82.50	9-1999
CCBC	Pikie, Giant	gold scale, tack eyes	NIB	$275.00	4-2000
CCBC	Pikie, Giant	rainbow, tack eyes	NIB	$235.83	5-1999
CCBC	Pikie, Giant	rainbow, tack eyes, PTCB	NIB	$249.00	1-2001
CCBC	Pikie, Giant Jointed	830, red head, orange spots, tack eyes	NIB	$146.80	3-2000
CCBC	Pikie, Giant Jointed	800, tack eyes	NIB	$122.50	4-1999
CCBC	Pikie, Giant Jointed	834, blue flash, tack eyes, 2PCCB	NIB	$57.00	8-1999
CCBC	Pikie, Giant Jointed	830, red head, orange spots, glass eyes, bad joint chips	EX-/IB	$410.59	6-1999
CCBC	Pikie, Giant Jointed	black scale, tack eyes	NIB	$148.00	4-2001
CCBC	Pikie, Giant Jointed	black scale, tack eyes, PTCB	EX/IB	$92.01	11-1999
CCBC	Pikie, Giant Jointed	black scale, tack eyes, stamped box	EX-/IB	$77.00	3-2002
CCBC	Pikie, Giant Jointed	pikie, tack eyes, 2PCCB	EX/IB	$52.00	6-1999
CCBC	Pikie, Giant Jointed	pikie, tack eyes, NOT MET	NIB	$61.00	4-2000
CCBC	Pikie, Giant Jointed	purple eel, tack eyes	EX-	$220.00	5-2001
CCBC	Pikie, Giant Jointed	purple eel, tack eyes	NIB	$321.00	4-2001
CCBC	Pikie, Giant Jointed	silver flash, tack eyes	EX+/IB	$95.00	6-1999
CCBC	Pikie, Husky		NIB	$51.00	2-1999
CCBC	Pikie, Husky	2300, unimproved lip, big screw	EX	$60.00	3-1999
CCBC	Pikie, Husky	2302, red head, glass eyes	NIB	$78.00	10-1999
CCBC	Pikie, Husky	2302 Special, white, 2-hook	NIB	$1,000.00	3-1999
CCBC	Pikie, Husky	2302 Special, white, red chin, glass eyes	NIB	$690.00	2-2000
CCBC	Pikie, Husky	2303, natural mullet, glass eyes	EX	$200.00	10-1999
CCBC	Pikie, Husky	2303, red, white, glass eyes, decent pointer, NOT MET	VG/IB	$21.00	1-1999
CCBC	Pikie, Husky	2307, natural mullet	NIB	$300.00	10-1999
CCBC	Pikie, Husky	2307 Special, mullet, glass eyes	NIB	$609.00	9-2000
CCBC	Pikie, Husky	2313, black	NIB	$750.00	3-1999
CCBC	Pikie, Husky	2318, glass eyes, crisp box	NIB	$79.00	5-2001
CCBC	Pikie, Husky	2331, rainbow fire, glass eyes, label	NIB	$231.50	6-1999
CCBC	Pikie, Husky	2333W, black scale, tack eyes	NIB	$56.00	4-1999
CCBC	Pikie, Husky	2334W, blue flash, tack eyes	NIB	$55.00	4-1999
CCBC	Pikie, Husky	2335L Special, purple eel, glass eyes, 2-hook	NIB	$698.00	3-1999
CCBC	Pikie, Husky	2337, yellow flash, tack eyes	EX	$115.00	10-2000
CCBC	Pikie, Husky	blue flash, tack eyes, decal, Sioux?	Mint	$27.99	5-1999
CCBC	Pikie, Husky	blue mullet, glass eyes	EX-	$80.00	1-1999
CCBC	Pikie, Husky	blue mullet, glass eyes, 2307 label	NIB	$221.00	11-2001
CCBC	Pikie, Husky	glass eyes, 2318 label	NIB	$232.50	3-2000
CCBC	Pikie, Husky	glass eyes	EX/IB	$76.00	4-1999
CCBC	Pikie, Husky	glass eyes, 2318 label	NIB	$120.00	3-2000
CCBC	Pikie, Husky	glass eyes, NOT MET	NIB	$36.00	4-2000

BRAND	MODEL	SERIES / MFG. CODE / DESCRIPTION	GRADE	PRICE	DATE
CCBC	Pikie, Husky	glass eyes, catalog, 2302 label, crisp box	NIB	$128.00	11-2000
CCBC	Pikie, Husky	pearl, bright yellow, red spots, tack eyes, decal	Mint	$256.00	8-2000
CCBC	Pikie, Husky	perch, glass eyes, AL&W box & lure	VG+/IB	$28.00	10-2000
CCBC	Pikie, Husky	rainbow, glass eyes	EX+/IB	$210.00	2-1999
CCBC	Pikie, Husky	red head, glass eyes, label	NIB	$112.00	10-2000
CCBC	Pikie, Husky	red, white	NIB	$50.00	2-1999
CCBC	Pikie, Husky	silver flash	EX	$65.00	10-1999
CCBC	Pikie, Husky	silver flash, NOT MET	NIB	$75.00	2-1999
CCBC	Pikie, Jointed	13", black scale, glass eyes		$67.00	12-1998
CCBC	Pikie, Jointed	730, red, orange, black spots, glass eyes	EX	$131.39	3-1999
CCBC	Pikie, Jointed	2600, glass eyes, label	NIB	$71.00	8-1999
CCBC	Pikie, Jointed	2600, red head, orange spots, tack eyes	EX-	$35.00	6-1999
CCBC	Pikie, Jointed	2602, correct box	VG/IB	$16.00	1-1999
CCBC	Pikie, Jointed	2604, tack eyes	NIB	$50.00	8-2000
CCBC	Pikie, Jointed	2608, glass eyes, rainbow stencil	NIB	$140.49	11-1999
CCBC	Pikie, Jointed	2608, glass eyes, stencil	EX-/IB	$64.00	10-2000
CCBC	Pikie, Jointed	2614, tack eyes, PTCB	NIB	$40.00	9-1999
CCBC	Pikie, Jointed	2618, glass eyes, hang tag, catalog, great set	NIB	$78.00	7-1999
CCBC	Pikie, Jointed	2619, tack eyes	NIB	$49.00	1-1999
CCBC	Pikie, Jointed	2621, red, black eye shadow, tack eyes, PTCB	NIB	$305.00	8-2001
CCBC	Pikie, Jointed	2630, red head, orange, black spots, painted eyes, glass eyes	EX-	$46.00	8-2001
CCBC	Pikie, Jointed	2630, red, orange, black spots, glass eyes	EX-	$204.49	3-1999
CCBC	Pikie, Jointed	2632	NIB	$154.02	11-1999
CCBC	Pikie, Jointed	2632, fireplug, stencil	EX/IB	$96.04	10-1999
CCBC	Pikie, Jointed	2638, pearl, tack eyes, Sioux City	NIB	$151.00	9-2000
CCBC	Pikie, Jointed	2639, tiger stripe, tack eyes, PTCB	NIB	$200.00	8-2001
CCBC	Pikie, Jointed	2643, strawberry, tack eyes, PTCB	NIB	$300.00	8-2001
CCBC	Pikie, Jointed	2644, whitefish, tack eyes, PTCB	NIB	$300.00	8-2001
CCBC	Pikie, Jointed	AL&W, perch, double jointed, glass eyes	Mint	$87.50	9-1999
CCBC	Pikie, Jointed	black scale	EX-	$145.00	2-2001
CCBC	Pikie, Jointed	deep yellow flash, glass eyes	VG	$50.00	3-1999
CCBC	Pikie, Jointed	fireplug, glass eyes	Mint	$123.15	11-1999
CCBC	Pikie, Jointed	frog, tack eyes	EX	$58.00	4-1999
CCBC	Pikie, Jointed	glass eyes, 2602 stencil	EX/IB	$46.00	1-2000
CCBC	Pikie, Jointed	glass eyes, 2602 stencil, crisp box	EX/IB	$46.00	1-2000
CCBC	Pikie, Jointed	grey & red bar code stripe, tack eyes, NOT MET	EX	$162.00	7-2000
CCBC	Pikie, Jointed	grey & red bar code stripe, tack eyes, NOT MET	EX	$162.00	7-2000
CCBC	Pikie, Jointed	Peters Special, 2600, metal tail	VG	$196.52	4-1999
CCBC	Pikie, Jointed	Peters Special, 2605WSS, dace, metal tail	EX/IB	$247.38	3-1999
CCBC	Pikie, Jointed	Peters Special, blue mullet, glass eyes, fluted tail	EX	$363.00	9-1999
CCBC	Pikie, Jointed	Peters Special, golden shiner, glass eyes	EX	$112.50	4-2000
CCBC	Pikie, Jointed	Peters Special, goldfish scale, glass eyes, unmarked box	EX-	$660.00	8-2002
CCBC	Pikie, Jointed	Peters Special, pearl, glass eyes	EX	$350.00	10-1999
CCBC	Pikie, Jointed	Peters Special, shad, NOT MET	NIB	$1,000.00	4-2001

BRAND	MODEL	SERIES / MFG. CODE / DESCRIPTION	GRADE	PRICE	DATE
CCBC	Pikie, Jointed	Peters Special, silver scale, red metal tail	EX	$511.33	3-1999
CCBC	Pikie, Jointed	pickerel, 2600R, silver glitter, red, glass eyes	NIB	$361.00	6-1999
CCBC	Pikie, Jointed	pickerel, red tail, glass eyes	VG+	$127.00	5-2000
CCBC	Pikie, Jointed	pikie, DLT, one tie under chin	Mint	$81.00	9-1999
CCBC	Pikie, Jointed	pikie, line tie under chin	NIB	$250.00	8-1999
CCBC	Pikie, Jointed	rainbow	NIB	$81.00	4-1999
CCBC	Pikie, Jointed	rainbow, glass eyes, 2608 stencil	NIB	$100.00	10-2000
CCBC	Pikie, Jointed	rainbow, glass eyes, 2608 stencil	NIB	$127.00	5-2000
CCBC	Pikie, Jointed	rainbow, silver back	AVG	$35.00	11-2000
CCBC	Pikie, Jointed	rainbow trout, plastic, photo finish	NIB	$68.09	12-1999
CCBC	Pikie, Jointed	red head, orange spots, glass eyes	EX	$228.00	5-1999
CCBC	Pikie, Jointed	red head, sparkles, glass eyes	EX	$237.50	11-1999
CCBC	Pikie, Jointed	tiger stripe, tack eyes	VG	$32.55	3-1999
CCBC	Pikie, Jointed	tiger stripe, tack eyes, PTCB	NIB	$56.59	10-1999
CCBC	Pikie, Jointed Husky	2318, crisp box	NIB	$95.00	11-1999
CCBC	Pikie, Jointed Husky	3000, PAL plastic in photo, alewife	EX-/IB	$299.00	12-2001
CCBC	Pikie. Jointed Husky	3000 Special, mullet, glass eyes	EX-/IB	$101.00	6-1999
CCBC	Pikie, Jointed Husky	3000WS, strawberry, fake glass eyes	EX+/IB	$128.50	5-1999
CCBC	Pikie, Jointed Husky	3001, glass eyes, 3001 papers	NIB	$52.00	10-2000
CCBC	Pikie, Jointed Husky	3001, perch, nice box	NIB	$70.00	1-1999
CCBC	Pikie, Jointed Husky	3002	EX/IB	$80.99	4-1999
CCBC	Pikie, Jointed Husky	3007, natural mullet, glass eyes, label	NIB	$145.02	11-1999
CCBC	Pikie, Jointed Husky	3007, natural mullet, label	NIB	$332.00	7-2000
CCBC	Pikie, Jointed Husky	3008	EX-/IB	$200.00	10-1999
CCBC	Pikie, Jointed Husky	3033, black scale, glass eyes	EX-	$175.00	10-1999
CCBC	Pikie, Jointed Husky	3033, black scale, tack eyes, PTCB	NIB	$132.00	10-2000
CCBC	Pikie, Jointed Husky	blue mullet, NOT MET	NIB	$132.50	2-1999
CCBC	Pikie, Jointed Husky	blue mullet	EX-	$43.00	1-1999
CCBC	Pikie. Jointed Husky	mullet, glass eyes, 1 cup corroded, NOT MET	EX-	$46.00	4-2001
CCBC	Pikie, Jointed Husky	yellow spots, tack eyes	EX	$76.00	1-1999
CCBC	Pikie, Jointed Midget	rainbow	NIB	$112.72	2-2000
CCBC	Pikie, Jointed Midget	rainbow, blue back	EX+	$202.50	1-2000
CCBC	Pikie, Jointed Snook	3400	EX/IB	$46.10	4-1999
CCBC	Pikie, Jointed Snook	5501W, tack eyes, PTCB	NIB	$26.50	1-1999
CCBC	Pikie, Jointed Snook	5502, 2 red heads/w, both in stamped boxes	NIB	$218.51	4-1999
CCBC	Pikie, Jointed Snook	5502, glass eyes	NIB	$51.69	5-1999
CCBC	Pikie, Jointed Snook	5502, glass eyes	NIB	$137.50	3-2000
CCBC	Pikie, Jointed Snook	5503 Special	NIB	$460.00	3-2000
CCBC	Pikie, Jointed Snook	5507, glass eyes	NIB	$198.00	8-1999
CCBC	Pikie, Jointed Snook	5507 Special, metal tail	NIB	$539.00	5-1999
CCBC	Pikie, Jointed Snook	5508, glass eyes, label	EX-/IB	$105.00	2-2001
CCBC	Pikie, Jointed Snook	5508, rainbow, 5508 box for jointed	EX-	$200.00	10-1999
CCBC	Pikie, Jointed Snook	5531, rainbow fire, glass eyes, catalog	EX/IB	$125.00	6-1999
CCBC	Pikie, Jointed Snook	pearl, tack eyes, back stencil in gold, light hook drag	EX-	$204.00	10-2001
CCBC	Pikie, Jointed Snook	red head, gold, repainted?, NOT MET	VG+	$73.00	4-2000
CCBC	Pikie, Jointed Striper	6800, glass eyes, NOT MET	Mint	$280.00	1-2001

BRAND	MODEL	SERIES / MFG. CODE / DESCRIPTION	GRADE	PRICE	DATE
CCBC	Pikie, Jointed Striper	6802, tack eyes	NIB	$32.00	6-1999
CCBC	Pikie, Jointed Striper	6818	EX	$1,225.00	10-1999
CCBC	Pikie, Jointed Striper	6818, silver flash, glass eyes	EX/IB	$52.07	4-1999
CCBC	Pikie, Jointed Striper	6819, frog, tack eyes, joint chip, 6819 PTCB	EX-/IB	$100.00	9-2002
CCBC	Pikie, Jointed Striper	6833, tack eyes	NIB	$76.00	10-2000
CCBC	Pikie, Jointed Striper	6839, blue flash, glass eyes, 2PCCB, papers	NIB	$125.00	12-1998
CCBC	Pikie, Jointed Striper	blue flash	EX	$210.00	10-1999
CCBC	Pikie, Jointed Striper	fireplug, glass eyes	VG	$125.55	8-1999
CCBC	Pikie, Jointed Striper	frog, tack eyes	VG	$76.00	6-1999
CCBC	Pikie, Jointed Striper	frog, tack eyes, 6819W PTCB	EXIB	$103.50	2-1999
CCBC	Pikie, Jointed Striper	glass eyes, 6807 label	NIB	$415.00	12-2001
CCBC	Pikie, Jointed Striper	rainbow, blue back, glass eyes	NIB	$433.00	5-2000
CCBC	Pikie, Jointed Striper	rainbow, glass eyes	EX+	$100.00	6-1999
CCBC	Pikie, Kingfisher	bumblebee, glass eyes, metal back plate	EX-	$520.00	9-1999
CCBC	Pikie, Kingfisher	KF118, silver flash	NIB	$1,500.00	9-1999
CCBC	Pikie, Kingfisher	KF130, pikie with plate, strawberry, big	EX/IB	$696.86	8-1999
CCBC	Pikie, Kingfisher	KF130, strawberry, metal flash plate	EX/IB	$696.86	8-1999
CCBC	Pikie, Kingfisher	KF135 Special, tiger stripe, glass eyes, plate, nice box	VG-/IB	$213.62	2-2000
CCBC	Pikie, Kingfisher	tiger stripe, glass eyes	EX-	$405.00	2-2000
CCBC	Pikie, Kingfisher	white	EX	$1,100.00	9-1999
CCBC	Pikie, Midget	2213, glass eyes, back stencil, 2213 stamp	NIB	$76.00	11-2000
CCBC	Pikie, Midget Jointed	4202, 4202 label	NIB	$561.00	1-2002
CCBC	Pikie, Salt Water	703SW, glass eyes, PTCB	NIB	$137.00	1-2001
CCBC	Pikie, Salt Water	718SW, tack eyes	NIB	$63.00	11-2000
CCBC	Pikie, Salt Water	734SW, 2-hook, tack eyes	NIB	$103.51	11-1999
CCBC	Pikie, Snook	18, side screw, NRA, box	NIB	$430.00	1-2000
CCBC	Pikie, Snook	black, white, glass eyes	VG+	$297.50	1-1999
CCBC	Pikie, Snook	blue flash, glass eyes	VG	$25.00	9-2001
CCBC	Pikie, Snook	blue mullet, glass eyes, box #?	NIB	$242.50	1-2000
CCBC	Pikie, Snook	mullet, glass eyes, unmarked box, NOT MET	EX	$102.00	1-2002
CCBC	Pikie, Snook	natural mullet, glass eyes, label	NIB	$336.00	3-2000
CCBC	Pikie, Snook	purple eel	EX+	$476.44	2-2000
CCBC	Pikie, Snook	rainbow, tack eyes, NOT MET	Mint	$59.00	12-2001
CCBC	Pikie, Snook	red, white, glass eyes, label box	NIB	$85.00	6-1999
CCBC	Pikie, Snook	silver flash, glass eyes	Mint	$55.00	2-2001
CCBC	Pikie, Snook	3400	EX/IB	$150.00	10-1999
CCBC	Pikie, Snook	3402, mint box	NIB	$213.50	7-1999
CCBC	Pikie, Snook	3403 Special, silver shiner	EX/IB	$78.11	2-1999
CCBC	Pikie, Snook	glass eyes, 3401 label	NIB	$202.00	10-2000
CCBC	Pikie, Snook	3400, glass eyes	NIB	$40.00	2-2001
CCBC	Pikie, Snook	3404, poor box	EX/IB	$125.00	10-1999
CCBC	Pikie, Snook	3408, rainbow, glass eyes	NIB	$270.59	6-1999
CCBC	Pikie, Striper	6901, tack eyes, PTCB, no top	NIB	$43.00	12-1998
CCBC	Pikie, Striper	6902W, red, white, tack eyes	NIB	$35.00	1-1999
CCBC	Pikie, Striper	6918, tack eyes, PTCB	NIB	$51.00	10-2000
CCBC	Pikie, Striper	6907, mullet, label box	VG+/IB	$113.50	4-1999

BRAND	MODEL	SERIES / MFG. CODE / DESCRIPTION	GRADE	PRICE	DATE
CCBC	Pikie, Striper	6919, silver flash	EX-	$125.00	10-1999
CCBC	Pikie, Striper	6931, fireplug, tag	NIB	$188.49	10-1999
CCBC	Pikie, Striper	rainbow fire	NIB	$600.00	5-2000
CCBC	Pikie, Striper	rainbow fire, glass eyes, unmarked box, NOT MET	Mint	$886.00	3-2000
CCBC	Pikie, Striper	silver flash, glass eyes	NIB	$243.00	9-2001
CCBC	Pikie, Tarpon	4002, 2 single hooks	EX/IB	$797.43	4-1999
CCBC	Pikie, Tarpon	4002, glass eyes, single hooks, vg+ box	EX-/IB	$600.00	10-1999
CCBC	Pikie, Tarpon	4002, trebles, hooks rusty	NIB	$305.00	5-1999
CCBC	Pikie, Tarpon	4018, trebles, hooks, label box	NIB	$1,700.00	5-1999
CCBC	Pikie, Tarpon	mullet, single hooks	EX-	$579.00	9-1999
CCBC	Pikie, Tarpon	red, white, glass eyes, single hooks	EX-	$421.00	8-1999
CCBC	Pikie, Three Jointed	red head, orange, black spots, plastic	EX-	$67.00	4-2001
CCBC	Plunker	3201 label	NIB	$77.50	1-2000
CCBC	Plunker	3204 label	NIB	$100.00	2-2002
CCBC	Plunker	3204, tack eyes, PTCB	NIB	$36.55	1-1999
CCBC	Plunker	black, 3213 box	VG/IB	$34.00	1-1999
CCBC	Plunker	black, glass eyes	EX-	$48.00	12-1998
CCBC	Plunker	black, glass eyes, nice box	NIB	$131.99	12-1999
CCBC	Plunker	black scale, tack eyes, PTCB, NOT MET	NIB	$86.00	10-2000
CCBC	Plunker	fire?, glass eyes	EX	$134.09	5-1999
CCBC	Plunker	frog, glass eyes	Mint	$135.00	9-1999
CCBC	Plunker	glass eyes, 3213 stencil	EX/IB	$66.52	10-1999
CCBC	Plunker	glass eyes, 3213 stencil	NIB	$77.00	11-1999
CCBC	Plunker	glass eyes, 3213 stencil box	NIB	$62.00	3-2002
CCBC	Plunker	glass eyes, 3213 stencil	NIB	$112.50	10-1999
CCBC	Plunker	glass eyes, 3218 label	NIB	$45.00	9-2000
CCBC	Plunker	golden shiner, glass eyes	EX-	$50.00	8-2002
CCBC	Plunker	golden shiner, glass eyes, 3204 stencil	NIB	$117.00	8-2001
CCBC	Plunker	Henry Dills with letter from Heinzerling, NOT MET	VG	$810.00	4-1999
CCBC	Plunker	lip chip, 3204 label	EX-/IB	$41.00	3-2002
CCBC	Plunker	perch, glass eyes	EX	$21.00	8-2002
CCBC	Plunker	pearl, glass eyes	VG+	$104.00	5-2001
CCBC	Plunker	pikie, glass eyes	EX-	$21.00	8-2002
CCBC	Plunker	pikie, glass eyes, label	NIB	$55.00	8-2000
CCBC	Plunker	rainbow fire, glass eyes, decent	VG+	$154.00	10-2001
CCBC	Plunker	rainbow, glass eyes	EX	$175.00	7-2000
CCBC	Plunker	rainbow, tack eyes	EX	$51.35	1-1999
CCBC	Plunker	red head, glass eyes, crisp box & catalog	NIB	$115.00	3-2001
CCBC	Plunker	red, white	EX+	$49.99	12-1998
CCBC	Plunker	red-winged blackbird, 2 cracked eyes	VG+	$61.00	8-2002
CCBC	Plunker	red-winged blackbird, glass eyes	AVG+	$154.48	7-1999
CCBC	Plunker	Special Order, no-scale perch, glass eyes	EX	$205.38	4-1999
CCBC	Plunker	white, black, glass eyes	EX-	$229.00	4-2000
CCBC	Plunker	white scale	VG-	$39.00	1-1999
CCBC	Plunker	white scale, stencil	NIB	$331.66	12-1999

BRAND	MODEL	SERIES / MFG. CODE / DESCRIPTION	GRADE	PRICE	DATE
CCBC	Plunker	yellow, black spots, tack eyes	EX	$25.00	2-2000
CCBC	Plunker	yellow spots, decal	Mint	$41.00	11-2000
CCBC	Plunker	yellow spots, glass eyes	EX	$168.30	2-1999
CCBC	Plunker	yellow, red, black spots, glass eyes, 3214 stencil	EX/IB	$266.99	10-1999
CCBC	Plunker (or Castriola)	couple pointers, 3131 stencil	EX/IB	$151.00	3-2002
CCBC	Plunker (or Injured Minnow)	1500, glass eyes, small chip, PTCB	EX/IB	$71.00	5-1999
CCBC	Plunker, Husky	5800, lip chip, rest nice		$129.00	6-1999
CCBC	Plunker, Husky	5801, 5801 label, glass eyes	NIB	$332.00	3-2001
CCBC	Plunker, Husky	perch, glass eyes, NOT MET	EX/IB	$158.00	6-1999
CCBC	Plunker, Husky	pikie, glass eyes	EX	$129.00	6-1999
CCBC	Plunker, Husky	red head, glass eyes	VG+	$78.00	4-2000
CCBC	Plunker, Husky	silver mullet, glass eyes	EX+	$338.33	5-1999
CCBC	Plunker, Musky	golden shiner, NOT MET	EX-	$154.00	10-2001
CCBC	Plunker, Musky	rainbow, glass eyes, NOT MET	EX	$405.00	3-2000
CCBC	Plunker, Snook	7102, glass eyes	NIB	$380.00	9-2000
CCBC	Plunker, Snook	7107, painted eyes, PTCB	NIB	$169.16	9-1999
CCBC	Plunker, Snook	7134B, blue flash & buck tail, glass eyes, NOT MET	NIB	$262.00	4-2001
CCBC	Plunker, Snook	7134BT, glass eyes	NIB	$182.00	9-2000
CCBC	Plunker, Snook	black, white, glass eyes	AVG	$67.00	4-2000
CCBC	Plunker, Spinning	golden shiner?, plastic	EX	$25.75	6-1999
CCBC	Polly Wiggle	brown pollywog	VG	$102.00	9-2000
CCBC	Polly Wiggle	pollywog	VG+	$71.00	9-1999
CCBC	Polly Wiggle	red, white	EX	$311.58	11-1999
CCBC	Pop 'N Dunk	blue head, red body, NOT MET	EX-	$202.00	4-2000
CCBC	Pop 'N Dunk	dace	AVG	$26.50	1-2000
CCBC	Pop 'N Dunk	perch	VG	$42.41	1-1999
CCBC	Pop 'N Dunk	perch, tack eyes, NOT MET	EX	$41.00	6-1999
CCBC	Pop 'N Dunk	red, black	EX-	$623.00	4-1999
CCBC	Pop 'N Dunk	red, black head, glass eyes	EX-	$400.00	3-1999
CCBC	Pop 'N Dunk	red, white, glass eyes, label	NIB	$175.00	9-1999
CCBC	Pop 'N Dunk	red-winged blackbird	EX-	$112.50	9-1999
CCBC	Pop 'N Dunk	red-winged blackbird, glass eyes	EX+	$306.00	8-2001
CCBC	Pop 'N Dunk	red-winged blackbird, glass eyes	VG+	$104.00	9-2000
CCBC	Pop 'N Dunk	red-winged blackbird, small chips inside, rest nice	EX-	$69.00	4-2000
CCBC	Pop 'N Dunk	silver flash & pikie, glass eyes	EX-	$76.00	6-2000
CCBC	Pop 'N Dunk	white scale	EX	$202.00	11-2000
CCBC	Pop 'N Dunk	white scale	EX-	$302.00	4-2000
CCBC	Pop 'N Dunk	white scale, big tail chip	VG	$62.00	12-2000
CCBC	Pop-It, Flyrod		VG-	$38.50	1-1999
CCBC	Pop-It, Flyrod	101, yellow, on ugly card	NOC	$287.00	6-1999
CCBC	Popper	red, white, painted eyes, name on back	EX-	$159.50	6-1999
CCBC	Popper	yellow, painted eyes, long, salt water	VG-	$36.50	7-1999
CCBC	River Rustler	3700 intro tag, catalog, nice box	NIB	$178.00	11-2000
CCBC	River Rustler	glass eyes, 3702 stencil	EX/IB	$316.00	9-2000
CCBC	River Rustler	perch, glass eyes	EX	$162.50	9-1999

BRAND	MODEL	SERIES / MFG. CODE / DESCRIPTION	GRADE	PRICE	DATE
CCBC	River Rustler	red head, glass eyes, big nose chip	AVG	$27.50	1-2000
CCBC	River Scamp	dace, glass eyes	EX	$57.99	5-1999
CCBC	River Scamp	dace, glass eyes	EX	$135.00	9-2000
CCBC	River Scamp	golden shiner, glass eyes, uncataloged	EX	$293.88	3-2000
CCBC	River Scamp	red side	EX+	$123.61	10-1999
CCBC	River Scamp	red side	VG+	$47.00	4-2001
CCBC	River Scamp	glass eyes, 4318 label box	NIB	$192.00	11-2001
CCBC	River Scamp	tack eyes?, 4305 label	NIB	$227.50	8-1999
CCBC	Sail Shark	x2, 2 different on bubble pack cards	NOC	$26.00	5-2001
CCBC	Sarasota	pikie	AVG	$67.00	4-1999
CCBC	Sarasota	pikie	VG-	$120.50	10-1999
CCBC	Sarasota	pikie	VG-	$150.00	5-2000
CCBC	Sarasota	silver flash, glass eyes, side hooks, nice except belly	VG+	$328.00	10-2002
CCBC	Sarasota	silver flash, glass eyes, side hooks	EX	$730.00	11-1999
CCBC	Sarasota	silver flash, glass eyes, unmarked box	NIB	$400.00	2-1999
CCBC	Sarasota	white, red chin	AVG	$41.00	2-2000
CCBC	Sarasota Special	silver flash, glass eyes, 2 side hooks, NOT MET	VG-	$191.39	6-1999
CCBC	"Seven Thousand"	7000, fireplug, NOT MET	VG+	$152.00	4-2000
CCBC	"Seven Thousand"	7000, green, black ribs	EX	$103.00	4-2000
CCBC	"Seven Thousand"	7000, rainbow fire	EX-	$311.00	5-2000
CCBC	"Seven Thousand"	7000, rainbow fire, bead eyes	VG-	$206.50	3-2000
CCBC	"Seven Thousand"	7000, tan, green	EX-	$88.00	4-2000
CCBC	"Seven Thousand"	7000, white	EX	$131.00	3-2002
CCBC	"Seven Thousand"	7000, 7018, no feelers, NOT MET	Mint	$128.00	5-1999
CCBC	"Seven Thousand"	7000, pikie, NOT MET	Mint	$153.50	5-1999
CCBC	"Seven Thousand"	7000?, red head, bead eyes, NOT MET	EX	$187.50	2-2000
CCBC	"Seven Thousand"	crawdad type, torn 7001 label	NIB	$331.00	2-2002
CCBC	Silver Side	perch, painted eyes, like Devilshorse	EX	$125.00	11-1999
CCBC	Silver Side	silver flash, painted eyes, like Devilshorse	EX	$125.00	11-1999
CCBC	Skipper	strawberry, big hook drag on belly	VG+	$334.00	10-2000
CCBC	Spook, Chugger	large gold eyes, Banner box & catalog	NIB	$30.00	5-2000
CCBC	Spoon-Tail	500, red head, painted eyes, ugly	EX	$202.00	8-2000
CCBC	Spoon-Tail	green, white, silver flakes	NIB	$67.00	6-1999
CCBC	Spoon-Tail	silver flash	EX	$87.00	10-2000
CCBC	Sucker	3900B, black	EX/IB	$750.00	4-1999
CCBC	Sucker	black sucker	Poor	$46.00	9-2001
CCBC	Sucker	nice	EX	$775.00	9-2002
CCBC	Sucker	NOT MET	EX-	$520.00	2-2000
CCBC	Sucker	yellow	EX-	$510.00	7-2000
CCBC	Sucker	yellow sucker, glass eyes	EX	$1,525.00	1-2000
CCBC	Sucker	yellow sucker, label	NIB	$1,607.00	2-2000
CCBC	Super 6 Assortment	vg lures, vg- box with lid reattached	VG-	$1,700.00	3-2001
CCBC	Surf Popper	silver flash, painted eyes	EX	$180.27	8-1999
CCBC	Surfster	4¼", red head, tack eyes	EX	$180.00	3-2000
CCBC	Surfster	6", red head/w, glass eyes	EX	$163.50	4-1999
CCBC	Surfster	7¼", perch, glass eyes, oversized box	VG/IB	$202.50	11-1999

BRAND	MODEL	SERIES / MFG. CODE / DESCRIPTION	GRADE	PRICE	DATE
CCBC	Surfster	7200, blue flash, tack eyes	EX	$51.57	4-1999
CCBC	Surfster	7200, blue flash, glass eyes	EX+	$131.00	5-2001
CCBC	Surfster	7200, PTCB	NIB	$219.50	9-1999
CCBC	Surfster	7207 Special, mullet, glass eyes	NIB	$405.00	6-1999
CCBC	Surfster	7218R	NIB	$160.50	1-1999
CCBC	Surfster	7218R Special, red around glass eyes	NIB	$200.00	7-1999
CCBC	Surfster	7218WP, tack eyes	NIB	$67.66	2-2000
CCBC	Surfster	7218, red eye shadow, glass eyes, NOT MET	EX	$102.00	11-2001
CCBC	Surfster	7234R, glass eyes, PTCB	NIB	$177.00	1-2001
CCBC	Surfster Husky	7318, PTCB	NIB	$449.00	2-2002
CCBC	Surfster Salt	7400, purple eel, glass eyes	VG	$127.50	4-1999
CCBC	Surfster Salt	7425 label, NOT MET	NIB	$218.00	10-2000
CCBC	Surfster Salt	7434, blue flash, glass eyes, rust	EX/IB	$155.50	4-1999
CCBC	Surfster Salt	7434, hook rust, 2PCCB	EX/IB	$153.61	1-1999
CCBC	Surfster	blue flash	EX	$59.21	1-1999
CCBC	Surfster	blue flash	EX	$200.00	10-1999
CCBC	Surfster	pearl, tack eyes	VG+	$57.00	8-2002
CCBC	Surfster	purple eel	G	$18.00	1-1999
CCBC	Surfster	purple eel, glass eyes, large	VG	$90.00	5-1999
CCBC	Tiny Tim	6400	NIB	$118.00	10-2000
CCBC	Tiny Tim	6401, 6401 label box	NIB	$102.50	8-1999
CCBC	Tiny Tim	6401, perch scale, painted eyes, label box	EX/IB	$96.00	9-1999
CCBC	Tiny Tim	6402, perch scale, painted eyes, label box	NIB	$158.05	9-1999
CCBC	Tiny Tim	6425, white scale, 6425 label	NIB	$255.00	3-2000
CCBC	Tiny Tim	6425, white scale, painted eyes, color catalog, 6425 stencil	NIB	$472.00	8-2001
CCBC	Tiny Tim	6427 label spotted	NIB	$354.02	4-1999
CCBC	Tiny Tim	fluorescent red, NOT MET	NIB	$112.00	7-2000
CCBC	Tiny Tim	perch, one chip	EX	$41.00	9-1999
CCBC	Tiny Tim	pikie	EX	$54.99	1-2000
CCBC	Tiny Tim	red head	NIB	$202.50	9-1999
CCBC	Tiny Tim	red, white, early	EX-	$90.99	2-1999
CCBC	Tiny Tim	red-winged blackbird	VG-	$42.00	3-2001
CCBC	Tiny Tim	red-winged blackbird, 2 small rough spots	VG-	$58.00	8-2002
CCBC	Tiny Tim	red-winged blackbird, painted eyes, back stencil	AVG	$88.75	1-2000
CCBC	Tiny Tim	spots, NOT MET	EX	$229.00	8-2000
CCBC	Tiny Tim	two 6400; one each: 6401, 6402, 6425	NIB	$712.00	8-2000
CCBC	Tiny Tim	white scale	EX-	$158.50	1-2000
CCBC	Tiny Tim	white scale	VG+	$63.50	1-1999
CCBC	Tiny Tim	white scale, gold stencil	VG+	$143.00	5-2000
CCBC	Tiny Tim	white scale, unmarked box, NOT MET	Mint	$181.50	8-1999
CCBC	Tiny Tim	x2; 1 pikie, 1 perch; 1 in correct label box	EX+/NIB	$210.00	6-1999
CCBC	Tiny Tim	yellow, 2 black spots	EX-	$71.00	2-1999
CCBC	Top-N-Pop	silver flash, plastic	EX	$53.00	10-2001
CCBC	Top Wiggle	yellow, plastic, 2PCCB	NIB	$35.00	5-1999
CCBC	Unfinished	x22, all different, silver scale, paint sticks some	Mint	$212.50	2-2000

BRAND	MODEL	SERIES / MFG. CODE / DESCRIPTION	GRADE	PRICE	DATE
CCBC	Wagtail Chub, Deluxe	802, glass eyes, 802 stencil	EX-/IB	$93.00	10-2000
CCBC	Wagtail Chub, Deluxe	806, golden shiner, ugly		$52.00	2-1999
CCBC	Wagtail Chub, Deluxe	frog, glass eyes, belly wear	VG-	$282.00	2-1999
CCBC	Wagtail Chub, Deluxe	gold flash	EX-	$266.00	5-1999
CCBC	Wagtail Chub, Deluxe	golden shiner	EX	$122.50	1-1999
CCBC	Wagtail Chub, Deluxe	goldfish, glass eyes	EX+	$611.00	8-2001
CCBC	Wagtail Chub, Deluxe	goldfish scale, glass eyes	Mint	$549.00	5-1999
CCBC	Wagtail Chub, Deluxe	natural chub, plain tail	EX-/IB	$222.22	3-2000
CCBC	Wagtail Chub, Deluxe	perch, early, fluted	VG	$68.00	5-2000
CCBC	Wagtail Chub, Deluxe	pikie, glass eyes, flat tail	VG-	$41.50	1-1999
CCBC	Wagtail Chub, Deluxe	red head	EX+	$135.00	10-1999
CCBC	Wee Dee		EX-	$510.00	12-1999
CCBC	Wee Dee	4800, bug finish, NOT MET	NIB	$1,115.00	10-1999
CCBC	Wee Dee	black scale, plastic	Mint	$34.90	9-1999
CCBC	Wee Dee	bug finish	EX	$615.00	11-1999
CCBC	Wee Dee	bug finish	EX	$637.33	3-1999
CCBC	Wee Dee	bug finish	EX-	$610.00	8-2000
CCBC	Wee Dee	bug finish, chip under 1 eye, nice	EX-	$455.00	9-2002
CCBC	Wee Dee	fire lacquer, plastic	Mint	$34.90	9-1999
CCBC	Wee Dee	frog	EX	$405.00	6-1999
CCBC	Wee Dee	frog	EX-	$415.02	9-1999
CCBC	Wee Dee	frog	G	$300.00	8-1999
CCBC	Wee Dee	frog, glass eyes	EX+	$746.00	8-2001
CCBC	Wee Dee	frog, glass eyes, nice	EX	$536.99	4-1999
CCBC	Wee Dee	frog, glass eyes, NOT MET	VG+	$306.00	6-2001
CCBC	Wee Dee	frog, plastic, plastic box & papers	NIB	$49.00	5-2002
CCBC	Wee Dee	frog, spots	VG+	$394.00	11-1999
CCBC	Wee Dee	frog, unmarked box	EX/IB	$500.00	10-2000
CCBC	Wee Dee	red, white	EX-	$975.00	10-1999
CCBC	Weed Bug	2800, weed bug finish, vg label box	EX+/IB	$1,290.00	10-1999
CCBC	Weed Bug	bug color, new weedguard	VG+	$515.52	1-1999
CCBC	Weed Bug	bug color, red bead eyes, weedguard missing	EX-	$296.00	12-1999
CCBC	Weed Bug	frog	EX	$430.33	3-1999
CCBC	Weed Bug	frog, belly chip, NOT MET	VG+ to EX-	$305.00	3-1999
CCBC	Weed Bug	frog, glass eyes	AVG	$157.51	2-2000
CCBC	Weed Bug	frog, glass eyes	EX-	$426.51	5-1999
CCBC	Weed Bug	frog, glass eyes	EX-	$462.00	2-2000
CCBC	Weed Bug	frog, glass eyes	EX-	$493.88	1-2000
CCBC	Weed Bug	frog, glass eyes, 2819 label	EX/IB	$695.00	2-2000
CCBC	Weed Bug	frog, glass eyes, small worm burn	VG	$191.00	5-2001
CCBC	Weed Bug	frog, glass eyes, stamped box, NOT MET	NIB	$503.00	3-1999
CCBC	Weed Bug	frog, NRA, unmarked box	AVG	$215.02	5-1999
CCBC	Weed Bug	frog, rusty hardware	EX	$450.00	11-1999
CCBC	Weed Bug	frog, short wires, 2819 label	EX	$800.00	10-1999
CCBC	Weed Bug	glass eyes, 2 papers, 2819 frog label	EX/IB	$692.32	3-2000
CCBC	Weed Bug	weed bug finish	EX-	$870.00	10-1999
CCBC	Weed Bug	white, glass eyes	EX-	$309.00	11-2000

BRAND	MODEL	SERIES / MFG. CODE / DESCRIPTION	GRADE	PRICE	DATE
CCBC	Weed Bug	white, red eyes	VG+	$317.11	12-1999
CCBC	Weed Bug	yellow, green, one bead eye	VG	$250.85	5-1999
CCBC	Weed Frog	frog, glass eyes	EX+	$539.00	8-2000
CCBC	Wiggle Diver	5041, red, yellow, plastic?	NIB	$66.00	9-1999
CCBC	Wiggle Diver	tiger stripe, wood	EX-	$70.00	3-1999
CCBC	Wiggle Fish	2400W, painted eyes, PTCB	NIB	$64.00	10-2000
CCBC	Wiggle Fish	2401, DLT, stencil box	EX/IB	$145.00	1-1999
CCBC	Wiggle Fish	2401, metal tail, Sioux City?	NIB	$99.99	5-1999
CCBC	Wiggle Fish	2402, glass eyes, DLT, great	EX+	$407.50	1-1999
CCBC	Wiggle Fish	2402, jointed	EX+	$125.00	10-1999
CCBC	Wiggle Fish	2402, red head, glass eyes, fluted	EX	$128.00	4-2000
CCBC	Wiggle Fish	2403 label	EX-/IB	$190.00	10-2000
CCBC	Wiggle Fish	2404, glass eyes	NIB	$280.00	9-2000
CCBC	Wiggle Fish	2405, tack eyes	VG	$58.50	1-1999
CCBC	Wiggle Fish	2418, frog, tack eyes, PTCB	NIB	$202.50	12-1998
CCBC	Wiggle Fish	Centennial	NIB	$46.00	8-1999
CCBC	Wiggle Fish	chub, glass eyes	EX	$102.50	5-1999
CCBC	Wiggle Fish	chub scale, 2-hook drags, rest nice	VG	$388.00	12-1999
CCBC	Wiggle Fish	Collector's Edition, perch	NIB	$42.00	6-1999
CCBC	Wiggle Fish	Commemorative	NIB	$57.00	11-2000
CCBC	Wiggle Fish	dace, glass eyes	VG+	$72.00	5-2000
CCBC	Wiggle Fish	glass eyes, 2400 stencil	EX/IB	$357.00	6-2002
CCBC	Wiggle Fish	glass eyes, red head label, NOT MET	EX/IB	$132.00	10-2000
CCBC	Wiggle Fish	gold tail, 2418 stencil	NIB	$178.50	8-1999
CCBC	Wiggle Fish	golden shiner	EX	$123.50	7-1999
CCBC	Wiggle Fish	golden shiner	EX-	$140.50	2-2000
CCBC	Wiggle Fish	golden shiner	VG-	$56.00	3-2001
CCBC	Wiggle Fish	golden shiner, fluted tail	EX-	$159.00	5-2000
CCBC	Wiggle Fish	golden shiner, glass eyes	EX-	$76.02	8-1999
CCBC	Wiggle Fish	golden shiner, glass eyes, fluted tail	VG	$51.00	5-2000
CCBC	Wiggle Fish	perch, glass eyes	VG+	$71.00	5-2000
CCBC	Wiggle Fish	perch, glass eyes, DLT	EX-	$91.25	4-1999
CCBC	Wiggle Fish	perch, glass eyes, jointed, DLT	EX-	$70.00	4-2000
CCBC	Wiggle Fish	perch, NOT MET	AVG	$34.55	1-1999
CCBC	Wiggle Fish	perch, tack eyes	EX	$72.55	2-2000
CCBC	Wiggle Fish	perch, tack eyes	VG-	$26.87	1-1999
CCBC	Wiggle Fish	pikie, big hook drag	G-	$327.22	10-1999
CCBC	Wiggle Fish	rainbow fire, primer rubbed on top	EX-	$1,385.00	4-2001
CCBC	Wiggle Fish	red, gold scales, silver nose, glass eyes	EX-	$1,594.50	12-1999
CCBC	Wiggle Fish	red head, tack eyes, blended	Mint	$69.00	2-2000
CCBC	Wiggle Fish	red head, unmarked lip, fluted tail, age lines	EX	$75.00	10-2000
CCBC	Wiggle Fish	red side, 2405 label	NIB	$481.00	11-1999
CCBC	Wiggle Fish	red side, box	VG+/IB	$139.00	5-1999
CCBC	Wiggle Fish	red side, glass eyes	EX-	$202.50	10-1999
CCBC	Wiggle Fish	red, white, glass eyes, DLT	VG+	$79.00	1-1999
CCBC	Wiggle Fish	shiner scale, tack eyes, back tag	EX	$49.01	11-1999
CCBC	Wiggle Fish	silver flash	EX	$140.00	10-1999

BRAND	MODEL	SERIES / MFG. CODE / DESCRIPTION	GRADE	PRICE	DATE
CCBC	Wiggle Fish	silver flash, tack eyes	Mint	$65.00	5-1999
CCBC	Wiggle Fish	tiny chip, 2418 special frog stencil	EX-/IB	$1,310.00	10-2000
CCBC	Wiggle Fish, Baby	golden shiner	EX-	$255.00	6-1999
CCBC	Wiggle Fish, Baby	golden shiner, DLT, fluted tail	EX	$260.00	8-1999
CCBC	Wiggle Fish, Baby	golden shiner, glass eyes, DLT	Mint	$271.00	7-1999
CCBC	Wiggle Fish, Baby	golden shiner, glass eyes, NOT MET	EX	$227.61	3-2000
CCBC	Wiggle Fish, Baby	perch, glass eyes, DLT, HPGM, fluted tail	EX	$762.00	4-2000
CCBC	Wiggle Fish, Husky		EX	$1,275.00	6-2001
CCBC	Wiggle Wizard	4500, red side	VG	$160.00	10-2000
CCBC	Wiggler	100, 101, DLT	EX/IB	$128.50	6-1999
CCBC	Wiggler	100, chub, box, NRA	NIB	$100.00	6-1999
CCBC	Wiggler	100, chub, DLT, label	EX/IB	$140.00	3-2001
CCBC	Wiggler	100, chub, glass eyes, DLT	EX+	$150.00	11-1999
CCBC	Wiggler	100, chub, glass eyes, stencil	VG+/IB	$84.00	10-2000
CCBC	Wiggler	100, chub, HPGM	EX-	$129.00	2-2002
CCBC	Wiggler	100, chub, HPGM, DLT	EX-	$104.01	5-1999
CCBC	Wiggler	100, chub, small chin chip	EX-/IB	$78.00	4-2000
CCBC	Wiggler	100, g stencil box	EX/IB	$135.09	2-2000
CCBC	Wiggler	100, golden shiner, glass eyes	VG+	$80.00	10-1999
CCBC	Wiggler	100, goldfish	EX-	$232.00	7-2001
CCBC	Wiggler	100, intro box	NIB	$2,001.00	9-1999
CCBC	Wiggler	100, intro box, beater	VG+/IB	$131.00	8-2000
CCBC	Wiggler	100, intro box, papers, nice	NIB	$700.00	3-2000
CCBC	Wiggler	100, old chub, glass eyes	NIB	$150.00	6-1999
CCBC	Wiggler	100, perch, glass eyes	EX	$87.99	10-1999
CCBC	Wiggler	100, perch, HPGM, beautiful	EX	$188.00	8-2002
CCBC	Wiggler	100, perch, HPGM, washer rig, early	EX-	$200.00	3-1999
CCBC	Wiggler	100, red, white, glass eyes, DLT, older	EX-	$37.00	1-1999
CCBC	Wiggler	100, vg- intro picture box	VG/IB	$565.55	1-2000
CCBC	Wiggler	100, white, black, glass eyes	EX	$480.00	2-2000
CCBC	Wiggler	101 intro box, pamphlet	EX/IB	$1,150.00	4-1999
CCBC	Wiggler	107, intro box, catalog, NOT MET	EX-/IB	$1,251.00	3-2001
CCBC	Wiggler	black, white	VG	$86.00	1-1999
CCBC	Wiggler	chub	EX	$93.00	1-1999
CCBC	Wiggler	chub, NOT MET	EX+	$77.00	8-2001
CCBC	Wiggler	green back	VG+	$112.00	7-2000
CCBC	Wiggler	intro box	EX/IB	$700.00	3-2000
CCBC	Wiggler	natural chub, vg- intro box, NOT MET	EX/IB	$685.00	6-1999
CCBC	Wiggler	pearl, glass eyes	EX	$470.00	9-2002
CCBC	Wiggler	washer rig, #2 intro picture box	EX/IB	$600.00	10-2000
CCBC	Wiggler, Baby	205, intro box, papers	NIB	$1,920.00	10-1999
CCBC	Wiggler, Baby	200, 205 green back, avg intro box	VG+/IB	$660.00	12-2000
CCBC	Wiggler, Baby	200, black, white, glass eyes, nice	EX	$355.00	8-1999
CCBC	Wiggler, Baby	200, chub, glass eyes, DLT, NOT MET	EX-	$63.00	4-2000
CCBC	Wiggler, Baby	200, golden shiner, glass eyes, DLT	EX	$125.00	11-1999
CCBC	Wiggler, Baby	200, perch, unmarked box, catalog	EX-/IB	$50.00	10-2000
CCBC	Wiggler, Baby	200, red side label, NRA box	NIB	$157.00	3-2001

BRAND	MODEL	SERIES / MFG. CODE / DESCRIPTION	GRADE	PRICE	DATE
CCBC	Wiggler, Baby	200 Special, silver scale, red, stencil	VG/IB	$91.00	3-2001
CCBC	Wiggler, Baby	200, Van Houten, red side label box	NIB	$1,275.00	11-1999
CCBC	Wiggler, Baby	206, goldfish scale	NIB	$685.00	5-1999
CCBC	Wiggler, Baby	212, all red, end label	NIB	$2,125.00	2-2002
CCBC	Wiggler, Baby	goldfish, DLT	EX	$152.22	10-1999
CCBC	Wiggler, Baby	perch	NIB	$162.50	8-1999
CCBC	Wiggler, Baby	perch, glass eyes, DLT	VG	$53.99	5-1999
CCBC	Wiggler, Creek Bug	1400, few pointers	EX-	$250.00	10-1999
CCBC	Wiggler, Creek Bug	1400, red, white	EX-/IB	$612.99	9-1999
CCBC	Wiggler, Creek Bug	gold, black ribs, small tail burn, shiny	EX- to VG+	$350.00	4-2000
CCBC	Wiggler, Creek Bug	black, glass eyes	EX	$265.00	4-2000
CCBC	Wiggler, Creek Bug	yellow, red wings	EX	$510.00	11-1999
CCBC	Wiggly Rind	metal	EX	$61.00	1-2001
Chain O Lakes	Musky Duck	papers, NOT MET	NIB	$142.50	5-1999
Chapman		#1 kidney, red, brass, NOT MET	VG-	$51.00	5-1999
Chapman		#2 teardrop, Chapman & Son, Theresa, NY	EX-	$150.00	10-2000
Chapman		metal fish, scale textured, front buzzer spinner	EX	$1,525.00	2-2001
Chapman		red 7 brass, NOT MET	VG-	$51.00	5-1999
Chapman	Allure	odd swivel, dents	VG-	$155.50	6-1999
Chapman	Kidney Spinner		VG	$76.00	10-1999
Chapman	Minnow Propeller	fish-shaped spoon with twisted tail fins	EX-	$300.00	1-2002
Chapman	Muskee Allure		EX	$500.00	4-2001
Chapman	Spinner		EX-	$96.00	1-2002
Chapman	Water Nymph	middle size	EX	$1,550.00	8-2002
Chapman	Various	2 different, #6 willow, buzz-notched, patent 3-84	EX-	$567.50	4-2000
Charmer		green, white stripe, NOT MET	VG	$536.00	10-2000
Charmer		orange, green stripe, glass eyes, 3-hook, rather ugly	VG+	$432.50	3-2000
Charmer	Midget	dark "puter" head, yellow tail, NO BIDS	EX	$2,000.00	8-2002
Charmer	Midget	no eyes	EX	$1,820.00	10-1999
Charmer	Minnow	brown, red, nice	VG+	$610.00	4-2001
Charmer	Minnow	gold with red stripe	EX-	$450.00	1-2002
Charmer	Minnow	missing 1½ props, checked, ugly	AVG	$230.00	4-2000
Charmer	Minnow	orange, green stripe, glass eyes	EX	$811.00	9-2002
Charmer	Minnow	orange, orange stripe	EX-	$881.00	2-2002
Charmer	Minnow	orange, red stripe	EX-	$1,300.00	4-2001
Charmer	Minnow	red, white, 3-hook, ugly line burns	G	$450.00	8-1999
Charmer	Minnow	white head, green stripe	EX-	$1,020.00	10-1999
Charmer	Minnow	white, red stripe	EX	$1,600.00	6-2001
Charmer	Minnow	white, red stripe	EX-	$1,250.00	5-2000
Charmer	Surface	orange, green	EX-	$600.00	3-1999
Charmer	Surface	white head, green spots, yellow tail, one bid	EX-	$1,800.00	8-2002
Chicago Tackle	Streamliner	1086, reel only	EX	$224.72	3-1999
Chicago Tackle	Wobbler	weird metal, Patent 1900	EX	$265.00	5-2000
Chix	Salmon	3-pack, blue gills, white	NIB	$151.00	6-1999
Cisco Kid		1353, yellow, brown squiggle, PTCB	NIB	$50.00	3-2002

BRAND	MODEL	SERIES / MFG. CODE / DESCRIPTION	GRADE	PRICE	DATE
Cisco Kid	10-pack	nice shipping box	NIB	$129.00	1-1999
Clark	Duckbill	600, yellow shore	NIB	$46.00	5-2001
Clark	Duckbill Water Scout	white shore	VG+	$68.75	2-2000
Clark	Duckling	scale pattern	VG-	$58.00	7-2002
Clark	Expert	glass eyes, 5-hook, hole props	VG+	$1,302.00	12-2000
Clark	Expert	green, white, 5-hook, hole props, many back digs		$360.00	8-2001
Clark	Popper Scout	silver scale, nice card & box	NIB	$54.00	8-2001
Clark	Popper Scout	yellow, red ribs	EX	$21.49	8-1999
Clark	Water Scout	32CS	NIB	$42.00	12-1998
Clark	Water Scout	300, black shore, tack eyes	EX-	$18.00	1-1999
Clark	Water Scout	317, black shore, tack eyes, great box & papers	NIB	$59.00	8-2001
Clark	Water Scout	3241, dent eyes, NIT	NIT	$207.00	3-2002
Clark	Water Scout	black, yellow, red spots, painted eyes?	NIB	$127.50	4-1999
Clark	Water Scout	frog, tack eyes, nice box	NIB	$68.00	3-2001
Clark	Water Scout	green perch, tack eyes	NIB	$59.00	10-2000
Clark	Water Scout	nice box, papers	EX/IB	$50.00	3-1999
Clark	Water Scout	perch	NIB	$26.00	4-2001
Clark	Water Scout	perch, duckbill, tack eyes	Mint	$88.00	11-2000
Clark	Water Scout	perch, indent red eyes, tube	NIT	$172.50	1-1999
Clark	Water Scout	perch scale, dent eyes	EX-	$30.00	3-1999
Clark	Water Scout	perch scale, nice box	NIB	$41.00	9-1999
Clark	Water Scout	perch scale, tack eyes	Mint	$23.50	7-1999
Clark	Water Scout	rainbow, box & papers	NIB	$66.99	12-1998
Clark	Water Scout	red head, white	NIB	$27.00	5-2001
Clark	Water Scout	scale pattern, oval indent eyes	EX	$28.95	12-1998
Clark	Water Scout	white shore, red spine	EX/IB	$49.99	4-1999
Clark	Water Scout Jr.	214, dent eyes, NIT	NIT	$217.00	3-2002
Cleopatra	Musky	articulated metal minnow, lamp shade, NOT MET		$720.00	11-1999
Clewell	Snakerbait		NIB	$1,350.00	10-1999
Clewell	Snakerbait	ugly	AVG	$149.50	1-1999
Clink	Salmon	red head, white, tail perfect, crisp box	NIB	$123.00	2-2002
Clinton	Wilt Champion Minnow		EX-	$2,500.00	10-1999
Clinton	Wilt Little Wonder		EX-	$2,200.00	10-1999
Coldwater	Ghost	luminous, avg picture box	AVG/IB	$449.00	10-2000
Coldwater	Hell Diver	big chip on back	AVG	$65.50	9-1999
Coldwater	Wiggler	strawberry, glass eyes, cracked, nice picture box	EX-/IB	$640.00	8-2002
Comstock	Flying Hellgramite	fake, NOT MET	EX	$1,475.00	12-2000
Cook	Colorado Moth		EX-	$255.00	10-2000
Cook	Colorado Moth	1⅛", brown, red	VG	$202.50	6-1999
Cook	Colorado Moth	1¾", nice color	EX	$290.05	4-1999
Cook	Colorado Moth	dull brown, mottled	EX	$136.50	4-1999
Cook	Colorado Moth	large buck type?	Mint	$405.00	8-1999
Cordell	Big-O	x2, 2 different, plastic, plastic box	NIB	$19.99	6-1999
Cordell	Big-O	x6, neat egg carton 6-pack	NIB	$127.50	3-2000

BRAND	MODEL	SERIES / MFG. CODE / DESCRIPTION	GRADE	PRICE	DATE
Crazy Legs		500, green	NIB	$31.50	5-1999
Crazy Legs	Various	mixed, 5 different	NIB	$120.00	3-1999
Cree-Duc		4", yellow, brown	NOC	$60.00	6-1999
Cumings, Ed	Marvelous Bass Getter	red head, like a Decker, plain label, vg+ 2PCCB	EX/IB	$622.00	11-2001
D.A.M.	Pikie, Ever Ready	perch, jointed, NOT MET	EX	$255.00	4-2002
D.A.M.	Wobbler, Baby Wooden	1618 Spinner, poor box	EX/IB	$50.00	7-1999
D.A.M.	Wobbler, Sea Devil	shiner scale, painted eyes, nice 2PCCB	NIB	$142.50	2-2000
Dalton		Special, Clearwater, Florida on belly	EX	$21.03	1-1999
Damyl	Spinner	perch crank bait, painted eyes, neat picture box	NIB	$258.30	1-2000
Damyl	Wobbler	pikie, painted eyes, neat picture box	NIB	$257.80	1-2000
Darby	Spring Bait	globe with bunch of wires & hooks	AVG	$105.00	1-2000
Decker	Bass Bait	brown box, papers	NIB	$1,027.99	4-1999
Decker	Bass Bait	yellow picture box	NIB	$455.00	4-1999
Decker	Surface	red, white, printing inside ex- box	EX/IB	$434.00	7-2002
Decker	Surface	globe, brown box, c.1908	EX/IB	$650.00	10-1999
Decker	Surface Water Casting Bass Bait	mouse shiny, vg+ picture box, papers	NIB	$620.00	11-2001
Decker	Surface Water Casting Bass Bait	mouse shiny, vg+ picture box, papers	NIB	$620.00	11-2001
Decker	Topwater	red, white	EX	$980.00	10-1999
Decker	Underwater	Manhattan	EX/IB	$2,870.00	10-1999
Delevan	North Channel Minnow	5-hook	EX-	$1,310.00	10-1999
Demon	Sail Shark	black head, clear, hard plastic box	NIB	$10.00	8-2000
Demon	Sail Shark	Demon's Sail Shark, gold CD, IKE box	NIB	$28.99	1-2000
Demon	Sail Shark	PB name on belly	NIB	$15.00	1-2001
Demon	Sail Shark	yellow, paper & box	EX/IB	$21.51	3-2000
Detroit Bait Co.	Bass Caller	bar perch	NIB	$294.00	3-2000
Detroit Bait Co.	Bass Caller	cream, crisp box & papers	VG+/IB	$227.00	3-2002
Detroit Bait Co.	North Channel Minnow	3-hook	VG	$255.00	2-2002
Detroit Bait Co.	North Channel Minnow	green with silver belly, 2 hooks missing, not bad	VG	$255.00	2-2002
Detroit Glass Minnow Tube Co.	Glass Minnow Tube		EX	$660.00	10-1999
Detroit Glass Minnow Tube Co.	Glass Minnow Tube	4¼", couple rusty hooks	EX-	$560.00	2-2002
Detroit Glass Minnow Tube Co.	Glass Minnow Tube	NOT MET	EX-	$560.00	3-1999
Detroit Glass Minnow Tube Co.	Glass Minnow Tube	sliding cap, ex- picture box, ex paper	NIB	$4,650.00	6-2001
Detroit Glass Minnow Tube Co.	Glass Minnow Tube	vg+ box, crisp papers	EX-/IB	$1,426.00	8-2002
Detroit Glass Minnow Tube Co.	Glass Minnow Tube	vg+ box, ex papers	EX-/IB	$2,500.00	7-2002
Detroit Glass Minnow Tube Co.	Weedless Wizard	frog, ex box, 2 papers	NIB	$2,313.00	10-2000
Diamond Mfg.	Ultra Casting	Pflueger Surprise, crackleback, superb box, Missouri	NIB	$1,295.00	9-2001
Dickens	Duplex Darter	red, white, nice box	NIB	$450.00	2-1999
Dineen	Spinning Minnow	hollow metal, Illinois item, ugly	EX	$381.00	2-2002

BRAND	MODEL	SERIES / MFG. CODE / DESCRIPTION	GRADE	PRICE	DATE
Doll	Top Secret	black, one white shad spot	VG+	$29.00	4-2000
Doll	Top Secret	perch, nice box & tag	NIB	$28.50	3-1999
Doll	Top Secret	shad	NIB	$20.53	1-2000
Doll	Top Secret	yellow, red	EX	$9.99	6-1999
Donaly Baits, Jim	Catchumbig Bait	woodpecker type with spinners, ugly	AVG	$1,400.00	1-2002
Donaly Baits, Jim	Jersey Wow	black, yellow design, 3 single hooks	EX	$565.00	4-1999
Donaly Baits, Jim	Jersey Wow	yellow, red, black, 1 treble	Mint	$710.00	4-1999
Donaly Baits, Jim	Red Fin	green, white, glass eyes, 3 metal flippers, NOT MET	VG	$295.00	4-2002
Donaly Baits, Jim	Red Fin	NOT MET	VG+	$710.00	5-1999
Donaly Baits, Jim	Red Fin Floater		VG-	$355.00	9-1999
Donaly Baits, Jim	Red Fin Floater	like Fishcake, 3-hook, very faded box	EX/IB	$950.00	3-2002
Donaly Baits, Jim	Red Fin Floater	yellow, black ribs	VG+	$230.00	4-1999
Donaly Baits, Jim	Red Fin Minnow		G+	$450.00	2-2002
Drake	Sea Bat	red head	NIB	$209.50	3-2000
Drake	Sea Bat	red, white	NIB	$168.00	4-2001
Dunk's	Pop 'N Dunk	red, white, glass eyes, nice 2PCCB	VG/IB	$76.00	6-1999
Edgren	Spinning Minnow	metal, nice picture box	NIB	$228.60	9-1999
Eger	Bullnose	silver flash, painted eyes	EX	$156.00	7-2000
Eger	Dillinger	white, red stripe, short fat type	NIB	$40.00	1-1999
Eger	Dillinger, Baby	201, white, black stripe, painted eyes	NIB	$34.52	9-1999
Eger	Dillinger, Master	308	NIB	$36.00	12-1998
Eger	Dillinger, Master	bar perch?, painted eyes, carved fish tail, #301 PTCB	NIB	$40.00	10-2001
Eger	Sergeant Sea Diver	red head, flitter, painted eyes	EX	$112.00	5-2001
Eger	Shrimp	ex Victory box	EX/IB	$464.00	2-1999
Eger	Spinner	cone-shaped body, Foss type blade	EX	$256.00	11-2001
Electrolure	Electrolure	Paul Bunyan type	EX/IB	$131.00	8-2000
Electrolure	Electrolure	red head, Illinois	EX	$25.00	10-2000
Ellis	Salmon Plug	white, silver scale	Mint	$51.00	1-1999
Eppinger	Husky Devle, Jr.	wood slide box, nice, NOT MET	EX-	$46.09	12-1999
Eppinger	Husky Devle, Winged	black & white scaled, wrong box	VG	$39.00	3-2001
Evans	Weed Queen	aluminum	G	$56.00	12-1999
Excel	Silver Streak	rubber minnow	NIB	$152.00	8-2000
Fenner	W.A.B. Weedless Automatic Bait	red, white	EX	$48.00	5-2000
Fin-Wing	Glow Wing		NIB	$141.49	3-2000
Fish-Rite	Auto hook setter	nice box	NIB	$21.60	8-1999
Fishtrap	700 Junior	red, white, spring hook, weedless, nice box	NIB	$27.00	8-2001
Flood	Florida Shiner		NIB	$590.00	10-1999
Flood	Florida Shiner	4¾", small, vg box	NIB	$400.00	6-2001
Flood	Florida Shiner	NOT MET	NIB	$387.99	9-1999
Flood	Florida Shiner	POBW, light stain on box	NIB	$285.00	10-2001
Flood	Minnow	papers	NIB	$317.00	12-1999
Florida Artifical Bait Company	Superstrike Shrimp	articulated shrimp, vg- picture box, 2 papers	NIB	$1,394.00	1-2002
Florida Artificial Bait Company	Superstrike Shrimp	green, 6 segment, celluloid	EX	$355.00	3-2001

BRAND	MODEL	SERIES / MFG. CODE / DESCRIPTION	GRADE	PRICE	DATE
Foss		#3, black, white, nice correctly marked tin box	NIB	$166.00	3-2002
Foss	Fan Dancer	#18, crisp box & papers	NIB	$48.00	3-2002
Foss	Frog	#12, nice blue tin box	EXIB	$61.00	9-2000
Foss	Minnow	white, glass eyes, hinged tin, papers	NIB	$50.00	1-1999
Foss	Skidder	picture, vg+ 2PCCB box	EX/IB	$455.00	1-2002
Foss	Skidder	red, ex- tin box	NIB	$102.00	1-2002
Foss	Tin Liz	gold, glass eyes	EX	$53.00	1-1999
Foss	Wiggler, Frog	#12	EX	$45.99	5-1999
Foss	Wiggler, Frog	#12, mint lure, avg tin box	AVG to Mint	$80.00	2-1999
Foss	Wiggler, Little Egypt	light blue, glass eyes, perfect	EX	$118.00	10-2001
Foss	Wiggler, Oriental	white, glass eyes, ex- blue hinged box, papers	EX/IB	$152.00	9-2002
Foss	Wiggler, Shimmy	#5 musky, red, vg red tin, papers	EX/IB	$66.51	2-2000
Four Brothers	Neverfail	3173, 5-hook, ex maroon box	EX/IB	$810.00	3-2001
Four Brothers	Neverfail	3173, rainbow, 5-hook, nice maroon box	EX/IB	$490.00	4-2001
Four Brothers	Neverfail	crackleback, 3-hook, maroon box	EX-/IB (G)	$356.09	9-1999
Francois	The Frog	ragged box	NIB	$133.50	4-1999
Freeport	Hook	trailer hook, ex wood box & papers	NIB	$660.00	6-1999
Gaide, C.J.W.	Bait	ugly, NOT MET	EX-	$383.00	2-2002
Gateway	River Master	HR5, rainbow, glass eyes, nice HR5 Gateway box	NIB	$103.00	9-2001
Gee Wiz	Frog		EX	$75.00	2-2000
Gee Wiz	Frog	4½", nice paper & box	NIB	$175.00	5-1999
Gee Wiz	Frog	23, nice box	NIB	$183.00	10-2000
Gee Wiz	Frog	no wheel	EX	$175.00	3-1999
Gee Wiz	Frog	small size	NIB	$202.50	4-1999
General Tool	Spoonfin	green, glass eyes	EX	$177.00	3-2001
Gen-Shaw	Wiggle Lure	nice paper, rough box, awful, NOT MET	Poor/IB	$42.00	6-1999
Glenwillow Products	Saf-T Lure	red head, tack eyes, mint lure & box	NIB	$92.00	9-2000
Goble Bait	Wiggler	smaller size, correct box	NIB	$1,500.00	4-2001
Goble Bait	Wiggler, Tulsa	poor papers	NIB	$1,400.00	11-2000
Go-Ite	Indiana	aluminum, agate guide	EX	$66.00	2-2002
Gopher	Gopher		NIB	$56.59	3-2000
Gowan	Bumble Bug		NIB	$36.02	5-1999
Gregory	Cleopatra Minnow	4 section, metal	EX	$820.00	9-2002
Gresh, Earl Parker	Bender	5¼", B-Flat shiner type, red, white, glass eyes	VG	$371.00	11-1999
Gresh, Earl Parker	Darter	red head, painted eyes, Gresh on belly, nice box	NIB	$208.00	7-2000
Gruber & Oliver	Glowurm	red, white, nice wood box	NIB	$185.05	1-2000
Gruber & Oliver	Glowurm	red, white, papers	EX	$152.50	5-1999
Gruber & Oliver	Glowurm	white, red stripe, box top missing	EX/IB	$275.00	4-1999
Gruber & Oliver	Glowurm	yellow, green stripe	EX+	$150.00	4-2000
Gudebrod	Blabber Mouth		NIB	$13.00	2-1999
H&I	Babe-Oreno	scramble finish, tack eyes	EX	$25.00	5-2001
H&I	Success Spinner	3-hook, nice box, c.1910	VG/IB	$260.00	3-2001
H&I Pflueger	Neverfail	crackleback, sienna, glass eyes, 3-hook, metal	EX/IB	$688.00	8-2001
H.H. Lure Co.	Scorpion	spinnerbait in great old 2PCCB, papers	NIB	$11.00	8-2001
Haas		3-jointed, corroded lip	EX-	$91.51	12-1999

BRAND	MODEL	SERIES / MFG. CODE / DESCRIPTION	GRADE	PRICE	DATE
Haas		4-segment minnow, some paint off lip	EX-	$185.00	5-1999
Haas	Beetle		VG	$250.00	10-2000
Haas	Liv-Minnow	scale	EX	$168.00	1-2001
Hagen	Spinner	metal lure, PTCB	NIB	$13.00	3-2002
Halik	Frog Jr.		EX-	$29.00	1-1999
Halik	Frog Jr.		EX/IB	$51.01	6-1999
Halik	Frog Jr.		NIB	$64.00	1-1999
Hampton	Kentucky Leader	shrink wrapped box	NIB	$61.00	6-2002
Handkamer	Jasper	no eyes, wood, made in Canada	VG	$34.00	2-2002
Hansen	Michigan Lifelike	5-hook	EX	$1,662.01	11-1999
Hansen	Michigan Lifelike	5-hook, chips & slivers	AVG	$910.00	1-2000
Hansen	Michigan Lifelike	5-hook, decent, 1-1-1997 photo?	AVG	$360.00	8-2002
Hansen	Spoonjack Minnow	green, yellow splatter finish	VG+	$463.89	7-1999
Hardy	St. George	3⅜", fly, Mark II check	EX-	$225.00	8-1999
Harlow	Spoon	patent 1888, nice	EX	$77.61	11-1999
Hayes	Feather Minnow	flyrod in nice box	NIB	$342.76	3-1999
Heddon		rainbow, fat body, L-rig, nice	EX	$243.00	8-2000
Heddon	0		VG+	$248.00	4-2000
Heddon	0	awful, NOT MET	Poor	$54.67	2-2000
Heddon	0	red & black	EX	$1,100.00	4-2001
Heddon	0	red, black spots, cup, unmarked, varnish flake	EX-	$1,100.00	10-1999
Heddon	0	red, black spots, small body, HPGM, c.1911	EX	$850.00	8-1999
Heddon	0	spots	VG	$333.33	3-2000
Heddon	0	spots, Up Bass box, nice, NOT MET	EX/IB	$910.00	1-2001
Heddon	0	spots, varnished over	Ugly	$60.00	6-1999
Heddon	0	strawberry, cup-rig	VG+ to EX-	$387.00	11-2000
Heddon	0	strawberry	EX-	$520.01	12-1999
Heddon	0	strawberry	EX-	$550.00	5-2000
Heddon	0	yellow spots	VG-	$150.00	4-1999
Heddon	0	yellow spots, tall marked Down Bass box	EX-/IB	$685.00	2-2000
Heddon	00		EX-	$409.00	4-2000
Heddon	00		VG	$266.00	4-2000
Heddon	00	awful	Poor	$100.00	4-2000
Heddon	00	awful, NOT MET	Poor	$97.00	2-2000
Heddon	00	great Down Bass box	EX/IB	$2,075.00	2-2000
Heddon	00	most paint there	AVG	$150.00	3-2000
Heddon	00	pine tree rf, NOT MET	EX-/IB	$675.00	3-2000
Heddon	00	red & black	EX-	$900.00	4-2001
Heddon	00	red, black spots	EX	$710.00	5-2001
Heddon	00	red, black spots, varnish	EX-	$1,600.00	10-1999
Heddon	00	red, black spots, varnish, chips	AVG+	$280.55	3-1999
Heddon	00	red spots, L-rig, decent	VG	$513.00	1-2001
Heddon	00	spots, awful	Ugly	$124.05	4-1999
Heddon	00	spots, vg Down Bass box, papers	EX/IB	$2,500.00	11-1999
Heddon	00	strawberry	EX-	$650.00	5-2000
Heddon	00	strawberry, cup	VG-	$240.00	8-2000
Heddon	00	strawberry, L-rig	VG+	$440.00	5-2000

BRAND	MODEL	SERIES / MFG. CODE / DESCRIPTION	GRADE	PRICE	DATE
Heddon	00	strawberry, L-rig, yellowed	VG+	$250.98	11-1999
Heddon	00	strawberry, POBW, problems	VG-	$200.00	12-1999
Heddon	00	strawberry, vg tall Down Bass box	EX-/IB	$970.00	5-2000
Heddon	00	strawberry, vg+ Down Bass box	EX/IB	$3,054.00	8-2000
Heddon	00	tall 002 Down Bass box	EX-/IB	$860.00	5-1999
Heddon	00	white spots, nice	EX-	$677.00	9-2002
Heddon	00	yellow spots	AVG	$198.00	10-2000
Heddon	00	yellow spots	VG+	$477.00	3-2002
Heddon	00	yellow spots, unmarked Down Bass box	VG+/IB	$410.00	9-1999
Heddon	00	yellow, red, black spots, cup rig	VG	$373.00	1-1999
Heddon	10	sienna, fat, HPGM, cup, unmarked	EX-	$1,000.00	10-1999
Heddon	10	strawberry, light casting minnow	VG+	$625.00	5-2000
Heddon	10	strawberry, like a small "00"	AVG	$414.00	11-1999
Heddon	10	white, spotted pointers	G	$255.00	12-1998
Heddon	10	yellow, red, black spots	VG-	$248.27	6-1999
Heddon	20	2/2, #20-8'-0-F-HD, H or E	EX-	$661.00	12-2001
Heddon	20	goldfish scale, glass eyes, Stanley prop	EX-	$500.00	12-2001
Heddon	20	red, glass eyes, cup, large touch-up		$89.00	7-2002
Heddon	20 Baby Dowagiac	RHF, 20RHF Banner box, papers	VG+/IB	$103.50	3-1999
Heddon	20 Baby Dowagiac	21 Down Bass box	VG+/IB	$300.00	1-2001
Heddon	20 Baby Dowagiac	crackleback	AVG	$36.00	12-1998
Heddon	20 Baby Dowagiac	crackleback, glass eyes, cup	VG+	$177.00	3-2001
Heddon	20 Baby Dowagiac	crackleback, vg intro box	EX/IB	$1,525.00	3-1999
Heddon	20 Baby Dowagiac	rainbow, cup, POBW	EX-	$285.00	5-2000
Heddon	20 Baby Dowagiac	rainbow, fat body, cup	EX-	$316.00	5-2000
Heddon	20 Baby Dowagiac	rainbow, glass eyes, 2HPGM, L-rig	EX-	$335.00	7-1999
Heddon	20 Baby Dowagiac	rainbow, glass eyes, belly chip but nice	EX-	$390.50	3-2000
Heddon	20 Baby Dowagiac	red, glass eyes, cup, not awful	G	$182.00	4-2001
Heddon	20 Baby Dowagiac	red head, silver scale, tack eyes	EX	$82.00	1-2000
Heddon	20 Baby Dowagiac	red head, silver scale, tack glass eyes	NIB	$154.00	12-1998
Heddon	20 Baby Dowagiac	tack eyes, Banner box	NIB	$150.00	1-1999
Heddon	20 Baby Dowagiac	white, glass eyes, POBW	VG	$193.50	12-1998
Heddon	20 Baby Dowagiac	white, red eyes, glass eyes, cup	VG	$208.50	1-2000
Heddon	20 Baby Dowagiac	white, red tip on tail, eye pointer, decent	G	$62.55	1-1999
Heddon	20 Baby Dowagiac	white, silver & gold sparkle, cup, POBW	EX	$616.00	7-2000
Heddon	100	103, aluminum, green back, cup	VG-	$207.00	8-2000
Heddon	100	103, aluminum "Why of it," wood box, papers	EX/IB	$1,685.00	1-2000
Heddon	100	103, aluminum, wood box	VG/IB	$1,025.00	5-1999
Heddon	100	104 wood box, crisp paper	NIB	$4,596.00	4-2000
Heddon	100	107 wood box, lid replaced, NOT MET	VG+/IB	$696.00	2-2002
Heddon	100	109L Down Bass box	VG+/IB	$212.50	8-1999
Heddon	100	109L Down Bass box	VG+/IB	$305.00	10-1999
Heddon	100	109P, L-rig, NOP	EX	$400.00	8-1999
Heddon	100	aluminum, cup, nice 153 wood box	EX-/IB	$1,580.45	1-2000
Heddon	100	avg 101 blue border box	EX-/IB	$850.00	4-2002
Heddon	100	bar perch, 2HPGM, cup, Down Bass box, papers	VG/IB	$540.00	8-1999
Heddon	100	bar perch, cup, vg+ white 109A Down Bass box	EX-/IB	$1,284.00	1-2000

BRAND	MODEL	SERIES / MFG. CODE / DESCRIPTION	GRADE	PRICE	DATE
Heddon	100	bar perch, decent rig, cup	VG-	$255.00	1-1999
Heddon	100	bar perch, fat, cup, unmarked props	EX-	$405.00	11-2000
Heddon	100	bar perch, HPGM, cup	EX-	$300.00	7-1999
Heddon	100	bar perch, HPGM, cup, avg unmarked wood box	VG+/IB	$686.05	10-1999
Heddon	100	bar perch, HPGM, cup, front prop marked	EX	$350.00	8-1999
Heddon	100	bar perch, L-rig, Down Bass box	NIB	$1,775.00	9-2000
Heddon	100	bar perch, L-rig, ugly belly, rest nice	VG	$300.00	2-1999
Heddon	100	bar perch, L-rig, unmarked Down Bass box	EX/IB	$384.00	10-2002
Heddon	100	blended red, black, HPGM, cup, unmarked	EX-	$430.00	8-1999
Heddon	100	blended white slate back, HPGM, cup	EX	$800.00	8-1999
Heddon	100	blue back, pretty	EX-	$872.00	1-2000
Heddon	100	blue scale, L-rig, NOT MET	VG	$265.00	2-2002
Heddon	100	blue, silver, 2HPGM, 2BW, cup	G	$232.50	5-1999
Heddon	100	copper, cup, thin	EX-	$855.00	12-1999
Heddon	100	crackleback, 2-piece, Brush box	NIB	$406.00	12-1999
Heddon	100	crackleback, 2-piece, hardware, Brush box	NIB	$356.00	10-2002
Heddon	100	crackleback, "2nd"	EX	$375.00	9-2000
Heddon	100	crackleback, 3BW, brass cups & ties	G	$370.00	12-2000
Heddon	100	crackleback, 3BW, NOT MET	VG+	$1,100.00	3-1999
Heddon	100	crackleback, 3 maybe 2? BW, nickel cups	AVG	$258.00	1-2002
Heddon	100	crackleback, blush, fat body, L-rig, Down Bass box	NIB	$740.00	9-2000
Heddon	100	crackleback, blush, L-rig	EX-	$375.00	10-1999
Heddon	100	crackleback, broad, L-rig, nice	EX	$355.55	12-1999
Heddon	100	crackleback, cracked eye, L-rig, okay	EX-	$153.00	5-2000
Heddon	100	crackleback, cup, Down Bass box	EX/IB	$408.78	3-2000
Heddon	100	crackleback, cup, tail chip, wood box	EX-/IB	$1,025.00	10-2000
Heddon	100	crackleback, fat, 2HPGM, cup, BW chipped	EX-	$375.00	3-1999
Heddon	100	crackleback, fat body, HPGM, cup, Missouri	EX+	$451.25	4-1999
Heddon	100	crackleback, fat body, L-rig	EX-	$192.00	5-2001
Heddon	100	crackleback, glass eyes, fat, L-rig, NOT MET	EX-	$202.52	6-1999
Heddon	100	crackleback, high forehead, 2BW, brass cups tie	EX	$800.00	10-1999
Heddon	100	crackleback, high forehead, 2BW, NOT MET	VG	$255.00	2-2002
Heddon	100	crackleback, high forehead, brass chips	Ugly	$280.70	11-1999
Heddon	100	crackleback, HPGM, cup, fat body	EX	$655.00	8-1999
Heddon	100	crackleback, HPGM, cup, nice wood box	EX/IB	$2,000.00	2-2000
Heddon	100	crackleback, HPGM, cup, tapered, unmarked	EX+	$765.00	8-1999
Heddon	100	crackleback, HPGM, cup, tapered, unmarked, crack?	EX-	$231.50	
Heddon	100	crackleback, HPGM, fat body, L-rig	EX-	$202.00	5-2001
Heddon	100	crackleback, L-rig	EX-	$242.50	1-2000
Heddon	100	crackleback, L-rig, ex Down Bass box, NOT MET	NIB	$472.00	7-2000
Heddon	100	crackleback, L-rig, marked front prop	VG	$132.50	5-1999
Heddon	100	cracklcback, nice wood box	EX/IB	$1,407.00	6-2000
Heddon	100	crackleback, sweeping gills, cup, unmarked	EX	$305.00	10-1999
Heddon	100	crackleback, wood box & paper nice	EX/IB	$1,575.00	5-2000
Heddon	100	crisp wood box	NIB	$2,125.00	1-2002

BRAND	MODEL	SERIES / MFG. CODE / DESCRIPTION	GRADE	PRICE	DATE
Heddon	100	fancy back, slim body, wood box	NIB	$2,751.00	9-2000
Heddon	100	fancy light green crackleback, fat, HPGM, cup	EX	$601.00	12-1999
Heddon	100	FG, NNOP, cup, pre-1910	VG	$305.00	1-1999
Heddon	100	frog scale, belly varnish	VG+	$375.00	5-2000
Heddon	100	frog scale, fat body, belly varnish	EX-	$510.00	3-2001
Heddon	100	frog scale, fat body, L-rig	EX-	$676.00	12-1998
Heddon	100	frog scale, L-rig	EX	$595.00	7-2000
Heddon	100	gold scale, L-rig, varnish loss	EX-	$405.00	7-1999
Heddon	100	goldfish, L-rig	EX-	$950.00	5-2000
Heddon	100	goldfish, L-rig, NOT MET	EX-	$425.00	3-2001
Heddon	100	good wood box	VG/IB	$512.00	3-2001
Heddon	100	green scale, broad scale, L-rig	VG	$255.00	6-1999
Heddon	100	green scale, L-rig, ugly varnish	AVG	$97.00	9-1999
Heddon	100	L-rig, marked 109 Up Bass box	EX-	$330.00	5-1999
Heddon	100	perch scale, L-rig, decent	VG+	$188.87	3-2000
Heddon	100	perch scale, L-rig, nice	VG+	$256.00	6-1999
Heddon	100	rainbow, cup	VG	$310.99	2-1999
Heddon	100	rainbow, cup, avg white pasteboard box	EX-/IB	$360.00	10-2002
Heddon	100	rainbow, cup, nice	EX to EX-	$287.86	1-2000
Heddon	100	rainbow, cup, nice 151 wood box	EX/IB	$1,878.73	1-2000
Heddon	100	rainbow, ex 100 wood box & papers	EX-/IB	$1,336.00	4-2002
Heddon	100	rainbow, fat, L-rig, avg unmarked box	EX	$302.00	11-2000
Heddon	100	rainbow, gleamer, fat body, L-rig	EX+	$458.53	1-2000
Heddon	100	rainbow, high forehead, brass,poor wood, NOT MET	VG-/IB	$751.00	1-2001
Heddon	100	rainbow, HPGM, BW, cup, missing plug	VG+	$92.00	4-2000
Heddon	100	rainbow, L-rig, big chips but not awful	AVG	$52.00	4-2000
Heddon	100	rainbow, L-rig, glass eyes, nice	EX	$355.00	11-1999
Heddon	100	rainbow, L-rig, marked	EX-	$280.00	8-1999
Heddon	100	rainbow, L-rig, some small chips	VG++	$191.00	8-2000
Heddon	100	rainbow, L-rig, varnish belly but nice	VG+	$130.00	4-2000
Heddon	100	rainbow, nice wood box	VG+/IB	$1,500.00	3-2001
Heddon	100	rainbow?, red stripe, copper eyes, L-rig	EX-	$202.49	10-1999
Heddon	100	rainbow, vg 101 wood box	VG+/IB	$535.00	12-2001
Heddon	100	red back, yellow, high forehead, 3 sweeping HPGM	VG-	$510.00	8-2001
Heddon	100	red, black HPGM, cup	VG	$139.00	5-2000
Heddon	100	red blend, POBW, ex- 104 wood box	EX-/IB	$1,600.00	10-2001
Heddon	100	red, cup, rig	EX	$405.00	3-2001
Heddon	100	red, cup, ugly	AVG	$231.50	1-2000
Heddon	100	red head, Stanley props, cup	EX	$749.00	5-2000
Heddon	100	red head, white & red tail, L-rig	EX	$522.00	3-2001
Heddon	100	red, L-rig, 104 Down Bass box, NOT MET	EX-/IB	$430.00	10-2000
Heddon	100	red, ugly	Poor	$76.00	12-1998
Heddon	100	salt flitter, fat, cup	EX+	$950.00	5-2000
Heddon	100	shiner scale, L-rig	VG+	$338.00	8-2000
Heddon	100	sienna crackleback, HPGM, 2BW, cup	EX-	$1,000.00	7-2000

BRAND	MODEL	SERIES / MFG. CODE / DESCRIPTION	GRADE	PRICE	DATE
Heddon	100	sienna crackleback, HPGM, cup, unmarked	G	$168.50	1-2000
Heddon	100	sienna, drags, chips, ugly	AVG	$167.50	2-1999
Heddon	100	sienna, HPGM, cup	EX-	$735.00	6-1999
Heddon	100	slate back, fat, HPGM, cup	EX-	$259.44	12-1999
Heddon	100	slate back, red eye shadow, HPGM, cup	EX	$810.00	4-2000
Heddon	100	slate, cup, wood box not marked	VG-/IB	$1,225.00	6-1999
Heddon	100	slate, red eyes	EX-	$575.00	5-2000
Heddon	100	vg+ wood box, $1,000.00 NOT MET	VG+/IB	$790.00	3-2001
Heddon	100	white, HPGM, cup, tiny varnish	EX-	$388.00	4-2000
Heddon	100	white, red eyes, fat body, cup	VG+	$300.00	3-1999
Heddon	100	white, wood box, NOT MET	VG-/IB	$810.00	9-1999
Heddon	100	wood box	EX/IB	$1,200.00	7-2000
Heddon	100	WYSIWYG, rainbow, HPGM, cup, "Gem"	EX	$126.00	8-1999
Heddon	100	yellow, high forehead, 2BW, brass cups	VG	$1,300.00	8-1999
Heddon	100	yellow, high forehead, brass, wood, NOT MET	VG-/IB	$1,505.02	11-1999
Heddon	101	L-rig, vg- Down Bass box	VG+/IB	$511.00	1-2001
Heddon	101	rainbow, blunt nose, ex marked wood box	EX/IB	$2,000.00	10-1999
Heddon	101	rainbow, blunt nose, vg+ marked wood box	EX/IB	$1,650.00	10-1999
Heddon	101	rainbow, fat, cup, name on props	VG+ to EX-	$425.00	10-1999
Heddon	103	aluminum, black HPGM, POBW, nice wood box, hf	VG+/IB	$2,550.00	12-2000
Heddon	104	blended red, cup, unmarked	EX	$700.00	10-1999
Heddon	104	solid red, POBW, L-rig, chip	EX-	$625.00	10-1999
Heddon	107	sienna crackleback, slim, cup, no name	EX	$1,000.00	10-1999
Heddon	109	cup, vg+ blue border Down Bass box	EX-/IB	$2,000.00	10-1999
Heddon	109	109D, cup, marked props	EX-	$500.00	10-1999
Heddon	109	109D, Down Bass box	EX-/IB	$500.00	10-1999
Heddon	150	2-piece, repainted, awful	Poor	$46.00	2-1999
Heddon	150	150P, painted eyes, papers, NOT MET	NIB	$153.00	3-2001
Heddon	150	150P, S-rig, Banner box	EX/IB	$154.01	9-1999
Heddon	150	150RSF, South Bend color, rough, NOT MET		$280.00	6-2001
Heddon	150	151 in nice wood box, papers	EX-	$1,810.00	2-1999
Heddon	150	151RB, rainbow, cup, vg+ wood box	VG+/IB	$935.00	12-2000
Heddon	150	154 Down Bass box, "154" looks bogus, NOT MET	NIB	$940.00	2-2002
Heddon	150	159L Up Bass box, NOT MET	EX-/IB	$600.00	3-1999
Heddon	150	159PL, L-rig, ex Up Bass box	NIB	$2,932.00	7-2002
Heddon	150	aluminum, cup, HPGM	VG+	$256.00	7-2002
Heddon	150	aluminum, L-rig, iffy paint job	EX	$455.00	4-2000
Heddon	150	bar perch, cup, fat	VG	$290.00	1-2000
Heddon	150	bar perch, cup, NOT MET	Poor	$66.00	2-2000
Heddon	150	bar perch, fat body, L-rig	EX-	$1,100.00	5-1999
Heddon	150	bar perch, L-rig	EX	$556.00	1-2001
Heddon	150	bar perch, L-rig	G	$120.00	12-1999
Heddon	150	bar perch, L-rig	VG	$282.77	2-2000
Heddon	150	bar perch, L-rig, decent	G+	$170.00	3-1999
Heddon	150	bar perch, L-rig, ex 159A Up Bass box	VG/IB	$510.00	12-2000

BRAND	MODEL	SERIES / MFG. CODE / DESCRIPTION	GRADE	PRICE	DATE
Heddon	150	bar perch, L-rig, Up Bass box	Both Mint	$2,700.00	1-1999
Heddon	150	bar perch, POBW, toilet	EX-	$550.00	5-2000
Heddon	150	black crackleback, L-rig	EX	$380.00	4-2000
Heddon	150	black sucker, brass, high forehead	EX-	$2,550.00	4-1999
Heddon	150	blended, aluminum, NOP, L-rig, thin body, varnish	EX-	$650.00	8-1999
Heddon	150	blended red head, cup, D. Double papers	G (EX?)	$811.00	5-1999
Heddon	150	blended red, fat body, L-rig	G	$161.00	12-1999
Heddon	150	blue crackleback, 2-piece, Brush box	EX/IB	$950.00	10-1999
Heddon	150	blue, cup, vg+ 159A Down Bass	VG+/IB	$2,700.00	11-2001
Heddon	150	bluish back, aluminum, HPGM	EX-	$799.00	8-2002
Heddon	150	bs. rainbow, brass, high forehead, 2BW	VG-	$2,025.00	4-1999
Heddon	150	crackleback, 3HPGM, cup	VG+	$285.00	7-1999
Heddon	150	crackleback, 3HPGM, L-rig	EX-	$300.00	1-1999
Heddon	150	crackleback, blush, L-rig, thin, pointed nose	EX	$555.00	6-1999
Heddon	150	crackleback, blush, L-rig, ugly belly varnish	VG	$200.00	8-1999
Heddon	150	crackleback, cup, HPGM, 1BW	Mint	$1,075.00	8-1999
Heddon	150	crackleback, cup, HPGM, POBW	VG	$151.00	12-1999
Heddon	150	crackleback, cup, much varnish flaking	G	$164.50	5-1999
Heddon	150	crackleback, faded wood box	VG+/IB	$1,450.00	5-2000
Heddon	150	crackleback, fat body, Up Bass box	EXIB	$535.00	4-1999
Heddon	150	crackleback, fat, HPGM, L-rig, c.1915, nice	EX	$352.00	9-2002
Heddon	150	crackleback, high forehead, 3BW, brass cups	VG-	$2,005.00	12-2001
Heddon	150	crackleback, HPGM, cup, props, unmarked, nice	EX+	$616.00	11-1999
Heddon	150	crackleback, HPGM, cup, unmarked	VG+	$284.88	9-1999
Heddon	150	crackleback, L-rig	EX-	$242.00	5-2001
Heddon	150	crackleback, L-rig	G	$166.50	3-1999
Heddon	150	crackleback, L-rig, 150 Up Bass box	EX/IB	$301.00	7-2001
Heddon	150	crackleback, L-rig, Down Bass box	EX-/IB	$501.57	2-2000
Heddon	150	crackleback, L-rig, Down Bass box, decent	G+/IB	$173.50	6-1999
Heddon	150	crackleback, L-rig, Up Bass box	VG/IB	$260.00	10-2000
Heddon	150	crackleback, painted eyes	EX	$126.00	1-1999
Heddon	150	crackleback, painted eyes	EX/IB	$158.00	1-2002
Heddon	150	crackleback, painted eyes	VG	$104.00	5-1999
Heddon	150	crackleback, painted eyes, PTCB	NIB	$112.50	3-2000
Heddon	150	crackleback, POBW, toilet, crisp Brush box, catalog	NIB	$432.00	2-2002
Heddon	150	crackleback, POBW, L-rig, Down Bass box, NOT MET	EX-/IB	$301.55	8-1999
Heddon	150	crackleback, poor picture	EX-	$200.00	1-1999
Heddon	150	crackleback, round body, cup, unmarked props	VG+	$375.00	3-1999
Heddon	150	crackleback, Up Bass box	EX-/IB	$417.00	8-2000
Heddon	150	crackleback, wood box & paper	EX/IB	$2,285.00	5-2001
Heddon	150	cup, 151 wood box, no writing, lid top	EX/IB	$1,450.00	5-1999
Heddon	150	cup, marked props, most paint gone, beater		$69.00	3-2001
Heddon	150	cup, rig, ugly	Poor	$153.00	1-1999

BRAND	MODEL	SERIES / MFG. CODE / DESCRIPTION	GRADE	PRICE	DATE
Heddon	150	fancy back, nice wood box	EX/IB	$1,426.00	5-2000
Heddon	150	flitter, cup, age lines, 159RH Up Bass box	VG+/IB	$460.00	2-2000
Heddon	150	flitter, HPGM, L-rig, marked props	EX-	$400.00	10-2000
Heddon	150	frog scale?	AVG	$91.00	12-1998
Heddon	150	frog scale, 2-piece, flawless	Mint	$2,850.00	5-2000
Heddon	150	frog scale, fat body, L-rig, belly varnish	VG+	$494.00	11-2000
Heddon	150	frog scale, L-rig	EX-	$810.00	6-2002
Heddon	150	frog scale, L-rig	VG-	$407.00	3-2001
Heddon	150	frog scale, L-rig, huge chips	Poor	$88.00	3-2000
Heddon	150	frog scale, L-rig, looks okay	VG-	$296.00	4-2001
Heddon	150	frog scale, L-rig, nice 159J Down Bass box	EX/IB	$1,400.00	8-1999
Heddon	150	frog, champagne eyes, fat, L-rig	VG	$422.00	2-2000
Heddon	150	frog, L-rig	EX	$910.00	9-1999
Heddon	150	frog, L-rig, NOT MET	EX	$560.00	10-2002
Heddon	150	frog, L-rig, varnish flake	VG	$485.00	12-1998
Heddon	150	gold, fat, HPGM, cup, 2 small ugly chips	VG-	$251.00	2-2000
Heddon	150	goldfish scale, L-rig, decent	VG+	$361.00	10-2001
Heddon	150	goldfish scale, L-rig, ugly belly	VG	$300.00	10-2000
Heddon	150	goldfish, fat body, L-rig	VG	$565.00	4-2000
Heddon	150	goldfish, L-rig	EX-	$1,850.00	5-2000
Heddon	150	green scale, fat body, L-rig, NOP	VG+	$375.00	8-1999
Heddon	150	green scale, fat, L-rig, pretty	EX- to EX	$810.00	3-2001
Heddon	150	green scale, L-rig	EX-	$393.00	3-2000
Heddon	150	green scale, L-rig	VG	$255.00	2-2000
Heddon	150	green scale, L-rig, NOP	EX+	$875.00	5-2000
Heddon	150	green, white, slim body, 3BW	AVG	$660.00	10-2002
Heddon	150	HPGM, L-rig, vg 159 Down Bass box, NOT MET	EX/IB	$610.00	10-2000
Heddon	150	HPGM, NOP, L-rig, missing hardware	Poor	$128.00	8-2000
Heddon	150	L-rig, 151 Up Bass box	EX-/IB	$305.00	7-2001
Heddon	150	L-rig, fat body, vg+ 152 tall Down Bass box	EX-/IB	$455.00	6-2002
Heddon	150	L-rig, high forehead, varnish	VG	$300.00	1-1999
Heddon	150	L-rig, nice 152 Down Bass box	EX/IB	$960.00	3-1999
Heddon	150	orange, black spots, L-rig	VG+	$1,025.00	6-2001
Heddon	150	orange, black spots, L-rig, marked props	VG-	$1,047.22	5-1999
Heddon	150	pearly gold, red eye shadow, L-rig	VG	$565.00	10-2000
Heddon	150	perch scale, L-rig	EX	$330.00	4-1999
Heddon	150	perch scale, L-rig, 159A Down Bass box	EX+/IB	$1,875.00	4-1999
Heddon	150	perch scale, L-rig, ugly varnish	VG	$280.55	3-2000
Heddon	150	perch scale, L-rig, wrong Down Bass box	VG	$251.05	8-1999
Heddon	150	poor pine tree box	EX-	$885.00	5-2000
Heddon	150	rainbow, 2-piece, belly stencil, marked	EX-	$244.56	9-1999
Heddon	150	rainbow, 2-piece, POBW	EX	$455.00	11-1999
Heddon	150	rainbow, 2-piece, zinc eyes	EX	$565.00	6-2000
Heddon	150	rainbow, 3HPGM, cup, ugly varnish	VG	$179.00	8-1999
Heddon	150	rainbow, cup	Poor	$66.00	10-2000
Heddon	150	rainbow, cup, unmarked Down Bass box	EX-	$300.00	7-1999
Heddon	150	rainbow, glass eyes	AVG	$75.00	1-1999

BRAND	MODEL	SERIES / MFG. CODE / DESCRIPTION	GRADE	PRICE	DATE
Heddon	150	rainbow, glass eyes, L-rig, belly varnish, NOT MET	EX-	$202.50	7-1999
Heddon	150	rainbow, HPGM, cup, light hook drag	EX-	$450.00	3-2000
Heddon	150	rainbow, HPGM, POBW, cup, unmarked	VG+	$188.37	9-1999
Heddon	150	rainbow, L-rig	EX	$310.00	4-2001
Heddon	150	rainbow, L-rig, fat body, varnish flakes	VG-	$203.50	11-1999
Heddon	150	rainbow, L-rig, light touch-up	VG*	$86.00	5-2000
Heddon	150	rainbow, L-rig, looks nice, junky box	EX	$204.00	10-2002
Heddon	150	rainbow, L-rig, NOT MET	VG	$180.50	10-1999
Heddon	150	rainbow, L-rig, vg- Down Bass box, decent	VG/IB	$255.00	12-1999
Heddon	150	rainbow, L-rig, vg unmarked box, NOT MET	EX/IB	$305.00	5-2001
Heddon	150	rainbow, large scrape on back, Down Bass box, NOT MET	AVG/IB	$177.00	3-2001
Heddon	150	rainbow, NOP, cup, fat body, varnish	AVG	$131.00	10-2000
Heddon	150	rainbow, painted eyes	AVG	$77.90	1-1999
Heddon	150	rainbow, painted eyes, PTCB catalog	NIB	$325.00	4-2000
Heddon	150	rainbow, painted eyes, vg Banner box	NIB	$213.00	5-2000
Heddon	150	rainbow, pine tree box, papers, NOT MET		$1,512.00	10-2001
Heddon	150	rainbow, round, cup, HPGM, poor wood box	EX/IB	$850.00	2-2000
Heddon	150	rainbow, S-rig, Banner box	NIB	$125.00	12-1999
Heddon	150	rainbow, thin body, cup, Up Bass box, nice, NOT MET	NIB	$522.00	3-2002
Heddon	150	red eyes & tail, 2-piece	EX-	$301.00	3-2000
Heddon	150	red head, painted eyes, catalog, NOT MET	EX/IB	$102.51	6-1999
Heddon	150	red head, painted eyes, S-rig, NOT MET	NIB	$102.00	4-2001
Heddon	150	red scale	EX	$1,200.00	4-2001
Heddon	150	red scale, glass eyes, L-rig, unmarked Down Bass box	AVG	$305.00	2-1999
Heddon	150	red scale, L-rig	G	$326.00	1-1999
Heddon	150	red scale, L-rig	VG	$213.00	10-2001
Heddon	150	red scale, L-rig	VG	$371.00	5-2000
Heddon	150	red scale, L-rig	VG+	$483.00	12-1999
Heddon	150	red scale, L-rig, ring ABW, pretty	EX	$1,975.00	9-1999
Heddon	150	red scale, unmarked Down Bass box	VG	$685.00	10-1999
Heddon	150	red, 2-piece, POBW	G	$148.00	5-2000
Heddon	150	red, cup	EX-	$750.00	5-2000
Heddon	150	red, dark back, HPGM, POBW, cup	VG	$191.50	5-1999
Heddon	150	red, fat, L-rig, NO BIDS	VG-	$355.00	12-1999
Heddon	150	red, HPGM, cup, NOP	EX	$900.00	8-1999
Heddon	150	red, huge belly chips, top okay	Fair	$75.00	1-1999
Heddon	150	red, white, painted eyes, age lines	EX	$97.00	1-1999
Heddon	150	S-rig, painted eyes, 150RHF Banner box	NIB	$187.00	1-2001
Heddon	150	saltwater, HPGM, cup, vg 159 pasteboard box, NOT MET	NIB	$898.00	10-2002
Heddon	150	saltwater, L-rig, NOT MET	EX	$356.00	1-2001
Heddon	150	saltwater, white flakes, L-rig, NOT MET	EX	$720.00	1-2001
Heddon	150	screamer lure, L-rig, vg 159D Down	NIB	$2,000.00	4-2000
Heddon	150	shiner scale, L-rig	EX+	$522.00	12-1999

BRAND	MODEL	SERIES / MFG. CODE / DESCRIPTION	GRADE	PRICE	DATE
Heddon	150	shiner scale, painted eyes	VG/IB	$96.00	4-1999
Heddon	150	sienna crackleback, cup, belly stencil, marked props	EX	$555.00	3-2002
Heddon	150	sienna crackleback, fat, HPGM, tail chip, cup	VG+	$456.00	1-2000
Heddon	150	sienna crackleback, HPGM, cup, poor wood box	EX-	$1,198.00	2-2002
Heddon	150	sienna crackleback, L-rig, small tail chip, nice	EX-	$627.00	5-2002
Heddon	150	sienna crackleback, L-rig, HPGM, pretty	EX-	$910.00	10-2001
Heddon	150	sienna crackleback, POBW, cup	EX-	$750.00	5-2000
Heddon	150	silver, HPGM, ugly varnish, looks gold		$1,000.00	9-2001
Heddon	150	slate, cup, HPGM, blunt nose, POBW	EX-	$330.00	12-2001
Heddon	150	slate, cup, HPGM, NOT MET	VG	$128.00	2-2002
Heddon	150	slate, cup, not awful	AVG	$100.00	2-1999
Heddon	150	slate, HPGM, cup, MP	VG-	$225.00	6-1999
Heddon	150	strawberry, L-rig, bad varnish, ugly	G	$351.00	11-2000
Heddon	150	vg 151 wood box	VG/IB	$788.00	11-2001
Heddon	150	vg+ pine tree box, lure belly varnish	VG+IB	$1,226.00	1-2001
Heddon	150	white, blush, red eyes, L-rig, marked props	EX-	$355.00	10-1999
Heddon	150	white, flitter, fat, L-rig	EX	$661.00	4-1999
Heddon	150	white, flitter, glass eyes, L-rig	EX+	$685.00	11-1999
Heddon	150	white, flitter, L-rig	Rough	$61.00	2-1999
Heddon	150	white, red eyes & tail, L-rig, 152 Down Bass box	NIB	$1,884.00	1-2000
Heddon	150	white, red eyes, L-rig	EX-	$349.00	7-2000
Heddon	150	white, red eyes, L-rig, POBW	EX-	$240.00	1-2002
Heddon	150	white, red head & tail, L-rig	EX-	$750.00	5-2000
Heddon	150	white, silver flakes, L-rig	EX-	$605.00	3-1999
Heddon	150	white, sparkles, HPGM, cup	EX-	$301.99	3-2000
Heddon	150	white, sparkles, L-rig, Down Bass box	EX/IB	$560.00	2-2000
Heddon	150	x2, one RHF & one OS; painted eyes, S-rig	EX	$330.50	8-1999
Heddon	150	yellow, black, H, L-rig, throat varnish	VG	$453.00	8-2000
Heddon	150	yellow, green back, fat, L-rig, NO BIDS	AVG	$355.00	12-1999
Heddon	150	yellow spots, painted eyes, pointers, NOT MET	VG+	$91.00	1-1999
Heddon	150	x2, frog, crackleback, L-rig, cup-rig	AVG	$187.00	10-2000
Heddon	151	great wood box, NOT MET	VG+/IB	$908.00	8-2000
Heddon	151	rainbow, HPGM, cup, unmarked wood box	EX/IB	$1,750.00	8-1999
Heddon	151	rainbow, L-rig, cup, Down Bass box	NIB	$1,350.00	10-1999
Heddon	151	rainbow, lure decent, nice wood box	VG+/IB	$1,077.00	11-2000
Heddon	152	red, white, red, L-rig, COBW	EX-	$1,000.00	10-1999
Heddon	152	slate, blunt nose, cup, vg wood box	EX/IB	$2,500.00	10-1999
Heddon	154	blended red, high forehead, cup, Down Bass box	VG/IB	$400.030	1-2000
Heddon	155	155YRB, early YRB, wood box type	VG+ to EX-	$1,500.00	10-1999
Heddon	159	159A, bar perch, L-rig, nice Up Bass box	EX-/IB	$636.00	11-2000
Heddon	159	159A, bar perch, L-rig, small flakes by eye	EX-	$800.00	10-1999
Heddon	159	159B, cup, tail chip, dent, ex Down Bass box	VG/IB	$669.00	12-2000
Heddon	159	159D Deluxe, green scale, L-rig, marked props	EX	$1,000.00	10-1999
Heddon	159	159D, 2-piece, COBW	EX-	$675.00	10-1999
Heddon	159	159H, red scale, no blush, L-rig, no name on box	EX	$2,000.00	10-1999
Heddon	159	159L, 2-piece, vg Brush box	EX+/IB	$900.00	10-1999

BRAND	MODEL	SERIES / MFG. CODE / DESCRIPTION	GRADE	PRICE	DATE
Heddon	159	159P, 2-piece, 159L Brush box	EX/IB	$950.00	10-1999
Heddon	159	159P, ring ABW	EX	$700.00	10-1999
Heddon	175	crackleback	AVG	$205.00	10-2000
Heddon	175	crackleback	EX	$1,550.00	5-2000
Heddon	175	crackleback, L-rig, NOT MET	VG-	$565.00	3-1999
Heddon	175	crackleback, NOT MET	VG+	$345.00	7-2000
Heddon	175	gray slate, 2BW, varnish	VG	$350.00	8-1999
Heddon	175	rainbow, cup	EX-	$1,325.00	5-2001
Heddon	175	rainbow, cup rig	VG+	$760.00	3-1999
Heddon	175	rainbow, cup rig, decent	VG+	$333.00	6-2001
Heddon	175	slate, HPGM, props, unmarked	EX-	$1,587.00	3-2001
Heddon	175	slate, NOT MET	VG	$463.00	9-2000
Heddon	175	yellowed white?	VG-	$393.50	3-2000
Heddon	200	3-pin, varnish, 200S Down Bass box	VG+/IB	$736.00	9-2000
Heddon	200	200SB, L-rig, tail cap, ugly varnish, Down Bass box, NOT MET	VG+/IB	$305.00	11-2000
Heddon	200	black, white, 3-pin, varnish flakes	VG	$246.50	5-1999
Heddon	200	black, white, L-rig, 3-screw collar	VG	$137.00	1-1999
Heddon	200	blue head, 2-pin, c.1912, Down Bass box	EX/IB	$1,500.00	2-2002
Heddon	200	blue head, 4-hook, 2 sides	VG+	$885.00	2-2000
Heddon	200	blue head, 4-hook, 2-pin, unmarked pine tree, vg+	EX-/IB	$3,500.00	11-2000
Heddon	200	blue head, 4-hook, 200SW Down Bass box	EX-/IB	$910.00	2-2002
Heddon	200	blue head, 4-hook, tail cap	VG	$710.00	3-2001
Heddon	200	blue head, L-rig, nice Up Bass box, catalog	NIB	$599.00	3-2000
Heddon	200	blue head, L-rig, Up bass, NOT MET	EX/IB	$350.00	8-2000
Heddon	200	blue head, nice 200BH Down Bass box	EX/IB	$513.00	9-2001
Heddon	200	blue head, no eyes, 2-piece, hardware, 200BH Up Bass box	NIB	$480.00	5-2000
Heddon	200	blue head, no eyes, L-rig, ugly varnish	VG	$127.00	5-2000
Heddon	200	blue head, sloped nose, 4-hook, tail cap, NOT MET	AVG	$169.00	3-2001
Heddon	200	blue head, sloped nose, repainted collar, NOT MET	EX	$1,006.00	8-2000
Heddon	200	blue head, type C, , double name caller, 3-pin	VG+	$153.00	8-2000
Heddon	200	frog, 3-pin, small chips, nice Up Bass box	VG+/IB	$205.00	4-2000
Heddon	200	frog, no eyes, 3-pin, tail cap, cup	G	$112.00	4-1999
Heddon	200	frog, no eyes, L-rig	EX-	$191.00	10-2000
Heddon	200	frog, no eyes, L-rig, Down Bass box	EX/IB	$307.00	1-2000
Heddon	200	frog, no eyes, L-rig, tail cap	EX-	$128.00	10-2000
Heddon	200	green scale, no eyes, L-rig	EX	$1,428.00	4-2000
Heddon	200	luminous, 3-hook, 200LUM Down Bass box	EX-/IB	$1,000.00	11-2000
Heddon	200	luminous, red, no eyes, bubbly	AVG	$117.00	12-1998
Heddon	200	red scale, no eyes, L-rig, decent	G	$866.00	5-2000
Heddon	200	red, white, glass eyes	EX	$237.50	2-1999
Heddon	200	red head, glass eyes, 2-piece, small wrinkle in paint	EX-	$306.00	2-2002
Heddon	200	red head, luminous, 200SL Down Bass box	EX-/IB	$500.00	9-2001

BRAND	MODEL	SERIES / MFG. CODE / DESCRIPTION	GRADE	PRICE	DATE
Heddon	200	sloped nose, brass tail & cups, NOT MET	VG	$510.00	6-2002
Heddon	200	solid red, repainted?, 2-pin	EX	$898.00	5-2000
Heddon	200	white, red & green spots, L-rig, tail cap	EX-	$800.00	12-1999
Heddon	210	210BF, glass eyes, NOT MET	EX-	$81.00	3-2001
Heddon	210	210BF, white eyes	NIB	$88.02	9-1999
Heddon	210	210BLH, painted eyes, 210BLH Banner box	NIB	$101.99	2-1999
Heddon	210	210BM, 2-piece, Brush box	NIB	$249.50	11-1999
Heddon	210	210GM		$29.50	2-1999
Heddon	210	210GM, 2-piece	EX	$82.00	2-2001
Heddon	210	210GM, 2-piece, worn box, NOT MET	EX+/IB	$104.00	3-2000
Heddon	210	210GM, looks poor	VG	$49.99	3-1999
Heddon	210	210GM, S-rig	EX	$81.00	3-2000
Heddon	210	219B, frog, glass eyes, 2-piece, Brush box, catalog	NIB	$698.00	5-1999
Heddon	210	219B, frog, no eyes, L-rig, Up Bass box, catalog	NIB	$568.00	5-1999
Heddon	210	blue head, glass eyes	VG	$61.00	3-1999
Heddon	210	blue head, glass eyes, Brush box	VG/IB	$100.00	6-1999
Heddon	210	blue head, glass eyes, Up Bass box	NIB	$521.99	2-1999
Heddon	210	frog, glass eyes	EX	$154.00	7-2000
Heddon	210	frog scale, L-rig	VG+	$830.00	1-2002
Heddon	210	frog, painted eyes	EX	$62.00	1-1999
Heddon	210	green scale, glass eyes, 2-piece	VG+	$212.00	1-2002
Heddon	210	L-rig, mint 219B Down Bass box	NIB	$405.00	3-1999
Heddon	210	luminous, awful chips, nice box, NOT MET	Poor/IB	$112.00	5-2001
Heddon	210	luminous, glass eyes	EX-	$375.00	1-1999
Heddon	210	luminous, red eyes & tail, 2-piece	EX+	$350.00	3-1999
Heddon	210	mouse	EX-	$103.50	1-1999
Heddon	210	mouse, ears & tail	VG	$61.99	4-1999
Heddon	210	mouse, S-rig	EX	$56.00	2-1999
Heddon	210	painted eyes, 210BF Banner box	NIB	$104.00	8-2002
Heddon	210	red head, 2-piece, glass eyes, Brush box	VG+/IB	$76.00	10-2001
Heddon	210	red head, glass eyes, 2-piece, NOT MET	EX+	$100.00	5-1999
Heddon	210	red head, painted eyes, S-rig	EX-	$37.00	11-2000
Heddon	210	red head, white, glass eyes	EX-	$66.00	1-1999
Heddon	210	red head, white, glass eyes, 2-piece, stencil	Mint	$179.50	1-2000
Heddon	210	red scale, no eyes, L-rig	VG	$340.00	3-2001
Heddon	210	red, white, Banner box	NIB	$152.00	1-1999
Heddon	210	red, white, glass eyes	VG	$45.00	1-1999
Heddon	210	red, white, glass eyes, 2-piece, NOT MET	EX	$62.00	1-1999
Heddon	210 Spook	210B	NIB	$133.50	12-1999
Heddon	210 Spook	210BF	NIB	$78.00	10-1999
Heddon	210 Spook	210BF	NIB	$82.00	6-1999
Heddon	210 Spook	210BH	NIB	$207.51	6-1999
Heddon	210 Spook	210BO	NIB	$197.51	6-1999
Heddon	210 Spook	210BO	NIB	$258.00	4-1999
Heddon	210 Spook	210SD	NIB	$141.00	3-1999
Heddon	210 Spook	210SS	NIB	$203.00	7-2000

BRAND	MODEL	SERIES / MFG. CODE / DESCRIPTION	GRADE	PRICE	DATE
Heddon	210 Spook	210SSD	NIB	$81.00	6-1999
Heddon	210 Spook	210BF, white eyes	NIB	$103.50	3-1999
Heddon	210 Spook	210BH	EX	$217.00	5-2000
Heddon	210 Spook	210BH	Mint	$194.00	8-2002
Heddon	210 Spook	210BH	NIB	$163.50	6-1999
Heddon	210 Spook	210BH	NIB	$212.50	2-1999
Heddon	210 Spook	210BH	NIB	$223.00	10-2002
Heddon	210 Spook	210BH	NIB	$229.00	4-1999
Heddon	210 Spook	210BH	NIB	$265.00	3-2000
Heddon	210 Spook	210Y	NIB	$127.50	6-1999
Heddon	210 Spook	black	EX+	$102.50	8-1999
Heddon	210 Spook	black	NIB	$137.00	4-2000
Heddon	210 Spook	black, J. Yates, NOT MET	EX	$84.00	2-1999
Heddon	210 Spook	black, white eyes	EX	$106.50	1-1999
Heddon	210 Spook	blue head, white	EX-	$160.00	11-2001
Heddon	210 Spook	bone, NOT MET	NIB	$107.00	1-2001
Heddon	210 Spook	bullfrog	EX	$61.00	7-2001
Heddon	210 Spook	chartreuse coach dog	EX	$86.89	2-1999
Heddon	210 Spook	coach dog	EX	$68.00	7-2001
Heddon	210 Spook	frog	Mint	$91.00	1-1999
Heddon	210 Spook	frog	VG	$56.55	1-1999
Heddon	210 Spook	orange dace, BSO, NOT MET	Mint	$325.00	4-1999
Heddon	210 Spook	shad	EX	$71.00	7-2001
Heddon	210 Spook	silver scale	EX+	$122.50	4-1999
Heddon	210 Spook	silver scale	Mint	$167.50	3-2000
Heddon	210 Spook	white, flitter, no code on box	NIB	$132.50	1-1999
Heddon	210 Spook	white, red eye shadow	EX	$105.00	10-2000
Heddon	210 Spook	x3, 3 different	NIB	$385.00	11-1999
Heddon	210 Spook	yellow	EX	$152.50	5-1999
Heddon	210 Spook	yellow	EX	$160.00	1-1999
Heddon	210 Spook	yellow	NIB	$127.50	4-1999
Heddon	210 Spook	yellow	NIB	$127.50	6-1999
Heddon	210 Spook	yellow coach dog	EX	$102.00	10-2002
Heddon	210 Spook	yellow coach dog	NIB	$106.00	10-2002
Heddon	210 Spook	yellow coach dog	NIB	$107.50	6-1999
Heddon	210 Spook	yellow coach dog	NIB	$125.00	8-2000
Heddon	210 Spook	yellow coach dog, no code on box	NIB	$125.50	1-1999
Heddon	250	green scale	VG	$450.00	10-2000
Heddon	250	red scale, L-rig, not awful	G	$360.00	5-2000
Heddon	250	strawberry, glass eyes	EX	$1,035.00	2-1999
Heddon	300	6-hook, marked repaint	New	$232.00	3-2002
Heddon	300	all varnish missing, was rainbow, now white	Fair	$156.00	7-2000
Heddon	300	blush crackleback, 2-hook	EX	$395.00	3-2002
Heddon	300	crackleback, HPGM, cup, unmarked, NOT MET	EX-	$300.00	9-1999
Heddon	300	crackleback, 2-hook, cup	EX-	$685.00	9-2000
Heddon	300	crackleback, 2-piece, chip POBW	EX-	$400.00	10-1999

BRAND	MODEL	SERIES / MFG. CODE / DESCRIPTION	GRADE	PRICE	DATE
Heddon	300	crackleback, 3-hook, round body, cup	EX	$775.00	5-2000
Heddon	300	crackleback, 3HPGM, flat L-rig	EX-	$300.00	8-1999
Heddon	300	crackleback, 5-hook, DL box	NIB	$5,600.00	1-2000
Heddon	300	crackleback, 6-hook	Fair	$1,052.50	1-1999
Heddon	300	crackleback, air gills, L-rig, x-holes		$157.50	8-1999
Heddon	300	crackleback, blush chin, L-rig	VG+	$255.00	8-1999
Heddon	300	crackleback, blush, L-rig	VG+	$229.00	8-2000
Heddon	300	crackleback, blush, L-rig, ugly belly varnish	VG	$137.50	8-1999
Heddon	300	crackleback, cup, $2,400.00 NOT MET	EX	$356.00	12-2000
Heddon	300	crackleback, cup, belly chip, decent	EX-	$204.00	7-2002
Heddon	300	crackleback, HPGM, cup, awful, ugly		$81.00	8-1999
Heddon	300	crackleback, HPGM, L-rig	EX-	$515.00	4-2001
Heddon	300	crackleback, HPGM, L-rig, NOT MET	EX-	$260.00	11-1999
Heddon	300	crackleback, HPGM, L-rig, NOT MET	VG+	$178.00	12-2000
Heddon	300	crackleback, long gill marks, cup, reserve	EX+	$2,400.00	11-2000
Heddon	300	crackleback, red chin, L-rig	VG+	$227.50	3-2000
Heddon	300	crackleback, thin, cup, NOT MET	EX-	$898.00	10-2000
Heddon	300	crisp 3023H Brush box	NIB	$1,200.00	9-2001
Heddon	300	frog spot, L-rig	EX-	$1500.00	9-2002
Heddon	300	frog spot, small tail sliver, L-rig	EX	$1500.00	9-2002
Heddon	300	high forehead, cup, unmarked	EX	$4,650.00	2-1999
Heddon	300	L-rig, bad bleed through, 2-piece, NOT MET	VG	$188.50	5-1999
Heddon	300	L-rig, crisp 302 Up Bass box & tissue NOT MET	NIB	$877.00	5-2002
Heddon	300	L-rig, fat body, HPGM, dull, rust	VG+	$300.00	12-1999
Heddon	300	natural scale, 6-hook, 585 with 2 minutes	EX-	$935.00	9-1999
Heddon	300	perch scale, 6-hook, 2-piece	EX-	$490.00	6-2001
Heddon	300	perch scale, 6-hook, 2-piece, NOT MET	EX-	$433.00	1-2002
Heddon	300	perch scale, 7-hook, 2-piece	EX-	$600.00	6-2002
Heddon	300	pike scale, 6-hook	EX-	$787.77	3-2000
Heddon	300	poor 301 white box	VG-/IB	$518.00	4-2000
Heddon	300	rainbow, 4-hook L-rig	EX-	$1,100.00	11-2001
Heddon	300	rainbow, 6-hook, L-rig	VG+	$1,205.00	3-2000
Heddon	300	rainbow, 7-hook, 2-piece	VG+	$910.00	3-2001
Heddon	300	rainbow, cup, fat, NOT MET	VG	$183.00	10-2000
Heddon	300	rainbow, cup, HPGM, ugly varnish, unmarked	VG-	$178.50	9-1999
Heddon	300	rainbow, cup, POBW	EX	$1,025.00	11-1999
Heddon	300	rainbow, cup, ugly varnish, otherwise nice	VG	$255.00	11-1999
Heddon	300	rainbow, green back, 3-hook	VG+	$775.00	5-2000
Heddon	300	rainbow, L-rig, decent, NOT MET	VG+	$260.00	11-2001
Heddon	300	rainbow, L-rig, marked, NOT MET	EX-	$240.50	9-1999
Heddon	300	rainbow, L-rig, NOT MET	EX	$510.00	7-1999
Heddon	300	rainbow, L-rig, one bid $1065.00	EX	$1,090.00	11-2000
Heddon	300	red eyes & tail, L-rig	EX-	$798.00	2-2000
Heddon	300	red head, cup rig, varnish loss, NOT MET	EX-	$205.00	3-1999
Heddon	300	red, L-rig, repainted?	EX-	$645.00	5-1999
Heddon	300	SB, 2-piece, unmarked props	EX-	$800.00	8-2001
Heddon	300	slate back, cup, thin, NOT MET	EX-	$765.00	10-2000

BRAND	MODEL	SERIES / MFG. CODE / DESCRIPTION	GRADE	PRICE	DATE
Heddon	300	slate, cup, HPGM, large crunch, age lines	AVG	$124.00	9-2000
Heddon	300	strawberry	VG-	$158.50	5-1999
Heddon	300	strawberry, 3-hook, L-rig	VG+	$325.00	5-2000
Heddon	300	strawberry, 6-hook, 2-piece, decent	EX-	$600.00	5-2002
Heddon	300	strawberry, 300SX3 Brush box	NIB	$2,125.00	6-2000
Heddon	300	strawberry, HPGM, L-rig, Down Bass box	VG+/IB	$760.00	6-1999
Heddon	300	white, cup, HPGM, ugly varnish	G	$166.00	1-2001
Heddon	300	white, glitter, 2-hook, hook drags, L-rig	VG+	$589.00	6-2001
Heddon	300	white, L-rig, spotty varnish, NOT MET	G	$296.00	2-1999
Heddon	300	white, red eye shadow, L-rig	EX-	$197.00	7-2002
Heddon	300	white, red eyes, 3-hook, 2-piece	EX-	$334.00	9-2000
Heddon	300	white, red eyes, 6-hook	VG	$585.00	3-2000
Heddon	300	white, red eyes, L-rig	EX-	$283.88	4-1999
Heddon	300	white, red eyes, L-rig	EX-	$390.00	11-2000
Heddon	300	white, red eyes, L-rig	VG+	$264.00	4-2000
Heddon	300	white, red eyes, L-rig, age lines, decent	VG+	$206.00	1-2002
Heddon	300	white spots, 6-hook, toilet	VG+	$566.00	4-2001
Heddon	300	XRY, 6-hook	VG+	$1,501.00	1-1999
Heddon	300	yellow, cup, unmarked props	G	$129.00	7-2002
Heddon	300	yellow spots, 2-piece	AVG	$188.00	10-2000
Heddon	300	pike scale, 3-hook, 2-piece, POBW, big burn	VG	$410.00	9-2001
Heddon	302	slate back, cup, POBW	EX	$1,350.00	10-1999
Heddon	309	XRY, 2-piece	EX	$1,000.00	10-1999
Heddon	400	aluminum, all brass, hook drag, 3BW, POBW	VG	$800.00	8-1999
Heddon	700 Musky Minnow	3-hook, swaybelly, 3BW, paint over/under it?	VG	$457.00	10-2001
Heddon	700 Musky Minnow	5-hook, round body, POBW, ex 701 intro box	NIB	$23,600.00	4-2002
Heddon	700 Musky Minnow	bar perch, 3-hook, swaybelly, decent	VG	$2,348.00	8-2002
Heddon	700 Musky Minnow	bar perch, swaybelly, 3-hook, 4BW, decent	VG	$1,116.00	10-2001
Heddon	700 Musky Minnow	crackleback, 3-hook, swaybelly, ugly belly, NOT MET	VG-	$685.00	3-2002
Heddon	700 Musky Minnow	crackleback, HPGM, big chip, cup, NOT MET		$2,247.00	12-2000
Heddon	700 Musky Minnow	crackleback, HPGM, swaybelly, nice	VG+	$3,050.00	1-2002
Heddon	700 Musky Minnow	perch, old, heavy L-rig, 4BW, COBW	VG+	$6,327.50	11-1999
Heddon	700 Musky Minnow	pikie, 3-hook, L-rig	VG-	$1,302.00	2-1999
Heddon	700 Musky Minnow	rainbow, 3-hook, swaybelly, could be worse	AVG	$1,550.00	5-2002
Heddon	700 Musky Minnow	rainbow, 3-hook, decent	VG+	$1,683.00	2-2000
Heddon	700 Musky Minnow	rainbow, swaybelly	VG-	$1,401.00	7-2002
Heddon	700 Musky Minnow	sienna, 3-hook, huge slice out belly		$630.00	10-2000
Heddon	700 Musky Minnow	sienna, 3-hook, overspray, big chips, awful	Poor	$560.00	8-1999
Heddon	700 Musky Minnow	sienna crackleback, 3-hook, 5 touch-ups, repaired, NOT MET		$1,326.00	12-2001
Heddon	700 Musky Minnow	sienna crackleback, 3-hook, NOT MET	VG+	$2,850.00	2-2000
Heddon	700 Musky Minnow	sienna crackleback, 3-hook, swaybelly	VG-	$2,500.00	6-2001
Heddon	700 Musky Minnow	sienna crackleback, ugly, NOT MET	AVG	$375.00	3-2002
Heddon	700 Musky Minnow	sienna perch, 5-hook, swaybelly, big chips, ugly	AVG	$5,200.00	2-2002
Heddon	700 Musky Minnow	sienna, rainbow, round body, 5 large hooks	EX-	$13,100.00	8-2002
Heddon	700 Musky Minnow	swaybelly, 3-hook, g 701 Musky Vamp box, NOT MET	VG+/IB	$1,229.00	11-2001

BRAND	MODEL	SERIES / MFG. CODE / DESCRIPTION	GRADE	PRICE	DATE
Heddon	700 Musky Minnow	bar perch, 3-hook, swaybelly	VG+	$3,451.00	2-2000
Heddon	700 Musky Minnow	bar perch, POBW2, swaybelly, cup	VG	$2,735.00	10-1999
Heddon	700 Musky Minnow	crackleback, 3-hook, 4BW, swayback	Mint	$5,500.00	5-2000
Heddon	700 Musky Minnow	crackleback, 3-hook, bad varnish on belly	AVG	$885.55	2-2000
Heddon	700 Musky Minnow	crackleback, blush, 3-hook, swaybelly, ugly varnish	VG	$1,300.00	8-2001
Heddon	700 Musky Minnow	fancy sienna	EX-	$4,850.00	4-2001
Heddon	Artistic Minnow	20, crackleback, white box	EX- /IB	$1,225.00	4-1999
Heddon	Artistic Minnow	51, blended gold, white 2PCCB	EX/IB	$960.00	5-1999
Heddon	Artistic Minnow	51, blended gold, white box	EX/IB	$960.00	4-1999
Heddon	Artistic Minnow	51, ex buoy, ex paper, NOT MET	EX-/IB	$1,175.00	8-1999
Heddon	Artistic Minnow	blended gold pointers	VG	$175.00	7-2001
Heddon	Artistic Minnow	gold	EX-	$151.00	10-2000
Heddon	Artistic Minnow	green back, gold digs, NOT MET	G	$76.00	1-1999
Heddon	Artistic Minnow	green, gold, buoy weight, rough label, papers	EX/IB	$1,600.00	5-2000
Heddon	Artistic Minnow	sienna	EX	$178.19	2-1999
Heddon	Artistic Minnow	sienna	VG+	$126.00	7-2000
Heddon	Artistic Minnow	sienna, buoy weight & papers, vg box	NIB	$1,375.00	9-2001
Heddon	Artistic Minnow	sienna, buoy weight	EX	$402.61	2-1999
Heddon	Artistic Minnow	sienna crackleback	EX	$300.00	1-1999
Heddon	Artistic Minnow	sienna crackleback, beater box	EX-	$775.00	5-2000
Heddon	Artistic Minnow	sienna, tail chip, otherwise okay	VG-	$112.50	1-1999
Heddon	Artistic Minnow	sienna,vg- white box, papers taped	NIB	$972.00	4-2001
Heddon	Artistic Minnow	white box, buoy weight, nice	NIB	$1,755.00	2-2000
Heddon	Bass Bug	58, Up Bass box	EX/IB	$280.00	11-1999
Heddon	Bass Bug	58, wood, NOT MET	Mint	$42.55	5-1999
Heddon	Bass Bug	60, tiny, Down Bass box	NIB	$1,428.00	8-2000
Heddon	Bass Bug Spook	875BW, wood, on nice card, window box	NIB	$426.00	12-2001
Heddon	Bass Bug Spook	974BW, card, window box, NOT MET	NIB	$66.00	8-2001
Heddon	Bass Bug Spook	974WR, card, 2PCCB Banner box	NIB	$80.00	5-2000
Heddon	Bass Bug Spook	975BR, crisp window box & card	NIB	$200.00	8-2002
Heddon	Bass Bug Spook	975DG, mint card & window box	NIB	$261.00	5-2000
Heddon	Bass Bug Spook	975WR, on card, NOT MET	NIB	$75.50	5-2000
Heddon	Bass Bug Spook	975WR, window box, NOT MET	NOC/IB	$79.00	6-1999
Heddon	Bass Bug Spook	975Y, mint card & window box	NIB	$261.00	5-2000
Heddon	Bass Bug Spook	brown	EX-	$27.55	7-1999
Heddon	Bass Bug Spook	brown, NOT MET	EX	$36.00	6-1999
Heddon	Basser	8501, L-rig, crisp Down Bass box, papers, NOT MET	NIB	$361.00	11-2001
Heddon	Basser	8502, Down Bass box	EX/IB	$157.00	3-2002
Heddon	Basser	8502, Down Bass box	NIB	$255.00	3-2001
Heddon	Basser	8502LUM, luminous, vg Brush box	AVG/IB	$41.00	10-2000
Heddon	Basser	8509J, frog scale, Down Bass box	NIB	$836.00	3-1999
Heddon	Basser	8509K, goldfish scale, ex Down Bass box	NIB	$635.00	7-2002
Heddon	Basser	8509L, 2-piece, Brush box	NIB	$263.00	9-1999
Heddon	Basser	8509L, perch scale, L-rig?, crisp Brush box	NIB	$303.00	8-2001
Heddon	Basser	8509M, 2-piece, Brush box	NIB	$247.50	1-2000

BRAND	MODEL	SERIES / MFG. CODE / DESCRIPTION	GRADE	PRICE	DATE
Heddon	Basser	8509M, mint Up Bass box	NIB	$716.00	3-1999
Heddon	Basser	8509M, heavy duty L-rig, Brush box	NIB	$415.00	4-1999
Heddon	Basser	8509P, crisp Down Bass box	NIB	$286.00	6-2001
Heddon	Basser	deep green scale, glass eyes, L-rig	EX+	$140.00	3-2001
Heddon	Basser	frog scale, Down Bass box, unmarked?	EX-	$410.99	8-1999
Heddon	Basser	frog scale, glass eyes, heavy L-rig	EX+	$456.00	3-2001
Heddon	Basser	frog scale, L-rig	EX-	$550.00	5-2000
Heddon	Basser	frog scale, L-rig, glass eyes	EX-	$299.76	10-1999
Heddon	Basser	frog scale, L-rig, NOT MET	EX	$143.00	6-2002
Heddon	Basser	goldfish scale, L-rig, NOT MET	EX	$256.00	10-2002
Heddon	Basser	green scale, ex- Up Bass box	NIB	$274.00	10-2001
Heddon	Basser	green scale, Up Bass box, NOT MET	EX/IB	$168.00	7-2000
Heddon	Basser	orange, black spots, glass eyes, NOT MET	EX-	$481.00	9-2002
Heddon	Basser	red head, glass eyes, 2-piece, nice	VG	$26.00	4-2000
Heddon	Basser	red head, glass eyes, L-rig	EX	$76.00	8-2001
Heddon	Basser	red head, L-rig	EX	$43.00	5-2000
Heddon	Basser	red head, L-rig, ex- Brush box	NIB	$116.00	10-2001
Heddon	Basser	red head, painted eyes, navy numbers	NIB	$150.00	4-1999
Heddon	Basser	red scale	EX+	$760.00	6-1999
Heddon	Basser	red, white, painted eyes, S-rig	EX	$57.00	1-1999
Heddon	Basser	SB, L-rig	EX-	$129.00	1-2002
Heddon	Basser	shiner scale, 2-piece	EX-	$62.80	3-2000
Heddon	Basser	shiner scale, glass eyes	Fair	$19.00	1-1999
Heddon	Basser	strawberry, glass eyes, S-rig, original wood	Mint	$192.00	10-2002
Heddon	Basser	strawberry, painted eyes, original	Mint	$89.88	6-1999
Heddon	Basser	white, gold glitter, glass eyes, 2-piece	EX	$256.29	5-1999
Heddon	Basser	x2; one 8509P, one 9L, 2-piece, Brush box	VG+/IB	$315.00	6-1999
Heddon	Basser Deluxe	Allen Stripey, glass eyes	Mint	$291.00	8-2000
Heddon	Basser Deluxe	luminous, salmon lure in wrong 8519P box	EX	$300.00	7-2002
Heddon	Basser Jr.	shiner scale, glass eyes, "Plunking"	EX	$381.56	2-2000
Heddon	Basser, Daddy	perch scale, rough lip edge, NOT MET	VG+	$658.00	8-2002
Heddon	Basser, Head-On	frog scale, not awful	AVG	$155.00	4-2000
Heddon	Basser, Head-On	goldfish scale	EX	$505.00	1-2002
Heddon	Basser, Head-On	green scale	EX-	$152.00	7-2000
Heddon	Basser, Head-On	green scale	VG+	$51.00	2-1999
Heddon	Basser, Head-On	natural scale	EX-	$168.00	2-2002
Heddon	Basser, Head-On	orange, black spots	VG+	$600.00	11-2001
Heddon	Basser, Head-On	perch scale	EX-	$154.49	8-1999
Heddon	Basser, Head-On	pike scale	EX	$155.00	10-2000
Heddon	Basser, Head-On	(M) pike scale	EX	$160.00	1-2001
Heddon	Basser, Head-On	pike scale, 8509P Up Bass box	VG-	$81.00	1-1999
Heddon	Basser, Head-On	(M) pike scale, unmarked Down Bass box, NOT MET	EX/IB	$114.00	4-2000
Heddon	Basser, Head-On	red scale, L-rig, unmarked box	EX-	$380.00	5-2000
Heddon	Basser, Head-On	(P) shiner scale, glass eyes, fat, L-rig	EX-	$228.50	5-1999
Heddon	Basser, King	PAS, teddy bear, string	EX-	$50.00	3-1999
Heddon	Basser, King	white shore, pearl?, tack bead eyes, rope	EX-	$44.51	1-2000

BRAND	MODEL	SERIES / MFG. CODE / DESCRIPTION	GRADE	PRICE	DATE
Heddon	Basser, King	XRYTB, glass eyes, breakaway, Brush box	NIB	$162.00	7-2000
Heddon	Big Bud	clear with dice inside	NOC	$58.00	3-2002
Heddon	Big Chug		EX	$90.00	7-2000
Heddon	Big Chug	GDS, mackerel	EX	$175.00	3-1999
Heddon	Big Chug	silver scale, NOT MET	VG	$24.99	4-1999
Heddon	Big Chug	white, red ribs	EX+	$40.51	9-1999
Heddon	Big Chug	XRY	EX	$150.00	3-1999
Heddon	Big Hedd	9330BJY, 12-pack, NOT MET	NIB	$80.00	3-1999
Heddon	Big Hedd	9330CD, 5⁄8 oz.	NIB	$23.00	7-2000
Heddon	Big Hedd	9330XBW	NIB	$39.99	2-1999
Heddon	Big Hedd	BGL, NOT MET	NIB	$32.00	4-1999
Heddon	Big Hedd	black coach dog	NIB	$96.00	12-1998
Heddon	Big Hedd	chrome, fluorescent orange shore	EX	$360.00	2-2002
Heddon	Big Hedd	rainbow?, yellow, black dots	VG+	$305.00	5-2002
Heddon	Big Joe	spots	EX-/IB	$300.88	3-1999
Heddon	Big Mary	10, white, sparkles	EX	$480.00	5-2001
Heddon	Big Mary	808RH, glitter, avg lure, Up Bass box	AVG/IB	$87.00	8-1999
Heddon	Big Mary	red head, glitter, vg+ 802 Down Bass box, NOT MET	NIB	$357.00	10-2001
Heddon	Big Mary	red head, yellow, glitter, glass eyes	EX-	$88.00	10-2000
Heddon	Big Mary	red, white glitter, glass eyes, prop?	EX-	$177.50	2-1999
Heddon	Bucktail, Surface	green back rainbow	EX-	$950.00	5-2000
Heddon	Bucktail, Surface	white, blue, crackleback, high forehead	EX-	$950.00	5-2000
Heddon	Bucktail, Surface	rainbow, vg white 401 pasteboard box, taped	VG+/IB	$2,725.00	2-2002
Heddon	Bug, Bubbling	90YB	EX	$99.00	5-2002
Heddon	Bug, Bubbling	black, yellow stripes, big chips	AVG	$170.00	2-2000
Heddon	Bug, Bubbling	copper, green, bad belly chip, rest nice		$153.00	12-2001
Heddon	Bug, Bubbling	red head	VG	$103.00	7-2001
Heddon	Bug, Bubbling	red, white	EX	$310.00	4-2001
Heddon	Bug, Bubbling	yellow, black, NOT MET	EX	$272.00	1-2001
Heddon	Bug, Westchester	green	EX	$686.00	8-2002
Heddon	Catalina	crackleback, wrapped line ties	EX-	$830.00	10-2001
Heddon	Chugger	2 different XBWs, red head, gold eyes	EX	$42.00	5-1999
Heddon	Chugger	14KCD	EX	$129.00	2-2001
Heddon	Chugger	14KCD?	EX	$138.00	9-2000
Heddon	Chugger	14KCD, white eyes	EX	$305.00	11-2000
Heddon	Chugger	9540, 9450L box (wrong) BRS	NIB	$81.00	5-2000
Heddon	Chugger	9540, brown scale, yellow eyes, brso	NIB	$218.00	5-2000
Heddon	Chugger	9540CDYS	NIB	$172.00	9-2000
Heddon	Chugger	9540CDYS, white eyes, 1PCWB	NIB	$130.00	7-2000
Heddon	Chugger	9540GFBS, white eyes, window box	NIB	$73.00	10-2000
Heddon	Chugger	9540GRA	NIB	$107.00	9-2000
Heddon	Chugger	9540OYG	NIB	$56.00	5-1999
Heddon	Chugger	9540SP, red, silver foil, 9540-SP Banner box	EX/IB	$48.52	3-2000
Heddon	Chugger	9540SWBS	NIB	$122.50	2-1999
Heddon	Chugger	9540VCD	NIB	$87.00	10-2001
Heddon	Chugger	9540VCD	NIB	$127.00	9-2000

BRAND	MODEL	SERIES / MFG. CODE / DESCRIPTION	GRADE	PRICE	DATE
Heddon	Chugger	9540WTGYB	NIB	$81.00	2-1999
Heddon	Chugger	9540YFSL	NIB	$359.00	10-2002
Heddon	Chugger	beige, gold shore ribs, yellow eyes	EX	$153.00	5-2000
Heddon	Chugger	black head & tail, clear, red, white, yellow spots, white eyes	EX	$79.00	4-2000
Heddon	Chugger	black, gold eyes	EX-	$41.00	3-1999
Heddon	Chugger	black, gold foil, gold eyes	EX	$95.50	4-1999
Heddon	Chugger	black, gold foil, gold eyes	EX-	$34.50	2-2000
Heddon	Chugger	black, orange spots & eyes	EX	$91.00	6-1999
Heddon	Chugger	black, orange spots, glass eyes	EX	$117.50	4-2000
Heddon	Chugger	black, silver, reflector, gold eyes	EX-	$20.55	3-1999
Heddon	Chugger	blue shore, gold eyes	Mint	$127.00	7-2002
Heddon	Chugger	BLGF, gold eyes, NOT MET	EX	$51.00	9-2000
Heddon	Chugger	bone, yellow eyes, black eye shadow	EX	$151.00	4-2000
Heddon	Chugger	brown & caramel to silver scales, white eyes	EX	$215.00	3-2002
Heddon	Chugger	BRS	EX	$100.00	9-2000
Heddon	Chugger	BRS, NOT MET	EX-	$54.00	9-2000
Heddon	Chugger	CDF	EX-	$100.00	9-2000
Heddon	Chugger	CDF, red eyes	NIB	$47.00	10-2000
Heddon	Chugger	chartreuse spots, gold eyes	VG	$61.01	5-1999
Heddon	Chugger	chrome, blue scale	EX	$82.59	3-2000
Heddon	Chugger	clear blue scale, red gills	EX	$100.00	2-2001
Heddon	Chugger	clear white, black spots, gold foil	EX	$100.00	6-1999
Heddon	Chugger	clear yellow, black spots, white eyes	EX	$64.00	4-2000
Heddon	Chugger	clear, green back, lime, red spots	EX	$103.59	10-1999
Heddon	Chugger	clear, white eyes	Mint	$56.50	6-1999
Heddon	Chugger	CPS	NIB	$159.00	9-2000
Heddon	Chugger	CRA	EX	$122.00	9-2000
Heddon	Chugger	crackleback	EX	$182.50	6-1999
Heddon	Chugger	crawdad?, brown, white eyes	EX	$305.00	8-1999
Heddon	Chugger	CRWS	EX	$172.00	9-2000
Heddon	Chugger	foil inset	EX	$71.00	6-1999
Heddon	Chugger	foil inset	EX-	$96.00	6-1999
Heddon	Chugger	frog scale, red head, gold eyes	EX	$170.50	10-1999
Heddon	Chugger	frog, white eyes	EX	$72.00	4-2000
Heddon	Chugger	GDS	EX	$208.00	9-2000
Heddon	Chugger	GFB, gold eyes	NIB	$88.00	10-2000
Heddon	Chugger	GFBS, white eyes	NIB	$88.00	10-2000
Heddon	Chugger	GLDS	NIB	$160.00	8-2000
Heddon	Chugger	gold, black spots, gold foil, gold eyes	EX-	$60.00	4-1999
Heddon	Chugger	gold, dark bronze scale, white eyes	EX	$89.88	3-2000
Heddon	Chugger	green scale, white, gold eyes	EX	$200.00	10-1999
Heddon	Chugger	GYH, silver scale	EX	$198.00	8-2000
Heddon	Chugger	KCD, NOT MET	NIB	$122.50	2-2000
Heddon	Chugger	LBL	EX	$169.00	9-2000
Heddon	Chugger	NBL	EX	$49.00	9-2000
Heddon	Chugger	natural striper	EX	$125.00	11-1999

BRAND	MODEL	SERIES / MFG. CODE / DESCRIPTION	GRADE	PRICE	DATE
Heddon	Chugger	NPY	NIB	$78.00	8-2000
Heddon	Chugger	orange, black ribs	EX	$255.00	11-1999
Heddon	Chugger	PC	NIB	$207.00	8-2000
Heddon	Chugger	perch, 2-piece	EX+	$40.00	2-1999
Heddon	Chugger	pike scale, white eyes	EX	$177.00	10-2000
Heddon	Chugger	rainbow, white eyes	EX	$162.50	1-2000
Heddon	Chugger	red, clear, gold foil	EX	$51.00	4-2000
Heddon	Chugger	red, gold foil	EX	$60.00	1-1999
Heddon	Chugger	red, gold foil	EX	$62.00	4-1999
Heddon	Chugger	red, silver foil, gold eyes	EX	$52.00	12-1999
Heddon	Chugger	red, tex. silver insert	EX	$68.01	5-1999
Heddon	Chugger	SD, clear belly	EX	$118.00	9-2000
Heddon	Chugger	SD, NOT MET	EX-	$47.00	9-2000
Heddon	Chugger	SFBS, white eyes	NIB	$47.00	10-2000
Heddon	Chugger	SFSXS	NIB	$104.00	8-2000
Heddon	Chugger	SFSXS, silver head & tail, silver foil inset	EX	$156.00	11-1999
Heddon	Chugger	SFSXS, white eyes	NIB	$77.00	10-2000
Heddon	Chugger	SFYS, white eyes	NIB	$93.00	10-2000
Heddon	Chugger	silver shad, orange eyes	Mint	$95.00	6-2000
Heddon	Chugger	silver, silver scale, white spots, yellow eyes, NOT MET	EX	$115.00	10-2000
Heddon	Chugger	SSRHYB, gold eyes	EX	$114.00	4-2000
Heddon	Chugger	strawberry, horribly oxidized		$156.00	10-2000
Heddon	Chugger	tiger stripe, white eyes	EX	$72.00	11-1999
Heddon	Chugger	two XRYs, gold eyes, PTCB	NIB	$46.53	8-1999
Heddon	Chugger	WCD, NOT MET	EX	$51.00	9-2000
Heddon	Chugger	white & black zebra, white eyes	EX	$103.00	3-2001
Heddon	Chugger	white, black spots	EX	$89.00	3-1999
Heddon	Chugger	XBW	Mint	$12.50	2-1999
Heddon	Chugger	XRYBB	EX-	$59.80	2-2000
Heddon	Chugger	XRYBB, white eyes	NIB	$121.00	10-2000
Heddon	Chugger	YCD, gold eyes	EX	$56.00	11-2000
Heddon	Chugger	YCD, NOT MET	EX-	$51.00	9-2000
Heddon	Chugger	XRS, NOT MET	EX	$31.00	9-2000
Heddon	Chugger	yellow bird, black wings	EX	$455.00	10-2001
Heddon	Chugger	yellow shad	EX	$73.00	4-1999
Heddon	Chugger	yellow, black spots, red eyes	VG+	$128.00	7-2000
Heddon	Chugger	yellow, black spots, silver foil insert	EX-	$53.00	8-2001
Heddon	Chugger	yellow, black tiger stripe	EX	$150.00	5-1999
Heddon	Chugger	zebra	EX-	$80.00	2-2000
Heddon	Chugger Jr.	9520BB, black, triangle box, NOT MET	NIB	$18.49	3-1999
Heddon	Chugger Jr.	9520BRS, gold eyes	NIB	$52.00	6-1999
Heddon	Chugger Jr.	9520SJ	NIB	$41.00	5-2001
Heddon	Chugger, Jr.	9520UY, chrome, chartreuse	NIB	$26.00	2-1999
Heddon	Chugger Jr.	green, yellow spots, gold eyes	EX	$66.59	3-2000
Heddon	Chugger Jr.	natural blue gill, Brazos buy	EX	$51.00	3-1999
Heddon	Chugger Jr.	red, white, yellow spots	EX	$33.50	1-1999

BRAND	MODEL	SERIES / MFG. CODE / DESCRIPTION	GRADE	PRICE	DATE
Heddon	Chugger Jr.	yellow bird, black wings	EX	$367.00	10-2001
Heddon	Chugger Jr.	yellow bird, black wings	EX	$417.00	10-2001
Heddon	Chugger Jr.	yellow, silver foil	VG	$32.00	1-1999
Heddon	Chugger Jr.	x3; white, black spots, orange, black spots, red foil	EX-	$104.00	7-1999
Heddon	Chugger Spook	159 different Spooks, NOT MET	EX-/NIB	$11,800.00	12-2000
Heddon	Chugger Spook	shad, red gills, yellow eyes	EX	$42.00	9-2001
Heddon	Chugger Spook	yellow bird	EX	$467.00	1-2002
Heddon	Coast Minnow		EX-	$2,600.00	4-2001
Heddon	Coast Minnow	6½", spots, HPGM, varnish, decent	VG-	$921.00	4-2000
Heddon	Coast Minnow	green scale back, orange belly, beautiful	EX-	$2,283.00	10-2000
Heddon	Coast Minnow Musky	7", strawberry, light varnish	EX	$2,550.00	4-1999
Heddon	Cobra	9930SF, PTCB	NIB	$20.50	1-1999
Heddon	Cousin	shad	Mint	$26.00	2-1999
Heddon	Cousin II	7735RS, silver scale	NIB	$26.65	6-1999
Heddon	Cousin II	bass	EX	$22.50	2-1999
Heddon	Cousin II	red, black spots	EX	$26.50	1-1999
Heddon	Crackle Back	8050GBC, crackleback	NIB	$35.26	5-1999
Heddon	Crackle Back	crackleback, blue, green, NOT MET	EX	$12.50	5-1999
Heddon	Craw Shrimp	3 different, NOT MET	EX	$61.08	4-1999
Heddon	Craw Shrimp	375AMR window box	NIB	$52.00	1-2000
Heddon	Craw Shrimp	amber, black	EX	$21.50	5-1999
Heddon	Craw Shrimp	amber, red spots	Mint	$25.49	6-1999
Heddon	Craw Shrimp	black, red	EX	$62.50	12-1998
Heddon	Craw Shrimp	blue	EX	$87.15	3-2000
Heddon	Craw Shrimp	dark	EX	$42.00	2-1999
Heddon	Craw Shrimp	green, black	VG	$27.50	2-1999
Heddon	Craw Shrimp	natural brown, clear	EX	$28.00	8-2001
Heddon	Craw Shrimp	root beer color	EX	$55.00	12-1998
Heddon	Crazy Crawler	3 different, tiny, 3-color eyes, common colors	EX	$71.00	8-1999
Heddon	Crazy Crawler	4 different, nice S-rig	VG+ to EX-	$134.00	1-1999
Heddon	Crazy Crawler	320BF, 3-color eyes, way too high	EX	$41.00	7-1999
Heddon	Crazy Crawler	320RHY, 3-color eyes	EX/IB	$13.50	2-1999
Heddon	Crazy Crawler	320XRS, tiny, 3-color eyes, PTCB	NIB	$38.00	12-2001
Heddon	Crazy Crawler	2100BF, 2-piece, black eyes, catalog	NIB	$111.00	4-1999
Heddon	Crazy Crawler	2100BF, 2-piece, Brush box	NIB	$150.50	8-1999
Heddon	Crazy Crawler	2120BF, 2-piece, red eyes, Banner box	NIB	$146.50	5-1999
Heddon	Crazy Crawler	2100BF, Banner box, catalog	NIB	$75.00	8-1999
Heddon	Crazy Crawler	2120BF, Banner box, crisp paper, catalog, NO BIDS		$50.00	1-2001
Heddon	Crazy Crawler	2100BF, Banner box, paper, catalog	NIB	$131.38	6-1999
Heddon	Crazy Crawler	2100BF, Banner box, papers	NIB	$66.00	6-2001
Heddon	Crazy Crawler	2120BF, black eyes, Brush box, catalog	NIB	$46.00	10-2000
Heddon	Crazy Crawler	2120BF, chip, age lines	AVG	$21.00	1-1999
Heddon	Crazy Crawler	2120BF, conetail	VG+	$155.00	4-2002
Heddon	Crazy Crawler	2100BF, Donaly clips	Mint	$200.00	6-1999
Heddon	Crazy Crawler	2100BF, Donaly clips	NIB	$256.51	5-1999

BRAND	MODEL	SERIES / MFG. CODE / DESCRIPTION	GRADE	PRICE	DATE
Heddon	Crazy Crawler	2100BF, S-rig	EX+	$25.00	10-2000
Heddon	Crazy Crawler	2100BF, S-rig, Brush box, papers	NIB	$104.09	2-2000
Heddon	Crazy Crawler	2120BF, S-rig, decent	VG	$16.00	4-1999
Heddon	Crazy Crawler	2120BF, NOT MET	EX-/IB	$42.00	1-1999
Heddon	Crazy Crawler	2120, black shore, red eyes	EX-	$162.50	10-1999
Heddon	Crazy Crawler	2100BWH, 2-piece	EX	$88.57	9-1999
Heddon	Crazy Crawler	2100BWH, Banner box	NIB	$92.00	11-1999
Heddon	Crazy Crawler	2100BWH, black eyes, unmarked Brush box	EX/IB	$89.99	9-1999
Heddon	Crazy Crawler	2100BWH, Donaly clips, crisp Brush box	NIB	$260.59	4-1999
Heddon	Crazy Crawler	2100BWH, intro paper, black eyes	NIB	$128.49	4-1999
Heddon	Crazy Crawler	2100BWH, S-rig	EX-	$38.99	2-1999
Heddon	Crazy Crawler	2100CM, small tail chip, nice	VG+	$536.00	5-2001
Heddon	Crazy Crawler	2100CM, colors faded, NOT MET	VG	$275.00	2-2002
Heddon	Crazy Crawler	2100GM	NIB	$144.49	10-1999
Heddon	Crazy Crawler	2100GM	VG	$30.50	1-1999
Heddon	Crazy Crawler	2100GM, 2-piece, Brush box	EX-/IB	$52.00	12-1999
Heddon	Crazy Crawler	2100GM, Brush box	NIB	$142.50	7-1999
Heddon	Crazy Crawler	2100GM, crisp Banner box	NIB	$188.00	8-2000
Heddon	Crazy Crawler	2100GM, Donaly clips	EX	$87.00	8-2000
Heddon	Crazy Crawler	2100GM, green, intro Brush box	EX/IB	$204.50	2-2000
Heddon	Crazy Crawler	2100GM, S-rig	EX	$61.00	4-1999
Heddon	Crazy Crawler	2100GW	EX	$169.00	1-2000
Heddon	Crazy Crawler	2100GW	NIB	$315.00	5-2000
Heddon	Crazy Crawler	2100GW	NIB	$332.00	12-2000
Heddon	Crazy Crawler	2100GW	VG	$103.50	1-1999
Heddon	Crazy Crawler	2100GW, Donaly clips	EX	$180.00	10-2000
Heddon	Crazy Crawler	2100GW, Donaly clips	EX	$256.00	4-2000
Heddon	Crazy Crawler	2100GW, Donaly clips	EX-	$213.51	3-1999
Heddon	Crazy Crawler	2100GW, intro paper & catalog	NIB	$343.00	10-2002
Heddon	Crazy Crawler	2100WBH	VG	$25.00	1-1999
Heddon	Crazy Crawler	2100XBW, avg box	VG+/IB	$202.56	11-1999
Heddon	Crazy Crawler	2100XBW, black eyes	VG+	$333.00	7-2000
Heddon	Crazy Crawler	2100XBW, red eyes	EX	$370.59	3-1999
Heddon	Crazy Crawler	2100XBW, red eyes	EX	$665.00	8-1999
Heddon	Crazy Crawler	2100XRS	NIB	$130.00	8-1999
Heddon	Crazy Crawler	2100XRS, 3-color eyes, intro papers	EX/IB	$127.50	1-1999
Heddon	Crazy Crawler	2100XRS, Banner box, paper, catalog	NIB	$142.29	6-1999
Heddon	Crazy Crawler	2100XRS, red eyes, Brush box, papers	NIB	$260.01	5-1999
Heddon	Crazy Crawler	2100XRW, 2-piece, XRS Brush box, intro paper	NIB	$154.00	4-2000
Heddon	Crazy Crawler	2100XRW, bad age lines	Decent	$23.50	1-1999
Heddon	Crazy Crawler	2100XRW, Banner box	NIB	$163.77	1-2000
Heddon	Crazy Crawler	2100XRW, Banner box, catalog, nice	NIB	$103.50	2-1999
Heddon	Crazy Crawler	2100XRW, crisp Banner box	NIB	$104.00	8-2000
Heddon	Crazy Crawler	2100XRY	Mint	$394.00	1-2000
Heddon	Crazy Crawler	2100XRY	Rough	$56.00	11-2000
Heddon	Crazy Crawler	2100XRY, red eyes	EX-	$226.00	10-2000
Heddon	Crazy Crawler	2100YRH	NIB	$86.00	2-1999

BRAND	MODEL	SERIES / MFG. CODE / DESCRIPTION	GRADE	PRICE	DATE
Heddon	Crazy Crawler	2100YRH	NIB	$152.50	5-1999
Heddon	Crazy Crawler	2100YRH, Banner box	NIB	$61.01	6-1999
Heddon	Crazy Crawler	2100YRH, Banner box	NIB	$78.01	8-1999
Heddon	Crazy Crawler	2100YRH, S-rig	NIB	$100.99	4-1999
Heddon	Crazy Crawler	2100YRH, tape on Banner box	NIB	$86.00	9-1999
Heddon	Crazy Crawler	2102XS, Donaly, intro papers	EX/IB	$255.99	4-1999
Heddon	Crazy Crawler	2120BWH, 2 different; 1 fat, 1 regular, 1 box	EX/IB	$152.00	4-1999
Heddon	Crazy Crawler	2120BWH, Banner box	NIB	$53.00	5-2000
Heddon	Crazy Crawler	2120BWH, Banner box, catalog, nice	NIB	$112.50	2-1999
Heddon	Crazy Crawler	2120BWH, Banner box, paper	VG/IB	$53.00	5-1999
Heddon	Crazy Crawler	2120BWH, Banner box, small peel on box top	NIB	$51.00	10-2001
Heddon	Crazy Crawler	2120BWH, red eyes, S-rig?	EX+	$41.00	3-2000
Heddon	Crazy Crawler	2120BWH, S-rig	AVG	$41.00	1-1999
Heddon	Crazy Crawler	2120BWH, S-rig	EX	$41.50	1-1999
Heddon	Crazy Crawler	2120, chipmunk, pretty, nice	EX-	$443.00	8-2001
Heddon	Crazy Crawler	2120CM, colors faded, NOT MET	VG-	$138.00	2-2002
Heddon	Crazy Crawler	2120, glow worm	EX-	$143.00	1-1999
Heddon	Crazy Crawler	2120GM	EX/IB	$135.50	7-1999
Heddon	Crazy Crawler	2120GM	NIB	$65.00	2-1999
Heddon	Crazy Crawler	2120GM	VG+	$36.00	1-1999
Heddon	Crazy Crawler	2120GM, Banner box, NOT MET	EX/IB	$49.00	6-2001
Heddon	Crazy Crawler	2120GM, Banner box, papers, nice	NIB	$66.00	1-2002
Heddon	Crazy Crawler	2120GW	EX-	$152.00	9-2000
Heddon	Crazy Crawler	2120GW, conetail	EX	$515.00	12-1999
Heddon	Crazy Crawler	2120GW, intro papers	EX/IB	$271.01	7-1999
Heddon	Crazy Crawler	2120RHW	EX	$61.00	2-1999
Heddon	Crazy Crawler	2120RHY	EX	$66.00	2-1999
Heddon	Crazy Crawler	2120, shore, yellow, red eyes	EX-	$157.00	10-1999
Heddon	Crazy Crawler	2120WRH, 2120YRH Banner box	EX/IB	$41.00	1-2001
Heddon	Crazy Crawler	2120WRH, conetail	EX	$203.00	2-2002
Heddon	Crazy Crawler	2120XBW	EX-	$189.00	2-2002
Heddon	Crazy Crawler	2120XBW	EX-	$313.77	1-2000
Heddon	Crazy Crawler	2120XBW, nice	EX	$306.00	3-1999
Heddon	Crazy Crawler	2120XBW, NOT MET	VG+	$203.00	3-1999
Heddon	Crazy Crawler	2120XBW, red eyes	EX	$238.50	2-2000
Heddon	Crazy Crawler	2120XBW, red eyes	EX	$271.06	1-2000
Heddon	Crazy Crawler	2120XBW, red eyes	EX-	$453.00	1-1999
Heddon	Crazy Crawler	2120XBW, red eyes, intro, catalog	EX/IB	$450.00	5-1999
Heddon	Crazy Crawler	2120XRS, Banner box	NIB	$69.00	11-1999
Heddon	Crazy Crawler	2120XRS, Banner box, catalog	NIB	$85.00	8-1999
Heddon	Crazy Crawler	2120XRS, Banner box, papers	NIB	$60.00	1-2002
Heddon	Crazy Crawler	2120XRS, conetail	EX	$205.00	2-2002
Heddon	Crazy Crawler	2120XRS, conetail	VG	$133.50	12-1999
Heddon	Crazy Crawler	2120XRS, conetail, intro papers, NOT MET	NIB	$265.00	4-2002
Heddon	Crazy Crawler	2120XRS, S-rig, Banner box	NIB	$84.00	10-1999
Heddon	Crazy Crawler	2120XRS, yellow, red eyes, intro papers	EX/IB	$91.00	2-2000
Heddon	Crazy Crawler	2120XRW	EX-	$21.00	1-1999

BRAND	MODEL	SERIES / MFG. CODE / DESCRIPTION	GRADE	PRICE	DATE
Heddon	Crazy Crawler	2120XRY	AVG	$46.51	4-1999
Heddon	Crazy Crawler	2120XRY	AVG	$314.18	3-1999
Heddon	Crazy Crawler	2120XRY, black eyes	EX+	$324.99	4-1999
Heddon	Crazy Crawler	2120XRY, decent Brush box	EX-/IB	$217.00	3-2002
Heddon	Crazy Crawler	2120XRY, red eyes	EX+	$362.00	3-2000
Heddon	Crazy Crawler	2120XRY, red eyes	EX-	$192.50	6-1999
Heddon	Crazy Crawler	2120XRY, red eyes	VG-	$164.50	12-1999
Heddon	Crazy Crawler	2120XRY, red eyes, Brush box	NIB	$432.00	2-2000
Heddon	Crazy Crawler	2120XRY, red eyes, not awful	AVG	$42.00	9-1999
Heddon	Crazy Crawler	2120YRH, black eyes, 2-piece	EX	$53.00	1-1999
Heddon	Crazy Crawler	2120YRH, black eyes, 2-piece	EX	$54.50	5-1999
Heddon	Crazy Crawler	2120YRH, Brush box, catalog	NIB	$125.00	1-1999
Heddon	Crazy Crawler	2120YRH, catalog, papers	NIB	$102.50	4-1999
Heddon	Crazy Crawler	2120YRH, fat body, NOT MET	EX/IB	$78.50	1-1999
Heddon	Crazy Crawler	2120YRH, red eyes, 2-piece	EX	$50.00	8-1999
Heddon	Crazy Crawler	2120YRH, S-rig	Mint	$35.00	5-2001
Heddon	Crazy Crawler	2122LUM, luminous, 1 flake, crisp papers, never wet	EX/IB	$305.00	11-2001
Heddon	Crazy Crawler	black shore, white eyes	EX	$650.00	8-2001
Heddon	Crazy Crawler	BWH, zinc eyes	EX	$250.00	8-2001
Heddon	Crazy Crawler	frog, tiny, 3-color eyes	EX	$20.52	1-1999
Heddon	Crazy Crawler	red head, silver shore	VG	$406.00	5-2002
Heddon	Crazy Crawlers	x3; one BF, one XRS, one YRH	EX	$152.00	1-1999
Heddon	Crazy Crawler	XRS, fat body	G	$17.50	1-1999
Heddon	Crazy Crawler	XRS, tiny, 3-color eyes	EX	$15.00	8-2002
Heddon	Crazy Crawler	YRH, zinc eyes	EX	$300.00	8-2001
Heddon	Crazy Crawler, Musky		G	$89.00	4-1999
Heddon	Crazy Crawler, Musky	2150BF	EX	$260.00	12-1999
Heddon	Crazy Crawler, Musky	2150BF	EX-	$300.00	10-1999
Heddon	Crazy Crawler, Musky	2150BF, Banner box	NIB	$406.00	11-2000
Heddon	Crazy Crawler, Musky	2150BF, Banner box, NOT MET	NIB	$405.03	6-1999
Heddon	Crazy Crawler, Musky	2150BF, Banner box, NOT MET again	NIB	$307.00	8-1999
Heddon	Crazy Crawler, Musky	2150BF, nice Banner box, NOT MET	EX/IB	$256.00	8-2001
Heddon	Crazy Crawler, Musky	2150BF, NO BIDS	NIB	$525.00	7-1999
Heddon	Crazy Crawler, Musky	2150CM, "N" backwards in "HEDDON"?	EX	$1,500.00	3-2002
Heddon	Crazy Crawler, Musky	2150GM	VG+	$182.49	4-1999
Heddon	Crazy Crawler, Musky	2150GM Banner box, NOT MET	EX-/IB	$231.00	3-2001
Heddon	Crazy Crawler, Musky	2150RH, red eyes	EX-	$300.00	9-2000
Heddon	Crazy Crawler, Musky	2150RHW, decent, NOT MET	VG+	$168.09	3-1999
Heddon	Crazy Crawler, Musky	2150WRH, Banner box	EX/IB	$148.00	9-2001
Heddon	Crazy Crawler, Musky	2150WRH, black eyes	EX/IB	$370.00	10-2000
Heddon	Crazy Crawler, Musky	2150XRW, black eyes	EX	$650.00	1-1999
Heddon	Crazy Crawler, Musky	2150YRH, 3-color eyes	EX-	$177.00	1-2002
Heddon	Crazy Crawler, Musky	2150YRH, Banner box	EX+/IB	$307.00	8-2001
Heddon	Crazy Crawler, Musky	2150YRH, black eyes	EX-	$183.00	11-2000
Heddon	Crazy Crawler, Musky	2150YRH, black eyes	Mint	$285.00	2-2000
Heddon	Crazy Crawler, Musky	2150YRH, red eyes, Brush box, NOT MET	NIB	$330.00	9-1999

BRAND	MODEL	SERIES / MFG. CODE / DESCRIPTION	GRADE	PRICE	DATE
Heddon	Crazy Crawler, Musky	2150YRH, red eyes, NOT MET	EX	$228.00	5-2000
Heddon	Crazy Crawler, Musky	BF, red eyes	VG+	$137.00	6-2002
Heddon	Crazy Crawler, Musky	RHY, black eyes	Mint	$314.00	7-2002
Heddon	Crazy Crawler, Musky	rough 2150WRH Banner box	EX/IB	$113.00	5-2002
Heddon	Crazy Crawler, Musky	WRH, red eyes	VG	$113.00	5-2002
Heddon	Crazy Crawler, Musky	WRH, toilet, Donaly clips	EX	$626.00	4-2001
Heddon	Crazy Crawler, Musky	YRH, Donaly hardware, bleed through	VG+	$269.00	8-2001
Heddon	Crazy Crawler, Musky	YRH, red eyes, NOT MET	EX	$180.00	10-2001
Heddon	Crazy Crawler Spook	9120CYG, modern Smith color	EX	$38.01	4-1999
Heddon	Crazy Crawler Spook	9120, flocked mouse	VG	$22.00	6-1999
Heddon	Crazy Crawler Spook	9120GR	NIB	$1,600.00	10-2000
Heddon	Crazy Crawler Spook	9120GR, plastic	NIB	$2,850.00	9-2000
Heddon	Crazy Crawler Spook	9120YRH, green, triangle bubble pack	NOC	$33.00	11-2000
Heddon	Crazy Crawler Spook	YRH, marked "2nd"	EX	$20.50	8-1999
Heddon	Darting Zara	BF, nail in mouth	EX	$550.00	5-2000
Heddon	Darting Zara	frog, glass eyes	EX	$493.00	4-2000
Heddon	Darting Zara	frog, glass eyes, 2-piece, wood	VG+	$130.00	5-1999
Heddon	Darting Zara	frog, glass eyes, Lurebob, NO BIDS	EX	$399.00	2-2000
Heddon	Darting Zara	rainbow?, glass eyes, 2-piece, dent, wood	VG	$112.00	4-1999
Heddon	Darting Zara	silver scale	EX-	$250.00	7-2001
Heddon	Darting Zara	silver scale, glass eyes, wood	EX	$132.49	2-1999
Heddon	Darting Zara	silver scale, painted eyes, prop	EX	$41.01	5-1999
Heddon	Darting Zara	XRW, gold eyes, NOT MET	NIB	$61.06	1-2000
Heddon	Darting Zara	XRW, prop, gold eyes	EX	$40.00	2-1999
Heddon	Darting Zara Spook	frog, gold eyes, no prop	EX-	$43.43	11-1999
Heddon	Deep-O-Diver	ex intro box, varnish a bit ugly	VG+/IB	$450.00	5-2002
Heddon	Deep-O-Diver	goldfish scale	VG+	$147.50	3-2000
Heddon	Deep-O-Diver	white, black spots, avg intro box, NOT MET	EX-/IB	$356.00	11-2000
Heddon	Deep-O-Diver	yellow, black spots	VG+	$96.00	8-2000
Heddon	Deep-O-Diver Deluxe	green scale	VG+	$85.00	4-2000
Heddon	Dowagiac Spook	amber center, white red spots ends	EX	$227.00	8-2000
Heddon	Dowagiac Spook	clear, glass eyes	EX	$657.58	10-1999
Heddon	Dowagiac Spook	common color, glass eyes	EX	$93.00	1-2002
Heddon	Dowagiac Spook	perch scale, glass eyes	EX-	$108.50	9-1999
Heddon	Dowagiac Spook	perch, glass eyes	EX	$100.00	3-1999
Heddon	Dowagiac Spook	shiner scale, glass eyes	EX-	$82.50	9-1999
Heddon	Dowagiac Spook	strawberry, painted eyes	EX	$71.00	8-2002
Heddon	Dowagiac Spook	strawberry, painted eyes	EX	$112.00	2-2002
Heddon	Dowagiac Spook	strawberry, painted eyes	EX-	$20.51	5-1999
Heddon	Dowagiac Spook	strawberry, painted eyes	Mint	$37.00	12-1999
Heddon	Dowagiac Spook	XBW, glass eyes	EX-	$305.00	8-1999
Heddon	Dowagiac Spook	XBW, glass eyes	EX-	$366.00	11-2001
Heddon	Dowagiac Spook	XRW, glass eyes, Flesh box	EX/IB	$96.00	1-2000
Heddon	Dowagiac Spook	XRY, painted eyes	VG	$12.50	1-1999
Heddon	Dowagiac Spook, Super	9109XRG, glass eyes, P?, crisp Brush box	NIB	$193.00	6-2001
Heddon	Dowagiac Spook, Super	amber spots, 9100S Up Bass box, papers	NIB	$809.99	2-2000
Heddon	Dowagiac Spook, Super	clear amber, spots, glass eyes, curved	VG+	$42.23	4-1999

BRAND	MODEL	SERIES / MFG. CODE / DESCRIPTION	GRADE	PRICE	DATE
Heddon	Dowagiac Spook, Super	glass eyes, L-rig, crisp Fish Flesh box	NIB	$125.00	10-2000
Heddon	Dowagiac Spook, Super	painted eyes	NIB	$48.85	4-1999
Heddon	Dowagiac, Super	perch, glass eyes	EX	$80.52	4-1999
Heddon	Dowagiac, Super	perch, glass eyes, toilet	EX	$46.51	5-1999
Heddon	Dowagiac, Super	shiner scale, glass eyes, 1 eye broken	EX-	$56.00	1-1999
Heddon	Dummy-Double	1509B, frog, L-rig, NOT MET	EX-	$1,725.00	8-2001
Heddon	Dummy-Double	1509S, avg Down Bass box, crisp paper	VG+/IB	$1,703.78	1-2000
Heddon	Dummy-Double	bar perch	AVG	$390.00	1-1999
Heddon	Dummy-Double	crackleback, L-rig	EX-	$1,400.00	8-2002
Heddon	Dummy-Double	crackleback, L-rig, 23 bids	EX-	$3,250.00	4-2000
Heddon	Dummy-Double	football rig, ugly	AVG	$512.00	4-2000
Heddon	Dummy-Double	football rig, wrong rear	VG+	$457.00	1-2001
Heddon	Dummy-Double	frog, L-rig, heavy age lines	VG-	$1,025.00	10-2000
Heddon	Dummy-Double	frog, no hooks	G	$2,282.00	8-2000
Heddon	Dummy-Double	frog, no side hooks, football rig	AVG	$2,283.00	8-2000
Heddon	Dummy-Double	L-rig, decent, NOT MET	VG	$431.00	11-2001
Heddon	Dummy-Double	lure, 3 good hooks	Poor	$510.00	7-2000
Heddon	Dummy-Double	orange spots, decent	VG+	$725.00	11-1999
Heddon	Dummy-Double	rainbow	AVG	$500.00	5-1999
Heddon	Dummy-Double	red, black spots, football rig	EX-	$3,100.00	4-1999
Heddon	Dummy-Double	slate, red eyes, NOT MET	VG	$775.00	2-1999
Heddon	Dummy-Double	SB, football rig, papers, unmarked box	VG+/IB	$1,400.00	3-2002
Heddon	Dummy-Double	spots, fairly ugly, NOT MET	VG-	$500.00	7-1999
Heddon	Dummy-Double	spots, football rig	VG	$1,200.00	8-2002
Heddon	Dummy-Double	spots, football rig	VG+	$1,277.00	3-2000
Heddon	Dummy-Double	spots, football rig, huge chip		$575.00	6-2002
Heddon	Dummy-Double	spots, L-rig	VG+	$1,225.00	4-1999
Heddon	Dummy-Double	spots, ugly, NOT MET	VG-	$365.00	8-1999
Heddon	Dummy-Double	strawberry	EX-	$2,200.00	5-2000
Heddon	Dummy-Double	white spots, L-rig	VG-	$436.00	2-2002
Heddon	Dummy-Double	yellow, red, green spots, L-rig	VG	$598.00	3-1999
Heddon	Dummy-Double	yellow spots, football rig, huge belly chip, rest okay		$1,000.00	12-2000
Heddon	Dummy-Double	yellow spots, L-rig	VG+	$737.00	10-2000
Heddon	Dying Flutter	2 different, frog, black, silver, white eyes	EX	$22.00	1-1999
Heddon	Dying Flutter	3 different	NIB	$35.01	1-1999
Heddon	Expert	aluminum, ugly	AVG	$510.00	1-2000
Heddon	Expert	blue head, sloped nose, brass cup, tail cap.	VG	$786.00	9-2000
Heddon	Expert	blue head, w/, red collar	VG+	$1,654.00	1-2000
Heddon	Expert, Underwater	short & fat, sweeping gills, tiny	AVG	$2,550.00	10-2000
Heddon	Expert, Underwater	white, 2BW, huge, tiny props	VG	$1,725.00	10-2000
Heddon	Expert, Underwater	white, gold wash still on hardware	EX-	$3,001.00	2-2002
Heddon	Expert, Underwater	#3, white, 2BW, small belly chips	VG++	$3,738.00	1-2002
Heddon	Fidget	402, blue headed crackleback	EX	$575.00	3-2002
Heddon	Fish, Spoony	5¾"	EX	$238.50	2-1999
Heddon	Fish, Spoony	large size, NOT MET	EX	$157.00	1-1999
Heddon	Fisher, Baby Game	5402 Up Bass box, papers	NIB	$227.00	12-2000

BRAND	MODEL	SERIES / MFG. CODE / DESCRIPTION	GRADE	PRICE	DATE
Heddon	Fisher, Baby Game	blue scale	VG+	$175.00	10-2000
Heddon	Fisher, Baby Game	blue scale, small worm burn on top tail	VG	$371.00	3-2001
Heddon	Fisher, Baby Game	red eyes & tail	EX	$76.00	2-2001
Heddon	Flaptail	7000GM, Banner box	NIB	$78.50	9-1999
Heddon	Flaptail	7000L, painted eyes	NIB	$55.55	5-1999
Heddon	Flaptail	7002, Brush box, glass eyes, small chip	VG/IB	$50.00	4-1999
Heddon	Flaptail	7002, glass eyes, 2-piece, Brush box	NIB	$174.49	5-1999
Heddon	Flaptail	7009SS, 2-piece, Brush box, nice	EX-/IB	$75.00	10-2001
Heddon	Flaptail	flyrod, 710Y Up Bass box	NIB	$180.00	10-2000
Heddon	Flaptail	flyrod, black, white	EX	$138.02	4-1999
Heddon	Flaptail	flyrod, black, white wings	EX	$309.00	9-1999
Heddon	Flaptail	flyrod, gold?	EX	$103.00	5-2000
Heddon	Flaptail	flyrod, red head	EX	$45.00	11-2000
Heddon	Flaptail	flyrod, red head	EX	$68.00	8-2000
Heddon	Flaptail	flyrod, red head	VG+	$42.00	3-2000
Heddon	Flaptail	flyrod, red, white	EX	$90.00	4-2001
Heddon	Flaptail	flyrod, red, white, pointers, cracks	AVG	$35.00	1-1999
Heddon	Flaptail	flyrod, vg 710BR Up Bass box	NIB	$291.00	4-2000
Heddon	Flaptail	flyrod, yellow, NOT MET	EX	$52.99	6-1999
Heddon	Flaptail	flyrod, yellow, NOT MET	EX-	$66.99	5-1999
Heddon	Flaptail	flyrod, yellow, on card, no box	NOC	$71.50	12-1999
Heddon	Flaptail	frog, 2-piece, flaw on back, burn?	VG+	$129.00	1-2001
Heddon	Flaptail	glass eyes, (P) pike scale, 2-piece, looks nice	EX	$122.50	6-1999
Heddon	Flaptail	L, S-rig, big eyes	EX-	$39.00	10-2000
Heddon	Flaptail	mouse, light belly drag	EX+	$100.00	10-2000
Heddon	Flaptail	perch scale, glass eyes, S-rig	EX	$77.00	11-2000
Heddon	Flaptail	perch, glass eyes, 2-piece	EX	$147.50	5-1999
Heddon	Flaptail	red head, glass eyes	EX	$52.50	3-2000
Heddon	Flaptail	red head, glass eyes, 2-piece	EX	$102.00	3-2001
Heddon	Flaptail	red, white, glass eyes	EX+	$100.00	1-1999
Heddon	Flaptail	shiner scale, glass eyes, 2-piece	EX	$98.00	5-2000
Heddon	Flaptail	SS, glass eyes, 2-piece	Mint	$107.50	9-1999
Heddon	Flaptail Bug	rough 720WR box	NIB	$102.50	6-1999
Heddon	Flaptail Jr.	chipmunk, NOT MET	EX-	$430.00	1-2000
Heddon	Flaptail Jr.	green scale?, glass eyes, 2-piece	EX+	$132.50	1-1999
Heddon	Flaptail Jr.	grey mouse, 2-piece	EX	$81.00	2-2002
Heddon	Flaptail Jr.	natural scale, glass eyes	EX	$123.51	6-1999
Heddon	Flaptail Jr.	perch scale, glass eyes, 2-piece	EX	$131.38	2-2000
Heddon	Flaptail Jr.	pike scale, glass eyes	Mint	$127.50	6-1999
Heddon	Flaptail Jr.	shiner scale, glass eyes	EX	$89.01	5-1999
Heddon	Flaptail Jr.	shiner scale, glass eyes	Mint	$250.00	2-2000
Heddon	Flaptail Jr.	silver scale	EX	$39.00	4-2001
Heddon	Flaptail Musky	7040GM Banner box	NIB	$207.55	4-1999
Heddon	Flaptail Musky	7040PAS, painted eyes, avg Banner box	EX/IB	$75.00	10-2000
Heddon	Flaptail Musky	7050PAS, painted eyes, Banner box	NIB	$56.00	10-1999
Heddon	Flaptail Musky	7050PAS, painted eyes, red Brush box	NIB	$81.00	3-2000
Heddon	Flaptail Musky	7050RH, painted eyes, Banner box papers	NIB	$56.00	11-1999

BRAND	MODEL	SERIES / MFG. CODE / DESCRIPTION	GRADE	PRICE	DATE
Heddon	Flaptail Musky	7059CP, glass eyes, nice Flesh box	NIB	$986.00	3-2001
Heddon	Flaptail Musky	glass eyes, toilet, 7052 Brush box	NIB	$382.00	10-2000
Heddon	Flaptail Musky	mouse	G	$31.77	2-1999
Heddon	Flaptail Musky	natural scale	EX-	$128.55	4-1999
Heddon	Flaptail Musky	red & white, glass eyes, unmarked Brush box	EXIB	$157.50	1-1999
Heddon	Flaptail Musky	red head, glass eyes	EX-	$77.00	6-2002
Heddon	Flaptail Musky	SB, teddy eyes, small chip	EX-	$250.00	1-2001
Heddon	Flaptail Musky	SD, painted eyes?, crisp Brush box	NIB	$187.00	9-2000
Heddon	Flaptail Musky	strawberry, teddy bear, glass eyes	EX	$361.00	2-2000
Heddon	Flaptail Vamp	goldfish scale, red, white, flapper	EX	$300.00	1-1999
Heddon	Flaptail Vamp	shiner scale, fat body, L-rig	EX	$325.00	8-1999
Heddon	Flipper	140, Stanley props, nicks, NOT MET		$261.00	5-2001
Heddon	Flipper	149, perch scale, avg Down Bass box	EX-/IB	$536.00	6-2002
Heddon	Flipper	149M, great box	NIB	$2,820.00	11-2000
Heddon	Flipper	fat body, Stanly props, 3 double hooks, red eyes & tail	VG+	$521.00	4-2001
Heddon	Flipper	frog spot, awful worm burn, $650.00 NOT MET		$153.00	8-2002
Heddon	Flipper	green scale, NOT MET	Poor	$56.00	4-2000
Heddon	Flipper	JRH, frog scale, tail chip	VG	$800.00	8-2000
Heddon	Flipper	natural scale	EX-	$1,200.00	5-2000
Heddon	Flipper	perch scale, L-rig	EX	$372.00	2-2002
Heddon	Flipper	red eyes & tail	EX-	$350.00	7-2001
Heddon	Flipper	shiner scale, L-rig, NOT MET	EX-	$315.00	8-2000
Heddon	Flipper	strawberry, age lines, no missing paint	VG	$475.00	11-1999
Heddon	Flipper	strawberry, unmarked Down Bass box	AVG/IB	$178.00	10-2002
Heddon	Flipper	white, bullseye, otherwise nice	EX-	$114.00	5-2001
Heddon	Flipper	white, red eye shadow, Heddon prop, NOT MET	VG	$135.00	10-2001
Heddon	Flipper	white, red nose	AVG	$69.00	2-2002
Heddon	Florida Special	10, white, red eyes, L-rig, NOT MET	VG	$143.00	10-2000
Heddon	Florida Special	19S, yellow, glitter, HPGM, L-rig	EX-	$500.00	10-1999
Heddon	Florida Special	green scale	EX-	$300.00	10-2000
Heddon	Florida Special	green scale	VG+	$525.00	5-2000
Heddon	Florida Special	red scale, 2 3/4", decent	VG	$307.00	5-2000
Heddon	Florida Special, Baby	green scale	VG+ to EX-	$575.00	5-2000
Heddon	Flyrod	4 poor condition, runtie, punkie, flaptail	Poor	$153.00	2-1999
Heddon	Game Fisher	5501, rainbow, L-rig, Down Bass box, nice	NIB	$238.00	8-1999
Heddon	Game Fisher	5502, crisp Up Bass box, nice	NIB	$315.00	4-2000
Heddon	Game Fisher	5502, L-rig, Down Bass box	EX-/IB	$195.00	1-2000
Heddon	Game Fisher	5502, nice Down Bass box	NIB	$255.00	5-1999
Heddon	Game Fisher	5509M, unmarked Down Bass box	EX-/IB	$200.00	10-1999
Heddon	Game Fisher	5509D, Up Bass box	EX/IB	$242.50	7-1999
Heddon	Game Fisher	5509D, vg Down Bass box	EX-/IB	$112.00	10-2000
Heddon	Game Fisher	green scale	EX	$34.00	6-2000
Heddon	Game Fisher	green scale	G	$37.00	1-1999
Heddon	Game Fisher	green scale, glass eyes, expert thinks fake	VG-	$578.00	2-2002
Heddon	Game Fisher	pike scale, L-rig	Mint	$177.00	1-2000
Heddon	Game Fisher	pike scale, vg unmarked Down Bass box	EX-	$151.00	8-1999
Heddon	Game Fisher	rainbow	EX	$106.00	10-2001

BRAND	MODEL	SERIES / MFG. CODE / DESCRIPTION	GRADE	PRICE	DATE
Heddon	Game Fisher	rainbow	EX-	$51.00	5-2000
Heddon	Game Fisher	rainbow	VG-	$35.00	1-1999
Heddon	Game Fisher	rainbow	VG-	$50.00	1-1999
Heddon	Game Fisher	red head & tail	EX	$133.50	1-2000
Heddon	Game Fisher	red eyes & tail	VG	$27.00	3-2000
Heddon	Game Fisher	red, white	EX	$73.00	1-1999
Heddon	Game Fisher	shiner scale	VG	$48.00	1-1999
Heddon	Game Fisher	shiner scale	VG+	$38.00	4-2000
Heddon	Game Fisher	shiner scale, Down Bass box	NIB	$228.37	2-1999
Heddon	Game Fisher	shiner scale, L-rig, nice	EX	$125.00	3-1999
Heddon	Game Fisher	two red eyes & tail, green scale	EX-	$113.00	6-2000
Heddon	Game Fisher	white, red	EX	$57.00	5-2000
Heddon	Game Fisher	x2; 1 shiner scale, 1 red & white; both nice	EX	$188.01	9-1999
Heddon	Game Fisher	x2; rainbow, 1 small & 1 large; nice	EX	$203.55	2-2000
Heddon	Game Fisher, Baby	5400S	EX-	$1,138.00	12-2000
Heddon	Giant Runt	red head, 2PCCB, papers	NIB	$812.00	12-1998
Heddon	Go-Deeper	orange spots, painted eyes	NIB	$80.00	1-1999
Heddon	Go-Deeper Crab	red, white, painted eyes, Banner box	NIB	$56.00	9-1999
Heddon	Go-Deeper Crab	D1900NC, painted eyes, S-rig, catalog	EX/IB	$40.00	5-1999
Heddon	Hardin Whiz	POBW, belly stencil, floppy, NOT MET	VG	$355.00	1-2001
Heddon	Hardin Whiz	shiner scale	EX	$1,245.00	7-2000
Heddon	Hedd Hunter	9320CD	NOC	$37.00	2-2000
Heddon	Hedd Hunter	9320NPB	NOC	$37.00	2-2000
Heddon	Hedd Hunter	9350NSN, Rapala shape	NOC	$34.63	2-2000
Heddon	Hedd Plug, Improved	3 different, flourescent, NOT MET	NIB	$122.50	8-1999
Heddon	Hedd Plug, Magnum	4½", fluorescent orange, black spots		$100.00	3-1999
Heddon	Hedd Plug, Magnum	4½", musky color	EX+	$100.00	3-1999
Heddon	Hedd Plug, Magnum	pike scale, lime green?	EX	$150.00	5-2002
Heddon	Hedd Plug	3 different	EX	$132.50	4-1999
Heddon	Hedd Plug	chartreuse, green, rainbow scale	Mint	$49.99	3-1999
Heddon	Hedd Plug	chartreuse, silver scale	EX	$42.00	1-1999
Heddon	Hedd Plug	chrome, big size	EX-	$28.00	6-2001
Heddon	Hedd Plug	natural striper, photo finish	EX	$103.50	1-2000
Heddon	Hedd Plug	pearl	EX	$61.00	6-1999
Heddon	Hep Spinners	easel display board, 3 lures	EX	$32.00	1-1999
Heddon	Hi-Tail		EX-	$40.99	1-1999
Heddon	Hi-Tail	5 different, all with white eyes	EX	$168.51	8-1999
Heddon	Hi-Tail	6 different, NOT MET	EX	$203.00	1-1999
Heddon	Hi-Tail	105B, gold eyes, topkick covered	NIB	$106.00	4-2000
Heddon	Hi-Tail	black	EX+	$46.90	12-1998
Heddon	Hi-Tail	black	VG	$37.00	1-1999
Heddon	Hi-Tail	black, gold eyes	EX	$62.00	5-1999
Heddon	Hi-Tail	black, white eyes	EX	$48.00	8-2001
Heddon	Hi-Tail	Budweiser decal, scrape	VG-	$150.00	5-2001
Heddon	Hi-Tail	Budweiser, NOT MET	AVG	$307.00	3-1999
Heddon	Hi-Tail	checkerboard	EX	$370.00	3-2001
Heddon	Hi-Tail	checkerboard	EX+	$416.00	4-2002

BRAND	MODEL	SERIES / MFG. CODE / DESCRIPTION	GRADE	PRICE	DATE
Heddon	Hi-Tail	frog	Mint	$66.50	2-1999
Heddon	Hi-Tail	frog	NIB	$69.00	2-1999
Heddon	Hi-Tail	frog, white eyes, NOT MET	EX	$36.06	1-2000
Heddon	Hi-Tail	Indy 500	EX+	$380.00	12-2001
Heddon	Hi-Tail	(P) pike scale, white eyes	EX	$39.00	5-1999
Heddon	Hi-Tail	perch	EX	$46.00	2-1999
Heddon	Hi-Tail	perch	EX	$66.08	2-1999
Heddon	Hi-Tail	perch	EX-	$51.00	1-1999
Heddon	Hi-Tail	perch scale	NIB	$69.00	1-2002
Heddon	Hi-Tail	perch, white eyes	EX	$46.10	4-1999
Heddon	Hi-Tail	perch, white eyes	EX-	$51.00	5-1999
Heddon	Hi-Tail	perch, white eyes	Mint	$49.99	5-1999
Heddon	Hi-Tail	perch, white eyes	Mint	$63.89	3-1999
Heddon	Hi-Tail	red & white	VG	$25.00	1-1999
Heddon	Hi-Tail	red & white, gold eyes, "Heddon" only	VG+	$44.50	4-1999
Heddon	Hi-Tail	red & white, white eyes	EX	$50.00	6-1999
Heddon	Hi-Tail	red & white, white eyes	Mint	$61.00	4-1999
Heddon	Hi-Tail	red head, white eyes	EX	$51.00	5-1999
Heddon	Hi-Tail	silver scale	EX	$28.25	1-1999
Heddon	Hi-Tail	silver scale	EX	$40.00	12-1998
Heddon	Hi-Tail	silver scale	EX	$41.00	1-1999
Heddon	Hi-Tail	silver scale	EX-	$41.00	3-1999
Heddon	Hi-Tail	silver scale	EX-	$46.00	3-1999
Heddon	Hi-Tail	silver scale	Mint	$40.00	4-2000
Heddon	Hi-Tail	silver scale	VG	$41.00	3-1999
Heddon	Hi-Tail	silver scale, unlisted	EX-	$585.00	6-1999
Heddon	Hi-Tail	silver scale, white eyes, NOT MET	EX	$35.02	7-1999
Heddon	Hi-Tail	store display with 4 colors, 12 lures	NOC	$600.00	5-2000
Heddon	Hi-Tail	x12, stand up display, 6 colors x2	NOC	$691.00	3-2000
Heddon	Hi-Tail	XRY, white eyes, NOT MET	EX	$356.00	4-2002
Heddon	Hi-Tail	yellow, white eyes	EX	$41.00	6-1999
Heddon	Hi-Tail	yellow, white eyes	VG+/IB	$48.78	5-1999
Heddon	Hi-Tail	yellow, yellow eyes	EX	$78.25	3-1999
Heddon	Hi-Tail	XRY, NOT MET	EX	$338.00	3-2002
Heddon	Ice-Spook	perch, 459L Up Bass box, Ice Spook paper	NIB	$2,402.00	10-2001
Heddon	Killer	400, blue & white, vg+ picture box	EX-/IB	$6,750.00	6-2001
Heddon	Killer	402, sienna crackleback	VG+	$400.00	1-2001
Heddon	Killer	402, yellow crackleback, skullcap, glass eyes	EX	$611.00	4-2000
Heddon	Killer	450, lavender, 3BW, repainted?	VG+	$1,480.00	9-2000
Heddon	Killer	450, red & white, vg- picture box, NOT MET	EX-/IB	$5,001.00	12-2000
Heddon	Killer	450, red, white & red	EX	$850.00	10-1999
Heddon	Killer	450, red, white & red, 1BW, repainted?	EX	$1,200.00	8-1999
Heddon	Killer	450, red, white & red, $500.00 NOT MET	EX	$240.00	5-2000
Heddon	Killer	aluminum, 3BW, avg intro picture box	EX-/IB	$5,000.00	10-1999
Heddon	Killer	red, white & red, NOT MET	AVG	$233.50	1-1999
Heddon	Killer Surface Minnow	402, rainbow, varnish flaking	VG-	$175.00	8-2002
Heddon	Killer Surface Minnow	white crackleback, NOT MET	EX	$797.00	3-2001

BRAND	MODEL	SERIES / MFG. CODE / DESCRIPTION	GRADE	PRICE	DATE
Heddon	Laguna Runt	10SSB, glass eyes, POBW, vg+ Up Bass box	EX-/IB	$189.00	8-2001
Heddon	Laguna Runt	L10XBP, painted eyes, Brush box	NIB	$102.50	1-2000
Heddon	Laguna Runt	L10XPB, painted eyes, crisp Brush box	NIB	$114.50	2-1999
Heddon	Laguna Runt	pearl, painted eyes	Mint	$41.00	7-2002
Heddon	Little Joe	red head, glitter, glass eyes, NOT MET	EX	$212.49	10-1999
Heddon	Little Mary	ex- 802 Down Bass box	EX-/IB	$400.00	10-1999
Heddon	Lucky 13	2500BRS	NIB	$128.00	8-2001
Heddon	Lucky 13	2500GRA	NIB	$107.00	9-2000
Heddon	Lucky 13	2509PLRH, no eyes, Brush box	EX-/IB	$167.50	8-1999
Heddon	Lucky 13	black & white, tack glass eyes, tough color	EX-	$61.00	8-1999
Heddon	Lucky 13	Charlie Campbell Frog	EX	$113.00	5-2000
Heddon	Lucky 13	goldfish scale, no eyes, cup, varnish	AVG	$78.00	10-2000
Heddon	Lucky 13	green scale, no eyes, 2-piece	NIB	$141.00	7-2002
Heddon	Lucky 13	JRH, glass eyes, S-rig, Brush box	NIB	$127.00	8-2002
Heddon	Lucky 13	long lip, L-rig, 2501 Brush box	EX/IB	$300.00	1-1999
Heddon	Lucky 13	long lip, L-rig, 2502 Up Bass box	NIB	$300.00	9-2001
Heddon	Lucky 13	red & white, no eyes, long lip, L-rig	EX-	$102.50	5-1999
Heddon	Lucky 13	red head, frog scale, glass eyes, S-rig	EX	$30.00	10-2000
Heddon	Lucky 13	red head, frog scale, no eyes	EX	$344.00	11-2001
Heddon	Lucky 13	red head, frog scale, no eyes, L-rig	EX-	$243.01	2-2000
Heddon	Lucky 13	red head, frog scale, tack glass eyes	NIB	$102.50	2-1999
Heddon	Lucky 13	red head, no eyes, long lip	EX-	$165.00	12-2000
Heddon	Lucky 13	red scale, no eyes	VG	$163.51	6-1999
Heddon	Lucky 13	red scale, no eyes	VG+	$325.00	5-2000
Heddon	Lucky 13?	silver scale, blue eyes & back, no stencil?	EX-	$401.00	4-2002
Heddon	Lucky 13	SS, painted eyes, S-rig, wood	Mint	$61.00	7-2002
Heddon	Lucky 13	W2500PRH, "Original," S-rig	NIB	$32.00	11-2000
Heddon	Lucky 13	XBW, painted eyes	EX	$202.00	5-2000
Heddon	Lucky 13	XRYBB, painted eyes, thin lip chip	EX-	$265.00	11-2000
Heddon	Lucky 13, Baby	frog, glass eyes	AVG	$12.50	1-1999
Heddon	Lucky 13, Baby	perch, no eyes	EX-	$425.00	1-1999
Heddon	Lucky 13, Baby	photo natural bass?	EX	$54.00	4-2000
Heddon	Lucky 13 Jr.	3409H, Wiggle King, fair intro box	AVG/IB	$267.00	5-2000
Heddon	Lucky 13 Spook	GRA, fluorescent green crawfish	NIB	$75.00	3-2002
Heddon	Lucky 13 Spook	natural bass?	Mint	$89.00	3-2002
Heddon	Lucky 13 Spook	NF, natural frog	NIB	$152.00	3-2002
Heddon	Lucky 13 Spook	pikie photo finish	EX	$204.00	8-2000
Heddon	Lucky 13 Spook	XRY, white eyes, S-rig, tail bell rig	Mint	$290.00	6-2002
Heddon	Lucky 13 Spook	yellow coach dog?	EX	$35.00	1-1999
Heddon	Lucky 13 Spook	yellow coach dog?	Mint	$76.00	1-1999
Heddon	Lucky 13 Spook	yellow tiger	Mint	$518.00	12-2001
Heddon	Lucky 13 Spook, Baby	South Bend color, silver	EX-	$355.00	11-2000
Heddon	Luny Frog		AVG	$42.00	2-2000
Heddon	Luny Frog		EX	$86.50	6-1999
Heddon	Luny Frog		EX	$96.00	1-1999
Heddon	Luny Frog		EX	$110.00	6-2000
Heddon	Luny Frog		EX-	$57.00	5-2000

BRAND	MODEL	SERIES / MFG. CODE / DESCRIPTION	GRADE	PRICE	DATE
Heddon	Luny Frog		VG	$62.55	1-1999
Heddon	Luny Frog		VG-	$66.00	2-1999
Heddon	Luny Frog	3509, red head, ex Up Bass box	EX-/IB	$1,326.99	2-2000
Heddon	Luny Frog	3509B, closed legs	Mint	$150.00	10-1999
Heddon	Luny Frog	3509BB, Up Bass box	NIB	$355.00	7-1999
Heddon	Luny Frog	closed legs	EX	$350.00	5-1999
Heddon	Luny Frog	lip chips, NOT MET		$61.66	2-1999
Heddon	Luny Frog	meadow frog	EX+	$134.00	10-2000
Heddon	Luny Frog	nice box	EX/IB	$305.00	4-2000
Heddon	Luny Frog	nice Up Bass box	NIB	$243.00	4-2001
Heddon	Luny Frog	nice Up Bass box	NIB	$430.00	1-2000
Heddon	Luny Frog	NOT MET	mint	$103.50	2-2000
Heddon	Luny Frog	open leg		$85.00	2-1999
Heddon	Luny Frog	open leg	EX-	$102.00	4-2000
Heddon	Luny Frog	red & white	EX	$1,075.00	12-1999
Heddon	Luny Frog	red head	VG+	$408.00	5-2001
Heddon	Luny Frog	red head, NOT MET	VG	$349.00	9-2000
Heddon	Luny Frog	red head, toes of one foot broken off	VG	$260.00	3-2001
Heddon	Luny Frog, Baby		EX	$123.50	2-1999
Heddon	Luny Frog, Baby	head, black, silver spots	EX-	$71.00	4-2000
Heddon	Luny Frog, Little		EX	$78.77	9-1999
Heddon	Luny Frog, Little		EX	$99.00	1-2000
Heddon	Luny Frog, Little		EX	$129.00	8-2000
Heddon	Luny Frog, Little		EX	$225.99	4-1999
Heddon	Luny Frog, Little		EX+	$152.50	5-1999
Heddon	Luny Frog, Little		VG+	$79.55	2-2000
Heddon	Luny Frog, Little	mint hang tag, ex 3409B Up Bass box	NIB	$561.00	10-1999
Heddon	Luny Frog, Little	perfect 3209B Down Bass box, hang tag, receipt	NIB	$481.00	7-1999
Heddon	Luny Frog, Little	wrong 3327 box, neat papers	NIB	$280.00	3-1999
Heddon	Luny Frog, Little	worm burn on belly, top okay		$52.77	2-1999
Heddon	Meadow Mouse	4000	EX/IB	$36.01	4-1999
Heddon	Meadow Mouse	4000, black & white, L-rig	VG+	$406.22	8-1999
Heddon	Meadow Mouse	4000GM Up Bass box	NIB	$270.50	11-1999
Heddon	Meadow Mouse	4000, green?, leather ears, tail, nice	EX	$103.50	6-1999
Heddon	Meadow Mouse	4000, white, red blush, green stripe, nice ears	EX	$192.00	8-2001
Heddon	Meadow Mouse	4000WM, L-rig	EX-	$155.00	3-2002
Heddon	Meadow Mouse	9800BLM, black	NIB	$36.00	1-1999
Heddon	Meadow Mouse	9800GM, NOT MET	NIB	$30.00	12-1999
Heddon	Meadow Mouse	9800W	NIB	$57.00	3-1999
Heddon	Meadow Mouse	black & white, earliest version, beautiful	EX	$611.00	2-1999
Heddon	Meadow Mouse	black & white, L-rig, pretty	EX	$535.11	5-1999
Heddon	Meadow Mouse	black, white head, L-rig	VG+	$405.00	10-2001
Heddon	Meadow Mouse	brown, L-rig, bead nose?	EX	$152.50	5-1999
Heddon	Meadow Mouse	chipmunk, wrong box 9800DL	EX	$91.04	6-1999
Heddon	Meadow Mouse	crisp 4000BM Brush box	NIB	$500.00	5-2001
Heddon	Meadow Mouse	L-rig, 4000GM Up Bass box	EX/IB	$202.50	8-1999
Heddon	Meadow Mouse	L-rig, wrong F4000GM Banner box	EX/IB	$189.02	7-1999

BRAND	MODEL	SERIES / MFG. CODE / DESCRIPTION	GRADE	PRICE	DATE
Heddon	Meadow Mouse	molded ears, plastic	VG+	$27.00	1-1999
Heddon	Meadow Mouse	red stripe on back, 4000WM Up Bass box	NIB	$510.00	2-2000
Heddon	Meadow Mouse	white, later plastic version	Mint	$50.00	7-2002
Heddon	Midget Digit	110XRS, painted eyes, wood, nice box	EX/IB	$104.50	9-1999
Heddon	Midget Digit	9020XRW window	NIB	$18.00	2-1999
Heddon	Midget Digit	green shore	NIB	$35.00	2-1999
Heddon	Midget Digit	yellow, black spots, red eyes	VG+	$181.00	7-2000
Heddon	Midget Digit	wood, ex B119LUM Brush box, varnish flakes, NOT MET	EX-/IB	$80.00	10-2001
Heddon	Ms. Mary	808, red head, rust cup	EX-	$300.00	10-1999
Heddon	Multiple Metal Minnow		EX	$425.00	12-1999
Heddon	Multiple Metal Minnow		EX	$900.00	4-2001
Heddon	Multiple Metal Minnow	hooks replaced, $500.00 NOT MET	EX	$355.00	5-2000
Heddon	Multiple Metal Minnow	nickel, NOT MET!	EX	$711.00	2-1999
Heddon	Multiple Metal Minnow	rough hooks	VG+	$458.00	8-2002
Heddon	Multiple Metal Minnow	silver	EX	$358.00	1-2002
Heddon	Munk Mouse	chipmunk, light drag	VG+	$152.50	1-1999
Heddon	Munk Mouse	crisp F4200CM Brush box , rev. lip, 2-piece	NIB	$433.88	11-1999
Heddon	Musky, Prowler	6¼", mackerel, NOT MET	VG	$41.99	6-1999
Heddon	Musky, Prowler	7075B, NOT MET	NIB	$41.50	5-1999
Heddon	Musky, Prowler	7050BWB, ⅝ oz.	NIB	$51.00	5-1999
Heddon	Musky, Prowler	7075SU	NIB	$57.00	4-2000
Heddon	Musky, Prowler	yellow, silver stripe	NIB	$46.00	2-2000
Heddon	Musky Surfacer	natural scale	EX-	$339.00	6-2002
Heddon	Musky Surfacer	shiner scale	EX	$1,850.00	5-2000
Heddon	Musky Surfacer	strawberry, only 1 prop, NOT MET	EX-	$333.00	8-2002
Heddon	Musky Surfusser	350, green scale, 1 side nice, 1 side ugly	VG	$620.00	8-2000
Heddon	Musky Surfusser	350, green scale, hook drag, chip	VG	$400.00	9-2000
Heddon	Musky Surfusser	350, natural scale, 359CP	VG/IB	$361.00	8-1999
Heddon	Musky Surfusser	350, natural scale, green	VG+	$433.00	10-2000
Heddon	Musky Surfusser	350, natural scale, hook drag, ugly belly	VG-	$178.50	11-1999
Heddon	Musky Surfusser	350, natural scale, small tail chip	EX-	$562.51	12-1999
Heddon	Musky Surfusser	350, red head, glass eyes, NOT MET	EX-	$383.00	5-1999
Heddon	Musky Surfusser	350SB, nice	EX-	$735.00	11-1999
Heddon	Musky Surfusser	350, yellow spots	EX-	$898.00	9-1999
Heddon	Musky Surfusser	352, toilet, Fish Flesh box	NIB	$1,026.00	2-2001
Heddon	Plug Deluxe, Salmon	red head, golden shiner, Up Bass box	EX-	$143.50	2-1999
Heddon	Polly Runt	Shiner scale, glass eyes, 2-piece	EX-	$323.58	4-1999
Heddon	Pop-Eye	chrome, plastic	NIB	$15.50	5-1999
Heddon	Pop-Eye Frog	box	NIB	$99.99	1-1999
Heddon	Pop-Eye Frog	on card in 85GF window box	NIB	$133.50	3-1999
Heddon	Pop-Eye Frog	unmarked window box	Mint	$76.00	2-1999
Heddon	Popper, Brush	4 different	NIB	$81.00	4-1999
Heddon	Popper, Brush	5440RFY, large size	NIB	$36.51	2-2000
Heddon	Popper, Brush	large size	NIB	$19.10	3-1999
Heddon	Popper Spook	4 different	VG	$16.06	3-1999
Heddon	Popper Spook	5 different flyrods	VG-/EX	$76.51	6-1999

BRAND	MODEL	SERIES / MFG. CODE / DESCRIPTION	GRADE	PRICE	DATE
Heddon	Popper Spook	930XRW, on card in window box	NIB	$76.00	5-1999
Heddon	Popper Spook	green, rough box	NIB	$29.00	1-1999
Heddon	Popper Spook	XRS	EX-	$31.00	3-2002
Heddon	Pork Rind Minnow	red, glass eyes, nice Down Bass box	NIB	$229.10	1-2000
Heddon	Pork Rind, Stanley	(M) pike scale, odd heart-shaped metal lip	EX	$361.00	8-2000
Heddon	Pork Rind, Stanley	shiner scale, glass eyes	EX	$60.00	10-2000
Heddon	Pork Rind, Stanley Weedless Perfection	12-pack, hooks on cards, nice	NIB	$300.00	11-1999
Heddon	Prowler	3½", brown crackleback	EX	$129.00	9-2000
Heddon	Prowler	3½", perch	EX	$66.77	4-1999
Heddon	Prowler	4½", BGL	EX	$11.50	1-1999
Heddon	Prowler	7205BWB	NIB	$18.21	1-1999
Heddon	Prowler	7025BWX	NIB	$16.50	1-1999
Heddon	Prowler	7025SSD, ⅜ oz.	NIB	$22.50	6-1999
Heddon	Prowler	green scale?	EX	$31.00	4-1999
Heddon	Punkie	BG, one hook	EX	$261.00	7-2000
Heddon	Punkie	rough 980SD box, NOT MET	NIB	$140.00	3-2001
Heddon	Punkie	sunfish	EX	$225.00	8-2000
Heddon	Punkie-Spook	BGL	Mint	$190.00	2-2000
Heddon	Punkie-Spook	sunfish	EX	$186.00	5-2001
Heddon	Punkie-Spook	sunfish, treble, no iris	EX	$167.50	2-2000
Heddon	Punkin-Spin	382NP	NIB	$155.00	1-2002
Heddon	Punkin-Spin	382NP, chrome	NIB	$191.00	3-2000
Heddon	Punkin-Spin	382NP, chrome	NIB	$282.50	7-1999
Heddon	Punkin-Spin	382PRL, NOT MET	NIB	$127.00	10-2000
Heddon	Punkin-Spin	blue scale, chrome	EX-	$131.38	2-2000
Heddon	Punkin-Spin	chrome	EX	$142.49	8-1999
Heddon	Punkin-Spin	chrome	EX	$255.99	3-1999
Heddon	Punkin-Spin	chrome, NO BIDS	EX+	$150.00	10-1999
Heddon	Punkin-Spin	ivory	EX	$162.00	6-2000
Heddon	Punkin-Spin	pearl, one bid	EX+	$150.00	10-1999
Heddon	Punkin-Spin	Smokey Joe	Mint	$91.00	7-2002
Heddon	Punkin-Spin	white pearl	Mint	$300.00	11-1999
Heddon	Punkin-Spin	white, ugly	Poor	$32.99	3-1999
Heddon	Punkin-Spin	yellow pearl	EX	$139.00	9-2000
Heddon	Punkin-Spin	yellow pearl	Mint	$170.00	6-1999
Heddon	Punkin-Spin	yellow pearl	NIB	$162.50	3-2000
Heddon	Punkin-Spin	yellow pearl, one bid	EX+	$130.00	10-1999
Heddon	Punkinseed	2-piece, tail, 9630SUN Banner box	NIB	$123.71	2-1999
Heddon	Punkinseed	20 different, 8-740s, 5-730s, plastic, NOT MET	VG-to Mint	$1,935.00	5-1999
Heddon	Punkinseed	380BGL	VG	$40.00	1-1999
Heddon	Punkinseed	320BGL, big scales, white eyes	EX+	$86.00	6-1999
Heddon	Punkinseed	320SUN, gold eyes	EX	$76.00	6-1999
Heddon	Punkinseed	380, 7 different, gold eyes, NOT MET	EX	$565.00	11-2000
Heddon	Punkinseed	380, blue chrome, NOT MET	EX	$393.55	10-1999
Heddon	Punkinseed	380BGL, gold eyes	EX	$48.00	1-1999
Heddon	Punkinseed	380BGL, gold eyes	EX	$67.01	5-1999

BRAND	MODEL	SERIES / MFG. CODE / DESCRIPTION	GRADE	PRICE	DATE
Heddon	Punkinseed	380BGL, gold eyes	NIB	$113.51	12-1999
Heddon	Punkinseed	380CRA	NIB	$137.50	4-1999
Heddon	Punkinseed	380CRA, gold eyes	AVG	$38.50	3-1999
Heddon	Punkinseed	380CRA, white eyes	NIB	$88.56	2-1999
Heddon	Punkinseed	380, perch?	EX	$80.00	12-1998
Heddon	Punkinseed	380SD, orange eyes	EX	$153.50	12-1999
Heddon	Punkinseed	380, strawberry	EX	$610.00	3-1999
Heddon	Punkinseed	380, strawberry, NOT MET	EX	$687.99	10-1999
Heddon	Punkinseed	380SUN	EX	$56.56	1-1999
Heddon	Punkinseed	380SUN	VG	$40.00	1-1999
Heddon	Punkinseed	320SUN, flyrod	EX	$315.00	6-1999
Heddon	Punkinseed	380SUN, gold eyes	EX	$80.99	3-1999
Heddon	Punkinseed	380SUN, gold eyes	EX-	$51.50	2-1999
Heddon	Punkinseed	380XBW, gold eyes	EX	$64.53	2-1999
Heddon	Punkinseed	380XBW, gold eyes	EX+	$111.00	11-2000
Heddon	Punkinseed	380XBW, white eyes, bell rig	EX	$113.00	2-1999
Heddon	Punkinseed	380XRW, gold eyes	EX	$132.00	1-1999
Heddon	Punkinseed	380XRY	EX	$91.00	2-1999
Heddon	Punkinseed	380XRY	EX+	$103.51	5-1999
Heddon	Punkinseed	380XRY	VG	$41.53	5-1999
Heddon	Punkinseed	380XRY, gold eyes	Mint	$108.00	1-1999
Heddon	Punkinseed	380XRY, gold eyes	Mint	$128.05	10-1999
Heddon	Punkinseed	380XRY, red eye shadow	EX	$136.00	4-2000
Heddon	Punkinseed	380XRY, white eyes	Mint	$113.61	6-1999
Heddon	Punkinseed	730BGL, mouth, 2-piece, S-rig	EX	$163.52	1-2000
Heddon	Punkinseed	730BGL, 2-piece, S-rig, Banner box	NIB	$200.50	3-2000
Heddon	Punkinseed	730BGL, 2-piece, S-rig, Banner box	NIB	$224.51	5-1999
Heddon	Punkinseed	730CRA	EX	$152.50	7-1999
Heddon	Punkinseed	730CRA, 2-piece	EX	$150.00	10-1999
Heddon	Punkinseed	730CRA, 2-piece	EX+	$208.50	6-1999
Heddon	Punkinseed	730CRA, chin tie, 2-piece	EX	$188.35	1-2000
Heddon	Punkinseed	730CRA, chin tie, 2-piece	Mint	$212.50	5-1999
Heddon	Punkinseed	730CRA, mouth, 2-piece, Brush box	NIB	$333.88	8-1999
Heddon	Punkinseed	730CRA, orange eyes, S-rig	EX	$112.50	12-1999
Heddon	Punkinseed	730CRA, S-rig, Brush box	EX/IB	$142.50	2-2000
Heddon	Punkinseed	730L, POBW, tough color in a 730	EX	$540.00	1-2002
Heddon	Punkinseed	730ROB, chin tie, 2-piece	EX-	$405.02	1-2000
Heddon	Punkinseed	730SUN	NIB	$281.00	4-2000
Heddon	Punkinseed	730SUN, awful glue spot	Poor	$23.36	2-1999
Heddon	Punkinseed	730SUN, catalog	EX-/IB	$415.01	3-1999
Heddon	Punkinseed	730SUN, mouth	EX-	$157.50	4-1999
Heddon	Punkinseed	730SD	G	$50.00	1-1999
Heddon	Punkinseed	730, white shore, black ribs, 2-piece	EX-	$838.00	1-2002
Heddon	Punkinseed	730XBW	EX	$203.50	4-1999
Heddon	Punkinseed	730XBW, Brush box	NIB	$384.00	1-1999
Heddon	Punkinseed	730XBW, catalog	NIB	$382.00	4-1999
Heddon	Punkinseed	730XBW, mouth, 2-piece, S-rig	EX	$270.02	1-2000

BRAND	MODEL	SERIES / MFG. CODE / DESCRIPTION	GRADE	PRICE	DATE
Heddon	Punkinseed	730XBW, NOT MET	EXIB	$204.00	7-2000
Heddon	Punkinseed	730XBW, POBW	G	$61.00	8-1999
Heddon	Punkinseed	730XBW, ugly	VG-	$112.50	1-1999
Heddon	Punkinseed	730XRS	EX-	$560.00	4-1999
Heddon	Punkinseed	730XRS, chin tie, 2-piece	VG+	$610.00	6-1999
Heddon	Punkinseed	730XRW, "Sinker" odd stencil	EX	$406.00	10-2000
Heddon	Punkinseed	730XRW, S-rig, Banner box, NOT MET	NIB	$725.00	7-2000
Heddon	Punkinseed	730XRY, 2-piece, S-rig, bleed	EX	$150.00	4-2000
Heddon	Punkinseed	730XRY, 2-piece, S-rig, catalog, Banner box	NIB	$394.00	4-2001
Heddon	Punkinseed	730XRW, S-rig, catalog, inspection tag, Banner box	NIB	$1,080.00	8-1999
Heddon	Punkinseed	730XRY, 2-piece, S-rig, NOT MET	VG+	$104.50	5-1999
Heddon	Punkinseed	740, 740 sunfish?	G	$147.50	9-1999
Heddon	Punkinseed	740BGL	EX+/IB	$280.00	2-1999
Heddon	Punkinseed	740BGL	EX-/IB	$143.00	8-2000
Heddon	Punkinseed	740BGL	G	$70.00	1-1999
Heddon	Punkinseed	740BGL	VG+	$152.51	2-1999
Heddon	Punkinseed	740BGL, avg box, NOT MET	G/IB	$228.00	12-1998
Heddon	Punkinseed	740BGL, chin tie, avg- Brush box	VG+/IB	$250.00	4-1999
Heddon	Punkinseed	740BGL, POBW	EX/IB	$256.00	2-1999
Heddon	Punkinseed	740BGL, POBW, chin tie, chip, CRA box	EX	$118.00	1-1999
Heddon	Punkinseed	740BOZ, gold scale?, blue eyes,	VG-	$154.05	6-1999
Heddon	Punkinseed	740CRA	EX-	$158.50	7-1999
Heddon	Punkinseed	740CRA	EX/IB	$380.00	1-1999
Heddon	Punkinseed	740CRA, 2-piece, POBW	EX	$180.50	9-1999
Heddon	Punkinseed	740CRA, blue eyes, POBW, NOT MET	EX	$127.00	12-1999
Heddon	Punkinseed	740CRA, Brush box	EX/IB	$425.00	7-1999
Heddon	Punkinseed	740CRA, POBW	EX	$102.00	8-1999
Heddon	Punkinseed	740CRA, POBW	EX	$175.00	7-1999
Heddon	Punkinseed	740CRA, POBW, chin tie, NOT MET	EX-	$83.00	8-1999
Heddon	Punkinseed	740CRA, stain on one side, nice Brush box	VG/IB	$191.16	8-1999
Heddon	Punkinseed	740, green perch?, chin tie	EX+	$535.00	8-1999
Heddon	Punkinseed	740K, red shore, NOT MET	EX-	$960.00	2-2000
Heddon	Punkinseed	740L, POBW	EX-	$272.99	11-1999
Heddon	Punkinseed	740, perch scale	EX	$127.00	8-2002
Heddon	Punkinseed	740, perch scale, NOT MET	EX+	$253.00	12-2001
Heddon	Punkinseed	740, perch scale, POBW, NOT MET	EX	$330.00	9-2001
Heddon	Punkinseed	740, red shore, goldfish, ugly burn	Fair	$442.00	4-2000
Heddon	Punkinseed	740ROB	EX-/IB	$273.00	10-1999
Heddon	Punkinseed	740ROB	NIB	$411.50	2-1999
Heddon	Punkinseed	740ROB	NIB	$620.00	4-1999
Heddon	Punkinseed	740ROB, nose chip, shiny	EX-/IB	$230.00	8-2000
Heddon	Punkinseed	740ROC or 740L	EX	$310.00	2-2000
Heddon	Punkinseed	740ROC, 2-piece, chin tie	EX-	$255.01	8-1999
Heddon	Punkinseed	740ROC, NOT MET	NIB	$270.00	2-2000
Heddon	Punkinseed	740ROC, red eyes, nice, NOT MET	VG+	$61.00	12-1999
Heddon	Punkinseed	740SD	EX-	$96.00	3-2000

BRAND	MODEL	SERIES / MFG. CODE / DESCRIPTION	GRADE	PRICE	DATE
Heddon	Punkinseed	740SD, 2-piece, NOT MET	EX	$128.50	8-1999
Heddon	Punkinseed	740SD, old shad color, nice	EX-	$175.00	3-1999
Heddon	Punkinseed	740SH, 2-piece, chin tie, Brush box	NIB	$380.00	10-2000
Heddon	Punkinseed	740SHA, couple chips, catalog	VG/IB	$235.00	6-1999
Heddon	Punkinseed	740SUN, POBW	EX-	$144.00	3-2001
Heddon	Punkinseed	740SUN	NIB	$325.00	8-2000
Heddon	Punkinseed	740SUN, NOT MET	EX-	$142.60	3-2000
Heddon	Punkinseed	740SUN, POBW	EX	$255.00	5-1999
Heddon	Punkinseed	740SUN, shiny	EX	$258.88	2-2000
Heddon	Punkinseed	740SUN, worm burn on tail, NOT MET	Decent	$71.00	8-1999
Heddon	Punkinseed	740SYN, POBW, nice	EX-	$154.00	6-2001
Heddon	Punkinseed	740XBW, 2-piece, POBW, chin tie	VG+	$237.50	8-1999
Heddon	Punkinseed	740XBW, ring around BW	EX	$675.11	6-1999
Heddon	Punkinseed	740XRW	EX	$260.55	6-1999
Heddon	Punkinseed	740XRW	EX	$338.00	10-1999
Heddon	Punkinseed	740XRW	EX-	$291.00	3-2000
Heddon	Punkinseed	740XRW, 2-piece	VG+	$114.57	1-2000
Heddon	Punkinseed	740XRW, 2-piece, NOT MET	EX-	$210.00	5-1999
Heddon	Punkinseed	740XRW, 2-piece, POBW	VG	$168.50	6-1999
Heddon	Punkinseed	740XRW, 2-piece, ugly varnish	G	$102.51	2-1999
Heddon	Punkinseed	740XRW, chin tie	VG-	$168.50	6-1999
Heddon	Punkinseed	740XRW, POBW	EX-	$180.27	8-1999
Heddon	Punkinseed	740XRW, red line, chin tie	EX+	$200.00	10-2000
Heddon	Punkinseed	740XRY, 740ROB box	NIB	$1,180.00	4-1999
Heddon	Punkinseed	742XS, 2-piece, Brush box	NIB	$550.00	10-2001
Heddon	Punkinseed	742XS, Brush box	EXIB	$1775.00	4-1999
Heddon	Punkinseed	742XS, "floater," white shore	NIB	$338.00	4-2002
Heddon	Punkinseed	740XSK, goldfish shore, chin tie, Brush box	NIB	$3,719.00	12-2000
Heddon	Punkinseed	980SUN, flyrod on card	NOC	$255.00	1-1999
Heddon	Punkinseed	8630SUN, gold eyes, 740XRW box	EX to VG+	$161.38	12-1999
Heddon	Punkinseed	9630, bar perch?	Mint	$578.00	3-1999
Heddon	Punkinseed	9630BGL	EX	$65.00	1-1999
Heddon	Punkinseed	9630BGL	VG	$46.00	1-1999
Heddon	Punkinseed	9630BGL Banner box	NIB	$123.51	2-2000
Heddon	Punkinseed	9630BGL Banner box	NIB	$137.00	1-1999
Heddon	Punkinseed	9630BGL, gold eyes, Banner box	EXIB	$117.50	3-1999
Heddon	Punkinseed	9630BGL, gold eyes, Banner box	NIB	$112.00	10-2000
Heddon	Punkinseed	9630BGL, gold eyes, S-rig, PTCB	NIB	$105.00	11-2000
Heddon	Punkinseed	9630BGL, S-rig, bell rig tail	NIB	$129.49	5-1999
Heddon	Punkinseed	9630BGL, S-rig, PTCB	NIB	$149.00	5-1999
Heddon	Punkinseed	9630, bluegill, rear bell rig, gold eyes	VG-	$42.23	2-1999
Heddon	Punkinseed	9630CD	EX	$48.09	1-1999
Heddon	Punkinseed	9630CD	EX	$275.00	3-1999
Heddon	Punkinseed	9630CD	EX-	$53.00	1-1999
Heddon	Punkinseed	9630CD	EX-	$147.00	3-2001
Heddon	Punkinseed	9630CD	Mint	$331.00	9-2000
Heddon	Punkinseed	9630CD	NIB	$475.00	9-1999

BRAND	MODEL	SERIES / MFG. CODE / DESCRIPTION	GRADE	PRICE	DATE
Heddon	Punkinseed	9630CD	VG	$62.67	3-1999
Heddon	Punkinseed	9630CD, 9630CRA Banner box, orange eyes	NIB	$202.50	4-1999
Heddon	Punkinseed	9630CD, 9630CRA Banner box	NIB	$127.00	1-1999
Heddon	Punkinseed	9630CD, gold eyes, red gills	VG+	$96.00	6-1999
Heddon	Punkinseed	9630CD,Whopper Stopper card	NOC	$385.00	3-1999
Heddon	Punkinseed	9630, coach dog	EX+	$350.00	11-1999
Heddon	Punkinseed	9630CRA, bell rig	EX	$49.99	9-1999
Heddon	Punkinseed	9630CRA, gold eyes, S-rig	EX-	$62.99	2-1999
Heddon	Punkinseed	9630CRA,NOT MET	EX	$66.00	1-1999
Heddon	Punkinseed	9630CRA, orange eyes	NIB	$81.00	4-2000
Heddon	Punkinseed	9630, crappie, white eyes	Mint	$78.77	11-1999
Heddon	Punkinseed	9630GRA, on Whopper Stopper card	NOC	$705.00	11-2000
Heddon	Punkinseed	9630, green scale?	Mint	$1,135.00	1-2002
Heddon	Punkinseed	9630, green scale, green & black triangle box	NIB	$598.88	6-1999
Heddon	Punkinseed	9630, green scale, red eyes, black shadow, bell rig	NIB	$511.00	4-1999
Heddon	Punkinseed	9630RH, flitter	EX	$836.00	5-2000
Heddon	Punkinseed	9630RH, flitter, gold eyes, $1,200.00 NOT MET	EX	$735.00	2-2002
Heddon	Punkinseed	9630RH, ugly, NOT MET	VG-	$225.05	8-1999
Heddon	Punkinseed	9630SD	EX	$56.78	1-1999
Heddon	Punkinseed	9630SD	EX/IB	$106.49	3-1999
Heddon	Punkinseed	9630SD, gold eyes	EX-	$71.50	12-1999
Heddon	Punkinseed	9630SD, NOT MET	NIB	$67.00	9-2000
Heddon	Punkinseed	9630SD, old plastic slide box	NIB	$153.00	7-2000
Heddon	Punkinseed	9630SD, S-rig, bell rig, rub	VG	$51.00	2-1999
Heddon	Punkinseed	9630SD, white eyes, PTCB	NIB	$77.00	10-2000
Heddon	Punkinseed	9630SD, yellow eyes	EX-	$53.68	1-1999
Heddon	Punkinseed	9630SD, yellow eyes, older	VG+	$75.00	3-1999
Heddon	Punkinseed	9630, shad?, grey scale, white, orange eyes	EX-	$810.00	4-1999
Heddon	Punkinseed	9630SSD	NOC	$75.00	5-1999
Heddon	Punkinseed	9630SSD, gold eyes, bell rig	EX-	$71.00	6-1999
Heddon	Punkinseed	9630SUN	EX-	$43.00	3-2001
Heddon	Punkinseed	9630SUN	NIB	$83.00	1-1999
Heddon	Punkinseed	9630SUN	NIB	$177.50	7-1999
Heddon	Punkinseed	9630SUN	VG	$45.50	2-1999
Heddon	Punkinseed	9630SUN Banner box	EX/IB	$127.29	12-1999
Heddon	Punkinseed	9630SUN Banner box	NIB	$136.00	2-2002
Heddon	Punkinseed	9630SUN Banner box	NIB	$147.00	1-1999
Heddon	Punkinseed	9630SUN Banner box	VG+/IB	$76.00	9-1999
Heddon	Punkinseed	9630SUN, bell rig, PTCB	NIB	$79.00	7-2000
Heddon	Punkinseed	9630SUN, gold eyes	EX+	$43.55	12-1999
Heddon	Punkinseed	9630SUN, gold eyes, Banner box	NIB	$102.00	10-2000
Heddon	Punkinseed	9630SUN, gold eyes, Banner box & papers	EX/IB	$85.00	12-2001
Heddon	Punkinseed	9630SUN, gold eyes, Banner box, catalog	NIB	$160.50	9-1999
Heddon	Punkinseed	9630SUN, gold eyes, PTCB	NIB	$104.52	4-1999
Heddon	Punkinseed	9630SUN. gold, window box?	NIB	$127.00	8-2000
Heddon	Punkinseed	9630SUN, NOT MET	NIB	$117.00	6-1999
Heddon	Punkinseed	9630SUN, S-rig, Banner box	NIB	$192.50	5-1999

BRAND	MODEL	SERIES / MFG. CODE / DESCRIPTION	GRADE	PRICE	DATE
Heddon	Punkinseed	9630SUN, S-rig, Banner box	VG/IB	$81.00	6-1999
Heddon	Punkinseed	9630SUN, white eye, bell rig	EX	$52.00	3-2000
Heddon	Punkinseed	9630XBW, gold, 2-piece, S-rig, Brush box	NIB	$333.88	8-1999
Heddon	Punkinseed	9630XBW, gold eyes	EX-	$54.00	8-2002
Heddon	Punkinseed	9630XBW, gold eyes, 2-piece	EX-	$67.00	4-2000
Heddon	Punkinseed	9630XBW, gold eyes, Banner box	NIB	$152.00	1-2002
Heddon	Punkinseed	9630XBW, gold eyes, extra holes		$53.00	4-1999
Heddon	Punkinseed	9630XBW, S-rig	EX	$147.50	6-1999
Heddon	Punkinseed	9630XRW	EX-	$86.85	1-1999
Heddon	Punkinseed	9630XRW	NIB	$203.51	5-1999
Heddon	Punkinseed	9630XRW, gold, 2-piece, catalog, Banner box	NIB	$360.01	5-1999
Heddon	Punkinseed	9630XRW, gold eyes, 2-piece, S-rig	EX	$330.00	4-2000
Heddon	Punkinseed	9630XRW, gold eyes, avg box	NIB	$318.50	3-2000
Heddon	Punkinseed	9630XRW, gold eyes, Banner box & papers	NIB	$192.00	1-2002
Heddon	Punkinseed	9630XRW, gold eyes, S-rig, bell rig	EX	$255.00	4-2000
Heddon	Punkinseed	9630XRW, gold eyes, S-rig, catalog	NIB	$360.01	5-1999
Heddon	Punkinseed	9630XRY	EX	$128.00	2-1999
Heddon	Punkinseed	9630XRY	NIB	$167.50	1-2000
Heddon	Punkinseed	9630XRY, 2 bell rig, PTCB	NIB	$82.50	12-1999
Heddon	Punkinseed	9630XRY, bell rig	Mint	$90.00	2-1999
Heddon	Punkinseed	9630XRY, cream eyes, bell rig, no seam	NIB	$125.56	3-1999
Heddon	Punkinseed	9630XRY, gold eyes	EX-/IB	$77.00	6-1999
Heddon	Punkinseed	9630XRY, gold eyes, S-rig	EX	$90.99	3-1999
Heddon	Punkinseed	9630XRY, white eyes, bell rig	NIB	$103.50	4-1999
Heddon	Punkinseed	9630XRY, white eyes, S-rig, bell rig	NIB	$200.00	6-2000
Heddon	Punkinseed	BGL, flyrod	EX+	$168.00	10-2000
Heddon	Punkinseed	BGL, flyrod	Mint	$367.00	6-1999
Heddon	Punkinseed	BGL, flyrod, 1-hook	EX	$214.00	10-2000
Heddon	Punkinseed	BGL, flyrod, 2 big pointers	VG	$114.00	4-2000
Heddon	Punkinseed	BGL, flyrod, treble hook	EX	$270.00	3-1999
Heddon	Punkinseed	BGL, flyrod, treble hook	Mint	$356.99	5-1999
Heddon	Punkinseed	brown shore, unique silver ribs	EX	$2,184.99	10-1999
Heddon	Punkinseed	coach dog	NIB	$430.00	2-2000
Heddon	Punkinseed	CRA, flyrod	EX	$231.38	1-2000
Heddon	Punkinseed	CRA, flyrod	EX	$256.00	5-1999
Heddon	Punkinseed	CRA, flyrod	EX-	$131.00	10-2000
Heddon	Punkinseed	CRA, flyrod, treble	EX+	$256.00	6-1999
Heddon	Punkinseed	CRA, flyrod, treble	EX-	$162.00	10-2000
Heddon	Punkinseed	CRA, flyrod, treble, NOT MET	EX	$187.50	5-1999
Heddon	Punkinseed	CRA, S-rig, bell rig	VG	$62.00	5-1999
Heddon	Punkinseed	early shad, 2-piece, 740SUN box	EX-/IB	$149.00	3-2001
Heddon	Punkinseed	flyrod, 980CRA, PTCB	NIB	$305.00	9-2001
Heddon	Punkinseed	flyrod, bluegill, ugly	AVG to Poor	$123.52	5-1999
Heddon	Punkinseed	flyrod, crappie, 3-hook	EX	$330.01	3-1999
Heddon	Punkinseed	flyrod, crappie, treble hook	EX	$195.00	11-2000
Heddon	Punkinseed	flyrod, rock bass	EX+	$257.00	2-2002
Heddon	Punkinseed	flyrod, rock bass?	EX	$260.99	6-1999

BRAND	MODEL	SERIES / MFG. CODE / DESCRIPTION	GRADE	PRICE	DATE
Heddon	Punkinseed	flyrod, shad	EX	$152.00	3-2002
Heddon	Punkinseed	flyrod, shad	EX	$159.00	4-2000
Heddon	Punkinseed	flyrod, shad	EX	$242.00	3-2002
Heddon	Punkinseed	flyrod, shad	EX	$265.00	8-1999
Heddon	Punkinseed	flyrod, shad	EX	$267.00	5-1999
Heddon	Punkinseed	flyrod, shad, NOT MET	EX-	$124.00	3-2000
Heddon	Punkinseed	flyrod, shad, one hook	EX	$310.00	3-1999
Heddon	Punkinseed	flyrod, shad, window box, NOT MET	NIB	$243.00	12-2000
Heddon	Punkinseed	flyrod, shad, worn box	NIB	$179.00	1-2001
Heddon	Punkinseed	flyrod, sunfish	NIB	$355.00	11-1999
Heddon	Punkinseed	flyrod, white shore, glass eyes, 1-hook	EX	$1,000.00	10-2000
Heddon	Punkinseed	flyrod, sunfish, treble, NOT MET	Mint	$159.00	1-2001
Heddon	Punkinseed	flyrod x5, easy colors, NOT MET	EX	$1,400.99	7-1999
Heddon	Punkinseed	gold, 2-piece, 9630XBW Banner box, papers	NIB	$293.01	12-1999
Heddon	Punkinseed	orange eyes, Banner box	NIB	$102.00	10-2000
Heddon	Punkinseed	red head, flitter, NOT MET	VG+	$355.00	10-2000
Heddon	Punkinseed	rock bass, floater, chin tie, NOT MET	EX	$167.00	6-2002
Heddon	Punkinseed	SD, flyrod	EX	$157.50	1-2000
Heddon	Punkinseed	SUN, flyrod	EX	$137.50	3-1999
Heddon	Punkinseed	SUN, flyrod	EX	$189.00	3-1999
Heddon	Punkinseed	SUN, flyrod, treble, puckered lip	EX-	$201.50	6-1999
Heddon	Punkinseed	two 380SUNs, gold eyes	Mint	$104.00	12-1999
Heddon	Punkinseed	two 730s, three 740s, all nice NOT MET	EX- to EX	$570.00	10-2001
Heddon	Punkinseed	two BGLs, white eyes	EX+	$103.51	10-1999
Heddon	Punkinseed	x2; one 380BGL, one 730CRA	EX	$159.06	4-1999
Heddon	Punkinseed	x2; one 740BGL, one 740ROC	VG+	$304.00	4-1999
Heddon	Punkinseed	x2; one 9630BGL, one 9630CRA	VG-	$63.00	1-1999
Heddon	Punkinseed	XRW, flyrod, beautiful, NOT MET	EX+	$810.00	12-2001
Heddon	Punkinseed	BGL, flyrod, "shiner scale," a joke	EX	$244.00	2-2002
Heddon	Punkinseed	BGL, flyrod, treble hook	EX	$260.00	3-2000
Heddon	Punkinseed	BGL, flyrod, treble hook	EX-	$260.55	2-2000
Heddon	Punkinseed	S-rig, mouth tie, XRY Brush box & catalog	NIB	$341.00	6-2002
Heddon	Punkinseed	SUN, flyrod, 3-hook, unmarked Brush box	NIB	$400.99	4-1999
Heddon	Punkinseed	XRW, flyrod, 1-hook, nice	EX	$721.00	11-2000
Heddon	Punkinseed, Floating	740CRA	EX	$160.00	8-2000
Heddon	Punkinseed, Floating	740BGL, POBW	EX	$160.00	8-2000
Heddon	Punkinseed, Tiny	6 different, gold eyes, no hardware	EX	$232.00	6-2002
Heddon	Punkinseed, Tiny	380BGL	NIB	$67.01	9-1999
Heddon	Punkinseed, Tiny	380CRA, gold eyes	NIB	$123.51	11-1999
Heddon	Punkinseed, Tiny	380SUN, gold eyes	NIB	$96.99	9-1999
Heddon	Punkinseed, Tiny	380XBW	NIB	$209.50	3-2000
Heddon	Punkinseed, Tiny	380XBW, gold eyes, PTCB	NIB	$180.00	12-2001
Heddon	Punkinseed, Tiny	380XRW, gold eyes	EX+	$257.00	9-1999
Heddon	Punkinseed, Tiny	380XRY	NIB	$99.99	3-1999
Heddon	Punkinseed, Tiny	380XRY	NIB	$117.50	8-1999
Heddon	Punkinseed, Tiny	BGL, gold eyes	EX	$66.00	9-2000
Heddon	Punkinseed, Tiny	blue scale, red spots	Mint	$385.00	8-2002

BRAND	MODEL	SERIES / MFG. CODE / DESCRIPTION	GRADE	PRICE	DATE
Heddon	Punkinseed, Tiny	chartreuse shore	Mint	$636.00	7-2002
Heddon	Punkinseed, Tiny	CRA, gold eyes	Mint	$71.00	4-2000
Heddon	Punkinseed, Tiny	CRA, white eyes, rusty hooks	Mint	$38.00	8-2002
Heddon	Punkinseed, Tiny	crappie, gold eyes	EX	$81.00	8-1999
Heddon	Punkinseed, Tiny	FLS, grey scale, black spot, silver eyes	NOC	$650.00	11-2000
Heddon	Punkinseed, Tiny	fluorescent, chartreuse	Mint	$671.00	8-2002
Heddon	Punkinseed, Tiny	golden shiner, no belly stencil, NOT MET	Mint	$2,385.00	3-2000
Heddon	Punkinseed, Tiny	GRA, NOT MET	EX-	$777.00	12-2000
Heddon	Punkinseed, Tiny	NPB, chrome	EX	$499.00	2-2000
Heddon	Punkinseed, Tiny	OGG, 1980s Japanese color	NOC	$660.00	2-2002
Heddon	Punkinseed, Tiny	OGG, hot chartreuse, gold ribs	NOC	$735.00	10-2001
Heddon	Punkinseed, Tiny	one each: 1BGL, 1SUN; white eyes	Mint	$132.51	9-1999
Heddon	Punkinseed, Tiny	OOG, chartreuse, gold ribs, NOT MET	EX	$305.00	3-2001
Heddon	Punkinseed, Tiny	SD, gold eyes	EX	$103.50	3-1999
Heddon	Punkinseed, Tiny	strawberry spots, gold eyes, small chips	EX-	$359.00	2-2002
Heddon	Punkinseed, Tiny	SUN, gold eyes	Mint	$50.00	3-2000
Heddon	Punkinseed, Tiny	SUN, white eyes , 3 bids over $70.00	Mint	$86.00	4-2000
Heddon	Punkinseed, Tiny	SUN, white eyes, 12 bids	EX	$117.50	11-1999
Heddon	Punkinseed, Tiny	XBW, gold eyes	EX	$148.00	9-2000
Heddon	Punkinseed, Tiny	yellow coach dog, gold eyes	EX	$517.00	10-2000
Heddon	River Runt	2-piece, 110GWH Brush box	EX/IB	$182.00	2-2002
Heddon	River Runt	2-piece, 119R Brush box, NOT MET	NIB	$164.00	10-2002
Heddon	River Runt	2-piece, small 110BWH Up Bass box	NIB	$360.00	3-2000
Heddon	River Runt	4 different Spook Glows, NOT MET	EX	$163.00	7-2000
Heddon	River Runt	4 different Spook Glows, one each: XGY, XLB, XOY, XYS	EX-	$151.00	9-2001
Heddon	River Runt	9 different, common, all with catalogs, nice	NIB	$362.00	8-1999
Heddon	River Runt	12-pack of all 4 Spook Glow colors	NIB	$2,778.00	1-2000
Heddon	River Runt	110, 2-piece, BW, NOT MET	EX+	$275.00	11-2000
Heddon	River Runt	110, black, 119G	EX-/IB	$202.00	10-2000
Heddon	River Runt	110, dace, glass eyes, 2-piece	VG to EX	$134.09	5-1999
Heddon	River Runt	110, dace, glass eyes, 2-piece	VG+	$52.00	1-2000
Heddon	River Runt	110, dace, L-rig, heavy crazing, NOT MET	VG+	$66.00	3-2000
Heddon	River Runt	110, glass eyes, 2-piece, L-rig, NOT MET	VG	$59.00	5-2000
Heddon	River Runt	110, glass eyes, L-rig, decent	VG+	$62.00	6-1999
Heddon	River Runt	110, glass eyes, small eye crack, 2-piece, L-rig	EX+	$147.50	5-1999
Heddon	River Runt	110, green scale, glass eyes	EX	$158.56	10-1999
Heddon	River Runt	110, natural scale, 2-piece	Mint	$261.00	4-2000
Heddon	River Runt	110, L-rig, 119L Up Bass box	VG/IB	$301.00	7-2001
Heddon	River Runt	110, natural scale, 2-piece, NOT MET	EX-	$75.99	3-2000
Heddon	River Runt	110, natural scale, glass eyes, one eye cracked	VG	$63.00	8-1999
Heddon	River Runt	110, perch scale	EX+	$165.00	5-2000
Heddon	River Runt	110, perch, glass eyes	Mint	$182.49	2-1999
Heddon	River Runt	110, rainbow, 2-piece, small #111 Up Bass box	NIB	$227.50	3-2000
Heddon	River Runt	110, rainbow, glass eyes	VG+	$381.00	4-1999
Heddon	River Runt	110, red, glass eyes	EX+	$430.33	2-2000

BRAND	MODEL	SERIES / MFG. CODE / DESCRIPTION	GRADE	PRICE	DATE
Heddon	River Runt	110, red head, glass eyes, 2-piece, poor box	EX/IB	$104.00	5-1999
Heddon	River Runt	110, red head, silver flakes, glass eyes	EX	$110.00	12-1998
Heddon	River Runt	110, red head, silver flitter, glass eyes	Mint	$139.88	6-1999
Heddon	River Runt	110, shiner scale, glass eyes	VG+	$56.00	10-2000
Heddon	River Runt	110, silver herring, glass eyes	Mint	$700.00	2-2000
Heddon	River Runt	110, white, black, glass eyes, 2-piece, NOT MET	VG-	$76.00	5-1999
Heddon	River Runt	110, shiner scale	Mint	$137.50	2-2000
Heddon	River Runt	110P, glass eyes, L-rig, ugly age lines	VG+	$125.00	5-2000
Heddon	River Runt	111, rainbow, glass eyes, 2-piece, Up Bass box	EX/IB	$300.00	10-1999
Heddon	River Runt	112 Brush box	EX-/IB	$91.00	3-2000
Heddon	River Runt	112, small Down Bass box	NIB	$203.25	2-2000
Heddon	River Runt	119N, dace, 2-piece, Up Bass box	EX/IB	$171.00	11-2000
Heddon	River Runt	119L, name on box	EX	$160.00	10-1999
Heddon	River Runt	119M, 2-piece	EX	$87.00	11-2000
Heddon	River Runt	119N, 2-piece, Brush box, NOT MET	NIB	$228.00	9-2000
Heddon	River Runt	119R, 2-piece, Brush box	EX-/IB	$150.00	11-2000
Heddon	River Runt	119R, glass eyes, Up Bass box	NIB	$390.00	5-2000
Heddon	River Runt	9010SFR	NIB	$51.01	7-1999
Heddon	River Runt	9010XBL, white eyes, Daisy box	NIB	$98.50	5-1999
Heddon	River Runt	9010XGF, white eyes, Daisy box	NIB	$48.02	5-1999
Heddon	River Runt	9110, rainbow	NIB	$39.00	3-1999
Heddon	River Runt	9110, red head, S-rig	NIB	$38.00	3-2001
Heddon	River Runt	9110SGXGY, crackleback, black, red	NIB (1/3)	$130.16	6-1999
Heddon	River Runt	9110SGXYS	EX-/IB	$74.00	1-2002
Heddon	River Runt	9110SRXBY, papers	NIB	$129.49	12-1999
Heddon	River Runt	9110SRXLB, nice box	EX/IB	$76.00	8-2001
Heddon	River Runt	9110XRG, gold eyes, papers	NIB	$25.57	8-1999
Heddon	River Runt	9112 Brush box	NIB	$29.51	2-2000
Heddon	River Runt	9119GWH, black, white, nice box	VG-/IB	$115.91	12-1999
Heddon	River Runt	9119L, perch scale, glass eyes, Up Bass box	EX/IB	$152.50	4-1999
Heddon	River Runt	9119XRS, Brush box	EX-	$43.52	5-1999
Heddon	River Runt	9400WL, Centennial	NIB	$36.00	3-1999
Heddon	River Runt	9430L, jointed	NIB	$36.00	4-1999
Heddon	River Runt	BRS, yellow eyes	EX	$58.00	7-2000
Heddon	River Runt	FF9010GB	NIB	$68.00	10-2000
Heddon	River Runt	luminous, fat black ribs, 9119XBW box, blistered		$290.00	1-2002
Heddon	River Runt	OS, 6 red, silver, black, silver	EX	$164.50	2-1999
Heddon	River Runt	rainbow, 2-piece	EX-	$52.51	6-1999
Heddon	River Runt	SS, 2 red & white flitters	EX-	$21.00	1-1999
Heddon	River Runt	XRG, XRW Brush box	EX	$16.00	1-1999
Heddon	River Runt	XRY, teddy bear eyes, string	EX	$228.50	1-2000
Heddon	River Runt	baby bass, white eyes	EX	$30.00	10-2001
Heddon	River Runt	black, 2 piccc, NOT MET		$76.00	5-1999
Heddon	River Runt	black, gold eyes, 2-piece	EX	$129.00	4-2000
Heddon	River Runt	clear plum, black ribs	EX	$59.00	7-2000

BRAND	MODEL	SERIES / MFG. CODE / DESCRIPTION	GRADE	PRICE	DATE
Heddon	River Runt	dace, painted eyes, POBW, wood	VG+	$86.00	5-1999
Heddon	River Runt	natural, photo, gold, green, orange, gold eyes	EX	$75.00	4-2001
Heddon	River Runt	one each: 9400P, 9400SD, 9400RH, 9400M	EX/IB	$103.55	1-1999
Heddon	River Runt	one each: BHWS, XRY 2-piece, XRS 2-piece	NIB	$89.00	2-1999
Heddon	River Runt	one each: flitter, snaker, midget, all 2-piece	EX	$48.00	2-1999
Heddon	River Runt	perch, glass eyes	EX	$149.00	1-1999
Heddon	River Runt	red, gold foil	VG	$32.00	4-2000
Heddon	River Runt	shiner scale, 2-piece	Mint	$128.50	3-2000
Heddon	River Runt	Spook Glow orange, yellow ribs	Mint	$72.00	8-2000
Heddon	River Runt	Spook Ray red, black ribs, gold eyes	EX	$72.00	6-2000
Heddon	River Runt	Waterwave R&W, Everlasting	EX+	$300.00	12-2001
Heddon	River Runt	x3, P, jointed red-head, red-head	NIB	$62.00	2-1999
Heddon	River Runt	XBW, deep m, deep jointed	NIB	$98.00	2-1999
Heddon	River Runt, Floating	BF, white eyes	EX	$46.00	3-2001
Heddon	River Runt, Floating	BF, white eyes	EX	$53.01	3-1999
Heddon	River Runt, Floating	black, 2-piece, NOT MET	Mint	$56.00	6-1999
Heddon	River Runt, Floating	CD, chartreuse, silver, NOT MET	EX	$178.00	9-2000
Heddon	River Runt, Floating	dace, 2-piece	EX	$35.00	2-2001
Heddon	River Runt, Floating	dace, 2-piece, rusty	EX-	$86.52	8-1999
Heddon	River Runt, Floating	dace, jointed, 2-piece	EX-	$65.00	7-2002
Heddon	River Runt, Floating	FFGB	Mint	$54.00	7-2002
Heddon	River Runt, Floating	FFGR	Mint	$77.00	7-2002
Heddon	River Runt, Floating	FFRG, no-lip	EX	$104.50	4-1999
Heddon	River Runt, Floating	FFSB	Mint	$43.00	7-2002
Heddon	River Runt, Floating	FFSR	Mint	$54.00	7-2002
Heddon	River Runt, Floating	frog, yellow belly, white eyes, Pradco?	EX	$86.00	4-2000
Heddon	River Runt, Floating	golden shiner, Banner box	NIB	$104.25	2-1999
Heddon	River Runt, Floating	GW, puckered	Poor	$46.00	11-1999
Heddon	River Runt, Floating	jointed, POBW, box	EXIB	$51.01	3-1999
Heddon	River Runt, Floating	pearl shore, jointed, box, catalog	NIB	$46.50	1-1999
Heddon	River Runt, Floating	pink shore, white eyes	EX	$7.50	1-1999
Heddon	River Runt, Floating	red eyes & tail, luminous?, 2-piece, blister	VG+	$76.00	7-2002
Heddon	River Runt, Floating	red head, gold eyes, jointed, Banner box, NOT MET	NIB	$29.09	9-1999
Heddon	River Runt, Floating	red nose, silver tail, stripes, sparkles, NOT MET		$55.00	7-2000
Heddon	River Runt, Floating	red, silver scale, silver flitter inside	EX	$102.50	8-1999
Heddon	River Runt, Floating	red water wave, everlasting color	EX	$315.00	6-1999
Heddon	River Runt, Floating	red, white, everlasting color, 2-piece	VG	$177.00	6-2001
Heddon	River Runt, Floating	red, white, gold eyes, jointed	EX	$29.00	5-1999
Heddon	River Runt, Floating	red, white, marble, 2-piece, sunken eyes	EX+	$212.50	8-1999
Heddon	River Runt, Floating	silver glitter liner, red head & tail	EX	$76.00	3-1999
Heddon	River Runt, Floating	silver scale, gold eyes, jointed, 2-piece?	EX-	$133.81	3-2000
Heddon	River Runt, Floating	silver scale, jointed	EX-	$133.81	3-2000
Heddon	River Runt, Floating	BRS, white eye	EX	$33.50	6-1999
Heddon	River Runt, Floating	GFS, 2-piece, stripe	EX+	$57.00	10-2000
Heddon	River Runt, Floating	rainbow, 2-piece, Brush box	NIB	$60.00	8-1999
Heddon	River Runt, Floating	SP, no-lip, red, gold, NOT MET	EX	$163.16	3-1999

BRAND	MODEL	SERIES / MFG. CODE / DESCRIPTION	GRADE	PRICE	DATE
Heddon	River Runt, Floating	XRW, jointed	VG+	$24.50	2-1999
Heddon	River Runt, Floating	XRY	EX	$14.49	1-1999
Heddon	River Runt, Floating	XRY, gold eyes, jointed	EX-	$26.65	5-1999
Heddon	River Runt, Floating	XRY, gold eyes, jointed, Banner box	NIB	$39.99	9-1999
Heddon	River Runt, Floating	XRY, green & black triangle box	NIB	$11.01	6-1999
Heddon	River Runt, Floating	XRY, white eyes, b&g box	NIB	$11.01	7-1999
Heddon	River Runt, Floating	XRY, red belly stencil, 2-piece	VG+	$44.00	7-2002
Heddon	River Runt, Floating Spook	9400GR, C0, ½ oz.	NIB	$50.00	1-2002
Heddon	River Runt, Floating Spook	9400RB	VG/IB	$40.00	10-1999
Heddon	River Runt, Floating Spook	9400RB Banner box	NIB	$31.50	9-1999
Heddon	River Runt, Floating Spook	9400RH Runt box	NIB	$37.55	9-1999
Heddon	River Runt, Floating Spook	9400SRXRW, pink shore	NIB	$51.00	5-1999
Heddon	River Runt, Floating Spook	9409XRS Brush box	EX/IB	$32.00	2-1999
Heddon	River Runt, Floating Spook	9400XRW, S-rig, gold eye	NIB	$35.00	4-2001
Heddon	River Runt, Floating Spook	9409XRY, 2-piece	NIB	$41.00	5-2001
Heddon	River Runt, Floating Spook	9400XRY, 2-piece, catalog	NIB	$42.00	7-2002
Heddon	River Runt, Floating Spook	9409XRY Brush box, 2-piece	EX/IB	$17.30	2-2000
Heddon	River Runt, Floating Spook	9430XRY, jointed	NIB	$32.00	3-2002
Heddon	River Runt, Floating Spook	E9400RW, waterwave, catalog	NIB	$325.00	10-2002
Heddon	River Runt, Floating Spook	jointed, S-rig, newer, ex 9439XRG Brush box	NIB	$47.00	7-2002
Heddon	River Runt, Floating Spook	poor blistered 9409XWB box, NOT MET	VG/IB?	$148.00	8-2002
Heddon	River Runt, Go-Deeper	9XYB, scoop lip	EX-	$463.00	7-2002
Heddon	River Runt, Go-Deeper	black, white ribs, square lip	Mint	$30.00	1-1999
Heddon	River Runt, Go-Deeper	D9010SRXCW	NIB	$207.00	2-2002
Heddon	River Runt, Go-Deeper	GFRD9010, NOT MET	NIB	$74.00	7-2001
Heddon	River Runt, Go-Deeper	orange crackleback, modern lip	EX	$37.00	5-2000
Heddon	River Runt, Go-Deeper	RBXRS, m flitter	NIB	$105.00	2-1999
Heddon	River Runt, Go-Deeper	red head, gold eyes, step lip, Banner box	NIB	$39.99	9-1999
Heddon	River Runt, Go-Deeper	red head, white flitter, square lip	EX	$51.00	1-1999
Heddon	River Runt, Go-Deeper	red, silver foil	EX	$41.15	5-1999
Heddon	River Runt, Go-Deeper	SGOY, stair	EX	$46.00	6-1999
Heddon	River Runt, Go-Deeper	strawberry, 2-piece, scoop lip, sunken eyes	EX+	$203.50	8-1999
Heddon	River Runt, Go-Deeper	strawberry spots, square lip	VG+	$29.50	1-1999
Heddon	River Runt, Go-Deeper	XGF in 9119GW brush box	NIB	$134.00	2-2002
Heddon	River Runt, Go-Deeper	XRS, scoop lip, wrong 9010P box	EXIB	$20.50	2-1999
Heddon	River Runt, Go-Deeper	XRY, scoop lip	Mint	$21.00	8-1999
Heddon	River Runt, Go-Deeper	yellow coach dog, angle lip, NOT MET	EX	$22.50	1-1999
Heddon	River Runt, Midget	2 different, goldfish, pearl	EX	$105.01	8-1999
Heddon	River Runt, Midget	9010GCB, gold eyes, Banner box	NIB	$237.00	9-2000
Heddon	River Runt, Midget	9010P, 9010P Banner Box	NIB	$37.00	1-1999
Heddon	River Runt, Midget	9019XBW, 2-piece, catalog	NIB	$47.00	7-2002
Heddon	River Runt, Midget	black, 2-piece?, NOT MET		$28.27	5-1999
Heddon	River Runt, Midget	black, gold eyes, S-rig	EX	$24.99	2-1999
Heddon	River Runt, Midget	black, gold foil, NOT MET	EX	$43.09	6 1999
Heddon	River Runt, Midget	black, gold reflector	VG	$30.00	9-1999
Heddon	River Runt, Midget	black, silver foil, NOT MET	EX	$27.17	7-1999
Heddon	River Runt, Midget	early silver herring	EX	$155.00	1-2001

BRAND	MODEL	SERIES / MFG. CODE / DESCRIPTION	GRADE	PRICE	DATE
Heddon	River Runt, Midget	FF9010GB, Mahinske, NOT MET	NIB	$46.00	8-1999
Heddon	River Runt, Midget	FF9010SR, Mahinske, NOT MET	NIB	$61.00	8-1999
Heddon	River Runt, Midget	golden shiner, unmarked box	EX-/IB	$46.00	4-2000
Heddon	River Runt, Midget	goldfish?, S-rig, newer, Jacomet seller	EX	$68.00	10-1999
Heddon	River Runt, Midget	orange crackleback, white eyes, NOT MET	EX	$36.66	8-1999
Heddon	River Runt, Midget	pearl, gold eyes	EX	$41.00	6-1999
Heddon	River Runt, Midget	rainbow, gold eyes	EX	$31.01	6-1999
Heddon	River Runt, Midget	red, silver foil, NOT MET	EX	$66.00	6-1999
Heddon	River Runt, Midget	silver herring	EX-	$99.00	3-1999
Heddon	River Runt, Midget	silver herring, 2-piece, early, nice	Mint	$112.00	8-2002
Heddon	River Runt, Midget	SRBW, yellow ribs, NOT MET	NIB	$35.00	2-1999
Heddon	River Runt, Midget	strawberry, gold eyes, chips	AVG	$24.50	1-1999
Heddon	River Runt, Midget	white, gold eyes, poor box, 18 bids	EX	$229.00	7-2000
Heddon	River Runt, Midget	XRY, gold eyes	EX-	$12.00	1-1999
Heddon	River Runt, Midget Go-Deeper	D9010, red, silver glitter, stair lip	EX	$104.50	9-1999
Heddon	River Runt, Midget Go-Deeper	D9010SFB, stair lip	EX	$58.00	9-1999
Heddon	River Runt, Midget Go-Deeper	D9110SP, red, silver, silver sparkles	NIB	$113.00	7-2000
Heddon	River Runt, Midget Go-Deeper	D9010SRXBY	EXIB	$42.00	10-2000
Heddon	River Runt, Midget Go-Deeper	FFSB	EX	$49.99	4-1999
Heddon	River Runt, Midget Go-Deeper	XRG, scoop lip	Mint	$42.99	1-1999
Heddon	River Runt, No-Snag		EX	$127.50	1-1999
Heddon	River Runt, No-Snag	9XGF, 2-piece	EX	$57.00	7-2002
Heddon	River Runt, No-Snag	9119XGF	NIB	$182.00	10-2000
Heddon	River Runt, No-Snag	avg D9119L Brush box	NIB	$52.00	7-2002
Heddon	River Runt, No-Snag	D9119RH, flitter, ex Brush box	NIB	$152.00	7-2002
Heddon	River Runt, No-Snag	dace	EX	$56.55	2-2000
Heddon	River Runt, No-Snag	dace	Mint	$104.01	10-1999
Heddon	River Runt, No-Snag	dace	NIB	$177.50	3-2000
Heddon	River Runt, No-Snag	ex D9119XRY Brush box & paper	NIB	$64.00	7-2002
Heddon	River Runt, No-Snag	ex N9112 box, papers, catalog	NIB	$95.00	5-2000
Heddon	River Runt, No-Snag	GFS, NOT MET	EX	$66.00	2-2001
Heddon	River Runt, No-Snag	goldfish shore	EX	$135.00	8-2000
Heddon	River Runt, No-Snag	green scale	EX-	$293.00	7-2002
Heddon	River Runt, No-Snag	(M) pike scale, wrong box	EX	$52.00	4-2000
Heddon	River Runt, No-Snag	N9110, dace	NIB	$202.50	10-1999
Heddon	River Runt, No-Snag	N9110S, no hook guards	NIB	$384.00	6-2001
Heddon	River Runt, No-Snag	N9119P	EX/IB	$74.00	5-2000
Heddon	River Runt, No-Snag	N9119R	NIB	$123.00	7-2000
Heddon	River Runt, No-Snag	N9119XGF, papers	EX/IB	$112.50	5-1999
Heddon	River Runt, No-Snag	N9119XGF, papers, crisp	NIB	$178.00	8-2001
Heddon	River Runt, No-Snag	N9110XRG	EX/IB	$37.00	5-2000
Heddon	River Runt, No-Snag	N9119XRS	NIB	$57.00	6-1999
Heddon	River Runt, No-Snag	natural or pike?	EX	$93.92	2-1999
Heddon	River Runt, No-Snag	natural scale, light rust	EX-	$83.00	10-2000
Heddon	River Runt, No-Snag	PAS	EX-	$585.00	3-2002
Heddon	River Runt, No-Snag	perch scale	EX	$31.00	3-2000
Heddon	River Runt, No-Snag	perch, N9119P box	VG/IB	$49.99	5-1999

BRAND	MODEL	SERIES / MFG. CODE / DESCRIPTION	GRADE	PRICE	DATE
Heddon	River Runt, No-Snag	red head, flitter	EX	$71.00	3-2001
Heddon	River Runt, No-Snag	red head, flitter	EX	$118.60	2-2000
Heddon	River Runt, No-Snag	red head, white glitter	EX	$93.00	4-2000
Heddon	River Runt, No-Snag	shiner scale	EX	$37.50	1-1999
Heddon	River Runt, No-Snag	shiner scale	EX	$77.99	2-2000
Heddon	River Runt, No-Snag	shiner scale	Rough	$20.00	8-2002
Heddon	River Runt, No-Snag	white	EX	$261.51	3-2000
Heddon	River Runt, No-Snag	XBW	EX	$45.00	5-2000
Heddon	River Runt, No-Snag	XBW	EXIB	$40.00	4-1999
Heddon	River Runt, No-Snag	XBW, nice Brush box	NIB	$95.50	8-1999
Heddon	River Runt, No-Snag	XBX, nice box, catalog & No-Snag paper	EXIB	$51.00	5-2002
Heddon	River Runt, No-Snag	XGF	EX-	$66.00	1-1999
Heddon	River Runt, No-Snag	XGF	VG	$76.00	12-1998
Heddon	River Runt, No-Snag	XGF, closed guard	EX	$65.01	6-1999
Heddon	River Runt, No-Snag	XGF, closed guard	EX	$73.75	6-1999
Heddon	River Runt, No-Snag	XRG	Mint	$43.75	3-1999
Heddon	River Runt, No-Snag	XRS	Mint	$49.99	6-1999
Heddon	River Runt, No-Snag	XRS, Brush box	EX/IB	$76.33	3-2000
Heddon	River Runt, No-Snag	XRY	EX	$50.00	3-1999
Heddon	River Runt, No-Snag	XRY	EX-	$31.50	8-1999
Heddon	River Runt, No-Snag	XRY	Rough	$21.00	8-2002
Heddon	River Runt, No-Snag	XRY	VG	$36.00	1-1999
Heddon	River Runt, No-Snag	XRY, Brush box	EX/IB	$56.33	3-2000
Heddon	River Runt, No-Snag	XRS, $75.00 NOT MET	NIB	$41.00	6-2001
Heddon	River Runt, No-Snag	XRS, small closed guard	EX	$41.00	3-2000
Heddon	River Runt, Salmon	8859XRX, white shore?, teddy bear eyes	NIB	$615.00	2-2002
Heddon	River Runt, Salmon	red head, spots, 2-piece, 8859SPRH Brush box	NIB	$1,393.00	9-2000
Heddon	River Runt, Salmon	shiner scale, tack bead eyes, NOT MET	NIB	$331.00	3-2001
Heddon	River Runt, Salmon	XRW, glass eyes, teddy bear eyes	VG+	$150.00	9-1999
Heddon	River Runt, Sinking	9XBW, 2-piece	NIB	$47.00	7-2002
Heddon	River Runt, Sinking	9XRG	Mint	$41.00	7-2002
Heddon	River Runt, Sinking	9XRS, 2-piece	NIB	$47.00	7-2002
Heddon	River Runt, Sinking	9XRSXL, early type, narrow lip	VG	$30.00	7-2002
Heddon	River Runt, Sinking	9010BHY, Daisy box	NIB	$49.99	3-1999
Heddon	River Runt, Sinking	9010GFR	EX	$31.00	9-1999
Heddon	River Runt, Sinking	9010GFR	VG-	$22.01	9-1999
Heddon	River Runt, Sinking	9010M, 2-piece, catalog	NIB	$40.00	7-2002
Heddon	River Runt, Sinking	9010S, S-rig, crisp catalog, hang tag	NIB	$78.00	4-2000
Heddon	River Runt, Sinking	9010SEXBY, black, white, yellow ribs	NIB	$56.200	12-1998
Heddon	River Runt, Sinking	9110L, gold eyes	NIB	$35.99	7-1999
Heddon	River Runt, Sinking	9110, red head, 2-piece	EXIB	$35.00	2-1999
Heddon	River Runt, Sinking	9110SGXGY	EX	$100.00	8-1999
Heddon	River Runt, Sinking	9110SP, red, silver flitter inside	NIB	$168.00	12-1998
Heddon	River Runt, Sinking	9019XBY, 2-piece, paper	NIB	$43.00	7-2002
Heddon	River Runt, Sinking	9119XRG, Brush box	EXIB	$45.01	2-1999
Heddon	River Runt, Sinking	9110XRW	EXIB	$15.50	12-1998
Heddon	River Runt, Sinking	9110XRY, gold eyes	NIB	$25.00	7-1999

BRAND	MODEL	SERIES / MFG. CODE / DESCRIPTION	GRADE	PRICE	DATE
Heddon	River Runt, Sinking	9330, red head, jointed	NIB	$46.00	7-1999
Heddon	River Runt, Sinking	9330RHF, silver scale, jointed	NIB	$151.00	10-2000
Heddon	River Runt, Sinking	9330XRY, jointed	NIB	$29.00	3-2002
Heddon	River Runt, Sinking	9430XRS, jointed	NIB	$61.00	3-2001
Heddon	River Runt, Sinking	black, silver foil	EX-	$46.26	2-2000
Heddon	River Runt, Sinking	black, silver reflector, box	NIB	$40.00	1-1999
Heddon	River Runt, Sinking	black, white ribs, Runt box	EX	$31.50	1-1999
Heddon	River Runt, Sinking	blue shore, white eyes, window box	NIB	$90.99	12-1999
Heddon	River Runt, Sinking	CBO, white eyes, NOT MET	EX-	$31.99	3-1999
Heddon	River Runt, Sinking	clear, orange spots	EX	$225.00	6-1999
Heddon	River Runt, Sinking	FF9010GFYBS	EX-	$145.00	3-2002
Heddon	River Runt, Sinking	FFGB	Mint	$67.00	7-2002
Heddon	River Runt, Sinking	FFGR	Mint	$78.00	7-2002
Heddon	River Runt, Sinking	FFRGF, red, gold foil	EX-	$24.00	8-2002
Heddon	River Runt, Sinking	FFSB	Mint	$67.00	7-2002
Heddon	River Runt, Sinking	FFSR	Mint	$63.00	7-2002
Heddon	River Runt, Sinking	glow worm, 2-piece	EX	$150.00	6-1999
Heddon	River Runt, Sinking	green scale, gold eyes	EX	$202.00	10-2000
Heddon	River Runt, Sinking	GW, no picture	Mint	$127.50	2-2000
Heddon	River Runt, Sinking	jointed, 9330L Banner box, NOT MET	NIB	$29.00	10-2000
Heddon	River Runt, Sinking	luminous, bad bubbling	Poor	$152.00	7-2000
Heddon	River Runt, Sinking	neon green shore	EX-	$41.00	1-1999
Heddon	River Runt, Sinking	OCB, $20.00 postage	EX+	$32.00	4-2000
Heddon	River Runt, Sinking	orange crackleback, white eyes	EX	$35.13	3-2000
Heddon	River Runt, Sinking	orange crackleback, white eyes	EX	$46.01	6-1999
Heddon	River Runt, Sinking	orange crackleback, white eyes, NOT MET	EX	$46.51	8-1999
Heddon	River Runt, Sinking	pearl, gold eyes	EX	$53.52	5-1999
Heddon	River Runt, Sinking	pike scale, 2-piece	NIB	$40.00	7-2002
Heddon	River Runt, Sinking	pink shore in 9400SP box	EX	$67.00	7-2000
Heddon	River Runt, Sinking	red head	NIB	$24.50	3-1999
Heddon	River Runt, Sinking	red, black, Spook Glow, white eyes	EX	$50.00	2-1999
Heddon	River Runt, Sinking	red, clear, silver flitter, insert, NOT MET	EX	$65.50	5-1999
Heddon	River Runt, Sinking	red, gold foil	Mint	$41.00	11-2000
Heddon	River Runt, Sinking	red, white waterwave	EX-	$256.75	8-1999
Heddon	River Runt, Sinking	SG, red, black ribs	EX	$51.00	3-2000
Heddon	River Runt, Sinking	SGRB	EX	$79.00	2-1999
Heddon	River Runt, Sinking	SGXOY	EX	$60.00	3-1999
Heddon	River Runt, Sinking	SGXRO, NOT MET	EX	$41.00	3-1999
Heddon	River Runt, Sinking	SGXRO, NOT MET	EX	$42.00	2-1999
Heddon	River Runt, Sinking	SGXYS	NIB	$74.00	7-2002
Heddon	River Runt, Sinking	Spook Glow green, yellow ribs	EX	$56.00	10-2001
Heddon	River Runt, Sinking	Spook Ray red, orange, black ribs	EX	$65.00	12-1998
Heddon	River Runt, Sinking	spots, pearl, 9110RB box	EX	$179.51	4-1999
Heddon	River Runt, Sinking	strawberry, gold eyes, catalog	NIB	$117.50	7-1999
Heddon	River Runt, Sinking	strawberry, gold eyes, jointed, S-rig	EX	$190.00	3-2000
Heddon	River Runt, Sinking	strawberry, gold eyes, S-rig	EX	$51.06	5-1999
Heddon	River Runt, Sinking	transparent white, black spots, silver foil	EX-	$80.00	7-2000

BRAND	MODEL	SERIES / MFG. CODE / DESCRIPTION	GRADE	PRICE	DATE
Heddon	River Runt, Sinking	XBW	NIB	$31.00	7-2002
Heddon	River Runt, Sinking	XRS	NIB	$26.00	7-2002
Heddon	River Runt, Sinking	XRS, gold eyes, jointed, Banner box, NOT MET	NIB	$26.00	9-1999
Heddon	River Runt, Sinking	XRS, jointed, Banner box	NIB	$26.50	1-1999
Heddon	River Runt, Sinking	XRY, gold eyes	EX-	$10.00	1-1999
Heddon	River Runt, Sinking Go-Deeper	gold eyes, stair	NIB	$42.00	12-1998
Heddon	River Runt Spook	E9400RW, everlasting red, white Waterwave	EX	$199.00	2-2002
Heddon	River Runt Spook	silver	EX	$81.00	4-1999
Heddon	River Runt Spook, Go-Deeper	D9110RH, gold eye, square lip	NIB	$35.00	2-1999
Heddon	River Runt Spook, Go-Deeper	D9110SRXRW, crisp	NIB	$63.00	10-2001
Heddon	River Runt Spook, Go-Deeper	D9110XBW	EX/IB	$25.06	7-1999
Heddon	River Runt Spook, Go-Deeper	D9110XBW, banner box	NIB	$45.00	1-1999
Heddon	River Runt Spook, Go-Deeper	D9110XBW, papers	NIB	$103.51	2-2000
Heddon	River Runt Spook, Go-Deeper	D9119GWH, black, white, puckered, nice box	AVG/IB	$113.61	12-1999
Heddon	River Runt Spook, Go-Deeper	D9119XRY, scoop lip, 9119XRY Brush	NIB	$66.50	9-1999
Heddon	River Runt Spook, Go-Deeper	D9119XRY, scoop lip, catalog	EX/IB	$47.00	7-2002
Heddon	River Runt Spook, Go-Deeper	DD9400BRS, brown crawdad, red angle lip	NIB	$50.00	2-1999
Heddon	River Runt Spook, Go-Deeper	DD9400CBO	NIB	$56.75	3-1999
Heddon	River Runt Spook, Go-Deeper	D9430M, jointed	NIB	$37.00	5-1999
Heddon	River Runt Spook, Midget	goldfish scale, tan stripe, gold eyes, NOT MET	Mint	$181.00	12-2001
Heddon	River Runt Spook, Sinking	crackleback, gold eyes	EX	$102.00	10-2001
Heddon	River Runt Spook, Sinking	XBW, correct box	EX	$26.00	1-1999
Heddon	River Runt, Tiny	353SDN, natural shad	NIB	$27.00	12-1998
Heddon	River Runt, Tiny	353SUC, natural sucker	NIB	$67.00	1-1999
Heddon	River Runt, Tiny	black, silver foil, glass eyes	EX	$77.51	2-2000
Heddon	River Runt, Tiny	black, silver foil, glass eyes	EX	$77.99	2-2000
Heddon	River Runt, Tiny	natural shad	NIB	$27.55	2-1999
Heddon	River Runt, Tiny	PTCB	NIB	$16.50	1-1999
Heddon	River Runt, Tiny	XBW	Mint	$98.00	8-2002
Heddon	River Runt, Tiny Go-Deeper	black, silver foil, glass eyes	EX	$80.99	2-2000
Heddon	Runtie	950XRS, OCIB	NIB	$141.00	1-2002
Heddon	Runtie	flyrod	EX+	$69.00	1-1999
Heddon	Runtie	flyrod, dace	EX	$71.01	6-1999
Heddon	Runtie	flyrod, red head	EX	$96.00	3-2002
Heddon	Runtie	flyrod, shiner scale, a little wrinkly	EX-	$76.00	3-2002
Heddon	Runtie	flyrod, wood, NOT MET	EX	$266.00	6-2000
Heddon	Runtie	one each: flyrod, shiner scale XRW; 8859XRX Brush box	EX	$115.00	1-2002
Heddon	Runtie	red head, white	EX	$56.00	4-1999
Heddon	Runtie	shiner scale, wood	VG	$222.50	7-1999
Heddon	Runtie	XRG, flyrod	EX	$122.51	1-2000
Heddon	Runtie	XRG, flyrod, NOT MET	Mint	$109.50	6-1999
Heddon	Runtie Spook	flyrod, 950XBW gold stencil	EX	$404.00	1-2002
Heddon	Runtie Spook	red head, NOT MET	EX	$76.50	7-1999
Heddon	Runtie Spook	shiner scale	EX-	$51.99	9-1999
Heddon	Runtie Spook	XRG	Mint	$107.49	7-1999

BRAND	MODEL	SERIES / MFG. CODE / DESCRIPTION	GRADE	PRICE	DATE
Heddon	Runtie Spook	XRS	EX	$66.00	1-2000
Heddon	Runtie Spook	yellow	EX	$162.00	5-2000
Heddon	Shark Mouth Minnow	red head flitter, cast aluminum?	EX	$513.00	10-2001
Heddon	Saltwater Special	600, 3⅜", red head, glass eyes	EX	$120.50	3-2000
Heddon	Saltwater Special	red head flitter	EX	$325.00	5-2000
Heddon	Scissortail		VG	$28.00	2-1999
Heddon	Scissortail	3 different	EX	$89.88	4-1999
Heddon	Scissortail	9830P, Banner box	NIB	$57.00	3-1999
Heddon	Scissortail	9830XBW	NIB	$39.80	2-1999
Heddon	Scissortail	one each: M, XRS, red head; all ex	EX	$64.66	4-2000
Heddon	Scissortail	OS, catalog	NIB	$71.00	10-2001
Heddon	Scissortail	pike scale	EX	$27.00	8-2001
Heddon	Scissortail	red, white	EX	$23.35	5-1999
Heddon	Scissortail	shiner scale, missing hook	EX	$21.01	2-1999
Heddon	Scissortail	XRY	EX	$61.00	10-1999
Heddon	Sea Runt	YRH, painted eyes	Mint	$43.00	7-2002
Heddon	Shrimpy Spook	½ whiskers	EX	$290.00	8-1999
Heddon	Shrimpy Spook	9009NS Up Bass box	EX/IB	$250.00	10-2000
Heddon	Shrimpy Spook	natural shrimp	EX+	$350.00	7-2001
Heddon	Shrimpy Spook	nice	EX	$300.00	4-1999
Heddon	Shrimpy Spook	NOT MET	EX-	$149.00	9-2000
Heddon	Shrimpy Spook	red, white flitter, st. tail	EX	$305.00	3-1999
Heddon	Shrimpy Spook	whiskers, eyes okay	VG+	$227.50	3-1999
Heddon	Skipper	red eyes & tail	VG-	$348.00	9-2000
Heddon	Slope Nose	3-pin, L-rig		$356.00	9-2000
Heddon	Slope Nose	blue head, 1-pin, c.1903, chips, NOT MET	VG	$587.00	9-2000
Heddon	Slope Nose	blue head, 4-hook, 2-pin, red collar, tailcap	VG+	$1000.00	4-2000
Heddon	Slope Nose	blue head, avg picture box, decent lure, collar repainted	VG+/IB	$610.00	7-2002
Heddon	Slope Nose	blue head, NOT MET	EX-	$550.00	11-2000
Heddon	Slope Nose	blue head, pinned collar, brass tail	AVG	$201.00	6-2002
Heddon	Slope Nose	black, white, red collar, rare papers	EX-	$2,060.00	12-1999
Heddon	Slope Nose	poor picture box	EX-/IB	$1274.00	10-2000
Heddon	Sonar	26 different, salesman marked, odd colors	Mint	$56.01	2-1999
Heddon	Sonar	x3; two 433GFs, one 431SFs	NIB	$16.00	1-1999
Heddon	Sonic	14KCD	VG	$61.25	4-1999
Heddon	Sonic	385L, 12-pack with 9 lures	NIB	$90.00	5-1999
Heddon	Sonic	385L, PTCB	NIB	$15.50	2-1999
Heddon	Sonic	385SF	NIB	$17.00	1-1999
Heddon	Sonic	388PUM, natural punkinseed	NIB	$27.00	4-2000
Heddon	Sonic	9385SD, yellow scale	NIB	$23.02	1-1999
Heddon	Sonic	baby bass	Mint	$34.00	1-1999
Heddon	Sonic	black scale, chrome	Mint	$21.50	2-1999
Heddon	Sonic	blue scale, chrome	VG	$20.50	1-1999
Heddon	Sonic	checkerboard, NOT MET	EX	$228.00	11-2000

BRAND	MODEL	SERIES / MFG. CODE / DESCRIPTION	GRADE	PRICE	DATE
Heddon	Sonic	clear yellow, black spots	EX	$61.00	3-2000
Heddon	Sonic	coach dog, gold bolt	Mint	$26.00	2-1999
Heddon	Sonic	frog, gold eyes, 325BAR box	EX	$43.00	6-1999
Heddon	Sonic	GBP	NOC	$30.00	4-1999
Heddon	Sonic	Johnson Outboard logo, NOT MET	EX	$112.00	7-2000
Heddon	Sonic	Johnson Seahorse logo	EX	$355.00	4-1999
Heddon	Sonic	natural shad	NIB	$28.50	2-1999
Heddon	Sonic	NSN, photo perch?	EX	$46.00	10-2001
Heddon	Sonic	orange crackleback	EX	$30.00	3-2000
Heddon	Sonic	perch	VG	$9.75	1-1999
Heddon	Sonic	perch, molded hangers	Mint	$36.00	1-1999
Heddon	Sonic	shad	Mint	$14.00	2-1999
Heddon	Sonic	shad, paint raised on BW	EX	$10.50	1-1999
Heddon	Sonic	white, black bolt, newer	NOC	$45.99	6-1999
Heddon	Sonic	x15, stand-up display, common colors	EX	$500.00	10-2000
Heddon	Sonic	yellow coach dog?	EX	$36.80	2-1999
Heddon	Sonic	yellow, black coach dog	Mint	$22.50	2-1999
Heddon	Sonic	yellow, black coach dog, gold eyes	Mint	$33.00	1-1999
Heddon	Sonic, Firetail	2 black coach dogs	EX	$31.00	2-1999
Heddon	Sonic, Firetail	SD, black, green triangles card	NOC	$13.00	8-2001
Heddon	Sonic, Super	1999 Smith color	Mint	$257.51	7-1999
Heddon	Sonic, Super	9385BC, black crappie, PTCB	NIB	$20.50	1-1999
Heddon	Sonic, Super	985C, plastic lid box	NIB	$19.00	7-2000
Heddon	Sonic, Super	9385CD	NIB	$19.00	1-1999
Heddon	Sonic, Super	9385CR, PTCB	NIB	$46.00	1-1999
Heddon	Sonic, Super	9385CS, crystal shad	NIB	$22.00	8-2001
Heddon	Sonic, Super	9385GFB, gold foil black?	NIB	$53.00	8-2001
Heddon	Sonic, Super	9385GRA	NIB	$71.25	3-2000
Heddon	Sonic, Super	9385L, Abu Record	NIB	$31.00	3-1999
Heddon	Sonic, Super	9385LC, natural perch	NIB	$56.00	3-2000
Heddon	Sonic, Super	9385L, PTCB	NIB	$18.00	4-1999
Heddon	Sonic, Super	9385NP, nickel plate	NIB	$52.00	8-2001
Heddon	Sonic, Super	9385NRT, natural trout	NIB	$98.00	10-2001
Heddon	Sonic, Super	9385NSD, nickel shad, black scale back	NIB	$53.00	8-2001
Heddon	Sonic, Super	9385PUM	NIB	$76.51	3-2000
Heddon	Sonic, Super	9385RFL	NIB	$50.00	8-2002
Heddon	Sonic, Super	9385SUC, natural sucker	NIB	$134.02	3-2000
Heddon	Sonic, Super	9386SD, natural shad	NIB	$30.00	4-2000
Heddon	Sonic, Super	albino	EX+	$76.00	3-2000
Heddon	Sonic, Super	black scale, bronze chrome	EX	$41.00	2-1999
Heddon	Sonic, Super	CS, gold eyes	EX	$25.21	2-1999
Heddon	Sonic, Super	GLDS	EX-	$36.46	4-1999
Heddon	Sonic, Super	GPB, gold, black back	EX+	$33.00	2-1999
Heddon	Sonic, Super	gold spots	EX	$51.00	8-2002
Heddon	Sonic, Super	gold spots	EX+	$60.00	1-1999
Heddon	Sonic, Super	green scale, black coach dog	EX	$56.50	2-1999
Heddon	Sonic, Super	natural redfish	Mint	$325.00	4-2002

BRAND	MODEL	SERIES / MFG. CODE / DESCRIPTION	GRADE	PRICE	DATE
Heddon	Sonic, Super	orange crackleback	Mint	$52.00	8-1999
Heddon	Sonic, Super	pearl scale	EX	$27.00	5-1999
Heddon	Sonic, Super	purple bar scale	EX	$67.00	4-2000
Heddon	Sonic, Super	red head, blue tail, silver scale	EX	$16.00	2-1999
Heddon	Sonic, Super	V9385GF, gold flitter	NIB	$70.00	2-1999
Heddon	Sonic, Top	300NGL, natural bgl	NIB	$89.88	4-1999
Heddon	Sonic, Top	bar fish	EX	$36.00	1-1999
Heddon	Sonic, Top	black scale	EX+	$47.00	5-1999
Heddon	Sonic, Top	blue scale, purple?	EX	$31.67	6-1999
Heddon	Sonic, Top	perch, yellow scale?	EX	$22.00	1-1999
Heddon	Sonic, Top	purple scale	NIB	$61.00	3-1999
Heddon	Sonic, Top	yellow	NIB	$35.00	6-1999
Heddon	Sonic, Ultra	325BAR, nice PTCB	NIB	$52.71	1-1999
Heddon	Sonic, Ultra	325SD, nice PTCB	NIB	$42.00	1-1999
Heddon	Spin Diver	bar perch	VG-	$760.00	7-1999
Heddon	Spin Diver	bar perch, $700.00 NOT MET	VG	$390.00	1-2002
Heddon	Spin Diver	bar perch, NOT MET	AVG	$362.85	1-1999
Heddon	Spin Diver	bar perch, ugly	AVG	$265.00	4-2001
Heddon	Spin Diver	bar perch, wood, chip on tail, NOT MET	VG-	$485.00	8-2001
Heddon	Spin Diver	correct 3002 Down box	EX-/IB	$1,649.00	3-2001
Heddon	Spin Diver	crackleback	EX-	$405.00	1-2002
Heddon	Spin Diver	crackleback	VG+	$649.00	4-2001
Heddon	Spin Diver	crackleback, problems with belly varnish	VG+	$1,136.00	7-2000
Heddon	Spin Diver	deluxe red scale, small chip on back, touch-up	VG	$1,125.00	9-2001
Heddon	Spin Diver	frog	EX-	$1,825.00	3-2001
Heddon	Spin Diver	frog	EX-	$2,427.00	5-2001
Heddon	Spin Diver	frog scale, small touch-up on tail	VG+	$921.00	7-2002
Heddon	Spin Diver	frog spot	EX	$1,750.00	4-2001
Heddon	Spin Diver	frog, not awful	AVG	$285.00	6-2000
Heddon	Spin Diver	frog, small nose chip, light rub on tail	EX-	$1,075.00	10-2001
Heddon	Spin Diver	frog, ugly, NOT MET	AVG	$180.00	5-1999
Heddon	Spin Diver	frog, varnished tail & belly	VG-	$1,055.00	5-1999
Heddon	Spin Diver	goldfish scale, NOT MET	VG+	$1,044.00	3-2000
Heddon	Spin Diver	goldfish, beater, NOT MET		$228.00	5-2000
Heddon	Spin Diver	green scale	AVG	$348.00	3-2002
Heddon	Spin Diver	green scale	VG	$1,126.01	4-1999
Heddon	Spin Diver	green scale, decent	VG+	$898.88	1-2000
Heddon	Spin Diver	green scale, nice	EX-	$580.00	9-2002
Heddon	Spin Diver	green scale, one rough side, one nice side	½ VG+	$263.00	5-2000
Heddon	Spin Diver	green scale, ugly	Poor	$305.00	7-2001
Heddon	Spin Diver	rainbow	Fair	$142.00	1-1999
Heddon	Spin Diver	rainbow, missing spinner, hook	Poor	$109.16	9-1999
Heddon	Spin Diver	rainbow, small nose chip, light varnish, NOT MET	EX-/VG+	$660.00	6-2001
Heddon	Spin Diver	red eyes & tail, heavy varnish flaking, otherwise okay	VG-	$404.00	3-2000
Heddon	Spin Diver	rainbow, varnish, $700.00 NOT MET	EX-	$660.00	6-2001

BRAND	MODEL	SERIES / MFG. CODE / DESCRIPTION	GRADE	PRICE	DATE
Heddon	Spin Diver	red eyes & tail, poor box	EX/IB	$889.00	10-2002
Heddon	Spin Diver	red eyes & tail, white	VG+	$900.00	5-2000
Heddon	Spin Diver	red eyes & tail, white, varnish loss but still nice	VG+	$685.00	4-2002
Heddon	Spin-Diver	red scale, decent, NOT MET	VG	$234.00	5-2002
Heddon	Spin Diver	red scale, decent	VG	$462.00	4-2001
Heddon	Spin Diver	red, white with correct 3002 box	EX-	$1,700.00	4-2001
Heddon	Spin Diver	strawberry	Rough	$289.00	8-1999
Heddon	Spin Diver	strawberry, ugly	AVG	$350.00	4-2001
Heddon	Spin Diver	white, red eyes & tail	EX-	$1,554.00	1-2000
Heddon	Spook, Baby Crab	eye missing	EX-	$31.00	8-2001
Heddon	Spook, Crab	luminous, nice 9909LC Brush box & catalog	NIB	$293.88	11-1999
Heddon	Spook, Super	strawberry, painted eyes	EX	$31.00	1-1999
Heddon	S.O.S. 140	140L, glass eyes, chip between eyes, okay	VG	$51.01	2-1999
Heddon	S.O.S. 140	frog spot, glass eyes, 2-piece	EX	$374.00	9-2002
Heddon	S.O.S. 140	green scale, 2-piece	EX	$163.00	4-2001
Heddon	S.O.S. 140	painted eyes, 140L Banner box	NIB	$75.00	10-2000
Heddon	S.O.S. 140	painted, 140P Banner box	NIB	$86.00	10-2000
Heddon	S.O.S. 140	perch, painted eyes	EX	$42.00	2-1999
Heddon	S.O.S. 140	red head, glass eyes, 2-piece, NOT MET	Mint	$105.02	5-1999
Heddon	S.O.S. 140	red head, L-rig	EX-	$63.00	1-2002
Heddon	S.O.S. 140	red, white, glass eyes, 2-piece	Mint	$106.50	10-1999
Heddon	S.O.S. 140	shiner scale	EX	$132.50	1-1999
Heddon	S.O.S. 140	shiner scale, glass eyes, 2-piece	Mint	$114.00	11-2000
Heddon	S.O.S. 140	shiner scale, glass eyes, 2-piece, belly dent	EX-	$51.00	9-2000
Heddon	S.O.S. 160	160, green scale, L-rig	EX	$133.50	8-1999
Heddon	S.O.S. 160	160P, L-rig, decent	VG+	$51.01	6-1999
Heddon	S.O.S. 160	169N Up Bass box, nice, NOT MET	NIB	$305.00	12-2001
Heddon	S.O.S. 160	dace, L-rig	EX	$176.00	8-2002
Heddon	S.O.S. 160	silver scale	EX-	$127.00	10-2000
Heddon	S.O.S. 160	silver scale, 2-piece	EX	$104.00	1-2001
Heddon	S.O.S. 160	shiner scale, 2-piece	EX	$92.50	3-1999
Heddon	S.O.S. 160	shiner scale, glass eyes, L-rig	EX-	$122.00	3-1999
Heddon	S.O.S. 160	shiner scale, glass eyes, L-rig, 1-pointer	EX-	$101.00	10-2000
Heddon	S.O.S. 170	2-piece, 179P Brush box	NIB	$302.00	11-2000
Heddon	S.O.S. 170	170P, tan back, L-rig, $3,000.00 NOT MET	EX+	$1,331.00	3-2000
Heddon	S.O.S. 170	frog spot, L-rig, lots of pointers	G	$262.00	10-2001
Heddon	S.O.S. 170	green scale, 2-piece	EX-	$168.50	1-1999
Heddon	S.O.S. 170	green scale, L-rig	VG+	$121.00	11-2001
Heddon	S.O.S. 170	L-rig, 179N Up Bass box, NOT MET	EX-/IB	$178.00	3-2002
Heddon	S.O.S. 170	perch scale, 2-piece, NOT MET	EX-	$122.50	12-1999
Heddon	S.O.S. 170	pike scale, glass eyes, 2-piece	VG+	$127.50	6-1999
Heddon	S.O.S. 170	red head, 2-piece, big varnish flake, ugly bleed	VG+	$107.00	12-2000
Heddon	S.O.S. 170	red head, 2-piece, small dent, nice	EX	$157.51	2-2000
Heddon	S.O.S. 170	red head, L-rig	EX-	$160.00	3-1999
Heddon	S.O.S. 170	red head, white, L-rig	VG	$97.00	4-1999
Heddon	S.O.S. 170	red, white, 2-piece, looks super	EX	$126.50	3-1999
Heddon	S.O.S. 170	shiner scale, 2-piece	Mint	$305.00	2-2002

BRAND	MODEL	SERIES / MFG. CODE / DESCRIPTION	GRADE	PRICE	DATE
Heddon	S.O.S. 170	shiner scale, 2-piece, NOT MET	EX-	$70.00	7-2000
Heddon	S.O.S. 170	shiner scale, glass eyes, L-rig	EX-	$225.00	5-1999
Heddon	S.O.S. 170	shiner scale, L-rig	VG	$88.00	4-1999
Heddon	S.O.S. 370	black sucker, L-rig, Heddon props, beater		$160.00	8-2001
Heddon	S.O.S. 370	pike scale, cup rig, Stanley props	EX-	$765.00	6-2002
Heddon	S.O.S. 370	pike scale, Stanley props, mint	EX+	$939.00	2-2002
Heddon	S.O.S. 370	really a 160 green scale, L-rig	EX-	$305.00	3-2001
Heddon	S.O.S. 370	red head, cup rig, Stanley props	EX-	$617.00	8-2002
Heddon	S.O.S. 370	red head, L-rig, Heddon props	EX	$1,009.00	9-2001
Heddon	S.O.S. 370	red head, Stanley props	VG-	$355.00	11-1999
Heddon	S.O.S. 370	red head, Stanley props	VG-	$670.00	2-2000
Heddon	Spoony Frog	frog, 50% paint loss on legs	VG-	$134.06	8-1999
Heddon	Spoony Frog	frog, awful paint		$27.00	1-1999
Heddon	Spoony Frog	frog color, minor chips on feet	EX-	$198.50	7-1999
Heddon	Spoony Frog	frog finish, 8209B Up Bass box	EX/IB	$462.00	5-2002
Heddon	Spoony Frog	gold, NOT MET	VG	$26.00	1-1999
Heddon	Spoony Frog	silver	EX	$20.52	11-1999
Heddon	Spoony Frog	silver, NOT MET	EX	$36.25	2-2000
Heddon	Stanley	#70, pike scale, glass eyes, skitter attached, rough box	NIB	$350.00	2-2002
Heddon	Stanley, King	299M, pike scale, 299M Up Bass box	NIB	$87.00	9-2002
Heddon	Stingaree	9930, red head	NIB	$34.00	8-2002
Heddon	Stingaree	9930, red head, PTCB	NIB	$26.99	2-1999
Heddon	Stingaree	complete set of 12, only one 330XRY box	EX	$610.00	2-2002
Heddon	Stingaree	frog, large size	EX-	$36.00	5-1999
Heddon	Stingaree	perch	EX-	$26.00	2-1999
Heddon	Stingaree	red, white	NIB	$52.01	3-1999
Heddon	Stingaree	wood, unmarked	AVG	$132.50	2-1999
Heddon	Stingaree	XBW	EX+	$19.60	2-1999
Heddon	Stingaree	XRY	EX	$27.00	2-1999
Heddon	Stingaree, Tiny	frog	VG	$15.57	1-1999
Heddon	Stingaree, Tiny	perch	EX	$25.57	2-1999
Heddon	Stingaree, Tiny	x2; one perch scale, one XRY	EX	$34.00	8-2002
Heddon	Sucker, Black	5-hook, many hook drags	AVG	$3,050.00	2-2000
Heddon	Sucker, Black	attractive	EX-	$2,850.00	8-2002
Heddon	Sucker, Black	beautiful	EX	$5400.00	9-2002
Heddon	Sucker, Black	hooks, cups missing on side	AVG	$651.00	3-1999
Heddon	Sucker, Black	huge chip between eyes, NOT MET	Fair	$339.00	11-1999
Heddon	Sucker, Black	L-rig, bottom tail missing, decent otherwise	VG-	$1,028.00	2-2002
Heddon	Sucker, Black	more white than normal, nice	VG+	$2,807.00	4-2002
Heddon	Sucker, Black	no primer left except on back	Poor	$400.00	1-2002
Heddon	Sucker, Black	odd color, much varnish	AVG	$2,638.00	9-2000
Heddon	Sucker, Black	POBW, nice	EX-	$4,351.00	1-2002
Heddon	Sucker, Black	ugly varnish, NOT MET	AVG	$710.00	2-2002
Heddon	Surface Minnow	402, white, crackleback, forehead, NOT MET	EX	$768.00	6-2001

BRAND	MODEL	SERIES / MFG. CODE / DESCRIPTION	GRADE	PRICE	DATE
Heddon	Surface Minny	260, green scale, glass eyes, NOBP, toilet	VG+	$364.00	9-2000
Heddon	Surface Minny	260, perch scale, 2-piece, NOT MET	EX	$407.00	5-2001
Heddon	Surface Minny	269L, vg 261 Up Bass box	EX/IB	$650.00	10-1999
Heddon	Surface Minny	red eyes & tail	EX-	$875.00	5-2000
Heddon	Swimming Minnow	800, spots	VG	$275.00	2-2000
Heddon	Swimming Minnow	800, strawberry	EX	$1,750.00	5-2000
Heddon	Swimming Minnow	802, nice Up Bass box	VG+/IB	$182.00	10-2001
Heddon	Swimming Minnow	900	EX	$2,750.00	4-2000
Heddon	Swimming Minnow	900, bad varnish, no chips, NOT MET	AVG	$158.00	9-2000
Heddon	Swimming Minnow	900SB, chips	VG-	$500.00	7-2001
Heddon	Swimming Minnow	900, spots	VG-	$422.00	12-1998
Heddon	Swimming Minnow	900, spots, ugly edge rubs, bad	Fair	$256.00	3-2000
Heddon	Swimming Minnow	900, white, red spots, big belly chips, NOT MET	G	$760.55	3-1999
Heddon	Swimming Minnow	900, yellow spots, $500.00 NOT MET	VG+	$405.00	4-2001
Heddon	Swimming Minnow	900, yellow spots, decent, NOT MET	VG+	$447.00	4-2000
Heddon	Swimming Minnow	900, yellow spots, HPGM, rough box	EX-/IB	$1,900.00	5-2000
Heddon	Tadpolly	2-piece, 5002 Brush box	NIB	$222.50	10-1999
Heddon	Tadpolly	6000, green scale, huge chips	Fair	$28.76	1-1999
Heddon	Tadpolly	5000, 2-different, black head, yellow crackleback	EX-	$579.00	4-1999
Heddon	Tadpolly	5000, crab, L-rig	EX-	$158.49	1-2000
Heddon	Tadpolly	5000, crackleback, L-rig, varnish	EX-	$150.00	8-1999
Heddon	Tadpolly	5000, green scale, L-rig, beautiful	EX+	$500.00	1-1999
Heddon	Tadpolly	5000, nice Down Bass box	EXIB	$510.50	2-2000
Heddon	Tadpolly	5000, rainbow	EX-	$320.75	3-1999
Heddon	Tadpolly	5000, strawberry, 2-piece	EX-	$256.00	7-2000
Heddon	Tadpolly	5000, strawberry, L-rig, bell plate, light age lines	EX+	$450.00	12-1999
Heddon	Tadpolly	5000, yellow, black back stripe, NOT MET	VG+	$291.95	12-1999
Heddon	Tadpolly	5000BH, yellow, bad varnish, rest okay	VG	$390.00	3-2000
Heddon	Tadpolly	5000D	EX/IB	$290.00	2-2000
Heddon	Tadpolly	5000D, bar perch, Down Bass box	EX/IB	$505.00	9-2002
Heddon	Tadpolly	5000D, L-rig, intro box	VG+IB	$380.00	6-1999
Heddon	Tadpolly	5000, red head, blended	EX+	$312.00	3-2002
Heddon	Tadpolly	5009D, Down Bass box, special card & paper	NIB	$1,077.99	3-2000
Heddon	Tadpolly	5009D Up Bass box	VG-IB	$73.10	3-2000
Heddon	Tadpolly	6000, crackleback, L-rig	VG+	$150.00	8-1999
Heddon	Tadpolly	6000, frog, decent	VG	$93.00	1-2001
Heddon	Tadpolly	6000, goldfish scale, L-rig	EX-	$448.99	2-2000
Heddon	Tadpolly	6000, green scale, L-rig	EX-	$250.00	8-1999
Heddon	Tadpolly	6000, perch scale, glass eyes, heart, Down Bass box	NIB	$612.00	8-2000
Heddon	Tadpolly	6000, red scale	VG	$208.00	6-2000
Heddon	Tadpolly	6000, white flitter	EX	$700.00	12-1999
Heddon	Tadpolly	bar perch, Down Bass box	VG+IB	$525.00	5-2000
Heddon	Tadpolly	crackleback	EX-	$300.00	10-2001
Heddon	Tadpolly	crackleback, ex but wrong 5009P Up Bass box	EX	$500.00	10-1999
Heddon	Tadpolly	crisp 5009D Brush box	EXIB	$280.00	11-1999

BRAND	MODEL	SERIES / MFG. CODE / DESCRIPTION	GRADE	PRICE	DATE
Heddon	Tadpolly	ex- 5009D intro box	EXIB	$750.00	10-1999
Heddon	Tadpolly	flawless 5009M Down Bass box	NIB	$562.00	9-1999
Heddon	Tadpolly	frog scale, cracked eyes	AVG	$68.00	1-1999
Heddon	Tadpolly	frog, glass eyes, L-rig	VG+	$203.51	8-1999
Heddon	Tadpolly	frog, varnish flakes on belly, avg intro box	EX-IB	$300.00	10-2002
Heddon	Tadpolly	green scale, L-rig	VG	$99.99	2-1999
Heddon	Tadpolly	gir, L-rig, 5002 Down Bass box	NIB	$390.01	10-1999
Heddon	Tadpolly	intro Box	VGIB	$565.87	4-1999
Heddon	Tadpolly	nice goldfish scale, ex- 5009K intro box	EX-IB	$1,201.00	2-2002
Heddon	Tadpolly	rainbow, 2-piece, small belly chip at hook, nice	VG+	$81.25	4-2000
Heddon	Tadpolly	rainbow, pointers, intro box	VG+	$650.00	3-1999
Heddon	Tadpolly	red eyes & tail, 6000 intro box	EXIB	$513.00	5-2000
Heddon	Tadpolly	red scale, intro box	EXIB	$600.00	4-1999
Heddon	Tadpolly	shiner scale, glass eyes	EX+	$462.50	2-2000
Heddon	Tadpolly	shiner scale, glass eyes, age lines	EX+	$182.00	9-2002
Heddon	Tadpolly	spots	AVG	$42.76	7-1999
Heddon	Tadpolly	white, flitter, glass eyes	VG+	$82.00	10-2001
Heddon	Tadpolly	white, glass eyes	VG-	$53.00	3-1999
Heddon	Tadpolly	white, glass eyes	VG-	$74.00	1-1999
Heddon	Tadpolly	white, red eyes, L-rig	VG	$75.00	1-1999
Heddon	Tadpolly	small back chip, crisp 5009A Down Bass box	EX-IB	$430.00	8-2001
Heddon	Tadpolly	vg+ 6009D intro box	EXIB	$613.03	1-2000
Heddon	Tadpolly, Baby	green scale, ugly belly varnish, NOT MET	EX-	$91.00	3-2002
Heddon	Tadpolly, Baby	red scale, intro box	EX-/IB	$560.00	5-1999
Heddon	Tadpolly, Bottlenose	yellow spots	VG+	$328.00	4-2001
Heddon	Tadpolly, Magnum	clear	EX	$31.99	2-1999
Heddon	Tadpolly, Runt	SB, glass eyes, NOT MET	VG+	$536.00	1-2000
Heddon	Tadpolly, Spook	½ oz. Pepsi	EX	$86.00	8-1999
Heddon	Tadpolly, Spook	red & white Banner box, 2PCCB	NIB	$27.88	2-1999
Heddon	Tadpolly, Spook	red bullfrog	NIB	$21.50	2-1999
Heddon	Tease, Tiny	natural scale	VG+	$192.45	4-1999
Heddon	Tease, Tiny	perch	EX	$407.00	3-1999
Heddon	Tease, Tiny	red head, white, cup	EX-	$66.00	1-2000
Heddon	Tiger	3 sizes	EX-	$81.00	3-1999
Heddon	Tiger	4", black, gold	EX	$10.60	2-1999
Heddon	Tiger	4", tiger stripe	EX	$34.00	5-2000
Heddon	Tiger	4½", clear, black, gold, insert	EX	$51.00	5-1999
Heddon	Tiger	4¼" black, silver	EX	$13.01	2-1999
Heddon	Tiger	4¼", gold, stripes	VG	$11.00	2-1999
Heddon	Tiger	5", blue flash flitter	EX	$41.01	2-1999
Heddon	Tiger	5¼", clear, sparkles on back	EX	$338.00	4-2000
Heddon	Tiger	1010TG	NIB	$35.00	5-2000
Heddon	Tiger	1020 TG	NIB	$26.85	4-1999
Heddon	Tiger	1020TG, 3¾"	EX	$12.45	4-1999
Heddon	Tiger	1040GSCD, 5"	NIB	$191.00	2-2000
Heddon	Tiger	CDF but stripes	EX	$75.00	10-2000
Heddon	Tiger	purple, silver reflector	NIB	$32.01	4-1999

BRAND	MODEL	SERIES / MFG. CODE / DESCRIPTION	GRADE	PRICE	DATE
Heddon	Tiger	one each: 1030Y, 1030GF	NIB	$56.01	5-1999
Heddon	Tiger, Big	1040TG	NIB	$54.01	2-2000
Heddon	Tiger, Big	PM	Mint	$53.00	4-2000
Heddon	Tiny Spook	310BGL	NIB	$143.00	5-2001
Heddon	Tiny Spook	red head	EX	$66.00	2-2000
Heddon	Tiny Spook	XRY	EX+	$81.00	9-1999
Heddon	Torpedo	120, green scale	Mint	$650.00	5-2000
Heddon	Torpedo	120M, Stanley props	Mint	$480.00	3-2001
Heddon	Torpedo	120M, Stanley props, NOT MET	EX-	$178.50	5-1999
Heddon	Torpedo	122	EX	$250.00	10-1999
Heddon	Torpedo	129D, L-rig	EX-	$275.00	10-1999
Heddon	Torpedo	130, crackleback, L-rig	EX	$1200.00	7-2001
Heddon	Torpedo	130?, green scale, glass eyes, L-rig	EX	$202.50	5-1999
Heddon	Torpedo	130, green scale, glass eyes, nice	EX-	$238.15	2-1999
Heddon	Torpedo	130, green scale, nice	EX-	$126.51	1-2000
Heddon	Torpedo	130L, shiner scale, painted eyes, catalog	NIB	$66.00	5-1999
Heddon	Torpedo	130P Banner box, painted eyes, catalog	NIB	$124.00	10-2001
Heddon	Torpedo	130, pike scale, glass eyes, toilet-rig	EX	$223.00	5-2001
Heddon	Torpedo	139PYB, mint Up Bass box	NIB	$700.00	2-1999
Heddon	Torpedo	blue scale, glass eyes, marked props	EX	$535.00	3-2001
Heddon	Torpedo	blue scale, vg Up Bass box, tail chip	NIB	$1,400.00	5-2000
Heddon	Torpedo	dace, ex- wrong 139M Brush box	EX/IB	$375.00	10-1999
Heddon	Torpedo	green scale, L-rig	EX	$301.00	2-2002
Heddon	Torpedo	nice 122 Down Bass box	EX/IB	$250.00	9-2001
Heddon	Torpedo	rainbow, painted eyes	Mint	$51.00	7-2002
Heddon	Torpedo	white, black ribs, glass eyes, no props	EX	$250.00	9-1999
Heddon	Torpedo	XWB, glass eyes, POBW	EX-	$150.00	8-1999
Heddon	Torpedo	yellow, silver flakes	EX-	$480.00	12-1998
Heddon	Torpedo, Magnum	362LC	NOC	$83.00	2-1999
Heddon	Torpedo, Magnum	BF	EX-	$84.00	2-1999
Heddon	Torpedo, Magnum	BF, white eyes	EX	$61.51	6-1999
Heddon	Torpedo, Magnum	BF, white eyes	EX	$84.00	1-1999
Heddon	Torpedo, Magnum	blue shore	EX	$580.00	6-2001
Heddon	Torpedo, Magnum	frog	EX	$77.00	1-1999
Heddon	Torpedo, Magnum	frog, white eyes	NOC	$77.00	12-1998
Heddon	Torpedo, Magnum	hot bar perch	EX	$541.00	12-1998
Heddon	Torpedo, Magnum	modern Smith color	EX	$56.01	3-1999
Heddon	Torpedo, Magnum	modern Smith color, red CD	EX	$80.99	3-1999
Heddon	Torpedo, Magnum	natural perch?, photo finish	Mint	$110.00	1-2000
Heddon	Torpedo, Magnum	natural striper	EX	$137.00	10-2000
Heddon	Torpedo, Magnum	natural striper	NIB	$77.00	4-1999
Heddon	Torpedo, Magnum	orange, black spots, modern	EX	$46.00	4-1999
Heddon	Torpedo, Magnum	pale yellow coach dog	Mint	$31.00	5-1999
Heddon	Torpedo, Magnum	perch?	EX	$200.50	2-1999
Heddon	Torpedo, Magnum	perch, white eyes, 2 others	EX	$102.50	3-1999
Heddon	Torpedo, Magnum	purple shore, red eye shadow	EX	$3,500.00	9-2001
Heddon	Torpedo, Magnum	red, white	EX+	$405.00	1-1999

BRAND	MODEL	SERIES / MFG. CODE / DESCRIPTION	GRADE	PRICE	DATE
Heddon	Torpedo, Magnum	red head, white eyes, window box	NIB	$278.00	10-2001
Heddon	Torpedo, Magnum	SS, white eyes	Mint	$335.00	12-2001
Heddon	Torpedo, Magnum	SS, white eyes, PTCB	NIB	$182.50	6-1999
Heddon	Torpedo, Magnum	strawberry	EX+	$203.50	12-1999
Heddon	Torpedo, Magnum	white, blue eyes	EX-	$406.00	3-1999
Heddon	Torpedo, Magnum	white, blue eyes	NIB	$285.35	12-1998
Heddon	Torpedo, Magnum	white, blue eyes	NIB	$355.00	2-1999
Heddon	Torpedo, Magnum	white shore, white eyes, NOT MET	EX	$83.00	10-2000
Heddon	Torpedo, Magnum	x2, frog, striper	EX	$112.50	9-1999
Heddon	Torpedo, Magnum	XBS, white eyes	EX	$410.00	9-1999
Heddon	Torpedo, Magnum	XRS, white eyes	EX	$83.01	9-1999
Heddon	Torpedo, Magnum	XRW	VG	$82.00	4-1999
Heddon	Torpedo, Magnum	XRY	EX	$305.00	3-2000
Heddon	Torpedo, Magnum	XRY, white eyes	NIB	$525.00	4-2001
Heddon	Torpedo, Stanley	pikie scale, glass eyes, cup rig	Mint	$650.00	3-2000
Heddon	Torpedo, Tiny	0360VY, 8 bids	NIB	$46.59	3-2000
Heddon	Torpedo, Tiny	22 different	EX+	$134.50	2-1999
Heddon	Torpedo, Tiny	black, gold foil, gold eyes	Mint	$41.50	4-1999
Heddon	Torpedo, Tiny	CD, black belly stencil, gold eyes	EX	$47.00	4-2001
Heddon	Torpedo, Tiny	weird bluish-black color	EX	$11.00	1-1999
Heddon	Vamp	7500M, Spook, painted eyes, NOT MET	NIB	$77.50	5-1999
Heddon	Vamp	7500PG, tack eyes, Banner box	EX-/IB	$223.00	3-2001
Heddon	Vamp	7500S, L-rig, Up Bass box	EX-/IB	$372.00	10-2000
Heddon	Vamp	7502, glass eyes, 2-piece, Brush box	NIB	$300.00	10-1999
Heddon	Vamp	7502RET, glass eyes, L-rig, ex Up Bass box	NIB	$151.50	12-1999
Heddon	Vamp	7509D, green scale, Up Bass box, nice	NIB	$197.00	5-2001
Heddon	Vamp	7509M, Down Bass box	NIB	$350.00	3-2000
Heddon	Vamp	7509M, glass eyes, 2-piece, Brush box	EX/IB	$200.00	10-1999
Heddon	Vamp	7509M, L-rig, Down Bass box	EX/IB	$325.00	4-1999
Heddon	Vamp	7509M, L-rig, Up Bass box	EX/IB	$131.50	1-2000
Heddon	Vamp	7509P, age lines	EX-	$100.00	10-1999
Heddon	Vamp	7509P, L-rig, Up Bass box	VG-/IB	$79.01	6-1999
Heddon	Vamp	7509PL, pearl, 2-piece	VG/IB	$191.38	5-1999
Heddon	Vamp	7509RET, 2-piece, Brush box	EX-/IB	$170.27	1-2000
Heddon	Vamp	9502 Down Bass box	EX+/IB	$205.00	1-1999
Heddon	Vamp	blue scale	Fair	$56.01	2-2000
Heddon	Vamp	blue scale, 7509X Down Bass box	EX-/IB	$1,275.00	3-1999
Heddon	Vamp	blue scale, L-rig	VG+	$375.00	6-1999
Heddon	Vamp	crackleback, L-rig, red eye shadow, belly crack, nice	EX-/VG+	$405.00	11-2001
Heddon	Vamp	crackleback, plastic tack eyes, "Original"	EX+	$150.00	7-2001
Heddon	Vamp	dace, glass eyes, 2-piece	VG+	$176.00	3-2001
Heddon	Vamp	frog scale	EX+	$875.00	5-2000
Heddon	Vamp	frog scale, glass eyes	EX-	$525.00	1-1999
Heddon	Vamp	frog scale, L-rig	VG-	$128.50	2-2000
Heddon	Vamp	frog scale, L-rig, beautiful	EX	$1,425.00	7-2000
Heddon	Vamp	frog spots, L-rig	EX-	$284.00	8-2002

BRAND	MODEL	SERIES / MFG. CODE / DESCRIPTION	GRADE	PRICE	DATE
Heddon	Vamp	frog, L-rig	VG+	$353.00	5-2001
Heddon	Vamp	green head, yellow blue head, white yellowed?, glass eyes, L-rig	EX-	$1,275.00	4-2000
Heddon	Vamp	green pike scale, 2-piece	EX+	$175.00	8-1999
Heddon	Vamp	green scale, glass eyes	VG-	$60.00	1-1999
Heddon	Vamp	green scale, glass eyes, 2-piece	EX	$117.00	2-2001
Heddon	Vamp	green scale, glass eyes, L-rig	EX	$154.00	3-2002
Heddon	Vamp	green scale, glass eyes, small nose chip	VG	$35.00	1-1999
Heddon	Vamp	green scale, L-rig	EX	$122.49	5-1999
Heddon	Vamp	green scale, L-rig, pretty	EX	$63.00	3-2002
Heddon	Vamp	L-rig, 8500M Down Bass box	NIB	$312.55	1-2000
Heddon	Vamp	L-rig, ex 7509R Down Bass box	NIB	$1,025.00	12-2000
Heddon	Vamp	Luny Frog, glass eyes, L-rig	Mint	$1,313.00	4-1999
Heddon	Vamp	Luny Frog, L-rig	VG-	$201.00	3-2001
Heddon	Vamp	Luny Frog, L-rig, NOT MET	VG-	$88.75	8-1999
Heddon	Vamp	(M) pike scale, Down Bass box, p. catalogue	EX-/IB	$255.00	5-1999
Heddon	Vamp	(M) pike scale, L-rig	EX	$93.00	5-2000
Heddon	Vamp	natural scale, L-rig	EX	$187.00	8-2000
Heddon	Vamp	natural scale, L-rig	EX-	$139.00	5-2000
Heddon	Vamp	orange, black spots	EX-	$306.00	10-2002
Heddon	Vamp	orange, black spots, corroded hardware, unmarked Down Bass box	EX-	$907.50	7-1999
Heddon	Vamp	orange, black spots, glass eyes, L-rig	EX	$1,975.00	4-2001
Heddon	Vamp	(P) shiner scale, glass eyes, odd S-rig, Banner box	NIB	$193.05	2-2000
Heddon	Vamp	(P) shiner scale, L-rig, Up Bass box nice	NIB	$325.00	10-2001
Heddon	Vamp	(P) shiner scale, red head, L-rig	VG+	$170.27	1-2000
Heddon	Vamp	PAS, glass eyes, 2-piece, decent	VG	$31.00	10-2000
Heddon	Vamp	perch, painted eyes, jointed, Banner box	EX-	$32.00	1-1999
Heddon	Vamp	pike scale, L-rig	EX	$104.00	11-2000
Heddon	Vamp	pike scale, L-rig	EX	$142.50	3-2000
Heddon	Vamp	pike scale, L-rig	EX-	$78.77	3-2000
Heddon	Vamp	pike scale, painted eyes	EX+	$21.50	1-1999
Heddon	Vamp	pike, glass eyes, Down Bass box missing end	VG/IB	$72.00	2-1999
Heddon	Vamp	rainbow, glass eyes	EX-	$74.79	12-1998
Heddon	Vamp	rainbow, jointed, glass eyes, nose chip	G	$28.00	1-1999
Heddon	Vamp	rainbow, L-rig, ex Up Bass box	EX-/IB	$182.50	12-1999
Heddon	Vamp	rainbow, Roundnose, agelines	VG	$450.00	9-2000
Heddon	Vamp	rainbow, tack eyes	EX	$41.00	8-1999
Heddon	Vamp	rainbow, tack eyes, S-rig	EX	$53.00	3-2001
Heddon	Vamp	red head flitter	EX+	$305.00	3-1999
Heddon	Vamp	red head flitter, L-rig	EX	$229.00	5-2000
Heddon	Vamp	red head Luny Frog, toilet, NOT MET	EX	$699.00	10-2000
Heddon	Vamp	red, frog spot, glass eyes, 2-piece, NOT MET	VG-	$201.00	5-1999
Heddon	Vamp	RHF, glass eyes, 2-piece	EX-	$112.50	9-1999
Heddon	Vamp	round nose, rainbow L-rig	EX-	$888.00	10-2000
Heddon	Vamp	round nose, Zara body, rainbow, glass eyes, L-rig	VG+	$1,000.00	2-2000
Heddon	Vamp	SB, painted eyes	NOC	$56.00	9-2000

BRAND	MODEL	SERIES / MFG. CODE / DESCRIPTION	GRADE	PRICE	DATE
Heddon	Vamp	strawberry, glass eyes	EX	$79.99	8-1999
Heddon	Vamp	strawberry, glass eyes	EX-	$142.50	3-2000
Heddon	Vamp	strawberry, glass eyes, 2-piece, heavy checking	VG	$50.00	2-2000
Heddon	Vamp	strawberry, L-rig, nice	EX	$99.00	11-2000
Heddon	Vamp	strawberry, painted eyes	EX	$33.50	6-1999
Heddon	Vamp, Baby	7409M, L-rig, sharp Down Bass box	EX/IB	$238.04	9-1999
Heddon	Vamp, Baby	Allen Stripey, chips, NOT MET	G	$68.00	6-2000
Heddon	Vamp, Baby	crackleback, 2-piece, POBW	EX-	$931.00	3-2001
Heddon	Vamp, Baby	frog scale, glass eyes, L-rig	EX-	$265.00	1-2001
Heddon	Vamp, Baby	frog, glass eyes, L-rig, Down Bass box, paper	NIB	$1,525.00	5-1999
Heddon	Vamp, Baby	glass eyes, L-rig, (P) shiner scale, Down Bass box & catalog	NIB	$284.00	9-2000
Heddon	Vamp, Baby	goldfish scale, L-rig	EX-	$405.00	3-2001
Heddon	Vamp, Baby	L-rig, 7409M Down Bass box	EX-/IB	$196.00	9-2000
Heddon	Vamp, Baby	L-rig, crisp 7409D Down Bass box	NIB	$365.00	2-2002
Heddon	Vamp, Baby	red eyes & tail, L-rig	EX	$160.00	4-2000
Heddon	Vamp, Baby	red eyes & tail, L-rig	Mint	$180.50	5-1999
Heddon	Vamp, Baby	red head, white, silver flakes	VG	$95.00	12-1998
Heddon	Vamp, Baby	white, red eyes & tail, repainted?	Mint	$156.03	3-1999
Heddon	Vamp, Baby Surface	silver scale, 2-piece, glass eyes, NOT MET	EX-	$76.00	8-2000
Heddon	Vamp, Flap-Tail Musky	SS, glass eyes, toilet	EX	$228.00	2-2001
Heddon	Vamp, Giant	7550PAS	EX-/IB	$200.00	10-1999
Heddon	Vamp, Giant Jointed	7350RHT, painted eyes, Banner box	NIB	$100.00	8-1999
Heddon	Vamp, Giant Jointed	7352, glass eyes, Brush box	NIB	$179.25	6-1999
Heddon	Vamp, Giant Jointed	7352, glass eyes, Brush box	NIB	$227.00	10-2000
Heddon	Vamp, Giant Jointed	7359PAS Brush box	EX/IB	$227.50	7-1999
Heddon	Vamp, Giant Jointed	red eyes & tail, glass eyes, large Brush box, catalog	NIB	$292.00	10-2000
Heddon	Vamp, Giant Jointed	shiner scale, painted eyes, Banner box	NIB	$122.50	5-1999
Heddon	Vamp, Giant Jointed	red, white, glass eyes, rough Brush box	NIB	$163.11	4-1999
Heddon	Vamp, Giant Jointed	7359PAS	EX/IB	$141.00	5-2000
Heddon	Vamp, Great	PAS, glass eyes, toilet	EX+	$578.88	5-1999
Heddon	Vamp, Great	SS?, Blue Herring, $125.00 NOT MET	VG	$68.00	5-2000
Heddon	Vamp, Great	shiner scale, glass eyes, toilet, NOT MET	VG	$212.50	4-1999
Heddon	Vamp, Great	strawberry, glass eyes, toilet	EX-	$423.88	5-1999
Heddon	Vamp, Jointed	7300RET, L-rig	EX	$152.00	4-2000
Heddon	Vamp, Jointed	7509D, NOT MET	EX/IB	$118.49	3-2000
Heddon	Vamp, Jointed	7309L, L-rig, nice Up Bass box	NIB	$255.00	12-1999
Heddon	Vamp, Jointed	7352 Brush box, catalog	NIB	$445.00	2-2001
Heddon	Vamp, Jointed	7359M, large red border, Up Bass box	NIB	$265.01	11-1999
Heddon	Vamp, Jointed	crackleback, glass eyes, L-rig	AVG	$90.00	5-1999
Heddon	Vamp, Jointed	green scale, Brush box	EX/IB	$247.50	1-2000
Heddon	Vamp, Jointed	green scale, glass eyes, Brush box	NIB	$325.00	11-1999
Heddon	Vamp, Jointed	L-rig, 7309P Brush box	EX/IB	$162.50	3-2000
Heddon	Vamp, Jointed	natural pike?		$19.73	5-1999
Heddon	Vamp, Jointed	natural scale, glass eyes, L-rig, nice	EX	$179.00	11-2000
Heddon	Vamp, Jointed	white, red tail, glass eyes	Rough	$21.00	2-1999

BRAND	MODEL	SERIES / MFG. CODE / DESCRIPTION	GRADE	PRICE	DATE
Heddon	Vamp, Jointed	XRY, painted eyes, wood	EX	$26.56	3-2000
Heddon	Vamp, Jointed Musky	7", natural scale, glass eyes, L-rig	EX-	$164.50	7-1999
Heddon	Vamp, Jointed Musky	7609M, 8", glass eyes, L-rig, nice Down Bass box	EX-/IB	$2285.00	9-2002
Heddon	Vamp Kingfish Spook	KF9759YBS Brush box (+$500.00)	NIB	$1,500.00	1-2001
Heddon	Vamp, Musky	6", frog, glass eyes	VG+	$2,550.00	2-2000
Heddon	Vamp, Musky	6", natural scale, NOT MET	VG+	$202.00	4-2001
Heddon	Vamp, Musky	6", pike scale, $595.00 NOT MET	EX	$370.00	5-2002
Heddon	Vamp, Musky	6", pike scale, NOT MET	EX+	$430.00	4-2001
Heddon	Vamp, Musky	6", shad, glass eyes, red gills	VG+	$207.00	6-2002
Heddon	Vamp, Musky	6", toilet seat, vg+ 7550S Brush box	EX/IB	$457.00	7-2000
Heddon	Vamp, Musky	8", green scale, varnish flakes	VG	$925.00	5-2000
Heddon	Vamp, Musky	8", nice Down Bass box, asking price	EX-/IB	$2,400.00	8-2002
Heddon	Vamp, Musky	8", pike scale, glass eyes, corroded metal, nice	EX-	$769.99	11-1999
Heddon	Vamp, Musky	8", pike scale, nice	EX-	$710.00	3-2002
Heddon	Vamp, Musky	8", shiner scale, 2 big chips	G	$261.00	8-1999
Heddon	Vamp, Musky	8" shiner scale, glass eyes, L-rig, NOT MET	VG+	$503.00	8-2002
Heddon	Vamp, Musky	7352, glass eyes, jointed, Brush box	NIB	$227.00	10-2000
Heddon	Vamp, Musky	7352RH, jointed, glass eyes, 2-piece, Brush box	NIB	$247.27	10-1999
Heddon	Vamp, Musky	7600, 8", all paint gone from forehead, L-rig, M		$56.00	9-2000
Heddon	Vamp, Musky	7600, 8", natural scale, glass eyes, L-rig	AVG	$360.00	12-1999
Heddon	Vamp, Musky	7600P, L-rig, hook drag, avg Down Bass box, NOT MET	EX-IB	$2,235.00	12-2000
Heddon	Vamp, Musky	heavy L-rig, rough 7559M Up Bass box	NIB	$718.00	11-2000
Heddon	Vamp, Musky	L-rig, vg- 7550S Up Bass box, nice	EX/IB	$600.00	8-2002
Heddon	Vamp, Musky	spots, bite marks	VG-	$105.38	12-1998
Heddon	Vamp, Musky	toilet seat, "Great Vamp" 7559R Brush box, NOT MET	NIB	$382.00	2-2002
Heddon	Vamp, Round Nose	rainbow	EX	$1,900.00	4-2001
Heddon	Vamp Spook	7000M Banner box	NIB	$53.50	1-1999
Heddon	Vamp Spook	9509P, glass eyes, hang tag, ex+ Up Bass box	NIB	$430.00	7-1999
Heddon	Vamp Spook	9750L Banner box, navy stock numbers	NIB	$84.00	4-1999
Heddon	Vamp Spook	9750RHF banner box	NIB	$109.50	1-1999
Heddon	Vamp Spook	9750XRY, molded plastic lip, new	NIB	$101.00	3-1999
Heddon	Vamp Spook	frog, vertical center mold, fake?	EX	$250.00	7-2000
Heddon	Vamp Spook	Glow Worm, decent	VG+	$115.00	8-2002
Heddon	Vamp Spook	(M) pike scale, navy numbers on box	NIB	$150.00	6-1999
Heddon	Vamp Spook	pearl?, silver scale, white eyes	EX	$241.00	3-2002
Heddon	Vamp Spook	pike scale, gold eyes	EX-	$17.50	2-1999
Heddon	Vamp Spook	poor 9759GW Flesh box, NOT MET	EX/IB	$264.00	3-2002
Heddon	Vamp Spook	rainbow, gold eyes, wrong box	EX	$88.59	6-1999
Heddon	Vamp Spook	red eyes & tail, glass eyes hook drag but nice	VG+	$51.00	4-2000
Heddon	Vamp Spook	red eyes & tail, Fish Flesh box	EX/IB	$222.59	8-1999
Heddon	Vamp Spook	red head, glass eyes	VG	$72.50	12-1998
Heddon	Vamp Spook	red head, vg Banner box	NIB	$52.01	2-1999
Heddon	Vamp Spook	red, silver, flitter inside	EX	$102.50	9-1999
Heddon	Vamp Spook	RHF, glass eyes, Up Bass box, NOT MET	EX/IB	$136.00	3-2001
Heddon	Vamp Spook	shiner scale, glass eyes	EX	$128.00	8-2000

BRAND	MODEL	SERIES / MFG. CODE / DESCRIPTION	GRADE	PRICE	DATE
Heddon	Vamp Spook	shiner scale, glass eyes, NOT MET	EX/IB	$230.00	12-2000
Heddon	Vamp Spook	strawberry, gold eyes	EX	$66.00	4-2000
Heddon	Vamp Spook	strawberry, plastic lip, painted eyes, surface, NOT MET	EX	$71.00	7-2000
Heddon	Vamp Spook	XBW gold eyes	EX	$69.00	2-1999
Heddon	Vamp Spook	XRB, gold eyes	VG+	$96.55	10-1999
Heddon	Vamp Spook	XRW, gold eyes, 2-piece	Mint	$46.00	4-2000
Heddon	Vamp Spook	XRY Banner box, gold eyes	NIB	$33.00	9-2000
Heddon	Vamp Spook, Jointed	9XRK	EX	$343.00	7-2002
Heddon	Vamp Spook, Jointed	9XRW, 2-piece, beautiful	EX	$137.00	8-2002
Heddon	Vamp Spook, Jointed	green scale, glass eyes, metal lip, wrong box	EX	$305.00	11-2000
Heddon	Vamp Spook, Jointed	natural scale	EX-	$60.00	11-1999
Heddon	Vamp Spook, Jointed	XRG, 2-piece	EX-	$128.05	9-1999
Heddon	Vamp Spook, Surface	silver flitter filling, red head	EX	$177.50	4-1999
Heddon	Vampire	7509M, Down Bass box	EX/IB	$182.50	5-1999
Heddon	Vampire	(M) pike scale, very nice	EX	$87.00	10-2000
Heddon	Vampire	perch scale, L-rig	EX-	$102.50	1-2000
Heddon	Vampire	pike scale, L-rig	EX	$92.00	8-2002
Heddon	Vampire	pike scale, nice	EX-	$83.00	2-2000
Heddon	Vampire	strawberry	EX-	$99.00	4-2000
Heddon	Various	Vamp & Flaptail; both red head, painted eyes	EX+	$76.00	10-1999
Heddon	Various	x5; one each: Flaptail, Zaragossa, Chugger, Crawler; wood	VG-	$71.00	9-1999
Heddon	Walton Feather Tail	#42, blush eyes, POBW	EX-	$250.00	10-1999
Heddon	Walton Feather Tail	#49G, black	EX+	$275.00	10-1999
Heddon	Walton Feather Tail	black, NOT MET	EX	$217.00	8-2000
Heddon	Walton Feather Tail	(M) pike scale, glass eyes, nice	EX	$150.00	5-2000
Heddon	Walton Feather Tail	pike scale, NOT MET	EX	$59.00	5-2000
Heddon	Walton Feather Tail	rainbow, glass eyes, gleamer	EX-	$364.00	1-2000
Heddon	Walton Feather Tail	red, white	VG	$86.00	1-1999
Heddon	Wee Tad	590BRSJO	NIB	$260.00	9-2001
Heddon	Wee Willie	strawberry, glass eyes	VG+	$305.00	11-1999
Heddon	Wee Willie	white, flitter, cup rig, vg- unmarked Up Bass box	NIB	$425.00	11-2001
Heddon	Wee Willie	yellow head, white, flitter, glass eyes, Brush box	NIB	$500.00	3-2001
Heddon	Weedless Widow	222, POBW, Brush box, NO BIDS	NIB	$49.99	6-1999
Heddon	Weedless Widow	green scale, no eyes	EX-	$52.00	6-1999
Heddon	Weedless Widow	yellow, sparkles	EX	$54.00	9-2000
Heddon	Widget	9 different, nice	EX- to EX	$310.00	11-1999
Heddon	Widget	300BF window box, on card	NIB	$177.00	2-2000
Heddon	Widget	BF	EX+	$50.00	3-2001
Heddon	Widget	black, spotted, NOT MET	EX	$71.01	8-1999
Heddon	Widget	mouse	EX	$124.72	5-1999
Heddon	Widget	mouse	VG+	$64.55	11-1999
Heddon	Widget	perch scale, NOT MET	EX-	$52.00	4-2000
Heddon	Widget	perch scale, red window box	NIB	$143.00	7-2000
Heddon	Widget	silver, red, black spots	Mint	$75.00	8-1999
Heddon	Widget	SS, red head	EX	$66.00	10-2001

BRAND	MODEL	SERIES / MFG. CODE / DESCRIPTION	GRADE	PRICE	DATE
Heddon	Wiggle King	2000, red & white blended	VG	$127.50	11-1999
Heddon	Wiggle King	(M) pike scale, no eyes, belly stencil, unmarked Down Bass box	VG-	$285.00	11-2000
Heddon	Wiggle King	red head, belly decal, ugly varnish	AVG	$75.00	11-1999
Heddon	Wiggle King	red scale, painted eyes?, cup	EX-	$406.00	5-2000
Heddon	Wiggle King	shiner scale	NIB	$2,000.00	4-2000
Heddon	Wiggle King	strawberry, intro slant head	VG+	$750.00	5-2000
Heddon	Wiggler	1600, crackleback, inchworm	EX-	$179.50	12-1998
Heddon	Wiggler	1602, crisp tall Down Bass box, hang tag, crab paper	NIB	$1,225.00	1-2002
Heddon	Wiggler	red head, hang tag, papers, tall Down Bass box	NIB	$779.00	9-2001
Heddon	Wiggler	red, white, "Wiggler" on side, Down Bass box	EX/IB	$293.88	8-1999
Heddon	Wiggler, Baby Crab	1900, 1900 Brush box	VG+/IB	$70.00	3-2000
Heddon	Wiggler, Baby Crab	1900, crackleback, 1900 Down Bass box	EX/IB	$330.00	3-1999
Heddon	Wiggler, Baby Crab	1900, crackleback, L-rig, Up Bass box	EX/IB	$202.50	2-2000
Heddon	Wiggler, Baby Crab	1900, crackleback, NOT MET	EX	$148.00	10-2000
Heddon	Wiggler, Baby Crab	1900 Deluxe, red scale, unmarked box	EX-/IB	$260.00	5-2000
Heddon	Wiggler, Baby Crab	1900, green scale, L-rig	EX	$320.00	6-1999
Heddon	Wiggler, Baby Crab	1902, crisp Brush box	NIB	$330.00	4-1999
Heddon	Wiggler, Baby Crab	1909B, ex- Down Bass box, NOT MET	VG+/IB	$122.00	10-2002
Heddon	Wiggler, Baby Crab	1909J, Down Bass box nice	EX-/IB	$408.00	4-2002
Heddon	Wiggler, Baby Crab	1950 Deluxe, red scale	EX-	$156.00	6-2000
Heddon	Wiggler, Baby Crab	1959P, Brush box, 2-piece, tiny nose chip	EX/IB	$282.00	10-2000
Heddon	Wiggler, Baby Crab	crab, later	EX+	$370.00	5-2000
Heddon	Wiggler, Baby Crab	crackleback	EX-	$350.00	5-2000
Heddon	Wiggler, Baby Crab	fancy red scale, pork rind pin on back	EX+	$538.00	9-2000
Heddon	Wiggler, Baby Crab	frog	EX-	$48.00	3-2001
Heddon	Wiggler, Baby Crab	frog, tag, Down Bass box, intro paper	EX/IB	$330.00	1-1999
Heddon	Wiggler, Baby Crab	goldfish, bad varnish, ugly	VG-	$58.00	4-2000
Heddon	Wiggler, Baby Crab	L-rig, unmarked Down Bass box	EX-/IB	$234.00	5-2002
Heddon	Wiggler, Baby Crab	natural scale, age lines but nice	EX-	$1,000.00	7-2001
Heddon	Wiggler, Baby Crab	perch scale	VG-	$80.00	1-1999
Heddon	Wiggler, Crab	3½", strawberry	VG	$141.19	1-1999
Heddon	Wiggler, Crab	1800P, L-rig	EX	$423.00	5-1999
Heddon	Wiggler, Crab	1800S, Down Bass box, nice	VG+/IB	$229.00	5-2002
Heddon	Wiggler, Crab	1809B, frog, intro Down Bass box	EX/IB	$400.00	8-2000
Heddon	Wiggler, Crab	1809D, crisp "crab" Down Bass box	EX/IB	$337.00	5-2000
Heddon	Wiggler, Crab	1809J, frog scale	VG-	$158.00	5-2000
Heddon	Wiggler, Crab	crab, U-collar, unmarked intro box	EX-/IB	$300.00	8-1999
Heddon	Wiggler, Crab	crackleback, Down Bass intro box, NOT MET	VG+/IB	$140.00	7-2000
Heddon	Wiggler, Crab	crackleback, glass eyes	VG+	$153.00	1-2001
Heddon	Wiggler, Crab	crackleback, glass eyes, L-rig	VG	$91.99	5-1999
Heddon	Wiggler, Crab	frog, small, L-rig, varnish	VG	$53.00	10-2000
Heddon	Wiggler, Crab	frog, vg "crab" Down Bass box, papers	VG/IB	$168.00	11-2000
Heddon	Wiggler, Crab	green scale, no eyes, 1600 body	VG+	$400.00	2-2002
Heddon	Wiggler, Crab	green scale, poor Down Bass box, NOT MET	EX-/IB	$105.00	9-2000
Heddon	Wiggler, Crab	inchworm, frog, glass eyes, L-rig	VG+	$177.00	7-2000

BRAND	MODEL	SERIES / MFG. CODE / DESCRIPTION	GRADE	PRICE	DATE
Heddon	Wiggler, Crab	rainbow scale, age lines	EX-	$598.00	8-2002
Heddon	Wiggler, Crab	red head & tail, not marked, luminous?	EX-	$400.00	8-2002
Heddon	Wiggler, Crab	red head blended white, glitter	VG	$272.75	3-1999
Heddon	Wiggler, Crab	red, white, L-rig, unmarked Up Bass box	VG+/IB	$125.00	7-1999
Heddon	Wiggler, Crab	white, glass eyes, leather tail	EX+	$227.51	6-1999
Heddon	Wiggler, Crab	yellow, black, small, L-rig	EX	$284.00	11-2000
Heddon	Wiggler, Crab	yellow spots, Down Bass intro box, catalog	EX-/IB	$300.00	10-2000
Heddon	Wiggler, Deep Diving	1600, crackleback, L-rig, vg Down Bass box	NIB	$520.00	12-1999
Heddon	Wiggler, Deep Diving	1600, crackleback, pigtail	VG	$163.00	1-1999
Heddon	Wiggler, Deep Diving	1600, inchworm, white, red flakes, varnish	VG	$150.00	3-2000
Heddon	Wiggler, Deep Diving	1600, inchworm, yellow, black, red spots	VG+	$79.00	8-1999
Heddon	Wiggler, Deep Diving	1600, rainbow, inchworm, tall unmarked Down Bass box, NOT MET	EX-/IB	$315.00	10-2001
Heddon	Wiggler, Deep Diving	1600, red, white, inchworm, NOT MET	AVG	$46.00	1-1999
Heddon	Wiggler, Deep Diving	1600S, Deep S, avg Down Bass box	VG+/IB	$365.00	10-2000
Heddon	Wiggler, Deep Diving	1600SB, unmarked Down Bass box, varnish	VG-/IB	$102.00	11-2000
Heddon	Wiggler, Deep Diving	1600S, NOT MET	EX-/IB	$408.03	1-2000
Heddon	Wiggler, Deep Diving	1600, strawberry, bottom cup, pigtail line tie	EX	$400.00	3-1999
Heddon	Wiggler, Deep Diving	1600, white, L-rig nice	EX	$229.48	3-2000
Heddon	Wiggler, Deep Diving	1600, yellow spots, ex- tall Down Bass box	EX/IB	$1,400.00	12-2001
Heddon	Wiggler, Deep Diving	1602, mint box, hang tag, papers	NIB	$1,225.00	1-2002
Heddon	Wiggler, Deep Diving	1609S, tall Down Bass box, side hooks	EX-/IB	$305.00	11-2000
Heddon	Wiggler, Deep Diving	frog, pigtail	EX	$331.00	8-2000
Heddon	Wiggler, Deep Diving	strawberry, side hooks	VG+	$375.00	5-2000
Heddon	Wiggler, Deep Diving	yellow, strawberry, 3 side hooks , L-rig	VG+	$104.00	5-2000
Heddon	Wiggler, Midget Crab	frog, 2-piece	EX	$250.00	10-1999
Heddon	Wiggler, Near Surface	1609B, 1609B tall Down Bass Wiggler box	EX/IB	$1,330.00	10-1999
Heddon	Wiggler, Near Surface	1700, blue scale, several pointers, ugly	VG-	$431.00	11-2000
Heddon	Wiggler, Near Surface	1700, goldfish, inchworm, tie	EX-	$1,200.00	10-2001
Heddon	Wiggler, Near Surface	1700, strawberry, glass eyes, cup	VG	$158.00	1-1999
Heddon	Wiggler, Near Surface	1700, strawberry, pigtail line tie, paper, 1705 Down Bass box	NIB	$1,027.00	1-2001
Heddon	Wiggler, Near Surface	1700, strawberry, pigtail, L-rig	VG	$176.00	3-1999
Heddon	Wiggler, Near Surface	1700, Vamp plus 5-hook	Poor	$155.00	1-1999
Heddon	Wiggler, Near Surface	inchworm, frog, glass eyes, varnish	VG	$118.00	5-2000
Heddon	Wiggler, Near Surface	inchworm, yellow spots, cracked eye	EX-	$550.00	5-2000
Heddon	Wiggler, Surface	1700, yellow, black, red spots, pigtail	EX-	$230.50	8-1999
Heddon	Wilder-Dilg	#2, Mannfeld Coaxer, vg unmarked Heddon box	NIB	$462.00	5-2001
Heddon	Wilder-Dilg	#3, Venable's Charmer, picture box		$200.00	9-1999
Heddon	Wilder Dilg	#4, Kemper's Char, glass eyes, ex box	EX/IB	$812.00	8-2000
Heddon	Wilder-Dilg	#6, bass size, Down Bass box, card	NIB	$861.00	8-2000
Heddon	Wilder-Dilg	#6, in rough picture box	EX/IB	$87.05	2-2000
Heddon	Wilder-Dilg	#6, Wilder's Fancy, great box	NIB	$1,002.00	8-2000
Heddon	Wilder-Dilg	#7, crisp Up Bass box	NIB	$225.00	2-2000
Heddon	Wilder-Dilg	#8, Zane Grey, picture box, card	EX/IB	$271.05	3-1999
Heddon	Wilder-Dilg	#12, Bob Davis card, Up Bass box	NIB	$433.00	1-2002
Heddon	Wilder-Dilg	#12, yellow, Down Bass box	EX/IB	$113.02	3-1999

BRAND	MODEL	SERIES / MFG. CODE / DESCRIPTION	GRADE	PRICE	DATE
Heddon	Wilder-Dilg	#33, trout, Down Bass box, card, NOT MET	NOB	$237.00	10-2001
Heddon	Wilder-Dilg	crisp Down Bass box	NIB	$255.00	9-1999
Heddon	Wilder-Dilg	ex- Irving Cobb picture box	NIB	$627.00	6-2002
Heddon	Wilder-Dilg	intro box	NIB	$356.50	4-1999
Heddon	Wilder Dilg	Venable's Charmer, nice picture box	NIB	$450.00	6-2002
Heddon	Wilder-Dilg	lure is awful, vg odd box		$305.00	1-1999
Heddon	Wilder-Dilg	red, #30 Down Bass box	NIB	$431.00	3-2000
Heddon	Wilder-Dilg	red, avg picture box	EX/IB	$204.55	11-1999
Heddon	Wilder-Dilg	red, Down Bass box	NIB	$326.00	7-1999
Heddon	Wilder-Dilg	red, yellow	Mint	$34.00	1-2000
Heddon	Wilder-Dilg	Venable's Charmer	EX/IB	$148.00	1-1999
Heddon	Wilder-Dilg	vg Bob Davis picture box, NOT MET	EX/IB	$177.50	1-2000
Heddon	Wilder-Dilg	vg+ Bob Davis picture box	NIB	$277.99	1-2000
Heddon	Wilder-Dilg	vg+ unmarked Down Bass box, NOT MET	NIB	$85.00	6-2002
Heddon	Wilder-Dilg	white, vg+ Up Bass box	VG/IB	$145.00	7-2000
Heddon	Wilder-Dilg	Zane Gray, nice box	EX/IB	$610.00	8-2000
Heddon	Wilder-Dilg	Bryan Glory, rough picture box, papers	NIB	$138.55	2-2000
Heddon	Wilder-Dilg Spook	XRS, NOT MET	Mint	$22.27	8-1999
Heddon	Woodpecker	1001, red head, blue border, Down Bass box, luminous paper	EX-/NIB	$3,550.00	4-2002
Heddon	Woodpecker	1001, red head, hand marked box Heddon tissue, NOT MET		$1,025.00	2-2002
Heddon	Wounded Spook	2 different, perch XRY, gold eyes	EX	$90.00	3-1999
Heddon	Wounded Spook	2XRY, red head, gold eyes	EX	$75.00	3-1999
Heddon	Wounded Spook	9140SD, white eyes, PTCB	NIB	$80.00	10-2000
Heddon	Wounded Spook	9140XRS, gold eyes	NIB	$81.00	4-1999
Heddon	Wounded Spook	9140XRW, 2PCCB, 2-piece rig	NIB	$151.50	1-1999
Heddon	Wounded Spook	9140XRY	EXIB	$71.00	4-1999
Heddon	Wounded Spook		Mint	$44.51	1-1999
Heddon	Wounded Spook	BF, gold eyes	VG+	$69.99	4-1999
Heddon	Wounded Spook	crackleback	EX	$345.00	6-1999
Heddon	Wounded Spook	frog	EX-	$61.00	1-1999
Heddon	Wounded Spook	frog, white eyes	EX	$25.02	12-1999
Heddon	Wounded Spook	frog, white eyes	EX	$28.08	8-1999
Heddon	Wounded Spook	frog, white eyes	EX	$52.00	4-2000
Heddon	Wounded Spook	frog, white eyes	VG	$56.00	3-1999
Heddon	Wounded Spook	frog, white eyes	EX-	$26.01	8-1999
Heddon	Wounded Spook	gold eyes, 9140XRY Banner box	NIB	$37.00	6-2000
Heddon	Wounded Spook	gold eyes, L-rig	Mint	$66.00	9-2000
Heddon	Wounded Spook	gold eyes, L-rig, $5.00	EX	$27.51	7-1999
Heddon	Wounded Spook	gold eyes, L-rig, crisp box & catalog	NIB	$89.00	1-2001
Heddon	Wounded Spook	gold eyes, L-rig, NOT MET	Mint	$46.53	6-1999
Heddon	Wounded Spook	GRA	EX	$335.00	1-2002
Heddon	Wounded Spook	green, pink, white	EX	$26.50	12-1998
Heddon	Wounded Spook	perch scale, white eyes	Mint	$44.00	5-2001
Heddon	Wounded Spook	perch, box papers	NIB	$40.00	2-1999
Heddon	Wounded Spook	perch, gold eyes	EX-	$29.00	9-1999

BRAND	MODEL	SERIES / MFG. CODE / DESCRIPTION	GRADE	PRICE	DATE
Heddon	Wounded Spook	perch, white eyes	EX	$18.51	5-1999
Heddon	Wounded Spook	perch, white eyes	EX	$34.00	8-1999
Heddon	Wounded Spook	perch, white eyes	Mint	$20.00	4-1999
Heddon	Wounded Spook	PSTB, frog, white eyes	NIB	$46.00	1-2000
Heddon	Wounded Spook	red head, flitter, gold eyes	Mint	$61.00	8-1999
Heddon	Wounded Spook	red head, yellow eyes	EX	$89.50	6-1999
Heddon	Wounded Spook	red, white, gold eyes	EX	$71.01	2-1999
Heddon	Wounded Spook	RHF, gold eyes	EX	$92.00	8-1999
Heddon	Wounded Spook	RHF, gold eyes, 2PCCB	NIB	$112.50	5-1999
Heddon	Wounded Spook	shad	NIB	$40.00	8-2000
Heddon	Wounded Spook	shad, white eyes	EX	$55.00	6-1999
Heddon	Wounded Spook	shad, white eyes	EX	$100.00	8-2001
Heddon	Wounded Spook	shad, white eyes	EX-	$32.07	2-1999
Heddon	Wounded Spook	shad, white eyes	VG	$22.50	12-1999
Heddon	Wounded Spook	shad, white eyes, PTCB	NIB	$89.00	11-1999
Heddon	Wounded Spook	white eyes, L-rig, PTCB	VGIB	$47.00	5-1999
Heddon	Wounded Spook	XBW	VG	$37.99	12-1998
Heddon	Wounded Spook	XBW, recessed gold eyes	EX	$67.00	4-2000
Heddon	Wounded Spook	XBW, white eyes	EX	$47.00	4-2000
Heddon	Wounded Spook	XBW, white eyes	EX	$89.00	2-2000
Heddon	Wounded Spook	XBW, white eyes, window box	NIB	$65.00	3-2000
Heddon	Wounded Spook	XRS, gold eyes	EX	$39.00	4-1999
Heddon	Wounded Spook	XRS, gold eyes, box	VGIB	$53.00	4-1999
Heddon	Wounded Spook	XRS, white eyes	VG	$30.00	1-2000
Heddon	Wounded Spook	XRW, gold eyes	EX	$87.00	1-1999
Heddon	Wounded Spook	XRW, gold eyes	EX+	$46.50	3-1999
Heddon	Wounded Spook	XRW, gold, sunken eyes	EX	$22.25	11-1999
Heddon	Wounded Spook	XRW, recessed eyes, S-rig	EX	$77.00	1-1999
Heddon	Wounded Spook	XRY, gold eyes	EX	$26.51	4-1999
Heddon	Wounded Spook	XRY, gold eyes	EX	$50.99	3-1999
Heddon	Wounded Spook	XRY, gold eyes	EX	$52.02	6-1999
Heddon	Wounded Spook	XRY, gold eyes	EX-	$33.50	1-2000
Heddon	Wounded Spook	XRY, gold eyes	VG	$17.54	2-2000
Heddon	Wounded Spook	XRY, gold eyes	VG	$69.99	4-1999
Heddon	Wounded Spook	XRY, white eyes	EX-	$31.51	4-1999
Heddon	Wounded Spook	XRY, white eyes, NOT MET	VG-	$9.99	5-1999
Heddon	Wounded Spook	XRY, white eyes, ugly	VG-	$28.89	3-1999
Heddon	Wounded Spook	9140L Banner box, gold eyes	NIB	$56.00	4-2000
Heddon	Wounded Spook	gold eyes, 9140XRW Banner box	EXIB	$63.00	4-2000
Heddon	Zara	frog scale, painted eyes, wood, no hardware	EX	$16.00	7-2002
Heddon	Zara	frog, wood	Mint	$37.00	5-1999
Heddon	Zara II	chrome, white eyes	NIB	$233.00	9-2001
Heddon	Zara II	frog, gold eyes	NIB	$37.00	10-2001
Heddon	Zara II	GRA	EX	$61.00	4-1999
Heddon	Zara II	red	EX+	$36.00	1-1999
Heddon	Zara II	scale, red ribs	EX	$75.00	2-1999
Heddon	Zara II	yellow, 2 black dots, red gills	EX	$91.50	6-1999

BRAND	MODEL	SERIES / MFG. CODE / DESCRIPTION	GRADE	PRICE	DATE
Heddon	Zara II	9240ORH, looks red to me	NIB	$134.00	12-2000
Heddon	Zara II	9240XBL	NIB	$42.00	8-2001
Heddon	Zara, Baby	crackleback, gold eyes	EX	$123.06	6-1999
Heddon	Zara, Drop	silver scale	NOC	$52.50	1-1999
Heddon	Zara-Spook	2 different, XRB, clear, chin tie, no hole	EX	$133.50	4-1999
Heddon	Zara-Spook	1 molded, 1 S-rig; blueshore, nose tie	EX	$20.50	3-2000
Heddon	Zara-Spook	2 nose ties, 1 chin tie, no hole; natural bluegill, GD?	EX-	$65.99	6-1999
Heddon	Zara-Spook	13 different swaybacks	EX- to Mint	$800.00	7-2002
Heddon	Zara-Spook	17 Pradcos	EX	$156.00	3-1999
Heddon	Zara-Spook	9250SS, white eyes	NIB	$32.00	6-1999
Heddon	Zara-Spook	9250XRW	NIB	$50.00	3-1999
Heddon	Zara-Spook	9255C, blue shore, original chin tie	NIB	$63.00	8-1999
Heddon	Zara-Spook	9255XBL triangle card	NOC	$84.00	5-2001
Heddon	Zara-Spook	9255XBW, swayback, original	NIB	$100.00	9-2000
Heddon	Zara-Spook	9256NF, Charlie Campbell, chin tie, swayback	NIB	$88.00	7-2000
Heddon	Zara-Spook	bar perch? chin tie, no hole, swayback	EX	$260.00	4-2000
Heddon	Zara-Spook	brown crawdad?, chin tie, no hole	EX	$120.50	6-1999
Heddon	Zara-Spook	baby bass, chin tie, no hole, swayback	EX	$94.00	5-2000
Heddon	Zara-Spook	baby bass, original chin tie, no hole	EX	$60.01	6-1999
Heddon	Zara-Spook	baby bass, swayback, chin tie, no hole	EX	$128.50	2-2000
Heddon	Zara-Spook	bass?, green, black, original	EX	$182.50	1-1999
Heddon	Zara-Spook	baby bass, luminous, chin tie, swayback	EX	$48.00	4-2001
Heddon	Zara-Spook	BB, swayback	NIB	$92.00	8-2000
Heddon	Zara-Spook	BF, white eyes & nose	EX	$46.99	1-1999
Heddon	Zara-Spook	BF, white eyes & nose, window box	NIB	$50.00	2-1999
Heddon	Zara-Spook	black, silver foil, nose tie	EX	$200.00	2-2000
Heddon	Zara-Spook	BRS	EX	$137.00	10-2002
Heddon	Zara-Spook	BRS, chin tie, swayback	EX	$114.00	10-2001
Heddon	Zara-Spook	BRS, swayback NOT MET	EX	$79.00	3-2002
Heddon	Zara-Spook	CD, green scale, luminous belly, chin tie, no hole	EX	$70.00	4-2000
Heddon	Zara-Spook	Charlie Campbell, natural mullet?, chin tie, no hole	VG+	$68.00	5-1999
Heddon	Zara-Spook	Charlie Campbell, natural yellow mullet?, chin tie, no hole	VG+	$71.00	5-1999
Heddon	Zara-Spook	Charlie Campbell, baby bass, chin tie, no hole	EX	$142.00	12-1998
Heddon	Zara-Spook	Charlie Campbell, frog, chin tie, no hole	EX	$69.00	2-2000
Heddon	Zara-Spook	Charlie Campbell, natural bass, swayback	EX	$53.00	8-2001
Heddon	Zara-Spook	Charlie Campbell, natural striper, chin	EX	$41.00	3-1999
Heddon	Zara-Spook	Charlie Campbell, shad, chin tie, NOT MET	EX	$104.00	4-2000
Heddon	Zara-Spook	chrome, black scale, nose tie	NIB	$69.00	4-1999
Heddon	Zara-Spook	chrome, original chin tie, no hole	VG	$73.00	4-1999
Heddon	Zara-Spook	clear, chin tie, no hole	EX	$137.50	12-1998
Heddon	Zara-Spook	clear, chin tie, swayback	EX	$55.00	6-2002
Heddon	Zara-Spook	clear, chin tie, swayback	EX	$178.50	3-2000
Heddon	Zara-Spook	clear, heavy duty hardware	EX+	$80.50	4-2000
Heddon	Zara-Spook	clear, nose tie, molded hardware	EX	$56.00	5-1999

BRAND	MODEL	SERIES / MFG. CODE / DESCRIPTION	GRADE	PRICE	DATE
Heddon	Zara-Spook	clear, nose tie, molded hardware	EX	$86.00	5-1999
Heddon	Zara-Spook	clear, white eyes, chin-no hardware	Mint	$62.00	2-1999
Heddon	Zara-Spook	Cohiba Cuban Cigar special order	NOC	$11.00	2-1999
Heddon	Zara-Spook	Color-C-lector, 6-pack	NIB	$217.50	12-1998
Heddon	Zara-Spook	Color-C-lector, black, red, silver, EBSCO	NOC	$12.49	2-1999
Heddon	Zara-Spook	crawdad, Florida brown, original	VG	$126.00	1-1999
Heddon	Zara-Spook	crawdad, original	EX	$102.50	8-1999
Heddon	Zara-Spook	clear, nose	NIB	$132.50	1-1999
Heddon	Zara-Spook	clear, white eyes & nose, heavy duty	EX-	$107.50	1-1999
Heddon	Zara-Spook	Dowluck special order	NOC	$11.01	2-1999
Heddon	Zara-Spook	FF9250GR, NOT MET	NIB	$137.50	10-1999
Heddon	Zara-Spook	FFGB		$86.00	12-1998
Heddon	Zara-Spook	FFGB	EX	$86.00	12-1998
Heddon	Zara-Spook	FFGR, NOT MET	EX	$112.51	3-1999
Heddon	Zara-Spook	frog, Charlie Campbell	EX	$67.00	1-1999
Heddon	Zara-Spook	frog, Charlie Campbell, no hole	EX	$39.87	9-1999
Heddon	Zara-Spook	frog, chin tie, no hole	EX	$107.50	4-1999
Heddon	Zara-Spook	frog, chin tie, no hole, NOT MET	EX	$73.00	2-2000
Heddon	Zara-Spook	frog, gold eyes, chin tie, no hole	EX	$79.00	5-1999
Heddon	Zara-Spook	frog, gold eyes, chin tie, no hole	Mint	$100.00	5-1999
Heddon	Zara-Spook	frog, gold eyes, chin tie, swayback	EX	$72.00	5-2001
Heddon	Zara-Spook	frog scale, looks like a Pradco lure	EX	$232.00	6-2000
Heddon	Zara-Spook	frog, wood	EX	$16.00	1-1999
Heddon	Zara-Spook	GD color, chin tie, no hole	EX	$41.00	6-1999
Heddon	Zara-Spook	GRA, swayback, chin tie, no hole	NIB	$79.00	2-2002
Heddon	Zara-Spook	green, red, black spots, chin tie	NIB	$185.00	3-1999
Heddon	Zara-Spook	green scale baby bass, chin tie, swayback	EX	$44.00	4-2001
Heddon	Zara-Spook	green scale coach dog, chin tie, no hole	EX-	$191.38	2-2000
Heddon	Zara-Spook	GR luminous belly, chin tie, no hole	EX	$70.00	4-2000
Heddon	Zara-Spook	KCH, 6 stripes, chin tie, swayback	EX	$242.00	4-2001
Heddon	Zara-Spook	MG, gold musky, chin tie, no hole	NOC	$167.50	1-1999
Heddon	Zara-Spook	MG, gold scale musky	NOC	$133.50	2-1999
Heddon	Zara-Spook	MG, swayback, chin tie, no hole	NIB	$236.00	2-2002
Heddon	Zara-Spook	natural bluegill, Charlie Campbell, chin tie, no hole	EX	$167.50	12-1999
Heddon	Zara-Spook	natural chrome shad, chin tie, no hole, clear silver foil, NOT NET	EX	$76.00	2-2000
Heddon	Zara-Spook	natural frog, chin tie, no hole, original	EX	$143.50	4-1999
Heddon	Zara-Spook	natural green perch, chin tie, no hole	EX	$153.28	2-2000
Heddon	Zara-Spook	natural shad?, Charlie Campbell, chin tie, no hole	EX	$157.10	12-1999
Heddon	Zara-Spook	natural striper, chin tie, no hole	EC	$38.00	5-2000
Heddon	Zara-Spook	natural striper, NOT MET	EX	$110.00	4-2001
Heddon	Zara-Spook	NSP, natural spotted bass, Charlie Campbell	EX	$138.00	12-1999
Heddon	Zara-Spook	NVRB, natural rainbow chrome	NIB	$67.00	3-2000
Heddon	Zara-Spook	perch?, chin tie, swayback,	VG	$114.00	7-2002
Heddon	Zara-Spook	photo frog, chin tie, no hole, NOT MET	EX	$51.00	6-1999

BRAND	MODEL	SERIES / MFG. CODE / DESCRIPTION	GRADE	PRICE	DATE
Heddon	Zara-Spook	purple, chin tie, no hole, washer eyes	EX	$50.00	1-1999
Heddon	Zara-Spook	red, gold foil, gold eyes	EX	$102.70	11-1999
Heddon	Zara-Spook	red, gold, flitter inside	EX	$247.50	7-1999
Heddon	Zara-Spook	red, gold foil, nose tie	EX-	$87.00	2-2002
Heddon	Zara-Spook	red, white, chin tie, no hole	EX-	$71.00	5-1999
Heddon	Zara-Spook	red, white, molded hardware	NIB	$26.51	4-1999
Heddon	Zara-Spook	red, white, white eye, nose tie	EX	$36.00	2-1999
Heddon	Zara-Spook	red, white, white eyes, nose tie	EX-	$43.99	1-1999
Heddon	Zara-Spook	red head	NIB	$69.00	12-1998
Heddon	Zara-Spook	red head, white eyes, flitter, nose tie	EX/IB	$18.50	10-1999
Heddon	Zara-Spook	S9250SFB	NIB	$200.00	2-2002
Heddon	Zara-Spook	shad, nose tie	EX	$77.02	1-1999
Heddon	Zara-Spook	silver, glitter filled	EX	$261.00	12-1998
Heddon	Zara-Spook	silver scale, gold eyes, nose tie	VG	$31.00	1-1999
Heddon	Zara-Spook	silver scale, white eyes, nose tie	EX-	$14.01	8-1999
Heddon	Zara-Spook	special order kamikaze quality tackle	NOC	$24.50	2-1999
Heddon	Zara-Spook	SS	NIB	$46.05	12-1998
Heddon	Zara-Spook	SS, chin tie, swayback	EX	$37.00	2-2002
Heddon	Zara-Spook	SS, chin tie, swayback, 4-seam, no hole nose	Mint	$41.00	8-2002
Heddon	Zara-Spook	SS, gold eyes, Banner box	NIB	$40.00	1-2000
Heddon	Zara-Spook	SS, gold eyes, nose tie	EX-	$22.05	4-1999
Heddon	Zara-Spook	SS, gold eyes, spoon, Banner box	NIB	$22.00	11-1999
Heddon	Zara-Spook	SS, nose tie	EX-	$41.99	1-1999
Heddon	Zara-Spook	SS, nose tie	EXIB	$19.00	1-1999
Heddon	Zara-Spook	SS, nose tie, molded hook hangers	EX+	$22.16	5-1999
Heddon	Zara-Spook	SS, nose tie, molded hook hangers	NIB	$22.51	8-1999
Heddon	Zara-Spook	SS, chin tie, no hole, original	EX	$85.00	4-1999
Heddon	Zara-Spook	SS, white eyes, heavy salt rig	NIB	$41.00	3-1999
Heddon	Zara-Spook	SS, white eyes, nose tie	EX-	$10.49	8-2001
Heddon	Zara-Spook	SS, wood	NOC	$18.00	2-1999
Heddon	Zara-Spook	SSXRY, chin tie, no hole	VG	$24.94	12-1998
Heddon	Zara-Spook	x2; one red fish flash, one black flash flash; Banner box	VG/IB	$124.72	6-1999
Heddon	Zara-Spook	x2; XRW, red head, glass eyes, nose tie, washer eyes	VG	$76.95	2-1999
Heddon	Zara-Spook	x2; XRYSS, glass eyes, nose tie	EX	$71.00	2-1999
Heddon	Zara-Spook	x3, red head, XRY, BF	VG	$162.00	12-1998
Heddon	Zara-Spook	x3; one red head, one XRY, one SS	VG	$82.00	12-1998
Heddon	Zara-Spook	x3; one XRY, one XBL, one SS nose	EX-	$65.00	2-1999
Heddon	Zara-Spook	white. gold eyes, nose tie	VG	$16.51	8-1999
Heddon	Zara-Spook	XBW, chin tie, no hole	VG	$59.50	3-1999
Heddon	Zara-Spook	XBW, chin tie, no hole	VG+	$68.00	5-1999
Heddon	Zara-Spook	XBW, gold eyes	EX	$57.50	8-1999
Heddon	Zara-Spook	XBW, white eyes, nose tie, NOT MET	EX	$32.00	3-1999
Heddon	Zara-Spook	XRB	EX	$54.10	1-1999
Heddon	Zara-Spook	XRB	NIB	$80.00	12-1998
Heddon	Zara-Spook	XRB, chin tie, no hole	EX-	$51.00	6-1999

BRAND	MODEL	SERIES / MFG. CODE / DESCRIPTION	GRADE	PRICE	DATE
Heddon	Zara-Spook	XRB, gold eyes, nose tie	EX	$33.00	6-1999
Heddon	Zara-Spook	XRB, white eyes	EX	$22.00	10-1999
Heddon	Zara-Spook	XRB, white eyes	NIB	$81.01	12-1998
Heddon	Zara-Spook	XRS, clear, chin tie, swayback	EX	$65.00	5-2001
Heddon	Zara-Spook	XRS, white eyes, chin tie, swayback	Mint	$79.00	11-1999
Heddon	Zara-Spook	XRW	EX	$52.01	12-1998
Heddon	Zara-Spook	XRW	NIB	$82.00	12-1998
Heddon	Zara-Spook	XRW, nose tie, molded hook hangers	EX	$26.01	5-1999
Heddon	Zara-Spook	XRW, nose tie, molded hook hangers	NIB	$24.01	8-1999
Heddon	Zara-Spook	XRY	NIB	$44.00	5-2002
Heddon	Zara-Spook	XRY	NIB	$66.00	12-1998
Heddon	Zara-Spook	XRY, 2PCCB, gold eyes	NIB	$152.50	12-1998
Heddon	Zara-Spook	XRY, chin tie, swayback	EX	$44.00	2-2002
Heddon	Zara-Spook	XRY, chin tie, swayback	EX	$59.00	6-2002
Heddon	Zara-Spook	XRY, gold eyes, Banner box	NIB	$52.00	1-1999
Heddon	Zara-Spook	XRY, gold eyes, nose tie	EX-	$46.99	1-1999
Heddon	Zara-Spook	XRY, gold eyes, nose tie	VG	$40.00	1-1999
Heddon	Zara-Spook	XRY, nose tie	EX	$41.00	1-1999
Heddon	Zara-Spook	XRY, nose tie	EX-/IB	$36.00	1-1999
Heddon	Zara-Spook	XRY, nose tie, molded hook hangers	NIB	$23.01	8-1999
Heddon	Zara-Spook	XRY, white eyes, nose tie	EX	$18.50	4-1999
Heddon	Zara-Spook	XRY, white eyes, nose tie	Mint	$30.70	2-1999
Heddon	Zara-Spook	XRY, white eyes, nose tie	VG	$10.51	4-1999
Heddon	Zara-Spook	XRY, white eyes, nose tie	VG	$33.99	1-1999
Heddon	Zara-Spook	XRY, white eyes, PSTB	NIB	$51.01	1-2000
Heddon	Zaragossa	0001 Centennial, sienna	NIB	$77.00	1-1999
Heddon	Zaragossa	6500SO, painted eyes, Banner box	NIB	$125.00	6-1999
Heddon	Zaragossa	6509DYB, yellow belly, 2-piece, Brush box	EX/IB	$504.99	11-1999
Heddon	Zaragossa	6509K, Down Bass box, L-rig, NOT MET	NIB	$2,550.00	12-1999
Heddon	Zaragossa	6509P	VG+	$375.00	10-1999
Heddon	Zaragossa	6509PRH	EX-	$700.00	10-1999
Heddon	Zaragossa	6509PRH2H, 2-piece, CA, BW, Brush box, NOT MET	NIB	$525.00	1-2000
Heddon	Zaragossa	6509RH2H, red head, 2-piece, flitter, Brush box	EX/IB	$699.00	5-2002
Heddon	Zaragossa	BF, painted eyes, Banner box	NIB	$75.75	3-1999
Heddon	Zaragossa	blue scale, glass eyes, L-rig	VG+	$536.00	12-1999
Heddon	Zaragossa	blue scale, L-rig, Buy It Now?	EX	$2,250.00	8-2002
Heddon	Zaragossa	Centennial, BB	NIB	$81.00	1-2002
Heddon	Zaragossa	Centennial, F, not BF, glass eyes	NIB	$101.00	1-2002
Heddon	Zaragossa	Centennial, crackleback	NIB	$29.00	1-1999
Heddon	Zaragossa	Centennial, frog	NIB	$26.00	1-1999
Heddon	Zaragossa	Centennial, frog	NIB	$29.67	1-1999
Heddon	Zaragossa	Centennial, frog	NIB	$32.00	1-1999
Heddon	Zaragossa	Centennial, frog	NIB	$42.00	1-1999
Heddon	Zaragossa	Centennial, frog, glass eyes	NIB	$36.00	7-2000
Heddon	Zaragossa	Centennial, green scale, glass eyes	NIB	$30.00	8-1999
Heddon	Zaragossa	Centennial, white shore	NIB	$42.50	1-1999

BRAND	MODEL	SERIES / MFG. CODE / DESCRIPTION	GRADE	PRICE	DATE
Heddon	Zaragossa	Centennial, X6500WGNS	NIB	$49.05	7-1999
Heddon	Zaragossa	Centennial, yellow spots	NIB	$96.00	3-2001
Heddon	Zaragossa	Centennials, 6 different	NIB	$261.50	5-1999
Heddon	Zaragossa	crackleback, L-rig	EX-	$650.00	10-1999
Heddon	Zaragossa	Deluxe, green scale, L-rig, snub nose tie	EX-	$425.00	3-1999
Heddon	Zaragossa	goldfish scale, blunt nose	VG+	$2,200.00	5-2000
Heddon	Zaragossa	green scale, glass eyes, L-rig	EX-	$280.00	1-2000
Heddon	Zaragossa	green scale, glass eyes, L-rig	VG+	$91.55	9-1999
Heddon	Zaragossa	late dace, toilet	EX-	$405.00	10-2002
Heddon	Zaragossa	L-rig, nice Down Bass box	NIB	$725.00	9-2001
Heddon	Zaragossa	painted eyes, Banner box	VGIB	$62.00	1-1999
Heddon	Zaragossa	perch scale, 2-piece	VG+	$201.00	8-1999
Heddon	Zaragossa	red scale, L-rig, no chin tie	VG-	$1,300.00	11-2000
Heddon	Zaragossa	silver scale, painted eyes, original	Mint	$20.50	3-2000
Heddon	Zaragossa	strawberry, glass eyes, L-rig	VG-	$187.00	8-2000
Heddon	Zaragossa	white, red eyes, extra hook screwed in	EX+	$140.50	11-1999
Heddon	Zaragossa	white, red eyes, L-rig	VG+	$216.00	3-2001
Heddon	Zaragossa, Baby	SO, Banner box, NOT MET	NIB	$316.88	3-1999
Heddon	Zaragossa Jr.	rainbow, glass eyes, for Japan	EX	$96.00	8-2000
Heddon	Zig-Wag	2 different Luny Frogs; 1 red head, 1 natural	G	$220.37	4-1999
Heddon	Zig-Wag	5", herring, painted eyes	Mint	$96.00	9-2002
Heddon	Zig-Wag	8300, red head, natural scale, old stencil	EX	$263.00	8-1999
Heddon	Zig-Wag	8300, shiner scale, old stencil, L-rig	EX+	$100.55	8-1999
Heddon	Zig-Wag	8302 Up Bass box	VG+IB	$60.00	4-1999
Heddon	Zig-Wag	8309M, Down Bass ad box	EX/IB	$255.00	4-1999
Heddon	Zig-Wag	avg Up Bass box	EX-/IB	$64.99	10-1999
Heddon	Zig-Wag	crackleback	EX-	$525.00	8-1999
Heddon	Zig-Wag	frog, glass eyes	Poor	$27.00	2-1999
Heddon	Zig-Wag	Luny Frog, glass eyes, one medium chip	EX	$306.00	1-1999
Heddon	Zig-Wag	perch scale, older L-rig	Mint	$314.99	8-1999
Heddon	Zig-Wag	pike scale, Down Bass box	NIB	$310.00	3-2000
Heddon	Zig-Wag	red head, glass eyes, L-rig, Up Bass box	NIB	$90.00	6-1999
Heddon	Zig-Wag	red head, green scale, 2-piece, Brush box	NIB	$256.51	2-2000
Heddon	Zig-Wag	red head, green scale, belly stencil, very nice	EX+	$240.60	12-1999
Heddon	Zig-Wag	red head, L-rig, Up Bass box	EX/IB	$127.50	2-2000
Heddon	Zig-Wag	red head, natural scale, glass eyes	EX-	$86.00	11-2000
Heddon	Zig-Wag	red head, natural scale, glass eyes	Mint	$200.00	9-1999
Heddon	Zig-Wag	red head, natural scale, L-rig	VG+	$30.00	10-2000
Heddon	Zig-Wag	red head, pike scale, ex hang tag	Mint	$293.00	4-2001
Heddon	Zig-Wag	red, white, 8302 Up Bass box	EX/IB	$80.50	1-1999
Heddon	Zig-Wag	red, white, glass eyes, L-rig, pretty, too cheap	EX+	$81.07	8-1999
Heddon	Zig-Wag Junior	PRH, painted eyes	Mint	$34.00	7-2002
Heddon	Zig-Wag, King	8369, A. Stripey, 1 cracked eye, Brush box	EX/IB	$127.50	4-2000
Heddon	Zig-Wag, King	8369PLXR, red head, Brush box	EX/IB	$203.50	7-1999
Heddon	Zig-Wag, King	8369PAS, Brush box	NIB	$318.00	5-2001
Heddon	Zig-Wag, King	8369PBH, glass eyes, POBW	NIB	$140.00	10-2000

BRAND	MODEL	SERIES / MFG. CODE / DESCRIPTION	GRADE	PRICE	DATE
Heddon	Zig-Wag, King	blue scale	EX	$171.00	8-2000
Heddon	Zig-Wag, King	white, glass eyes, POBW	EX-	$152.50	1-2000
Heddon	Zig-Wag, King	XRW, pearl?, string hook	EX-	$237.50	1-2000
Heddon	Zig-Wag, King	XRW, painted eyes, Banner box	NIB	$75.00	3-2000
Heddon	Zig-Wag, King Salmon	8350P string, crisp Brush box & catalog	NIB	$134.00	11-2000
Helin	Fishcake	2 frog & 1 yellow with red spots	VG	$25.00	1-1999
Helin	Fishcake	4 assorted	EX	$51.00	11-1999
Helin	Fishcake	6-pack, assorted, 2 flourescent	NIB	$114.00	4-2000
Helin	Fishcake	6-pack, five lures (four #9s, one #11)	NIB	$164.50	6-1999
Helin	Fishcake	#7, black spots, black prop	NIB	$20.50	6-1999
Helin	Fishcake	#7, red, white	NIB	$22.05	12-1999
Helin	Fishcake	#7, yellow, red spots	NIB	$20.00	6-1999
Helin	Fishcake	#9B	NIB	$27.60	6-1999
Helin	Fishcake	#9, fluorescent orange, black spots, pointers, dirt	VG	$24.50	3-1999
Helin	Fishcake	#9FR	NIB	$33.00	4-1999
Helin	Fishcake	#9, gold scale, black	NIB	$32.00	6-1999
Helin	Fishcake	#9, orange, red spots	Mint	$30.56	2-1999
Helin	Fishcake	#11	NIB	$39.00	4-1999
Helin	Fishcake	#11, black, glitter	Mint	$11.50	5-1999
Helin	Fishcake	#11F	NIB	$38.00	5-1999
Helin	Fishcake	#11, fluorescent orange	EX	$10.99	12-1999
Helin	Fishcake	#11, orange, black spots	NIB	$29.95	2-1999
Helin	Fishcake	#11, silver	NIB	$30.99	2-1999
Helin	Fishcake	black scale	Mint	$16.01	3-1999
Helin	Fishcake	x2; 1 frog, 1 black with orange spots	Mint	$47.00	3-1999
Helin	Flatfish	6" orange, black stripe, red spots, wood	EX	$36.01	3-1999
Helin	Flatfish	12-pack, dealer display window boxes	NIB	$161.50	3-1999
Helin	Flatfish	flyrod, F7, white, 2PCCB, 1945	NIB	$15.50	5-1999
Helin	Flatfish	S3, frog, tag burn, 2 crisp 1937-1938 papers	NIB	$51.00	3-2002
Helin	Flatfish	x56, plastic, no hooks, special display board	New	$455.00	3-2000
Helin	Swimmerspoon	4 different	NIB	$33.00	12-1999
Helin	Swimmerspoon	white, red, black spots	NIB	$18.26	5-1999
Hendryx	Minnow, Serpentine	correct Bings Bucktail box	EX-	$500.00	10-1999
Hendryx	Minnow, Serpentine	green, spiral thing, ugly	VG	$400.00	1-2000
Hendryx	Spinner, American	5", ball type	VG+	$32.00	6-1999
Henning	Minnow Tube	glass, unmarked wood box, NOT MET	EX	$1,075.00	7-1999
Hinckley	Phantom Float	polished aluminum, January 12, 1905, cleaned	EX	$286.00	10-2000
Hinckley	Phantom, Yellow Bird Fish	#3, vg+ white pasteboard box	AVG/IB	$334.00	8-2001
Hinckley	Yellow Bird	1897 patent	VG	$76.50	8-1999
Hinkle	Lizard	green, black	EX	$86.00	5-2000
Hinkle	Lizard	green scale	EX+	$97.00	5-2000
Hoage	Magnetic Weedless	brown, green	EX	$24.99	5-1999
Hoage	Magnetic Weedless	red head, black	EX	$39.88	8-1999
Hoage	Magnetic Weedless	red, white	EX	$29.00	6-1999
Hoage	Spoon Fin		EX	$400.00	10-1999
Hoage	Spoon Fin	green, yellow, glass eyes	EX	$100.00	10-2000
Hobbs Supply	Bon-Net	rainbow, glass eyes, 6-hook, nice box	VG/IB	$242.50	2-2000

BRAND	MODEL	SERIES / MFG. CODE / DESCRIPTION	GRADE	PRICE	DATE
Hom-Arts	Skipper	rainbow	NIB	$46.00	4-2000
Homemade	Bomber	12", huge, red, white	EX	$28.00	1-1999
Howe's	Vacuum Bait	dragonfly	VG	$406.00	1-1999
Howe's	Vacuum Bait	dragonfly, white, black?, no eyes	EX+	$473.98	4-1999
Howe's	Vacuum Bait	white, red gills, nice tin box, NOT MET	VG-/IB	$224.50	6-1999
Howe's	Vacuum Bait	white, tin box, nice paper, NOT MET	EX-/IB	$536.00	2-2001
Howe's	Vacuum Bait	white, vg- tin box	EX/IB	$780.00	10-1999
Hub	Muk-Ka-Choc	yellow, black spots, NOT MET	EX	$102.00	5-2000
Hungry-Jack			EX-	$501.00	3-2002
Hungry-Jack		NOT MET	VG+	$356.99	5-1999
Illingsworth		#5, MK-2, spin, ½ bail, bakelite sides	VG+	$187.00	10-2001
Immell	Chippewa	3½", crackleback	VG	$204.00	8-2002
Immell	Chippewa	3½", rainbow	EX	$965.00	9-2002
Immell	Chippewa	4", crackleback, side spots, vg- box, NOT MET	VG/IB	$690.00	10-2002
Immell	Chippewa	#99, crackleback, ex- intro box	VG+/IB	$3,450.00	6-2001
Immell	Chippewa	bass size, brown, sienna	EX+	$1,650.00	4-2001
Immell	Chippewa	bass, chips, NOT MET	G	$229.50	1-2000
Immell	Chippewa	bass, rainbow	EX-	$700.00	12-1999
Immell	Chippewa	bass size, crackleback, nice box	NIB	$3,250.00	12-2001
Immell	Chippewa	pike, brown sienna	EX	$999.00	11-1999
Immell	Chippewa	pike size, rainbow, avg box, chips, but nice	VG/IB	$1,025.00	5-2002
Immell	Chippewa	pike size, red, aluminum, correctly marked box	NIB	$3,600.00	4-2001
Immell	Chippewa	pike size, red, big chips, NOT MET	AVG	$167.50	11-1999
Immell	Chippewa	rainbow, avg "pike" box, wants $2,100, NOT MET	EX/IB	$870.00	3-2002
Immell	Chippewa	red, orange, NOT NET	AVG	$237.50	8-1999
Immell	Chippewa	sienna, awful belly, NOT MET	AVG+	$257.00	10-2000
Immell	Chippewa	silver, red back, glass eyes, nice	EX-	$430.34	2-2000
Immell	Musky, Chippewa	crackleback	G	$1,550.00	5-2002
Immell	Musky, Chippewa	Ever seen an excellent one? Now you have!	EX	$3,000.00	4-2001
Immell	Musky, Chippewa	white with spots, chips metal strip NO BIDS	EX-	$2,000.00	8-2002
Immell	Chippewa	4", rainbow, pike size, vg Blair box	NIB	$4,506.00	3-2001
Immell	Chippewa	4", sienna crackleback	AVG	$175.00	2-2002
Immell	Chippewa Musky	white, ugly, NOT MET	VG-	$380.00	1-2002
Immell	Chippewa	bass, sienna, yellow, awful	Poor	$177.50	4-1999
Immell Chippewa		3", red?, no middle hook	VG	$228.00	8-2000
Immell Chippewa	Bass	sienna crackleback	G	$270.00	3-1999
Immell Chippewa	Bass	white	EX-	$890.00	10-1999
Immell Chippewa	Musky	crackleback, chips, NOT MET	G	$775.00	3-1999
Immell Chippewa	Musky	red, 7 yellow big chips, NOT MET	AVG	$305.00	5-1999
Immell Chippewa	Pike	crackleback	EX-	$970.00	10-1999
Immell Chippewa	Pike	crackleback, ugly	Fair	$275.00	3-1999
Immell Chippewa	Pike	missing belly hook, awful	Poor	$250.00	5-1999
Interchangeable Bait Co.	Bubble Sally	with pills & papers, NOT MET	NIB	$48.00	8-2001
Isle Royale	Wobblit	#3333H, Bass-Oreno type, red head, painted eyes	NIB	$36.00	5-2000

BRAND	MODEL	SERIES / MFG. CODE / DESCRIPTION	GRADE	PRICE	DATE
Jacobs	Polly-Frog	4¼", wood with hair legs, neat	EX	$159.00	8-2001
James, W.H.		metal fish spin, patent January 27th, 1874	AVG	$88.00	1-1999
Jamison	Coaxer	#1, frog finish, ex- box (text only on box top)	NIB	$485.00	8-2002
Jamison	Coaxer	#1 in 2PCBB, c.1916	VG+	$177.50	5-1999
Jamison	Coaxer, Underwater	decent pasteboard box, NOT MET	EX/IB	$230.00	2-2002
Jamison	Jamison's # 1500	strawberry, nice	EX	$27.08	2-1999
Jamison	Mascot	red, white	EX+	$200.00	8-1999
Jamison	Mascot, Winged	#2, nice ex- pasteboard box	EX/IB	$380.00	2-2002
Jamison	Mascot, Winged	red head	EX	$103.00	3-2001
Jamison	Mouse, Struggling		EX	$112.50	1-2000
Jamison	Mouse, Struggling	painted eyes, NOT MET	EX-	$102.50	2-2000
Jamison	Wig-L-Twin	black, gold scales	EX	$37.00	1-1999
Jamison	Wig-L-Twin	brown head & wings, silver scale	Mint	$122.50	3-2000
Jamison	Wig-L-Twin	brown scale	EX-	$34.33	1-2000
Jamison	Wig-L-Twin	perch	EX	$36.51	5-1999
Jamison	Wig-L-Twin	red head	EX	$38.00	3-2001
Jamison	Wig-L-Twin	red, white	EX	$26.01	2-1999
Jamison	Wig-L-Twin	white, black head	EX	$103.00	4-2000
Jamison	Wiggler, Surface	flyrod, bar perch	VG	$46.00	5-1999
Jamison	Wiggler, Surface	flyrod, bar perch, nice box marked yellow perch	NIB	$295.00	2-2000
Jamison, W.J.	Frog, Hasting's Weedless Rubber		VG+	$75.00	4-2000
Jamison, W.J.	Weedless Frog	legs missing, nice picture box	IB	$900.00	8-2001
Jennings	Torpedo	glass bead eyes, metal spiral body	VG	$497.00	3-1999
Jennings	Torpedo	metal barber pole type spinner	VG	$407.00	4-1999
Jenson	Frogleg Kicker		NIB	$41.00	1-2000
Jenson	Frogleg Kicker		NIB	$58.25	2-1999
Jenson	Frogleg Kicker	bass size	EX	$29.00	7-1999
Jersey	Expert	weird chin spinner, 3 single hooks	EX	$3,170.00	10-1999
Jersey	Wow	blackshore, one treble	EX-	$388.88	1-2000
Johnson	Automatic Striker	2"	EX	$500.00	10-1999
Johnson	Automatic Striker	2"	NIB	$2,100.00	10-1999
Johnson	Automatic Striker	3", vg+ box, papers	EX/IB	$1,600.00	11-2000
Johnson	Automatic Striker	6½"	EX/IB	$1,580.00	10-1999
Johnson	Automatic Striker	large, huge chip on tail, rest ex		$438.00	5-1999
Johnson	Automatic Striker	large size, ex front, poor back, jointed, NOT MET	Poor	$202.50	6-1999
Johnson	Automatic Striker	large, some tail paint missing	VG-	$300.00	5-1999
Johnson	Automatic Striker	medium size	EX	$585.00	3-2000
Johnson	Automatic Striker	small size	EX	$497.00	7-1999
Johnson	Automatic Striker	small size	EX	$535.25	11-1999
Johnson	Automatic Striker	small size, painted eyes, hair gone	VG+	$270.00	10-2000
Johnson	Automatic Striker	white, black stripes	VG-	$257.00	2-1999
Johnson	Automatic Striker Junior	beige, brown stripe	EX	$431.00	11-1999
Johnson	Automatic Striker Junior	black, white, no eyes	VG+	$354.00	3-2000
Johnson	Automatic Striker Junior	on card	NIB	$1,031.88	5-1999
Johnson	Striker Minnow	small size	VG-	$200.00	5-1999
Jumping Jo		scale	NIB	$31.00	4-1999

BRAND	MODEL	SERIES / MFG. CODE / DESCRIPTION	GRADE	PRICE	DATE
K & K	Minnow, Animated	g rare maroon picture box	EX-/IB	$6,500.00	12-2001
K & K	Minnow, Animated	green, jointed, ugly chips	AVG	$150.00	1-2002
K & K	Minnow, Animated	jointed, probably never wet but huge chips, NOT MET	Poor	$202.00	12-2001
K & K	Minnoette	ugly	AVG	$125.00	8-1999
Kalamazoo	Minnow	#1, 3-hook, nice shape	EX	$4,307.00	9-1999
Kalamazoo	Minnow	#1, lime green back, silver belly, 3-hook	EX-	$835.00	10-2000
Kalamazoo	Minnow	#2, 4 doubles, 1 treble missing	EX	$5,357.00	9-2000
Kalamazoo	Minnow	#2, lime green back, silver belly, 5-hook	EX-	$1,714.00	10-2000
Kaufmann	Harkauf Topwater Minnow	green, white, painted eyes	EX	$612.00	8-2000
Kautzky	Musky Ike	red, white	EX	$15.00	3-1999
Kautzky	Shark Ike	3 different, old plastic box	NIB	$33.00	4-1999
Kautzky	Shark Ike	4 different	NIB	$38.77	1-2000
Kautzky	Shark Ike	6-pack	NIB	$63.50	6-1999
Kautzky	Shark Ike	#166, red head, gold scale	NIB	$9.99	4-1999
Kautzky	Shark Ike	black, yellow ribs	NIB	$9.99	4-1999
Kautzky	Shark Ike	orange, black spots, PTCB	NIB	$15.51	11-1999
Kautzky	Shark Ike	red head, on card	NIB	$12.51	3-2000
Kautzky	Shark Ike	red, white, intro card	NIB	$26.00	5-1999
Kautzky	Shark Ike	silver	NIB	$13.00	7-1999
Kautzky	Top Ike	red, white, NOT MET	NIB	$21.00	3-1999
Kautzky	Top Ike	yellow, red spots, NOT MET	EX	$10.50	7-1999
Keeling		silver-green, glass eyes, 5-hook	AVG	$361.00	2-2000
Keeling	Crab	black, white	EX+	$150.00	8-1999
Keeling	Expert	5-hook, round body, hole props, looks odd	EX+	$511.00	10-2001
Keeling	Expert	large bowtie props, glass eyes	VG	$1,082.50	3-1999
Keeling	Expert	no eyes, HPGM, screw hangers	EX-	$430.00	7-1999
Keeling	Expert	red, HPGM, 5-hook, hole props	VG+	$638.00	10-1999
Keeling?	Expert	silver, 5-hook, "expert" on side	VG+	$850.00	5-2000
Keeling	Expert	yellow, no eyes, 2HPGM	VG-	$392.00	6-1999
Keeling	Expert, Baby		VG+	$375.00	10-1999
Keeling	Expert, Musky	5", 3-hook, 4BW, props missing & broke	VG	$785.00	9-2002
Keeling	Flapper	4½", green scale, no eyes	EX-	$82.55	12-1999
Keeling	Flapper	450, rainbow, no eyes	EX	$125.00	3-1999
Keeling	General Tom	bar fish, glass eyes, spinner?	VG-	$159.00	1-2000
Keeling?	Pikie	Zaragossa type, glass eyes	EX	$152.50	10-1999
Keeling	Tom Thumb Surface	strawberry, glass eyes, rough box	EX/IB	$255.77	3-1999
Keeling	Wiggler, Tom Thumb	3 different	Rough	$20.50	3-1999
Keeling	Wiggler, Tom Thumb	dark green scale, great box & paper	NIB	$500.00	8-1999
Keeling	Wiggler, Tom Thumb	pigtail lure with box, Hobbs buy	Poor	$67.00	3-1999
Keeling	Wiggler, Tom Thumb	rainbow, big chips, Hobbs buy	Poor	$47.00	3-1999
Keeling	Wiggler, Tom Thumb	red, white, fair box, Newby bought	EX/IB	$200.00	7-2000
Keeling	Wiggler, Tom Thumb	yellow scale, heavy age lines, papers	NIB	$163.00	1-2001
Keeling	Zara, Baby	pikie, glass eyes	EX+	$300.00	8-1999
Keen	Kicker Frog		EX	$1,025.00	11-2001
Kent		green, white, 5-hook	AVG	$1,275.00	10-2002
Kent	Floater	frog, glass eyes, small tail chip, NOT MET	EX-	$400.00	8-2001

BRAND	MODEL	SERIES / MFG. CODE / DESCRIPTION	GRADE	PRICE	DATE
Kent	Floater Frog	copper, black spots, original	VG	$4,406.00	2-2002
Kent	Frog	back repainted		$153.50	1-1999
Kent	Frog	glass eyes, 6 spots, one small chip	EX-	$472.00	8-2002
Ketchall	Wobbler	red, white, age lines but nice	EX	$71.00	8-2002
Ketchum	Frog Casting Frame Gang	hooks replaced, decent box	NIB	$80.00	1-1999
Ketchum	Frog Casting Frame Gang	rough box	EX/IB	$102.00	4-2000
Kimmich	Mouse	bead eyes, in picture box	EX/IB	$575.00	1-1999
Kimmich	Mouse	great box & papers, Snipers	NIB	$526.10	11-1999
Kimmich	Mouse	nice box, hair a little rough	EX/IB	$472.00	4-2001
King	Chub	3½"	NIB	$34.00	3-2001
Kingfisher		Bass-Oreno type, red, white, tack eyes, decent newer box	EX-/IB	$22.50	11-1999
Kingfisher		chub scale, 3-hook, NOT MET	EX/IB	$256.00	11-1999
Kingfisher		white, glass eyes, HPGM, 3-hook, unmarked props	EX-/IB	$405.00	3-1999
L & S	Baby Cat	gold, black, window box	NIB	$25.39	1-1999
L & S	Bass Master	2519, green, yellow, sparkles, clear eyes, window box	NIB	$44.00	6-2001
L & S	Musky Master	J435	EX	$24.75	1-1999
L & S	Musky Master	common color, gold, orange eyes, black box	NIB	$137.00	5-2001
L & S	Musky Master	perch, opaque red eyes	EX	$55.00	12-2000
L & S	Musky Master	scale, opaque eyes	EX-	$55.00	5-2001
L & S	Musky Master	yellow, green scale, clear eyes, NOT MET	EX	$29.00	1-2001
L & S	Panfish Master	#0032	NIB	$8.74	1-1999
L & S	Panfish Master	nice box with papers	NIB	$16.50	12-1998
L & S	Pike Master	3021, blue scale	NIB	$22.17	1-1999
L & S	Pike Master	common color, orange eyes	EX	$10.00	5-2001
L & S	Pike Master	silver, black back, ribs	NIB	$27.80	2-1999
L & S	Trout Master	opaque eyes	EX	$18.00	4-2001
L & S	Various	5 common colors	EX-	$52.50	1-1999
Labouff	Creeper	green	VG	$34.00	1-1999
LaMay	Creeper	frog, modern, 2PCCB, NOT MET	NIB	$25.00	10-2000
Land-Em		spring papers, plain box	EXIB	$449.00	1-2000
Lane		3 different; spinner, spoon	NOC	$7.99	5-1999
Lane	Minnow, Automatic	paint flaking	VG	$2,100.00	8-2002
Lane	Wagtail	silver, green	Mint	$655.00	8-2000
Lane	Wagtail Shinner	CCBC lip?	EX-	$183.50	5-1999
Lane	Wagtail Wobbler		EX	$376.00	11-1999
Lane	Wagtail Wobbler		EX-	$318.00	1-2000
Larson	Weed Splitter	black head, scale pattern, odd weedless hooks	EX	$21.00	8-2002
Lauby		4¼", white, black back, spots, nice	EX	$127.50	8-1999
Lauby		pike size, spots	EX-	$157.00	1-2000
Lauby	Flyrod	strawberry, thick body	EX-	$132.50	1-200
Lauby	Flyrod	strawberry, thin body	EX-	$153.50	1-2000
Lauby	Spoon, Weedless Wonder	3½", yellow, black spots, nice box & papers	NIB	$709.00	5-2001
Lauby	Spoon, Weedless Wonder	4", red head, with flippers	EX-	$74.00	4-2000
Lauby	Spoon, Weedless Wonder	strawberry	VG+	$68.00	10-2000
Lauby	Spoon, Weedless Wonder	white, spots, nicks around hook guard	VG	$87.00	3-2000

BRAND	MODEL	SERIES / MFG. CODE / DESCRIPTION	GRADE	PRICE	DATE
Lazy Ike	Sail Shark	105	NIB	$32.03	7-1999
Lazy Ike	Sail Shark	205	NIB	$14.01	7-1999
Lazy Ike	Sail Shark	235	NIB	$26.01	7-1999
Lazy Ike	Sail Shark	240	NIB	$15.01	7-1999
Lazy Ike	Sail Shark	245	NIB	$31.01	7-1999
Lazy Ike	Sail Shark	265	NIB	$15.01	7-1999
Lazy Ike	Sail Shark	purple, chrome	NIB	$27.50	7-2001
LeBoeuf	Creeper	frog	EX/IB	$72.00	8-2000
LeBoeuf	Creeper	light frog	NIB	$75.00	12-1999
LeBoeuf	Creeper	light frog, 2PCCB	NIB	$56.00	6-2001
Leo Wise	Mouse	grey hair, bead eyes, sponge tail	EX	$410.00	11-1999
Leon Tackle	Chase-A-Bug	gray waterwave	EX	$84.00	3-1999
Lews		BB1L, Speed Spool	Mint	$69.00	9-2000
Lews		BB1, Speed Spool	VG	$51.00	2-1999
Live Action	Frog	nice box	NIB	$237.50	2-2000
Lloyd	Hungry-Jack		EX-	$356.01	3-1999
Lloyd	Hungry-Jack	NOT MET	EX-	$279.00	8-1999
Luhr Jenson	Dogwalker		EX	$27.00	1-1999
Lur-All	Beetle Bug	164 on card in box	NIB	$51.00	6-1999
Lurette	Glass Tube	#2		$925.00	7-2001
Macatawa	Musky Frog	cool	NIB	$165.00	1-1999
Makinen		6-pack, 6 different, common lures, graphics inside lid	EX/IB	$480.00	3-2002
Makinen	Holi-Comet	frog, jointed, catalog, NOT MET	NIB	$17.50	6-1999
Makinen	Holi-Comet	pikie	EX/IB	$60.00	1-1999
Makinen	Waddle Bug	NOT MET	NIB	$37.00	4-1999
Makinen	Wonderlure		NIB	$42.30	10-1999
Manitou	Minnow	dark green, wrench, papers	NIB	$3,190.00	10-1999
Manitou	Minnow	green, yellow belly, wrench & paper	NIB	$2,000.00	8-2000
Manitou	Minnow	red, hook drag	VG+	$1,082.00	3-2002
Manitou	Minnow	wrench & papers, NOT MET	NIB	$2,107.00	9-1999
Mann, J.H.		spinner, Syracuse, New York, bent	AVG	$83.00	10-2000
Mann, J.H.	Dancer	frog, finned Zara type	EX	$63.00	12-1998
Mann, J.H.	Dancer	shad, finned Zara type	NOC	$10.51	2-1999
Mann, J.H.	Dancer	Zara type, frog	NOC	$26.97	2-1999
Mann, J.H.	Frog	black	NIB	$51.00	2-1999
Mann, J.H.	Frog	green pearl, black spots	EX	$42.00	2-1999
Mann, J.H.	Frog?	hourglass shape, rear spinner	NIB	$57.00	1-1999
Mann, J.H.	Frog	yellow, black spots		$42.00	2-1999
Mann, J.H.	Hackleback	finned Wounded Spook	EX	$48.00	12-1998
Mann, J.H.	Hard Worm	four different	EX	$42.00	11-2000
Manning	Tasty Shrimp		EX	$34.00	3-1999
Marathon		9 lures, 1947 book	NIB	$42.00	1-1999
Marathon	Joe's Deep Runner	x3, Froelich plastic lures, 3 different colors	Mint	$66.00	3-2002
Marathon	Musk-E-Monk	rainbow, tack eyes, 2PCCB	VG/IB	$65.00	12-1998
Marathon	Waterfrog	glass eyes, hair frog	NIB	$56.00	8-2000
Marsh	Marvel	Florida, yellow shore, vg+ plastic box	NIB	$60.00	3-2001

BRAND	MODEL	SERIES / MFG. CODE / DESCRIPTION	GRADE	PRICE	DATE
Martin		7", green scale, black, white, NOT MET	NIB	$27.00	5-2001
Martin	Lizzard	#25G, rough corners on box	NIB	$52.00	1-2000
Martin	Lizzard	#51SW, white, black spots & line	NIB	$46.00	5-1999
Martin	Lizzard	green perch	NIB	$76.00	4-1999
Martin	Lizzard, Fetchi	red head, painted eyes	NIB	$23.49	4-2000
Martin	Tad	green scale, "tad" on belly	EX	$66.00	1-2001
Marvelus	Neverfail	3-hook, white, vg box	VG+/IB	$406.00	9-2001
Mason		4", silver herring, NOT MET	NIB	$102.00	5-2001
Mason		4", white herring, NOT MET	NIB	$102.00	5-2001
Mason		4", yellow, red gills	NIB	$250.00	5-2001
Mason	Salmon Plug	white, crisp box & paper	NIB	$189.00	1-2001
Mason	Salmon Plug	white, crisp box & paper	NIB	$197.00	1-2001
Mason	Salmon Plug, Deluxe	silver herring, painted eyes, great box & papers	NIB	$225.00	8-2001
Mason	Salmon Plug, Deluxe	white Herring, Seattle, Washington	NIB	$333.00	9-2000
Mason	Salmon Plug, Deluxe	yellow Herring, Seattle, Washington	NIB	$355.00	9-2000
Master		pikie type, glass eyes?	EX	$22.50	1-2000
Master	Snook Jr.	DD, pikie type, yellow spray, glass eyes, ugly	NIB	$421.00	2-2001
McCagg	Barney	side hook, large, black, green scale, stripe, nice	NIB	$165.00	10-2000
Medley	Wigglefish	green, yellow stripes	VG	$155.00	10-2000
Medley	Wiggly Crawfish	green, silver, red	VG+	$137.00	3-2001
Medley	Wiggly Crawfish	red, yellow	EX-	$160.00	3-2001
Medley	Wiggly Crawfish	yellow, brown	EX-	$148.00	3-2001
Medley	Wiggly Crawfish	yellow, red, brown	EX-	$150.00	3-2001
Meek		#2 Tournament, aluminum, tiny handle, Max Hartstall, 1910	EX	$1,375.00	6-2002
Meisselbach	Okeh	625	EX	$100.00	4-2001
Mepps	Harley-Davidson	Mepps with decal, 13 bids	NIB	$41.00	9-1999
Mermade		4 different, NOT MET	EX-	$71.00	4-1999
Mermade	MerMinnow	spoon, NOT MET	Mint	$9.99	1-1999
Mermade	Scatback	2PCCB	NIB	$137.50	3-1999
Mermade	Scatback	papers	NIB	$20.00	5-1999
Michigan	Lifelike	3-hook	AVG	$600.00	3-2001
Michigan	Lifelike	5-hook, ex picture box & paper	NIB	$8,000.00	12-2001
Michigan	Lifelike	awful, NOT MET	Poor	$431.00	4-1999
Michigan	Lifelike	c.1910, circular hardware	EX+	$1,680.00	10-1999
Michigan	Lifelike	ugly	AVG	$565.00	10-1999
Milam & Sons		#5, cracked ivory handle, small nicks on left side	EX-	$1,380.00	5-2002
Milam, B.C.		#3, six o'clock, 2 clicks, NOT MET	EX-	$895.00	8-2001
Miller's	Reversible Minnow	red head, white, NOT MET	G	$860.00	5-1999
Miller's	Reversible Minnow	yellow, gold spots, Neverfail hardware	Mint	$6,000.00	12-2001
Miller's	Reversible Spinner	in 2PCCB picture box	VG/IB	$1,100.00	12-1998
Millsite	Basser	yellow, black spots	NIB	$24.00	5-2000
Millsite	Daily Double	1 large, 3 small	VG+	$46.52	3-2000
Millsite	Daily Double	3 different	EX	$57.00	3-1999
Millsite	Daily Double	4 different	EX	$36.25	3-1999
Millsite	Daily Double	8401, perch	NIB	$27.80	3-1999
Millsite	Daily Double	flyrod, yellow, black spots	EX	$150.00	7-2000

BRAND	MODEL	SERIES / MFG. CODE / DESCRIPTION	GRADE	PRICE	DATE
Millsite	Daily Double	frog, NOT MET	NIB	$11.51	6-1999
Millsite	Daily Double	perch?	EX	$28.00	1-1999
Millsite	Daily Double	pikie, black head	EX/IB	$20.50	5-1999
Millsite	Daily Double	red, white	EX	$11.49	1-1999
Millsite	Daily Double	silver, black spots, NOT MET	EX-	$9.99	5-1999
Millsite	Paddle Bug	671, red, white	NIB	$29.99	6-1999
Millsite	Paddle Bug	brown scale	EX-	$20.49	6-1999
Millsite	Paddle Bug	perch scale	VG	$31.50	12-1998
Millsite	Paddle Bug	pikie	VG	$15.58	2-1999
Millsite	Paddle Bug	red, black scale	EX	$62.99	2-2000
Millsite	Paddle Bug	red, NOT MET	EX/IB	$26.00	2-2000
Millsite	Paddle Bug	red, white, with hang tag	EX	$28.50	2-1999
Millsite	Paddle Bug	red, white, with tag	Mint	$20.50	2-1999
Millsite	Paddle Bug	silver flash	AVG	$27.01	2-1999
Millsite	Paddle Bug	yellow	EX+	$31.05	5-1999
Millsite	Rattle Bug			$18.76	1-1999
Millsite	Rattle Bug	black, red	EX	$39.00	8-1999
Millsite	Rattle Bug	brown	EX-	$24.00	3-1999
Millsite	Rattle Bug	brown, yellow	EX	$36.00	1-1999
Millsite	Rattle Bug	gold, NOT MET	EX-/IB	$21.00	5-1999
Millsite	Rattle Bug	green scale	EX	$21.07	5-1999
Millsite	Rattle Bug	orange	EX-	$12.50	2-1999
Millsite	Rattle Bug	red, black lines	EX	$48.00	8-2001
Millsite	Rattle Bug	red, white		$11.10	1-1999
Millsite	Rattle Bug	red, white, early indent eyes, nice 2PCCB	NIB	$41.00	3-2001
Millsite	Rattle Bug	red, white, PTCB	EX/IB	$27.25	3-2000
Millsite	Rattle Bug	yellow, black	EX	$36.52	2-1999
Millsite	Rattle Bug	yellow, black spots, small chip	EX-	$42.00	1-2001
Millsite	Rattle Bug	yellow, black, wrong box	EX/IB	$47.00	12-1998
Millsite	Rattle Bug	yellow, red, 2PCCB, nice papers	EX-/IB	$104.00	8-2001
Millsite	Wig Wag	blue scale	VG+	$25.00	8-1999
Millsite	Wig Wag	red, black spots	EX	$10.00	1-2000
Millsite	Various	2 different Runt types; one 530, one 530T?	NIB	$38.09	4-1999
Millsite	Various	3 Runt types, common colors, PTCB	NIB	$27.03	9-1999
Millsite	Various	4 different Runt types	EX	$16.00	3-2001
Millsite	Various	6 common, mixed grades		$27.00	7-1999
Millsite	Various	28 different, common, Salesman display, NOT MET	EX	$362.00	3-2000
Millsite	Various	x2; 1 Paddle Plug, 1 Rattle Bug	EX	$47.00	3-1999
Minnow Tube	Unknown	3-hook, nice harness	VG	$760.00	3-1999
Mitchell		300, mint box & goodies	NIB	$80.00	2-1999
Mitchell		400	VG	$14.50	1-1999
Mity Atom	Mity Atom	black, white, wood?	EX	$30.30	6-1999
Modern Sporting Goods	Froglegs	molded front legs, great box, knife & fork	NIB	$152.00	5-2001
Moonlight		3000, frog, glass eyes, 2-hook, surface?	EX	$405.00	11-1999

BRAND	MODEL	SERIES / MFG. CODE / DESCRIPTION	GRADE	PRICE	DATE
Moonlight		green, white, 5-hook, tiny cups, ugly age lines & chips	AVG	$424.00	10-1999
Moonlight		red, 5-hook, nice	VG+	$585.77	5-1999
Moonlight		Surf-Oreno type, grey crackleback, glass eyes, unmarked box, nice	NIB	$481.00	5-2000
Moonlight	Aristocrat Torpedo	white, red ribs, glass eyes	EX-	$136.00	4-2000
Moonlight	Bass Seeker	bar perch, glass eyes	EX	$148.00	6-2000
Moonlight	Bass Seeker	perch, sparkles, glass eyes	EX	$113.00	10-2000
Moonlight	Crawfish	belly weight & legs	EX	$520.00	4-1999
Moonlight	Dreadnought	black, white	EX-	$3,738.00	3-2000
Moonlight	Floating Bait	#1, luminous, great woodpecker box	EX/IB	$815.00	5-2000
Moonlight	Floating Bait	3-pack, self glowing night bait	NIB	$1,620.00	3-1999
Moonlight	Floating Bait	luminous, very early box & papers	EX/IB	$500.00	5-2001
Moonlight	Minnow, Surface	white, glass eyes, 3-hooker, NOT MET	AVG	$100.00	8-1999
Moonlight	Mossback	1103, Surf-Oreno type, POBW, vg box	EX/IB	$610.00	8-2002
Moonlight	Pikaroon	4", bar perch	EX	$352.00	4-2000
Moonlight	Pikaroon	4", bar perch, glass eyes	EX-	$405.00	3-2000
Moonlight	Pikaroon	4⅛"	EX-	$164.00	2-2002
Moonlight	Pikaroon	5", in correct box, $1,600.00	EX	$1,600.00	4-2001
Moonlight	Pikaroon	5¼", bar perch, glass eyes, nice	EX-	$356.00	11-2000
Moonlight	Pikaroon	5¼", black, yellow belly, 3-hook	VG	$83.00	8-2000
Moonlight	Pikaroon	bar perch, 1-hook, $2,500.00	Mint	$2,500.00	4-2001
Moonlight	Pikaroon	bar perch, glass eyes, worm burn, NOT MET	AVG	$51.00	2-2000
Moonlight	Pikaroon	black, in #1003 box	EX/IB	$407.00	8-1999
Moonlight	Pikaroon	blue scale	EX	$605.00	3-2001
Moonlight	Pikaroon	green scale, decent box, NOT MET	VG/IB	$232.50	2-2000
Moonlight	Pikaroon	green, black stripe	VG	$127.50	8-1999
Moonlight	Pikaroon	orange, black spots	EX	$628.00	2-2002
Moonlight	Pikaroon	orange, black spots, 1-hook	EX	$1,825.00	8-1999
Moonlight	Pikaroon	orange, white, black spots, $850.00	EX+	$850.00	4-2001
Moonlight	Pikaroon	perch, tack eyes, NOT MET	VG-	$51.00	2-2000
Moonlight	Pikaroon	rainbow, nice	EX-	$255.00	11-1999
Moonlight	Pikaroon	red head	EX-	$185.00	9-2000
Moonlight	Pikaroon	red head, glass eyes, NOT MET	VG	$79.00	2-2000
Moonlight	Pikaroon	yellow, black eye shadow, glass eyes	EX-	$228.60	2-2000
Moonlight	Pikaroon	yellowed white, black eyes	EX-	$281.10	3-2000
Moonlight	Pikaroon, Jointed	4",	Fair	$48.50	5-1999
Moonlight	Pikaroon, Jointed	gold scale over black, poor box, NOT MET	VG+/IB	$290.00	8-1999
Moonlight	Pikaroon, Jointed	green scale, glass eyes, NOT MET	AVG	$54.00	2-2000
Moonlight	Pikaroon, Jointed	green scale, nice	VG+	$202.50	11-1999
Moonlight	Pikaroon, Jointed	in correct box ($775.00)	NIB	$750.00	4-2001
Moonlight	Pikaroon, Jointed	red head, glass eyes, NOT MET	EX	$83.00	4-2000
Moonlight	Pikaroon, Jointed	red, white, glass eyes, nice	EX-	$455.00	4-1999
Moonlight	Pikaroon, Jointed	shiner scale, small chip by eye	EX-	$275.00	5-2000
Moonlight	Polly-Wog	bar perch, glass eyes	VG	$362.00	10-2001
Moonlight	Polly-Wog	green, black		$425.00	4-2001
Moonlight	Polly-Wog	rainbow, in box		$950.00	4-2001

BRAND	MODEL	SERIES / MFG. CODE / DESCRIPTION	GRADE	PRICE	DATE
Moonlight	Spinning Bait	yellow, painted eyes, POBW	EX-	$235.00	8-2002
Moonlight	Torpedo	green scale, glass eyes	EX-	$219.00	5-2000
Moonlight	Weedless	#2, great woodpecker type box	EX/IB	$532.22	9-1999
Moonlight	Wiggler, Ladybug		EX	$900.00	4-2001
Moonlight	Wiggler, Ladybug	yellow, black spots, gold centers, painted eyes	VG	$300.00	6-1999
Moonlight	Wobbler	3¾", white, 5-hook, cup, ugly	EX-	$262.63	12-1999
Moonlight	Wobbler	luminous, in nice unmarked box	EX/IB	$310.00	7-2000
Moonlight	Wobbler	rainbow, brown back, cup faced, glass eyes, hook drag on back	VG-	$71.00	10-2000
Moonlight	Woodpecker	luminous, 3 side hooks	EX-	$360.00	10-1999
Moonlight	Woodpecker	luminous, ugly age line	EX-	$150.00	1-2000
Moonlight	Woodpecker, Midget	luminous	VG+	$69.50	1-2000
Moonlight	Zig-Zag	3-pack; 1 red & yellow, 1 red & white, 1 luminous, perch?	NIB	$2,358.33	3-1999
Mouse Bait Co.	Mouse	Fort Worth, Texas	VG	$68.00	6-1999
Mueller-Perry	Crazy Legs	2 mint, one in box with papers	NIB	$36.76	3-1999
Muskovie-Bomb	Muskovie-Bomb	red head, spring loaded, plain box	NIB	$43.00	8-2001
Musky Sucker	Flexie	7½", dirty box	NIB	$33.00	9-2001
Myers & Spellman	Minnow		EX	$380.00	10-1999
Nelson	Nature		NIB	$86.51	1-1999
Nemo	Bass Bait		EX	$600.00	4-2001
Nemo	Bass Bait	yellow	EX	$850.00	10-1999
Ness	Niftie Minnie	celluloid tube	VG	$1,025.00	2-2002
Ness	Niftie Minnie	celluloid tube, 5-hook	EX-	$1,025.00	2-2002
Ness	Niftie Minnie	glass tube, marked prop	EX	$1,600.00	8-2001
North Channel	Minnow	black, white, NOT MET	EX	$867.00	3-2001
Novelty Lure Co.	Sam-Bo		NIB	$52.26	2-1999
Ol' Skipper	Legs Wobbler	1604T, scale finish	NIB	$73.00	8-2001
Oliver & Gruber	Glowurm	crisp papers	EX	$81.00	8-2002
Oliver & Gruber	Glowurm	red, white	EX+	$139.50	1-2000
Oliver & Gruber	Glowurm	red, white	Mint	$87.00	3-2001
Oliver & Gruber	Glowurm	red, white, nice wood box	NIB	$185.05	1-2000
Oliver & Gruber	Glowurm	red, white, with papers	EX	$152.50	5-1999
Oliver & Gruber	Glowurm	white, red ribs, papers, NOT MET	EX	$90.00	4-2000
Oliver & Gruber	Glowurm	white, red stripes, missing box top	EXIB	$275.00	4-1999
Oliver & Gruber	Glowurm	yellow, green stripes	EX+	$150.00	4-2000
Oliver & Gruber	Glowurm	yellow, green, nice wood box	NIB	$344.00	9-2001
Olson	Salmon Plug		EX/IB	$90.00	4-2001
Optimus	Minnow	South Bend Hex, 3-hook, ex box	EX/IB	$935.00	6-2002
Orchard Industries	Bottom Scratcher	red head, thick plastic box	NIB	$41.00	8-2001
Orchard Industries	Bottom Scratcher	spotted ape, NOT MET	Mint	$12.50	8-1999
Orchard Industries	Bottom Scratcher	spotted ape, papers	NIB	$16.00	4-2001
Orchard Industries	Bottom Scratcher	WBH	NIB	$16.00	9-2001
Oscar Meyer	Wiener	3¼", novelty	EX	$49.01	2-2000
Oscar the Frog	Oscar the Frog		NIB	$490.00	10-1999
Outing	Bassy Getum	black bass finish	VG	$77.55	3-2000
Outing	Du-Getum	frog, 2PCCB, papers	NIB	$400.00	12-1998

BRAND	MODEL	SERIES / MFG. CODE / DESCRIPTION	GRADE	PRICE	DATE
Outing	Du-Getum	grass frog	NIB	$430.75	5-1999
Outing	Du-Getum	grass frog, rough box	NIB	$222.50	6-1999
Outing	Du-Getum	large	NIB	$380.00	10-1999
Outing	Du-Getum	nice box, papers rough	NIB	$307.99	9-1999
Outing	Du-Getum	small	NIB	$355.00	10-1999
Outing	Du-Getum	white frog, 1 large & 1 small, mint boxes	NIB	$715.00	12-1999
Outing	Getum	700AR, NOT MET	NIB	$285.00	10-2002
Outing	Getum	pale frog, mint red & blue box, papers	NIB	$372.00	5-2001
Outing	Pikie Getum	rainbow, 2 small chips	EX-	$151.00	1-1999
P & K		redwinged blackbird, musky size, black, yellow wings, NOT MET	NIB	$76.00	4-1999
P & K	Amazin' Maizie	#42RW, red & white	NIB	$32.00	3-1999
P & K	Bright Eyes	yellow, red	EX/IB	$13.49	1-1999
P & K	Bright Eyes	x2; 1 frog, 1 shiner, NOT MET	NIB	$37.00	5-1999
P & K	Whirl-A-Way	#0GS, black scale?, crisp box	NIB	$43.00	3-2001
P & K	Whirl-A-Way	black, 2PCCB	EX/IB	$49.00	7-2002
Pal	Electro	like Bunyan, amber, decent box, NOT MET	EXIB	$61.00	10-2000
Pardee		3-hook	Mint	$8,000.00	12-2001
Pardee	Musky	5-hook, paint on hubs, box bottom only	EXI1/2B	$10,000.00	6-2001
Paulson	Minnow, Combination	red head, glass eyes, papers	NIB	$1,165.00	10-2000
Paulson	Minnow, Combination	red, white, crisp paper & box	NIB	$510.00	5-2001
Paw Paw		301, perch, tack eyes, nice yellow & black photo box	NIB	$153.00	9-2001
Paw Paw		3200, white, glass eyes, 3215 photo box	NIB	$168.00	11-1999
Paw Paw		flyrod, gold, black, 3 small boxes with flies, nice	NIB	$197.50	5-1999
Paw Paw	3-hook	rainbow	NIB	$102.50	12-1998
Paw Paw	3-hook	rainbow, tack eyes	EX	$104.00	10-2000
Paw Paw	3-hook	rainbow, tack eyes	EX-	$47.00	6-1999
Paw Paw	3-hook	rainbow, tack eyes, 3-hook, Lucky Lure box	NIB	$117.00	10-2000
Paw Paw	Bass Seeker	red head, c.1927, crisp box	NIB	$291.00	9-2000
Paw Paw	Bass Seeker	red, white, glass eyes, great box	NIB	$153.70	9-1999
Paw Paw	Bass Seeker	shiner scale, photo box	EX/IB	$102.00	10-1999
Paw Paw	Bass-Oreno	natural chub	EX	$26.00	8-2001
Paw Paw	Bonehead	swamp minnow pikie, rhinestone eyes	EX	$50.00	7-2000
Paw Paw	Bullfrog	red, white	EX	$645.00	8-2000
Paw Paw	Bullhead	brown, black, tack eyes, chip, NOT MET	VG	$102.50	2-2000
Paw Paw	Bullhead	gold, black, pikie, tack eyes, ugly	AVG	$64.00	5-1999
Paw Paw	Bullhead	green, yellow, superb picture box, Bullhead papers	NIB	$535.00	5-2001
Paw Paw	Bullhead	red head, tack eyes	AVG	$56.00	10-2000
Paw Paw	Bullhead	red, silver, avg #3505 box	VG/IB	$128.00	3-1999
Paw Paw	Bullhead	red, white, tack eyes	EX	$182.50	6-1999
Paw Paw	Bullhead	red, white, tack eyes, NOT MET	EX	$157.50	8-1999
Paw Paw	Caster	3½", RT	EX	$103.00	3-2000
Paw Paw	Caster	2", green scale, copper back & sides	EX-	$86.00	10-1999
Paw Paw	Caster	5½", pike shape, jointed, tack eyes, huge touch up, ugly		$76.00	1-2000

BRAND	MODEL	SERIES / MFG. CODE / DESCRIPTION	GRADE	PRICE	DATE
Paw Paw	Caster	bass color, small	EX	$38.00	4-2000
Paw Paw	Casting Frog	#75 PTCB	NIB	$227.50	1-2000
Paw Paw	Crawdad	feelers & legs intact	Mint	$162.50	8-1999
Paw Paw	Crawdad	hanging BW, correct box, tough paperwork	EXIB	$800.00	4-2001
Paw Paw	Crawdad	pike scale, painted eyes, Lucky Lure box	NIB	$204.52	1-2000
Paw Paw	Crawfish	natural	EX-	$51.00	5-2000
Paw Paw	Dreadnought	rainbow trout, many pointers	VG-	$151.00	7-2000
Paw Paw	Fish Spoon	#1, great picture box	NIB	$61.00	8-1999
Paw Paw	Floater- Sinker	803	NIB	$51.00	8-2000
Paw Paw	Frog, Croaker	real skin, NOT MET	EX	$120.00	5-1999
Paw Paw	Go-Getter	rainbow trout	VG	$57.00	1-1999
Paw Paw	Injured Minnow	frog, tack eyes, 4401 box	EX-/IB	$50.00	2-1999
Paw Paw	Injured Minnow, Great	pikie, glass eyes	EX	$372.00	4-2001
Paw Paw	Lippy Joe	frog	EX	$75.00	8-2001
Paw Paw	Lippy Joe	Allen Stripey, jointed	EX	$50.00	8-2001
Paw Paw	Minnow	3350, green scale, gold spots, tack eyes	Mint	$255.00	4-2000
Paw Paw	Minnow, Aristocrat	2400, floater, shiner	NIB	$25.75	1-1999
Paw Paw	Minnow, Caster Mud	Caster?, large, tack eyes, mottled	EX	$102.60	1-2000
Paw Paw	Minnow, Musky	shad scale	EX	$108.00	8-2001
Paw Paw	Minnow, Surface	pikie, gold spots	EX	$108.00	5-2000
Paw Paw	Mouse	4741, yellow, black stripe, painted eyes, PTCB	NIB	$45.40	4-1999
Paw Paw	Mouse	red head, G & O Lucky box	EX-/IB	$102.00	11-2000
Paw Paw	Mouse, Hair	yellow head, natural, bucktail	EX/IB	$265.00	6-1999
Paw Paw	Mouse, Hair	spinnered, red head, ex Lucky Lure box	NIB	$280.00	1-2000
Paw Paw	Mouse, Musky	4", silver	VG	$290.51	4-1999
Paw Paw	Mouse, Musky Hair	5½", white head, small nose chip	EX-	$361.10	1-2000
Paw Paw	Pikie	perch, tack eyes, crisp red & white Lucky Lure box	NIB	$128.50	9-1999
Paw Paw	Pikie	pikie color, tack eyes, grooved head, nice	EX	$18.00	7-2001
Paw Paw	Pikie	pikie, tack eyes, great picture box	NIB	$153.60	8-1999
Paw Paw	Pikie	red head, white, pearl, tack eyes, orginal, crisp black box	NIB	$378.58	12-1999
Paw Paw	Pikie	strawberry, plastic	Mint	$154.00	8-2001
Paw Paw	Pikie	4¼", white, flitter, tack eyes	EX	$25.12	2-1999
Paw Paw	Pikie Getum	black, sparkles, rhinestone eyes	Mint	$85.00	8-2001
Paw Paw	Pikie Getum	perch, rhinestone eyes	Mint	$44.00	8-2001
Paw Paw	Pikie Getum	red head, rhinestone eyes	Mint	$46.00	8-2001
Paw Paw	Pikie Getum	shad, rhinestone eyes	Mint	$75.00	8-2001
Paw Paw	Pikie, Fluted	rainbow fire	EX-	$48.50	4-2000
Paw Paw	Pikie, Musky	red head	Mint	$53.00	10-2000
Paw Paw	Platypus	pikie, Flapjack hook hangers	EX	$226.00	4-2000
Paw Paw	Platypus	PTCB, plastic	NIB	$159.00	8-2000
Paw Paw	Plenty Sparkle	gold scale, rhinestones on belly	EX	$131.00	8-2001
Paw Paw	Plunker	fluorescent red, tack eyes	EX	$166.00	10-2001
Paw Paw	Plunker	perch, tack eyes, black & yellow picture box	NIB	$152.50	9-1999
Paw Paw	Punkinseed	green shad scale, tack eyes	VG+	$41.00	6-1999
Paw Paw	River Type	rainbow, tack eyes	EX	$66.00	1-2000

BRAND	MODEL	SERIES / MFG. CODE / DESCRIPTION	GRADE	PRICE	DATE
Paw Paw	River Type	rainbow, tack eyes	EX	$69.54	12-1999
Paw Paw	Surf-Oreno	red, white, tack eyes, great picture box	NIB	$150.00	8-1999
Paw Paw	Surf-Oreno Type	red head, glass eyes, black & yellow box	NIB	$177.50	10-1999
Paw Paw	Trout-Caster	natural chub, tack eyes, beautiful	EX+	$120.27	1-2000
Paw Paw	Trout-Caster	perch, tack eyes, beautiful	EX+	$68.56	1-2000
Paw Paw	Trout-Caster	mud minnow, NOT MET	EX-	$79.00	11-2000
Paw Paw	Weedless Wow	frog splatter with papers	NIB	$225.00	1-2002
Paw Paw	Weedless Wow	red head, glass eyes, nice	VG+	$152.00	1-2001
Paw Paw	Weedless Wow	silver flash, POBW, NOT MET	EX-	$76.55	2-2000
Paw Paw	Weedless Wow	splatter	VG	$85.00	4-1999
Paw Paw	Wobbler, Spoon Belly	pike body, pearly side spinners	EX	$255.00	8-2001
Paw Paw	Wotta-Frog		VG	$27.00	1-1999
Paw Paw	Wotta-Frog	3¾"	EX	$81.00	3-1999
Paw Paw	Wotta-Frog	4", NOT MET	EX	$61.00	1-1999
Paw Paw	Wotta-Frog	large	EX	$65.00	8-1999
Paw Paw	Wotta-Frog	large	NIB	$82.00	9-1999
Paw Paw	Wotta-Frog	large, PTCB, NOT MET	EX-/IB	$66.00	11-2000
Paw Paw	Wotta-Frog	regular	EX	$56.00	7-2002
Paw Paw	Wotta-Frog	Victory Finish, large	EX	$130.13	12-1999
Paw Paw	Wotta-Frog	weedless, rubber legs, weed guard, NOT MET	VG+	$72.00	11-2000
Peckinpaugh	Mouse	flyrod, brown, bead eyes, cute	EX	$81.00	11-2000
Pepper	5-hook	green, white belly, heavy age lines, ugly	VG-	$304.00	4-2000
Pepper	3-hook	green, yellow, glass eyes, NOT MET	G	$164.00	3-2001
Pepper	Minnow, Metal	HPGM	EX	$141.50	6-1999
Pepper	Minnow, New Century	silver, 3-hook	VG	$360.00	2-2002
Pepper	Minnow, New Century	silver, no eyes, 3-hook	EX-	$365.00	2-2002
Pepper	Minnow, Revolving	vg+ box	NIB	$5,900.00	6-2001
Pepper	Mouse	flyrod, on spinner, NOT MET	EX	$21.00	11-2000
Pepper	Roamer	green, yellow, glass eyes, 3-hook, screw eye hangers	VG	$154.00	9-2002
Pepper	Roman Redtail	ex- wood box	NIB	$3,500.00	12-2001
Pepper	Spinner, New Crown		EX	$455.00	6-1999
Pepper	Spoon	NOT MET	NOC	$16.50	5-1999
Perry, Buck	Spoon Plug	5-pack with papers	NIB	$31.00	1-1999
Perry, Buck	Spoon Plug	14 different, mostly mint	EX	$66.00	3-2002
Pfeiffer	Minnow	green, gold, open mouth, bag	NIB (bag)	$114.49	5-1999
Pfeiffer	Minnow Tube, Glass	ex- box, papers	EX/IB	$3,580.00	10-1999
Pfeiffer	Minnow Tube, Glass	nice picture box & papers	NIB	$4,600.00	12-2001
Pfeiffer	Minnow Tube, Glass	vg+ picture box, nice paper	EX/IB	$4,900.00	6-2001
Pfeiffer	Spin Dilly	brown, orange, flitter	EX	$100.00	2-1999
Pfieffer	Minnow Tube, Glass		NIB	$3,400.00	2-2000
Pflueger	Ball Spinner	Alligator, marked #7	EX-	$104.00	2-1999
Pflueger	Ball Spinner	glass bead eyes	EX	$62.00	6-1999
Pflueger	Ballerina (or O-Boy)	5439 Scramble finish, painted eyes, ring around BW	NIB	$177.00	2-2002
Pflueger	Breakless Devon Minnow	269NP, vg #3 Canoe box	NIB	$61.00	1-2002
Pflueger	Catalina	5571	EX	$450.00	10-1999

BRAND	MODEL	SERIES / MFG. CODE / DESCRIPTION	GRADE	PRICE	DATE
Pflueger	Catalina	crackleback, small, old HPGM, NOT MET	EX-	$400.00	9-2002
Pflueger	Catalina	strawberry, large, old HPGM NOT MET	EX-	$610.00	9-2002
Pflueger	Catalina	yellow, green, glass eyes, vg+ 5571 canoe box, NOT MET	NIB	$300.00	8-2001
Pflueger	Catalina	5", metalized, glass eyes, NOT MET	EX-	$381.98	1-2000
Pflueger	Catalina	2787, metalized musky	EX	$680.00	10-1999
Pflueger	Champion	brass eyes	EX+	$237.00	9-2000
Pflueger	Champion	white, brass eyes, shiny but plain	EX	$179.50	1-2000
Pflueger	Champion	white, brass tack eyes	EX+	$175.00	10-1999
Pflueger	Competitor	green?, brass tack eyes, 5-hook	EX	$362.99	8-1999
Pflueger	Competitor	green back, blended yellow, tack eyes, 5-hook	EX+	$629.00	9-1999
Pflueger	Competitor	green, yellow belly, metal tack eyes, 5-hook	EX	$230.00	6-2000
Pflueger	Conrad Frog	nice, NOT MET	EX-	$71.50	6-1999
Pflueger	Conrad Frog	single, weedless, NOT MET	EX	$70.00	1-2002
Pflueger	Conrad Frog	sinker, NOT MET	EX-	$77.00	7-1999
Pflueger	Crystal Minnow	chip on tail, NOT MET	VG	$820.00	7-2000
Pflueger	Crystal Minnow	luminous, still glows	EX	$2,020.00	12-2001
Pflueger	Electric Minnow	red head, glass eyes, Neverfail Monarch prop	EX-	$316.00	4-2000
Pflueger	Floating Metalized Minnow	button tack eyes?	EX-	$137.50	4-1999
Pflueger	Floating Monarch Minnow	crackleback, HPGM, 2-hook, cup	EX-	$510.00	11-2001
Pflueger	Floating Monarch Minnow	gray, large, HPGM, white belly chip	VG	$88.00	7-2002
Pflueger	Floating Monarch Minnow	perch, HPGM, NOT MET	EX	$310.00	3-2001
Pflueger	Floating Monarch Minnow	small, white, red blush	AVG	$77.00	7-2002
Pflueger	Floating Monarch Minnow	yellow		$1,450.00	4-2001
Pflueger	Globe	2 medium red & white, red head, pikie, musky	VG	$35.00	1-1999
Pflueger	Globe	2¾", yellow, gold, 3750 Canoe papers	NIB	$87.00	11-1999
Pflueger	Globe	2¾", luminous, 3750 Canoe papers	NIB	$82.01	11-1999
Pflueger	Globe	2¾", red, white, 3750 Canoe papers	NIB	$114.50	11-1999
Pflueger	Globe	3½", canoe box, NOT MET	EX/IB	$34.00	1-1999
Pflueger	Globe	3¾", luminous, gold dots, papers	NIB	$85.00	1-2002
Pflueger	Globe	3704, pike, red head, large	NIB	$87.00	10-2000
Pflueger	Globe	3704, pikie, red head	VG/IB	$42.00	1-1999
Pflueger	Globe	luminous	VG	$33.00	3-1999
Pflueger	Globe	luminous, Canoe box & papers	EX/IB	$75.00	3-1999
Pflueger	Globe	luminous, side hook, nice maroon box, paper	NIB	$960.00	10-2000
Pflueger	Globe	red, white, small, Canoe box	NIB	$102.50	8-1999
Pflueger	Globe	side hook, crisp blue 3750 box, paper	NIB	$235.50	3-2000
Pflueger	Globe	side hooks, Otter box, nice	NIB	$811.51	2-1999
Pflueger	Globe	white, small, side hook, Neverfail	EX-	$61.50	11-1999
Pflueger	Globe	x2, 1 with Neverfail		$50.00	12-1998
Pflueger	Globe	yellow, gold dots, small, rough Canoe box	EX-/IB	$40.00	10-1999
Pflueger	Globe	yellow, gold spots, Canoe box	NIB	$66.00	1-1999
Pflueger	Grasshopper	rubber, maroon box	NOC	$168.49	12-1999
Pflueger	Hellgramite	rubber, unmarked maroon box, NOT MET	NOC-/IB	$76.50	2-2000
Pflueger	Invincible Minnow	rubber?, on bucktail, no spinner	VG+	$78.77	12-1999
Pflueger	Kent Floater Frog	frog, glass eyes, belly nick but still nice	VG+	$380.00	8-2001
Pflueger	Kent Floater Frog	maroon #2 box	EXIB	$3,250.00	4-1999

BRAND	MODEL	SERIES / MFG. CODE / DESCRIPTION	GRADE	PRICE	DATE
Pflueger	Kent Floater Frog	glass eyes, diamond P prop, twisted wire	EX	$2,032.00	1-2000
Pflueger	Kent Frog	black frog, modern	NIB	$118.00	11-2000
Pflueger	Kent Frog	carved eyes, huge touch ups		$275.00	8-2002
Pflueger	Kent Frog	diamond P prop, NOT MET	Poor	$118.00	9-2001
Pflueger	Kent Frog	glass eyes	VG-	$442.50	2-1999
Pflueger	Kent Frog	glass eyes, huge hook drag, chip	AVG	$312.00	8-2000
Pflueger	Kent Frog	glass eyes, shiny	EX-	$750.00	3-2000
Pflueger	Kent Frog	large tack eyes	AVG	$232.00	10-2000
Pflueger	Kent Frog	modern 1999 version	NIB	$105.00	7-2000
Pflueger	Kent Frog	red lateral line, glass eyes, Neverfail, NOT MET	EX-	$755.00	1-2002
Pflueger	Ketchum	5-hook, Simmons Hardware, prop , marked	VG+	$576.99	6-1999
Pflueger	Kingfisher	crackleback, 3-hook, maroon 100 box	EX/IB	$410.00	2-2000
Pflueger	Kormish Frog	NO BIDS	NOC	$150.00	6-1999
Pflueger	Kormish Frog	ugly, NOT MET	NOC	$62.00	7-1999
Pflueger	Livewire		EX	$33.50	1-1999
Pflueger	Livewire	9453, 3¾", white, black ribs, painted eyes, PTCB	NIB	$41.50	4-1999
Pflueger	Livewire	5474, white, green, black ribs, painted eyes, PTCB	NIB	$60.00	6-1999
Pflueger	Livewire	pikie, painted eyes	EX	$109.29	2-2000
Pflueger	Livewire	red head, painted eyes, white & blue card, no writing?	NOC	$380.00	3-2001
Pflueger	Magnet	red, luminous, nice maroon bulldog	EX/IB	$850.00	8-2001
Pflueger	Magnet	white, agelines, NOT MET	EX	$137.50	1-2000
Pflueger	Magnet	x2; 1 luminous red head, 1 luminous	EX	$380.00	2-2000
Pflueger	Meadow Frog	cork or rubber, ugly	EX	$255.00	4-1999
Pflueger	Merit	3697, luminous, red, woodpecker type	EX/IB	$188.20	10-1999
Pflueger	Metalized Minnow	3 hook	VG+	$299.00	8-2002
Pflueger	Metalized Minnow	3-hook, maroon bulldog box	EX/IB	$1,480.00	11-1999
Pflueger	Metalized Minnow	3-hook, NOT MET	Mint	$405.00	5-2001
Pflueger	Metalized Minnow	cracks in metal, $450.00 NOT MET	G	$128.00	3-2001
Pflueger	Metalized Minnow	glass eyes, 3-hook, NOT MET	EX-	$237.84	5-1999
Pflueger	Metalized Minnow	silver, 5-hook, big belly dent, dog prop	VG+	$455.00	11-1999
Pflueger	Monarch	5-hook, crackleback, HPGM, bulldog, 1914	Mint	$600.00	10-1999
Pflueger	Monarch	aluminum, HPGM, 5-hook, round body	EX-	$950.00	5-2000
Pflueger	Monarch	bar perch, 5-hook, crisp box, dog paper, NOT MET	NIB	$1,527.00	6-2001
Pflueger	Monarch	rainbow, 3-hook, bulldog prop	VG+	$600.00	10-1999
Pflueger	Monarch	rainbow, 5-hook, fat body, nice	VG+	$725.00	5-2000
Pflueger	Monarch	rainbow, fat, 3-hook, bulldog Monarch prop	EX-	$400.00	1-2000
Pflueger	Monarch	rainbow, glass eyes, 3-hook bulldog prop	EX	$252.00	12-2001
Pflueger	Monarch	white, HPGM, gem clip, d. Pflueger prop	EX++	$2,000.00	10-1999
Pflueger	Monarch Metalized Minnow		EX	$1,250.00	4-2001
Pflueger	Monarch Minnow	sienna fire, maroon Monarch box	EX	$3,500.00	4-2001
Pflueger	Monarch, Underwater	2185, slate, crack at tail, gem clip, c.1910	VG	$650.00	10-1999
Pflueger	Monarch, Underwater	2195, red back stripe, 5-hook	EX-	$400.00	10-1999
Pflueger	Musky Minnow	5-hook, slate, HPGM	VG	$788.00	2-2002
Pflueger	Mustang	9509, blue mullet, plate, paper	NIB	$51.00	11-1999
Pflueger	Mustang	9540, sunfish scale, painted eyes	NIB	$26.00	5-1999

BRAND	MODEL	SERIES / MFG. CODE / DESCRIPTION	GRADE	PRICE	DATE
Pflueger	Mustang	9540, sunfish color, painted eyes	NIB	$77.53	2-1999
Pflueger	Mustang	5", red scale, painted eyes, nice	EX	$37.00	1-2001
Pflueger	Mustang	5", red, white, painted eyes, plates, Canoe box	NIB	$135.00	2-1999
Pflueger	Mustang	8903, silver, sparkle, green back, painted eyes, PTCB	NIB	$31.51	6-1999
Pflueger	Mustang	mullet scale, painted eyes, 9512 Canoe papers	NIB	$58.00	10-2001
Pflueger	Mustang	perch, plate, papers	NIB	$132.50	4-1999
Pflueger	Mustang	strawberry, painted eyes, PTCB	NIB	$52.00	8-2000
Pflueger	Mustang Musky	blue scale, painted eyes	NIB	$153.51	5-1999
Pflueger	Mustang Musky	eel, painted eyes	EXIB	$99.00	5-1999
Pflueger	Mustang Musky	sunfish, painted eyes	NIB	$172.50	5-1999
Pflueger	Neverfail	rainbow?, blue Canoe box, pretty	EXIB	$566.06	1-2000
Pflueger	Neverfail	rainbow, in correct box	NIB	$1,150.00	4-2001
Pflueger	Neverfail	sienna	EX+	$850.00	4-2001
Pflueger	Neverfail 3-hook	3105, frog scale, blush	EX-	$550.00	10-1999
Pflueger	Neverfail 3-hook	3165, frog	Mint	$525.00	10-1999
Pflueger	Neverfail 3-hook	3173 yellow perch, blue canoe box	EX/IB	$394.75	6-1999
Pflueger	Neverfail 3-hook	3195, red back stripe	EX	$490.00	10-1999
Pflueger	Neverfail 3-hook	3195, red back stripe, unmarked	EX+	$520.00	10-1999
Pflueger	Neverfail 3-hook	3196, red head	EX+	$350.00	10-1999
Pflueger	Neverfail 3-hook	ex- 3169 Four Brothers box	VG/IB	$700.00	10-1999
Pflueger	Neverfail 3-hook	Argyle back, red, black	EX/IB	$600.00	1-1999
Pflueger	Neverfail 3-hook	Argyle, painted eyes	EX-	$122.00	1-1999
Pflueger	Neverfail 3-hook	bar perch, bulldog prop, glass eyes, side spots, box & papers	Rough	$22.49	11-1999
Pflueger	Neverfail 3-hook	bar perch, glass eyes	EX	$209.49	12-1999
Pflueger	Neverfail 3-hook	bar perch, glass eyes	EX	$430.00	3-2000
Pflueger	Neverfail 3-hook	bar perch, glass eyes	VG-	$72.00	4-2000
Pflueger	Neverfail 3-hook	broad green scale, glass eyes, fat body	EX	$316.00	4-2000
Pflueger	Neverfail 3-hook	crackleback, cracked eyes, chipped nose	EX-	$150.00	4-2000
Pflueger	Neverfail 3-hook	crackleback, dog prop	VG+	$72.00	1-2002
Pflueger	Neverfail 3-hook	crackleback, flat plate, pretty	EX	$318.77	8-1999
Pflueger	Neverfail 3-hook	crackleback, glass eyes	Mint	$389.00	10-1999
Pflueger	Neverfail 3-hook	crackleback, glass eyes, fat Monarch body	VG+	$187.50	3-2000
Pflueger	Neverfail 3-hook	crackleback, glass eyes, HPGM, gleamer, gem clip	EX- to EX	$232.50	11-1999
Pflueger	Neverfail 3-hook	crackleback, glass eyes, HPGM, NOT MET	EX-	$81.25	11-1999
Pflueger	Neverfail 3-hook	crackleback, HPGM, fat body, dog prop	VG+	$300.00	1-2000
Pflueger	Neverfail 3-hook	crackleback, NOT MET	EX	$178.56	6-1999
Pflueger	Neverfail 3-hook	crackleback, see through, pre 1910	VG+	$75.00	10-2000
Pflueger	Neverfail 3-hook	crackleback, split box	EX/IB	$201.01	6-1999
Pflueger	Neverfail 3-hook	frog scale, glass eyes	EX	$383.00	7-2000
Pflueger	Neverfail 3-hook	frog scale, glass eyes	EX-	$356.00	4-2000
Pflueger	Neverfail 3-hook	frog, glass eyes, NOT MET	EX-	$176.00	12-1998
Pflueger	Neverfail 3-hook	frog scale, papers	NIB	$493.00	6-2001
Pflueger	Neverfail 3-hook	luminous, gold spots, glass eyes	EX-	$187.49	8-1999
Pflueger	Neverfail 3-hook	luminous, gold spots, marked prop	EX+	$325.00	12-1999

BRAND	MODEL	SERIES / MFG. CODE / DESCRIPTION	GRADE	PRICE	DATE
Pflueger	Neverfail 3-hook	natural perch scale, glass eyes	VG	$72.00	1-2000
Pflueger	Neverfail 3-hook	perch scale, glass eyes, crisp box, NOT MET	NIB	$390.00	4-2000
Pflueger	Neverfail 3-hook	perch scale, glass eyes, NOT MET	EX+	$280.00	8-2000
Pflueger	Neverfail 3-hook	perch, tack eyes	NIB	$103.49	4-1999
Pflueger	Neverfail 3-hook	rainbow	EX-	$177.50	6-1999
Pflueger	Neverfail 3-hook	rainbow, glass eyes	EX	$157.00	3-2002
Pflueger	Neverfail 3-hook	rainbow, glass eyes	EX	$212.50	6-1999
Pflueger	Neverfail 3-hook	rainbow, glass eyes	EX	$242.50	3-1999
Pflueger	Neverfail 3-hook	rainbow, glass eyes	EX-	$102.00	5-2000
Pflueger	Neverfail 3-hook	rainbow, glass eyes	VG+	$80.00	6-2000
Pflueger	Neverfail 3-hook	rainbow, glass eyes	VG+	$89.88	9-1999
Pflueger	Neverfail 3-hook	rainbow, glass eyes, bulldog OFP	EX-	$156.00	9-2000
Pflueger	Neverfail 3-hook	rainbow, in canoe 2PCCB	EX/IB	$385.00	12-1998
Pflueger	Neverfail 3-hook	rainbow, painted eyes, S-rig, POBW, NOT MET	EX	$52.00	6-1999
Pflueger	Neverfail 3-hook	red back, white blended, maroon Regal box	NIB	$808.00	4-1999
Pflueger	Neverfail 3-hook	red head, painted eyes, PTCB	NIB	$181.19	3-2000
Pflueger	Neverfail 3-hook	red, white, glass eyes	EX+	$361.00	12-1999
Pflueger	Neverfail 3-hook	red, white, glass eyes, nice box	EX-/IB	$206.49	9-1999
Pflueger	Neverfail 3-hook	red, white, worm burn, 1 side ex	Fair to EX	$98.00	5-1999
Pflueger	Neverfail 3-hook	sienna crackleback, glass eyes, HPGM	EX-	$410.50	3-2000
Pflueger	Neverfail 3-hook	silver	EX+	$520.00	10-1999
Pflueger	Neverfail 3-hook	strawberry, glass eyes	EX-	$240.50	3-2000
Pflueger	Neverfail 3-hook	strawberry, glass eyes, repainted?	EX+	$383.58	2-2000
Pflueger	Neverfail 3-hook	strawberry, glass eyes, big chip on back	AVG	$44.00	10-2000
Pflueger	Neverfail 3-hook	white, gem clip, unmarked	EX	$366.01	10-1999
Pflueger	Neverfail 3-hook	white, glass eyes, unmarked	EX-	$340.00	8-1999
Pflueger	Neverfail 3-hook	white, glass eyes, vg maroon box, $450.00 NOT MET	EX-/IB	$220.00	6-2001
Pflueger	Neverfail 3-hook	x2, bulldog front prop	VG-	$223.00	10-2000
Pflueger	Neverfail 5-hook	3⅝ ", perch, glass eyes	Mint	$570.65	3-1999
Pflueger	Neverfail 5-hook	3104, natural pike, tack eyes?	NIB	$431.00	12-1999
Pflueger	Neverfail 5-hook	3107, chub scale	EX+	$725.00	10-1999
Pflueger	Neverfail 5-hook	3169, spots	VG	$250.00	10-1999
Pflueger	Neverfail 5-hook	3169 WH-GR-RED, strawberry	NIB	$767.00	1-1999
Pflueger	Neverfail 5-hook	3181, red, blue rim canoe, papers	EX-/IB	$500.55	2-2000
Pflueger	Neverfail 5-hook	3185, crackleback, blush gills	EX+	$415.00	10-1999
Pflueger	Neverfail 5-hook	bar perch, glass eyes, varnish otherwise okay	VG+	$147.00	10-2000
Pflueger	Neverfail 5-hook	bar perch, glass eyes, fat body	VG	$249.40	5-1999
Pflueger	Neverfail 5-hook	broad green scale	EX	$480.00	8-1999
Pflueger	Neverfail 5-hook	crackleback?, glass eyes	EX/IB	$275.00	9-1999
Pflueger	Neverfail 5-hook	crackleback, glass eyes, couple pointers	EX-	$203.00	5-2000
Pflueger	Neverfail 5-hook	crackleback, glass eyes, POBW, ugly	NIB	$305.00	1-1999
Pflueger	Neverfail 5-hook	crackleback, HPGM, chip at BW	EX-	$280.00	11-1999
Pflueger	Neverfail 5-hook	crackleback, unmarked prop	EX	$331.99	8-1999
Pflueger	Neverfail 5-hook	perch, painted eyes	VG	$91.00	4-1999
Pflueger	Neverfail 5-hook	rainbow, glass eyes	EX+	$350.00	6-2000

BRAND	MODEL	SERIES / MFG. CODE / DESCRIPTION	GRADE	PRICE	DATE
Pflueger	Neverfail 5-hook	rainbow, glass eyes	EX	$290.00	4-1999
Pflueger	Neverfail 5-hook	rainbow, glass eyes	G	$92.00	2-1999
Pflueger	Neverfail 5-hook	rainbow, glass eyes	VG	$242.50	3-1999
Pflueger	Neverfail 5-hook	rainbow, glass eyes	VG+	$97.00	7-2000
Pflueger	Neverfail 5-hook	rainbow, glass eyes, NOT MET	EX	$380.00	9-1999
Pflueger	Neverfail 5-hook	rainbow, glass eyes, NOT MET	EX	$401.99	8-1999
Pflueger	Neverfail 5-hook	rainbow, NOT MET	EX	$363.00	8-1999
Pflueger	Neverfail 5-hook	red, yellow, crisp maroon see through target box	EX-/IB	$1,200.00	8-2001
Pflueger	Neverfail 5-hook	spots, gleamer but small scuff on back	VG+	$360.00	1-2000
Pflueger	Neverfail 5-hook	white, see through, Playfair wood box	EX-/IB	$1,724.00	5-2000
Pflueger	O' Boy	2¾", strawberry, glass eyes, marked lip	EX-	$200.00	8-1999
Pflueger	O' Boy	3½", red head, glass eyes, blue Canoe box, NOT MET	NIB	$202.50	2-2000
Pflueger	O' Boy	3½", strawberry, glass eyes, blue Canoe box	NIB	$648.00	2-2000
Pflueger	O' Boy	frog scale, glass eyes, blue canoe, paper	NIB	$699.00	2-2000
Pflueger	O' Boy	peanut butter, glass eyes	EX-	$140.25	2-2000
Pflueger	O' Boy	strawberry, glass eyes, nice	EX	$205.00	10-1999
Pflueger	O' Boy	strawberry, NOT MET	EX-	$158.00	11-2000
Pflueger	Pakron	red head	EX-	$280.00	10-1999
Pflueger	Pal-O-Mine	3¼", pikie, painted eyes	NIB	$76.00	11-1999
Pflueger	Pal-O-Mine	4", green, silver scale, glass eyes	EX+	$64.50	1-1999
Pflueger	Pal-O-Mine	4"?, pikie scale, nice box	NIB	$131.00	4-2000
Pflueger	Pal-O-Mine	6-pack, 5078, rainbow, pressed eyes	NIB	$184.00	7-2000
Pflueger	Pal-O-Mine	6-pack, silver sparkles, green back, NOT MET	NIB	$102.50	6-1999
Pflueger	Pal-O-Mine	5006, pikie, glass eyes, crisp box, papers	NIB	$227.50	1-2000
Pflueger	Pal-O-Mine	5040, sunfish, painted eyes, NOT MET	NIB	$44.00	2-1999
Pflueger	Pal-O-Mine	7604, natural pike, blue, glass eyes, NOT MET	NIB	$76.00	2-2000
Pflueger	Pal-O-Mine	9006, perch, PTCB, $35.00 reserve	NIB	$15.00	1-2000
Pflueger	Pal-O-Mine	blue scale, glass eyes?	EX-	$43.99	2-1999
Pflueger	Pal-O-Mine	blue scale, pressed eyes	NIB	$21.00	1-2001
Pflueger	Pal-O-Mine	crackleback, glass eyes	EX-	$54.00	10-2000
Pflueger	Pal-O-Mine	frog scale, glass eyes	Mint	$221.05	1-2000
Pflueger	Pal-O-Mine	frog scale, painted eyes	EX-	$198.00	6-2000
Pflueger	Pal-O-Mine	natural mullet, glass eyes, blue Canoe box	NIB	$355.00	2-2000
Pflueger	Pal-O-Mine	peanut butter?, painted eyes, large	Mint	$51.75	1-2000
Pflueger	Pal-O-Mine	perch, glass eyes, small	EX	$45.00	10-2000
Pflueger	Pal-O-Mine	pike, glass eyes, jointed shiner	AVG	$26.00	1-1999
Pflueger	Pal-O-Mine	pikie, tack eyes, modern, PTCB	NIB	$20.25	4-1999
Pflueger	Pal-O-Mine	rainbow, glass eyes, NOT MET	EX	$46.00	4-2000
Pflueger	Pal-O-Mine	rainbow, painted eyes	Mint	$36.00	11-1999
Pflueger	Pal-O-Mine	rainbow, painted eyes, small, PTCB	NIB	$51.00	3-1999
Pflueger	Pal-O-Mine	red head, sparkles, painted eyes, large, papers	NIB	$46.00	2-2000
Pflueger	Pal-O-Mine	S7033, plastic box, $35.00 reserve	NIB	$15.00	1-2000
Pflueger	Pal-O-Mine	strawberry, glass eyes	EX-	$62.00	2-1999
Pflueger	Pal-O-Mine	white flash, glass eyes, NOT MET	EX/IB	$62.00	2-1999
Pflueger	Pal-O-Mine	yellow perch, painted eyes	Mint	$42.00	11-2000

BRAND	MODEL	SERIES / MFG. CODE / DESCRIPTION	GRADE	PRICE	DATE
Pflueger	Pal-O-Mine, Mustang	scale patterns, painted eyes, PTCB	NIB	$47.00	5-2000
Pflueger	Pal-O-Mine, Pop Rite	blue scale, frog, painted eyes, PTCB	NIB	$41.00	5-2000
Pflueger	Phantom	ex- maroon box	EX/IB	$192.50	1-2000
Pflueger	Phantom	large	NIB	$200.00	4-2001
Pflueger	Phantom	Musky size, new OC/IB	NIB	$62.00	1-2000
Pflueger	Phantom	on ex card	EX/OC	$125.00	4-2001
Pflueger	Phantom	vg picture box	EX-/IB	$225.00	10-1999
Pflueger	Pilot Fly	1823, Royal Coachman #8	NOC	$25.00	2-2002
Pflueger	Pirate	white, green, 3-hook, cheap	VG	$32.00	1-2000
Pflueger	Playfair	bar perch, glass eyes, 5-hook, maroon Playfair box	NIB	$757.00	10-2000
Pflueger	Pop Rite	black, silver sparkles, t-bolt	EX	$41.00	5-2000
Pflueger	Razem	6096, red, white, NOT MET	VG/IB	$50.99	4-1999
Pflueger	Scoop	9303, silver sparkles, green back, glass eyes, Canoe box	EX/IB	$122.51	6-1999
Pflueger	Scoop	9355, Meadow Frog, glass eyes, 2PCCB	EX/IB	$125.49	11-1999
Pflueger	Spinner	scalloped, Abu Reflex, angled name	EX	$31.00	3-2000
Pflueger	Spinner	textured scale, angled name, c.1880	EX	$157.00	11-2000
Pflueger	Spinner	textured scale, musky size, painted frog	AVG	$41.00	3-2001
Pflueger	Spinner	textured scale, unmarked brass	EX	$137.00	7-2000
Pflueger	Spinner	textured, luminous, moth picture box, angled name	EX-	$63.00	8-2000
Pflueger	Spinner, American Ball	4½"	VG	$40.89	6-1999
Pflueger	Spinner, Fluted	fish design, NOT MET	EX	$102.00	11-2000
Pflueger	Spoon, Chum	6-pack, nice big box, 6 smaller mint boxes, NOT MET	NIB	$177.00	1-2002
Pflueger	Spoon, Maybug	glass beads	VG+	$1,525.00	5-1999
Pflueger	Spoon, Maybug	NOT MET	EX	$1,593.00	6-2001
Pflueger	Surprise	4", rainbow, glass eyes, 2-hook	EX+	$393.88	2-2000
Pflueger	Surprise	#4, rainbow, hole-eyes, superb 3973 maroon box	NIB	$1,053.00	9-2001
Pflueger	Surprise	3985, crackleback, lower lip chips	EX-	$305.00	10-1999
Pflueger	Surprise	golden shiner, glass eyes	EX	$287.00	5-2001
Pflueger	Surprise	golden shiner, glass eyes	EX	$700.00	4-2000
Pflueger	Surprise	rainbow, hole-eyes, Four Brothers, maroon box	VG-/IB	$355.00	10-2000
Pflueger	Surprise	belly chip, Four Brothers, maroon box	VG+	$610.00	3-1999
Pflueger	Surprise	crackleback, hole-eyes	EX	$525.00	5-2000
Pflueger	Surprise	crackleback, hole-eyes	VG-	$127.53	2-2000
Pflueger	Surprise	golden shiner	EX+	$750.00	4-2001
Pflueger	Surprise	luminous, glass eyes	EX	$256.00	10-2000
Pflueger	Surprise	luminous, hole-eyes, NOT MET	EX-	$257.52	1-2000
Pflueger	Surprise	white hole eye	EX-	$425.00	5-2000
Pflueger	Surprise	white lure, Four Brothers, crisp maroon box	NIB	$1,088.00	10-2000
Pflueger	Surprise	3980, white, hole-eyes	EX+	$500.00	10-1999
Pflueger	Tantrum	6-pack, painted eyes, NOT MET	NIB	$122.50	5-1999
Pflueger	TNT	rainbow, metal	VG	$76.00	6-1999
Pflueger	TNT	metal, NOT MET	EX	$50.01	5-1999
Pflueger	Wiggler, Wizard	flyrod, strawberry	EX	$41.99	3-2000
Pflueger	Wizard	3-hook, NOT MET		$156.00	3-2000

BRAND	MODEL	SERIES / MFG. CODE / DESCRIPTION	GRADE	PRICE	DATE
Pflueger	Wizard	5-hook, earliest model, R & L prop	AVG	$141.00	7-2002
Pflueger	Wizard	luminous, PTCB, paper	NIB	$134.00	10-2000
Pflueger	Wizard	rainbow, 3-hook, HPGM, screw-eye hook hangers	VG-	$325.00	10-2002
Pflueger	Wizard	rainbow, painted eyes, chip by eye	VG+	$57.00	10-2000
Pflueger	Wizard	silver, 5-hook, marked prop , c.1903, NOT MET	VG+	$157.00	1-2001
Pflueger, South Bend	Pike-Oreno	tack eyes, Pflueger box with South Bend bait label	NIB	$65.00	4-1999
Phantom Minnow	Phantom		EX	$75.00	4-2001
Pico	Perch	12-pack, 4 different colors	NIB	$132.50	8-1999
Pico	Perch	bead eyed, clear, back, CD, gold foil	EX	$82.00	4-2000
Pico	Pop	ad lure, 1 bid	NIB	$10.00	5-2000
Point Jude		6", blue back, white, blister pack	NOC	$31.00	1-2002
Point Jude	Stri-Pert	large stripper crank, painted eyes	NIB	$165.50	5-1999
Pontiac	Minnow, Radiant	5-hook, water stain box, papers	NIB	$6,060.00	10-1999
Pontiac	Minnow, Radiant	dark back/red, POBW, NOT MET	VG	$510.99	10-1999
Pontiac	Minnow, Radiant	glass eyes, brass hardware	AVG	$134.00	8-2002
Pontiac	Minnow, Radiant	ugly box with label half gone, NOT MET	Poor/IB	$360.00	4-2002
Porter	Pop-Stop	Florida bait, plastic box	NIB	$10.00	7-2000
Porter	Spin-Hawk	3-pack, plastic box	NIB	$76.99	6-1999
R.K. Tackle	Hollowhead	4 different, NOT MET	NIB	$102.50	5-1999
R.K. Tackle	Hollowhead	mahogany, papers	NIB	$33.00	3-1999
Rapala	Deep Diver	90, like fat rap, large metal lip, 16 bids	NIB	$27.00	11-2000
Rapala	Fat Rap Shallow	8 different, perch, chartreuse, silver, gold, x2	NIB	$150.00	1-2001
Rapala	Various	assorted, 10 different	NIB	$34.51	3-1999
Reds	Shur-Catch	12-pack display card, spring hook	NOC	$76.00	5-1999
Rhodes		green, 3-hook, see through, body wire, c.1907	AVG	$177.50	11-1999
Rhodes		perch, glass eyes, 5-hook, see through rig	VG	$415.50	4-1999
Rhodes	New Winner	3-hook, wood, ex- A9059, Sh hardware, NOT MET	NIB	$2,400.00	11-2000
Rinehart	Jinx	2¼", white shore, 2PCCB	EX/IB	$22.50	5-1999
Rinehart	Jinx	5", BBS, red, white, blue back, shiner, 2PCCB	EX/IB	$37.17	6-1999
Rinehart	Jinx	5", LBR, red, white, 2PCCB	EX-/IB	$24.00	6-1999
Rinehart	Jinx	5", red, white, 2pccb LBR, white shore	EX/IB	$42.17	6-1999
Rinehart	Jinx	35 different, 3 boxes, display case	EX	$350.00	8-1999
Rinehart	Jinx	BS, musky size nice box	EX/IB	$51.00	2-1999
Rinehart	Jinx	red, yellow, small	EX	$34.91	12-1999
Rinehart	Jinx	small, white, red ribs, crisp box	NIB	$27.00	8-2000
Rinehart	Musky, Jinx	4 different, 2PCCB	NIB	$202.50	2-1999
Rinehart	Musky, Jinx	green perch?, hard plastic box	NIB	$42.00	8-2002
Rinehart	Musky, Jinx	nice box	NIB	$36.50	2-1999
Rinehart	Musky, Jinx	pikie?	EX	$35.57	6-1999
Rinehart	Musky, Jinx	perch scale	VG+	$18.00	3-2001
Rinehart	Musky, Jinx	rainbow	EX-	$37.00	2-1999
Rinehart	Musky, Jinx	silver head, blue	NIB	$43.00	9-1999
Rinehart	Musky, Jinx	spots, flitter, papers	NIB	$65.00	9-2000
Roberts	Mud Puppy	⅔, natural, glass eyes, cartoon box	NIB	$85.00	5-1999
Roberts	Mud Puppy	⅔, natural, glass eyes, cartoon box	NIB	$127.50	4-1999

BRAND	MODEL	SERIES / MFG. CODE / DESCRIPTION	GRADE	PRICE	DATE
Roberts	Mud Puppy	black, white, glass eyes, special order, cartoon box	NIB	$117.00	9-2000
Roberts	Mud Puppy	natural, glass eyes, large, catalog	EX/IB	$42.00	1-1999
Roberts	Mud Puppy, Little	glass eyes, picture box, red & white picture papers EX-	NIB	$205.00	6-2001
Roberts	Mud Puppy, Little	natural, decal eyes, picture box, papers	EX/IB	$58.00	3-2000
Roberts	Pupette	yellow, black	NIB	$35.00	2-2000
Rochester	Spinner	plain	NOC	$52.00	3-1999
Ropher	Fin-Dingo	perch in wrong 2PCCB	NIB	$92.50	12-1998
Rosegard	Salmon	yellow, red gills, nice box	NIB	$27.00	2-2002
Russo, C.	Chugger	9", goldfish scale, glass eyes	EX	$284.99	3-2000
Saf-T-Lure	Saf-T-Lure	green, white	EX	$43.00	10-2000
San Luco	Injured Minnow	christmas tree, nice box	NIB	$44.51	3-2000
Sat-Kot	Spoon, Springloaded	fish-shaped spoon	EX	$57.99	6-1999
Schaefer	Turbulent	green, red, white spots, 3 sections	EX-	$138.50	2-2000
Schaefer	Turbulent	red, yellow, 2 papers, $450.00 NOT MET	NIB	$305.00	6-2002
Schaefer	Turbulent	red, yellow, ugly double wood spinner	NIB	$293.88	11-1999
Schaefer	Turbulent	white, muticolored spots, 2 sections	EX+	$116.00	8-2001
Schroeders	Wonder Plug	basser type, glass eyes, double jointed	EX	$215.00	1-1999
Scooter Pooper	Scooter Pooper		EX-	$52.99	5-1999
Scooter Pooper	Scooter Pooper	papers, NOT MET	NIB	$127.50	12-1999
Scooter Pooper	Scooter Pooper	NOT MET	EX	$54.00	6-2000
Sea Gull	Pollywog	pristine in correctly marked mint box	NIB	$2,000.00	4-2001
Sears & Roebuck	Minnow, Winner Wooden	9006, crackleback, box++	EX/IB	$828.00	5-1999
Shakespeare	Barnacle Bill	green back, silver, flitter, glass eyes	EX	$750.00	10-1999
Shakespeare	Barnacle Bill	white	VG	$483.00	7-2002
Shakespeare	Barnacle Bill	white, black tail, flitter, glass eyes	EX	$309.00	3-2001
Shakespeare	Bass	a CCBC NRA box	NIB	$275.00	10-1999
Shakespeare	Buddy	6568	NIB	$107.50	3-2000
Shakespeare	Bug	SB, flyrod, metal lip marked Shakespeare	EX-	$77.00	1-2002
Shakespeare	Bug, Kazoo		NM	$300.00	10-1999
Shakespeare	Bug, Kazoo	strawberry, feathers, glass eyes	VG	$45.98	4-1999
Shakespeare	Chub, Kazoo	638, glass eyes	EX	$300.00	10-1999
Shakespeare	Darting Shrimp	brown back, copper, glass eyes, very nice	EX	$175.00	11-1999
Shakespeare	Darting Shrimp	copper, glass eyes, small joint chip	EX-	$250.00	12-1999
Shakespeare	Darting Shrimp	silver, glass eyes, nice	EX-	$224.50	8-1999
Shakespeare	Dopey	6603, black body, white head	NIB	$77.00	5-2001
Shakespeare	Dopey	6603YP, nice box, papers	NIB	$53.99	3-1999
Shakespeare	Egyptian Wobbler	6636, red head, glass eyes	EX/IB	$148.00	2-2001
Shakespeare	Evolution	4GAEA, crisp grey oval box	EX/IB	$621.00	10-2000
Shakespeare	Evolution	ex grey box	VG/IB	$500.00	10-1999
Shakespeare	Evolution	ex grey oval box	EX-/IB	$644.00	3-2001
Shakespeare	Evolution	small chips	EX-	$300.00	10-2002
Shakespeare	Fancy Back	#00, crackleback, green scale, glass eyes, 2-hook, twin prop	EX	$297.00	5-2000
Shakespeare	Favorite Floating Bait	red back, white, 2-hook, A prop, c.1906	EX	$3,000.00	6-2001
Shakespeare	Favorite Floating Bait	red, chipping around eyes, repainted?	EX-	$800.00	10-2000

BRAND	MODEL	SERIES / MFG. CODE / DESCRIPTION	GRADE	PRICE	DATE
Shakespeare	Favorite Floating Bait	red, glass eyes, screw eyes, plain	EX-	$432.51	1-2000
Shakespeare	Favorite Floating Bait	triangle body, no eyes, screw	EX	$150.00	10-1999
Shakespeare	Favorite Floating Bait	yellow perch, 3-hook, flat plate, c.1916	EX	$780.00	6-2001
Shakespeare	Favorite Floating Bait	yellow, high forehead	VG+/ to EX-	$3,550.00	12-2001
Shakespeare	Favorite Floating Bait	Zara type, strawberry, glass eyes	VG+	$305.00	8-1999
Shakespeare	Fisher Bait	bar perch, painted eyes	EX	$155.00	10-1999
Shakespeare	Fishylure	hard rubber, small tail chip	EX/OC	$325.00	10-1999
Shakespeare	Floater	#42, yellow, green back, 3-hook (2 on belly), high forehead, B prop	EX-	$1,200.00	6-2001
Shakespeare	Frog Skin	hard rubber, 3rd leg still there, ugly	VG	$1,360.00	10-1999
Shakespeare	Frog Skin	Eger?, glass eyes	EX-	$200.00	10-1999
Shakespeare	Frog, Rhodes	ex wood box	NIB	$5,000.00	12-2001
Shakespeare	Frog, Rhodes	g Kalamazoo 2PCCB	EX/IB	$2,900.00	10-1999
Shakespeare	Hydroplane	crackleback, 709 photo sides	EX-	$91.00	5-2000
Shakespeare	Hydroplane	early version	Mint	$210.00	12-2001
Shakespeare	Hydroplane	green scale	EX-	$205.00	3-2000
Shakespeare	Hydroplane	rainbow scale, photo finish	VG+	$95.00	10-2000
Shakespeare	Hydroplane	rainbow, NOT MET	EX	$187.50	1-2000
Shakespeare	Hydroplane	red, yellow, no washer	Mint	$355.00	10-1999
Shakespeare	Injun Joe	frog, glass eyes, decent	VG+	$48.00	1-2000
Shakespeare	Injun Joe	red head	EX+	$87.86	1-2000
Shakespeare	Injun Joe	silver, flitter, glass eyes	EX	$250.00	10-1999
Shakespeare	Jim Dandy Floater	green scale	VG+	$70.00	10-1999
Shakespeare	Jim Dandy Punkinseed	red head, no eyes, POBW	EX-	$60.00	10-1999
Shakespeare	Mermaid	red head	EX	$125.00	10-1999
Shakespeare	Midget, Spinner	6601GP, photo perch, pressed eyes	NIB	$52.00	10-2000
Shakespeare	Midget, Spinner	green scale, red, painted eyes	Mint	$100.00	10-1999
Shakespeare	Midget, Underwater	6600, sienna crackleback, glass eyes, photo side	VG+	$266.00	1-2000
Shakespeare	Midget, Underwater	gold crackleback/yellow scale	EX-	$380.00	10-1999
Shakespeare	Minnow, Floater	#00, like Artistic Minnow, sienna crackleback, B-prop	EX+	$600.00	10-1999
Shakespeare	Minnow, Floater	#31YP, 3-hook, photo finish, red box	EX-/IB	$400.00	10-1999
Shakespeare	Minnow, Floater	metalized, red, silver3-hook, flat, HPGM, B prop	EX	$2,050.00	10-199
Shakespeare	Minnow, Floater	SB, triangle body, J.Dandy?	EX-	$666.00	3-2001
Shakespeare	Minnow, Floater-Sinker	#44, bar perch, 5-hook, plate	EX-	$480.00	3-2000
Shakespeare	Minnow, Floater-Sinker	#44 black, silver, white, red, high forehead, B prop, back scratchs, c.1909	VG+	$800.00	6-2001
Shakespeare	Minnow, Floater-Sinker	#44, perch?, 5-hook, POBW, gem clip, B prop	EX-	$636.61	4-1999
Shakespeare	Minnow, Floater-Sinker	44SY, grey box VG, flat plate, PP, sweeping HPGM	EX-/IB	$1,900.00	6-2001
Shakespeare	Minnow, Floater-Sinker	#44, yellow, high forehead, gem clip, A prop, c.1906	VG	$1,600.00	6-2001
Shakespeare	Minnow, Metalized	3-hook, nickel	EX	$1,020.00	10-1999
Shakespeare	Minnow, Metalized	glass eyes, 5-hook	EX-	$415.00	6-2000
Shakespeare	Minnow, Midget Metalized	copper, B prop, c.1909	EX	$2,500.00	6-2001
Shakespeare	Minnow, New Shiner	#23, wood box, vg paper, poor label	EX-/IB	$1,500.00	12-2001
Shakespeare	Minnow, New Shiner	slate, wood label dirty, avg	EX/IB	$2,850.00	6-2001

BRAND	MODEL	SERIES / MFG. CODE / DESCRIPTION	GRADE	PRICE	DATE
Shakespeare	Minnow, Panatella	green scale, white eyes, HPGM, 3-hook, shallow cup	Mint	$1,250.00	5-2000
Shakespeare	Minnow, Rhodes	yellow, 3-hook, in early ex+ box	NIB	$4,800.00	12-2001
Shakespeare	Minnow, Rhodes	green stripes, 5 hook, gem clip	EX-	$358.00	3-2000
Shakespeare	Minnow, Rhodes	green, white, 2HPGM, 5-hook, flat plate	EX-	$350.00	10-1999
Shakespeare	Minnow, Rhodes	green-blue, white, 3-hook, prop, Rhode prop	EX-	$950.00	10-1999
Shakespeare	Minnow, Rhodes	red, yellow, 5-hook, flat plate, pointed prop	VG+	$370.00	10-1999
Shakespeare	Minnow, Rhodes	yellow, gem clip	EX+	$1,080.00	12-2001
Shakespeare	Minnow, Rhodes	yellow, glass eyes, 3-hook, M clip, c.1906	EX	$1,080.00	6-2001
Shakespeare	Minnow, Saltwater	721, painted eyes, POBW	VG+	$250.00	10-1999
Shakespeare	Minnow, Shiner	3-hook, ex- 43 wood box	EX/IB	$2,900.00	10-1999
Shakespeare	Minnow, Sinker	#03	EX	$700.00	4-2001
Shakespeare	Minnow, Sinker	2-hook, flat plate, B prop, 33SC ex wood box	EX/IB	$2,850.00	10-1999
Shakespeare	Minnow, Sinker	3-hook, metalized nickel, B prop	EX-	$705.00	3-2000
Shakespeare	Minnow, Sinker	#03, crackleback	EX	$394.00	5-2001
Shakespeare	Minnow, Sinker	#33, copper, 3-hook, ex wood box	EX/IB	$3,050.00	10-2000
Shakespeare	Minnow, Sinker	#33, crackleback, glass eyes, 3-hook	EX-	$155.00	6-1999
Shakespeare	Minnow, Sinker	#33, gold, metalized, B prop, flat plate, wood, stamp, ex- end label	EX/IB	$4,050.00	6-2001
Shakespeare	Minnow, Sinker	#33GY, flat plate, ex- grey box	NIB	$2,450.00	6-2001
Shakespeare	Minnow, Sinker	#33, rainbow, B prop, flat plate, ex labeled wood box	NIB	$4,100.00	6-2001
Shakespeare	Minnow, Sinker	#33, red, yellow, HPGM, 3-hook, gem clip, POBW	EX-	$650.00	10-1999
Shakespeare	Minnow, Sinker	#33SR, solid red, 3-hook	NIB	$1,550.00	10-1999
Shakespeare	Minnow, Sinker	#43, rainbow, 3-hook, gem clip, B prop	EX-	$700.00	12-2001
Shakespeare	Minnow, Sinker	#43, red, silver, yellow, white, 3-hook, long, B prop, gem clip, c.1909	EX-	$800.00	6-2001
Shakespeare	Minnow, Sinker	rainbow, glass eyes, HPGM, 3-hook, flat plate	EX	$247.00	6-2000
Shakespeare	Minnow, Sinker	sienna crackleback, 3-hook, flat plate, PP	EX	$900.00	6-2001
Shakespeare	Mouse	green, glass eyes, tail, tiny lip chip	EX	$56.00	1-2000
Shakespeare	Mouse	green, yellow, glass eyes	EX	$110.00	10-1999
Shakespeare	Mouse	red head, painted eyes	VG	$130.00	7-2000
Shakespeare	Mouse, Swimming	red, white, in plastic top box	NIB	$32.00	1-1999
Shakespeare	Musky Floater	51, yellow gills, high forehead, 1 of 3 known, clip, B prop	EX- to VG+	$5,200.00	12-2001
Shakespeare	Musky Floater	61, red, yellow gills, 2-hook, gem clip, belly chip, c.1907	EX-	$5,600.00	6-2001
Shakespeare	Musky Minnow	5½", green back, white, big glass eyes, 3HPGM, 5-hook, 2BW	VG	$2,392.00	4-2000
Shakespeare	Musky Minnow	5⅜", no hooks or rear prop	VG-	$645.57	3-2000
Shakespeare	Musky Minnow	64, crackleback, silver b, red side, 5-hook, flat plate, 3HPGM, PP, c.1916	EX-	$5,100.00	6-2001
Shakespeare	Musky Minnow	64, green, red, silver, flat plate, unmarked prop, c.1916	EX-	$5,000.00	12-2001
Shakespeare	Musky Minnow	64, white, 5-hook, 3HPGM, flat plate, PP, c.1916	VG+ to EX-	$3,800.00	6-2001
Shakespeare	Musky Minnow	64, white, flat plate, unmarked prop c1916	EX-/VG+	$3,500.00	12-2001
Shakespeare	Musky Minnow	green back, white, 5-hook, pnt, smooth prop	EX	$3,079.00	8-2002

BRAND	MODEL	SERIES / MFG. CODE / DESCRIPTION	GRADE	PRICE	DATE
Shakespeare	Musky Minnow	orange, yellow, sweeping HPGM, 5-hook, small chips	EX-	$2,600.00	10-1999
Shakespeare	Musky Minnow	rainbow, early		$3,350.00	
Shakespeare	Musky Minnow	white, 5-hook, flat plate, NOT MET	EX-	$510.00	10-2002
Shakespeare	Musky Minnow	white, sweeping HPGM, 5-hook	EX-	$4,000.00	10-1999
Shakespeare	Pad-Ler	3¼", red, white	Mint	$267.50	1-2000
Shakespeare	Pad-Ler	frog	EX	$100.00	7-2000
Shakespeare	Pad-Ler	frog, pressed eyes	EX	$158.00	4-2000
Shakespeare	Pad-Ler	gray mouse	VG	$58.00	2-1999
Shakespeare	Pad-Ler	red head	EX	$210.00	10-1999
Shakespeare	Pad-Ler Musky	frog	VG+	$125.00	9-2000
Shakespeare	Pad-Ler Musky	frog, NOT MET	EX-	$500.00	4-2000
Shakespeare	Paddler, Baby	red head, small chip	EX-	$30.00	10-1999
Shakespeare	Pikie Kazoo, Baby	637, red, white, glass eyes	EX	$58.00	1-1999
Shakespeare	Pikie Kazoo, Baby	red head, glass eyes	EX	$150.00	10-1999
Shakespeare	Punkin-Seed	green?, silver, ex paper	EX-	$1,700.00	12-2001
Shakespeare	Punkin-Seed	red back, aluminum, B prop	EX-	$1,320.00	10-1999
Shakespeare	Punkin-Seed	red back, silver, HPGM, ugly varnish	EX-	$411.98	3-2000
Shakespeare	Punkin-Seed Sinker	slate, no box, nice papers	EX-	$2,000.00	6-2001
Shakespeare	Reed Trolling Musky		EX-	$250.00	10-1999
Shakespeare	Revolution	1st model, marked rear prop	EX-	$214.50	9-1999
Shakespeare	Revolution	2 prop, round, NOT MET	EX	$281.00	5-2001
Shakespeare	Revolution	2nd model, acorn rear, Micky Mouse prop	EX	$300.00	8-1999
Shakespeare	Revolution	4 different; 2 Wordens, 2 Revolutions, 1 dent	EX	$1,176.00	1-2000
Shakespeare	Revolution	early model	EX-	$350.00	5-2000
Shakespeare	Revolution	ex 4SAR wood box	EX/IB	$2,000.00	10-1999
Shakespeare	Revolution	Mickey Mouse prop	EX-	$350.00	10-1999
Shakespeare	Revolution	nice bucktail patina, egg shaped tail, 2 prop	EX	$392.00	9-2001
Shakespeare	Revolution	oldest 1899 model	EX	$483.00	8-2000
Shakespeare	Revolution	reg. size, Mickey prop , round ball	EX	$300.00	3-2000
Shakespeare	Revolution	yellow, in black, silver, vg+	VG/IB	$3,650.00	6-2001
Shakespeare	Revolution, Baby	small dent	EX	$300.00	4-2000
Shakespeare	Revolution, Baby	vg- black picture box	EX/IB	$2,450.00	10-1999
Shakespeare	Revolution Musky	bow tie prop	EX-	$313.00	3-2002
Shakespeare	Revolution Musky	pointed prop, 1-hook, tip missing	EX	$1,280.00	10-1999
Shakespeare	Revolution Musky	red, white, some large chips but still nice	VG	$1,750.00	8-1999
Shakespeare	Sardinia	261, painted eyes, rough box, 1 bid	NIB	$250.00	7-2000
Shakespeare	Sardinia	glass eyes, POBW	VG	$650.00	10-1999
Shakespeare	Sea Witch	strawberry, crack on belly	VG+	$37.33	8-1999
Shakespeare	Slim Jim	43GWJ, g label box	EX/IB	$550.00	10-1999
Shakespeare	Slim Jim	6541, green scale, painted eyes	NIB	$57.01	11-1999
Shakespeare	Slim Jim	ex white intro box, c.1908	NIB	$2,850.00	6-2001
Shakespeare	Slim Jim	gray, pink belly, green stripes, tiny glass eyes	EX-	$233.00	6-2000
Shakespeare	Slim Jim	HPVL, STPHW, tiny glass eyes, 3-hook	VG+	$331.00	3-2002
Shakespeare	Slim Jim	perch, glass eyes, 3-hook, photo, decent	EX-	$86.01	3-2000
Shakespeare	Slim Jim	pressed eyes, 6541YP nice box	NIB	$154.00	11-2000
Shakespeare	Slim Jim	small eyes, 5-hook, grey box, NOT MET	VG/IB	$350.00	3-2001

BRAND	MODEL	SERIES / MFG. CODE / DESCRIPTION	GRADE	PRICE	DATE
Shakespeare	Slim Jim	yellow perch, 5-hook	VG+	$350.00	10-1999
Shakespeare	Slim Jim	perch, tiny eyes, 5-hook, plate	VG	$305.00	1-2000
Shakespeare	Slim Jim	red head, small eyes, 2-hook	EX-	$70.99	1-2000
Shakespeare	Slim Jim	red scale, small eyes, 3-hook, photo, big belly chip	VG	$96.00	1-2000
Shakespeare	Slim Jim Floater	red, green, glass eyes	EX-	$350.00	10-1999
Shakespeare	Spinner	ex correct wood box	EX/IB	$1,420.00	10-1999
Shakespeare	Spinner	ex? wood box, part label	EX/IB	$800.00	12-2001
Shakespeare	Spinner, Floating	4SYs, ex oval 2PCCB	EX/IB	$745.00	2-2000
Shakespeare	Spinner Lure Assortment	6 lures, painted eyes, large 2PCCB	NIB	$213.01	1-2000
Shakespeare	Spinner, Surface	yellow, gold spots, vg+ wood label, stamp	EX/IB	$1,200.00	6-2001
Shakespeare	Strike-It	reddish-brown scale, glass eyes, fin chip, photo	EX-	$125.00	11-2000
Shakespeare	Submarine, Floating	perch, tack eyes, red box	EX/IB	$380.00	10-1999
Shakespeare	Submarine, Floating	tack eyes, photo perch, red box	EX/IB	$350.00	10-1999
Shakespeare	Submerged	#3, perch, POBW, ring, small chips	VG+	$650.00	10-1999
Shakespeare	Sure	ex- black picture box	EX/IB	$2,750.00	10-1999
Shakespeare	Surface Wonder	44W, poor picture box	Poor/IB	$405.00	10-2000
Shakespeare	Tantalizer	glass eyes, ball hook	EX	$290.00	10-1999
Shakespeare	Tantalizer	glass eyes, photo perch	EX	$159.00	6-2000
Shakespeare	Tantalizer	green, yellow, glass eyes, photo	EX-	$140.00	10-1999
Shakespeare	Tantalizer	jointed, glass eyes, knob hook, photo pikie, small tail chip	EX-	$178.55	1-2000
Shakespeare	Tantalizer	natural pike, missing one eye	EX-	$96.00	11-2000
Shakespeare	Tantalizer	photo, big joint chip on belly, gleamer	VG	$87.00	1-2000
Shakespeare	Tantalizer	pressed eyes, ball hanger, photo perch	EX	$224.00	10-2000
Shakespeare	Tantalizer	red head, glass eyes	EX-	$160.00	6-2000
Shakespeare	Tantalizer	red head, white, glass eyes	EX-	$152.50	1-2000
Shakespeare	Tarpalunge	#6640, natural scale	NIB	$810.00	3-1999
Shakespeare	Underwater Minnow 3-hook	bar perch	VG+	$310.00	10-1999
Shakespeare	Underwater Minnow 3-hook	brown sienna, yellow belly	EX-	$525.00	5-2000
Shakespeare	Underwater Minnow 3-hook	copper, see through, nice	VG+	$152.00	8-2000
Shakespeare	Underwater Minnow 3-hook	crackleback, in wood Sears Roebuck box, NOT MET	EX-/IB	$462.00	6-2000
Shakespeare	Underwater Minnow 3-hook	crackleback, plate, unmarked prop	VG+	$217.00	1-2000
Shakespeare	Underwater Minnow 3-hook	gold, yellow perch, sweeping HPGM	EX	$600.00	10-1999
Shakespeare	Underwater Minnow 3-hook	green, white, pointed prop	VG+	$100.00	4-2000
Shakespeare	Underwater Minnow 3-hook	green, white, sweeping HPGM, flat plate	EX-	$550.00	10-1999
Shakespeare	Underwater Minnow 3-hook	rainbow, wood box with faded top	EX-/IB	$586.00	1-2000
Shakespeare	Underwater Minnow 3-hook	sienna, flat plate, unmarked prop	EX	$700.00	12-2001
Shakespeare	Underwater Minnow 3-hook	white, ex unmarked wood box	EX	$1,324.00	1-1999
Shakespeare	Underwater Minnow 3-hook	white, flat plate	VG+	$90.00	5-1999
Shakespeare	Underwater Minnow 3-hook	white, flat plate	EX	$500.00	10-1999
Shakespeare	Underwater Minnow 3-hook	white, high forehead, B prop, HPGM, RABW, NOT MET	EX-	$355.00	1-2000
Shakespeare	Underwater Minnow 3-hook	white, HPGM, flat plate, vg wood box	EX/IB	$1,260.00	2-2000
Shakespeare	Underwater Minnow 3-hook	white, sweeping HPGM, gem clip	EX-	$570.00	10-1999
Shakespeare	Underwater Minnow 5-hook	aluminum, unmarked wood box	NIB	$1,975.00	2-1999
Shakespeare	Underwater Minnow 5-hook	bar perch, plate, pointers	VG+	$537.50	1-2000

BRAND	MODEL	SERIES / MFG. CODE / DESCRIPTION	GRADE	PRICE	DATE
Shakespeare	Underwater Minnow 5-hook	bar perch, HPGM, plain prop	EX-	$695.00	10-1999
Shakespeare	Underwater Minnow 5-hook	crackleback, flat plate, unmarked prop pointed	Mint	$380.00	12-2001
Shakespeare	Underwater Minnow 5-hook	early green back, gem clip	EX-	$420.00	1-2000
Shakespeare	Underwater Minnow 5-hook	fancy back, pretty	EX-	$400.00	1-1999
Shakespeare	Underwater Minnow 5-hook	frog, clip, HPGM	AVG	$204.00	10-2000
Shakespeare	Underwater Minnow 5-hook	green, copper belly, missing 2 hooks, plate HPGM	EX-	$385.00	4-2002
Shakespeare	Underwater Minnow 5-hook	green scale, pressed eyes, cup, photo box	VG-	$240.00	3-2001
Shakespeare	Underwater Minnow 5-hook	green, white, HPGM, bad wood box, NOT MET	VG/IB	$935.51	3-2000
Shakespeare	Underwater Minnow 5-hook	green, white, sweeping HPGM, flat plate	VG	$625.00	10-1999
Shakespeare	Underwater Minnow 5-hook	green, white, vg unmarked wood box	VG+/IB	$1,055.00	1-2000
Shakespeare	Underwater Minnow 5-hook	green, yellow belly, high forehead, touched up	Rough	$500.00	8-2000
Shakespeare	Underwater Minnow 5-hook	greenback rainbow	VG-	$325.00	5-2000
Shakespeare	Underwater Minnow 5-hook	nice wood box, NOT MET	VG-/IB	$860.00	9-1999
Shakespeare	Underwater Minnow 5-hook	rainbow, HPGM, flat plate	EX-	$456.00	10-2000
Shakespeare	Underwater Minnow 5-hook	rainbow, HPGM, plate	VG-	$217.49	2-2000
Shakespeare	Underwater Minnow 5-hook	rainbow, oldest style?, ugly	Poor	$148.00	3-1999
Shakespeare	Underwater Minnow 5-hook	rainbow, plate hardware, scratches but decent	VG-	$179.01	1-2000
Shakespeare	Underwater Minnow 5-hook	red head, see through, checked paint	Odd	$47.00	5-2000
Shakespeare	Underwater Minnow 5-hook	red, see through, nasty chin		$162.00	1-1999
Shakespeare	Underwater Minnow 5-hook	sienna crackleback, PP, flat plate	EX-	$1,000.00	6-2001
Shakespeare	Underwater Minnow 5-hook	sienna, flat plate, unmarked prop	EX-	$900.00	12-2001
Shakespeare	Underwater Minnow 5-hook	white, HPGM, 1BW, gem clip	VG	$225.01	6-1999
Shakespeare	Underwater Minnow 5-hook	yellow, flat plate, unmarked prop, ex- grey box	NIB	$1,600.00	12-2001
Shakespeare	Underwater Minnow 5-hook	yellow perch, high forehead, g picture box, ex paper	EX-/IB	$4,250.00	12-2001
Shakespeare	Waukazoo	Shakespeare 1" OM prop	AVG	$90.00	11-2000
Shakespeare	Waukazoo Surface	white	EX-	$79.00	1-2002
Shakespeare	Whirlwind	#6, white, brass cup, flat plate	EX-	$510.00	1-2000
Shakespeare	Whirlwind	red	EX	$330.00	3-2001
Shakespeare	Whirlwind	red, gem clip	EX	$604.64	12-1999
Shakespeare	Whirlwind	red, hump prop	VG+	$360.00	2-2002
Shakespeare	Whirlwind	red, plain prop	EX	$670.00	6-2001
Shakespeare	Wobbler, Kazoo	6637, greenscale photo, glass eyes	Mint	$184.50	1-2000
Shakespeare	Wobbler, Kazoo	6637 photo, painted eyes, ball hook,	EX	$135.00	10-1999
Shakespeare	Wobbler, Kazoo	green/orange photo, glass eyes	EX	$235.00	10-1999
Shakespeare	Wobbler, Kazoo	perch, jointed, painted eyes, photo	EX-	$124.00	10-1999
Shakespeare	Wobbler, Kazoo	red head, glass eyes, ball hook hanger gleamer	EX	$112.50	1-2000
Shakespeare	Wobbler, King Fish	white, glass eyes, one side ex other worm burn		$45.99	3-2000
Shakespeare	Wobbler, Spoon Bill	black head, red, yellow, glass eyes	EX	$190.00	10-1999
Shakespeare	Worden Bucktail	2¼", silver, hook missing	EX	$188.88	2-2000
Shakespeare	Worden Bucktail	B prop	EX	$250.00	10-1999
Shakespeare	Worden Bucktail	b/s, aluminum, ex- picture box, crisp paper	EX/IB	$3,650.00	6-2001
Shakespeare	Worden Bucktail	patent appl. prop	EX	$250.00	10-1999
Shakespeare	Worden Bucktail	patent appl. prop, one ding	EX-	$250.00	10-1999
Shakespeare	Worden Bucktail	patent appl. prop, replaced tail	EX	$200.00	10-1999

BRAND	MODEL	SERIES / MFG. CODE / DESCRIPTION	GRADE	PRICE	DATE
Shakespeare	Worden Bucktail	yellow spots	EX-	$429.00	3-2000
Shimano	Calcutta	400, with box	EX/IB	$173.50	1-1999
Shur Katch	Injured Minnow	shiner scale, tack eyes, nice 1PCCB	NIB	$40.00	1-2000
Shur Strike	Anteater	peanut butter, glass eyes	EX-	$82.00	10-2001
Shur Strike	Bass-Oreno	BOT-2, glass eyes, small	EX/IB	$32.00	4-2000
Shur Strike	Bass-Oreno	dace?, silver scale over red, dark head	EX	$55.00	4-2000
Shur Strike	Bass-Oreno	peanut butter, glass eyes, small lip chip	EX-	$116.00	5-2000
Shur Strike	Bass-Oreno	peanut butter, notch head, NRA	EX/IB	$227.00	8-2000
Shur Strike	Bass-Oreno	perch?, tack eyes	EX	$22.50	1-1999
Shur Strike	Bass-Oreno	pikie, glass eyes, grooved head	EX-	$47.00	12-2000
Shur Strike	Bass-Oreno	pikie, glass eyes, grooved head	EX-	$53.00	2-2002
Shur Strike	Bass-Oreno	pikie, glass eyes, V-notch, nice	EX-	$103.51	1-2000
Shur Strike	Bass-Oreno	rainbow, glass eyes	VG-	$13.00	1-2001
Shur Strike	Bass-Oreno	red side?, glass eyes	EX	$76.00	12-2000
Shur Strike	Bass-Oreno	silver flash, glass eyes	EX	$31.30	4-2000
Shur Strike	Bass-Oreno	silver flash, glass eyes	EX	$41.00	1-2001
Shur Strike	Bass-Oreno	yellow scale, glass eyes	VG+	$22.30	5-2000
Shur Strike	Bass-Oreno	yellow shiner, glass eyes, small	EX	$46.50	11-1999
Shur Strike	Bass-Oreno, Baby	peanut butter, glass eyes	EX	$68.95	1-2000
Shur Strike	Bass-Oreno, Baby	shiner scale, glass eyes	EX-	$22.00	8-2002
Shur Strike	Bass-Oreno, Baby	silver scale, 2PCCB, nice	NIB	$32.22	5-1999
Shur Strike	Bass-Oreno type	black scale, tack eyes, ugly	AVG	$51.00	5-2001
Shur Strike	Bass-Oreno type	red side, glass eyes, pretty	EX	$43.00	3-2002
Shur Strike	Bass-Oreno type	shiner scale, glass eyes	Mint	$99.00	3-2002
Shur Strike	Crawdad	yellow, red, black stripes, glass eyes, Gateway	EX	$610.00	9-2001
Shur Strike	Darter	concave belly, orange scale	VG+	$118.00	8-1999
Shur Strike	Darter	peanut butter, glass eyes, 2 small chips, light drag	VG	$230.50	3-1999
Shur Strike	Darter	red head, glass eyes, concave belly	EX	$103.00	4-2000
Shur Strike	Flatface	orange scale, glass eyes	EX-	$87.55	10-1999
Shur Strike	Flatface	pike scale, $100.00 NOT MET	EX-	$15.00	10-2000
Shur Strike	Gar	pikie finish, like Torpedo, NOT MET	VG+	$72.00	6-2001
Shur Strike	Gar, Baby	Torpedo type, pikie	VG	$136.00	4-2001
Shur Strike	Husky Musky	white fish, glass eyes, unmarked, CCBC?	EX	$517.03	6-1999
Shur Strike	Injured Minnow	IM-2, red head, yellow & red box, NRA, nice	NIB	$103.00	8-2001
Shur Strike	Injured Minnow	red side, glass eyes, "Injured Tom"	EX	$85.00	12-1999
Shur Strike	Injured Minnow	x2; 1 regular, 1 petite; tack eyes, nice	EX	$34.00	3-1999
Shur Strike	Kingfisher	red, white, glass eyes	EX	$87.55	10-1999
Shur Strike	Kingfisher	yellow scale, glass eyes	VG	$32.00	1-2001
Shur Strike	Minnow, Surface	blue head, yellow, glass eyes	Mint	$128.05	8-1999
Shur Strike	Minnow, Surface	scale, red stripe, glass eyes, nice	EX	$129.00	12-2000
Shur Strike	Minnow, Wounded	peanut butter, glass eyes	EX-	$48.00	2-2002
Shur Strike	Mouse	black, white, glass eyes, decent tail	VG	$31.00	5-2000
Shur Strike	Mouse	black, white, tack eyes	EX	$33.50	10-1999
Shur Strike	Mouse	frog, glass eyes, decent tail	EX-	$40.00	5-2000
Shur Strike	Mouse	frog, glass eyes, smaller one, nice	EX	$57.00	2-2002
Shur Strike	Mouse	grey, bead eyes, bigger than usual, gleamer	EX+	$154.00	4-2000
Shur Strike	Pikie	4¼", chain pike, glass eyes, insert lip	EX	$41.01	10-1999

BRAND	MODEL	SERIES / MFG. CODE / DESCRIPTION	GRADE	PRICE	DATE
Shur Strike	Pikie	700, peanut butter, 2-hook, glass eyes, nice	EX-	$104.00	1-2001
Shur Strike	Pikie	blue head, glass eyes, 3-hook, decent	VG+	$61.00	1-2001
Shur Strike	Pikie	dace, tack eyes	EX	$29.00	9-2001
Shur Strike	Pikie	green scale, glass eyes	EX-	$55.00	10-2001
Shur Strike	Pikie	peanut butter, 3-hook, glass eyes	EX-	$139.00	1-2001
Shur Strike	Pikie	peanut butter, glass eyes, 1 eye cracked	EX	$51.00	12-2000
Shur Strike	Pikie	peanut butter, glass eyes, 3-hook	EX	$181.00	7-2002
Shur Strike	Pikie	peanut butter, glass eyes, small	EX	$130.50	11-1999
Shur Strike	Pikie	perch, glass eyes, sliver by eye, green box	EX-/IB	$32.00	2-2000
Shur Strike	Pikie	pikie, glass eyes	EX/IB	$34.10	2-2000
Shur Strike	Pikie	pikie scale, glass eyes, 2PCCB	NIB	$61.75	6-1999
Shur Strike	Pikie	red, white, glass eyes, crisp O7B box	NIB	$57.27	8-1999
Shur Strike	Pikie	shiner scale, black eye shade, 3-hook	NIB	$64.00	10-1999
Shur Strike	Pikie	shiner scale, glass eyes	EX	$43.00	8-2000
Shur Strike	Pikie	silver flash, glass eyes, round nose	EX	$79.00	10-2001
Shur Strike	Pikie	Western Auto chain pickerel	EX-/IB	$71.00	4-2000
Shur Strike	Pikie	yellow chain pike, glass eyes, small	EX	$52.50	11-1999
Shur Strike	Pikie	yellow scale, glass eyes	VG	$23.50	1-1999
Shur Strike	Pikie	yellow scale, glass eyes, large size	EX	$61.00	1-2002
Shur Strike	Pikie Type	perch, tack eyes, blue & orange HR-0 box	EX/IB	$46.00	8-1999
Shur Strike	Pikie Type	tack eyes, blue & orange PT-14 box	EX/IB	$45.00	8-1999
Shur Strike	Pikie, Baby	silver flash, tack eyes, round nose	Mint	$15.00	1-2001
Shur Strike	Pikie, Jointed	chain pike, glass eyes, large size	EX	$31.03	11-1999
Shur Strike	Pikie, Jointed	peanut butter, glass eyes	EX-	$100.89	12-1999
Shur Strike	Pikie, Jointed	pike scale, glass eyes	EX	$33.00	8-2000
Shur Strike	Pikie, Jointed	silver flash, glass eyes	EX	$24.89	1-2000
Shur Strike	Pikie, Jointed	yellow pikie, glass eyes	EX	$47.00	5-2000
Shur Strike	Pikie, Midget	redside scale, glass eyes	EX	$132.00	7-2000
Shur Strike	River Master	1 red head, 1 shiner scale; glass eyes, decent	EX-	$18.10	3-2000
Shur Strike	River Master	2 different, glass eyes, RR2 box	VG	$19.49	4-1999
Shur Strike	River Master	black, glass eyes	EX	$50.00	1-2001
Shur Strike	River Master	black, glass eyes, "Gateway," bad age lines	AVG	$9.00	12-1999
Shur Strike	River Master	black, white, glass eyes, ugly	VG-	$35.00	5-1999
Shur Strike	River Master	blue scale over black, tack eyes	EX	$28.00	9-2001
Shur Strike	River Master	chain pickerel, glass eyes	EX	$24.38	11-1999
Shur Strike	River Master	D943RH, glass eyes, blue & orange box	NIB	$57.00	10-2000
Shur Strike	River Master	Floating Tom, pikie, tack eyes	EX-	$11.00	1-2000
Shur Strike	River Master	frog, glass eyes, $179.00 my maximum bid	EX-	$107.50	5-2000
Shur Strike	River Master	frog, tack eyes	EX	$16.50	2-2000
Shur Strike	River Master	frog, tack eyes	EX	$34.00	1-2002
Shur Strike	River Master	frog, tack eyes, RR-5 box, NOT MET	EX/IB	$20.00	1-2001
Shur Strike	River Master	J. C. Higgins, red head, tack eyes	EX-	$15.50	2-2000
Shur Strike	River Master	pearl, glass eyes	VG	$41.00	4-1999
Shur Strike	River Master	pearl, glass eyes	VG+	$62.00	3-2001
Shur Strike	River Master	pearl, glass eyes, NOT MET	EX	$38.00	11-2000
Shur Strike	River Master	pearl, glass eyes, small	EX	$49.76	11-1999
Shur Strike	River Master	pearl, pink spots, glass eyes	EX	$92.00	7-2002

BRAND	MODEL	SERIES / MFG. CODE / DESCRIPTION	GRADE	PRICE	DATE
Shur Strike	River Master	perch?, glass eyes	EX	$36.00	4-1999
Shur Strike	River Master	pike scale, glass eyes	EX	$28.89	2-2000
Shur Strike	River Master	pike scale, glass eyes, NO BIDS	EX	$19.00	1-2001
Shur Strike	River Master	pike scale, glass eyes, poor box	VG+	$19.99	5-1999
Shur Strike	River Master	rainbow, glass eyes	VG	$12.00	1-2001
Shur Strike	River Master	rainbow, glass eyes, floater	EX	$85.00	5-2000
Shur Strike	River Master	rainbow, glass eyes, in Gateway box	EX/IB	$177.50	10-1999
Shur Strike	River Master	rainbow, glass eyes, unmarked box	EX/IB	$31.00	2-2000
Shur Strike	River Master	red head, glass eyes	EX-	$14.00	5-2000
Shur Strike	River Master	silver flash, tack eyes, NO BIDS	EX	$10.00	12-2000
Shur Strike	River Master	red head, shiner scale, glass eyes, ugly green & white box	VG+/IB	$40.00	10-1999
Shur Strike	River Master	red head, white, tack eyes	EX	$12.51	12-1999
Shur Strike	River Master	RR8, rainbow, glass eyes	EX/IB	$56.99	4-1999
Shur Strike	River Master	SB, tack eyes	EX	$40.00	3-2001
Shur Strike	River Master	SB, tack eyes	EX	$45.00	1-2001
Shur Strike	River Master	silver flash, glass eyes	EX	$36.00	3-2000
Shur Strike	River Master	strawberry, glass eyes	VG+	$46.00	9-1999
Shur Strike	River Master	strawberry, tack eyes	EX	$33.00	9-2001
Shur Strike	River Master	strawberry, tack eyes	EX	$56.00	8-2000
Shur Strike	River Master	yellow flash, tack eyes	EX	$26.00	10-2000
Shur Strike	River Master	yellow scale, green box	EXIB	$37.50	4-2000
Shur Strike	River Master	x2, pike scale, dace?, glass eyes, green box, red & black box	EXIB	$150.45	3-2000
Shur Strike	River Master Floater	black, Gateway	EX-	$61.08	1-2000
Shur Strike	River Master Floater	black, glass eyes, NOT MET	EX-	$32.50	3-2000
Shur Strike	River Master Floater	brown, flitter, glass eyes	EX-	$46.00	1-2002
Shur Strike	River Master Floater	green scale, tack eyes, green & white box	EX/IB	$91.00	8-2000
Shur Strike	River Master Floater	pikie, glass eyes	EX	$23.00	2-2000
Shur Strike	River Master Floater	pike scale, glass eyes	EX-	$16.00	2-2000
Shur Strike	River Master Floater	rainbow, Gateway	EX-	$106.05	1-2000
Shur Strike	River Master Floater	red head, shiner scale, glass eyes	EX	$52.77	8-1999
Shur Strike	River Master Floater	red head, unmarked box	EX/IB	$42.00	11-2001
Shur Strike	River Master Floater	yellow scale, glass eyes	EX-	$20.00	1-2002
Shur Strike	River Master Floater	yellow scale, glass eyes	EX-	$74.00	1-2001
Shur Strike	River Master Flyrod	shiner scale	EX	$200.00	10-1999
Shur Strike	River Master Jointed	black head, white scale?, tack eyes	EX	$43.75	4-2000
Shur Strike	River Master Jointed	green chain perch, glass eyes, #4307 box	EX-IB	$47.99	4-2002
Shur Strike	River Master Jointed	pearl, "Andy Anderson" paper	Mint	$232.27	3-1999
Shur Strike	River Master Jointed	pearl, Gateway, nice box	EX/IB	$190.00	12-2000
Shur Strike	River Master Jointed	yellow flash, red scale, stripe, tack eyes	VG+	$49.00	5-2001
Shur Strike	River Master Jointed	yellow flash, tack eyes	EX-	$20.00	8-2001
Shur Strike	River Master Jointed	yellow flash, tack eyes, NOT MET	EX-	$33.00	4-2001
Shur Strike	River Master Jointed Floater	green perch, glass eyes	EX-	$46.00	1-2001
Shur Strike	River Master Jointed Floater	green perch, glass eyes, rough box	EX-/IN	$36.00	4-2001
Shur Strike	River Master Jointed Floater	silver flash, glass eyes	EX-	$26.00	1-2001
Shur Strike	River Master Jointed Sinker	BWH, glass eyes, chip but not awful	VG	$41.00	1-2001

BRAND	MODEL	SERIES / MFG. CODE / DESCRIPTION	GRADE	PRICE	DATE
Shur Strike	River Master Jointed Sinker	red head, shiner scale, glass eyes	EX-	$22.00	10-2002
Shur Strike	River Master Sinker	frog, glass eyes, nice HR-19 box	VG/IB	$78.00	6-2001
Shur Strike	River Master Sinker	pikie, tack eyes	EX	$15.00	8-2000
Shur Strike	Slant Nose	yellow scale, glass eyes	EX	$52.00	5-2000
Shur Strike	Slope Nose	peanut butter, glass eyes	EX	$102.00	1-2001
Shur Strike	Slope Nose	pikie scale, like Magnet, NOT MET	EX	$89.00	4-2000
Shur Strike	Slope Nose	shiner scale	EX-	$130.00	10-2000
Shur Strike	Slope Nose	shiner scale, no eyes	VG+	$100.00	9-2000
Shur Strike	Spinner, Baby Surface	yellow scale, glass eyes, wrong box	NIB	$127.00	8-2000
Shur Strike	Spinner, Floating	black head, yellow, glass eyes	EX	$86.00	1-2002
Shur Strike	Surface Glider	black, gold	EX	$450.00	4-2001
Shur Strike	Surface Minnie	yellow scale, glass eyes, NOT MET	EX	$51.00	6-2000
Shur Strike	Surface Spinner	black, yellow, glass eyes	EX-	$77.00	9-2000
Shur Strike	Surface Spinner	peanut butter, glass eyes	EX-	$114.00	12-2000
Shur Strike	Surface Spinner	peanut butter, glass eyes, NRA red & yellow box	EX-/IB	$168.00	3-2000
Shur Strike	Surface Spinner	red, white, glass eyes	EX-	$42.00	1-1999
Shur Strike	Surface Spinner	shiner scale, glass eyes	VG++	$66.00	6-2000
Shur Strike	Surface Spinner, Crab	unique crab color & body, 2 props, no bid	EX-	$100.00	3-2002
Shur Strike	Tom, Floating	pikie, glass eyes, back stencil	EX	$36.00	3-2001
Shur Strike	Torpedo	glass eyes, NOT MET	EX-	$56.55	5-1999
Shur Strike	Torpedo	GM series, white, black stripes, glass eyes	EX-	$81.00	10-2001
Shur Strike	Underwater Minnow	3-hook	VG+	$204.00	7-2000
Shur Strike	Underwater Minnow	Babe-Oreno type, frog, glass eyes, repainted?	EX	$100.00	5-2001
Shur Strike	Underwater Minnow	chain pickerel, 3-hook	EX	$316.00	2-2002
Shur Strike	Underwater Minnow	golden shiner, 3-hook	VG	$249.99	1-1999
Shur Strike	Underwater Minnow	green, rainbow, glass eyes, 3-hook	VG+	$406.51	6-1999
Shur Strike	Underwater Minnow	green scale, glass eyes, 3-hook, oddly repainted?	NIB	$431.00	11-2000
Shur Strike	Underwater Minnow	peanut butter, 2-hook, frnt spinner, glass eyes	EX-	$83.00	6-2001
Shur Strike	Underwater Minnow	pickerel scale, glass eyes, 3-hook	EX/IB	$394.00	10-2000
Shur Strike	Underwater Minnow	pikie, glass eyes, 3-hook, not awful	G	$112.50	3-1999
Shur Strike	Underwater Minnow	pikie scale, glass eyes, 3-hook	EX/IB	$302.00	10-2000
Shur Strike	Underwater Minnow	pikie scale, glass eyes, 3-hook, round body, side hook	EX-	$410.00	2-2000
Shur Strike	Underwater Minnow	pikie, tack eyes, 3-hook, nice box	NIB	$156.00	11-2000
Shur Strike	Underwater Minnow	rainbow, glass eyes, 3-hook	Poor	$12.60	8-1999
Shur Strike	Underwater Minnow	rainbow, glass eyes, 3-hook, not awful	VG-	$176.00	5-2000
Shur Strike	Underwater Minnow	red head, tack eyes, 3-hook	EX-	$77.10	10-1999
Shur Strike	Vamp, Dolphin Nose	pikie scale, glass eyes, top nose tie	EX-	$53.00	12-2000
Shurbite	Frog	plastic	NIB	$127.50	1-1999
Shurbite	She Devil	red, yellow, nice picture box	NIB	$19.99	2-1999
Shurbite	She Devil	white, nice box, for "fan?"	NIB	$42.00	1-2001
Shurkatch	Bass-Oreno	gold, black bars, tack eyes, great box	NIB	$52.00	9-2000
Silver Creek Novelty Works	Pikeroon	5" green, white belly, decent box	NIB	$960.00	5-2001
Silver Creek Novelty Works	Pikeroon	red head, nice box	EX/IB	$1,630.00	5-2000
Simmons Hardware	Ketch-Em	red, black gills, glass eyes, 5-hook, Neverfail, vg box	EX-/IB	$457.00	11-2001

BRAND	MODEL	SERIES / MFG. CODE / DESCRIPTION	GRADE	PRICE	DATE
Silver Creek Novelty Works	Polly-Wog	Moonlight?, perch, glass eyes	EX-	$421.00	8-2002
Silver Creek Novelty Works	Polly-Wog	huge chips, shiny, avg box	Fair/IB	$202.50	4-2000
Skinner	Spinner	5 assorted	VG+	$27.01	5-1999
Skinner	Turkey Wing	spinner blade only, 1874 patent	EX	$240.00	8-2002
Skinner	Turkey Wing	#15, 2¼"	EX	$280.00	11-1999
Smithwick	Devil Horse	black, bubble pack	NOC	$31.00	10-2000
Smithwick	Top-N Bottom Stud Duck	yellow, white ribs	Poor	$36.00	10-2002
Snod-Lo	Flaptail, Musky	green, painted eyes, c.1980	EX	$150.00	1-2002
Sockdolager	Springhook	4½", uncocked	Mint	$332.00	7-2000
South Bend	Babe-Oreno	972SP, painted eyes, PTCB	NIB	$30.00	1-1999
South Bend	Babe-Oreno	973, luminous, intro box	EX/IB	$62.51	2-1999
South Bend	Babe-Oreno	973, red head, glass eyes, intro? box	NIB	$73.00	8-1999
South Bend	Babe-Oreno	blue head, red body, glass eyes	EX-	$42.00	10-1999
South Bend	Babe-Oreno	gold, red, no eyes, old box style	EX/IB	$52.00	1-1999
South Bend	Babe-Oreno	green scale, glass eyes	NIB	$168.09	3-1999
South Bend	Babe-Oreno	green scale, tack eyes, 910YP box	EX+	$46.50	2-1999
South Bend	Babe-Oreno	moon & stars box	EX/IB	$152.00	5-2000
South Bend	Babe-Oreno	Night Luming, intro box, papers	EX/IB	$182.50	2-2000
South Bend	Babe-Oreno	no eyes, 973YP intro box	NIB	$200.00	6-2000
South Bend	Babe-Oreno	no eyes, ex 972BH early box	EX-/IB	$380.00	11-2000
South Bend	Babe-Oreno	red head, glass eyes, aluminum	EX-/IB	$52.50	2-2000
South Bend	Babe-Oreno	red head, glass eyes, cartoon box	NIB	$132.50	2-2000
South Bend	Babe-Oreno	red head, sparkle, glass eyes	EX	$62.00	5-2000
South Bend	Babe-Oreno	red stripe, glass eyes, 973RS stars box	EX/IB	$187.00	6-2000
South Bend	Babe-Oreno	red, white, arrowhead, glass eyes	VG-	$30.00	5-1999
South Bend	Babe-Oreno	red, white, no eyes, old box, papers	NIB	$64.09	5-1999
South Bend	Babe-Oreno	RS, red stripe, glass eyes	EX/IB	$275.00	9-1999
South Bend	Babe-Oreno	strawberry, glass eyes, lip chips	VG	$27.00	5-1999
South Bend	Bass Bug	6 on card in cellophane	NOC	$305.00	6-2001
South Bend	Bass Bug Oreno	850-6, Yellow Sally, mint cellophane over card	NOC	$169.00	10-2001
South Bend	Bass Bug Oreno	850-1, golden, mint cellophane over card	NOC	$105.00	10-2001
South Bend	Bass-Oreno	39 different, 8 boxes, mostly no eyes or tack eyes	AVG- to VG	$414.00	9-2000
South Bend	Bass-Oreno	973, rainbow, no-eyes, nice early box	NIB	$104.00	11-2000
South Bend	Bass-Oreno	973FW, frog, tack eyes, catalog	NIB	$56.00	7-1999
South Bend	Bass-Oreno	B.A.S.S. Limited Edition, red, white, black, modern	NIB	$60.00	5-2000
South Bend	Bass-Oreno	black, red eye shadow, glass eyes	VG++	$91.00	6-2000
South Bend	Bass-Oreno	copper, black back stripe, glass eyes	VG+	$54.00	11-2000
South Bend	Bass-Oreno	copper, glass eyes	EX-	$70.00	3-1999
South Bend	Bass-Oreno	G973FO, orange fire lacquer	NIB	$59.00	9-1999
South Bend	Bass-Oreno	G973FO, painted eyes, hang tag, NOT MET	NIB	$53.00	4-2001
South Bend	Bass-Oreno	G973 NR, red fire lacquer, painted eyes, NOT MET	NIB	$42.00	9-1999
South Bend	Bass-Oreno	glass eyes, crisp moon & stars box	NIB	$230.00	7-2001
South Bend	Bass-Oreno	olive scale, no eyes, light hook drag	EX-	$41.00	4-2000

BRAND	MODEL	SERIES / MFG. CODE / DESCRIPTION	GRADE	PRICE	DATE
South Bend	Bass-Oreno	pagin scale, orange, gold, glass eyes, beautiful	EX	$391.00	6-2001
South Bend	Bass-Oreno	rainbow, no eyes, Jersey Q, 1-hook, early box	NIB	$350.00	9-2001
South Bend	Bass-Oreno	red head arrow, tack eyes, crisp box, catalog	NIB	$41.00	9-1999
South Bend	Bass-Oreno	red head, gold, sparkle, glass eyes	EX	$62.00	6-2000
South Bend	Bass-Oreno	red head, sparkle, tack eyes, nice box	NIB	$83.00	10-2000
South Bend	Bass-Oreno	red head, white, glass eyes	EX	$50.00	3-1999
South Bend	Bass-Oreno	red head, white, glass eyes	VG+	$20.00	3-1999
South Bend	Bass-Oreno	red scale, no eyes, intro box	EX/IB	$98.50	9-1999
South Bend	Bass-Oreno	red, no eyes, no washer, line tie, shallow cups	EX	$90.00	9-2002
South Bend	Bass-Oreno	RSF, glass eyes, general wear	VG+	$25.00	3-1999
South Bend	Bass-Oreno	vg+ Night Luming intro box	EX+/IB	$228.50	1-2000
South Bend	Bass-Oreno	white, red side, red back stripe, glass eyes	VG+	$54.00	11-2000
South Bend	Bass-Oreno	yellow, red stripe, glass eyes	EXIB	$130.22	9-1999
South Bend	Bass-Oreno	yellow spots, no eyes	NIB	$112.51	3-2000
South Bend	Bass-Oreno, Baby	blue head, no eye	VG	$129.00	1-2001
South Bend	Bass-Oreno, Better	rainbow in cellophane	NIB	$152.50	1-1999
South Bend	Bass-Oreno, King	997SFS, silver scale, painted eyes, PTCB	NIB	$42.99	1-2000
South Bend	Bug-Oreno	#820, black, white, glass eyes	EX	$209.00	11-2000
South Bend	Callmac Bug	#7, flyrod, great intro box	NIB	$363.88	4-1999
South Bend	Callmac Bug	#9 Bob Davis	NIB	$82.00	9-2000
South Bend	Callmac Bug	#25, flyrod, on NRA card	NOC	$127.50	6-1999
South Bend	Callmac Bug	Bob Davis, NOC, window box	NIB	$117.00	10-2000
South Bend	Callmac Bug	Zane Grey model, large box	EX/IB	$41.00	10-2000
South Bend	Coast-Oreno	985, tack eyes	NIB	$520.00	1-2000
South Bend	Coast-Oreno	rainbow?, yellow, red, brown, Ludy buy	EX	$308.00	7-2000
South Bend	Dart-Oreno	lure is just a hook, intro box with super graphics	NIB	$113.00	5-2001
South Bend	Dive-Oreno	952RW, tack eyes, crisp box	NIB	$27.00	8-2001
South Bend	Dive-Oreno	953, red head, tack eyes, obsolete	NIB	$33.76	2-1999
South Bend	Dive-Oreno	x12; 12-pack, red head arrow, nice 2PCCB	NIB	$255.00	8-2000
South Bend	Dragon-Oreno	flyrod, yellow	EX	$55.00	11-2000
South Bend	Fin-Dingo	sunfish?	VG	$30.01	4-1999
South Bend	Fin-Dingo	red, white, NO BIDS	VG	$19.99	5-1999
South Bend	Fish-Obite	1991RW, plastic	NIB	$23.00	8-2001
South Bend	Fish-Obite	red, black squiggle, plastic	EX-	$42.00	9-2000
South Bend	Fish-Oreno	953P, glass eyes, wow, crisp Guarantee box	NIB	$199.50	1-2000
South Bend	Fish-Oreno	953S, silver, glass eyes, intro box	NIB	$191.00	7-1999
South Bend	Fish-Oreno	953YP, tack eyes	NIB	$72.00	1-2001
South Bend	Fish-Oreno	959, red head, glass eyes, intro box	EX-/IB	$57.00	3-2000
South Bend	Fish-Oreno	copper, glass eyes	EX-	$77.25	5-1999
South Bend	Fish-Oreno	frog, glass eyes, intro box, tag, mint papers	NIB	$545.00	1-2000
South Bend	Fish-Oreno	Guarantee box, hang tag, catalog, paper	NIB	$406.00	5-2001
South Bend	Fish-Oreno	pikie, glass eyes, hang tag, intro box	EX-/IB	$141.50	7-1999
South Bend	Fish-Oreno	pike scale, hang tag, mint intro box	NIB	$483.00	3-2000
South Bend	Fish-Oreno	red head, glass eyes, Guarantee intro box, tag, catalog	NIB	$188.50	8-1999
South Bend	Fish-Oreno	red head, glass eyes, hang tag, intro box, catalog	NIB	$203.00	11-2000
South Bend	Fish-Oreno	red head, glass eyes, insurance, old box	EX/IB	$93.00	5-1999

BRAND	MODEL	SERIES / MFG. CODE / DESCRIPTION	GRADE	PRICE	DATE
South Bend	Fish-Oreno	red head, intro box	EX/IB	$76.00	3-2000
South Bend	Fish-Oreno	red head, orange, black spots, glass eyes	EX-	$189.00	4-2000
South Bend	Fish-Oreno	red, white, intro box, papers	NIB	$77.00	2-1999
South Bend	Fish-Oreno	yellow spots, glass eyes	EX-	$67.00	9-2000
South Bend	Floater, Weedless	Bing hooks	EX	$275.00	10-1999
South Bend	Flyrod		EX	$125.00	4-2001
South Bend	Hop-Oreno	yellow, #816 PTCB	EX-/IB	$76.00	2-2002
South Bend	Injured Minnow	rainbow?, glass eyes, nice	VG+	$53.00	2-2000
South Bend	Injured Minnow	silver flake, glass eyes	EX	$45.44	10-1999
South Bend	Ketch-Oreno	flyrod	Mint	$300.00	2-2002
South Bend	Ketch-Oreno	green scale?, flyrod	Mint	$300.00	2-2002
South Bend	Lunge-Oreno	966, 6", red head, hang tag	EX/IB	$261.10	11-1999
South Bend	Lunge-Oreno	966, red head	VG++/IB	$210.00	8-2000
South Bend	Lunge-Oreno, Musky	936, red head, glass eyes, plain box	VG+/IB	$407.00	10-1999
South Bend	Midget	brown stripe, 3-hook	EX	$330.00	10-1999
South Bend	Midget	strawberry, 3-hook	EX	$585.00	10-1999
South Bend	Min-Buck	2 different, 945, aluminum, 3-hook, OS, nice	VG+	$434.00	4-1999
South Bend	Min-Buck	943, 3-hook, NOT MET	VG+	$91.00	7-2000
South Bend	Min-Buck	HPGM, 5-hook, 4BW	VG+	$1180.00	3-1999
South Bend	Min-Buck	red, black stripe, hex?, glass eyes, 5-hook, decent	AVG	$100.00	11-2000
South Bend	Min-Buck	yellow hex, HPGM, 5-hook, POBW	EX-	$575.00	8-2002
South Bend	Min-Buck, Musky	crackleback, 5-hook, NOT MET	EX-	$1,285.00	9-2000
South Bend	Min-Buck?	red, black spots, hex?, glass eyes, HPGM, 3-hook	VG+	$238.00	1-2001
South Bend	Minnow	rainbow, glass eyes, cracked BW	NIB	$355.00	4-2000
South Bend	Minnow, Combination	hex finish, vg hackle	EX	$475.00	5-2000
South Bend	Minnow, Combination	perch, hook drags but still nice	VG	$127.00	3-2001
South Bend	Minnow, Combination	red, black hex finish, original tail	EX	$400.00	8-1999
South Bend	Minnow, Combination	white, black stripe, glass eyes	EX	$310.00	10-1999
South Bend	Minnow, Floater	921, red mask, white, glass eyes, old box	EX/IB	$460.55	9-1999
South Bend	Minnow, Floating	red mask, glass eyes	EX/IB	$460.55	9-1999
South Bend	Minnow, Midget	901, rainbow, crisp intro box	NIB	$761.00	6-2002
South Bend	Minnow, Midget	rainbow, black eye shadow, intro box, nice	NIB	$280.00	6-2002
South Bend	Minnow, Surface	hex pattern, glass eyes, 3-hook, old style	EX	$848.00	3-2000
South Bend	Minnow, Surface	white, red face mask, glass eyes	EX	$278.00	9-2002
South Bend	Min-Oreno	red head, yellow, nice box, token paperwork	NIB	$263.00	5-2001
South Bend	Mouse-Oreno	949, black, POBW, very nice box	EX/IB	$119.38	3-1999
South Bend	Mouse-Oreno	flyrod, grey, bead eyes	EX	$61.00	2-1999
South Bend	Musk-Oreno	green scale, glass eyes, Musk-Oreno box	NIB	$400.00	6-2000
South Bend	Musk-Oreno	red head, intro box	VG+/IB	$97.00	6-2001
South Bend	Musky	yellow, 5-hook, 4 staggered BW, fake?	AVG	$300.00	7-2000
South Bend	Musky Minnow	rainbow, brown back, 5-hook, cup, marked, nice	VG+	$860.00	8-1999
South Bend	Musky Minnow	spots, 4BW, ugly, NOT MET	VG	$417.00	4-2000
South Bend	Musky Minnow	x2; 1 Musk-Oreno, 1 Underwater Minnow; glass eyes, NOT MET	Repainted	$152.00	5-2000
South Bend	Musky Minnow	x2; 1 Pike-Oreno, 1 Musk-Oreno; copper, black back, glass eyes, NOT MET	Repainted	$36.00	5-2000

BRAND	MODEL	SERIES / MFG. CODE / DESCRIPTION	GRADE	PRICE	DATE
South Bend	Nip-I-Didee	fire plug	NIB	$36.00	2-1999
South Bend	Optics	12-pack, dealer display box	NIB	$300.00	3-1999
South Bend	Oreno Display	37 lures, salesman sample	EX	$2,751.00	5-1999
South Bend	Oreno-Popper	2 different, yellow, white	EX	$158.25	2-2000
South Bend	Panatella	915, red head, gold, 5-hook, glass eyes, full tail cap, paint	EX	$268.00	3-2002
South Bend	Panatella	915RSF, glass eyes, 5-hook, nice box	Mint/NIB	$565.00	1-2000
South Bend	Panatella	crackleback, 3-hook side, HPGM, repainted?	EX+	$472.00	2-2000
South Bend	Panatella	crackleback, glass eyes, tail chip but still nice	EX-	$103.00	10-2000
South Bend	Panatella	crackleback, tack eyes, 5-hook	EX	$153.00	10-2000
South Bend	Panatella	crackleback, tail cup	EX-	$375.00	10-1999
South Bend	Panatella	green scale, glass eyes, 5-hook, end cap	EX	$351.01	1-2000
South Bend	Panatella	red side, glass eyes, 3-hook	VG	$173.00	10-2000
South Bend	Panatella	red, white, glass eyes	EX-	$177.00	7-1999
South Bend	Panatella	RSF, blended red scale	EX-	$162.00	8-2000
South Bend	Panatella	RWR, glass eyes, 5-hook	VG-	$83.00	10-2000
South Bend	Panatella	yellow, brown stripe, no cup	EX	$440.00	10-1999
South Bend	Pike-Oreno	956P, tack eyes, NOT MET	NIB	$31.00	4-2001
South Bend	Pike-Oreno	956RW, tack eyes, NOT MET	NIB	$36.00	4-2001
South Bend	Pike-Oreno	958SPLGS, 5⅜", green scale, tack eyes	NIB	$254.00	5-2000
South Bend	Pike-Oreno	green scale, no-eye, thin, early model	VG+	$16.00	8-2002
South Bend	Pike-Oreno	red head, tack eyes, mint box, papers	NIB	$49.99	12-1999
South Bend	Pike-Oreno	red, white, arrow head, tack eyes	EX/IB	$41.00	5-1999
South Bend	Pike-Oreno, Jointed	960, 8", green scale?, tack eyes	Mint	$93.00	5-2000
South Bend	Pippin	flyrod new in tube	NIT	$50.00	3-2002
South Bend	Plug-Oreno	frog, tack eyes	EX	$305.00	2-2002
South Bend	Plug-Oreno	frog, tack eyes, POTE, small chip	EX-	$384.00	5-2000
South Bend	Plug-Oreno	red head, tack eyes, ring around BW	Mint	$350.00	10-2000
South Bend	Plug-Oreno	yellow spots, glass eyes	VG+	$378.00	2-2000
South Bend	Plug-Oreno	yellow spots, glass eyes, nice	VG+	$358.00	3-2002
South Bend	Plunk-Oreno	929F, flyrod type, lip chips	VG+/IB	$76.00	2-2000
South Bend	Plunk-Oreno	black, tack eyes, 2-hook, later type	EX	$86.00	1-2001
South Bend	Plunk-Oreno	flyrod, light frog, scratched	VG	$90.00	3-2002
South Bend	Plunk-Oreno	flyrod, light frog, white fly	EX	$225.00	5-2002
South Bend	Plunk-Oreno	frog, tack eyes	VG+ to EX-	$50.00	12-1999
South Bend	Plunk-Oreno	rainbow, tack eyes, rough fly	EX	$285.00	1-2001
South Bend	Plunk-Oreno	rainbow, tack eyes, slant face, 2-hook	VG+	$122.00	7-2002
South Bend	Plunk-Oreno	red head, tack eyes, 2-hook	EX	$87.00	1-2002
South Bend	Plunk-Oreno	red head, tack eyes, great fly	EX-	$54.99	9-1999
South Bend	Plunk-Oreno	red, white, 2-hook, slant face	EX	$125.00	7-2002
South Bend	Plunk-Oreno	YP, tack eyes, 1-hook	EX-	$57.00	8-2001
South Bend	Plunk-Oreno	flyrod, rainbow, varnish, 1 ding, lousy pictures		$77.00	3-2001
South Bend	Spin-I-Diddee	6-pack, 1917YP, PTCB, nice display	NIB	$237.00	11-2000
South Bend	Sun Spot	525CR nice yellow jumping fish box	NIB	$78.00	1-2002
South Bend	Super Snooper	G, 1960, FG, fire lacquer finish	NIB	$61.00	11-2000
South Bend	Surf-Oreno	963, rainbow	EX/IB	$177.39	3-1999

BRAND	MODEL	SERIES / MFG. CODE / DESCRIPTION	GRADE	PRICE	DATE
South Bend	Surf-Oreno	963, red head	NIB	$79.00	5-2000
South Bend	Surf-Oreno	963SF, green scale, glass eyes	NIB	$280.00	10-2000
South Bend	Surf-Oreno	973, red head, arrow, pressed eyes, papers	NIB	$38.00	8-1999
South Bend	Surf-Oreno	blue head, white, glass eyes	EX-/EX	$406.12	1-2000
South Bend	Surf-Oreno	black forehead, red	EX-	$305.00	10-1999
South Bend	Surf-Oreno	chub?, glass eyes, tube props, T-wire	EX-	$121.00	6-1999
South Bend	Surf-Oreno	crackleback	EX	$200.00	10-1999
South Bend	Surf-Oreno	crackleback, glass eyes	VG+	$87.00	6-1999
South Bend	Surf-Oreno	crackleback, reinforced prop, glass eyes, varnish	EX-	$125.00	8-2001
South Bend	Surf-Oreno	frog, glass eyes, beautiful	EX	$192.00	9-2000
South Bend	Surf-Oreno	frog, old type, 1 loose prop, poor old box	EX	$123.00	1-1999
South Bend	Surf-Oreno	gold scale, red bars, tack eyes	EX-	$37.55	1-1999
South Bend	Surf-Oreno	green scale, glass eyes	EX-	$83.59	1-2000
South Bend	Surf-Oreno	luminous, tack eyes	EX	$76.00	4-2000
South Bend	Surf-Oreno	luminous, tack eyes, few age lines, new in box	NIB	$57.00	8-2001
South Bend	Surf-Oreno	luminous, tack eyes, nice box	NIB	$95.00	5-2001
South Bend	Surf-Oreno	rainbow, glass eyes	VG+	$83.00	3-2000
South Bend	Surf-Oreno	rainbow, glass eyes, older, NOT MET	EX	$154.75	6-1999
South Bend	Surf-Oreno	rainbow, glass eyes, regular box	NIB	$255.00	10-2000
South Bend	Surf-Oreno	red, black eye shadow, stencil back	EX	$209.00	10-2000
South Bend	Surf-Oreno	red head, glass eyes	EX/IB	$66.88	3-2000
South Bend	Surf-Oreno	red head, gold, flitter, glass eyes	EX	$128.00	9-2002
South Bend	Surf-Oreno	red, white, reinforced, glass eyes	NIB	$129.01	12-1999
South Bend	Surf-Oreno	RFS, red scale, glass eyes, reinforced hardware	EX+	$209.00	10-2000
South Bend	Surf-Oreno	spotted, re-hardware, glass eyes, nice	EX	$202.00	1-2001
South Bend	Surf-Oreno	strawberry, glass eyes	EX-	$178.49	3-1999
South Bend	Surf-Oreno	strawberry, old 903GCBW box	EX/IB	$185.00	6-1999
South Bend	Surf-Oreno	yellow, strawberry, glass eyes	EX	$176.00	3-2001
South Bend	Surf-Oreno, Baby	96?, SF, repainted?, glass eyes, Bing hooks	NIB	$355.00	11-2001
South Bend	Surf-Oreno, Baby	962, red head, glass eyes	NIB	$76.00	10-2000
South Bend	Surf-Oreno, Baby	blue head, white, glass eyes	EX	$255.00	3-2000
South Bend	Surf-Oreno, Baby	copper, glass eyes, reinforced nose	EX-	$202.50	8-1999
South Bend	Surf-Oreno, Baby	frog, pressed eyes	VG+	$20.00	4-2000
South Bend	Surf-Oreno, Flyrod	brown back, scale	VG+	$43.00	8-2000
South Bend	Surf-Oreno, Flyrod	green scale, painted eyes, beautiful	EX+	$87.00	4-2000
South Bend	Surf-Oreno, Flyrod	red scale	EX	$65.00	1-1999
South Bend	Surf-Oreno, Midget	962, orange, black spots, glass eyes	EX-	$141.38	10-1999
South Bend	Surf-Oreno, Midget	962, red, silver, glass eyes	EX-	$129.52	10-1999
South Bend	Surf-Oreno, Midget	green scale, glass eyes, vg intro box	NIB	$415.00	2-2000
South Bend	Surf-Oreno, Midget	orange, black spots, glass eyes	VG	$113.62	8-1999
South Bend	Surf-Oreno, Midget	rainbow, glass eyes, reinfored	Mint	$367.88	5-1999
South Bend	Surf-Oreno, Midget	red, white, glass eyes, special box	EX/IB	$52.02	12-1998
South Bend	Surf-Oreno, Musky	greenscale, NOT MET	VG	$206.49	5-1999
South Bend	Surf-Oreno, Musky	red head, glass eyes, 6", NOT MET	VG	$66.00	11-2000
South Bend	Tarp-Oreno	blue mullet scale, carved eyes, ex- 979MS intro box	EX-/IB	$450.00	6-2002
South Bend	Tarp-Oreno	blue scale, painted eyes	EX	$174.01	7-1999

BRAND	MODEL	SERIES / MFG. CODE / DESCRIPTION	GRADE	PRICE	DATE
South Bend	Tarp-Oreno	green mullet scale, tack eyes	VG+	$225.00	6-2002
South Bend	Tarp-Oreno	pearl, tack eyes	VG+	$325.00	6-2002
South Bend	Tarp-Oreno	red head, aluminum, glass eyes, double hooks	VG-	$200.00	6-2002
South Bend	Tarp-Oreno	red head, carved eyes, ex- 979RW box	EX-/IB	$400.00	6-2002
South Bend	Tarp-Oreno	red head, glass eyes	VG	$175.00	6-2002
South Bend	Tarp-Oreno	red head, gold, glass eyes, 2-hook single, bottom of box	EX	$305.00	4-2001
South Bend	Tarp-Oreno	Tarpon Special, carved eyes, ex- 979RW box	EX/IB	$450.00	6-2002
South Bend	Tarp-Oreno	yellow spots, tack eyes	VG	$225.00	6-2002
South Bend	Tease-Oreno	11", red head, gold, no hardware	VG+	$56.00	5-1999
South Bend	Tease-Oreno	11", red head, painted eyes	NIB	$203.50	2-2000
South Bend	Tease-Oreno	11", white, sine wave, 2PCCB	EX/IB	$218.49	2-1999
South Bend	Tease-Oreno	11", Zane Grey, blue, black water waves	EX	$109.00	5-2001
South Bend	Tease-Oreno	frog, glass eyes, NOT MET	EX/IB	$76.05	4-1999
South Bend	Tease-Oreno	glass eyes, crisp 940YP box	EX-/IB	$47.00	3-2002
South Bend	Tease-Oreno	red head, tack eyes, rough box, NOT MET	EX-/IB	$129.00	5-2000
South Bend	Tease-Oreno	red, white, painted eyes	NIB	$331.00	1-1999
South Bend	Tease-Oreno	red, white, tack eyes	NIB	$77.00	12-1999
South Bend	Tease-Oreno	Zane Grey, tack eyes, silver, blue back, NOT MET	VG	$123.00	5-2000
South Bend	Tex-Oreno	rainbow, weedless	EX-	$62.00	11-2000
South Bend	Troll-Oreno	greenscale, glass eyes	EX-	$58.00	6-2002
South Bend	Trout-Oreno	971BH, NOT MET	EX/IB	$290.00	10-1999
South Bend	Trout-Oreno	red head, aluminum, crisp tiny intro box	NIB	$394.00	5-2001
South Bend	Truck-Oreno	red, white, nice box	NIB	$7,500.00	4-2002
South Bend	Truck-Oreno	yellow spotted color reproduction	EX	$199.00	6-1999
South Bend	Two-Oreno	red, white, window box, NOT MET	NIB	$77.53	3-1999
South Bend	Underwater Minnow	1 Bass-O, 1 Tease-O, red head, glass eyes, white, flitter, black wave, tack eyes	NIB	$149.00	5-1999
South Bend	Underwater Minnow	3-hook, 903RAIN intro box NOT MET	NIB	$960.00	5-2001
South Bend	Underwater Minnow	901, green scale, glass eyes, 3-hook, chip under eye	VG	$76.00	10-2000
South Bend	Underwater Minnow	903GCB, 3-hook, age lines	EX/IB	$325.00	1-2001
South Bend	Underwater Minnow	904, crackleback, glass eyes, 3-hook, nice	EX	$152.00	8-2001
South Bend	Underwater Minnow	905W, hex pattern, 5-hook, yellow box	EX-/IB	$335.00	1-2001
South Bend	Underwater Minnow	905YP, glass eyes, 5-hook, nice box, NOT MET	EX/IB	$280.00	11-2001
South Bend	Underwater Minnow	913, rainbow, glass eyes, 5-hook, brass tail cap, box rough	EX-/IB	$240.00	6-2000
South Bend	Underwater Minnow	915RSB, red scale blend, 5-hook	NIB	$515.00	5-1999
South Bend	Underwater Minnow	920, luminous, marked prop, NOT MET	EX	$334.00	11-2001
South Bend	Underwater Minnow	bar perch, glass eyes, 3-hook	AVG	$81.00	12-1998
South Bend	Underwater Minnow	chain pickerel, tack eyes, 3-hook	VG+	$43.00	4-2001
South Bend	Underwater Minnow	crackleback, 5-hook, nice	EX-EX	$296.00	3-1999
South Bend	Underwater Minnow	crackleback, glass eyes, 3-hook	VG	$87.00	5-2000
South Bend	Underwater Minnow	crackleback, glass eyes, 5-hook	EX+	$400.00	3-2000
South Bend	Underwater Minnow	flyrod, frog, bucktail, curved legs, NOT MET	EX	$21.00	11-2000
South Bend	Underwater Minnow	frog, glass eyes, 3-hook, belly chips	G	$60.23	4-1999
South Bend	Underwater Minnow	green back stripe, 3-hook	EX	$415.00	10-1999

BRAND	MODEL	SERIES / MFG. CODE / DESCRIPTION	GRADE	PRICE	DATE
South Bend	Underwater Minnow	Hex pattern, 3-hook	EX	$450.00	10-1999
South Bend	Underwater Minnow	perch, 3-hook	EX	$275.00	10-1999
South Bend	Underwater Minnow	perch, 5-hook	NIB	$665.00	10-1999
South Bend	Underwater Minnow	perch, 5-hook	VG+	$176.00	8-2000
South Bend	Underwater Minnow	rainbow, 5-hook	EX	$375.00	10-1999
South Bend	Underwater Minnow	rainbow, 5-hook, some small chips	VG-	$101.75	3-2000
South Bend	Underwater Minnow	rainbow, glass eyes, 3-hook	EX-	$200.00	6-1999
South Bend	Underwater Minnow	rainbow, glass eyes, 3-hook	VG	$62.00	11-2000
South Bend	Underwater Minnow	rainbow, glass eyes, HPGM, 3-hook, NOT MET	EX-	$140.50	3-2000
South Bend	Underwater Minnow	rainbow, HPGM, 3-hook, NOT MET	EX-	$188.00	10-2000
South Bend	Underwater Minnow	rainbow, HPGM, 5-hook	VG	$163.00	9-2000
South Bend	Underwater Minnow	red, black spots, 3-hook	VG	$221.00	4-2001
South Bend	Underwater Minnow	red, white, red, black eye shadow, glass eyes, 3-hook	EX-	$157.00	3-2001
South Bend	Underwater Minnow	red, white, tack eyes, 3-hook, decent	VG+	$36.81	11-1999
South Bend	Underwater Minnow	scale "SF," glass eyes, 3-hook, nice box, NOT MET	EX/IB	$157.00	8-2001
South Bend	Underwater Minnow	sienna, 5-hook, unmarked	EX	$710.00	10-1999
South Bend	Underwater Minnow	slate?, 5-hook	AVG	$69.00	12-1998
South Bend	Underwater Minnow	strawberry, 3-hook, nice old 952YP box	Ugly	$66.87	6-1999
South Bend	Underwater Minnow	strawberry, glass eyes, HPGM, 3-hook, unmarked, cup	EX-	$182.50	2-2000
South Bend	Underwater Minnow	white hex, 5-hook	EX-	$363.00	8-2000
South Bend	Underwater Minnow	white, dark green stripe, 3-hook	EX	$291.00	1-2000
South Bend	Underwater Minnow	white, red stripe, 3-hook	EX-	$355.00	1-2000
South Bend	Underwater Minnow	white, red stripe, 5-hook, chip otherwise nice	EX	$212.50	1-2000
South Bend	Underwater Minnow	yellow hex, glass eyes cracked, 3-hook	EX-	$317.00	8-2000
South Bend	Underwater Minnow	yellow perch, 3-hook	EX	$380.00	10-1999
South Bend	Underwater Minnow	yellow perch, glass eyes, shiny	EX	$233.00	3-2001
South Bend	Underwater Minnow	yellow spots, glass eyes, 3-hook, cup	EX	$223.50	2-2000
South Bend	Underwater Minnow	yellow, green back, 5-hook	Mint	$510.00	5-2000
South Bend	Underwater Minnow	x2, 5-hook, ugly	Poor	$90.00	10-2000
South Bend	Vacuum	#21, white, red ribs, huge eye chip, nice box, NOT MET		$305.00	2-2000
South Bend	Vacuum	dragonfly, papers	NIB	$2,305.00	10-1999
South Bend	Vacuum	red, black spots, varnish flaking	VG	$416.00	3-1999
South Bend	Vacuum	white, paint off cups, ex #1 box	NIB	$813.00	3-2002
South Bend	Vacuum	white, red gills?	VG	$70.00	11-2000
South Bend	Weedless	bucktail	EX	$100.00	4-2001
South Bend	Whirl-Oreno	butterfly, 935 box	VG/IB	$300.00	2-2000
South Bend	Whirl-Oreno	butterfly, NOT MET	EX	$283.00	3-2001
South Bend	Whirl-Oreno	frog	VG	$142.50	5-1999
South Bend	Whirl-Oreno	frog	VG+	$157.00	8-2000
South Bend	Whirl-Oreno	frog, nice hair	EX-	$100.00	8-1999
South Bend	Whirl-Oreno	red head	EX-	$223.71	3-2000
South Bend	Whirl-Oreno	red, white, NOT MET	EX+	$153.49	6-1999
South Bend	Whirl-Oreno	red, white	VG-	$66.01	12-1999
South Bend	Whirl-Oreno	red, white, 20 % paint loss on one side	AVG	$48.77	7-1999

BRAND	MODEL	SERIES / MFG. CODE / DESCRIPTION	GRADE	PRICE	DATE
South Bend	Whirl-Oreno	red, white, decent	VG	$93.00	10-2000
South Bend	Whirl-Oreno	red, white, nice	VG+	$129.50	1-1999
South Bend	Whisker	flyrod, new on card, unmarked yellow window box	NIB	$96.00	9-2002
South Bend	Wiz-Oreno	967, red head, crisp intro box	NIB	$255.00	8-1999
South Bend	Woodpecker, Weedless	red head	EX-	$229.17	1-2000
South Coast	Minnow		EX	$420.00	10-1999
Southern Bait Co.	Stick	perch, PTCB	NIB	$48.00	4-2001
Sparks, Jack	Hair Mouse	jointed, spinner, NOT MET	EX	$37.00	5-2001
Spider		muti-spring loaded	NIB	$100.00	6-1999
Spiral		orange	NIB	$458.75	1-2000
Springfield Novelty	Reel		NIB	$185.00	10-1999
Springfield Novelty	Reel	barber pole style	NIB	$204.40	3-1999
Springfield Novelty	Reel	gold, black, extra large dealer poster	NIB	$547.99	1-2000
Springfield Novelty	Reel	silver, red stripe	NIB	$281.50	2-2000
Springfield Novelty	Reel	white, black stripe	NIB	$383.00	1-2000
Staley Johnson	Twin Min	brown scale?, box vg & papers	NIB	$165.00	3-2002
Staley Johnson	Twin Min	nice 2pccb	NIB	$149.00	12-1998
Staley Johnson	Twin Min	one large chip, nice box	VG/IB	$105.00	10-2000
Staley Johnson	Twin Min	papers, mint box	NIB	$332.52	6-1999
Steeles	Wigglefrog	in tube	NIT	$165.00	3-1999
Sterling		3 hook, Pflueger hardware, Reese	EX/IB	$333.00	8-2000
Sterling	Neverfail	bar perch, 3-hook, maroon box	EX- to -VG/IB	$569.00	9-1999
Stevens Carrie	Royal Tiger	fly, autographed on card	EX	$256.00	5-1999
Stewart	Pad Hopper		NIB	$125.00	1-1999
Stewart	Pad Hopper	300	NIB	$177.00	12-1998
Stewart	Pad Hopper	light frog	EX-	$67.00	8-1999
Stewart	Pad Hopper	small lip chip	VG	$32.00	3-1999
Storm	Glop	golden shiner?	EX	$37.00	12-1999
Storm, Bud	Glop	black, weird	EX	$52.00	8-1999
Storm, Bud	Glop	coach dog	EX	$72.00	2-2002
Stormy	Petrel	flyrod, black	EX	$222.00	11-2000
Stormy	Petrel	frog color, nice box, NOT MET	NIB	$431.00	1-2002
Stormy	Petrel	frog, large size, nice box, only 1 bid	NIB	$430.00	2-2002
Stormy	Petrel	frog, vg box	VG+/IB	$121.00	10-2000
Stream-Eze	Mermaid	flyrod, silver crown, brown hair, green tail	Mint	$51.00	5-2000
Stream-Eze	Mermaid	gold, PTCB	NIB	$36.00	6-1999
Stream-Eze	Virgin Mermaid	black	EX-	$25.00	10-1999
Stream-Eze	Virgin Mermaid	flyrod, red, green, tiny box	NIB	$70.00	8-1999
Stream-Eze	Virgin Mermaid	NOT MET	EX	$34.00	7-1999
Stream-Eze	Virgin Mermaid	with box, NOT MET	EX-	$20.00	1-1999
Strike King	Bass King	red head, no eyes, nice 8546 box	NIB	$123.00	9-2000
Strike-Master	Killer	white, glass eyes, brass cups	EX	$128.00	6-2000
Strike-Master	Surface Glider Minnow	red head, silver, glass eyes, nice	EX	$308.33	1-2000
Strike-Master	Surface Killer	red head, glass eyes, NOT MET	EX-	$105.50	3-2000
Strike-Master	Water Waltzer	black, white head	VG/IB	$90.00	1-2002
Strikee	Minnow	3½"	Mint	$32.80	6-1999

BRAND	MODEL	SERIES / MFG. CODE / DESCRIPTION	GRADE	PRICE	DATE
Surebite	She Devil	red, yellow, Al Sisco box	EX/IB	$37.50	3-2000
Survivor		bleeder type, red, white	NIB	$575.00	10-1999
Szabo	Cree-Duc	2½", brown, white, NOT MET	NOC	$42.99	6-1999
Szabo	Cree-Duc	brown, white	EX	$33.23	12-1998
Szabo	Cree-Duc	white, black	VG	$38.73	1-1999
T & W	Flutter Jack Jr.	nickel, black hair, picture box	NIB	$34.77	1-1999
Tango, Rush		mottled, $50.00 box	NIB	$176.89	8-1999
Tango, Rush		mottled, nice box	NIB	$139.00	11-2000
Tango, Rush		white, red & green mottling	EX	$70.00	4-2000
Tango, Rush	Midget	victory finish	Mint	$355.00	1-2000
Tango, Rush	S.O.S.	yellow, victory finish	EX-	$100.00	8-1999
Tango, Rush	Swimming Minnow	red head, white, prize box #8	NIB	$182.50	4-1999
Tango, Rush	Swimming Minnow	red head, yellow, prize box	NIB	$197.50	4-1999
Tango, Rush	Tango, Trout	6-pack, 6 different, superb box with picture inside	NIB	$2,326.00	1-2002
Ted Smallwoods	Plug	darter type, decal eyes, ugly	EX	$109.00	4-2002
Tempter	Frog		EX	$150.00	10-2000
Tempter	Frog	with legs	EX	$182.50	6-1999
Thompson	Doll Top Secret	shad	NIB	$18.39	12-1999
Thoren	Minnow Chaser	one medium sized chip, new but rear lure		$180.00	6-2001
Thoren	Minnow Chaser	red, white, NOT MET	EX	$380.08	6-1999
Tiede	Doodler		NIB	$15.50	1-1999
Tillicum	Salmon Plug	5", pearl	EX	$35.00	4-2001
Tillicum	Tyee Salmon Plug	7", rainbow, painted eyes, no hooks	Mint	$305.00	1-2001
Trenton	Spin Diver	scale pattern, Kentucky	EX	$24.00	6-2000
True Temper	Bass Pop	frog, glass eyes	EX	$222.50	1-1999
True Temper	Crippled Shad		VG	$11.50	1-1999
True Temper	Crippled Shad	shad, NOT MET	EX	$14.00	11-2000
True Temper	Crippled Shad	speed shad?, orange, black spots	Mint	$125.00	6-1999
True Temper	Crippled Shad	speed shad window box	NIB	$18.05	6-1999
True Temper	Speed Shad	#103, pearl	NIB	$16.50	1-1999
True Temper	Speed Shad	red, white	NIB	$26.29	2-1999
Turner	Spider	multi-spring hook	NIB	$77.00	9-2000
Turner	Spider	multi-spring hook	NIB	$113.50	1-1999
Turner	Spider	multi-spring hook, 1949	NIB	$104.00	4-2000
Turner	Spider	multi-spring hook, papers	NIB	$159.15	8-1999
Tuttle	Bass, Devil Bug	nice box	EX/IB	$64.79	7-1999
Tuttle	Devil Bug	mouse, raggy box, NOT MET	VG-/IB	$27.00	6-1999
Tuttle	Devil Bug	nice picture box	NIB	$127.50	2-1999
Tuttle	Devil Bug	red box	EX-/IB	$135.83	2-2000
Tuttle	Mouse, Devil Bug	vg- picture intro box	EX-/IB	$55.55	8-1999
U.S. Specialty	Rush Tango	mottled, 1PCCB	NIB	$179.50	11-1999
U-Get-Em	Underwater Minnow	crackleback, by Pflueger, 3-hook, maroon box, NOT MET	NIB	$1,228.00	6-1999
Uniline	Spinno Minnow	#4, shiner, crisp box	NIB	$95.00	2-2000
Uniline	Spinno Minnow	#5, charcoal, gold	NIB	$159.00	3-2001
Uniline	Spinno Minnow	#504, shiner scale, NOT MET	NIB	$68.77	5-1999
Uniline	Spinno Minnow	#505, black, white	NIB	$117.51	5-1999

BRAND	MODEL	SERIES / MFG. CODE / DESCRIPTION	GRADE	PRICE	DATE
Uniline	Spinno Minnow	#506, light green scale	NIB	$199.99	4-1999
Uniline	Spinno Minnow	#507, blue bugger	NIB	$213.50	4-1999
Uniline	Spinno Minnow	#508, goldfish	NIB	$126.50	4-1999
Uniline	Spinno Minnow	#508, goldfish scale	NIB	$127.50	9-1999
Uniline	Spinno Minnow	#511, yellow scale	NIB	$96.50	6-1999
Uniline	Spinno Minnow	#514, pike scale	NIB	$83.00	9-2000
Uniline	Spinno Minnow	frog	NIB	$75.00	11-1999
Uniline	Spinno Minnow	frog, great picture box	NIB	$113.41	4-1999
Uniline	Spinno Minnow	gold scale, very nice 501 box	NIB	$81.00	3-1999
Uniline	Spinno Minnow	rainbow	EX	$86.55	4-1999
Uniline	Spinno Minnow	rainbow, fair box	EX/IB	$104.00	4-2000
Uniline	Spinno Minnow	rainbow?, green, white?	VG	$36.00	4-1999
Uniline	Spinno Minnow	red, white, decent box	VG/IB	$52.00	3-1999
Uniline	Spinno Minnow	shiner scale, nice box	NIB	$81.05	3-1999
Uniline	Spinno Minnow	white, yellow	EX/IB	$53.00	6-1999
Uniline	Spinno Minnow	silver scale, blue, yellow	VG	$58.00	4-1999
Vann-Clay	Minnow	spring loaded head c 1920s	VG	$860.00	2-2002
Vann-Clay	Minnow, Retrievable	red, side hook, unique?	G	$975.00	5-2000
Vann-Clay	Zaragossa	perch	EX	$1250.00	10-1999
Vaughn	Vaughn's Lure		NIB	$320.00	10-1999
Vaughn	Vaughn's Lure	black, minnow body, twirly head	EX	$200.00	10-2000
Vaughn	Vaughn's Lure	black, nice picture box	NIB	$326.00	5-2000
Vaughn	Vaughn's Lure	black, rainbow head, tail chip, c. 1946	NIB	$356.00	9-2000
Vaughn	Vaughn's Lure	red, white, nice box	EX-/IB	$295.00	2-2000
Vom Hofe, E.	Perfection Fly Reel	#2, German silver, rubber, 2" x ⅞", nice case, January 23 '83	EX/IC	$4,255.00	5-2002
Vom Hofe, E.	Perfection Fly Reel	German silver, rubber, 3"x2"x⅞", torn case, January 23 '83	EX/IC	$4,600.00	5-2002
Vom Hofe, J.		raised pillar fly, (brass?) 1903 patent, l nice	EX-	$511.50	2-200
Walton	Speed Bait	12 props, weird	EX	$210.00	6-2001
Water Scouts, B.C.	Little Eddie	like Clarks Scout, black, white, plastic box	NIB	$44.00	6-1999
Weber	Al Foss Shimmy Wiggler	red, white	NIB	$25.00	9-1999
Weber	Beetle	x22, nice Lur-All assortment	EX	$103.00	10-2000
Weber	Dive-N-Wobble	DFR21, No.D, white, sparkle, small	NIB	$105.00	3-2001
Weber	Dive-N-Wobble	orange spots	NIB	$65.50	4-2000
Weber	Dr. Henshall	hairy bass fly on great card	NOC	$23.00	9-2000
Weber	Dr. Henshall Bass Bug	grey, spider box	EX/IB	$43.55	6-1999
Weber	Dr. Henshall Bass Bug	white, red, spider box	EX/IB	$52.55	6-1999
Weber	Flip-Frog		NIB	$15.00	6-1999
Weber	Lifelike Beetle	3 different, new on round card, plastic box	NIB	$33.00	8-2001
Weber	Pop-Akel	fire in rough box NOT MET	NIB	$12.00	7-2000
Weber	Pop-Wobble	mouse	EX-	$26.00	12-1998
Weber	Streamer Flies	x20, styrofoam display, looks like frame	EX	$15.00	9-1999
Weber	Swim King	black frog	NIB	$81.00	11-2000
Weber	Swim King	yellow frog	EX	$32.00	3-1999
Weed King	Weedless Plug	hidden hooks	NIB	$170.01	12-1998
Weezel	Sparrow		NIB	$103.00	9-2000
Weezel	Sparrow	nice picture box	NIB	$129.00	7-1999

BRAND	MODEL	SERIES / MFG. CODE / DESCRIPTION	GRADE	PRICE	DATE
Welch & Graves	Minnow Tube, Glass	NOT MET	EX	$810.00	9-1999
Welch & Graves	Minnow Tube, Glass	wood box	NIB	$1,775.00	5-1999
Weller		143, chub, 3-jointed, nice box with paper	NIB	$207.00	4-2000
Weller	Professor	lousy spoon in picture box	NIB	$41.00	1-2002
Western Auto	Shur Strike Pikie	perch scale, nice box	NIB	$62.25	6-1999
Whopper Stopper		yellow, black ribs, jointed, NOT MET	Mint	$25.00	11-1999
Whopper Stopper	Bayou Boogee Top	5 different in boxes	NIB	$66.25	3-1999
Whopper Stopper	Bayou Boogee Top	funny little prop bait	EX	$24.00	2-1999
Whopper Stopper	Dog Walker	like Zara Spook, frog	EX	$21.50	1-1999
Whopper Stopper	Dog Walker	perch	NOC	$20.50	1-1999
Whopper Stopper	Hellraiser		NIB	$19.99	2-1999
Whopper Stopper	Hellraiser	#5G, round props, small 300 size	NOC	$19.80	4-1999
Whopper Stopper	Hellraiser	#10, (XBW), large 500 size, printed props	NOC	$26.00	4-1999
Whopper Stopper	Hellraiser	#304S, silver scale	NIB	$21.00	2-1999
Whopper Stopper	Hellraiser	#365, round props	NOC	$7.00	3-1999
Whopper Stopper	Hellraiser	#365, yellow, green stripes	NOC	$7.00	2-1999
Whopper Stopper	Hellraiser	red head, white	NIB	$11.00	1-2000
Whopper Stopper	Hellraiser	clear, screw in line tie	EX	$19.99	6-1999
Whopper Stopper	Hellraiser	frog, large	NOC	$33.00	11-1999
Whopper Stopper	Hellraiser	red, white, beater	EX-	$19.99	2-1999
Whopper Stopper	Hellraiser	red, white, plastic box	NIB	$10.50	6-1999
Whopper Stopper	Hellraiser	white shore	NOC	$9.00	2-1999
Whopper Stopper	Hellraiser	x2	EX+	$108.50	1-1999
Whopper Stopper	Hellraiser	x2	NOC	$67.00	2-1999
Whopper Stopper	Lizard	eel looking lure, hard plastic box	NIB	$32.50	11-1999
Whopper Stopper	Scrambler	Zara type, pikie, with props	NOC	$21.50	3-1999
Wilcox	Wiggler	maroon, red, very nice, NOT MET	EX-	$3201.00	9-2002
Wilcox	Wiggler	NO BIDS	AVG	$1,800.00	2-2000
Wilcox	Wiggler	Type 2, 3-hook, ugly color	EX	$4,880.00	6-2001
Wilcox	Wiggler	Type 2, frog, NOT MET	VG	$1,750.00	6-1999
Wilcox	Wiggler	ugly, NOT MET	Fair	$760.00	3-1999
Wilford	Croaker Bass Bait	woodpecker type, white, jointed, bad pictures		$300.00	8-2001
Williams, Ted	Ny Buck	jigs counter display, Miami, Florida, ugly	Poor	$721.00	5-2000
Wilson	Bassermizer	blended red head	EX	$550.00	5-2000
Wilson	Bassermizer	red, white	EX	$360.00	4-1999
Wilson	Bassermizer	red, white, NOT MET	EX+	$370.00	6-1999
Wilson	Six-In-One	bar perch	EX	$550.00	5-2000
Wilson	Wobbler, Fluted	bar perch	EX	$128.50	4-1999
Wilson	Wobbler, Fluted	neat 2PCCB picture	EXIB	$132.50	3-1999
Wilson	Wobbler, Winged	white	EX	$85.00	5-2000
Winchester	Bass Fly	snelled on card	NOC	$172.00	4-1999
Winchester	Multi-Wobbler	9200, rainbow?, glass eyes, decent, NOT MET	VG	$180.50	9-1999
Winchester	Multi-Wobbler	9201, green	VG	$275.00	1-1999
Winchester	Multi-Wobbler	9201, green, gold back, yb, papers	NIB	$793.00	9-2000
Winchester	Multi-Wobbler	9202, green, NOT MET	EX	$277.00	3-2000
Winchester	Multi-Wobbler	9204, red	AVG	$202.50	1-1999
Winchester	Multi-Wobbler	9206, rainbow, crisp box & paper, NOT MET	NIB	$1,675.00	10-2000

BRAND	MODEL	SERIES / MFG. CODE / DESCRIPTION	GRADE	PRICE	DATE
Winchester	Multi-Wobbler	crackleback	EX-	$316.00	3-1999
Winchester	Multi-Wobbler	gold, brown back stripe	EX	$400.00	10-2000
Winchester	Multi-Wobbler	green, gold side, NOT MET	EX-	$304.89	5-1999
Winchester	Multi-Wobbler	green parrot in nice box	EXIB	$776.00	2-1999
Winchester	Multi-Wobbler	rainbow, crisp box, packers slip	NIB	$1,277.00	6-2002
Winchester	Multi-Wobbler	rainbow, several small chips, NOT MET	AVG	$179.00	10-2000
Winchester	Multi-Wobbler	red head, looks decent	VG+	$233.00	4-2000
Winchester	Multi-Wobbler	white, red eyes	EX	$376.10	11-1999
Winchester	Spinner	9611	EX-	$41.00	6-2002
Winchester	Spinner	9623	EX	$66.00	3-2000
Winchester	Underwater Minnow	3-hook	EX-	$1,500.00	4-1999
Winchester	Underwater Minnow	3-hook, repainted, mint	REPAINT	$325.00	12-1999
Winchester	Underwater Minnow	9012, green back, gold, 3-hook	VG+	$383.00	4-2000
Winchester	Underwater Minnow	9015, crackleback, glass eyes, 3-hook, NOT MET	VG-IB	$810.00	4-1999
Winchester	Underwater Minnow	9016 crackleback, 3-hook, small chip	VG+	$406.00	11-2000
Winchester	Underwater Minnow	awful, chips, 3-hook, no hooks, #9215 on prop	Poor	$204.00	4-2000
Winchester	Underwater Minnow	blood red, 3-hook, ex box	NIB	$2,400.00	12-2001
Winchester	Underwater Minnow	crackleback, 3-hook, box missing end flap, papers	NIB	$1,000.00	7-2000
Winchester	Underwater Minnow	dark red, 3-hook	EX	$1,350.00	10-1999
Winchester	Underwater Minnow	dark red, 3-hook, ex- unmarked box	EXIB	$2,500.00	6-2001
Winchester	Underwater Minnow	green, 3-hook	Poor	$90.98	5-1999
Winchester	Underwater Minnow	no eyes, 3-hook, cheap, prop marked, NOT MET	EX	$153.50	3-2000
Winchester	Underwater Minnow	parrot finish, 3-hook	EX	$1,150.00	8-2002
Winchester	Underwater Minnow	rainbow 3-hook	EX	$1,000.00	12-2001
Winchester	Underwater Minnow	rainbow, 3-hook, POBW	EX-	$1,650.00	10-1999
Winchester	Underwater Minnow	rainbow, 3-hook, marked prop	EX	$688.00	10-2000
Winchester	Underwater Minnow	rainbow, 3-hook, tiny tail chip	EX	$1,400.00	6-2001
Winchester	Underwater Minnow	rainbow, (repainted?), 3-hook, Mahinski sell	EX	$810.00	3-2000
Winchester	Underwater Minnow	red, 3-hook	EX-	$1,200.00	5-2000
Winchester	Underwater Minnow	red, 3-hook	Mint	$650.00	12-2001
Winchester	Underwater Minnow	red, white, 3-hook, cheap, line tie, large body	Poor	$74.00	1-1999
Winchester	Underwater Minnow	white, brown back stripe, red chin, 3-hook	EX-	$431.00	10-2000
Winnie	Michigan Stump Dodger	perch, metal eyes, nice picture box	EXIB	$1,300.00	4-2002
Winnie	Michigan Stump Dodger	red, white, metal eyes, age lines, nice picture box	EX-IB	$1,176.00	4-2002
Winters	Bass Bait		EX	$650.00	4-2001
Woods	Arkansas Wiggler	like Spoon Plug, metal, nice picture box	NIB	$61.00	5-2000
Woods	Dipsy Doodle	perch	NIB	$15.50	1-1999
Woods	Dipsy Doodle	yellow scale, like one on box	NIB	$80.00	1-1999
Woods	Doodler	#616, black, picture box, catalog	NIB	$51.00	5-2000
Woods	Doodler	shad scale, plastic lure, vg+ #604 box	NIB	$100.00	8-2001
Woods	Doodler	YSB1215, yellow, silver bars, catalog, nice	NIB	$88.00	9-2000
Woods	Expert	2½", green, white, pre-1904, NOT MET	EX-?	$511.00	9-2002
Woods	Expert	5-hook	VG-	$515.00	5-1999
Woods	Expert	aluminum, 5-hook, ex- wood box	EXIB	$4,000.00	12-2001

BRAND	MODEL	SERIES / MFG. CODE / DESCRIPTION	GRADE	PRICE	DATE
Woods	Expert	aluminum, 5-hook, ex- wood box with label	EXIB	$4,000.00	6-2001
Woods	Expert	aluminum, HPGM, NOT MET	VG	$257.00	5-2001
Woods	Expert	(brown back?), 5-hook, "the expert"	EX	$1,300.00	12-2001
Woods	Expert	gold, round body, #1 removable hooks	EX-	$800.00	1-1999
Woods	Expert	green, 5-hook, hole props, 2BW, re-hooks	VG	$391.00	5-2001
Woods	Expert	green white, 3-hook, "expert"	EX	$1,200.00	12-2001
Woods	Expert	green, white, 3-hook, #1 hooks	EX	$1500.00	6-2001
Woods	Expert	green, white, 5-hook, #1 detachable hooks	EX-	$1,500.00	6-2001
Woods	Poppa-Doodle	1997, re-issue	NIB	$15.00	4-2001
Woods	Spot Tail	703, red head, papers, 2PCCB picture box	NIB	$203.00	1-2000
Woods	Spot Tail	black in box, one more nice	EXIB	$20.25	1-1999
Woods	Various	3 different	EX	$17.45	3-1999
Woods	Various	4 different, common, one box & catalog	EX	$52.86	1-1999
Woods	Various	6-pack, nice display, PTCB	NIB	$102.50	4-1999
Woods	Various	one 005 Doodler perch, one 1001 Deep-R-Doodle	NIB x 2	$310.00	4-1999
Worden	Minnow, Combination	aluminum, ex white box, original string tie	EXIB	$4,600.00	6-2001
Worden	Minnow, Combination	aluminum, line tie, ex white box	EXIB	$4,500.00	12-2001
Worden	Underwater Minnow	green, 3-hook, 1 chip, pretty, NOT MET	EX-	$464.00	11-1999
Worden	Underwater Minnow	ugly, 5-hook, screw hook holders, awful	Poor	$160.50	10-1999
Worth	Flutter Fin	2 different	VG	$26.00	6-1999
Worth	Flutter Fin	6 different colors	NIB	$202.85	3-1999
Worth	Flutter Fin	black, white scales	Mint	$19.50	1-1999
Worth	Flutter Fin	orange, black scales	EX	$17.77	7-1999
Wright McGill	Bass-Nabber	black, white, glass eyes, NOT MET	VG+	$76.00	3-2000
Wright McGill	Bass-O-Gram	2½", green, yellow, glass eyes	EX-	$370.00	2-2000
Wright McGill	Bass-O-Gram	red head	EX-	$199.00	9-2000
Wright McGill	Bass-O-Gram	red head & tail, glass eyes, belly crack	Nice	$300.00	3-1999
Wright McGill	Bug-A-Boo	1½", black, white	EX-	$17.00	1-1999
Wright McGill	Crawdad	gold, brown	EX	$86.00	8-1999
Wright McGill	Crawfish	green, bead eyes	EX	$96.00	1-2000
Wright McGill	Crawfish	softshell, rough #551 box	EXIB	$76.00	3-2000
Wright McGill	Flapper Crab		EX	$75.00	4-1999
Wright McGill	Flapper Crab	1¾", grey, no legs	EX	$132.50	1-2000
Wright McGill	Flapper Crab	2", no legs	EX	$86.00	1-2000
Wright McGill	Flapper Crab	2", yellow, nice	Mint	$170.50	1-2000
Wright McGill	Flapper Crab	missing legs	EXIB	$103.00	1-1999
Wright McGill	Flapper Crab	missing legs	EXIB	$165.00	9-1999
Wright McGill	Flies	x24, salesman display, NO BIDS	EX	$200.00	6-1999
Wright McGill	Fly Rod Bait		EX	$100.00	4-2001
Wright McGill	Fly Rod Bait	super nice	EX	$155.00	11-2000
Wright McGill	Fly Rod Nature Faker	bead, eyes	VG	$28.00	1-1999
Wright McGill	Granger	8040, 8', ⅜, nice tube & bag, plastic on handle	NIT	$978.00	3-2002
Wright McGill	Hijacker	gold scale, nice box	EXIB	$13.50	4-2000
Wright McGill	Hijacker	red, white	NIB	$24.99	6-1999
Wright McGill	Horsefly	flyrod, glass eyes, ugly	Poor	$20.00	6-1999
Wright McGill	Miracle Minnow	#470W	NIB	$25.99	2-2000
Wright McGill	Miracle Minnow	#472J18	NIB	$15.50	5-1999

BRAND	MODEL	SERIES / MFG. CODE / DESCRIPTION	GRADE	PRICE	DATE
Wright McGill	Miracle Minnow	#472J7	NIB	$27.00	5-1999
Wright McGill	Mouse, Baby	lint covered, ugly, NOT MET	EX?	$189.50	1-2000
Wright McGill	Nicky Mouse	I sniped $103.79, but problem	EX	$103.50	9-1999
Wright McGill	Nicky Mouse	grey, nice whiskers and eyes	EX-	$291.00	2-2000
Wright McGill	Open Mouth Shiner	red, white, ugly	AVG	$62.00	12-1999
Wright McGill	Skipper, Fly Rod	yellow, black stripe, glass eyes	EX+	$109.01	5-1999
Wright McGill	Swim Mouse	ugly, NOT MET	AVG	$30.50	8-1999
Wyers	Devon	3CM, c.1910, safety box	NIB	$100.00	7-2000
Wynne	Ol' Skipper	Lucky Tail Wobbler ex- box top	EXIB	$49.00	8-2002
Wynne	Ol' Skipper	red, white, 1603 box	NIB	$46.00	2-1999
Zink	Screwtail	black, white	EX	$77.76	1-2000
Zink	Screwtail	green, yellow	EX-	$99.00	7-2000
Zink	Screwtail	red, white	EX	$84.00	4-1999
Zink	Screwtail	red, white	EX-	$76.00	4-1999
Zink	Screwtail	red, white	VG+	$66.50	1-1999
Zink	Screwtail	red head, papers	NIB	$255.00	1-2000
Zink	Screwtail	yellow, black, stripe	NIB	$190.00	7-1999
Zumski	Whiptail Sucker	glass eyes, grey, NOT MET	VG+	$103.50	1-1999
	Bug-N-Bass	frog	EX	$406.00	2-2002

PHOTO GALLERY

We have included approximately 242 photos showing lures from the very old (Pflueger 1890s Muskellunge Minnow, Heddon cup hardware prototype, Wobbler, Vacuum Bait, etc.) to some of the very last of the Heddons that have already become both popular and expensive (Wee Tads, Preyfish, Cracklebacks, etc.). We have chosen not to give a value to the lures shown as they are in our respective collections (most in author Lewis's collection) and have not been marketed recently, with only a few exceptions. Also, the whole purpose of our book is to give exact prices of items actually sold and not just approximations based upon general sales patterns. However, we also thought it necessary to have a photo essay of lures to show the uninitiated some possibilities and to show the more advanced collectors some lures that they may not have considered in the past.

Few of the photos in this book have appeared in print before. However, they were all taken by author Lewis (with six exceptions taken by author Kolbeck) for his multi-volume work on *Modern Fishing Lure Collectibles*, of which Volumes 1 and 2 have already been published by Collector Books and are available from either author Lewis (see address in his Introduction) or the publisher. We have tried to select a wide array of lures, other collectibles, a few reels of interest, and many different eras.

The reader can expect to find in the photo essay the classic lures from most of the major companies. In other words, South Bend often brings to mind such lures as Babe-Orenos and Fish-Obites. Creek Chub reminds us of Wigglers and Pikies and Plunkers. Shakespeare had its classic Swimming Mouse. Pflueger had its early rubber minnows and great five hook minnows, in addition to others. Heddon is always associated with River Runts, Punkinseeds and Crazy Crawlers, in addition to its early lures prior to 1940. Paw Paw made many great lures but its hardware examples often set Paw Paw baits off from others, so the hardware is shown in detail. In addition to the foregoing companies, Weber Lifelike Fly Company of Stevens Point, Wisconsin (author Kolbeck's home), was instrumental in the development of fly rod baits and fly fishing techniques, and thus the flies are shown along with some of the rarer and more unusual Weber items.

Finally, we have attempted to give a good cross-section of other lure companies, large and small, that have contributed to our ability to find lures to collect anywhere from twenty to one hundred years later. As the purpose of this book is not illustration per se, our photo numbers had to be limited and somewhat arbitrary. However, we hope that the photos give the reader an idea of the broad spectrum of lures available today for the collector. The photos should also help collectors identify some hardware types, box types, common company colors, standard company lures, some unusual finds, and just some colorful baits for all to behold. It is recommended that the collector invest in as many pictorial lure guides as possible to become familiar with the lures, reels and rods available to collect. Though biased, we can both recommend starting with *Modern Fishing Lure Collectibles*, Volumes 1 and 2, by author Russell E. Lewis for a very good overview of collectibles related to fishing. Also, the books contain a very detailed annotated bibliography of additional recommended books on lure collecting.

Two early Dolls. Note the flat-painted eyes, the small screw hardware compared to the Heddon painted models, and the traditional Doll colors. Some of the early ones also had a line tie clip as shown on the large Doll. But, all together, look for the foregoing combination and you should have one of the earliest Dolls.

These fly rod baits were left over in the Weber archives in a two-piece cardboard box containing one gross of lures in assorted colors and two sizes. These were only made in Dylite plastic after 1956. These have usually been selling for $6.00 to $15.00 and I think are worth at least $20.00 in their condition. As with most lures, the frog patterns sold the quickest, and those indeed brought over $20.00 in many cases.

Another rare color, Yellow Shore, 2100 XYS, in two-piece hardware.

Another great lure sold to me by John Kolbeck, a Dive-N-Wobl, new in a box with original hang tag never removed, in orange spotted version. This is one of the only bass type plugs ever sold by Weber, and its value is negotiable. Out of the box these trade for $30.00 to $50.00 depending on condition, but they are very uncommon. If people knew what they were, they would command more money. This one cost me $150.00 new in the box. Model DB 12, Series D in wrong DB16 box. The lure body is 3¾" long, unique through body cloth hardware with 108-pound tensile strength, and painted eyes.

Side view of Bear Creek wooden decoy.

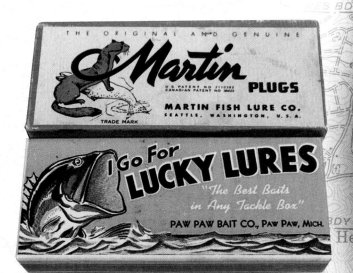

Two nice lure box examples.

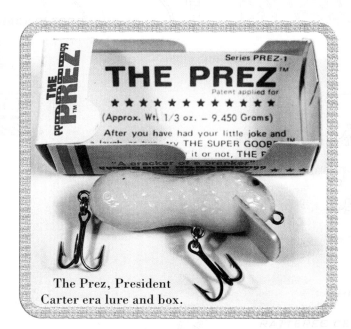

The Prez, President Carter era lure and box.

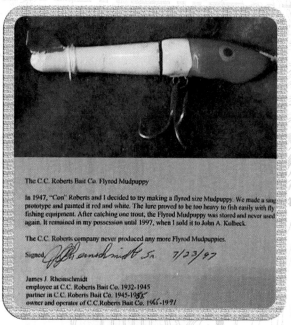

Rare prototype C.C. Roberts Fly Rod Mudpuppy.
(Photo courtesy J. Kolbeck)

Rare Weber Lifelike Fly Co. "Stoneakle." *(Photo courtesy J. Kolbeck)*

Rare Weber
Lifelike Fly Co.
"Juneakle."
(Photo courtesy J. Kolbeck)

Rare Weber Lifelike Fly Co. "Hellgrammite."
(Photo courtesy J. Kolbeck)

Rare Weber Lifelike Fly Co.
"Helgramakle." *(Photo courtesy J. Kolbeck)*

Rare
Weber Life-
like Fly Co.
"Bumbilakle."
(Photo courtesy J. Kolbeck)

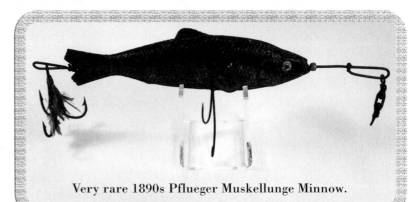

Very rare 1890s Pflueger Muskellunge Minnow.

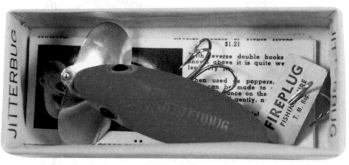

1950s Arbogast Jitterbug in rare Fireplug color in box.

Two 1950s – early 1960s, Lucky Lady Lures,
Los Angeles, California.

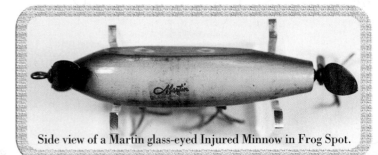

Side view of a Martin glass-eyed Injured Minnow in Frog Spot.

Shad River-Runt Spook in two-piece cardboard box.

Rarest of the Heddon Sonics, two Top Sonics.

P-K Fly Rod rubber mouse.

Neon Mickey Salmon Plug from Pacific Northwest.

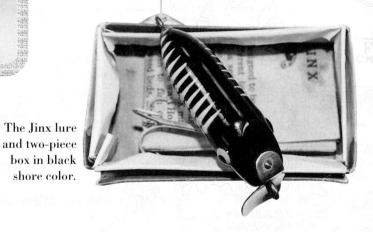

The Jinx lure and two-piece box in black shore color.

The Real Lure and its tube, New York.

1960s Eddie Pope Hot-Shot on collectible card.

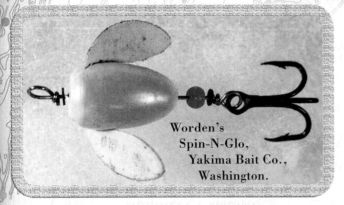

Worden's
Spin-N-Glo,
Yakima Bait Co.,
Washington.

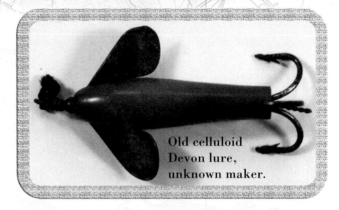

Old celluloid
Devon lure,
unknown maker.

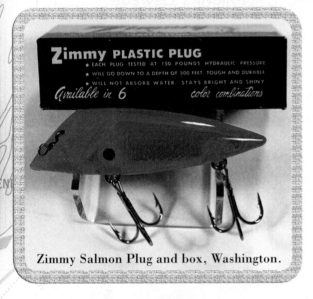

Zimmy Salmon Plug and box, Washington.

Two nice Millsite translucent lures, Howell, Michigan.

Close-up of a Millsite 100-
Series Floater in Cardinal.

A Millsite Daily Double with tag.

Predecessor of
100-Series, Millsite
Wig-Wag with tag.

Close-up of a hang tag for the
Millsite Daily Double.

A dozen assorted Frost Flies from G.W. Frost & Sons.

Very rare Weber "Grasshopper" card
from Weber archives.

Close-up of #371
G.W. Frost Polar
Bear Streamers.

Last versions of Weber
"Muddler Minnows," new in packs.

Demon Lure
Co., San
Antonio, Texas,
"Sail Shark."

Box for
Weber No.
300 Futurist
Fly Reel,
rare.

Back and front of prototype "Re-treevit" type fly reel found in Weber archives.

Weezels in a box, fly rod size,
Cincinnati, Ohio.

Barracuda lure patch, Florida.

Harrison
Industries,
Bill Plummer frog.

Arbogast Hula Dancer
in frog pattern.

Clockwise from upper left. Rare Colorado Moth,
Tin Liz, Cool Ripple Frog, two Marathons.

Rare Arbogast Tin Liz two-piece cardboard box.

Rare (but, poor shape) Arbogast
Hula Dancer two-piece box.

Arbogast Hustler in
common Arbogast
color pattern.

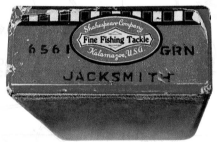

Two-piece
cardboard box
for Shakespeare
"Jacksmith" lure.

Wooden carved eye Pflueger Poprite #8500 lure in box.

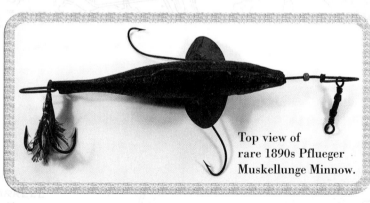

Top view of
rare 1890s Pflueger
Muskellunge Minnow.

Bottom view of rare 1890s Pflueger Muskellunge Minnow.

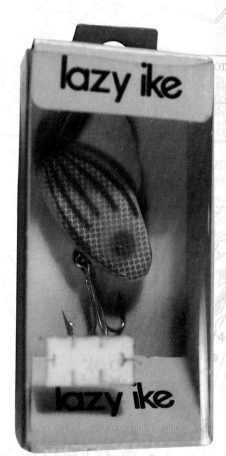

Dura-Pak version of
Sail Shark by Lazy Ike.

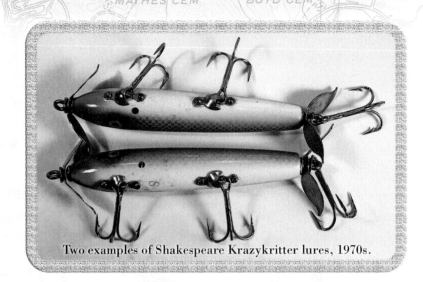

Two examples of Shakespeare Krazykritter lures, 1970s.

Hong Kong Shakespeare box for 1970s wooden lures.

Dura-Pak version of Sail Shark by Creek Chub Bait Co.

Thompson "Doll Top Secret" in Heddon Barfish.

Luhr Jensen Alaskan Plug on 1960s card, Oregon.

Lur-All Beetle Bug new in box on card, rare, 1930s.

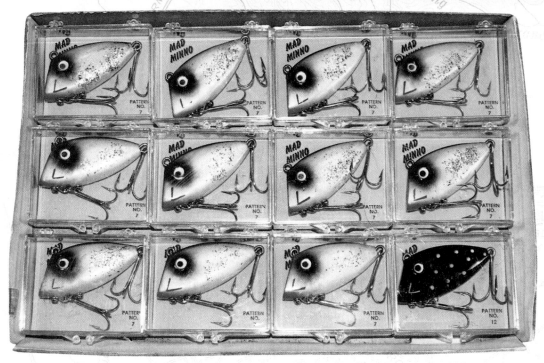

Dealer dozen Buckeye Baits (Ohio) Mad Minnos.

Thompson "Doll Top Secret" in Heddon Blue Chrome.

Rainbow trout color Buckeye Baits Bug-N-Bass.

Common colors in Fin-Dingos, Ropher, and South Bend.

Patch and Hellbender combination.

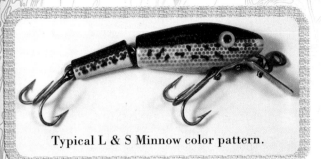

Typical L & S Minnow color pattern.

J.C. Higgins (Sears Roebuck & Co.) wooden lure.

J.C. Higgins (Sears Roebuck & Co.) box back.

Dealer dozen Hildebrandt Spinners new in box, Indiana.

Early Helin Company Flatfish two-piece box, Detroit.

Collectible Helin "Swimmerspoon."

Examples of two South Bend two-piece bait boxes.

South Bend Babe-Oreno box for a R/W lure.

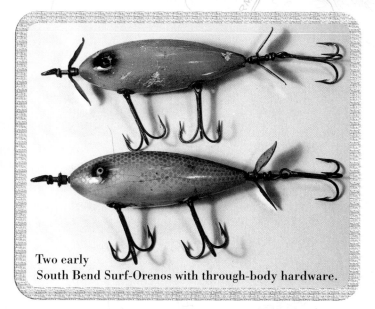

Two early
South Bend Surf-Orenos with through-body hardware.

South Bend GE
wooden Babe-Oreno
from box.

South Bend
Pike-Oreno
box for a
957P.

Pike color tack-eyed South Bend Pike-Oreno from box.

South Bend Fish-Oreno, glass-eyed,
chip, missing metal line tie.

Early but poor condition
South Bend glass-eyed Minnow.

Collectible Tenite South Bend
Fish-Obite, "Guaranteed Lure."

A rare Michigan plastic bait, "The Game Fish Lure" and box.

Small R/W Creek Chub glass-eyed
Ding Bat with metal line tie.

An early box for a dozen Weezel Spinning Rex Spoons.

Another CCBC
Dingbat,
glass-eyed,
line tie.

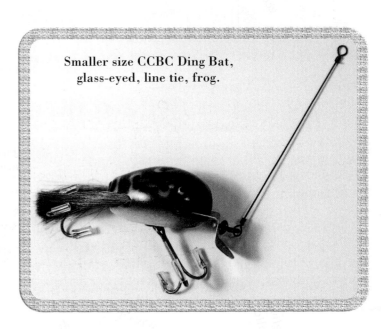

Smaller size CCBC Ding Bat,
glass-eyed, line tie, frog.

Larger size CCBC
Ding Bat, glass-eyed,
line tie, frog.

A Golden Shiner
#5600 CCBC Dinger,
late 1930s – early 1950s.

Two classic CCBC colors
in Pikies, Golden Shiner, and Silver Flash.

Classic CCBC glass-eyed Pikie Minnows, single line ties.

Creek Chub Plunker
in Rainbow, glass eyes.

Creek Chub two-piece box examples, one printed, one stamped.

Two CCBC Pikie boxes, one
printed, one stamped.

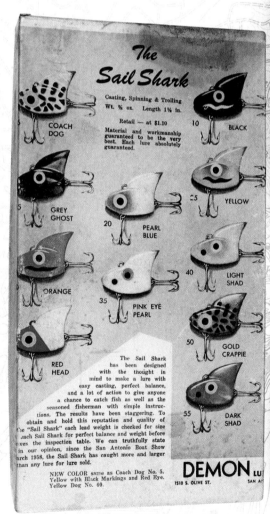

Very rare dealer carton for
Demon Lure's "Sail Shark."

Pico Lures "Side-Shad" new in box, San Antonio, Texas.

Counter display of Lazy Ike "Shark Ike" lures.

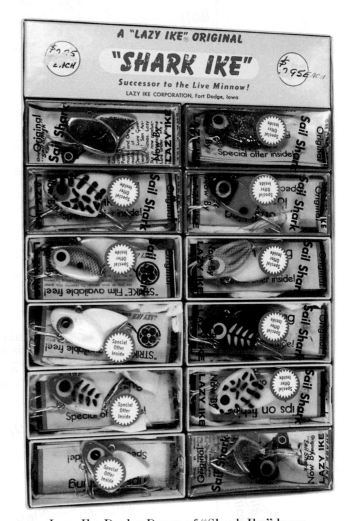

Lazy Ike Dealer Dozen of "Shark Ike" lures.

Two-piece Paw Paw lure box, red and green version.

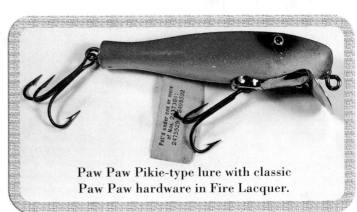

Paw Paw Pikie-type lure with classic Paw Paw hardware in Fire Lacquer.

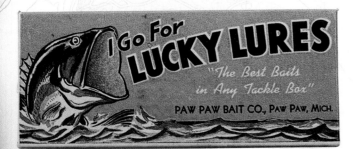

Two-piece Paw Paw lure box, blue and white version.

Paw Paw wooden lure in great Rainbow pattern.

CCBC Baby Pikie, wood, glass-eyed, double line tie, Golden Shiner.

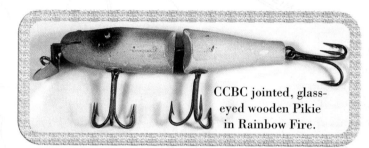

CCBC jointed, glass-eyed wooden Pikie in Rainbow Fire.

Heddon Centennial Edition box from 1994.

Heddon Sonic in a Heddon/Daisy box, common color.

Back of a Heddon/Daisy box, Victor period.

J.C. Higgin's wooden Pikie, new in box.

Box back of lure shown at left.

Patent pending version of "Voo-Doo lure," new in box.

Wooden Plunker, Arnold.

Unner-Flash lure.

Wooden Plunker, Arnold.

Just Five Favorite Baits
THAT'S MY TACKLE BOX!
Says TONY ACCETTA

U. S. PROFESSIONAL BAIT and FLY CASTING CHAMPION

They give the Advantages of 1001 Baits
Here is one of them

WEED-DODGER
PAT. NO. 2,145,283

An entire tackle box in five lures! Accetta box.

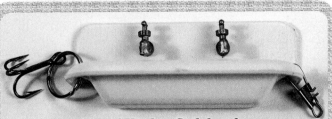

**Flyrod Kitchen Sink lure by
Lutito Lure & Novelty, Denver, Colorado.**

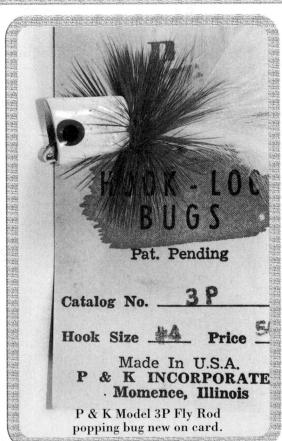

HOOK - LOC
BUGS
Pat. Pending

Catalog No. _____ 3P

Hook Size ___ Price 5

Made In U.S.A.
P & K INCORPORATE
Momence, Illinois

P & K Model 3P Fly Rod popping bug new on card.

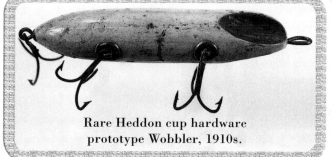

Rare Heddon cup hardware
prototype Wobbler, 1910s.

Heddon wooden "Weedless Widow"
showing "paint off belly weight."

Heddon "River Runts," gold eye is earlier model.

Heddon "Go-Deeper Crab" in
wood with metal line tie.

Heddon River Runts.

Heddon River Runt Spook
Sinker showing early hardware.

Collectible short production
Heddon Preyfish, large size.

Rare Heddon
Wee Tads from 1982.

Heddon wooden Widgets from the 1950s.

Heddon Crackleback in
Orange Crackleback color, large size.

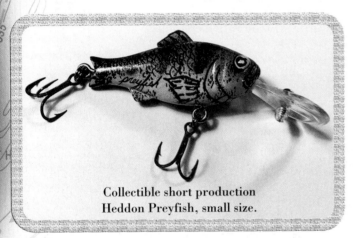

Collectible short production
Heddon Preyfish, small size.

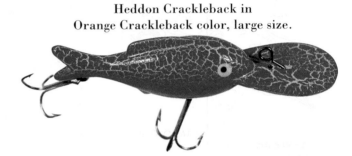

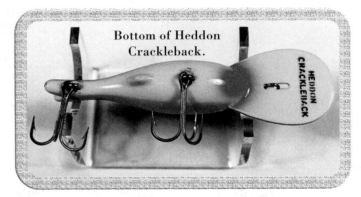

Bottom of Heddon
Crackleback.

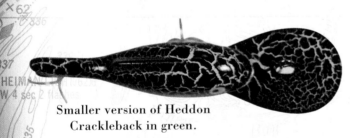

Smaller version of Heddon
Crackleback in green.

Two Heddon Scissortails from the 1960s.

Newer version of Heddon Mouse, brown fur model.

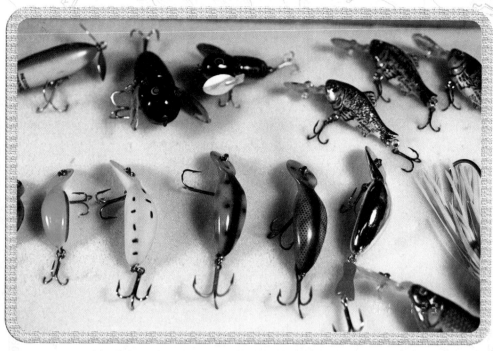

Collectible plastic Heddons. Top row: one Wounded Spook, one Crazy Crawler, three small Preyfish, one Brush Popper, one large Preyfish. Bottom row: Tadpolly Spooks.

A Heddon Chugger Spook from the 1960s or 1970s.

A close-up of a Heddon Spin-Fin #3 size, 1960s.

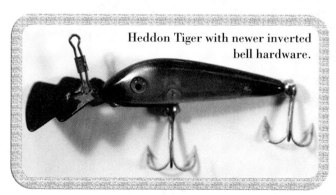

Heddon Tiger with newer inverted bell hardware.

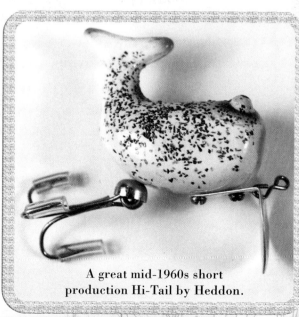

A great mid-1960s short production Hi-Tail by Heddon.

Heddon Tadpolly Spook from 1950s with gold eyes and black pupils.

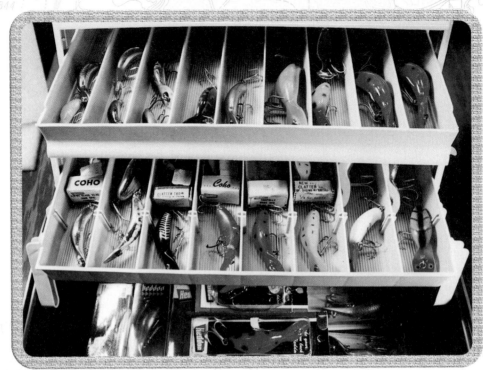

Plastic Heddon collectible Tadpolly Spooks from the 1950s – 1980s.

Heddon Sounder #702 FY,
one of Heddon's last spoons.

Heddon Sculpin #712, Heddon's
another late run spoon.

Late run but collectible colors for Zara Spooks.

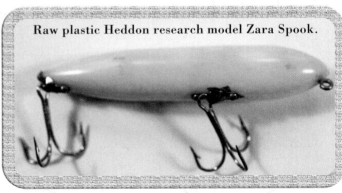

Raw plastic Heddon research model Zara Spook.

Late run but collectible colors for Zara Spooks.

Rare Heddon SK-4 Sonic kit in shipping carton.

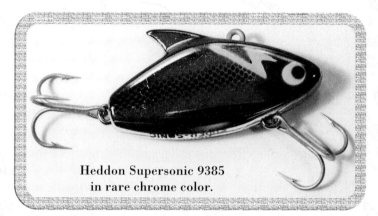

Heddon Supersonic 9385
in rare chrome color.

Heddon
Sonic 385 GR,
rare color.

Heddon Supersonic brown and
gold "Vibraflash" new in box.

Everyone's favorite:
Heddon Punkinseeds!

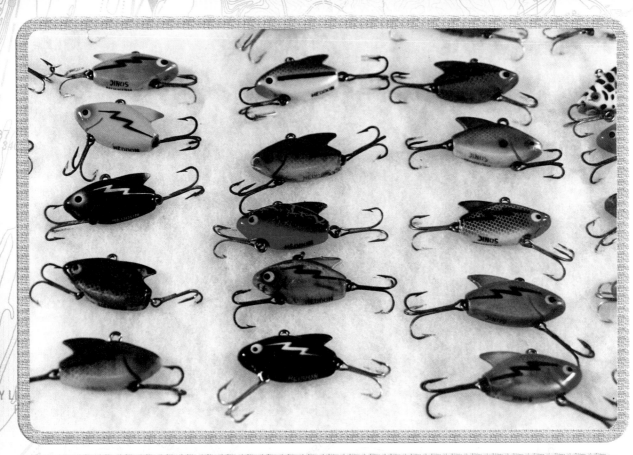

A few Heddon 385 Sonics, common to rare.

Doll Top Secret and Heddon plastic Punkinseed with transitional hardware.

Close-up of Heddon plastic Punkinseed in photo at left.

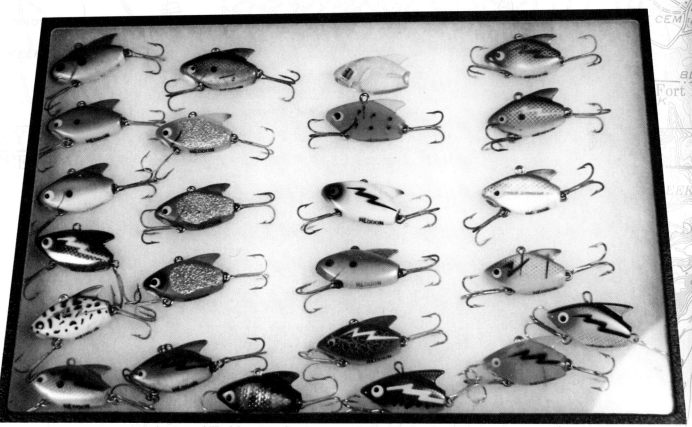

A tray of Heddon 385 Sonics, rare Vibraflash, clear, and orange.

Crazy Crawlers by Heddon, a staple since 1940!.

Early Heddon wood Crazy Crawlers surrounding a 1950s plastic.

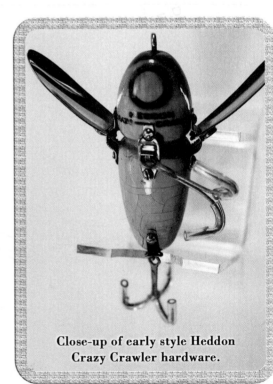

Close-up of early style Heddon Crazy Crawler hardware.

Top view of the rare Heddon 2120 Crazy Crawler in Chipmunk pattern.

Heddon 2100 in common color and 2120 in bullfrog.

Bottom view of the rare Heddon 2120 Crazy Crawler in Chipmunk pattern.

Heddon Musky Crawlers, a 2100 and two 2120.

An early Langley "De-Liar" in Patent Pending box.

Late 1950s two-piece box with two spools of line.

205

Miscellaneous metal lures from the 1960s found in storage in a hardware store.

Folk Lure of a "Banana Lure" (plastic fruit with hooks).

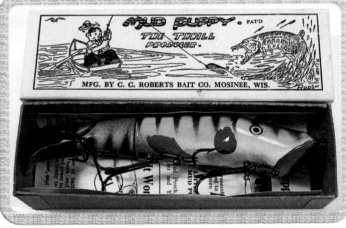

C.C. Roberts Bait Co. Mud Puppy in cartoon box.

Very old Jacob's "Chunk" lure, Vicksburg, Michigan.

Bottom of a Shakespeare Swimming Mouse.

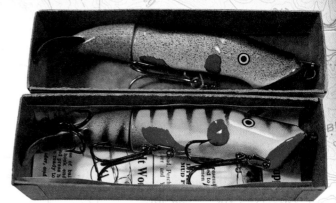

Two examples of Mud Puppy lures with painted eyes.

JACOBS'
WEEDLESS RUBBER CHUNK
Manufactured by
E. L. JACOBS
VICKSBURG, MICHIGAN

Two-piece cardboard box for lure shown on
previous page, bottom left; very rare.

A difficult to find South Bend Mouse.

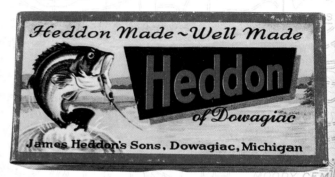

Standard Heddon box of the 1940s
and into the early 1950s.

Great Paw Paw box and lure combination, perfect 10.

A Weber frog with bead
eyes, hair lure from
1940s – 1950s.

Tru-Temper Side Shad
bought by Bomber.

A Helin "Fish Cake," very
collectible wooden lure.

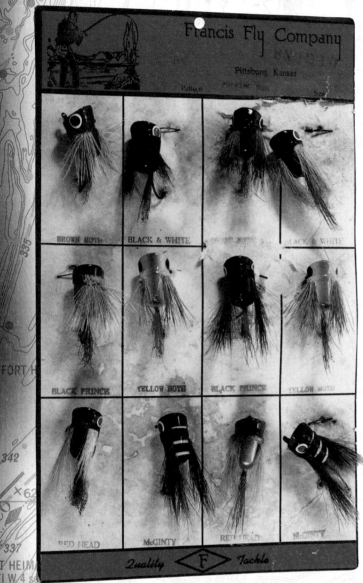

Rare Francis Fly Co., Pittsburgh, Kansas, display card.

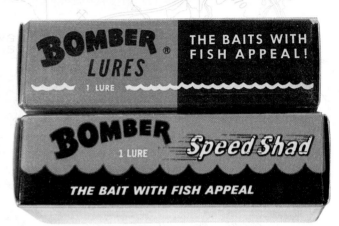

Bomber Bait Co. box examples.

One example of an Eagle Claw box with a Bug-A-Boo.

Second version of patented Helin Fly-Rod Flatfish box.

"Patented" version of Helin Fly Rod Flatfish box.

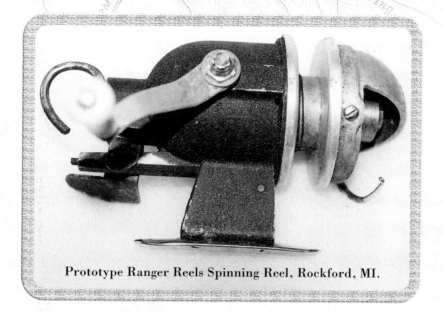

Prototype Ranger Reels Spinning Reel, Rockford, MI.

Contents of Helin box with
papers and wooden fly rod lure.

Bagley's patch for jacket, collectible recent baits.

Ranger Reels
baitcaster, early 1950s.

Prototype Ranger Reel spinning reel,
never produced, 1940s – 1950s.

Unique Frank Borman presentation reel by Mitchell.

Borman Garcia Mitchell #408 on an UMCO box.

One of dozens of collectible Ambassadeur Reels.

Close-up of a J.C. Higgins #312 fly reel, 1960s.

Abu Garcia casting plug (practice plug).

A nice collectible UMCO #173 US.

Abu Garcia 1973 plastic lure, Droop Snoop.

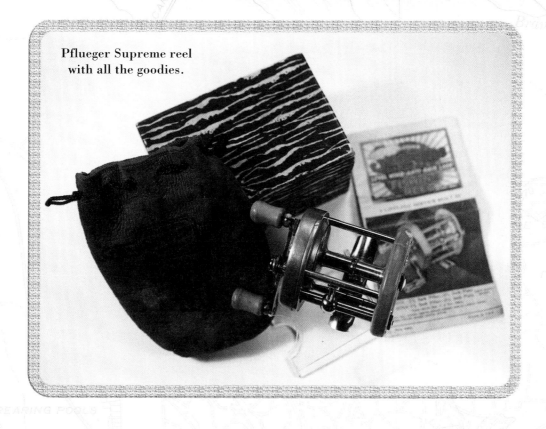

Pflueger Supreme reel
with all the goodies.

A Shakespeare
President reel and
its box and extras.

A collectible Zebco Cardinal Spinning reel.

THE W. & J. MADE FOR ANGLER'S PLAY

Early metal spoon in two-piece box made in Detroit.

RANDALL DECOYS
- HAND MADE
- PERFECTLY BALANCED
- GUARANTEED
"PREFERRED BY OLD TIMERS"

RANDALL DECOYS
- HAND MADE
- PERFECTLY BALANCED
- GUARANTEED
"PREFERRED BY OLD TIMERS"

Randall Fish Decoy boxes, two-piece cardboard.

Beautiful wooden Barracuda Bait underwater minnows.

Rare pink Johnson "Princess" reel.

SHUR·STRIKE minnows HIGH IN QUALITY

SHUR-STRIKE MINNOWS
HIGH IN QUALITY

QUALITY and ACTION FULLY GUARANTEED
Western Auto Stores

Side view of two Shur-Strike (CCBC) boxes and a rare Western Auto box.

Two Shur-Strike (CCBC) boxes and a rare Western Auto box.

End view of Shur-Strike box with glass-eyed River Master.

Rare Shurkatch one-piece cardboard box, New York.

Author Lewis's display of Mermaid "Dolly Bobber" inserts, The bobbers normally have an inner tube around them.

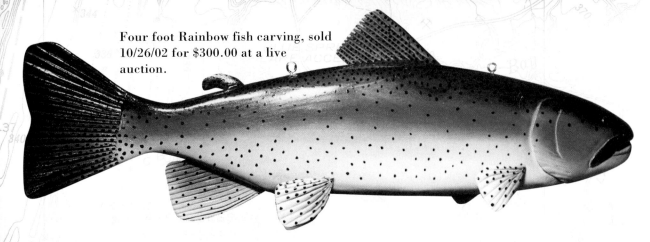

Four foot Rainbow fish carving, sold 10/26/02 for $300.00 at a live auction.

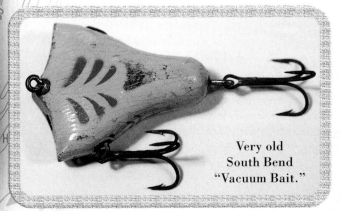

Very old South Bend "Vacuum Bait."

Pflueger 5-hook minnow with "Neverfail" hardware.

Another view of the 1890s Pflueger Muskellunge Minnow.

Bottom of 5-hook minnow shown above. PFLUEGER is stamped on front prop only.

An example of a Pflueger lure box.

An example of a Pflueger reel box.

An example of a Pflueger box.

An example of a Pflueger box.

An example of a Pflueger box.

Classic CCBC Wiggler, double line tie, with evidence of "success."

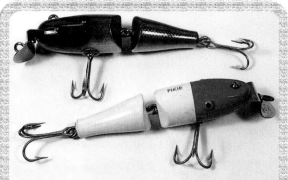

Glass-eyed and tack-eyed CCBC jointed Pikies, double line tie & single line tie.

Classic CCBC colors in two typical Pikies.

A CCBC and a J.C. Higgins version of Injured Minnows.

Classic and common CCBC two-piece boxes for above lures.

CCBC Plunker box in printed version for Rainbow lure shown earlier on page 196.

Collectible Lazy Ike "Chug Ike" lure, KC-2 frog.

Box end for a 1970s Chug Ike.

Close-up of a Keel-Fish and its papers.

Close-up of Keel-Fish box bottom.

Full view of P-K Popping, new on card.

South Bend Fish-Obite in rare black and white color.

Prototype Pflueger (Enterprise)
Ideal Bass Fly sent to Weber.

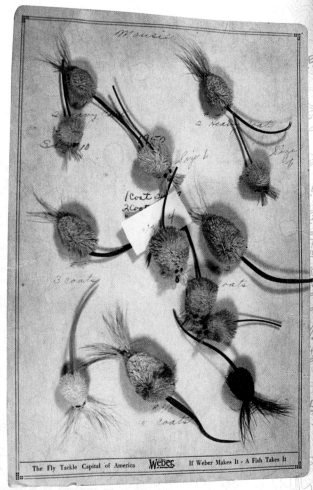

One-of-a-kind Archival Weber "Mousie Assortment."

Weber's sample for Pflueger
found in Weber archives.

Weber Slaymaker's Select
Seven Streamers in box.

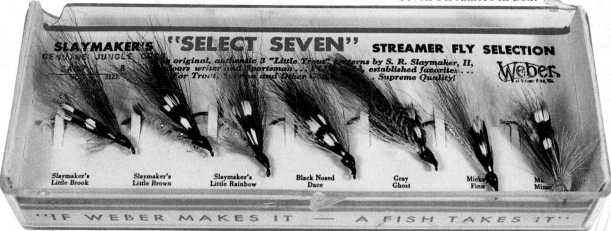

Heddon with one Bug-N-Bass; left row from top to bottom: Scissortail, Baby Zara, Scissortail, Dowagiac Spooks; right row from top to bottom: Small Bug-N-Bass by Buckeye Baits, Heddon Mouse, small Flap-tail Mouse, Tiny Lucky 13, Deep 6, Scissortail.

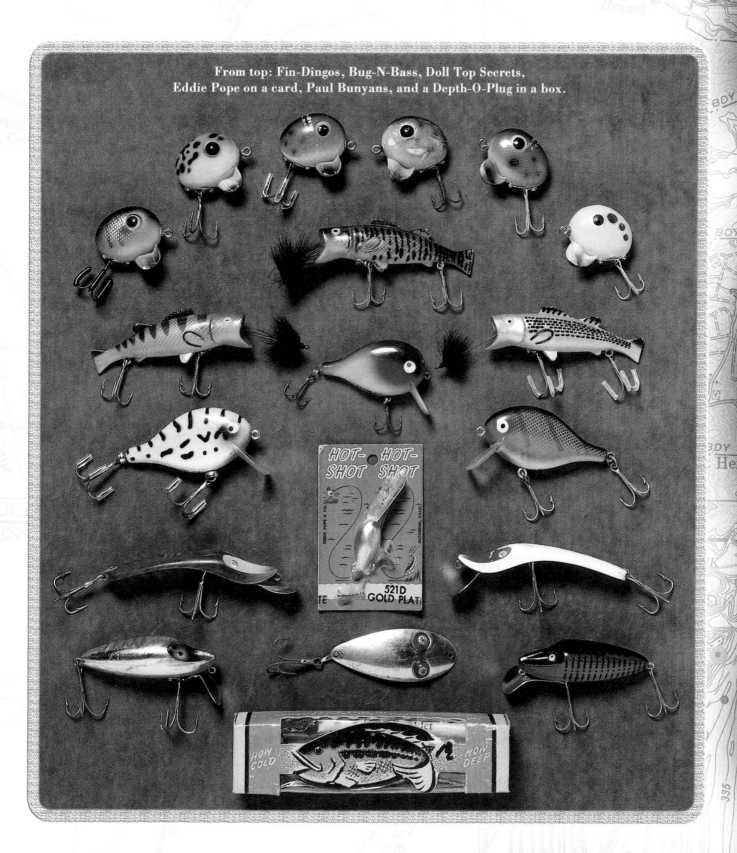

From top: Fin-Dingos, Bug-N-Bass, Doll Top Secrets,
Eddie Pope on a card, Paul Bunyans, and a Depth-O-Plug in a box.

Bombers surrounding a Lucky Lady; a row of Fin-Dingos, including a Ropher box and the white Ropher in a South Bend tube; Shur-Strike River Master; Shakespeare Dapper Dan; Paul Bunyan Weaver; boxed Plastic Pikie in frog; and another River Master; Christmas Tree Waterdog (wooden) and its box.

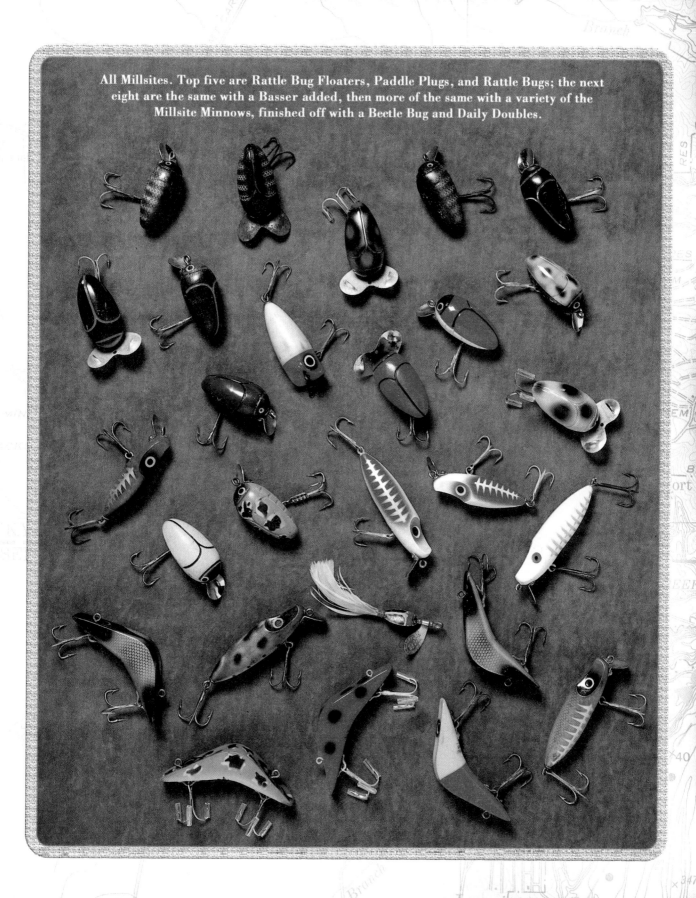

All Millsites. Top five are Rattle Bug Floaters, Paddle Plugs, and Rattle Bugs; the next eight are the same with a Basser added, then more of the same with a variety of the Millsite Minnows, finished off with a Beetle Bug and Daily Doubles.

This is the very first box for a "Spook" or "Fish-Flesh" bait. This is a box for a 9759D Vamp Spook.

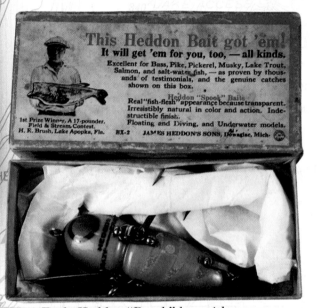

Early Heddon "Brush" box with a rare color 2100 Glo-Worm Crazy Crawler with the early two-piece hardware.

Details of a Daisy-era Sonic slide top box showing a 9385 CD, Super Sonic, and the box insert.

The harder to find 9630 XRW in gold eyes with surface hardware, compared to another 9630 SD with yellow eyes and surface hardware.

A crisp introductory "Brush" box (BX-2 noted on box) for a 2120 Crazy-Crawler, also advertising "Spook" baits, and a crisp upward leaping bass box with a 2100 Crazy-Crawler.

Details of another type of Daisy-era Sonic box, one-piece cardboard with cellophane insert. This is a very rare color Sonic, the 385 SDGS.

New-in-the-box with paper insert surface hardware wooden 2100 in red/yellow, YRH, that was in upward leaping bass box above.

Surface hardware
and mouth color on
2100 Crazy-Crawler.

Two-piece hardware on the 2120.

Earliest box and black/white, BWH, 2120 new inside.

An example of a River Runt
with two-piece hardware.

A nice comparison of some of the many variations one finds in
the plastic Model 9630s, this shows three different hardware
styles, different eyes, different stenciling, and note the red
blush under the upper model that is missing from an otherwise
identical model on the bottom. These are all Crappie 9630s.

Clockwise from top, the large wooden floating Model 740 in early
two-piece hardware in Crappie; a common colored Sunfish, SUN,
in the small plastic Model 380; the Model 730 smaller wooden sinker
in tough to find Yellow Shore, XRY with surface belly hardware
and two-piece tail hardware; a standard color Crappie in the plastic
Model 9630 CRA; and two examples of the Fly Rod Punkie Spook,
one in Crappie and one in Bluegill.

BRAND	MODEL / SERIES	DESCRIPTION	GRADE	PRICE	DATE
	2:1	ball handle, 1871 Terry patent reel seat	VG	$215.00	4-1999
	40	fly reel, German silver & rubber, unmarked, nice	EX	$415.00	9-2000
Abbey & Imbrie		ball casting reel, no mention of condition	VG	$157.00	10-2000
Abbey & Imbrie	2/00	raised pillar, filed foot	VG	$132.00	10-2000
Abbey & Imbrie	Silver King 82	300 yards, nice box	EX/IB	$51.00	2-2000
Abbey & Imbrie	Vom Hofe Compensating	ex wood box with interior label, NOT MET	EX-/IB	$405.00	6-2002
Able	1	in pouch, NOT MET	Mint	$257.00	1-1999
Able	TR-2	spare spool	EX	$271.01	3-1999
Abu		spin casting reel, like Cardinal, name on side	EX-	$142.50	2-1999
Abu	33DLX	deluxe, gold & black, wood box, NOT MET	NIB	$358.00	3-1999
Abu	75	75th Anniversary, wood box & goodies NOT MET	NIB	$243.00	5-2000
Abu	136	spin casting reel	EX	$20.00	1-1999
Abu	170		NIB	$89.00	8-2001
Abu	222		VG	$200.00	4-1999
Abu	222	spin casting reel, ugly green, rinky dink	NIB	$212.50	12-1999
Abu	225	spinning reel	Mint	$290.00	12-1998
Abu	290		NIB	$56.00	3-1999
Abu	333	spin reel	EX-	$107.50	5-1999
Abu	444	black & grey	EX/IB	$207.50	3-1999
Abu	444	looks similar to Zebco Cardinal 4	EX	$76.00	10-2000
Abu	444	spinning reel	EX-	$90.00	12-1998
Abu	444A	service	EX	$204.00	8-2000
Abu	444A	spinning reel, looks like Cardinal	EX-	$202.00	12-1998
Abu	500DLX	deluxe, wood box, NOT MET	EX/IB	$738.00	3-1999
Abu	501	nice box	NIB	$152.00	9-2000
Abu	501	spin casting reel, underslung	EX/IB	$177.50	3-1999
Abu	503	closed-face spinning reel, underslung	NIB	$405.00	1-2000
Abu	503	spin casting reel	EX	$73.00	5-1999
Abu	503	spin casting reel, black & gold, underslung	Mint	$147.50	1-1999
Abu	505		EX	$79.00	7-2000
Abu	505		EX	$112.50	3-1999
Abu	505		EX+	$202.50	3-1999
Abu	505		VG	$153.50	3-1999
Abu	505	closed-face spinning reel, underslung	EX-	$213.50	3-1999
Abu	505	spin casting reel, black & red	EX-	$122.50	1-1999
Abu	505	spin casting reel, black & red, underslung	EX-	$130.00	1-1999
Abu	505	spin casting reel, underslung	NM	$190.00	12-1998
Abu	506		EX	$83.00	7-2000
Abu	506		EX	$128.50	3-1999
Abu	506		VG	$86.00	5-2000
Abu	506	spin casting reel	EX-	$52.00	5-1999
Abu	506	spin casting reel, underslung	EX	$76.00	8-1999
Abu	506M		Mint	$202.50	1-1999
Abu	506M	closed-face spinning reel, underslung	EX/IB	$179.00	4-2000
Abu	507		EX	$183.50	4-1999
Abu	507	blue box	NIB	$190.00	9-1999
Abu	507	spin casting reel, black & silver?, underslung	EX-	$126.00	1-1999

BRAND	MODEL / SERIES	DESCRIPTION	GRADE	PRICE	DATE
Abu	507	spin casting reel, oiler & goodies	VG/IB	$154.50	6-1999
Abu	520	closed-face spinning reel	EX-	$79.00	8-1999
Abu	1000	stainless steel, modern	EX	$102.50	1-1999
Abu	1000	white, single-knob	NIB	$108.00	9-2000
Abu	1000C	black, modern	EX-	$47.00	1-1999
Abu	1044	closed-face spinning reel, extra spool & goodies	NIB	$123.50	6-1999
Abu	1044	spin casting reel, underslung	EX-	$54.00	1-1999
Abu	1500C		EX	$114.50	8-1999
Abu	1500C		NIB	$232.00	5-1999
Abu	1500C	all goodies	NIB	$193.50	6-1999
Abu	1500C	case	EX	$192.45	3-1999
Abu	1500C	NOT MET	EX	$113.00	7-1999
Abu	1500C	NOT MET	EX-	$85.00	1-2000
Abu	1500C	serial number 771200, goodies	NIB	$293.00	6-2002
Abu	1500(C?)	silver	EX-	$125.00	3-1999
Abu	1500CDLX	deluxe, black & gold, wood box, NOT MET	NIB	$860.00	3-2001
Abu	1750	clicker broke	EX	$151.50	9-1999
Abu	1750	free spool reel red	EX-	$50.00	6-1999
Abu	1750A		EX	$97.00	9-1999
Abu	1750A		Mint	$165.83	5-1999
Abu	1750A		VG	$51.00	5-1999
Abu	1750A	free spool reel	EX+	$91.00	8-2002
Abu	2000		EX	$150.00	9-1999
Abu	2000		Mint	$187.50	5-1999
Abu	2000	direct drive	EX-	$114.00	9-2001
Abu	2050	narrow spool, pouch	VG	$150.00	1-1999
Abu	2050	nice box & goodies	NM/IB	$333.00	6-1999
Abu	2050	pouch	EX	$117.56	2-1999
Abu	2500	direct drive	EX-	$277.00	9-2001
Abu	2600	free spool reel, SD, red & white spacers	EX-	$140.00	1-1999
Abu	2650		EX	$177.50	8-1999
Abu	3000		VG+	$35.00	8-2001
Abu	3000	brown	EX	$222.50	6-1999
Abu	2100 Sport		EX/IB	$311.99	6-1999
Abu	2500C		EX	$83.00	3-1999
Abu	2500C		EX	$102.50	1-1999
Abu	2500C		EX	$110.00	5-1999
Abu	2500C		EX-	$67.00	7-2000
Abu	2500C		EX-	$105.49	6-1999
Abu	2500C		Mint	$122.50	2-1999
Abu	2500C		NIB	$171.00	7-1999
Abu	2500C		NIB	$183.55	3-1999
Abu	2500C		VG	$102.50	3-1999
Abu	2500C		VG	$127.50	12-1998
Abu	2500C	2 pearl	EX	$135.00	12-1998
Abu	2500C	all goodies	NIB	$276.01	2-1999
Abu	2500C	all goodies	NIB	$305.00	12-1998
Abu	2500C	box, case & parts	EX/IB	$172.00	9-1999

BRAND	MODEL / SERIES	DESCRIPTION	GRADE	PRICE	DATE
Abu	2500C	near mint	EX+	$152.50	1-1999
Abu	2500C	NOT MET	EX	$71.00	4-2000
Abu	2500C	NOT MET	EX-	$114.00	9-2000
Abu	2500C	pouch	Mint	$256.80	1-2000
Abu	2500C	silver	EX	$83.00	3-1999
Abu	2500(C?)	short twin handle	EX-	$147.50	11-1999
Abu	3500C	modern	NIB	$150.00	1-1999
Abu	3500C	modern, no-knob	EX	$92.00	12-1998
Abu	3500C	silver, modern, no-knob	EX	$107.49	2-1999
Abu	4000	red	EX	$138.50	6-1999
Abu	4000	suede pouch & goodies, nice	EX	$157.50	1-1999
Abu	4000D		EX	$222.00	9-2000
Abu	4000D		EX	$234.00	3-1999
Abu	4000D		EX	$325.00	11-1999
Abu	4000D		EX+	$261.00	10-2000
Abu	4000D		EX-	$193.00	1-1999
Abu	4000D		Mint	$285.00	4-2000
Abu	4000D		VG	$45.00	4-1999
Abu	4000D		VG	$91.00	7-1999
Abu	4000D		VG	$138.50	4-1999
Abu	4000D		VG	$150.01	8-1999
Abu	4000D		VG	$242.50	1-1999
Abu	4000D		VG+	$167.00	10-2000
Abu	4000D		VG+	$169.50	4-1999
Abu	4000D		VG+	$200.00	11-2001
Abu	4000D	bad boat rash	AVG	$162.50	2-1999
Abu	4000D	bad boat rash, NOT MET	VG-	$152.00	4-1999
Abu	4000D	boat rash	VG-	$112.50	5-1999
Abu	4000D	bronze	EX-	$192.00	8-2000
Abu	4000D	brown	VG+	$107.00	5-2001
Abu	4000D	copper	EX-	$152.00	4-2000
Abu	4000D	copper	EX-	$165.00	10-1999
Abu	4000D	double black handle	Mint	$436.00	1-1999
Abu	4000D	not really gold	VG+	$183.00	2-2002
Abu	4000D	NOT MET	G	$77.00	5-2000
Abu	4000D	papers	EX+/IB	$520.00	1-2000
Abu	4500		VG	$172.51	7-1999
Abu	4500	NOT MET	Mint	$212.00	11-2001
Abu	4500	red	EX-	$200.00	9-2000
Abu	4500	red	EX-	$206.00	9-2000
Abu	4500	red	EX	$225.01	8-1999
Abu	4500	red	EX+	$356.02	6-1999
Abu	4500	red	Mint	$263.00	10-1999
Abu	4500	red, 3-screw, pouch	EX	$228.00	8-2000
Abu	4500	red, power handle	EX	$261.99	11-1999
Abu	4500C	modern	EX	$45.95	2-1999
Abu	4500C		EX	$105.00	3-2000
Abu	4500C		NIB	$280.00	3-1999

BRAND	MODEL / SERIES	DESCRIPTION	GRADE	PRICE	DATE
Abu	4500C		NIB	$371.00	11-1999
Abu	4500C		VG+	$125.50	3-1999
Abu	4500C		VG-	$71.00	6-1999
Abu	4500C	spare spool	EX-	$127.50	6-1999
Abu	4500C	x2, both with spare spools	EX	$255.00	3-1999
Abu	4500CB	box	EXIB	$76.53	2-1999
Abu	4500CS	modern	NIB	$136.60	3-1999
Abu	4500D	green, NOT MET	Mint	$510.00	2-2002
Abu	4600C	black with red thumb bar	EX	$303.00	1-1999
Abu	4600C	newer type	NIB	$41.01	12-1998
Abu	4600C	red thumb bar	EX	$204.50	11-1999
Abu	4600C	red thumb bar, box & papers	VG+/IB	$255.50	2-1999
Abu	4600C	red thumb bar, goodies	EXIB	$132.50	7-1999
Abu	4600CB	red, smooth side, NOT MET	EX	$43.00	10-2000
Abu	4600CS	NOT MET	EX	$102.50	1-1999
Abu	5000		VG	$44.52	12-1998
Abu	5000		VG	$50.00	1-1999
Abu	5000	3-screw	VG	$67.00	1-1999
Abu	5000	3-screw, all accessories	NM	$176.00	1-1999
Abu	5000	2 pearl handles, 4-screw, case	VG	$60.00	12-1998
Abu	5000	3-screw, 2 black handles, boat rash	VG	$95.00	12-1998
Abu	5000	3-screw, case & goodies	VG	$55.55	1-1999
Abu	5000	3-screw, case & goodies, mint	NIC	$212.50	2-1999
Abu	5000	3-screw, case, double-knob handle	VG	$115.50	2-1999
Abu	5000	3-screw, double-knob handle	VG+	$81.00	1-1999
Abu	5000	3-screw, pretty	EX	$43.50	11-1999
Abu	5000	4-screw	Mint	$129.00	10-2000
Abu	5000	4-screw	VG	$81.05	2-1999
Abu	5000	4-screw, broken handle	EX	$46.00	1-1999
Abu	5000	4-screw, case	EX	$168.51	12-1998
Abu	5000	4-screw, case, oil hole, nice	EX/IB	$50.00	8-1999
Abu	5000	4-screw, case, parts & oiler	Mint	$182.50	3-1999
Abu	5000	4-screw, goodies	NIB	$456.00	7-1999
Abu	5000	4-screw, goodies & pouch	NIP	$158.00	10-2000
Abu	5000	4-screw, NOT MET	EX/IB	$230.00	6-1999
Abu	5000	4-screw, oil holes, goodies	EX/IP	$184.50	5-1999
Abu	5000	4-screw, pouch	EX	$348.00	7-2000
Abu	5000	4-screw, smooth sides	AVG	$42.00	1-1999
Abu	5000	pearl double-knob handle, 4-screw, goodies & case	NIC	$167.50	3-1999
Abu	5000	handles: 2 red, 2 pearl, 1 black	VG	$82.00	12-1998
Abu	5000	pearl, 3-screw, double-knob handle, all accesories	NM	$200.75	1-1999
Abu	5000	pouch	EX-/IP	$80.00	8-2000
Abu	5000	pearl double-knob handle, 4-screw, accessories	EX	$187.00	1-1999
Abu	5000	pearl double-knob handle, 4-screw, goodies	EX	$197.00	1-1999
Abu	5000	pearl double-knob handle, 4-screw, pouch & accessories	EX/IP	$128.00	10-2000

BRAND	MODEL / SERIES	DESCRIPTION	GRADE	PRICE	DATE
Abu	5000	case & all goodies, mint	NIB	$231.49	4-1999
Abu	5000	case & goodies only	EX	$51.00	2-1999
Abu	5000	case & parts tube	EX	$143.00	1-2001
Abu	5000	double-knob handle	VG	$87.00	12-1998
Abu	5000	Garcia, black label, no goodies	NIB	$150.00	4-1999
Abu	5000	pearl double-knob handle, 3-screw, case & goodies	Mint	$201.00	12-1999
Abu	5000	pearl double-knob handle, 3-screw, goodies, NOT MET	NIP	$95.00	4-2000
Abu	5000	pearl double-knob handle, 4-screw, case, catalog	EX+	$165.50	11-1999
Abu	5000	pearl double-knob handle, 4-screw, goodies	VG	$115.00	1-1999
Abu	5000	single handle	VG	$41.00	12-1998
Abu	5000	with case	EX	$75.00	1-1999
Abu	5000	with case	VG	$62.00	1-1999
Abu	5000	wrong handle	VG	$51.00	1-1999
Abu	5000A	2 pearl handles, box & goodies	EX/IB	$212.00	1-1999
Abu	5000A	3-screw	NIB	$285.01	5-1999
Abu	5000A	4-screw, all goodies	NIB	$380.00	6-1999
Abu	5000B	3-screw	EX-	$96.00	8-2000
Abu	5000B	3-screw, counter balance handle	VG+	$132.00	1-1999
Abu	5000B	3-screw, nice display box	NIB	$255.00	8-2001
Abu	5000C		EX-	$222.50	2-1999
Abu	5000C		VG	$78.02	2-1999
Abu	5000C		VG	$86.00	1-1999
Abu	5000C	047200, near mint	EX/IB	$152.50	2-2000
Abu	5000C	3-screw	VG+	$96.00	12-1998
Abu	5000C	4-screw, aluminum arbor, no Abu pouch	EX+/IP	$522.00	4-2001
Abu	5000C	4-screw, case & papers	NM	$360.00	3-1999
Abu	5000C	75th Anniversary, NOT MET	NIB	$153.03	3-1999
Abu	5000C	75th Anniversary, polished chrome	NIB	$250.00	3-1999
Abu	5000C	75th Anniversary, stainless steel	NIB	$225.00	12-1998
Abu	5000C	black	EX	$202.50	9-1999
Abu	5000C	black, case only, with parts	EX	$25.00	2-1999
Abu	5000C	black, works good	AVG	$33.00	1-1999
Abu	5000C	black, wrong handle	VG+	$85.00	1-1999
Abu	5000C	black, wrong handle	VG-	$62.00	1-1999
Abu	5000C	box & goodies	EX/IB	$212.50	5-1999
Abu	5000C	box & goodies	NIB	$355.00	7-1999
Abu	5000C	box & goodies, small rub on edge	EX/IB	$261.00	2-1999
Abu	5000C	case & goodies	Mint	$345.00	11-1999
Abu	5000C	counter balance handle	EX-	$112.50	12-1998
Abu	5000C	leather case included	VG	$132.00	1-1999
Abu	5000C	leather pouch	Mint	$355.00	3-1999
Abu	5000C	no goodies	Mint	$313.00	2-1999
Abu	5000C	papers	EX/IB	$232.50	7-1999
Abu	5000C	pouch, box & goodies	EX/IB	$179.51	1-1999
Abu	5000C	serial number 730402, nice	Mint	$142.00	6-2002

BRAND	MODEL / SERIES	DESCRIPTION	GRADE	PRICE	DATE
Abu	5000C	serial number 83983, papers	EX	$158.50	1-1999
Abu	5000C	wrong handle	EX	$128.50	12-1998
Abu	5000CDL	1996 version, wood box & goodies	NIB	$355.00	3-1999
Abu	5000CDL	box & goodies	NIB	$910.00	4-1999
Abu	5000CDL	no box, boat rash	VG	$445.00	2-1999
Abu	5000CDL	serial number 86-0 89-90, wood box & goodies	NIB	$406.60	2-2000
Abu	5000CDL	teak box & goodies, c.1990	NIB	$510.00	2-2000
Abu	5000CDL	wood box	EX/IB	$380.00	1-2001
Abu	5000CDL	wood box	NIB	$520.00	2-1999
Abu	5000CDL	wood box	NIB	$570.00	1-1999
Abu	5000CDL	wood box	NIB	$620.00	12-1999
Abu	5000CDL	wood box	NIB	$950.00	8-2000
Abu	5000CDL	wood box & all goodies	NIB	$710.00	5-1999
Abu	5000CDL	wood box & goodies	NIB	$355.00	6-2002
Abu	5000D		AVG	$56.00	12-1998
Abu	5000D		EX-	$91.00	12-1998
Abu	5000D		EX-	$103.50	8-1999
Abu	5000D		Mint	$244.85	11-1999
Abu	5000D		NIB	$256.00	11-2000
Abu	5000D		NIB	$305.00	3-1999
Abu	5000D		VG	$55.00	12-1998
Abu	5000D		VG	$66.50	1-1999
Abu	5000D		VG	$67.00	1-1999
Abu	5000D		VG	$70.00	3-1999
Abu	5000D		VG	$76.00	1-1999
Abu	5000D		VG+	$41.00	8-2000
Abu	5000D		VG-	$58.00	1-1999
Abu	5000D	3 handles only	VG	$38.50	1-1999
Abu	5000D	all goodies	NIB	$305.00	8-1999
Abu	5000D	blue & teal	VG+	$273.45	11-1999
Abu	5000D	box & goodies	NIB	$356.00	4-2000
Abu	5000D	case & parts	VG	$87.50	12-1998
Abu	5000D	champagne color	EX-	$710.00	7-2002
Abu	5000D	double pearl handle, click	VG	$81.00	1-1999
Abu	5000D	gold, papers	NIB	$2,850.00	11-1999
Abu	5000D	green	EX-	$136.00	1-2001
Abu	5000D	green, NOT MET	NIB	$178.00	9-2002
Abu	5000D	minor boat rash	VG+	$66.00	4-1999
Abu	5000D	NOT MET	EX	$139.00	4-1999
Abu	5000D	pouch & box	NIB	$187.00	3-2001
Abu	5000D	ragged box	EX/IB	$130.00	6-1999
Abu	5000DLX	deluxe, a little ugly	VG-	$330.00	3-1999
Abu	5000DLX	deluxe, all goodies but reel is rough	AVG/IB	$255.00	6-1999
Abu	5000DLX	deluxe, black & gold, boat rash	VG	$197.00	10-2000
Abu	5000DLX	deluxe, in box with goodies	EX/IB	$711.00	5-1999
Abu	5000DLX	deluxe, level wind worn, looks decent	VG?	$169.50	7-1999
Abu	5000DLX	deluxe, some roughness	EX	$601.00	1-1999
Abu	5000DLX	deluxe, wood box & all goodies	NIB	$910.00	11-2000

BRAND	MODEL / SERIES	DESCRIPTION	GRADE	PRICE	DATE
Abu	5000DLX	deluxe, wood box & goodies, NOT MET	EX/IB	$810.00	4-2000
Abu	5001C		EX	$96.00	3-1999
Abu	5001C		EX-	$104.00	3-2001
Abu	5001C		NIB	$315.00	5-1999
Abu	5001C		VG	$120.00	10-2000
Abu	5001C		VG	$152.50	1-1999
Abu	5001C	3-screw	EX/IB	$125.00	8-2000
Abu	5001C	4 used reels	VG	$455.00	2-1999
Abu	5001C	black	EX-	$84.00	6-2001
Abu	5001C	goodies	EX/IP	$368.50	1-2000
Abu	5001C	pouch	EX	$162.00	7-2000
Abu	5500	bronze	EX-	$172.00	8-2001
Abu	5500	bronze	VG+	$307.50	6-1999
Abu	5500	bronze, goodies	EX/IB	$395.00	8-2001
Abu	5500	brown	EX	$255.00	10-2000
Abu	5500	brown	EX-	$222.50	3-2000
Abu	5500	brown	EX-	$268.00	4-2001
Abu	5500	brown	NIB	$610.00	4-2000
Abu	5500	brown	NM	$341.66	3-1999
Abu	5500	brown	VG	$127.50	4-1999
Abu	5500	brown	VG-	$242.49	1-2000
Abu	5500	brown, a lot of boat rash	Fair	$81.00	1-1999
Abu	5500	brown, case	EX-	$370.00	10-1999
Abu	5500	brown, pouch & papers	Mint	$405.00	9-2000
Abu	5500	gold, NOT MET	EX	$1,274.99	12-1998
Abu	5500	maroon	VG+	$204.00	11-2001
Abu	5500	serial number 760301, maroon	EX	$376.00	9-1999
Abu	5500	red	EX	$167.50	3-1999
Abu	5500	red	EX	$233.50	3-1999
Abu	5500	red	EX	$256.00	11-1999
Abu	5500	red	EX	$415.00	11-1999
Abu	5500	red	EX/IB	$371.00	8-2001
Abu	5500	red	NIB	$700.00	2-2002
Abu	5500	red	VG	$202.49	6-1999
Abu	5500C	Abu Garcia box, no goodies	NIB	$518.99	4-1999
Abu	5500C	black	EX-	$89.00	2-1999
Abu	5500C	black	EX-	$207.50	2-1999
Abu	5500C	blue & grey	NIB	$820.00	12-1999
Abu	5500C	case & goodies	EX-	$168.50	4-1999
Abu	5500C	power handle	EX-	$95.99	2-1999
Abu	5500C	rough	AVG	$46.01	3-1999
Abu	5500C	serial number 730401	EX-	$154.00	2-2001
Abu	5500C	serial number 771103, goodies	NIB	$338.00	6-2002
Abu	5500C	serial number 790303, goodies	NIB	$283.00	6-2002
Abu	5500C	serial number 800804, black, goodies	NIB	$380.00	6-2002
Abu	5500C	silver	Rough	$61.00	12-1998
Abu	5500C	x2, both steel blue	EX	$800.00	2-1999
Abu	5500C		EX-	$160.00	7-2000

BRAND	MODEL / SERIES	DESCRIPTION	GRADE	PRICE	DATE
Abu	5500C		EX-	$56.00	6-1999
Abu	5500C		Mint	$182.00	8-2001
Abu	5500C		VG	$103.38	12-1998
Abu	5500C		VG+	$162.50	4-1999
Abu	5500CDL	teak box	NIB	$4,000.00	2-2002
Abu	5500D	green	EX	$225.00	10-2002
Abu	5500D	NOT MET	EX-/IB	$212.50	8-1999
Abu	5500D	serial number 771100	EX	$202.52	1-1999
Abu	5600C	red thumb bar	EX	$96.00	4-1999
Abu	5600C	red thumb bar	EX	$127.50	3-1999
Abu	5600C	red thumb bar	VG	$71.00	7-1999
Abu	5600C	red thumb bar	VG+	$112.50	4-1999
Abu	5600C	red thumb bar	VG-	$103.49	3-1999
Abu	5600C	red thumb bar, rebuilt	VG	$135.00	12-1998
Abu	5600CDL	662/1000, fancy box	NIB	$350.00	4-1999
Abu	5600CDL	795/1000, fancy box, modern	NIB	$197.50	4-1999
Abu	6000		VG	$51.00	12-1998
Abu	6000	3-screw	EX	$90.99	9-1999
Abu	6000	3-screw, case	EX	$191.00	1-1999
Abu	6000	4-screw	EX	$80.00	12-1998
Abu	6000	4-screw	EX	$95.00	12-1998
Abu	6000	4-screw, box & pouch	EX/IB	$97.50	1-1999
Abu	6000	4-screw, case	EX	$150.00	3-1999
Abu	6000	4-screw, leather case & box	EX/IB	$91.00	12-1998
Abu	6000	a lot of rubs	G	$37.00	2-1999
Abu	6000	case, parts & box	EX	$66.00	12-1998
Abu	6000	counter balance handle	EX-	$80.00	1-1999
Abu	6000	counter balance handle, 4-screw, case & goodies	EX/IB	$150.00	3-1999
Abu	6000	counter balance handle, 4-screw, goodies	NIP	$302.00	3-2001
Abu	6000	no serial number	VG-	$58.00	3-1999
Abu	6000	round ball handle, 4-screw, papers & mint goodies	NIB	$346.00	10-2000
Abu	6000	serial number 020902, 4-screw, old counter balance handle	EX	$96.00	2-1999
Abu	6000	service	EX	$315.00	8-2000
Abu	6000C		EX+	$182.50	3-1999
Abu	6000C		NIB	$328.00	3-1999
Abu	6000C	3-screw, NOT MET	EX	$61.00	10-2001
Abu	6000C	black	VG+	$61.00	9-2000
Abu	6000C	black	Mint	$225.35	2-1999
Abu	6000C	box & all goodies	NIB	$268.00	3-2000
Abu	6000C	case only, goodies	Mint	$50.00	3-1999
Abu	6000C	red?, 4-screw, DP & counter balance handle	EX	$107.49	2-1999
Abu	6001C		VG	$102.51	5-1999
Abu	6001C	1987 model	NIB	$142.79	4-1999
Abu	6001C	serial number 87	NIB	$129.50	1-2000
Abu	6500	brown, in nice box	NIB	$670.00	9-2002
Abu	6500	red	NIB	$355.00	7-1999

BRAND	MODEL / SERIES	DESCRIPTION	GRADE	PRICE	DATE
Abu	6500	red, counter balance handle, 3-screw	Mint	$455.00	2-1999
Abu	6500	serial number 700201, red, high speed	EX-	$265.00	12-2001
Abu	6500C		EX	$168.00	12-1998
Abu	6500C		EX/IB	$107.50	3-1999
Abu	6500C	750902, pouch & goodies	EX/IP	$310.00	9-2000
Abu	6500C	black?	NIB	$366.00	12-1998
Abu	6500C	box, pouch & all goodies	NIB	$357.00	3-2001
Abu	6500C	silver?, box & goodies	NIB	$416.50	2-1999
Abu	6500C	serial number 730801	EX	$229.00	6-2002
Abu	6500C	silver	EX-	$144.50	1-1999
Abu	6500C	pouch	EX	$168.30	2-1999
Abu	6500C	purple & silver	EX-	$330.00	2-2000
Abu	6500C3	bubble pack	NOC	$65.00	1-1999
Abu	6500C3	left-handed	EX	$63.51	1-1999
Abu	6600C	red thumb bar	VG+	$285.00	1-2001
Abu	6600CL	click	EX	$71.00	1-1999
Abu	7000		EX	$98.00	2-1999
Abu	7000		NIB	$207.50	5-1999
Abu	7000		NM	$271.00	1-1999
Abu	7000		VG+	$91.00	2-1999
Abu	7000	box & papers	VG	$118.49	1-1999
Abu	7000	disassembled, parts only	VG	$76.98	2-1999
Abu	7000	green, "Pro Shop"	NIB	$177.50	3-1999
Abu	7000	maroon	Mint	$93.79	1-1999
Abu	7000	NOT MET	NIB	$132.00	8-2001
Abu	7000	red	EX-	$87.00	1-1999
Abu	7000C	black, NOT MET	NIB	$96.00	9-2000
Abu	7000C	synchronized, modern	NIB	$134.24	3-1999
Abu	8000	red, 3-speed	EX	$227.00	8-2001
Abu	8600		EX	$122.00	8-2001
Abu	8600	deep sea	EX	$136.00	10-2000
Abu	10000C		NIB	$197.00	8-2001
Abu	10000CDL	goodies	NIB	$400.00	3-2001
Abu	Ambassadeur 8600		VG+	$152.00	3-2001
Abu	Abu-Matic 80	small dent, screws & box	VG/IB	$51.00	3-1999
Abu	Abu-Matic 120	NOT MET	EX	$18.00	1-1999
Abu	Abu-Matic 120 Ultra-Mag XL 1V	serial number 850100	Mint	$151.00	6-2002
Abu	Abu-Matic 170		NIB	$102.50	3-1999
Abu	Abu-Matic 170	NOT MET	EX	$20.50	1-1999
Abu	Abu-Matic 1075		EX-	$31.00	4-1999
Abu	Ambassadeur	Anniversary, chrome, NOT MET	NIB	$256.00	8-2000
Abu	Ambassadeur 30	leather case & papers	NIB	$158.05	7-1999
Abu	Cardinal 3		Mint	$224.00	1-1999
Abu	Cardinal 3	beige & black, spool, all goodies	NIB	$215.00	4-1999
Abu	Cardinal 3	brown	EX	$190.00	7-1999
Abu	Cardinal 3	grey & black, spool	EX	$224.50	1-1999
Abu	Cardinal 3	spare spool, box & goodies	EX/IB	$187.50	8-1999

BRAND	MODEL / SERIES	DESCRIPTION	GRADE	PRICE	DATE
Abu	Cardinal 4		AVG	$71.00	9-1999
Abu	Cardinal 4		EXIB	$152.50	10-1999
Abu	Cardinal 4		Mint	$157.50	1-2000
Abu	Cardinal 4	beige frame, black rotor	EX+	$204.49	6-1999
Abu	Cardinal 4	beige frame, black rotor	EX-	$122.50	6-1999
Abu	Cardinal 4	crisp box & goodies	NIB	$97.00	6-2001
Abu	Cardinal 4X	beige & dark brown	VG	$195.00	4-1999
Abu	Cardinal 4X	grey, maroon rotor	EX	$198.00	3-2001
Abu	Cardinal 4X	rare	EX	$132.51	8-1999
Abu	Cardinal 4X	spare spool, goodies & crisp box	NIB	$311.00	5-2001
Abu	Cardinal 6		VG	$76.00	1-1999
Abu	Cardinal 6	similar to Zebco, papers	NIB	$250.00	10-2001
Abu	Cardinal 33	1 type 750100	EX	$202.50	8-1999
Abu	Cardinal 33	2 type 750600s	NIB	$180.50	8-1999
Abu	Cardinal 33	3 type 761000s	NIB	$204.50	8-1999
Abu	Cardinal 33	oiler, spool & goodies	EX/IB	$100.00	4-2000
Abu	Cardinal 33	rough box, NOT MET	Mint	$151.00	4-2000
Abu	Cardinal 33	spare spool	NIB	$94.00	9-2000
Abu	Cardinal 33	spin casting reel, like Zebco	EX	$89.55	5-1999
Abu	Cardinal 40		NIB	$155.40	2-2000
Abu	Cardinal 40		VG/IB	$81.00	11-2000
Abu	Cardinal 40	blue & white	EX	$67.00	7-2000
Abu	Cardinal 44	express, rare UK Tournament Special	NIB	$467.00	11-2000
Abu	Cardinal 44	serial number 37200	EX	$168.50	9-1999
Abu	Cardinal 44	spin casting reel	VG+	$93.00	5-1999
Abu	Cardinal 54	nice box & goodies	NIB	$107.00	4-2000
Abu	Cardinal 55	skirted spool	EX	$49.50	8-1999
Abu	Cardinal 60		NIB	$191.40	1-2000
Abu	Cardinal 60A	brown & black	EX	$116.50	1-1999
Abu	Cardinal 66	spare spool	NIB	$135.05	8-1999
Abu	Cardinal 77		EX/IB	$102.50	10-1999
Abu	Cardinal 77	cream & green, NOT MET	Mint	$66.00	10-2000
Abu	Cardinal 77	spare spool	NIB	$142.50	8-1999
Abu	Cardinal 77X		VG	$57.99	6-1999
Abu	Cardinal 77X	goodies	NIB	$152.00	2-2000
Abu	Cardinal 77X	NOT MET	EX-	$77.00	1-1999
Abu	Cardinal 154	spin casting reel		$38.50	1-1999
Abu	Cardinal 154	spin reel	Mint	$61.00	5-1999
Abu	Cardinal 157	Garcia	EX	$61.50	4-1999
Abu	Cardinal 222	spinning reel, green	VG	$217.50	6-1999
Abu	Cardinal 753		NIB	$32.00	1-1999
Abu	Cardinal C4X		EX	$86.02	3-1999
Abu	Cardinal C4X	spare spool	NIB	$101.00	8-2001
Abu	CT Mag-Elite 6500C3		NIB	$130.50	1-1999
Abu	Diplomat 178		VG	$76.00	6-1999
Abu	Diplomat 601M	spin casting reel	NIB	$36.00	5-1999
Abu	Fast Cast 1	spin casting reel	NIB	$52.99	5-1999
Abu	Morrum MM	wood box & goodies	NIB	$310.00	6-2002

BRAND	MODEL / SERIES	DESCRIPTION	GRADE	PRICE	DATE
Abu	Record 600	spin casting reel	VG	$192.50	7-1999
Abu	Record 1800A	NOT MET	VG	$91.00	1-1999
Abu	Record 1800C	bag & box	EX-/IB	$93.00	8-1999
Abu	Record 5000	paperwork & goodies, very nice	NIB	$548.00	11-1999
Abu	Record Flyer 3000	great access, box, spool in tube, etc.	NIB	$736.00	9-2000
Abu	Record Sport 2100	narrow spool	VG+	$237.50	6-1999
Abu	Record Standard	nice box	NIB	$228.50	8-1999
Abu	T6600CL	Tournament	NIB	$91.00	1-1999
Abu	Various	one 5001C & one 6001C, NOT MET	EX-	$1,625.00	8-1999
Abu-Garcia	Ambassadeur 30	saltwater & goodies	EX/IB	$158.05	7-1999
Airex		Lionel 12-pack, spool & nice box	NIB	$212.00	8-2000
Airex	Larchmont	Lionel pouch & goodies	NIB	$141.50	3-2000
Airex	Larchmont	parts, all goodies & mint box	NIB	$107.00	12-1998
Airex	Larchmont	spin reel	EX-	$15.00	8-2001
Airex	Vagabond	Lionel pouch & goodies	EX/IB	$44.00	8-2001
Alcedo	2C		AVG	$36.00	12-1998
Alcedo	2CS	spin reel, Italy	EX-	$50.00	8-2001
Alcedo	Micron		EX	$90.00	2-1999
Alcedo	Micron		EX-	$92.00	4-2000
Alcedo	Micron		NIB	$155.00	11-1999
Alcedo	Micron		VG	$63.75	1-1999
Alcedo	Micron	bent leg version, spare spool, 1946	EX	$320.00	2-2002
Alcedo	Micron	blue?	EX	$197.00	1-2002
Alcedo	Micron	box & goodies	EX/IB	$202.50	5-1999
Alcedo	Micron	pouch & spare spool	EX	$175.00	10-2000
Alcedo	Micron	nice box	EX/IB	$157.50	2-2000
Alcedo	Micron	nice box & papers	EX+/IB	$168.00	4-2000
Alcedo	Micron	nice box, papers & spare spool	NIB	$185.00	10-2000
Alcedo	Micron C4		EX-	$143.00	1-1999
Allcock	Aerial	3", ventilated spool, c.1910	EX-	$550.00	8-2002
Allcock	Aerial	4", ventilated narrow spool, trade mark, c.1920	EX	$610.00	8-2002
Allcock	Aerial	4", ventilated wide spool, no trade mark, c.1920	EX-	$545.00	8-2002
Allcock	Black Knight		EX/IB	$102.50	1-1999
Allcock	Pattern 9 Centerpin	made only in 1939	EX-	$484.00	9-2001
Allcock-Stanley		spin reel, early, ugly, NOT MET	VG+	$77.00	4-2000
Anthony		3½", German silver, S-handle, 250 yards	VG	$731.00	4-2000
Ari't Hart	F4	pouches & 2 spare spools, NOT MET	Mint	$365.00	9-2000
Arjon	Champion	red, leather pouch, Sweden, pretty	NIP	$830.00	10-2000
Arjon	Commander	gold	EX	$400.00	10-2000
Arjon	Commander	leather pouch, parts, tubes, papers	NIP	$355.00	8-2002
Arjon	Commander	pouch & goodies	NIP	$1,093.00	4-2001
Armax		bait casting reel, plain	VG	$63.00	1-1999
Ayers & Son	St. John's	fly reel, brass or German silver, pretty	EX	$77.00	1-2002
Bache Brown	Spinster Mark VI	spinning reel	EX-	$69.00	1-1999
Benjamin-Sellar	Thumzey	BCLW, missing end cap	EX	$750.00	8-2002
Bluegrass		casting, level wind, German silver, case, nice	EX	$385.00	-2000

BRAND	MODEL	SERIES / MFG. CODE / DESCRIPTION	GRADE	PRICE	DATE
Bogdan	3/0	3¾"	EX-	$921.00	2-2001
Bogdan		(50?), 3⅛" x 1⅛"	Mint	$1,725.00	9-2000
Bogdan	#1 Salmon	c.1977, NOT MET	EX-	$1,326.00	6-1999
Bogdan	Salmon Multiplier 1	NOT MET	EX	$1,225.00	4-2001
Bourne & Bond		Kentucky, nice	EX	$147.50	2-2000
Bradford Bradford &		fly reel, Boston, decent, NOT MET	VG+	$1,225.00	8-2001
Bronson	Coronet 25N	nice	EX	$62.00	7-1999
Bronson	Invader 26	ask price	EX	$350.00	1-2001
Car Gem	17	sealed bag	NIB	$45.00	8-1999
Carpenter Rod Co.		trout, 2⅜" x ½₁₂", beautiful	EX	$665.00	2-2002
Centaure		large spinning reel	EX-	$85.00	8-1999
Chamberlain, Cartridge & Target Co.	Hunter		VG	$310.00	3-1999
Chicago	Streamliner		EX	$100.00	6-1999
Chicago	Streamliner	metal side plate, nice case, NOT MET	EX/IC	$175.00	6-1999
Chicago	Streamliner	rod	VG	$115.00	4-1999
Chicago	Streamliner 1788	gentleman, no tip	VG	$200.00	4-1999
Chubb, T.M.		small fly reel, German silver, raised pillar, 1886 patent	VG+	$1,782.00	9-2002
Clerk		round ball-handle, nice toning	VG+	$381.00	5-2000
Clerk	4	2¼", n. silver, slightly filed foot	VG+	$760.00	8-2002
Coit		3 colors, your choice, crisp boxes	NIB	$199.00	3-2002
Conroy		2¾", counter-balance handle	VG	$155.00	4-2001
Conroy		bait casting reel, extended seat, simple, NOT MET	EX-	$351.00	1-2001
Conroy		brass casting reel, lots of honest wear, looks okay	G (6/7)	$410.00	8-2001
Conroy, Bissett & Malleson		fly reel, 4½", brown color	VG	$449.00	3-2000
Coptes	Mosquito Kid	spinning reel	EX	$153.50	6-1999
Coxe	10C	Bronson papers & goodies	NIB	$53.00	11-2001
Coxe	14/0	cradle, NOT MET	EX-	$761.00	10-1999
Coxe	15	serial number 36, pouch, paper	EX/IB	$360.00	9-2000
Coxe	25-2	German silver & bakelite	EX-	$98.00	2-1999
Coxe	25-2	tiny knob chip	EX	$104.38	2-1999
Coxe	25-3	German silver, nice marked pouch	EX/IP	$90.00	2-2002
Coxe	25-3	wood arbor	EX-	$57.00	7-1999
Coxe	25-23	silver & black	VG+	$183.00	1-1999
Coxe	25C	leather pouch, vg+ correct 2PCCB	EX/IB	$77.00	2-2002
Coxe	25N	narrow spool, pouch & box, NOT MET	NIB	$250.00	5-1999
Coxe	25N	pretty	EX	$57.00	3-2001
Coxe	25N	pretty	EX	$74.73	10-1999
Coxe	25N-2	German silver, nice case	EX	$214.50	1-1999
Coxe	30C	more modern style, nice box	NIB	$66.00	5-1999
Coxe	315L		VG	$53.88	1-1999
Coxe	950	500 yards, crisp box & papers, NOT MET	NIB	$102.00	8 2002
Coxe	36861	silver, rubber, beautiful, NOT MET	EX+	$611.02	3-2000
Coxe	Coronet 25	Bronson case	EX/IC	$40.00	8-1999
Coxe	Coronet 25	case	EX/IC	$47.76	7-1999

BRAND	MODEL	SERIES / MFG. CODE / DESCRIPTION	GRADE	PRICE	DATE
Coxe	Coronet 25	ex marked pouch	EX/IP	$60.00	8-2002
Coxe	Coronet 25	oiler, papers & leather pouch	EX/IP	$63.00	7-1999
Coxe	Invader	missing end cap	EX	$228.00	4-2001
Coxe	Invader 26	free spool reel, red & white	Mint	$409.00	9-2000
Coxe	Invader 26	free spool reel, star drag, red & white spacers	EX	$339.00	3-2001
Coxon	Aerial	3½", 4-spoke, NOT MET	EX	$870.00	8-2002
Cozzone		3", saltwater, German silver & rubber	EX-	$73.00	8-2000
Cozzone	36381	150 yards, German silver		$70.00	12-1999
Crack	300	nice box	NIB	$299.00	5-2001
D.A.M.	220		VG-	$29.50	2-1999
D.A.M.	238	spinning reel	EX	$78.75	2-1999
D.A.M.	250L	papers and box	EX/IB	$140.00	7-2000
D.A.M.	256 Automatic	spin casting reel, 10 bids	NIB	$776.00	3-2000
D.A.M.	270		NIB	$100.00	3-1999
D.A.M.	270	rough box & goodies	NIB	$80.00	1-1999
D.A.M.	330?	220?	NIB	$80.00	1-2001
D.A.M.	330	papers	EX	$27.00	10-2000
D.A.M.	330N	box & papers	EX/IB	$45.50	2-1999
D.A.M.	550		EX	$58.00	2-1999
D.A.M.	700B		NIB	$152.00	3-1999
D.A.M.	800B		EX	$83.00	9-2000
D.A.M.	1001	spare spool, spring, goodies	EX/IB	$76.01	6-1999
D.A.M.	1401	spare spool, spring, goodies	EX/IB	$71.01	6-1999
D.A.M.	4000	spin	EX-	$56.00	9-2000
D.A.M.	Effzeh 495	brass fly reel, NOT MET	EX-	$67.00	10-1999
D.A.M.	Quick 330		VG	$19.00	1-1999
D.A.M.	Quick Super 2-Speed	gear shift	EX-	$79.00	11-2001
Daiwa	Millionaire 3RM	box & papers	EX/IB	$43.50	1-1999
Daiwa	Millionaire 5HS	box & goodies	EX/IB	$83.00	5-2000
Daiwa	Millionaire II	500M 5.2:1	EX	$41.00	5-1999
Daiwa	TD1Hi	baitcasting reel	EX	$81.00	1-1999
Dingley		fly reel, 3", similar to Hardy Uniqua	EX-	$138.00	8-2001
Dingley		fly reel, 3", with silk line	Mint	$260.00	8-2002
Dreiser		built into wood handle, dated 1850, nice	EX-	$710.00	5-1999
Dukehart	Vom Hofe	3½", raised pillar, nice case	VG+	$211.50	6-1999
Eagle Claw		spinning reel, fair box	VG/IB	$56.00	2-1999
Emery John		tarpon fly reel, like Fin Nor	EX+	$279.00	11-2000
English		mahogany "trolling," wide casting reel, iron & wood, c.1770	EX-	$1,205.00	8-2002
Eppinger		bait casting reel, NOT MET	EX	$54.00	4-2000
Farlow		5½", wood & brass, reel seat signed	EX-	$130.00	7-2000
Farshure		spinning reel, weird looking	EX	$1,137.00	11-2001
Feurer Bros	Taurus 480	papers, 1975 receipt	NIB	$189.00	11-2000
Fin Nor		4", gold	EX-	$325.00	11-1999
Fin Nor	2.5/0	2.5/0	EX-	$466.01	3-1999
Fin Nor	2.5/0	2.5/0, retails for $1,669.00	EX	$405.00	1-1999
Fin Nor	3	spinning reel, NOT MET	EX	$207.00	1-1999
Fin Nor	3	wedding cake, NOT MET	EX	$860.00	10-2000

BRAND	MODEL	SERIES / MFG. CODE / DESCRIPTION	GRADE	PRICE	DATE
Fin Nor	4	fly reel, spare spool & goodies	NIB	$465.00	6-1999
Fin Nor	4C651	gold finish	Mint	$503.00	4-2001
Fin Nor	4.5/0	4.5/0, gold	EX-	$638.00	1-1999
Fin Nor	15/0	15/0, (German silver?), c.1938, NOT MET	EX-	$2,750.00	11-2000
Fin Nor	245		EX	$795.00	1-1999
Fin Nor	336		VG	$650.00	2-1999
Fin Nor	Ahab 8		EX	$124.17	1-1999
Fin Nor	CR45	fly reel, for 4, 5 & 6 lines	Mint	$152.00	1-1999
Fin Nor	Estima E.S. 200	new		$39.00	5-2001
Fin Nor	FR8		Mint	$311.00	5-2000
Fin Nor	FR10		Mint	$300.00	5-2000
Fin Nor	Lite S200	with rod	EX	$86.00	5-2001
Flo Line		pencil sharpener, looks new	Mint	$203.00	3-2002
Follett		fly reel, 3¾", open bird cage design	EX	$965.00	3-2000
Follett		fly reel, open Indiana style, ugly	VG+	$300.00	4-1999
Foss	3-25	NOT MET	EX	$406.00	10-2000
Fosters Ashbourne	Dingley D1	3¾", NOT MET	VG	$157.00	9-2002
Four Brothers	80 Delight	fly reel, German silver & hard rubber	EX-	$330.00	5-2000
Four Brothers	Delite	fly reel, bakelite nickel plate, brass rubbed	VG	$266.00	11-2001
Four Brothers	Delite	flyrod, hard rubber sides, bakelite, nickel plated brass	VG	$203.00	10-2001
Four Brothers	Sumco 2257	brass, nice	EX	$55.00	10-2001
Four Brothers	Sumco 2258		G	$35.00	1-1999
Fullilove, Frank	Crown	Kentucky style, c.1903, NOT MET	Mint	$3,550.00	2-2002
Garcia	408	in box	NM	$139.50	12-1998
Garcia	Abu 444	open-faced spinning reel	EX	$143.01	1-1999
Garcia	Abu Matic 40	nice box	EXIB	$46.60	1-1999
Garcia	Abu Matic 501	closed face spinning reel	NIB	$208.50	1-1999
Garcia	Cardinal 3	spool only	EX	$14.50	1-1999
Garcia	Mitchell 300	all goodies	NIB	$155.00	10-2000
Gates, George		salmon fly reel, 3½" x 1¼", tiny pictures, NOT MET	EX-	$1,058.00	2-2002
Gayle & Sons	3	Tournament, screw head broke off	VG	$1,335.00	11-1999
Gayle & Sons	3	aluminum pitted, NOT MET	VG	$810.00	12-1998
Go-Ite		5", agate, rough box & papers	EX/IB	$46.00	6-1999
Go-Ite		Indiana style	EX	$66.00	2-1999
Go-Ite		Indiana style, metal eye	EX-	$51.00	5-2000
Go-Ite		nice picture box	EX/IB	$129.01	5-1999
Great Lakes	Whirlaway		EX	$66.00	6-1999
Great Lakes	Whirlaway 75	papers	NIB	$66.00	9-2002
Grice & Young	Golden Eagle	4½"	EX	$74.00	11-2001
Grice & Young	Orlando Minor	manual side casting reel	EX/IB	$237.50	6-1999
H & I	Utica Automatic	fly reel, Little Finger, c.1912	VG	$162.50	10-1999
H & I	Vernely	fly reel, bakelite	NIB	$26.00	4-1999
Hardy		fly reel, Pfleuger Medalist type, dark brass, ivory handle, hand on rod trademark	VG-	$1,651.00	4-2001
Hardy		flyweight, in case	EX	$102.50	1-1999
Hardy		spinning reel, pouch, well used	VG-	$162.50	3-2000

BRAND	MODEL	SERIES / MFG. CODE / DESCRIPTION	GRADE	PRICE	DATE
Hardy	Altex 2 MK V	spinning reel	EX	$240.00	9-2001
Hardy	Bougle	3" aluminum	EX-	$2,000.00	6-2001
Hardy	Bougle	1998 re-issue, NOT MET	NIC	$306.75	6-1999
Hardy	Bougle Perfect	3¼", c.1921 – 1923	VG	$2,300.00	3-2000
Hardy	Cascapedia	4/0, marked case	EX/IC	$10,000.00	6-2001
Hardy	Cascapedia	4/0, salmon limited edition, NOT MET	NIB	$1,300.00	8-2002
Hardy	Duplicate Mark I	2⅞", well used		$278.00	1-1999
Hardy	Elarex	level wind bait casting, NOT MET	VG+	$114.00	6-2001
Hardy	Exalta	box and goodies	NIB	$224.50	1-1999
Hardy	LHR	light weight fly reel	VG	$84.00	1-1999
Hardy	LRH	trout	EX	$105.00	1-1999
Hardy	Perfect	2⅞", agate line guide	VG+	$610.00	9-2002
Hardy	Perfect	2⅞", box with plain paper label, ugly	EX-	$456.00	8-1999
Hardy	Perfect	2⅞", owned by "famous people," c.1923 – 1926	VG	$698.75	8-1999
Hardy	Perfect	3⅛", paint loss	VG	$319.00	1-1999
Hardy	Perfect	3⅝"	NIB	$530.00	8-1999
Hardy	Perfect	4", USA Duplicated Mark 2	EX	$330.00	3-1999
Hardy	Perfect	4", very nice box	EX/IB	$427.00	5-2000
Hardy	Perfect	50% loss of bluing	VG	$265.02	1-1999
Hardy	Perfect	fly reel, 2⅞", A&F, agate guide, spare pawl	EX-	$830.00	10-2000
Hardy	Perfect	missing agate line guide	VG	$588.00	4-2001
Hardy	Perfect Mark II	wide spool, c.1950, NOT MET	EX-	$242.50	5-1999
Hardy	Princess	3½", papers	Mint	$247.50	5-1999
Hardy	St. George Jr.	A&F, fancy case	EX	$1,032.00	10-2001
Hardy	St. John Spitfire	3⅞", NOT MET	VG+/IB	$307.00	1-1999
Hardy	Silex Major	4"	EX-	$384.00	12-1999
Hardy	Sunbeam	3", blue & cream box	NIB	$326.00	9-2000
Hardy	Sunbeam	lots of wear, NOT MET	VG	$177.00	8-2001
Hardy	Uniqua	2⅝", slight filing on foot, 1923	EX-	$260.00	2-1999
Hardy	Uniqua	3⅛", pre-1912	AVG	$305.00	2-2000
Hardy	Zenith	3⅝" x ⅝"	NIB	$127.50	8-1999
Harrington	350	modern design, NOT MET	EX	$51.00	10-2000
Heddon		automatic fly reel, rim rash, Banner box	EX-/IB	$95.00	10-1999
Heddon		baitcasting reel, no model number, level wind	EX-	$510.00	8-2002
Heddon	3-15	dull finish	EX	$180.00	10-1999
Heddon	3-15	German silver	EX	$270.00	10-1999
Heddon	3-15	Kentucky style, German silver	EX	$315.00	3-2002
Heddon	3-15	leather un pouch	EX	$225.00	4-2000
Heddon	3-25		EX	$291.00	4-2001
Heddon	3-25		EX-	$240.00	5-1999
Heddon	3-25	bag	VG+	$220.02	3-1999
Heddon	3-25	German silver	EX	$275.00	10-1999
Heddon	3-25	marked leather pouch, very nice	EX/IP	$350.00	1-2002
Heddon	3-30	magnesium spool, aluminum handle, white sapphire	EX+	$2,025.00	11-2001
Heddon	3-30	Tournament, NOT MET	EX	$765.00	2-2002
Heddon	3-30	unpolished German silver, jeweled, nice	EX	$750.00	3-2002
Heddon	3-30 ST	tournament handle	EX	$1,350.00	10-1999
Heddon	3-35	broken screw head	EX-	$155.00	7-1999

BRAND	MODEL	SERIES / MFG. CODE / DESCRIPTION	GRADE	PRICE	DATE
Heddon	3-35	dull finish	EX	$315.00	10-1999
Heddon	3-35	nice, NOT MET	EX	$227.50	5-1999
Heddon	3-35	NO BIDS	Mint	$222.22	10-1999
Heddon	3-35	prototype, extra bail & adjacent nut, NOT MET	EX	$505.00	8-2001
Heddon	3-35	satin	EX+	$307.00	7-1999
Heddon	3-35	Up Bass box	EX/IB	$511.00	2-2000
Heddon	4-18	click bad, replaced washer under screw		$2,450.00	10-1999
Heddon	35	NOT MET	EX	$382.00	12-1999
Heddon	40	Carter patents	EX	$950.00	10-1999
Heddon	45		EX	$257.00	4-2001
Heddon	45	Carter 1904 & 1905 patents, nice	EX	$336.00	11-2001
Heddon	45	Carter 1904 patent, NOT MET	VG	$212.00	6-2000
Heddon	45	Carter patents 1904 & 1905	EX	$580.00	10-1999
Heddon	45	Carter patents, take apart	EX-	$232.50	10-1999
Heddon	45	NOT MET	EX	$237.50	2-2000
Heddon	45	NOT MET	EX	$282.88	6-1999
Heddon	57	automatic fly reel, great Banner box	NIB	$87.00	10-2000
Heddon	100	spin casting reel	Mint	$86.00	12-1998
Heddon	105SS		EX	$100.00	8-2000
Heddon	152	spin casting reel	EX/IB	$20.50	1-1999
Heddon	236	spinning reel, box & papers	EX/IB	$37.17	12-1998
Heddon	236	spinning reel, box & papers	NIB	$37.00	12-1998
Heddon	320	fly reel & papers	NIB	$43.00	1-2001
Heddon	415	windshield wiper	EX	$2,680.00	10-1999
Heddon	450	trolling		$41.00	1-1999
Heddon	3200	box & all goodies	NIB	$202.50	5-1999
Heddon	3200 Mark IV	nice pouch	EX/IB	$76.00	8-2002
Heddon	Chief Dowagiac	nice box, great papers	EX-/IB	$224.00	3-1999
Heddon	Chief Dowagiac 4	nice box, papers	EX/IB	$335.00	3-2002
Heddon	Chief Dowagiac 4	nut buggered	VG+	$54.00	3-2001
Heddon	Dominator 420	Daisy, deep sea	NIB	$367.00	8-1999
Heddon	Heritage 35	pouch, goodies & paper	EX	$150.00	1-1999
Heddon	Heritage 30	2 hang tags, pouch	NIB	$310.00	11-2001
Heddon	Heritage 30	pouch	EX	$102.50	11-1999
Heddon	Heritage 30 Mark III	pouch & goodies, rubs	AVG	$86.00	1-1999
Heddon	Heritage 45	great box	NIB	$153.00	10-2000
Heddon	Imperial 125	fly reel, nice, NOT MET	EX	$179.00	7-2000
Heddon	Indian Chief 3	missing level wind & screw	?	$302.00	7-1999
Heddon	Lone Eagle 206	Down Bass box	NIB	$360.00	9-2000
Heddon	Lone Eagle 206	nice box	EX/IB	$255.00	8-2000
Heddon	Lone Eagle 206	ratty box	EX/IB	$71.00	5-2001
Heddon	Mark IV		EX	$75.00	4-2001
Heddon	Mark IV 3200		VG	$89.00	12-1998
Heddon	Mark IV 3200	box & all goodies	NIB	$265.00	1-1999
Heddon	P-41	bag & box	EX/IB	$86.00	3-2000
Heddon	P-41	black, papers	NIB	$77.00	9-2000
Heddon	P-41	black plate, removable ring, NOT MET	NIB	$154.00	8-2002
Heddon	P-41	black sides, pouch, crisp box	EX/IB	$86.00	3-2000

BRAND	MODEL	SERIES / MFG. CODE / DESCRIPTION	GRADE	PRICE	DATE
Heddon	P-41	gold	EX-	$56.00	5-1999
Heddon	P-41	gold, nice box	EX/IB	$178.00	1-2001
Heddon	P-41	silver, missing 2 screws	EX	$41.27	3-2000
Heddon	P-41N	narrow spool, black frame	EX	$41.05	8-1999
Heddon	Pal 25	pro-weight, gold	Mint	$86.00	9-2000
Heddon	Pal P-41	black, jeweled end caps	EX	$46.023	1-1999
Heddon	Pal Pro-weight 26	level wind, NOT MET	EX-	$54.00	4-2000
Heddon	Waltonian 31AB		EX	$344.00	4-2000
Heddon	White House 215	rough Up Bass box	VG/IB	$86.00	11-2000
Heddon	White House Angler		EX	$250.00	1-1999
Heddon	White House Angler	avg box, NOT MET	VG+/IB	$157.00	10-2000
Heddon	White House Angler	decent box	EX+/IB	$306.00	3-2001
Heddon	Winona 105-FF		VG	$40.00	9-1999
Heddon	Winona 105-SS	nice box & papers, extension piece	NIB	$256.00	4-2002
Heddon	Winona 108-48	picture box is a little rough	EX/IB	$50.00	3-2000
Hendryx	150	raised pillar, 1876, 1888, brass, silver gone	VG+	$100.00	4-2000
Hendryx	4907	80 yards, raised pillar	EX	$97.00	5-2000
Henshall	Van Antwerp	bait casting / fly reel, ugly design	EX-	$1,580.00	6-2001
Hermos	36381	250 yards, German silver		$38.88	12-1999
Herters		fly reel, unmarked D.A.M., single action	EX	$97.00	6-2000
Herters	703	fly reel	NIB	$227.50	2-2000
Herters	709	fly reel, box & goodies	NIB	$36.00	6-2001
Holzman		saltwater, German silver & rubber	EX	$3,050.00	10-2000
Horton	Bluegrass 3	NOT MET	EX-	$255.00	6-1999
Horton	Bluegrass 25 Simplex		EX	$460.00	4-1999
Horton-Bristol	10	level wind, German silver, gleamer	EX+	$391.00	5-2000
Horton Meek	3		NIB	$499.00	6-2001
Humpal	66	spin casting reel & Johnson 40	NIB	$164.00	12-1998
Hurd	Supercaster	2 stripped screws	VG	$75.00	1-2001
Hurd	Supercaster	case	VG	$255.00	3-1999
Hurd	Supercaster	in pouch	EX	$197.00	8-2001
Hurd	Supercaster	missing 2 screws, broken tip, case	AVG/IC	$100.00	3-2001
Hurd	Supercaster	no case, NOT MET	EX	$129.00	8-2000
Hurd	Supercaster	normal type?	EX	$305.00	4-2000
Hurd	Supercaster	pouch	NIP	$290.01	6-1999
Hurd	Supercaster	walnut, no rod tip	VG?	$193.38	4-1999
Hurd	Supercaster	with case	EX/IC	$150.00	2-2000
Hurd	Supercaster	with tip & case	EX-/IC	$150.00	7-2001
Hurd	Supercaster	wood	VG+	$119.00	10-1999
Hurd	Supercaster	wood, case	EXIC	$202.50	5-1999
Hurd	Supercaster	wood, case & vg box	NIB	$405.00	5-1999
Hurd	Supercaster	wood, NOT MET	EX	$178.00	2-1999
Hurd	Supercaster	wood, wrong handle	VG	$119.52	3-1999
J.T. Crouch & Sons	Tournament	beautiful, NOT MET	EX	$105.00	3-2001
Johnson	Fiskar	spin casting reel, underslung, nice display box & papers	NIB	$139.00	3-2002
Katchem		ice fishing, built-in, nice, NOT MET	EX-	$101.00	10-2000
Kilian	Neo Caster	crisp box & papers	NIB	$114.00	9-2000

BRAND	MODEL	SERIES / MFG. CODE / DESCRIPTION	GRADE	PRICE	DATE
Koph	Mills 3	December 16, 1981 patent embossed, foot sides, 1-piece	EX	$2,500.00	6-2001
Kosmic		300 yards, German silver & rubber, nice	EX	$121.50	3-2000
Kosmic		missing 2 screws	VG	$152.50	1-1999
Kovalovsky	16/0	type 2, NOT MET	EX+	$3,500.00	8-1999
Kovalovsky	245	type 2, grey	VG	$910.00	1-1999
Kovalovsky	36861	gold, some repairs, NOT MET	VG+	$1,805.00	3-2001
Kovalovsky	C	Tuna Club decal, NOT MET	Mint	$1,875.00	6-2001
Kozzone		deep sea, German silver	VG+	$99.00	6-1999
L & S	4610	(maybe spinning reel?), strange plastic, goodies	NIB	$535.00	12-2000
Lampson	LP1.5	fly reel, spare spool	Mint	$142.50	3-1999
Langley	Target 340	decent box	NIB	$210.00	3-2001
Langley	Target 340	green	VG+	$82.00	1-2002
Lasso		spinning reel, old & ugly, France	VG-	$74.00	4-2000
Lectro-Matic		spin casting reel, battery operated	EX	$75.00	1-1999
Lenz Machine Works		plastic & aluminum, strange with clear windows to view bearings	VG+	$315.00	2-2002
Leonard, H.L.		fly reel, German silver & brass, bi-metal	EX	$2,550.00	3-2000
Leonard, H.L.		fly reel, rubber & German silver silver, raised pillar, NOT MET	EX	$1,025.00	8-1999
Leonard Mills	44	fly reel, German silver, raised pillar, beautiful	EX	$1,260.00	8-2001
Lexington		Kentucky type	EX-	$330.59	6-1999
Luxor		spin reel	EX	$142.50	3-1999
Luxor		spinning reel	VG	$106.66	3-1999
Luxor		spinning reel, grey, initials scratched	VG-	$56.55	2-1999
Luxor		spinning reel, nice	EX-	$71.00	6-1999
Luxor	2	France	EX-	$112.00	8-2001
Luxor	3	spin reel, papers	EX/IB	$152.50	7-1999
Makoora	Big Game	Australia, 500 made	EX	$1,625.00	4-2000
Malloch		fly reel, ebonite, German silver, NOT MET	EX	$318.00	11-2000
Malloch		spinning reel, brass, rotating head, c.1884	EX-	$158.00	8-2001
Marine Record		spinning reel, Swiss	EX	$103.00	9-2000
Martin		fly reel, automatic, patent dates 1892 & 1895	VG+	$255.00	11-1999
Martin	72	big drag fly reel, fancy, papers	NIB	$75.00	6-2001
Marsters		ball type, brass, (c.1860s?), Brooklyn, New York	VG	$237.50	6-1999
Mascotte		spinning reel, blue & black	EX	$203.50	6-1999
Meek	3	beauty	EX	$361.00	4-2000
Meek	3	cork arbor, 2" x 1¹³⁄₁₆"	EX	$455.00	7-1999
Meek	3	Horton Manufacturing, balsa spool	EX	$325.51	2-2000
Meek	3	jeweled, click, drag	EX	$605.00	4-1999
Meek	3	tournament tri-handle	EX-	$430.76	2-199
Meek	7		EX-	$661.00	3-1999
Meek	25	Horton Manufacturing	EX	$250.00	8-2000
Meek	34	free spool reel, unpolished but decent	VG+	$202.00	10-2001
Meek	44	fly reel	AVG	$187.50	2-1999
Meek	55	fly reel, NOT MET	VG	$124.00	11-2000
Meek	Horton 2	jeweled end caps	EX	$685.00	9-1999
Meek	Bluegrass 25		EX-	$350.00	5-2001
Meek	Bluegrass 33	1905 Carter patent, $600.00, NOT MET	EX	$340.00	3-2001

BRAND	MODEL	SERIES / MFG. CODE / DESCRIPTION	GRADE	PRICE	DATE
Meek	Bluegrass 34	Horton Simplex free spool reel	VG	$180.00	8-2000
Meek & Sons	2	original patina	EX	$1,576.00	2-2001
Meek & Sons	4	filed seat, bent spool, NOT MET, okay		$310.00	2-2000
Meek & Sons	4	toned, looks nice	EX-	$701.00	8-2002
Meek & Sons	5	unmarked case, unpolished	EX	$1,100.00	9-2002
Meek & Sons	Bluegrass 3	3 o'clock	EX	$285.00	2-2002
Meek & Sons	Bluegrass 25		VG+	$358.00	1-1999
Meek & Sons	Bluegrass 25	"C" on foot	EX-	$350.00	5-1999
Meek & Sons	Bluegrass 33		VG	$200.00	2-1999
Meek & Sons	Bluegrass 33	Carter patent	EX	$267.00	4-1999
Meek & Sons	Bluegrass 33	NOT MET	VG	$177.50	6-1999
Meek, B. F.	6	c.1884	VG	$5,111.00	2-2002
Meek-Horton	4		EX	$382.88	7-1999
Meek-Horton	4	jeweled	EX	$405.00	6-1999
Meek-Horton	30	level wind, German silver, missing 1 screw	EX-	$158.00	5-2001
Meek-Horton	Bluegrass 3	2 clicks, NOT MET	EX	$306.00	7-1999
Meek-Horton	Bluegrass 3	NOT MET	EX	$295.00	2-2000
Meek-Horton	Tournament 3	1" spool, tiny handle, AL spool, NOT MET	EX-	$621.00	1-2002
Meek-Horton	Tournament 3	narrow spool, small handle, NOT MET	EX	$355.00	1-2001
Meek-Milam	1	foot filed	EX-	$3,412.00	10-2000
Meek-Milam	2	Lawrence Jones, NOT MET	EX	$3,000.00	1-2002
Meek-Milam	3	12 o'clock, 2 click, one replaced screw	EX-	$2,214.00	8-2001
Meek-Milam	4	brass	VG	$2,025.00	4-2000
Meisselbach		2½", unmarked, German silver & bakelite, pretty	EX	$167.50	6-1999
Meisselbach		automatic fly reel, 1914 patent	VG	$68.00	8-2000
Meisselbach		large, rubber & (German silver?)	EX-	$76.00	1-1999
Meisselbach	22	patented thumb brake	VG	$160.00	1-2002
Meisselbach	205	level wind, newer	NIB	$73.03	2-2000
Meisselbach	280	featherweight, open spool	VG+	$58.00	1-2001
Meisselbach	580	nice, NOT MET	EX+	$42.00	6-1999
Meisselbach	645	nice box	EX-/IB	$178.00	1-2001
Meisselbach	660	fly reel, automatic	EX/IB	$183.50	6-1999
Meisselbach	685	free spool, sapphire bearings, German silver, NOT MET	EX	$359.00	2-2002
Meisselbach	Expert	fly reel, plating loss, open design	VG	$157.00	7-2000
Meisselbach	Featherlight 260	fly reel	VG+	$53.00	8-2000
Meisselbach	Featherlight 260	nice box	NIB	$246.00	11-2001
Meisselbach	Flyer 645		EX	$148.45	8-1999
Meisselbach	Neptune	silver & bakelite	VG	$66.51	1-1999
Meisselbach	Rainbow 627	fly reel, nice box & paper	EX/IB	$322.00	8-2000
Meisselbach	Rainbow 631	fly reel, closed sides	VG+	$165.00	10-2000
Meisselbach	Rainbow 731	fly reel, all finish rubbed off	VG	$137.00	4-2000
Meisselbach	Ranger 130	in box	NIB	$227.75	3-1999
Meisselbach	Target 105	bait casting, cheap plastic, ratty box	EX/IB	$21.00	10-2000
Meisselbach	Tripart	Heddon Dowagiac	EX	$431.00	6-2001
Meisselbach	Tripart 580	1909 patent	EX	$61.00	1-1999
Meisselbach	Tripart 581	box & pocket catalog, nice	EX/IB	$141.00	2-1999
Meisselbach	Tripart 581	decent box	EX/IB	$87.00	3-2001

BRAND	MODEL	SERIES / MFG. CODE / DESCRIPTION	GRADE	PRICE	DATE
Meisselbach	Tripart 780	German Silver	EX	$381.00	1-2000
Mepps	Super Mecca		EX	$143.65	4-1999
Mepps	Super Mecca		VG+	$91.00	1-2001
Mepps	Super Mecca	box, papers & spare spool	EX/IB	$221.00	4-2000
Meyer, Lou	Flo-Line	pencil sharpener, rough paint	VG	$35.00	8-2001
Milam	2	wrong handle, nicely toned	EX	$1,225.00	4-2000
Milam	Rustic 3	drag does not work	VG	$416.88	4-1999
Milam & Son	5	large, NOT MET	EX-	$911.00	12-1998
Milam & Son	Kentucky Reel 5	Frankfort, Kentucky	VG+	$1,476.00	3-1999
Milam, B. C.	3	well used from picture	VG	$849.00	6-1999
Mills, William	2	Vom Hofe, saltwater, German silver, missing end cap	VG	$230.00	1-2001
Mitchell	300		EX-	$22.50	1-1999
Mitchell	300		EX-	$28.77	1-1999
Mitchell	300		NIB	$67.00	2-1999
Mitchell	300		VG	$23.00	1-1999
Mitchell	300	blue box & papers	EX/IB	$81.00	3-1999
Mitchell	300	box & ad	NIB	$43.00	1-1999
Mitchell	300	box & all goodies	NIB	$35.00	1-1999
Mitchell	300	clam box, no sleeve, all goodies	NIB	$78.00	6-2002
Mitchell	300	nice box	NIB	$42.50	12-1998
Mitchell	300	no bail spring	VG+	$23.50	12-1998
Mitchell	300	plastic box	NIB	$51.01	2-1999
Mitchell	300S	skirted, paper	NIB	$102.50	5-1999
Mitchell	301		VG/IB	$39.00	7-1999
Mitchell	302		EX-	$33.60	12-1998
Mitchell	302		VG	$32.02	1-1999
Mitchell	304	display box & crisp papers	NIB	$242.00	8-2001
Mitchell	304	manual	Mint	$82.00	4-1999
Mitchell	306		EX	$39.00	1-1999
Mitchell	308		EX-	$49.99	2-1999
Mitchell	308		EX-	$58.00	12-1998
Mitchell	308		EX	$58.00	2-1999
Mitchell	308		Mint	$56.00	5-1999
Mitchell	308		VG	$38.00	2-1999
Mitchell	308	mint box & goodies	NIB	$122.50	2-1999
Mitchell	308	NOT MET	EX	$52.55	2-2000
Mitchell	308	NOT MET	EX	$58.00	12-1998
Mitchell	308	spare spool	EX-	$31.00	2-1999
Mitchell	330		EX-	$32.00	1-1999
Mitchell	386		EX-	$50.00	12-1998
Mitchell	402	box & goodies	NIB	$169.50	1-1999
Mitchell	406	no goodies	NIB	$56.00	8-2001
Mitchell	408		EX	$84.77	4-1999
Mitchell	408		Mint	$118.00	2-2001
Mitchell	408		NIB	$83.00	3-2000
Mitchell	408		NM	$113.50	12-1998
Mitchell	408	308 box with papers	NIB	$122.51	5-1999
Mitchell	408	spare spool	EX	$85.00	2-1999

BRAND	MODEL	SERIES / MFG. CODE / DESCRIPTION	GRADE	PRICE	DATE
Mitchell	408	spare spool	VG+	$66.00	4-2000
Mitchell	408	spare spool, plastic clam box	NIB	$147.00	10-2001
Mitchell	409		EX	$65.00	1-1999
Mitchell	410	spare spool	EX	$46.00	1-1999
Mitchell	486	spin reel, extra large	EX	$100.00	1-1999
Mitchell	510	special rod needed	NM	$61.00	3-1999
Mitchell	510	with special rod, reel only fits this rod	EX	$153.00	6-2001
Mitchell	908	spin reel, ultralight, crisp box & papers	NIB	$104.00	1-2001
Mitchell	7130	fly reel	NIB	$41.00	1-1999
Mitchell	CAP		VG	$26.00	2-1999
Mitchell	Tournament	spinning reel, stacked spool, strange	Mint	$1,075.00	12-1999
National Specialities		Indiana type, broken wire	EX-	$137.50	8-1999
Newport	350	thumb brake, rubber & German silver, grubby	VG	$47.00	3-2001
Nordic	Supreme 45		NIB	$222.00	8-2000
N.Z. Sports Mfg.	Wilhous Brand	brass telephone latch, pretty	EX	$250.00	3-2001
Ocean City	109	narrow 1" spool, great box, NOT MET	NIB	$190.00	11-2000
Ocean City	245	609	EX-	$202.50	2-1999
Ocean City	981	box & papers	VG/IB	$31.00	1-1999
Old Pal	Electric	tackle box case, charger, battery, nice	EX/IB	$178.00	9-2002
Orvis	50A		NIB	$272.00	8-1999
Orvis	50A	spinning reel, pouch & manual	EX+	$213.50	1-1999
Orvis	50A	spin reel, ultralight, goodies	NIB	$200.00	6-2001
Orvis	100A		EX	$56.00	2-1999
Orvis	101	spin reel, left-handed, Italy	VG	$34.00	8-2001
Orvis	300	spin reel	Mint	$113.00	1-2001
Orvis	Battenkill 5/6	fly reel	VG	$76.00	2-1999
Orvis	Madison	3, 4 & 5 line with bag	Mint	$45.01	1-1999
Orvis	Perfect	fly reel, S-handle, counter balance marked Manchester, Vermont	VG	$836.26	6-1999
Peetz		65th Anniversary, salmon, mahogany & brass	EX	$86.00	1-1999
Peetz		mahogany, nice decal, Canada	EX	$47.00	3-2001
Peetz	wood	nice	EX	$50.00	3-2001
Peerless	2	3⅛", German silver, pretty	EX/IC	$350.00	11-2000
Penchon-Michel	Luxor	spin reel	EX	$50.00	4-2000
Penn	10	level wind	EX	$46.99	1-1999
Penn	12LT		Mint	$285.00	1-1999
Penn	25GLS	black	EX-	$65.00	10-2000
Penn	26M	green monofilament, box	EX	$102.50	1-1999
Penn	40GLS	graphite	EX	$102.98	1-1999
Penn	80W	brass, NOT MET	EX	$340.00	11-2000
Penn	115	9/0, nice box	NIB	$164.00	8-2002
Penn	275	NOT MET	VG	$70.00	6-1999
Penn	450SS	spinning reel, NOT MET	NIB	$76.00	5-1999
Penn	706	manual bail	EX-	$204.00	4-2000
Penn	706	spinning reel, large, green & white, handle & drag	EX	$148.00	4-2000
Penn	710	spin reel, green & white, drag knob	Mint	$49.00	10-2000
Penn	710	spin reel, green, goodies	NIB	$152.00	8-2001
Penn	712	spin reel	EX-	$33.95	1-1999

BRAND	MODEL	SERIES / MFG. CODE / DESCRIPTION	GRADE	PRICE	DATE
Penn	716	ultralight spin reel	Mint	$151.51	2-1999
Penn	5500SS	spinning reel, modern, BB, SS	Mint	$68.00	1-1999
Penn	8500SS	spinning reel, gold & black	Mint	$84.50	1-1999
Penn	International 12H	NOT MET	NIB	$250.00	3-1999
Penn	International 12T	modern	Mint	$285.00	11-2000
Penn	International 20		VG	$140.25	2-1999
Penn	International 30	650 yard line	EX	$242.50	5-1999
Penn	International 50		EX-	$280.00	1-1999
Penn	International 50	50th Anniversary 241	Mint	$850.00	1-2002
Penn	International 50	gold	EX-	$300.00	4-2001
Penn	International 50W		EX-	$290.00	3-1999
Penn	International 50W	ding on left side	EX-	$370.00	2-1999
Penn	International 80TX		Mint	$550.00	2-1999
Penn	International 80W		EX	$416.00	1-1999
Penn	International 80W		EX-	$380.00	3-1999
Penn	International II 130ST	box & all goodies, NOT MET	NIB	$925.00	8-1999
Penn	Levelmatic 930		EX	$58.00	1-1999
Penn	Levelmatic 940	box & papers	EX/IB	$96.07	1-1999
Penn	Peerless 9	box & goodies	EX/IB	$24.50	2-1999
Penn	Peerless N209		VG	$21.00	1-1999
Penn	Senator	1/0	EX	$90.00	6-1999
Penn	Senator	3/0	VG	$38.00	1-1999
Penn	Senator	3/0, c.1960, blue box	NIB	$146.00	1-2000
Penn	Senator	3/0, worn box	VG/IB	$46.00	1-1999
Penn	Senator	4/0	EX	$53.00	1-1999
Penn	Senator	4/0	VG	$57.00	1-1999
Penn	Senator	4/0, maroon box with papers	EX/IB	$66.00	1-1999
Penn	Senator	6/0, black, beautiful	EX	$54.00	2-1999
Penn	Senator	9/0	EX	$89.00	4-1999
Penn	Senator	10/0	VG	$124.00	1-1999
Penn	Senator	12/0, black & silver, NOT MET	EX	$128.00	1-1999
Penn	Senator	12/0, Star roller rod, NOT MET	EX-	$257.00	5-2001
Penn	Senator	14/0, silver & black	EX	$227.00	1-1999
Penn	Senator	16/0	EX	$405.00	10-1999
Penn	Senator	16/0	EX-	$511.00	10-2000
Penn	Senator	16/0	EX-	$538.00	5-2000
Penn	Senator 111	2/0, box & papers	NIB	$127.50	1-1999
Penn	Senator 112	3/0	EX/IB	$52.00	1-1999
Penn	Senator 112H	3/0	EX	$69.00	1-1999
Penn	Senator 112H	3/0, gold & red, pretty	EX-	$57.00	1-1999
Penn	Senator 112H, Special	3/0, red	NIB	$61.00	9-2000
Penn	Senator 113H	4/0	NIB	$84.00	2-1999
Penn	Senator 114H	4/0 or 6/0	EX	$48.00	4-2000
Penn	Senator 114HL		EX	$74.00	9-2000
Penn	Senator 115	9/0	EX/IB	$201.00	1-1999
Penn	Senator 115	9/0, excellent box	EX/IB	$202.00	8-2002
Penn	Spinfisher 704	green	EX	$53.00	10-2001
Penn	Spinfisher 706	no bail, box & papers	EX/IB	$265.00	6-1999

BRAND	MODEL	SERIES / MFG. CODE / DESCRIPTION	GRADE	PRICE	DATE
Penn	Spinfisher 712	green & white, drag & knob	EX	$51.00	4-2000
Penn	Spinfisher 716	green	VG	$44.00	3-2001
Penn	Squidder	box & goodies	NIB	$49.10	2-1999
Penn	Squidder 140		EX-	$35.00	1-1999
Penn	Squidder 140		EX/IB	$68.00	2-1999
Peters		Indiana	EX-	$160.00	4-2001
Pflueger		250 yards, Ohio, 1978, nice box	EX+/IB	$91.00	4-2000
Pflueger		1964, 100th Anniversary	EX	$43.00	6-1999
Pflueger		2800, no handle, release not working	EX-	$222.00	8-2001
Pflueger		Kentucky style, brass, diamond P, crosshatching	NIB	$404.50	1-1999
Pflueger	40	maroon box	EX	$123.00	1-1999
Pflueger	511		VG-	$56.00	1-1999
Pflueger	511	papers, NOT MET	EX+	$34.40	10-1999
Pflueger	611B	bronze color, mint	Mint	$142.50	2-1999
Pflueger	611B	free spool, brown, star drag	EX	$112.50	12-1998
Pflueger	1494	box	VG-	$115.00	2-1999
Pflueger	1494	oldest, maroon box & papers	NIB	$258.50	4-1999
Pflueger	1495	fly reel, old style, box	VG/IB	$121.50	4-1999
Pflueger	1576	leaping bass logo	EX-	$76.00	9-1999
Pflueger	1775?	free spool reel, narrow spool, leaping bass logo	Mint	$87.50	3-2000
Pflueger	1895	jewels, very nice	EX	$24.00	5-2000
Pflueger	2600	all accessories	NIB	$1,202.00	10-1999
Pflueger	2600	nice	EX	$566.00	3-1999
Pflueger	2800		EX-	$635.00	10-1999
Pflueger	2800		NIB	$709.00	11-2000
Pflueger	2800	goodies	NIB	$690.00	11-1999
Pflueger	2800	leaping bass logo	EX-	$193.00	2-2002
Pflueger	2800	noisy, release doesn't work, broken		$405.00	8-1999
Pflueger	2800 DF		Mint	$588.00	6-1999
Pflueger	8053X	raised pillar, brass, diamond P, Kentucky	NIB	$404.50	1-1999
Pflueger	Akerite 2068	saltwater type, lightweight, nice box	EX/IB	$61.00	3-2001
Pflueger	Akron	papers	NIB	$46.00	5-1999
Pflueger	Akron 1893L		EX	$24.50	1-1999
Pflueger	Atlapac	very nice tin box & bag	EX/IT	$420.00	1-2002
Pflueger	Atlas Portage	fly reel, raised pillar, looks like German silver, nice	EX-	$91.00	4-2000
Pflueger	Avalon	1909 patent	VG	$300.00	10-2000
Pflueger	Avalon 350	bulldog logo, 1909 patent	VG-	$300.00	10-2000
Pflueger	Buckeye		EX-	$141.38	8-1999
Pflueger	Buckeye		EX-	$153.50	9-1999
Pflueger	Buckeye		VG	$64.00	4-1999
Pflueger	Buckeye	handle replaced, for parts	Fair	$37.00	1-1999
Pflueger	Buckeye	light boat rash	VG+	$51.00	5-2001
Pflueger	Buckeye 80		VG+	$71.50	3-1999
Pflueger	Capitol 605J	tall maroon box	NIB	$160.50	4-1999
Pflueger	Capitol 1788	red end plate, large, pretty	EX	$77.00	9-2000
Pflueger	Delight	fly reel, 80 yards, German silver & rubber	EX-	$300.00	4-2000
Pflueger	Four Brothers Delight	60 yards, German silver & rubber	EX	$480.00	9-2000
Pflueger	Golden West	60 yards	EX	$635.00	6-2001

BRAND	MODEL	SERIES / MFG. CODE / DESCRIPTION	GRADE	PRICE	DATE
Pflueger	Golden West	fly reel	VG	$326.00	9-2000
Pflueger	Golden West	fly reel, 2½", big gouge from handle wear	VG	$380.00	8-1999
Pflueger	Golden West	fly reel, 2½", smallest size	EX+	$600.00	11-1999
Pflueger	Golden West 1878	bait casting reel	VG+	$50.00	12-1999
Pflueger	Golden West 7095	2½", "60" on foot, bulldog logo	EX	$662.00	8-2002
Pflueger	Hawkeye	2½", silver & rubber, missing endcap	EX-	$350.00	4-2000
Pflueger	Knobby 1963		NIB	$52.50	4-2000
Pflueger	Knobby 1963	free spool reel, star drag, red	EX	$93.00	1-1999
Pflueger	Knobby 1965	free spool reel, red, star drag	EX+/IB	$138.50	6-1999
Pflueger	Knobby Deluxe	red color, hang tag, papers & wrench	NIB	$203.00	10-2001
Pflueger	Medalist	agate, metal name tag	VG-	$284.00	8-2000
Pflueger	Medalist 1394	first model	VG	$205.00	8-2002
Pflueger	Medalist 1394	fly reel, reel seat filed, ugly	Poor	$66.76	1-1999
Pflueger	Medalist 1492	agate line guide, sculpter pillars	VG-	$65.60	8-1999
Pflueger	Medalist 1492	spare spool, NOT MET	EX	$33.00	8-1999
Pflueger	Medalist 1494	round line guide, amber handle	EX	$137.00	4-2001
Pflueger	Medalist 1494	silver?, Diamolite Line guide	EX	$128.00	3-2001
Pflueger	Medalist 1495		NIB	$86.00	11-1999
Pflueger	Medalist 1495	nice box	NIB	$46.00	1-1999
Pflueger	Nobby 1960	free spool reel, star drag, red	Mint	$200.00	1-1999
Pflueger	Norka	40 yards, c.1911, jeweled	EX	$1,225.00	2-2002
Pflueger	Pacron 3178	NOT MET	EX/IB	$44.83	5-2000
Pflueger	Pacron 3178	wire line type	EX	$37.00	11-2000
Pflueger	Progress	60 yards, gunmetal & silver, bulldog logo	EX	$163.00	8-2000
Pflueger	Progress	fly reel, brass	VG+	$101.00	6-1999
Pflueger	Progress	fly reel, raised pillar, dog on foot	EX	$152.00	10-2000
Pflueger	Progress	fly reel, vg brass		$80.75	2-1999
Pflueger	Progress 1783	fly reel, raised pillar, maroon box	EX/IB	$114.00	9-2000
Pflueger	Progress 1783	nice box	NIB	$181.94	3-2000
Pflueger	Progress 1784	fly reel, nice box & paper	VG+I/B	$91.60	3-2000
Pflueger	Progress 1923	fly reel, skeleton	EX-?	$107.50	4-1999
Pflueger	Redifor		VG	$224.50	1-1999
Pflueger	Redifor	German silver, jeweled, 1907 & 1914 patents	EX	$176.60	10-1999
Pflueger	Redifor	German silver, jeweled, bulldog logo	VG+	$177.50	1-1999
Pflueger	Redifor	Kentucky style, jeweled	EX	$251.38	1-2000
Pflueger	Redifor	NOT MET	EX	$128.50	8-1999
Pflueger	Rocket	bakelite spacer	EX	$122.50	6-1999
Pflueger	Rocket 1365F		EX/IB	$66.00	6-1999
Pflueger	Rocket 1375		NIB	$69.75	4-1999
Pflueger	Skilkast	1953, hang tag	NIB	$97.66	6-1999
Pflueger	Summit		Mint	$55.00	10-2000
Pflueger	Summit	1926 patent, g maroon box & goodies	EXIB	$224.00	11-2001
Pflueger	Summit	goodies	NIB	$81.00	10-2000
Pflueger	Summit	mint pouch (leather bag)	EX	$41.00	5-2000
Pflueger	Summit 1993L		EX-	$25.00	8-1999
Pflueger	Summit 1993L	crisp box & all goodies	NIB	$306.00	4-2000
Pflueger	Summit 1993L	light spool, nice box	EX/IB	$347.00	4-2000
Pflueger	Summit 1993L	pouch	EX+	$102.00	4-2000

BRAND	MODEL	SERIES / MFG. CODE / DESCRIPTION	GRADE	PRICE	DATE
Pflueger	Supreme	510, pouch, tool, oil, NOT MET	EX	$52.50	8-1999
Pflueger	Supreme	box & papers	VG/IB	$47.00	1-1999
Pflueger	Supreme	brown & gold, "last one made"	EX-	$626.00	9-2002
Pflueger	Supreme	first model, windshield wiper	EX-	$300.00	8-1999
Pflueger	Supreme	free spool, grey, wide spool, star drag, pouch	NIP	$55.00	11-2000
Pflueger	Supreme	free spool reel, hex drag	EX	$61.00	8-1999
Pflueger	Supreme	leather bag, extra cub handle & goodies	NIB	$159.10	6-1999
Pflueger	Supreme	missing part of level wind, replaced nut	AVG	$150.00	9-1999
Pflueger	Supreme	old, free spool type reel, Douglas patent	EX-	$250.00	4-1999
Pflueger	Supreme 510	box & goodies	NIB	$135.83	5-1999
Pflueger	Supreme 511		EX+	$66.00	6-1999
Pflueger	Supreme 611B	ballbearing	EX	$127.50	10-1999
Pflueger	Supreme 1573		VG	$17.50	12-1998
Pflueger	Supreme 1573	box & all goodies, beautiful	NIB	$206.40	2-1999
Pflueger	Supreme 1573	comfort grip, ring papers, cub handle, bass logo	NIB	$112.00	8-2000
Pflueger	Supreme 1573	free spool, goodies & 2PCCB	NIB	$73.00	1-1999
Pflueger	Supreme 1573	gold & black box with papers	VG/IB	$24.15	1-1999
Pflueger	Supreme 1573	mint in gold & black box with goodies	NIB	$280.00	1-1999
Pflueger	Supreme 1575	free spool reel, star drag	EX	$56.00	2-2000
Pflueger	Supreme 1576	wide spool, leaping bass logo, pouch	EX-/IB	$81.00	12-1999
Pflueger	Supreme 1577	free spool reel, narrow spool, plastic box	NIB	$114.00	3-2001
Pflueger	Supreme 1577	narrow spool, leaping bass logo	EX	$152.50	8-1999
Pflueger	Supreme 1577	narrow spool, leaping bass logo	NIB	$148.00	5-2000
Pflueger	Supreme 1793	all goodies, mint	NIB	$333.00	9-2001
Pflueger	Supreme 1973	all goodies, box is a little rough	EX-/IB	$35.00	4-2000
Pflueger	Supreme 1973?	cub handle, great box & goodies	NIB	$162.00	4-2000
Pflueger	Supreme, CK	brown, high speed, BB, star drag	EX	$505.00	6-2001
Pflueger	Supreme, DL, CK	high speed type	EX	$1,036.00	5-2001
Pflueger	Templar 400		VG+	$96.00	5-2000
Pflueger	Templer	German silver & rubber, Williams drag	EX	$172.00	10-2000
Pflueger	Templer	lightweight saltwater, German silver & hard rubber	EX-	$125.00	8-2000
Pflueger	Templer	November 18, 1909 patent	EX	$152.50	3-2000
Pflueger	Templer 350	1419 1/2, silver & rubber, bulldog logo	EX	$199.00	4-2000
Pflueger	Trump	c.1974, Arkansas, NOT MET	NIB	$33.78	5-1999
Pflueger	Trump 2	1943, 1944, brass	NIB	$167.50	3-1999
Pflueger	Trump 1942		NIB	$57.00	4-1999
Pflueger	Trump 1943	Arkansas box	NIB	$52.55	1-1999
Pflueger	Trump 1943	catalog	NIB	$36.51	1-2000
Pflueger	Trump 1943	crisp box & papers, cellophane intact	NIB	$125.00	1-2002
Pflueger	Trusty 1933	newer box, cellophane intact	NIB	$78.00	4-2000
Pflueger	Worth	January 22, 1907 – December 29, 1914	EX-	$261.00	3-2001
Pflueger	Worth	jeweled	EX	$150.00	6-2001
Pflueger	Worth 2963		EX-	$130.00	1-2002
Precision-Bilt	Mosquito		EX	$40.77	7-1999
Quick-O-Mat		spin reel, neat	EX	$109.00	11-2000
Rainbow	888	bait casting reel, Sweden, NOT MET	EX/IB	$163.00	10-2000
Record		fly reel, solid aluminum sides	EX-	$107.50	9-1999

BRAND	MODEL	SERIES / MFG. CODE / DESCRIPTION	GRADE	PRICE	DATE
Record	1500C		EX/IB	$90.10	11-1999
Record	1600		EX/IB	$232.51	10-1999
Record	1600C		EX/IB	$80.00	11-1999
Record	1600C		EX/IB	$135.30	10-1999
Record	1700	all goodies	EX/IB	$172.55	10-1999
Record	1700C		EX+/IB	$96.10	11-1999
Record	1800	all goodies	EX/IB	$153.50	10-1999
Record	1800	engraved end plates, leather case	VG	$355.00	9-1999
Record	1800	white agate bearing, nice	EX	$206.00	3-2000
Record	1800C		NIB	$255.00	2-2000
Record	1800C	nice box & goodies	NIB	$142.50	11-1999
Record	1900	nice box	NIB	$256.00	1-2000
Record	1900	pouch	EX	$320.00	8-2000
Record	2000		EX-	$178.50	3-1999
Record	2000	c.1942, box & goodies	VG	$1,728.00	2-2002
Record	5000		EX	$1,001.55	11-1999
Record	5000		VG+	$255.00	3-2000
Record	5000	case, papers & goodies	EX-	$405.99	2-1999
Record	5000	goodies	EX	$424.00	3-1999
Record	5000	goodies	EX/IP	$428.00	2-2000
Record	5000	no serial number, goodies	EX/IP	$787.00	2-2000
Record	5000	pouch	EX/IP	$455.00	2-2000
Record	5000	pouch & goodies	EX+	$660.00	1-2000
Record	5000	pouch & goodies	NIP	$610.00	1-2000
Record	5000	pouch, aluminum parts, tube	EX/IP	$510.00	10-2000
Record	5000	pouch & goodies	EX	$660.00	3-2000
Record	5000	pouch, rash	VG+	$404.99	11-1999
Record	5000 SG	first model made, pouch & goodies	EX/IP	$1,825.00	4-2001
Record	6000	pouch & goodies	EX/IP	$300.00	10-2000
Record	Ambassadeur 5000		VG	$520.50	1-1999
Record	Ambassadeur 5000		VG+	$535.00	9-1999
Record	Ambassadeur 5000	nice	EX	$688.00	7-2000
Record	Ambassadeur 5000	no serial number	EX	$599.00	6-1999
Record	Ambassadeur 5000	pre-Abu	EX-	$520.00	1-1999
Record	Ambassadeur 5000	rubs	VG-	$320.00	6-1999
Record	Ambassadeur 5000	SG, case & parts	EX-	$1075.00	5-2001
Record	Ambassadeur 5000 SG	goodies	EX/IP	$1,572.00	4-2001
Record	Ambassadeur 5000 SG	pouch & goodies	EX-	$960.00	5-2000
Record	Clipper 2300C	NLW, competition, pretty	EX	$227.50	9-1999
Record	Rullen	parts, all goodies & mint box	NIB	$612.00	12-1998
Record	Standard	fly reel, pewter, nice	EX-	$76.00	8-2000
Record Abu	6000	parts, grey spool & pouch	EX	$670.00	12-1998
Redifor		jeweled, NOT MET	VG	$179.00	4-2000
Redifor	Betzsel	jeweled caps, NOT MET	VG+	$177.50	6-1999
Reel Works	3	serial number 846, name engraved, NOT MET	EX-	$604.00	8-2002
Rinehart	Master Pumper	case, NOT MET	EX/IC	$260.00	11-1999
Rivers	Tournament 500	similar to Abu, NOT MET	VG+	$49.00	9-2001
Rivers Expert	Tournament	2 star drags, Sweden	EX-	$320.00	7-2000

BRAND	MODEL	SERIES / MFG. CODE / DESCRIPTION	GRADE	PRICE	DATE
Rock River		fly reel, Rockford, Illinois	NIB	$102.50	3-2000
Rocket	1355	NO BIDS	NIB	$175.00	3-2000
Ross	Cimarron C2		EX	$103.50	3-1999
Sage	508	fly reel, pouch	Mint	$156.00	1-1999
Schmelzer	Tournament	NOT MET	EX	$28.00	4-1999
Seamaster	Mark III	fly reel, saltwater, SS, pillar, c.1981	EX	$3,200.00	6-2001
Shakespeare		Style C	VG	$810.00	2-2002
Shakespeare		type B, double worm gear, pitting	VG	$206.00	2-2002
Shakespeare	3	type B, NOT MET	VG+	$250.00	1-2001
Shakespeare	3B	twin screw	VG+	$265.28	10-1999
Shakespeare	3M		VG-	$164.00	8-2000
Shakespeare	1798	spin casting reel	EX/IB	$29.71	5-1999
Shakespeare	1850	spin casting reel	EX/IB	$127.50	12-1999
Shakespeare	1924		NIB	$43.00	3-2000
Shakespeare	1924	small handle, arbor, pouch	EX	$150.00	10-1999
Shakespeare	1930	nice box & goodies	NIB	$48.00	10-2000
Shakespeare	1975	free spool reel, BC, red, white, blue, star drag, missing 1 logo	EX	$48.00	8-2002
Shakespeare	1981DC		EX	$222.50	10-1999
Shakespeare	2052		EX	$57.00	8-1999
Shakespeare	2052		Mint	$41.50	5-1999
Shakespeare	2062		VG	$28.50	2-1999
Shakespeare	2062	spin reel	NIB	$53.00	8-2000
Shakespeare	2091	spin reel, large	NIB	$60.00	2-1999
Shakespeare	B	parts only (most missing)	Poor	$143.00	8-2000
Shakespeare	Black Knight	cheap model, black rubber side plates, 1909	EX	$38.00	8-2001
Shakespeare	Criterion 1960		NIB	$50.00	7-2000
Shakespeare	Criterion FA	1960, left-handed	EX	$51.00	3-1999
Shakespeare	Favorite	60 yards, (German silver?), c.1910, decent	VG+	$52.00	10-2001
Shakespeare	Favorite 2	non-level wind, 1910, decent	VG+	$52.00	10-2001
Shakespeare	Hercules	200 yards, German silver & rubber, 1966, pretty	EX	$103.00	5-2000
Shakespeare	Marhoff	German silver, goodies	EX/IB	$60.00	8-2000
Shakespeare	Marhoff	hard plastic box	NIB	$205.00	2-2001
Shakespeare	Marhoff	hinged plastic case, 1964	EX/IB	$51.00	8-2000
Shakespeare	President	1970A	NIB	$197.50	1-2000
Shakespeare	President DF	free spool reel, star drag, engraving, 1980HB	EX-	$152.50	4-1999
Shakespeare	President GE	1970, SS, (German silver?), pillars, no raindrop, pretty	EX	$162.50	9-1999
Shakespeare	President II	1980	Mint	$247.00	12-1998
Shakespeare	President II	1980, black, NOT MET	VG+	$66.00	9-2000
Shakespeare	President II	fancy scroll	EX	$294.01	12-1998
Shakespeare	President II	spin reel, 2810DE	EX	$67.00	3-2001
Shakespeare	President II	US eagle logo, nice box & goodies	NIB	$179.00	8-2002
Shakespeare	President II 1980		EX-	$122.50	6-1999
Shakespeare	President II 1980	black, silver eagle logo, NOT MET	EX-	$117.50	4-2000
Shakespeare	President II 1981	blue oval, engraved	EX-	$181.50	9-1999
Shakespeare	President II 1981	crisp box & goodies	NIB	$187.00	4-2000
Shakespeare	President II 1982		VG	$142.50	4-1999

BRAND	MODEL	SERIES / MFG. CODE / DESCRIPTION	GRADE	PRICE	DATE
Shakespeare	President II 1982		VG+	$82.00	1-1999
Shakespeare	President II 1982	fancy scroll	VG	$89.00	4-1999
Shakespeare	President II 1984B	fancy scroll, eagle logo	Mint	$116.50	4-1999
Shakespeare	President II DB	1982	VG	$89.00	4-1999
Shakespeare	President II DB	lots of boat rash	(VG?)	$91.00	8-2001
Shakespeare	President II HB	eagle logo	EX	$169.50	10-1999
Shakespeare	Service 2	60 yards, narrow spool	VG	$81.00	4-1999
Shakespeare	Silver Swan	dark color, ugly, runs good	VG+	$41.00	8-2001
Shakespeare	Sportcast	free spool reel, 1982	EX	$50.00	3-1999
Shakespeare	Tournament 26		EX	$86.00	5-2000
Shakespeare	Tournament 1740HE	free spool, balsa arbor, beautiful	Mint	$129.00	8-1999
Shakespeare	Tournament 1910	50 yards, tiny handle, German silver	EX	$338.00	7-2000
Shakespeare	Tournament 1914		EX	$155.00	1-1999
Shakespeare	Tournament 1924	aluminum finish, tiny handle, NOT MET	EX-	$247.00	1-2002
Shakespeare	Wondercast 1795	spin cast reel	VG-	$52.50	4-1999
Shakespeare	Tournament 26	aluminum	EX	$69.00	2-2001
Shimano	Baitrunner 4500	spin reel	EX	$77.50	2-1999
Shimano	Bantam 10	black	EX	$32.00	1-1999
Shimano	Bantam 100		EX	$80.50	1-1999
Shimano	Bantam 100		EX-	$51.00	3-1999
Shimano	Bantam 100		VG+	$53.50	4-1999
Shimano	Bantam 100	silver	EX	$69.00	6-1999
Shimano	Bantam 100	silver	EX	$86.03	6-1999
Shimano	Bantam 100	spare spool & handle	Mint	$155.00	8-2000
Shimano	Bantam 100EX		NIB	$227.52	9-1999
Shimano	Bantam 100EX	box & goodies	EX/IB	$152.50	4-1999
Shimano	Bantam 100EX	wood handle	VG+	$121.00	1-1999
Shimano	Bantam 200	wood handles	EX	$101.99	3-1999
Shimano	Bantam 300		Mint	$180.00	7-2000
Shimano	Bantam 400		Mint	$152.00	7-2000
Shimano	Bantam 500		Mint	$152.00	7-2000
Shimano	Bantam 1000		NIB	$100.00	6-1999
Shimano	Bantam Citica 200		EX	$66.00	1-1999
Shimano	Bantam Mag 50SG	heavy, freshwater	EX	$42.50	3-1999
Shimano	Bantam Pro Mag 100X		EX	$44.00	3-2001
Shimano	BB1	Lew's Speed Spool, fish logo	Mint	$127.00	8-2002
Shimano	Calcutta 100		Mint	$110.00	1-1999
Shimano	Calcutta 100		NIB	$140.50	3-1999
Shimano	Calcutta 200	bag, papers	Mint	$132.50	2-1999
Shimano	Calcutta 250		EX-	$127.50	2-1999
Shimano	Calcutta 400		EX/IB	$152.50	3-1999
Shimano	Calcutta 700	gold, pretty	EX	$182.00	1-1999
Shimano	Coriolis		Mint	$51.00	1-1999
Shimano	Curado 201		EX	$93.00	3-1999
Shimano	Curado CU201		EX	$75.50	3-1999
Shimano	Spirex 1000		EX	$42.00	1-1999
Shimano	Stella 1000F		NIB	$386.00	5-2001
Shimano	Stella 2500F		NIB	$402.00	5-2001

BRAND	MODEL	SERIES / MFG. CODE / DESCRIPTION	GRADE	PRICE	DATE
Shimano	Stradic 2000FG		EX	$52.00	5-2001
Shimano	Synetre 2000FH		NIB	$63.00	5-2001
Shimano	TLD 10	nice box	NIB	$280.00	3-2002
Shimano	Triton TLD25L		EX-	$162.50	3-1999
South Bend	400		EX/IB	$37.00	10-2000
South Bend	450	in nice tin can, "Our Hardware"	VG/IC	$66.05	4-1999
South Bend	750	NOT MET	NIB	$61.00	4-1999
South Bend	900ABL	box	EX-/IB	$204.00	5-2000
South Bend	1000	German silver, nice leather pouch	EX-/IP	$34.00	8-2001
South Bend	1131A	reel used, intro box, papers & tag	AVG	$92.53	11-1999
South Bend	1131B	serial number 30041, 1907 patent	EX-	$82.67	1-2000
South Bend	1250	arbor, pouch & goodies	NIB	$100.00	9-2001
South Bend	1250 Model E	red marble grip & spacer	Mint	$70.00	5-2000
South Bend	2500	stainless, nice box	NIB	$373.00	10-2000
South Bend	Kentucky	left-handed, horseshoe marking, non-level, pouch	EX-	$717.67	1-2000
South Bend	Oreno 1155	fly reel	EX/IB	$67.00	2-2000
South Bend	Oreno 1196	fly reel, single action	EX	$46.00	4-2001
South Bend	Oreno Matic 1126	vg box	EXIB	$39.00	2-1999
South Bend	Perfect-Oreno 750	crisp box & papers	NIB	$80.00	8-2001
South Bend	St. Joe 1170	fly reel	EX-	$47.00	5-2000
South Bend	St. Joe 1170	fly reel, raised pillar	VG+	$48.00	8-2000
Stead	36770	German silver & rubber, back plate cracked	(EX-?)	$1,791.00	8-2002
Stevens		16/0, 7½", "86-16-0"	EX	$3,550.00	3-2000
Stockford			VG	$200.00	6-1999
Stork		fly reel	VG-	$153.00	2-1999
Talbot	3	outside jeweled caps	EX	$1,680.00	9-2000
Talbot	33	corner of seat bent, otherwise nice		$655.00	2-1999
Talbot	33	Nevada, Missouri, NOT MET	EX?	$1,302.00	2-2002
Talbot	35	as found, looks okay	EX	$1,452.00	12-1999
Talbot	50	#4 size, Nevada, Missouri	EX-	$3,000.00	8-2002
Talbot	Ben-Hur	Nevada, Missouri	EX	$3,975.00	11-1999
Talbot	Eli	Abercrombie & Fitch	EX	$871.00	10-1999
Talbot	Mars	Kansas City, Missouri, pouch, wrong handle, modern re	EX	$450.00	1-2002
Talbot	Meteor	Kansas City, Missouri		$448.33	3-1999
Talbot	Meteor	Kansas City, Missouri, 3 o'clock	EX	$513.00	2-2000
Talbot	Meteor	Nevada, Missouri	EX	$640.00	5-2001
Talbot	Meteor	Schmetzler Arms	EX	$811.00	9-1999
Talbot	Star	8.5/9, Schmelzer Arms, Kansas City, Missouri		$425.00	6-1999
Talbot	Star	Kansas City, Missouri, filed reel seat, nice	EX-	$330.50	5-1999
Talbot	Star	Marshall Fields & Co., not graded, looks okay	(EX-?)	$395.00	8-2002
Talbot	Tomahawk	Chicago, Illinois, NOT MET	EX	$635.00	7-2000
Talbot Vim	Tomahawk	Kansas City, Missouri, 3 0'clock, 1 click, polished	EX	$1,539.00	8-2001
Thommen	Record 400	spinning reel	VG	$25.00	1-1999
Thommen	Record 400	spinning reel, papers & nice box	NIB	$81.00	12-1998
Thommen	Record 50B	spinning reel, papers & nice box	NIB	$147.50	12-1998
Topper		spin reel	NIB	$78.00	1-2001
Turnbull		fly reel, 4½", heavy brass	EX	$361.00	6-1999

BRAND	MODEL	SERIES / MFG. CODE / DESCRIPTION	GRADE	PRICE	DATE
Val-Craft	350	fly reel, gold anodized aluminum, nice	EX	$137.50	1-1999
Vetco	Pioneer Model B #0001	crisp box & papers, NOT MET	NIB	$137.00	8-2002
Vom Hofe	521 6/0	silver & black, pretty	EX	$621.00	1-1999
Vom Hofe	621 4/0	needs cleaning but looks nice	EX?	$350.00	8-2001
Vom Hofe	36617	1896 patent, original case	VG+/IC	$305.00	5-2000
Vom Hofe	Dame Stoddard & Co	bay, box is a little rough	EX-/IB	$650.00	8-1999
Vom Hofe	Sam 7		EX-	$56.00	8-1999
Vom Hofe	Universal Star 6/0	July 14, 1896 & 1902 patents	EX	$350.00	3-1999
Vom Hofe, Ed.		2" fly reel, cloverleaf logo, German silver & rubber	EX	$1,436.00	10-2000
Vom Hofe, Ed.		4/0, fly reel, salmon	EX-	$1,550.00	2-1999
Vom Hofe, Ed.		6/0 EVH, perforated star drag	EX-	$370.00	2-1999
Vom Hofe, Ed.		16/0, original case, star drag	EX-	$11,500.00	8-2002
Vom Hofe, Ed.		ball handle, brass, stamped		$1,380.00	10-2000
Vom Hofe, Ed.		bay 1902 patent	VG+	$282.88	4-1999
Vom Hofe, Ed.		fly reel, 2¼", bakelite, unpolished, nice	EX-	$283.00	10-2001
Vom Hofe, Ed.	92	1902	EX	$510.00	1-1999
Vom Hofe, Ed.	200	decent, NOT MET	EX-	$127.00	10-2001
Vom Hofe, Ed.	423	4/0, fly reel, NOT MET	EX	$2,500.00	2-1999
Vom Hofe, Ed.	423	3/0, fly reel, $2,250.00 reserve met later	Mint	$1,825.00	4-1999
Vom Hofe, Ed.	491	1.0, snap missing on leather case	EX-/IC	$517.00	5-2002
Vom Hofe, Ed.	501	6/0, engraved name, silver & rubber	EX-	$500.00	5-2001
Vom Hofe, Ed.	504	#1 fly reel	EX	$3,000.00	10-2000
Vom Hofe, Ed.	504	#1 fly reel, German silver & rubber	EX-	$3,000.00	10-2000
Vom Hofe, Ed.	504	4/0, spool corroded	EX-	$1,500.00	2-2002
Vom Hofe, Ed.	521	6/0, German silver & rubber, beautiful	EX	$355.00	8-2000
Vom Hofe, Ed.	521	wrong handle, cracked side	VG+/IC	$287.00	5-2002
Vom Hofe, Ed.	521	wrong handle, marked leather case, rough	VG-	$144.00	5-2002
Vom Hofe, Ed.	521	wrong handle, marked leather case, rough	VG-	$287.00	5-2002
Vom Hofe, Ed.	621	1/0, foot ground down, NOT MET	EX	$584.00	11-2000
Vom Hofe, Ed.	621	2/0, 1896 patent	EX-	$455.00	9-2002
Vom Hofe, Ed.	621	6/0, ugly	AVG	$168.00	10-2000
Vom Hofe, Ed.	621	61	EX	$350.00	6-1999
Vom Hofe, Ed.	621	36617	EX	$284.00	11-2000
Vom Hofe, Ed.	992	bass reel 3", leather case, poor	EX-/IC	$575.00	5-2002
Vom Hofe, Ed.	36557	raised pillar, spool corroded, otherwise nice	VG+	$108.00	8-2001
Vom Hofe, Ed.	36678	1902 patent	EX	$550.00	3-2000
Vom Hofe, Ed.	Commander Ross 712	10/0, pretty	EX-	$2,025.00	4-2000
Vom Hofe, Ed.	Model Tobique 504	2/0, unmarked case, NOT MET	EX	$2,640.00	1-2000
Vom Hofe, Ed.	Mutiplier	#2, fly reel, 2¼ ratio	EX	$450.00	3-2000
Vom Hofe, Ed.	Regal 464		VG	$710.00	4-1999
Vom Hofe, Ed.	Regal 491	#1, box & hang tag, NOT MET	EX+/IB	$898.00	8-1999
Vom Hofe, Ed.	Restigouche 423	6/0, fly reel, pretty, NOT MET	EX/IC	$2,125.00	11-1999
Vom Hofe, Ed.	Restigue	4/0, fly reel, seat screws replaced, clicker	(EX?)	$1,725.00	7-1999
Vom Hofe, Ed.	Sam's Spoon	3 different	EX	$80.00	4-2000
Vom Hofe, Ed.	Sam's Spoon	one #5 & one #6	EX	$125.00	6-1999
Vom Hofe, J.		1/0, 1885 & 1889 patents, some screw damage	EX-	$465.00	4-1999
Vom Hofe, J.		#3, bait casting reel, J.P. Lovell Arms Co., 1886 & 1889 patents, raised pillar	EX	$290.00	3-2000

BRAND	MODEL	SERIES / MFG. CODE / DESCRIPTION	GRADE	PRICE	DATE
Vom Hofe, J.		2", early brass, cloverleaf, rubber, ugly	AVG	$148.00	9-2000
Vom Hofe, J.		#3, fly reel, Dame-Stoddard Co., Boston, Massachusetts, perforated outer rim	VG+	$2,275.00	4-2001
Vom Hofe, J.		#3, raised pillar, October 8, 1989 patent, NOT MET	VG	$99.02	6-1999
Vom Hofe, J.		#4, fly reel, 2⅛", Abbie & Imbrie imprint	VG+	$475.00	4-1999
Vom Hofe, J.		9/0, 1911 patent	EX	$402.00	10-2000
Vom Hofe, J.		casting reel, all metal	VG+	$91.00	3-2000
Vom Hofe, J.		fly reel, 2¼", raised pillar, rubber, 1889 patent	EX	$675.00	8-1999
Vom Hofe, J.		fly reel, German silver, rubber, very nice patina, smaller, 1889 patent	EX	$961.00	1-2002
Vom Hofe, J.		fly reel, large, Folsom Arms	EX-	$516.00	7-1999
Vom Hofe, J.		light, saltwater, 1885 patent, missing endcap	AVG	$51.00	9-2000
Vom Hofe, J.		raised pillar, unmarked, c.1890	VG-	$210.00	4-1999
Vom Hofe, J.		trout, 1¾" x 2", October 8, 1889 patent	EX+	$372.00	3-2001
Vom Hofe, J.	92		VG	$227.50	1-1999
Vom Hofe, J.	153	1911 patent	EX-	$310.00	6-1999
Vom Hofe, J.	B	4/0, George Eastman, pretty	EX	$510.00	9-1999
Vom Hofe, J.	Kentucky	German silver, rubber click button, 1889 patent	EX-	$450.00	6-2001
Vom Hofe, J.	JVH	raised pillar, 1886 patent	AVG	$133.50	4-1999
Vom Hofe, J.	Thomas J. Conroy	foot damage, not awful	AVG	$152.51	1-1999
Wakeman	Skeleton	1886 patent	EX	$744.00	4-2000
Walker		2/0, salmon, restored, NOT MET		$1,280.00	1-2000
Waltco	Ny-O-Lite	red & white	NIB	$70.00	8-1999
Waltco	Ny-O-Lite	white & brown	EX	$16.25	10-1999
Warren		casting reel, brass, round ball	VG+	$255.65	3-2000
Weber	Futurist	fly reel, small chip, screw replaced	Fair	$26.00	1-1999
Welch, Jack		handmade	EX	$1,015.00	6-2001
Wildon, D.D.	Kentucky DDS	one of 4 known	EX	$3,350.00	4-2001
Williams, Ted	450	spin reel	VG/IB	$51.00	5-2001
Williams, Ted	450	spin reel, (made by Alcedo?), vg box & paper	EX-/IB	$66.00	4-2000
Williams, Ted	550	spin reel, papers & soft pouch, Italy, nice	NIP	$103.00	8-2001
Williams, Ted	312	fly reel, single action, brown-bronze color	EX	$56.00	9-2002
Williams, Ted	430	casting reel	EX+	$97.00	4-2000
Williams, Ted	440	spin reel, nice Sears & Roebuck Co. box	EX/IB	$32.00	3-2001
Williams, Ted	470	fly reel, case, nice	EX/IC	$153.50	5-1999
Williams, Ted	535	casting reel, star drag, Sears & Roebuck Co.	EX-	$89.00	11-2001
Williams, Ted	540	spin casting reel	EX+	$50.00	10-2000
Williams, Ted	31231552	fly reel, single action, pouch & papers	NIP	$76.00	9-2000
Williams, Ted	IV	spinning reel	EX-/IB	$65.00	5-1999
Williams, Ted	Shakespeare President II?	bait casting / free spool reel, star drag	EX	$232.00	4-2000
Winchester		fly reel, small, awful punch pressed item	EX	$132.00	8-2000
Winchester	1119	25 yards, raised pillar, (gold plated?)	VG+	$112.00	11-2000
Winchester	1212	screw frame, better quality than usual	EX	$202.00	1-2002
Winchester	1236	fly reel	EX	$202.00	6-1999
Winchester	1236	fly reel, NOT MET	EX	$104.49	7-1999
Winchester	1236	fly reel, raised pillar, knob missing, cheap	EX-	$90.00	5-2000
Winchester	1336	fly reel, aluminum, ugly, NOT NET	VG	$76.00	3-2000
Winchester	2236		VG	$104.50	1-1999

BRAND	MODEL	SERIES / MFG. CODE / DESCRIPTION	GRADE	PRICE	DATE
Winchester	2644	awful box & reel, NOT MET	VG/IB	$660.50	2-2000
Wood	English	brass, nice	EX	$103.00	1-2001
Wright & McGill	Free-Line	like Whirl-Away, built-in bulb at base of rod	EX-	$86.00	8-2001
Yawman & Erbe		fly ree, automatic		$112.30	2-1999
Yawman & Erbe		fly reel, automatic, 1891 patent	AVG	$67.51	11-1999
Young, J.W.	Landex	fly reel, 3½"	G	$77.00	1-1999
Zangi	3V	spin reel, honest wear but runs well, it's mine	VG+	$286.00	8-2001
Zebco	11	x2, 1 vg & 1 ex		$40.00	1-1999
Zebco	22	nice box	EX/IB	$51.00	11-2000
Zebco	44	spin casting reel, underslung	NIB	$76.00	8-1999
Zebco	55		NIB	$136.00	10-2000
Zebco	55	yellow & red box	EX/IB	$59.00	8-2001
Zebco	Cardinal	x2, one #3 & one #4, 1 spare spool	VG	$172.28	5-1999
Zebco	Cardinal 3		EX	$76.00	10-2000
Zebco	Cardinal 3		EX	$132.00	4-2001
Zebco	Cardinal 3		EX	$165.33	8-1999
Zebco	Cardinal 3		EX-	$116.05	3-1999
Zebco	Cardinal 3		EX-	$91.00	10-1999
Zebco	Cardinal 3		EX-	$170.00	3-1999
Zebco	Cardinal 3		NIB	$194.00	7-2000
Zebco	Cardinal 3		NIB	$270.00	3-1999
Zebco	Cardinal 3		VG	$91.01	1-1999
Zebco	Cardinal 3		VG	$117.50	3-1999
Zebco	Cardinal 3	2 spare spools	EX-	$133.00	4-2000
Zebco	Cardinal 3	no bail	VG+	$66.50	5-1999
Zebco	Cardinal 3	green & white	EX	$60.00	8-2002
Zebco	Cardinal 3	spare spool	EX	$125.50	8-1999
Zebco	Cardinal 3	wear on reel foot	EX-	$150.00	2-1999
Zebco	Cardinal 4	bail doesn't work, turns rough	Poor	$67.00	8-2001
Zebco	Cardinal 4	box & papers	EX/IB	$167.50	2-1999
Zebco	Cardinal 4		AVG	$68.00	3-1999
Zebco	Cardinal 4		AVG	$75.00	3-1999
Zebco	Cardinal 4		EX	$55.00	10-1999
Zebco	Cardinal 4		EX	$60.00	9-1999
Zebco	Cardinal 4		EX	$92.99	7-1999
Zebco	Cardinal 4		EX	$98.51	6-1999
Zebco	Cardinal 4		EX	$107.51	8-1999
Zebco	Cardinal 4		EX	$118.38	7-1999
Zebco	Cardinal 4		EX	$132.50	2-1999
Zebco	Cardinal 4		EX	$140.00	12-1998
Zebco	Cardinal 4		EX+	$127.50	6-1999
Zebco	Cardinal 4		Mint	$111.00	1-2001
Zebco	Cardinal 4		Mint	$142.50	6-1999
Zebco	Cardinal 4		NIB	$227.00	4-2000
Zebco	Cardinal 4		VG	$50.00	7-1999
Zebco	Cardinal 4		VG	$72.77	6-1999
Zebco	Cardinal 4		VG	$75.00	9-1999
Zebco	Cardinal 4		VG	$73.00	6-1999

BRAND	MODEL	SERIES / MFG. CODE / DESCRIPTION	GRADE	PRICE	DATE
Zebco	Cardinal 4		VG+	$77.00	4-2000
Zebco	Cardinal 4		VG	$84.00	3-1999
Zebco	Cardinal 4		VG	$84.00	5-1999
Zebco	Cardinal 4		VG	$86.00	2-1999
Zebco	Cardinal 4		VG	$94.00	1-1999
Zebco	Cardinal 4		VG	$99.00	3-1999
Zebco	Cardinal 4		VG+	$94.02	9-1999
Zebco	Cardinal 4	Abu, dark green & light green	VG	$81.00	1-1999
Zebco	Cardinal 4	spare spool & papers	EX	$100.00	11-2000
Zebco	Cardinal 4	green box	NIB	$153.50	4-1999
Zebco	Cardinal 4	NOT MET	EX-	$81.00	5-1999
Zebco	Cardinal 4	NOT MET	NIB	$120.15	5-1999
Zebco	Cardinal 4	papers	Mint	$118.00	11-2000
Zebco	Cardinal 4	rod & reel blister pack	NOC	$255.00	1-2000
Zebco	Cardinal 4	spare spool	EX	$150.00	3-1999
Zebco	Cardinal 4	spare spool, foam box & parts	EX	$141.63	5-1999
Zebco	Cardinal 4	spool only, aluminum reproduction	EX	$31.00	8-1999
Zebco	Cardinal 4	spool only, in case	NIC	$31.00	2-1999
Zebco	Cardinal 4	ugly	AVG	$88.00	4-1999
Zebco	Cardinal 4	wrench & papers	NIB	$230.00	11-1999
Zebco	Cardinal 6		EX	$75.00	1-1999
Zebco	Cardinal 6		EX+	$76.00	3-1999
Zebco	Cardinal 6		VG	$70.00	1-1999
Zebco	Cardinal 6		VG	$83.00	9-1999
Zebco	Cardinal 6	spare spool	EX-	$76.00	4-1999
Zebco	Cardinal 6	NOT MET	NIB	$75.00	5-1999
Zebco	Cardinal 6	NOT MET	NIB	$91.00	3-1999
Zebco	Cardinal 6X	rough box, NOT MET	EX	$127.50	3-2000
Zebco	Cardinal 7	2 spare spools	EX	$109.00	8-2001
Zebco	Cardinal 7	Abu, NOT MET	EX	$100.50	4-1999
Zebco	Cardinal 7	spare spool	Mint	$125.00	3-1999
Zebco	Cardinal 7		AVG	$51.00	3-1999
Zebco	Cardinal 7		EX	$75.00	4-2001
Zebco	Cardinal 7		EX-	$68.57	3-1999
Zebco	Cardinal 7		EX/IB	$72.55	4-1999
Zebco	Cardinal 7		NIB	$94.00	7-2000
Zebco	Cardinal 7		VG	$48.99	6-1999
Zebco	Cardinal 7X	brown/white	VG-	$77.00	3-1999
Zebco	Cardinal 33	black, yellow & black box, 1955 papers	NIB	$56.00	7-1999
Zebco	Cardinal 33	modern	NIB	$202.50	4-1999
Zebco	Cardinal 554	papers	NIB	$87.00	6-2001
Zebco	Cardinal 557	Cardinal 57 box	NIB	$50.00	2-1999
Zwarg	Saugenay	2/0, fly reel	NM	$2,651.00	5-2000
Zwarg	36557	German silver & rubber, NOT MET	EX	$499.00	10-2000
Zwarg	36770	German silver, never polished, NOT MET	EX	$935.00	3-2000

BRAND	MODEL	SERIES / MFG. CODE / DESCRIPTION	GRADE	PRICE	DATE
Abu	Suecia 321	spin casting reel, glass, 2-piece	Mint	$81.00	10-2000
Abu	Tournament II	6', bait casting reel, 2-piece, pouch, nice	EX	$167.50	3-2000
Action Ind.	Action	square, maroon & white	EX	$20.50	5-2000
Armax	7286	3/2, fly rod	EX	$133.81	1-1999
Browning	312910	casting reel, tube & pouch	EX/IT	$395.00	2-2000
Browning	Dave Fritts	6', E-glass	Mint	$41.00	3-1999
Browning	Silaflex	6'6", casting reel, 2 piece	EX+	$201.50	12-1999
Browning	Silaflex	bait casting reel, custom case	EX	$312.00	11-1999
Browning	Silaflex 312920	bait casting reel, 2-piece	EX	$134.00	6-2002
Browning	Silaflex Medallion 23965	bag & tube, NOT MET	NIT	$110.07	11-1999
Champion		(Fat Boy?), pistol grip, bluish-white	EX	$432.00	9-2002
Davis	Special	9'	Mint	$310.00	9-1999
Dickerson		2/1, 4' – 7', no tube, no bag, loose ferrule, c.1962	EX	$900.00	12-1999
Dickerson	90182	3/2, 9', bag & tube	EX/IT	$2,275.78	8-1999
Dickerson	Special 8015	2/2, 8', tube & sock, 1 of only 16 made	EX/IT	$4,076.00	4-2001
Edwards E.		3/2, 8½', fly reel, bamboo, bag & tube	VG+	$465.65	6-1999
Fenwick		5½', medium, Featherweight All-Angle grip	EX-	$141.50	8-1999
Fenwick		custom bait casting, All-Angle grip, nice	EX	$152.52	8-1999
Fenwick		Featherweight All-Angle grip	EX-	$100.00	3-1999
Fenwick	FF60	6', 5 – 6 weight line, 2-piece, bag & tube	EX	$213.36	3-1999
Fenwick	FF756-4	fly reel, backpack, tube & case	NIT	$180.00	5-1999
Fenwick	FF807	8', 3⅜oz., 7 weight line, bag & tube, NOT MET	NIT	$77.00	6-1999
Fenwick	FF807	8', 7 weight line, bag & tube, mint	NIT	$126.50	8-1999
Fenwick	Lunker Stik 1155	5'6", 2¼ oz. shaft, ⅜ – ¾ oz.	EX	$305.00	8-2000
Fenwick	Lunker Stik 1255	5½'	EX	$150.00	10-2000
Fenwick	Lunker Stik 1255	bag	EX/IB	$144.50	8-1999
Fenwick	Lunker Stik 1256		EX-	$81.00	8-1999
Fenwick	Lunker Stik 1256	5½', ⅜ – 1¼ oz., 15 – 25 lb., regular grip	EX	$213.50	3-1999
Fenwick	Lunker Stik 1261	6', ⅜ – 1¼ oz., NOT MET	EX	$51.00	8-1999
Fenwick	Lunker Stik 1361		EX	$61.00	12-1999
Fenwick	Lunker Stik 1456	Fenwick grip	EX	$162.50	4-1999
Fenwick	Lunker Stik 1460	6', 8⅜ oz., 10 – 20 lb.	EX	$200.00	2-1999
Fenwick	Lunker Stik 1461	Champion grip, ceramic eyes	EX-	$75.00	12-1999
Fenwick	Lunker Stik 2000	2053, 5½', pistol grip, nice	EX	$510.00	10-1999
Fenwick	Lunker Stik 2000	2056, 10 – 20 lb. line, newer grip, 6 power	EX	$206.00	6-2001
Fenwick	Lunker Stik 2000	2060, 6', medium grip	Mint	$510.00	11-1999
Fenwick	Lunker Stik 2000BC		EX	$127.00	4-2000
Fenwick	Lunker Stik 2056	5½', ½ – 1 oz., newer	EX	$134.50	3-1999
Fenwick	Lunker Stik 207446	6'	EX	$200.00	2-1999
Fenwick	Lunker Stik PLC	5½', 11" rubber handle	Mint	$232.50	4-1999
Fenwick	Lunker Stik PLC55	5½', ½ - 1 oz.	EX/IC	$411.00	2-2000
Fenwick	Lunker Stik PLC60	2-piece, regular grip	Mint	$260.00	4-1999
Fenwick	Lunker Stik PLC65	6½'	EX	$303.50	3-1999
Fenwick	Lunker Stik PLC 65	2-piece	EX	$232.50	10-1999
Fenwick	Lunker Stik PLS 65	spinning reel, bag & tube	VG	$53.00	1-1999
French, P.		7', 2-2, fly rod, bag &case, NOT MET	Mint	$820.00	1-1999

BRAND	MODEL	SERIES / MFG. CODE / DESCRIPTION	GRADE	PRICE	DATE
Garcia	Conlon Companion 2621	casting reel, 2-piece, lightweight, blue	EX	$74.00	7-1999
Garcia	Conlon Five Star 2102	7', medium grip, agate eyes	NIbag	$67.00	4-2000
Gephart	700	4' – 6', casting reel, NOT MET	NIC	$51.00	10-2000
Goodwin	Granger	2/2, 7', "Victory," tube & bag	EX/IT	$725.00	6-1999
Goodwin	Granger	3/2, 8½', fly reel, bag & tube, "Victory" NOT MET	EX-	$305.75	8-1999
Granger	Deluxe	3/2, 8½', bag & tube, needs work	IT	$410.00	9-1999
H & I		3/1, 9', spinning reel, short tip, wrong eye, bag	EX	$100.00	8-2000
H & I	2411	7¾', fly reel, bag, very nice	EX+/IB	$46.00	11-1999
H & I	Chancellor	3/2, 8½', case, NOT MET	NIT	$416.00	3-2000
H & I	Tonka Queen	2/2, 7¾', tube & bag	NIT	$360.00	2-2000
H & I	Tonkin Prince	2/1, 7'	EX	$212.00	9-2001
Heddon		3/2, 8½', flymetal bamboo, bag	EX/IT	$255.00	3-2000
Heddon	9	2/1, bait casting reel, bag & brass top tube	NIT	$332.00	8-1999
Heddon	10	3/2, 8', 4 weight, 1½ ferrule	EX	$400.00	2-2002
Heddon	10	3/2, 8½', tube & bag, NOT MET	EX/IT	$178.50	1-2000
Heddon	10	8½', 2" F, HDH or E, plastic still on grip, bag	NIT	$500.00	1-2002
Heddon	14	8½'	EXR	$244.50	1-1999
Heddon	17	3/2, 7½', bag, Sci-Ang tube	NIT	$525.00	9-2000
Heddon	17	3/2, 8', tube & bag	EX/IT	$673.87	1-2000
Heddon	20	2/3 tips, 7', ½FHE, H or F, 1 tip short	EX-	$756.00	12-2001
Heddon	20	9', 2½ F	EX	$200.00	1-1999
Heddon	35	3/2, 9', restored	EX-	$267.00	3-2002
Heddon	50	3/2, 8', 1½F, 4 weight, 1 tip repaired, NOT MET	EX-/IT	$516.00	1-2002
Heddon	60	3/2, 9', restored, NOT MET		$500.00	1-2000
Heddon	211	6', lightweight, bait casting reel, hollow glass, newer	Mint	$108.51	5-1999
Heddon	261	5½', casting reel, glass tube & pouch	EX/IP	$170.00	4-2002
Heddon	400	5', 4F, casting reel, bamboo, 2-piece, revarnished	EX-/IT	$152.00	3-2001
Heddon	400	6', medium, bag, tag attached	Mint	$275.00	2-1999
Heddon	1000	3/1, 9', refinished	EX	$361.00	10-2001
Heddon	3151L	5', steel, bamboo color, nice pouch	NIP	$151.00	8-2001
Heddon	3151L	steel, bamboo color, walnut grip, case	NIC	$242.00	3-2000
Heddon	6783	6', brown glass	EX	$31.00	7-2000
Heddon	Black Beauty 17	3/2, 8½, pouch & tube, mint	NIT	$465.00	8-2000
Heddon	Black Beauty 17	3/2, 8½, very minty bag and tube	NIT	$434.00	7-2000
Heddon	Black Beauty 17	3/2, 9', sack, poor tube, refinished, nice	EX	$300.00	12-2001
Heddon	Black Beauty 17	8½', bag & tube	EX	$425.99	1-1999
Heddon	Black Beauty 17-8	1¾ , F-HD	NIS	$544.00	4-2001
Heddon	Black Beauty 75	8½', fly line, C-HCH, fiberglass	EX/IT	$50.00	9-2000
Heddon	Black Beauty 75	9', glass	Mint	$217.50	1-1999
Heddon	Black Pal 708	newer, fiberglass	Mint	$137.50	5-1999
Heddon	Deluxe 35	3/2, 9', 5 – 6 weight line	EX	$566.00	5-2002
Heddon	Deluxe 35	3/2, 9', 6 – 7 weight line, revarnished	EX	$350.00	9-2001
Heddon	Deluxe Peerless 35	3/2, 8½', 2 ferrule	EX-	$565.00	4-1999
Heddon	Expert 125	3/2, 8½', 2½' FH, CH or D, nice pouch	NIT	$400.00	3-2002
Heddon	Expert 125	3/2, 8½', center is 2" short	VG	$302.77	4-1999
Heddon	Expert 125	3/2, 9', tube & bag, NOT MET	Mint	$257.00	6-1999

BRAND	MODEL	SERIES / MFG. CODE / DESCRIPTION	GRADE	PRICE	DATE
Heddon	Featherlight 31	7'2", overvarnished, NOT MET	EX/IT	$560.00	3-2001
Heddon	Featherweight 14	2/2, 7½', 0-¾F, tube & bag	NIT	$690.00	2-2000
Heddon	Golden Mark 50	6½', 5 weight line, fly reel	Mint	$208.50	12-1999
Heddon	Mark IV	6', 2-piece, medium action, nice pouch & tube	NIT	$122.00	5-2002
Heddon	Mark IV 6903	6', 2-piece	EX	$76.00	2-2000
Heddon	Mark IV 6903	2-piece	EX	$81.00	4-1999
Heddon	Mark IV 8457	2/1, 8½', nice tube, plastic on cork	NIT	$150.00	3-2002
Heddon	Mark IV 8457	8½', fly reel, pouch	NIT	$71.00	4-2000
Heddon	Mark V	6'6", spin casting reel, walnut SS wraps, tube	EX/IC	$255.00	12-1999
Heddon	Musky Pal Special 6276	tobacco glass	Mint	$100.00	10-2001
Heddon	Musky Pal Spook 5123	5'	EX	$41.00	1-2000
Heddon	Musky Special 6276	5½', yellow fiberglass	EX	$6.00	3-2002
Heddon	Pal	3/5, 5', Pal P-41 reel	EX	$150.00	1-1999
Heddon	Pal	5'1", hollow tobacco glass	EX-	$64.00	3-2002
Heddon	Pal 130	6½, medium spinning reel	NIT	$82.75	4-1999
Heddon	Pal 718	71, spin reel	Mint	$20.50	5-1999
Heddon	Pal 816	6', 2-piece	EX	$67.12	5-1999
Heddon	Pal 5551	5½', case	EX/IC	$87.00	8-1999
Heddon	Pal Mark II 6803	6', 2-piece	NIT	$198.50	6-1999
Heddon	Pal Mark IV	6'	EX	$76.50	4-1999
Heddon	Pal Mark IV 8407	8½, tube, nice		$46.00	1-1999
Heddon	Pal Spook	bag & tube	NIT	$213.50	4-1999
Heddon	Pal Spook 3351	5½', bag	NIB	$191.72	4-1999
Heddon	Pal Spook 4451	4½', case	Mint	$192.50	1-1999
Heddon	Pal Spook 6651L	5½', lightweight, case	EX/IC	$202.50	9-1999
Heddon	Pal V 6918	6½', 2-piece	EX	$58.00	2-2000
Heddon	Power Plus Mark IV 6905		EX	$74.00	2-2002
Heddon	Premier	3/2, 9', HGH, aluminum tube, sock	EX/IT	$330.00	11-2000
Heddon	Premier 115	3/2, 7½', fly rod, tube & bag	EX/IT	$678.00	8-2001
Heddon	President 50	3/2, 9', 6 weight line, over varnished, bag & tube	EX	$643.00	5-2002
Heddon	President 150	7½', wraps poor, uneven sections	VG	$496.06	1-1999
Heddon	Thoroughbred 14	3/1	VG+	$207.50	7-1999
Heddon	Roto Tip	ice fishing	EX	$82.00	11-1999
Heddon	Spook 5551-4-L		EX-	$127.50	4-2000
Heddon	Superlative	T2270, 24K eyes	EX-	$345.47	4-1999
Heddon	Superlative 1170-7-L	spinning reel, 2-piece	NIT	$156.01	2-2000
Heddon	Superlative 2270L	5½', tube & papers	EX/IT	$325.00	11-1999
Heddon	Superlative 2270M	5½', medium, nice case	EX/IC	$283.00	11-1999
Heddon	Superlative T2270-XL	pouch, beautiful	NIP	$256.00	4-2000
Herters		8', fly reel, bamboo	EX	$138.00	3-1999
Howells,G.H	4438	2/2, 8', 6 weight line, tube & sock	NIT	$1,825.00	11-2000
Hurd		2 great pamphlets, tip only, cb. tube	EX	$405.00	4-1999
Hurd	Supercaster	walnut handle	VG	$155.25	1-1999
Hurd	Supercaster	wood, case	EX/IC	$308.00	8-1999
Jenkins	GA-70L	2/2, plugs, bag & tube, NOT MET	NIT	$811.00	11-1999
Jenkins,C.W.		2/2, bamboo, fly reel, plastic on grip, NOT MET	Mint	$835.00	10-1999
Johnson	Profile	Uniglass 800 8C64 (Philipson?)	EX	$610.00	6-2001

BRAND	MODEL	SERIES / MFG. CODE / DESCRIPTION	GRADE	PRICE	DATE
Kusse Ron		2/2, 8', fly reel, mint bag & tube, 6 – 7 weight line, beautiful	NIT	$1,500.00	8-2001
Leonard		2/2, 7', Maxwell era	Mint	$2,425.00	4-2000
Leonard	39DF-4	472P, 2/2, 7½', 4 weight line, bag & tube	EX/IT	$2,225.00	4-1999
Leonard	51S.D.F	3/2, 9', fighting grip, all goodies, mint	NIT	$896.00	9-2001
Leonard	Baby Catskill	2/2, 6', one tip 1" short, bag	EX/IT	$1,275.00	8-2000
Leonard, H.L.	53	3/2, 10', 7¾ oz., bag & tube	NIT	$600.00	8-1999
Leonard, H.L.	136	2/2, 6', 3 weight line, bag & tube	EX/IT	$1,550.00	4-1999
Montague	Clipper	3/1, tube	EX	$79.00	8-1999
Montague	Flash	3/1, 9'	EX	$230.50	1-1999
Montague	Manitou	3/2, 9', nice decal	EX	$333.00	8-2001
Montague	Rapidian	3/2, 8½', goodies	NIT	$290.00	5-1999
Montague	Rapidian	7½', 2/1	EX	$180.00	2-2000
Montague	Redwing	3/2, 7½', bag & tube	EX	$640.00	6-1999
Montague	Somers Point	5½', 2-piece, saltwater, extra heavy duty	EX/IT	$128.50	7-1999
Orchard Industries	Action	4½', fancy grip, maroon & white	EX	$63.00	1-2002
Orchard Industries	Action	5', white & red stripes	EX	$65.00	10-2000
Orchard Industries	Action	green & white, bakelite handle, round shaft	EX	$215.00	11-2001
Orchard Industries	Action	metal, red & white grip	EX	$104.00	10-2000
Orchard Industries	Action Rod 1680	2/1, 8', glass, pouch, NOT MET	NIP	$53.00	7-2000
Orchard Industries	Action Rod AS-47	case, NOT MET	NIC	$86.00	3-2000
Orvis		7'9", graphite, tube & bag, NOT MET	EX	$190.00	7-1999
Orvis	Battenkill	3/2, 6½', bag & tube	EX	$807.50	3-1999
Orvis	Battenkill	2/2, 7½', 4¼ oz, bag & tube	EXIT	$585.00	6-1999
Orvis	Battenkill	2/2, 7½', dented tube, otherwise nice, c.1970	EX/IT	$528.00	10-2001
Orvis	Battenkill	2/2, 7½', HDH, bag & tube, NOT MET		$480.00	4-1999
Orvis	Battenkill	2/2, 7½', tube & bag	EX+/IT	$600.00	2-2000
Orvis	Battenkill	8'6", bag & tube	EX+	$515.96	1-1999
Orvis	Battenkill	8½', 3/2, tube cap damaged	EX	$400.00	3-1999
Orvis	Battenkill Impregnated	3/2, 9', 8 – 9 weight line, dark, bag	EX/IB	$405.00	9-2001
Orvis	Golden Eagle	7½', glass, 6 weight line, bag & tube	EX+	$301.10	3-1999
Orvis	HLS2	9', 7 weight line, 2-piece	Mint	$167.00	1-1999
Orvis	Impregnated Special	2/1, 6½', tube & bag	EX/IT	$566.00	8-2000
Orvis	Limestone Special	2/2, 8½', tube & sock	NIT	$709.00	4-2001
Orvis	Madison	8½' 4¾ oz, 2/1, tube & bag	NIT	$612.00	2-2000
Orvis	Midge	2/2, 7½', 5 weight line, crisp sock & tube	NIT	$600.00	1-2002
Orvis	Mitey Mite	2/1, 5', bag & tube	EX/IT	$947.00	4-1999
Orvis	Penn's Creek	2/2, 7', 3⅜ oz., 4 weight line, sock	NIT	$895.00	10-2001
Orvis	Wes Jordan	8', 4¾ oz., fly reel, for a GBF, NOT MET	MIT	$890.00	8-1999
Payne		3/2, 7½', varnish is a little rough	EX-	$600.00	1-2002
Payne	98	2/2, 7', 2¹³⁄₁₆ oz., bag	EX/IT	$3,000.00	10-2002
Payne, E. F.	Abercrombie & Fitch	3/2, 9', replacement tip, c.1920s, NOT MET	EX/IT	$1,025.00	10-2001
Payne, Jim	200	3/2, 8', restored	MR	$2,426.00	4-2000
Payne, Jim	208	3/2,9', 5 – 6 line, restored	EX-	$1,502.50	8-1999
Pflueger		casting reel, steel	Mint	$56.26	8-1999
Pflueger	Supreme 121P	6', M, EEM, glass	NIC	$206.00	5-2000
Philipson		3/1, 8½', fly reel, bamboo, tube & bag	EX-	$178.50	8-1999

BRAND	MODEL	SERIES / MFG. CODE / DESCRIPTION	GRADE	PRICE	DATE
Philipson		fly reel, fiberglass, tube & bag, NOT MET	EX	$34.00	8-1999
Philipson	3M Basstamer BC50	5', 7½ – ⅜ oz. lures	Mint	$2,035.00	9-2002
Philipson	3M Basstamer BC56	5'6", 1 oz., missing reel lock	Mint	$1,705.00	9-2002
Philipson	8C64	6'4", glass, 2-piece, bag	EX	$1,325.00	3-1999
Philipson	Deluxe Swamp Fox DC60B	NOT MET	EX/IC	$1200.00	4-2001
Philipson	Eponite 76	custom built for Furrs	VG+	$730.00	10-1999
Philipson	Haywood Zephyr	7½', modern with old blank	NIT	$395.00	11-2000
Philipson	Johnson Profile 6C64	6'4", bait casting reel, 2-piece	EX	$910.00	3-2001
Philipson	Master G-M0652	5'5", spinning reel	EX	$172.50	12-1998
Philipson	P7OL	spinning reel	Mint	$257.00	3-1999
Philipson	P76F	7½', 5 weight line, sack, no tube	Mint	$193.05	4-1999
Philipson	P86F HDH	fly reel, 4¾ oz.	EX	$169.16	2-1999
Philipson	Pacemaker	3/2, 8½', tube & sock	EX-/IT	$373.00	8-2001
Philipson	Pacemaker	3/2, 9', sock & tube	EX/IT	$250.00	8-2002
Philipson	Pacemaker 18	6', bamboo, 2-piece, bend	VG	$470.00	2-1999
Philipson	Pacemaker 18	6', bamboo, 2-piece, bend	VG	$560.00	2-1999
Philipson	Pacemaker	3/2, 8½', cardboard tube	NIT	$510.00	12-1999
Philipson	Paragon 79 9-578 HCH	3/2, 9', bamboo	EX-	$200.00	8-1999
Philipson	PH60	modern reproduction, NOT MET	Mint	$417.66	2-2000
Philipson	Phillipson Peerless "5"	3/2, 8', 5 weight line, bag & tube	EX/IT	$892.00	4-2000
Philipson	Power-Kast	2/1, 6'3", (writing on handle?) (on rod?)	EX-	$425.00	10-2001
Philipson	Stream Knight SK64	spinning reel, 2-piece	NIT	$103.00	4-2001
Philipson	Uniglass 800	3/2, 8 weight line, bag & tube	EX	$128.51	1-1999
Prichard		1881 & 1889 patents, lemonwood, wood case	AVG	$206.14	6-1999
Record	49	5', baitcasting reel, medium grip, cheap	NIBag	$66.00	4-2001
Record	Corona	5½', 2-piece, sack, nice	EX	$187.00	8-2000
Sans Pariel	5 wt	2/2, tube	NIT	$1,700.00	10-2000
Schaff	Dickerson 7012	7', 2-piece, 4 weight line, fancy bag & tube, 1994	NIT	$1,575.00	5-2000
Shakespeare		7¾, fly reel, bag & tube	EX/IT	$41.00	11-1999
Shakespeare	Wonder Rod	3/1, fly reel, bag & aluminum tube	NIT	$69.00	8-2000
Shimano	Speedmaster 30 SM1753	7½', heavy flippin	EX	$108.00	5-2001
Silaflex	Perfexion 201	7½', fly reel, pre-Browning, tube & sack	EX	$330.00	7-1999
South Bend	13	3/2, 9½', over varnished, NOT MET	EX	$104.00	2-2002
South Bend	24	some probelms 3/2, ferrule crack	VG/IT	$54.00	4-2001
South Bend	26	2/1, 7½', refinished	EX/IT	$285.00	9-2001
South Bend	166-9	3/2, 9', HDH, tube, bag	EX/IT	$250.00	6-1999
South Bend	290	2/2, 7½'	EX	$255.00	7-2000
South Bend	290	2/2, 7½', bag & tube	EX/IT	$275.00	2-2000
South Bend	290	2/2, 7½', one tiptop missing, bag	EX/IT	$190.00	10-2000
South Bend	290	3/2, 7½', bamboo	VG+	$305.00	3-1999
South Bend	291	3/2, 7½', sock	NIT	$360.00	11-2000
South Bend	359	3/2, 9', bag	Mint	$127.50	8-1999
South Bend	359	3/2, 9', dry fly reel action	NIT	$150.00	10-2000
Summers, R. W.	735	2/2, 7'3", 4 – 5 weight line, c.1984, bag & tube	EX/IT	$2,075.00	9-2001
Thomas, F. E.	Special Browntone	8', bag & tube	EX	$1,825.00	4-1999
True Temper		5'7", yellow steel	NIC	$112.00	10-2000
Tycoon		8'1", deep sea trolling, extra heavy duty, bamboo	EX	$1,855.00	5-1999

BRAND	MODEL	SERIES / MFG. CODE / DESCRIPTION	GRADE	PRICE	DATE
Tycoon Tackle	Scion	6'10", over 5 lb., 1938	EX	$1,626.00	10-1999
Vom Hofe, J.	2	fly reel, seat bent	VG-	$406.00	1-1999
Walker, Richard	Mark IV	carp rod, revarnished, NOT MET	EX	$1,900.00	8-2002
Weber	Henshall	3/2, 8½', original bag, no tube	VG	$228.00	6-1999
Weber	Mastercraft 3500	8½', 35 made by Heddon, restored, NOT MET	EX	$170.00	1-2001
Weir, John		2/2, 9', custom, $5,000.00 NOT MET	NIT	$500.00	4-2001
Williams, Ted		spin casting reel, & pouches	NIC	$127.50	3-2000
Winchester		3/1, fly reel, steel, wood grip, NO BIDS	EX	$100.00	3-2000
Winston		7', fly rod, mint bag & tube	NIT	$406.53	3-1999
Winston	IM6	#6, 2/1, 8½', pouch & tube	EX/IT	$304.00	10-2000
Wright McGill	Granger	3/2, 9', bag & tube	EX/IT	$373.00	8-2002
Wright McGill	Granger Favorite	3/2, 8½'	EX	$495.00	5-2001
Wright McGill	Granger Favorite	3/1, 9', bag & tube	VG+	$210.00	1-1999
Wright McGill	Granger Favorite	3/2, 9', wrap still on grip, tube & sack	NIT	$1,000.00	9-1999
Wright McGill	Granger Special GS8040	3/2, 4 oz., 5 weight line, butt ¾" short, refinished		$660.00	9-2001
Wright McGill	Granger Victory	3/2, 8', restored	EX	$650.00	3-1999
Young Paul		2/1, 7½', dated June 1953, bag & tube	Mint	$1,275.00	8-1999
Young, Paul		2/2, 8', fly rod, 6 weight line, possibly over varnished, nice	EX/IT	$810.00	8-2001
Young, Paul	Perfectionist	2/2, 7½', restored	Mint	$2,700.00	4-2000
Young, Paul	Spinmaster	2/1, 6½'	EX	$482.00	2-2002

MISCELLANEOUS

ADVERTISEMENTS

BRAND	DESCRIPTION	GRADE	PRICE	DATE
Heddon	Lone Eagle Reel, 12" x 18", previously sold for $200.00	VG	$2,027.00	11-2000
Heddon	O. and O. Sporting Goods, ad on book of matches, Rochester, Minnesota	VG	$27.00	9-2002
South Bend	3' x 5' stand up display, "Fish & Feel Fit"	EX	$2,150.00	10-1999

BADGES

BRAND	DESCRIPTION	GRADE	PRICE	DATE
Childress	x6, all different, nice paint, c.1950	EX	$102.50	7-1999
Field & Stream	bass, 4 lb. 4 ozs.	EX	$66.00	2-1999
Field & Stream	not sure of fish type, 30 lb.	EX	$61.00	8-1999
Field & Stream	smallmouth bass, 4 lb. 11 ozs.	EX	$67.00	1-1999
Field & Stream	walleye, 9 lb. 5 ozs.	EX	$169.35	3-2000
Hagen	Rotor Bobber, papers included	NIB	$41.00	8-2001
Mermaid	novelty, black hair	EX	$25.77	7-1999
Olsen, Nels	bobber, 1901 patent, papers, unmarked box, Iowa item	NIB	$301.00	10-2001
Stamdie Products	Nibble Nabber, automatic strike	Mint	$510.00	8-2000

BOOKS

BRAND	DESCRIPTION	GRADE	PRICE	DATE
Taylor, Samuel	*Angling in All Its Branches*, 1st Edition, 1800, 298 pages	VG	$280.00	11-1999

BUG DOPES

BRAND	DESCRIPTION	GRADE	PRICE	DATE
Bickmore	repellent, 8 tins	NIB	$92.00	6-1999

CREELS

BRAND	DESCRIPTION	GRADE	PRICE	DATE
	split willow, single ribs, nice leather	EX-	$167.50	2-2000
Freeman/Mariner	fancy, modern	Mint	$1,826.00	2-2000
French	hoizontal supports, very nice	EX	$410.00	7-1999
Lawrence Co.	#5 strap, strap only	Mint	$292.89	6-1999
Lawrence Co.	#6 strap, metal name tag & stamp	EX-	$1560.89	3-1999
Lawrence Co.	split willow, straps machined	EX	$1550.00	6-1999
Macmonies	split willow, small repair, NOT MET	VG+	$1,825.00	5-1999
Sheldon	wide strips, Indian Head, wood top, ugly	EX	$271.00	6-1999
Simeonov	leather, c.1930, beautiful	EX+	$3,050.00	4-1999
Simeonov	modern, made in 1999	Mint	$2,700.00	4-1999
Turtle		NM	$1,500.00	4-2000
Turtle	carved turtle latch, turtle trademark, NOT MET	EX-	$232.50	11-1999
Turtle	nice cording, beautiful	EX	$635.00	1-1999
Turtle	tight weave, nice turtle latch, NOT MET	EX-	$330.00	12-2001
Turtle	trademark, exact one from book, $1,000.00 – $1,500.00	EX-	$550.00	8-2002

DECOYS

BRAND	DESCRIPTION	GRADE	PRICE	DATE
	18" carved trout, c.1880, in shadow box, nice	EX	$1,652.00	1-1999
Chautauqua	7⅜", ice spearing, glass eyes, leather tail, NOT MET	EX	$1,215.00	10-2001
Downey, A.J.	13¾" trout, c.1980, NOT MET	Mint	$305.00	1-2002
Heddon	4-point, bar perch	VG+	$910.00	10-2002
Heddon	4-point, bar perch, nice	EX-	$2,282.00	9-2000
Heddon	4-point, crackleback, (revarnished), NOT MET	EX	$1,775.00	5-2001
Heddon	4-point, green scale	EX-	$2,750.00	5-2000
Heddon	4-point, green scale	Rough	$382.00	9-2000
Heddon	4-point, green scale, belly varnish	EX-	$2,400.00	10-1999
Heddon	4-point, green scale, real ugly	AVG	$600.00	8-1999
Heddon	4-point, ice decoy	EX	$3400.00	4-2001
Heddon	4-point, L-rig	VG	$616.00	5-1999
Heddon	4-point, L-rig, nice	EX	$2,351.00	5-1999
Heddon	4-point, perch scale	AVG	$224.00	3-2002
Heddon	4-point, perch scale	EX	$1,313.00	1-2000
Heddon	4-point, perch scale	EX-	$1,691.66	9-1999
Heddon	4-point, perch scale	VG+	$920.00	9-1999

DECOYS (continued)

BRAND	DESCRIPTION	GRADE	PRICE	DATE
Heddon	4-point, perch scale, awful belly, rest ugly	Poor	$305.00	12-2001
Heddon	4-point, perch scale, belly varnish flaking	EX-	$1,500.00	1-2002
Heddon	4-point, perch scale, vg- Down Bass box, NOT MET	EX/IB	$1,375.00	9-2002
Heddon	4-point, rainbow, a few varnish flakes on top, many varnish flakes on belly	VG+	$1,136.00	8-2000
Heddon	4-point, rainbow, decent, NOT MET	VG+	$1,125.00	12-1999
Heddon	4-point, white, red eye shade, NOT MET	EX-	$1,225.00	11-2000
Heddon	Bat Wing, bar perch, 5BW, NOT MET	AVG	$712.00	11-2000
Heddon	Bat Wing, bar perch, missing piece of tail, ugly	AVG-	$2,500.00	11-2000
Heddon	Bat Wing, bar perch, pigtail line tie	VG	$3250.00	8-2002
Heddon	Bat Wing, overpaint, revarnished wing, NOT MET	Poor	$306.00	11-2000
Heddon	natural scale	Rough	$321.00	9-2000
Mizera	6¼", red head, white, red tail, ugly	VG-	$124.72	4-1999
Mizera	6¾" pike, solid silver, no pizzaz	EX	$130.00	10-1999
Mizera	9" pike, red, white	EX	$385.00	4-1999
Paw Paw	7½", replaced fin, NOT MET	AVG	$77.000	11-2000
Paw Paw	ice fishing, silver flash, revarnished	Rough	$224.00	11-2001
Stewert	8" bass, c.1980, signed	Mint	$271.78	3-1999

DISPLAYS

BRAND	DESCRIPTION	GRADE	PRICE	DATE
CCBC	14" x 10" stand-up counter, "Oh Man, What Action."	EX	$283.00	4-2001

EYES

BRAND	DESCRIPTION	GRADE	PRICE	DATE
CCBC	glass x 50, 15/64"	Mint	$76.00	3-2000
	glass on wires x 50, NOT MET	Mint	$32.00	5-1999

FLIES

BRAND	DESCRIPTION	GRADE	PRICE	DATE
Grey, Zane	streamer, authentication paper, framed	EX	$100.00	6-1999
Shakespeare	Otsego Bass, White Miller, super nice card	NOC	$17.00	11-2000

GAFFS

BRAND	DESCRIPTION	GRADE	PRICE	DATE
Marble	pincer type, spring	EX	$53.00	1-1999

GREASES

BRAND	MODEL	DESCRIPTION	GRADE	PRICE	DATE
Pflueger	Run Free	12-pack, each tube new in box	NIB	$96.00	1-2002

GRIPS

BRAND	MODEL	DESCRIPTION	GRADE	PRICE	DATE
Champion	All Angle		EX-	$50.00	1-2002
Featherweight	All Angle	cork dirty no end cap	AVG	$108.50	1-2000
Featherweight	All Angle	foam, NOT MET	VG+	$51.00	3-2000
Featherweight	All Angle	plastic still on cork	Mint	$222.50	12-1999
Featherweight	All Angle	(reproduction?), color odd	Mint	$125.00	11-1999
Featherweight	All Angle	small repair	VG+	$125.00	3-2000
Featherweight	All Angle		EX	$152.50	3-2000
Featherweight	All Angle		EX	$113.49	3-2000
Featherweight	All Angle		EX-	$125.00	3-2000
Featherweight	All Angle		EX	$122.50	6-1999
Featherweight	All Angle		EX	$155.50	8-1999
Featherweight	All Angle		VG+	$62.00	9-1999
Featherweight	Champion 6AP30	plastic bag	NIB	$78.00	9-2000
Featherweight	Champion	black pistol	EX	$222.50	6-1999
Featherweight	Champion	brown pistol	EX-	$152.50	3-2000
Featherweight	Champion	cork	EX	$69.00	6-2000
Featherweight	Champion	cork	VG	$49.99	5-1999
Featherweight	Champion	foam	EX	$58.00	4-2001
Featherweight	Champion	foam handle	EX	$46.00	10-2000
Featherweight	Champion	green pistol grip	EX	$350.00	8-1999
Featherweight	Champion	pistol grip	VG-	$78.00	5-1999
Featherweight	Champion	black pistol grip, spacers	EX	$367.00	5-1999
Featherweight	Champion	black pistol grip	EX	$301.15	8-1999
Featherweight	Champion	black pistol grip, spacers	EX	$376.00	5-1999
Featherweight	Champion	plastic still on cork	Mint	$151.00	12-1999
Featherweight	Champion	purple pistol grip	EX	$227.50	10-1999
Featherweight	Champion	walnut	EX	$90.00	6-2000
Featherweight	Champion	wood, probably not factory	EX	$103.50	8-1999
Featherweight	Champion	wrong Garcia endcap, NOT MET	VG	$51.22	6-1999
Featherweight	Champion		EX	$112.52	8-1999
Featherweight		pistol grip, brown	EX	$124.00	6-2000
Featherweight		11", pistol grip, burgundy	EX	$287.50	10-1999
Featherweight	Spinchucker 22A	rough box	NIB	$102.50	8-1999

HARPOONS

BRAND	DESCRIPTION	GRADE	PRICE	DATE
Vom Hofe, E.	10', 3 tips, German silver fittings	EX	$575.00	8-2000

HOOKS

BRAND	DESCRIPTION	GRADE	PRICE	DATE
	spring hook, patented September 7, 1997 & May 30, 1999	EX	$177.00	5-2001
G.W. Evans & Son	spring hook	EX	$561.51	10-1999
G.W. Evans & Son	multi-spring hook, nice shape	EX	$885.00	3-2000
Greer	patented lever, c.1900	EX	$28.00	8-2002

HOOKS (continued)

BRAND	DESCRIPTION	GRADE	PRICE	DATE
Henzel	weedless	NOC	$19.00	1-2002
Lite Striking	spring hook	NIB	$41.00	9-2000
Winchester	2PCCB, box is a little rough, very plain	VG	$200.00	4-1999
Yankee Doodle	spring hook	EX	$300.00	1-1999

JARS

BRAND	MODEL	DESCRIPTION	GRADE	PRICE	DATE
Foss	Pork Rind	glass, never opened, very nice	EX	$76.00	8-2001

KNIVES

BRAND	DESCRIPTION	GRADE	PRICE	DATE
Marbles	(fish knife?), rosewood fish decal inlaid, very worn		$536.89	7-1999

LINES

BRAND	MODEL	DESCRIPTION	GRADE	PRICE	DATE
Ashaway		ships wheel, wood spool with linen line	EX	$39.80	3-2000
Ashaway		silk flyline, great swaztika box, nice spool	NIB	$108.00	3-2001
CCBC	Lite Chub	awful, pigtail line tie, NOT MET		$167.82	5-1999
Hall		x27, all different, salesman sample, NOT MET	NIB	$145.05	6-1999
Hall		x33, all different, nice display, NOT MET	NIB	$81.00	5-1999
Hall		x35, all different, salesman sample, NOT MET	NIB	$200.00	6-1999
Heddon		2 different	EX	$26.50	1-1999
Heddon		monofilament, Daisy/Heddon	EX	$30.00	1-1999
Heddon	Dandy-Line	waterproof, pure Japanese silk	VG-	$305.00	3-1999
Heddon	Pal-On	2 plastic spools of braided line, picture box	NIB	$53.00	12-1999
Heddon	Pal-On	20 lb., twin spools, leaping bass	Mint	$91.00	8-1999
O'Hara	Fisherman's	24 spools, 25 yards, silk, 10 lb.	NIB	$30.75	6-1999
Vom Hofe, E.		27, 300 yards, wood, box, nice	EX/IB	$56.00	5-1999
Winchester	8612	16 lb., wood spool, holes punched	EX	$325.00	1-1999
Winchester	Vacation Special	wood, bass picture, holes, ugly	G	$130.49	8-1999

LINE DRYERS

BRAND	DESCRIPTION	GRADE	PRICE	DATE
Hardy	compact, fold-up, nice	EX	$455.00	2-2000
Hardy	newer looking	EX	$96.00	1-2002
Vom Hofe, E.	solid brass, folding 9" x 20" x 20", nice	EX	$338.00	6-2002

LINE SPOOLS

BRAND	MODEL	DESCRIPTION	GRADE	PRICE	DATE
Heddon	Simpson	wood, bass, hole, one side rough	AVG	$248.00	2-2000

MAGAZINES

BRAND	MODEL	DESCRIPTION	GRADE	PRICE	DATE
Field & Stream	1906		Fair	$48.77	2-1999
Outdoor Life	March 1930	great color cover	EX	$26.00	2-1999

MATCH SAFES

BRAND	DESCRIPTION	GRADE	PRICE	DATE
sterling silver	fancy scroll, fly fisherman, marked "Sterling"	EX	$209.00	1-2001

MINNOW BUCKETS

BRAND	MODEL	DESCRIPTION	GRADE	PRICE	DATE
Climax	Lifesaver 100	green, floating	EX+	$43.00	10-2001
Expert		oval, green, nice stencil of fish	EX-	$395.00	8-2002
Hartford		floating, $1,000.00 NOT MET	EX	$112.00	5-2002
Keen Kutter		2-piece, galvanized metal	Mint	$120.00	4-1999
Lucas		c.1917, nice graphics	VG+	$228.00	1-2001
Old Pal		hand aerator, red & blue logo, nice	EX-	$150.00	8-2002

MINNOW TRAPS

BRAND	MODEL	DESCRIPTION	GRADE	PRICE	DATE
Orvis		glass minnow, wood box	NIB	$380.00	5-1999
Witherspoon Simpson Glass Co.	Joy	glass, c.1935	EX	$87.00	5-2000

MOTORS

BRAND	MODEL	DESCRIPTION	GRADE	PRICE	DATE
Evinrude	1911	decent looking, stored since 1935	EX-	$985.00	2-2000

PAPERS

BRAND	MODEL	DESCRIPTION	GRADE	PRICE	DATE
Heddon	Dummy Double	box insert, line drawing of L-rig 1500	EX	$461.00	2-2002
Heddon		o & slopenose, bamboo rods on reverse, c.1912	EX	$382.00	1-2001

REEL SPOOLS

BRAND	MODEL	DESCRIPTION	GRADE	PRICE	DATE
Zebco	Cardinal 4	spool only	EX	$22.51	1-2000
Zebco	Cardinal 4	with case	NIC	$27.00	1-2000
Zebco	Cardinal 4	5 spools, new, NOT MET	Mint	$75.75	3-2000

SIGNS

BRAND	MODEL	DESCRIPTION	GRADE	PRICE	DATE
CCBC		25" x 37" tri-fold	VG	$2,625.00	12-1998
Heddon	Shore Minnow River Runts	4-Stooges, transparent panel, NOT MET	EX	$1,158.00	2-2002

SONAR

BRAND	MODEL	DESCRIPTION	GRADE	PRICE	DATE
Lawrence	LFP 300	green box, 762358 papers	Mint	$400.00	6-2000

SPEARS

BRAND	MODEL	DESCRIPTION	GRADE	PRICE	DATE
forged		7½", 6 tines, plain	EX	$62.00	4-1999
Moonlight	Paw Paw Fish Spear	#5, frog, 2-hook, 2 line ties, NOT MET	EX-	$635.00	4-2000
Pflueger	Ecko	7 frog spears, Zebra box	NIB	$57.00	8-2001

SPRING HOOKS

BRAND	MODEL	DESCRIPTION	GRADE	PRICE	DATE
Evans	Eagle Claw	8 hooks, c.1877, NOT MET	EX	$1,045.00	4-2002
Evans	Eagle Claw Fish Trap	c.1877, very nice but NOT MET	EX	$1,045.00	4-2002
Greer		lever patented, c.1900	EX	$28.00	8-2002

TACKLE BOXES

BRAND	MODEL	DESCRIPTION	GRADE	PRICE	DATE
Airex	Lionel Train Corporation 730		VG	$96.00	1-1999
Hardy Brothers		vest pocket, 7" x 5½" embossed leather fly case	EX	$345.00	6-2001
Heddon	Outing	red, black, crackleback, bass logo	VG	$202.50	1-1999
Heddon	Outing		VG	$78.00	1-2001
Kennedy	CO-155-AL	medium, aluminum, newer	EX	$32.00	4-1999
Kennedy	Hip Roof Great Lakes	grey liner, 6 trays, large compartments	Mint	$82.00	5-2001
Kennedy		large, brass hardware, aluminum trays	Mint	$262.00	6-1999
Tronick		wood, no medallion	EX	$200.00	9-2000
UMCO	1000A		Mint	$511.00	8-1999
UMCO	1000A	clean	EX	$67.66	8-1999
UMCO	1000A	small dent, clean trays	EX-	$76.00	1-1999
UMCO	1000A		VG	$132.50	1-1999
UMCO	1000U	green	VG+	$108.05	4-1999
UMCO	1000U	green	EX-	$94.00	5-1999
UMCO	1000U	musky with 5 decent lures	EX	$76.00	12-1998
UMCO	1000US	2 worm burns	EX-	$142.50	4-1999
UMCO	1000W	brown	VG+	$100.99	7-1999
UMCO	1000W		EX	$100.00	10-1999
UMCO	10B	14 compartments	EX	$16.50	1-1999
UMCO	10B		Mint	$11.49	8-1999
UMCO	131AS		Mint	$48.00	1-1999

TACKLE BOXES (continued)

BRAND	MODEL	DESCRIPTION	GRADE	PRICE	DATE
UMCO	133AS		EX-	$51.00	1-1999
UMCO	173A		EX	$62.00	1-1999
UMCO	175U	worm burn	G	$53.50	3-1999
UMCO	2000U	5 worm burns	VG	$131.50	4-1999
UMCO	204A	correct cardboard shipping box	NIB	$240.00	9-2001
UMCO	204R	large lure compartments	EX-	$123.49	3-2000
UMCO	205A	aluminum, 3 trays, no burns	EX+	$74.00	11-2000
UMCO	2080U	green, hard white plastic trays, NOT MET	Mint	$152.00	8-2002
UMCO	2080U	hard plastic trays, outer brown wood finish	EX	$132.00	10-2001
UMCO	3080-UPB	with cheap lures	EX	$680.00	2-1999
UMCO	3500U	Possum Belly	EX	$222.00	10-2000
UMCO	3500U	worm burns	VG	$270.00	4-1999
UMCO	3500UPB	double belly, NOT MET	EX	$202.00	6-2000
UMCO	3500US	missing 2 trays	EX	$214.50	3-1999
UMCO		4' x 9', pocket size	EX	$34.33	1-1999
UMCO	4500U	brown	EX	$216.00	11-2000
UMCO	4500UPB	no "UMCO," just code, made for Bass Pro Shops	Mint	$173.00	1-2002
UMCO	4500UPR	plastic trays	EX	$160.00	4-1999
UMCO	900W		Mint	$182.50	10-1999
UMCO	P9		Mint	$18.00	1-1999
UMCO	U2000	few worm burns, crack, NOT MET	VG	$58.77	7-1999
UMCO		vest pocket, 2 round & 1 oval compartment	EX	$45.00	1-1999
UMCO	204	aluminum	EX	$82.00	7-1999
UMCO	803	dirty trays	EX-	$69.00	3-2000
UMCO	1000	bigger trays	EX-	$62.00	7-2000
UMCO	1000	silver latches	EX	$178.05	3-2000
UMCO	3060	large, green Umcolite	EX-	$248.00	11-2001
UMCO	4500	80 good modern lures included	EX	$251.00	3-1999
Wheatley		small fly, 6 compartments	EX	$69.00	11-2000

TIN, SPLIT SHOT

BRAND	MODEL	DESCRIPTION	GRADE	PRICE	DATE
Abbey&Imbrie		split shot, round	EX-	$81.00	12-1999
Abbey&Imbrie		x2, celluloid	EX-	$160.00	10-2000
Burkhard		duck head, round, slide hole	EX	$306.02	2-2000
Houston	Split Shot	3/0, yellow, red letters	EX	$20.51	12-1999
Pflueger	BB	36 tins in display box, very nice	NIB	$102.50	4-1999
Shurkatch	36-pack	3 dozen box, nice	NIB	$115.00	10-2000
Trout Line		tobacco, fishing sceen	VG+	$616.00	10-2000
Winchester		round, shot tin, rotating hole, NOT MET	VG-	$178.00	3-1999
Winchester	9114	NOT MET	EX	$157.50	4-1999

TOYS

BRAND	MODEL	DESCRIPTION	GRADE	PRICE	DATE
Lakeside Toys Co.	Aquaphibian Terror Fish 8607	c.1960	NIB	$431.00	6-2001

WEATHERVANES

BRAND	DESCRIPTION	GRADE	PRICE	DATE
	cast iron fish, early 1900s	EX	$13,100.00	4-2002